CITIES IN CHANGE

CITIES IN CHANGE: STUDIES ON THE URBAN CONDITION

JOHN WALTON
DONALD E. CARNS
Northwestern University

BOSTON: Allyn and Bacon, Inc.

HT
151
.W32

Chapter opening photographs by Talbot Lovering and Tania D'Avignon.

Library of Congress Catalog Card Number: 72-81483.

To the authors
of the articles
that appear in this book

CONTRibUTiNG AUTHORS

Janet Abu-Lughod, professor of sociology, Northwestern University.
Michael Aiken, associate professor of sociology, University of Wisconsin.
Robert R. Alford, professor of sociology, University of Wisconsin.
Howard S. Becker, professor of sociology, Northwestern University.
Daniel Bell, professor of sociology, Harvard University.
Richard A. Berk, assistant professor of sociology and urban affairs, Northwestern University.
Robert Blauner, professor of sociology, University of California at Berkeley.
Hans Blumenfeld, research associate, Division of Town and Regional Planning, University of Toronto.
Kenneth Boulding, professor of economics, University of Michigan.
Donald E. Carns, assistant professor of sociology, Northwestern University.
V. Gordon Childe, director, Institute of Archaeology, University of London.
Henry Cohen, director, Center for New York City Affairs, and professor of urban affairs, New School for Social Research.
Robert Coles, member of the faculty, Harvard University.
Herbert Costner, professor of sociology, University of Washington.
Anthony Downs, formerly consultant to the National Advisory Commission on Civil Disorders.
Sheldon Goldenberg, graduate student in sociology, Northwestern University.
Andrew C. Gordon, assistant professor of sociology and urban affairs, Northwestern University.
Walter Gove, associate professor, Department of Sociology and Anthropology, Vanderbilt University.
Edward Greer, Department of Sociology, Wheaton College.
Scott A. Greer, professor of sociology and urban affairs, Northwestern University.
Philip M. Hauser, professor of sociology, The University of Chicago.
Irving Louis Horowitz, professor of sociology, Rutgers, The State University.
Bert F. Hoselitz, professor of economics and of the social sciences, The University of Chicago.

Jane Jacobs, freelance writer, author of *The Death and Life of American Cities* (1961) and other books.

William Kornhauser, professor of sociology, University of California, Berkeley.

Oscar Lewis, late professor of anthropology, University of Illinois.

Raymond W. Mack, professor of sociology, vice president and dean of faculties, Northwestern University.

Dennis C. McElrath, professor of sociology, University of California, Santa Cruz.

James R. McIntosh, associate professor of sociology, Lehigh University.

James Alan McPherson, Department of English, Iowa State University.

Stanley Milgram, professor of psychology, Graduate Center, The City University of New York.

Harvey Molotch, associate professor of sociology, University of California at Santa Barbara.

Daniel P. Moynihan, professor of education and urban politics, Graduate School of Education, Harvard University.

Frank J. Munger, professor of political science, Syracuse University.

Rhoads Murphey, professor, Department of Geography and Center for Chinese Studies, University of Michigan.

Peter H. Rossi, Department of Social Relations, The Johns Hopkins University.

Allan Schnaiberg, assistant professor of sociology and urban affairs, Northwestern University.

Peter Schrag, editor, *Change* magazine; editor-at-large, *Saturday Review.*

Joyce R. Starr, graduate student in Sociology, Northwestern University.

Gerald D. Suttles, associate professor of sociology, The University of Chicago.

Jon Van Til, Department of Sociology and Anthropology, Swarthmore College.

Sally Bould Van Til, Department of Sociology, Bryn Mawr College.

John Walton, associate professor of sociology and urban affairs, Northwestern University.

James Q. Wilson, professor of government and member of the faculty of public administration, Harvard University.

John Zeisel, assistant professor in the sociology of design, Harvard University; partner, Brolin-Zeisel Research and Design Associates, New York.

CONTENTS

chapter 7. the changing character of urban politics 451

chapter 8. cities and the future 629

PREfACE

A few years ago, due to the efforts of Scott Greer and David Minar, the departments of sociology and political science at Northwestern University initiated a
series of summer programs dealing with the urban phenomenon. These annual
sessions, which bear the name "Institute on Urbanism and Urbanization," typically attract a variety of undergraduate and graduate students from colleges in
the area as well as people from the local community.

During the summer of 1970, we found ourselves co-teaching one of these
institutes. We had individually offered such courses during the regular school
year, but team teaching and the variety of student interests allowed the kind of
interaction of ideas which suggested many interesting avenues for improvement.
Among these, we felt, was the possibility of bringing together under one cover a
new and balanced set of materials that would better reflect contemporary orientations to this field, which has changed so rapidly in recent years.

Although notable exceptions exist, our survey of the literature on cities
suggests that most books, especially readers, are either too issue-oriented (overly
topical) or are heavyweight collections apparently designed for technical use by
graduate students and practicing urban scholars. Many of these books and readers
tend to be static in their approach to cities; they are not particularly oriented to
change processes. Also, some of these offerings try to touch all or most bases in
the urban field rather than limiting themselves to a managable range of phenomena.

In our attempts to use other anthologies in the urban field, two problems
arise again and again. First, the compilers often include a great deal of older or
classical material. We are not suggesting that a careful reading of Georg Simmel,
Oswald Spengler, or Max Weber would not materially advance one's understanding of cities. But these materials have appeared time and again, and to put them
into yet another anthology seemed to us a waste of time, money, and the opportunity to present newer and equally interesting discussions of some perennial
issues. Second, many editors do not put much of themselves into their books.
These collections often lack an explicit general plan, introductions to the readings,

or an integration of themes, resulting in what the book trade calls a "non-book."

We have tried to avoid these shortcomings in two ways. First, this collection contains an introductory chapter that provides a plan of the themes, their integration, and suggested uses of the material. Following this general orientation, each chapter is introduced by a brief discussion of the articles it contains and how they fit together. Second, we have included a number of essays prepared especially for this volume. This stems from the fact that our survey of the literature revealed an absence of high-quality discussions of several issue areas we felt should be included within our framework. Having identified these areas, we were then fortunate in successfully persuading colleagues with special expertise to write essays that appear here for the first time.

We feel we have improved upon existing books by eliminating or alleviating many of the problems mentioned above.

One of the organizing principles of this book is *change*. This is reflected in the overall organization, which progresses from general views of cities, especially the historical city, to the final chapter, some glimpses into possible futures of cities. We have concentrated on change in other ways, notably by pairing chapters 4 and 5 plus chapters 6 and 7 such that, in the first case, older and then emerging life styles and views of urbanity are presented, and in the second pair of chapters, politics and domination are followed by newer, change-oriented forms of political and social response. This kind of organization permits the reader to follow threads through thematic sections of the book and to appreciate the dynamic character of urban social and political life.

As an adjunct to our change orientation, we have also included articles which deal with a comparative focus on cities—specifically, portraits of urban patterns not customarily found in the western world and descriptions of urban life which help dispel the belief that the United States is unique in its possession of urban problems.

In summary, this volume has grown out of our endeavors to teach about the rapidly changing field of urban studies from a coherent contemporary perspective. The readings cover a broad, yet integrated, range of topics. In each selection we have tried to combine good scholarship with interesting reading. In addition to many recent articles not previously reprinted, we have included original material reflecting some of the most up-to-date thinking on the emerging city. More generally, the emphasis is on change: past to present and present to the foreseeable future. Our principal aim is to provide the student with some understanding of this change process and how it affects his or her city, society, and world. We hope our colleagues and students will find the materials as interesting as have we.

CHAPTER 1

iNTROduCTiON

During the approximately ten thousand years of man's literate history on earth, and probably for a time before that, one ineluctable trend has characterized the organization of his life: he has joined with larger and larger clusters of other men into what we call today *cities*. Man's ability to leave the non-city is based, first of all, on his society's capacity to produce agricultural surplus, for cities are not self-sufficient in that most basic of ways. Over the course of human history, cities have enlarged their food base through conquest and, later, mechanization and scientific discovery; in either case, larger and larger cities resulted. Living as we do in the last half of the twentieth century, we are experiencing a logarithmic growth of urban places not only in the more developed western countries, but also in newly developing nations of the world. Each year a greater proportion of all societies is urbanizing so that the urban life form is becoming overwhelmingly the modal one for man.

The systematic study of cities began not very long ago. It was initiated by Europeans and Americans who were in the main born and raised in nonurban environments. To many of them, the city represented chaos or the potential of chaos, a problem in social disorganization which had to be either wished out of existence or reorganized such that man, requiring the small face-to-face intimate group, could survive in such an alien setting as a fast-paced, impersonal city. Yet to the everlasting credit of these early urban students, many of them (especially the so-called Chicago school in this country) transcended their rural backgrounds, took a realistic look at cities, and started us on the way toward a disciplined study of the urban condition.

Today, most scholars who study cities have been lifelong urban residents—as are the students who read books like this one. Accustomed to this life form since birth, we are attuned, in many important ways, to appreciate its rich diversity. We cannot afford, except in our private moments of fantasy or when we drop out, to escape the realities of urban structures, cultures, and social problems. We may conclude, if we wish, that cities are inherently alien to the nature of man, but we cannot ignore the fact that more and more people in all societies are choosing, or are forced, to live in such conditions.

Over the past ten years, hundreds of books and articles have been published which deal with aspects of the urban environment. Many, if not most, of these publications appeared in response to rapidly shifting foci in urban studies, shifts frequently brought on by public moods, fancies, and the expediencies of practical urban and national politics. Seen in these terms, urban pollution, ghetto riots, and the form and function of the Negro family are good examples of areas where this responsiveness of social science and journalism to the ups and downs of public interest is apparent. And this is a good thing. For, among other benefits, these publications codify and frequently extend this public interest over time, help increase the probability that concerted and effective action may result, and certainly provide rich source materials for countless college classes which deal with the urban scene. What they do not do, in most cases, is address themselves to elements of cities which exist at the most basic level of conceptualization: how urban people view their world; how urban consciousness expands to nonurban environments; how city people adapt their styles of life to the exigencies of urban living, including their dependence upon networks of contacts rather than spatial arrangements; and how hierarchical power relations are organized in the city to produce efficiency and inefficiency, justice or injustice, and the like.

We have assembled these articles because these basic themes form an indispensable part of our approach to the city. The plethora of issue-oriented books now available provide a glimpse of only one side of the urban problem; it is equally important to approach urban phenomena on levels which transcend (or underpin) specific issues, events, or social problems. Indeed, to gain an adequate understanding of these issues, it is necessary to understand some of these broader principles of urban life. To be sure, we have included a considerable amount of material dealing with issues and events, for example, urban riots and the antipollution movement. But we have done our best to integrate these into broader frameworks, to contextualize them in the fabric of our urban imagination.

Further, this collection reflects a growing concern in social science, a comparative perspective on social phenomena. Comparisons are made among many of the articles appearing in this book and between articles and chapters; these relate elements of cities in time and space, and occasionally both, to seek those aspects of cities which transcend the immediate and the narrow and, occasionally, provide a view of causal processes at work.

Third, the book is oriented around the idea of *change*. The title suggests our orientation: cities, like most social facts, are ever-changing entities, growing or declining, rearranging themselves internally, and are intimately tied to the larger societies of which they are a significant part. To the greatest extent possible, we present two sides of many urban situations: "now" and "coming." When this was not done, nevertheless the student should think in those terms.

Fourth, we have tried to include only pieces written for this volume or those that have not yet received enough exposure to have achieved the status of classics. Obviously, some of the articles (for example, those by Childe and Greer) have been around for a while, but they are indispensable. On the other hand, many standard essays, such as those by Louis Wirth on urbanism as a way of life and by Robert E. Park, have been omitted. These are readily available from a number of sources; indeed, many readers which appeared in the 1960s are prefaced by some of these classics.

Finally, we have tried to conclude this anthology with a sense of the future. Not only does prediction and a view of future urban forms follow logically from our orientation toward change, but the last chapter also stimulates the student to exercise his own imagination about the future of cities.

For, as we have said, cities are here to stay; indeed, they may well represent, in broadest perspective, the only significant human life form for the next few hundred years.

HOW TO USE THIS BOOK

Let us begin with some general points about the book, then examine its organization in detail.

First of all, consider the size of this book. Some forty articles plus introductions comprise a formidable task for any student. We suggest you read the Table of Contents carefully, and then read the chapter introductions. Select those chapters or articles which fit your current interests and which best supplement other books you are using. The rest of the reader will always be there, ready for you to go back to, to browse through, when your interests shift or some new urban crisis springs up in this country.

Second, we have tried to balance the book in its level of technicality. Some of the articles are written in a journalistic style, others in a more technical way. The less technical pieces should increase your understanding and your urban vocabulary. We have avoided unduly specialized or esoteric articles, for our orientation is toward understanding basic processes in cities.

Carefully scan each introduction (including this one) before reading articles in a chapter.

This book is organized into four sections, each of which is discussed below in some detail.

I.   Chapters 2 and 3 deal with the concept of *city* and the process of cities in the making, of people becoming urban in residence, and of whole societies urbanizing. Chapter 2 takes the student from the first cities, described by V. Gordon Childe, to what may be the last, Kenneth Boulding's view of cities in the international system of power politics and economics. On the way are selections on cities in newly developing and already developed parts of the world. Taken as a whole, this chapter is a logical introduction to the study of cities wherever or whenever they may exist. And Chapter 3 initiates our focus on change, although it is inherent in the progression of Chapter 2 also, for cities, their residents, and their surrounding societies are and have been in a state of flux, whether in the developed West or the developing Third World.

The introductions to chapters 2 and 3 summarize the contents and suggest salient approaches to the nature and emergence of cities. This unit of two chapters provides a take-off for several different points, among them an extensive study of new cities or cities in new states, the impact of becoming urban on migrants, and out of that a comparison or urban and nonurban milieus in terms of familism, human happiness and satisfaction, and the like. At this point, look at the next section on urban life styles, for many of these same themes are treated in detail there.

II.   Chapters 4 and 5 concern urban living, first in terms of the styles and conditions found in cities, and, second, with relation to patterns of change or trends which various writers feel are occurring in cities. The primary focus of this section is on cities in developed countries, especially the United States.

As noted above, themes which first emerge in section I can be picked up and traced in section II. In particular, the culture and ambience of cities receive some attention in both chapters 4 and 5, the central question being: Are cities unlivable? In Chapter 5, a city is discussed which *seems* to be civil, i.e., tolerant and habitable. Allied with this point, other articles discuss specific aspects of cities, pointing out how differentiated they are internally. Again, this theme, first stated in section I and now repeated, is to remind the student that it is not really valid to speak of "cities" as if they were homogeneous entities. A city is actually many cities—even many small towns in some cases—and certainly a great number of networks defined by mutual interests or conflicts. The richness found in diversity is a basic viewpoint of section II.

III.   Chapters 6 and 7 shift the focus somewhat, for they concern power and social change in cities. Here again, the emphasis is on internal diversity, but the interaction among individuals and the polity and economy becomes one of the central points, along with various arrangements of power relations to be found in cities, especially in the United States. In recent years, riots, social movements, and general urban unrest have been in the headlines more and more often. In this section, we have tried to make these changes more intelligible by showing how they are the result of power relationships and socioeconomic deprivation in cities. Or, put differently, when men lack power, they realize it and their interests are both objectively and subjectively threatened or denied; if this continues long enough, something will happen. What that something is will, of course, vary. Again, the emphasis is on change. Thus, Chapter 7 focuses on emerging processes of power and their effects.

If the student has followed the discussion to this point, he will realize that any number of themes were introduced in section I, described and analyzed in section II, and related to power and social change in section III. For example recent urban migrants are discussed in Chapter 3, characterized in chapters 4 and 5, and related to broad patterns of unrest and political control in chapters 6 and 7. This reader will be most useful when the student adopts this kind of strategy:

follow points through the book as they are developed, discussed, analyzed, and shown to change.

IV. Chapter 8 deals with the future of cities and urban societies. As mentioned before, it is a logical extension to the organization of the book as a whole. Thus, if the student is interested in minority groups who have only recently migrated to cities, he would first read about cities in general in Chapter 2; concentrate on the rural to urban shift in Chapter 3; read the characterizations of, for example, blacks in chapters 4 and 5; study the nature of powerlessness, power, and response in chapters 6 and 7; and conclude, in Chapter 8, with Downs's discussion of the future of the American ghetto. To be sure, not all themes can be threaded so neatly through the book, but the student will soon discover which can be traced in this way, and at the same time he may wish to stop off on the way to delve into some pocket of special interest to him.

Ultimately, any book is a personal statement, even an anthology. The selections in this book are our choice, of course, and we cannot please everyone. We have deemphasized some aspects of cities and emphasized others; for a book to cover everything would be an impossibility. But we feel the themes in this reader are some of the most fundamental and interesting for a clear and comprehensive understanding of modern cities. We hope the student will agree.

CHAPTER 2

CONTENTS

CONCEPTS of THE CITY

The concept "city" has not always meant what it does today, and probably will not mean the same thing in the future. As we use the term now, a city consists of a relatively dense population living off an agricultural hinterland, with or without manufacturing, but with some form of interdependence and specialization of functions. Cities have not been with us for long, especially when the entire sweep of man's existence is taken into account. It is this variability of viewpoints with which Chapter 2 deals, and the articles here are arranged in a logical progression of concepts of cities from pre-industrial roots in the late Bronze Age to modern megalopoli intimately tied to worldwide systems of politics, economics, and warfare.

The first selection, V. Gordon Childe's "The Urban Revolution" deals with the origins of the first cities in the fertile crescent of the Tigris-Euphrates rivers. Childe's books, including *What Happened in History* and *Man Makes Himself*, deal with the same theme in more detail. The earliest cities were apparently concentrations of households in or near a river delta, organized around a ruler who invoked an urban deity (that is, a place god) in whose name he ruled. The growth of a priestly class also provided systems of continuing control, including counting schemes to deal with crops, labor, and the like. Keep in mind that pre-industrial cities—that is, cities before the sixteenth or seventeenth centuries in the West—were dependent on an agricultural system which was, itself, not mechanized. This gave rise to severe limitations on the size a city could attain, and if a city grew beyond the limits of its supporting agricultural hinterland, some form of military conquest was necessary to broaden the food base. Such was the case of Rome: it grew as its hinterland increased through conquest, and also while the area immediately around Rome was stripped bare. Athens in the so-called Golden Age, on the other hand, had a fairly small agricultural area to support it and was, by today's standards, a very small city.

We have come to equate certain concepts in our study of cities, especially the development of industrialization and urbanization. That is, we expect to find that the growth of cities into large metropolitan centers is a function of the in-

creased scale of industrial production and its attendant control structures—
bureaucracies. The article by Rhoads Murphey, "Urbanization in Asia," is a reminder that many different factors are important in the process of urbanization,
among them the residue of colonial administration. A good part of Asia was
colonized by European powers in the nineteenth and twentieth centuries. India
is a prime example and is discussed by Murphey; others include Vietnam (French),
Indonesia (Dutch), and China (various powers). In each case, cities developed
without a wide-scale industrial base to support them. They exist today as monu-
ments to the colonial planter or mercantile class, but they represent urban opportunities for the rural poor nonetheless. This has given rise to the concept of under-
industrialization, or overurbanization—in either case the recognition that in
newly developing nations there are more people in urban places than can
be provided jobs, food, clothing, and shelter. And one should keep in mind
that developed nations, such as the United States, share the same problem,
largely stemming from patterns of systematic discrimination. Africa, Asia, and
Latin America have, at the same time, the most accelerating rates of urbanization, the highest birth rates, and the lowest levels of industrialization in the
world, and all this provides a very different view of urbanization than is found
in the West.

The third article, "The Urban Pattern" by Hans Blumenfeld, analyzes the
modern Western city. One of its central foci is concentration on post-industrial
patterns, i.e., the movement of manufacturing to satellite cities within the larger
metropolitan area and the concentration of service and control functions in the
central city. Allied with this is a view of cities as metropolitan regions encompassing large urban and nonurban hinterlands. It is, in a sense, the city writ large, or,
if one is inclined to the view, the end of the traditional city of factories and tenements and the development of the new city, a large, urbanized region tied together by a shrinking space-time ratio and by the electronics revolution in the
media. These themes are repeated in some detail in articles in chapters 4 and 5,
but it is Blumenfeld's treatment that ties them together into a coherent, predictive picture of the western city.

Finally, Kenneth Boulding's concluding article, "The City as an Element in
the International System," expands our view of cities back to a worldwide perspective. For the nations of the world are increasingly tied together in networks
of economic and political interdependence. To the extent that the city, wherever
it exists, is the focal point of a large area of productivity and political control, it
is also tied thereby quite directly into the international system of relations. Even
more to the point, Boulding shows how former virtues of cities (for example,
they were safer places than rural areas in times past) have changed to detriments,
especially with the advent of aerial warfare. Thus, the city is a kind of pawn in
the system of international power politics. To be sure, Boulding's analysis
is more broadly based than this. In fact, he shows us how certain patterns
are apparently worldwide in scope: the lack of a sense of community in large
cities, the flight from central cities, and the growth of suburbs and exurbs.

His conclusion, an appeal for an urban consciousness and especially for a sense of urban power in the world system, is a logical position if one assumes that cities are, for the foreseeable future, the major significant organized life form for modern man.

1

V. GORDON CHILDE, The Urban Revolution

The concept of "city" is notoriously hard to define. The aim of the present essay is to present the city historically—or rather prehistorically—as the resultant and symbol of a "revolution" that initiated a new economic stage in the evolution of society. The word "revolution" must not of course be taken as denoting a sudden violent catastrophe; it is here used for the culmination of a progressive change in the economic structure and social organization of communities that caused, or was accompanied by, a dramatic increase in the population affected—an increase that would appear as an obvious bend in the population graph were vital statistics available. Just such a bend is observable at the time of the Industrial Revolution in England. Though not demonstrable statistically, comparable changes of direction must have occurred at two earlier points in the demographic history of Britain and other regions. Though perhaps less sharp and less durable, these too should indicate equally revolutionary changes in economy. They may then be regarded likewise as marking transitions between stages in economic and social development.

Sociologists and ethnographers last century classified existing pre-industrial societies in a hierarchy of three evolutionary stages, denominated respectively "savagery," "barbarism" and "civilization." If they be defined by suitable selected criteria, the logical hierarchy of stages can be transformed into a temporal sequence of ages, proved archaeologically to follow one another in the same order wherever they occur. Savagery and barbarism are conveniently recognized and appropriately defined by the methods adopted for procuring food. Savages live exclusively on wild food obtained by collecting, hunting, or fishing. Barbarians on the contrary at least supplement these natural resources by cultivating edible plants and—in the Old World north of the Tropics—also by breeding animals for food.

Throughout the Pleistocene Period—the Paleolithic Age of archaeologists—all known human societies were savage in the foregoing sense, and a few savage tribes have survived in out of the way parts to the present day. In the archaeological record barbarism began less than ten thousand years ago with the Neolithic

V. Gordon Childe, "The Urban Revolution," *Town Planning Review,* vol. 21, no. 1 (April 1950), pp. 3–17. Reprinted by permission.

Age of archaeologists. It thus represents a later, as well as a higher stage, than savagery. Civilization cannot be defined in quite such simple terms. Etymologically the word is connected with "city," and sure enough life in cities begins with this stage. But "city" is itself ambiguous so archaeologists like to use "writing" as a criterion of civilization; it should be easily recognizable and proves to be a reliable index to more profound characters. Note, however, that, because a people is said to be civilized or literate, it does not follow that all its members can read and write, nor that they all lived in cities. Now there is no recorded instance of a community of savages civilizing themselves, adopting urban life or inventing a script. Wherever cities have been built, villages of preliterate farmers existed previously (save perhaps where an already civilized people have colonized uninhabited tracts). So civilization, wherever and whenever it arose, succeeded barbarism.

We have seen that a revolution as here defined should be reflected in the population statistics. In the case of the Urban Revolution the increase was mainly accounted for by the multiplication of the numbers of persons living together, i.e., in a single built-up area. The first cities represented settlement units of hitherto unprecedented size. Of course it was not just their size that constituted their distinctive character. We shall find that by modern standards they appeared ridiculously small and we might meet agglomerations of population today to which the name city would have to be refused. Yet a certain size of settlement and density of population is an essential feature of civilization.

Now the density of population is determined by the food supply which in turn is limited by natural resources, the techniques for their exploitation and the means of transport and food-preservation available. The last factors have proved to be variables in the course of human history, and the technique of obtaining food has already been used to distinguish the consecutive stages termed savagery and barbarism. Under the gathering economy of savagery, population was always exceedingly sparse. In aboriginal America the carrying capacity of normal unimproved land seems to have been from .05 to .10 per square mile. Only under exceptionally favorable conditions did the fishing tribes of the Northwest Pacific coast attain densities of over one human to the square mile. As far as we can guess from the extant remains, population densities of paleolithic and pre-neolithic Europe were less than the normal American. Moreover such hunters and collectors usually live in small roving bands. At best several bands may come together for quite brief periods on ceremonial occasions such as the Australian corroborrees. Only in exceptionally favored regions can fishing tribes establish anything like villages. Some settlements on the Pacific coasts comprised thirty or so substantial and durable houses, accommodating groups of several hundred persons. But even these villages were only occupied during the winter; for the rest of the year their inhabitants dispersed in smaller groups. Nothing comparable has been found in pre-neolithic times in the Old World.

The Neolithic Revolution certainly allowed an expansion of population and enormously increased the carrying capacity of suitable land. On the Pacific

Islands neolithic societies today attain a density of thirty or more persons to the square mile. In pre-Columbian North America, however, where the land is not obviously restricted by surrounding seas, the maximum density recorded is just under two to the square mile.

Neolithic farmers could of course, and certainly did, live together in permanent villages, though, owing to the extravagent rural economy generally practiced, unless the crops were watered by irrigation, the villages had to be shifted at least every twenty years. But on the whole the growth of population was not reflected so much in the enlargement of the settlement unit as in a multiplication of settlements. In ethnography neolithic villages can boast only a few hundred inhabitants (a couple of *pueblos* in New Mexico house over a thousand, but perhaps they cannot be regarded as neolithic). In prehistoric Europe the largest neolithic village yet known, Barkaer in Jutland, comprised fifty-two small, one-roomed dwellings, but sixteen to thirty houses was a more normal figure; so the average local group in neolithic times would average 200 to 400 members.

These low figures are of course the result of technical limitations. In the absence of wheeled vehicles and roads for the transport of bulky crops men had to live within easy walking distance of their cultivations. At the same time the normal rural economy of the Neolithic Age, what is now termed slash-and-burn or *jhumming*, condemns much more than half the arable land to lie fallow so that large areas were required. As soon as the population of a settlement rose above the numbers that could be supported from the accessible land, the excess had to hive off and found a new settlement.

The Neolithic Revolution had other consequences beside increasing the population, and their exploitation might in the end help to provide for the surplus increase. The new economy allowed, and indeed required, the farmer to produce every year more food than was needed to keep him and his family alive. In other words it made possible the regular production of a social surplus. Owing to the low efficiency of neolithic technique, the surplus produced was insignificant at first, but it could be increased till it demanded a reorganization of society.

Now in any Stone Age society, paleolithic or neolithic, savage or barbarian, everybody can at least in theory make at home the few indispensible tools, the modest cloths and the simple ornaments everyone requires. But every member of the local community, not disqualified by age, must contribute actively to the communal food supply by personally collecting, hunting, fishing, gardening or herding. As long as this holds good, there can be no full-time specialists, no persons nor class of persons who depend for their livelihood on food produced by others and secured in exchange for material or immaterial goods or services.

We find indeed today among Stone Age barbarians and even savages expert craftsmen (for instance flint-knappers among the Ona of Tierra del Fuego), men who claim to be experts in magic, and even chiefs. In paleolithic Europe too there is some evidence for magicians and indications of chieftainship in pre-neolithic times. But on closer observation we discover that today these experts are not full-time specialists. The Ona flintworker must spend most of his time hunting; he only adds to his diet and his prestige by making arrowheads for clients who reward him with presents. Similarly a pre-Columbian chief, though entitled to customary gifts and services from his followers, must still personally lead hunting and fishing expeditions and indeed could only maintain his authority by his industry and prowess in these pursuits. The same holds good of barbarian societies that are still in the neolithic stage, like the Polynesians where industry in gardening takes the place of prowess in hunting. The reason is that there simply will not be enough food to go round unless every member of the group contributes to the supply. The social surplus is not big enough to feed idle mouths.

Social division of labor, save those rudiments imposed by age and sex, is thus impossible. On the contrary community of employment, the common absorption in obtaining food by similar devices guarantees a certain solidarity to the group. For cooperation is essential to secure food and shelter and for defense against foes, human and subhuman. This identity of economic interests and pursuits is echoed and magnified by identity of language, custom and belief; rigid conformity is enforced as effectively as industry in the common quest for food. But conformity and industrious cooperation need no state organization to maintain them. The local group usually consists either of a single clan (persons who believe themselves descended from a common ancestor or who have earned a mystical claim to such descent by ceremonial adoption) or a group of clans related by habitual intermarriage. And the sentiment of kinship is reinforced or supplemented by common rites focused on some ancestral shrine or sacred place. Archaeology can provide no evidence for kinship organization, but shrines occupied the central place in preliterate villages in Mesopotamia, and the long barrow, a collective tomb that overlooks the presumed site of most neolithic villages in Britain, may well have been also the ancestral shrine on which converged the emotions and ceremonial activities of the villagers below. However, the solidarity thus idealized and concretely symbolized is really based on the same principles as that of a pack of wolves or a herd of sheep; Durkheim has called it "mechanical."

Now among some advanced barbarians (for instance tattooers or woodcarvers among the Maori) still technologically neolithic we find expert craftsmen tending towards the status of full-time professionals, but only at the cost of breaking away from the local community. If no single village can produce a surplus large enough to feed a full-time specialist all the year round, each should produce enough to keep him a week or so. By going round from village to village an expert might thus live entirely from his craft. Such itinerants will lose their membership of the sedentary kinship group. They may in the end form an analogous organization of their own—a craft clan, which, if it remain hereditary, may become a caste, or, if it recruit its members mainly by adoption (apprenticeship throughout Antiquity and the Middle Ages was just temporary adoption), may turn into a guild. But such specialists, by emancipation from kinship ties, have also forfeited the protection of the kinship organization which alone, under barbarism, guaranteed to its members security of person and property. Society must be reorganized to accommodate and protect them.

In pre-history specialization of labor presumably began with similar itinerant experts. Archaeological proof is hardly to be expected, but in ethnography metalworkers are nearly always full-time specialists. And in Europe at the beginning of the Bronze Age metal seems to have been worked and purveyed by perambulating smiths who seem to have functioned like tinkers and other itinerants of much more recent times. Though there is no such positive evidence, the same probably happened in Asia at the beginning of metallurgy. There must of course have been, in addition, other specialist craftsmen whom, as the Polynesian example warns us, archaeologists could not recognize because they worked in perishable materials. One result of the Urban Revolution will be to rescue such specialists from nomadism and to guarantee them security in a new social organization.

About 5,000 years ago irrigation cultivation (combined with stock-breeding and fishing) in the valleys of the Nile, the Tigris-Euphrates, and the Indus had begun to yield a social surplus, large enough to support a number of resident specialists who were themselves released from food-production. Water-transport, supplemented in Mesopotamia and the Indus valley by wheeled vehicles and even in Egypt by pack animals, made it easy to gather food stuffs at a few centers. At the same time dependence on river water for the irrigation of the crops restricted the cultivable areas while the necessity of canalizing the water and protecting habitations against annual floods encouraged the aggregation of population. Thus arose the first cities—units of settlement ten times as great as any known neolithic village. It can be argued that all cities in the old world are offshoots of those of Egypt, Mesopotamia and the Indus basin. So the latter need not be taken into account if a minimum definition of civilization is to be inferred from a comparison of its independent manifestations.

But some three millennia later cities arose in Central America, and it is impossible to prove that the Mayas owed anything directly to the urban civilizations of the Old World. Their achievements must therefore be taken into account in our comparison, and their inclusion seriously complicates the task of defining the essential preconditions for the Urban Revolution. In the Old World the rural economy which yielded the surplus was based on the cultivation of cereals combined with stock-breeding. But this economy had been made more efficient as a result of the adoption of irrigation (allowing cultivation without prolonged fallow periods) and of important inventions and discoveries—metallurgy, the plough, the sailing boat and the wheel. None of these devices was known to the Mayas; they bred no animals for milk or meat; though they cultivated the cereal maize, they used the same sort of slash-and-burn method as neolithic farmers in prehistoric Europe or in the Pacific Islands today. Hence the minimum definition of a city, the greatest factor common to the Old World and the New, will be substantially reduced and impoverished by the inclusion of the Maya. Nevertheless, ten rather abstract criteria, all deducible from archaeological data, serve to distinguish even the earliest cities from any older or contemporary village.

1.   In point of size the first cities must have been more extensive and more densely populated than any previous settlements, although considerably smaller than many villages today. It is indeed only in Mesopotamia and India that the first urban populations can be estimated with any confidence or precision. There excavation has been sufficiently extensive and intensive to reveal both the total area and the density of building in sample quarters and in both respects has disclosed significant agreement with the less industrialized Oriental cities today. The population of Sumerian cities, thus calculated, ranged between 7,000 and 20,000; Harappa and Mohenjo-daro in the Indus valley must have approximated to the higher figure. We can only infer that Egyptian and Maya cities were of comparable magnitude from the scale of public works, presumably executed by urban populations.

2.   In composition and function the urban population already differed from that of any village. Very likely indeed most citizens were still also peasants, harvesting the lands and waters adjacent to the city. But all cities must have accommodated in addition classes who did not themselves procure their own food by agriculture, stock-breeding, fishing, or collecting—full-time specialist craftsmen, transport workers, merchants, officials, and priests. All these were of course supported by the surplus produced by the peasants living in the city and in dependent villages, but they did not secure their share directly by exchanging their products or services for grains or fish with individual peasants.

3.   Each primary producer paid over the tiny surplus he could wring from the soil with his still very limited technical equipment as tithe or tax to an imaginary deity or a divine king who thus concentrated the surplus. Without this concentration, owing to the low productivity of the rural economy, no effective capital would have been available.

4.   Truly monumental public buildings not only distinguish each known city from any village but also symbolize the concentration of the social surplus. Every Sumerian city was from the first dominated by one or more stately temples, centrally situated on a brick platform raised above the surrounding dwellings and usually connected with an artificial mountain, the staged tower or ziggurat. But attached to the temples, were workshops and magazines, and an important appurtenance of each principal temple was a great granary. Harappa, in the Indus basin, was dominated by an artificial citadel, girt with a massive rampart of kiln-baked bricks, containing presumably a palace and immediately overlooking an enormous granary and the barracks of artisans. No early temples nor palaces have been excavated in

Egypt, but the whole Nile valley was dominated by the gigantic tombs of the divine pharoahs while royal granaries are attested from the literary record. Finally the Maya cities are known almost exclusively from the temples and pyramids of sculptured stone round which they grew up.

Hence in Sumer the social surplus was first effectively concentrated in the hands of a god and stored in his granary. That was probably true in Central America while in Egypt the pharaoh (king) was himself a god. But of course the imaginary deities were served by quite real priests who, besides celebrating elaborate and often sanguinary rites in their honor, administered their divine masters' earthly estates. In Sumer indeed the god very soon, if not even before the revolution, shared his wealth and power with a mortal viceregent, the "City-King," who acted as civil ruler and leader in war. The divine pharaoh was naturally assisted by a whole hierarchy of officials.

5.   All those not engaged in food-production were of course supported in the first instance by the surplus accumulated in temple or royal granaries and were thus dependent on temple or court. But naturally priests, civil and military leaders and officials absorbed a major share of the concentrated surplus and thus formed a "ruling class." Unlike a paleolithic magician or a neolithic chief, they were, as an Egyptian scribe actually put it, "exempt from all manual tasks." On the other hand, the lower classes were not only guaranteed peace and security, but were relieved from intellectual tasks which many find more irksome than any physical labor. Besides reassuring the masses that the sun was going to rise next day and the river would flood again next year (people who have not five thousand years of recorded experience of natural uniformities behind them are really worried about such matters!), the ruling classes did confer substantial benefits upon their subjects in the way of planning and organization.

6.   They were in fact compelled to invent systems of recording and exact, but practically useful, sciences. The mere administration of the vast revenues of a Sumerian temple or an Egyptian pharaoh by a perpetual corporation of priests or officials obliged its members to devise conventional methods of recording that should be intelligible to all their colleagues and successors, that is, to invent systems of writing and numeral notation. Writing is thus a significant, as well as a convenient, mark of civilization. But while writing is a trait common to Egypt, Mesopotamia, the Indus valley and Central America, the characters themselves were different in each region and so were the normal writing materials—papyrus in Egypt, clay in Mesopotamia. The engraved seals or stelae that provide the sole extant evidence for early Indus and Maya writing no more represent the normal vehicles for the scripts than do the comparable documents from Egypt and Sumer.

7.   The invention of writing—or shall we say the inventions of scripts—enabled the leisured clerks to proceed to the elaboration of exact and pre-

dictive sciences—arithmetic, geometry and astronomy. Obviously beneficial and explicitly attested by the Egyptian and Maya documents was the correct determination of the tropic year and the creation of a calendar, for it enabled the rulers to regulate successfully the cycle of agricultural operations. But once more the Egyptian, Maya and Babylonian calendars were as different as any systems based on a single natural unit could be. Calendrical and mathematical sciences are common features of the earliest civilizations and they too are corollaries of the archaeologists' criterion, writing.

8.   Other specialists, supported by the concentrated social surplus, gave a new direction to artistic expression. Savages even in paleolithic times had tried, sometimes with astonishing success, to depict animals and even men as they saw them—concretely and naturalistically. Neolithic peasants never did that; they hardly ever tried to represent natural objects, but preferred to symbolize them by abstract geometrical patterns which at most may suggest by a few traits a fantastical man or beast or plant. But Egyptian, Sumerian, Indus and Maya artist-craftsmen—full-time sculptors, painters, or seal-engravers—began once more to carve, model or draw likenesses of persons or things, but no longer with the naive naturalism of the hunter, but according to conceptualized and sophisticated styles which differ in each of the four urban centers.

9.   A further part of the concentrated social surplus was used to pay for the importation of raw materials, needed for industry or cult and not available locally. Regular "foreign" trade over quite long distances was a feature of all early civilizations and, though common enough among barbarians later, is not certainly attested in the Old World before 3000 B.C. nor in the New before the Maya "empire." Thereafter regular trade extended from Egypt at least as far as Byblos on the Syrian coast while Mesopotamia was related by commerce with the Indus valley. While the objects of international trade were at first mainly "luxuries," they already included industrial materials, in the Old World notably metal the place of which in the New was perhaps taken by obsidian. To this extent the first cities were dependent for vital materials on long distance trade as no neolithic village ever was.

10.   So in the city, specialist craftsmen were both provided with raw materials needed for the employment of their skill and also guaranteed security in a state organization based now on residence rather than kinship. Itinerancy was no longer obligatory. The city was a community to which a craftsman could belong politically as well as economically.

Yet in return for security they became dependent on temple or court and were relegated to the lower classes. The peasant masses gained even less material advantages; in Egypt for instance metal did not replace the old stone and wood tools for agricultural work. Yet, however imperfectly, even the earliest urban communities must have been held together by a short of solidarity missing from any neolithic village. Peasants, craftsmen, priests and rulers form a community, not only by reason of identity of language and belief, but also because each performs mutually complementary functions, needed for the well-being (as redefined under civilization) of the whole. In fact the earliest cities illustrate a first approximation to an organic solidarity based upon a functional complementarity and interdependence between all its members such as subsist between the constituent cells of an organism. Of course this was only a very distant approximation. However necessary the concentration of the surplus really were with the existing forces of production, there seemed a glaring conflict on economic interests between the tiny ruling class, who annexed the bulk of the social surplus, and the vast majority who were left with a bare subsistence and effectively excluded from the spiritual benefits of civilization. So solidarity had still to be maintained by the ideological devices appropriate to the mechanical solidarity of barbarism as expressed in the pre-eminence of the temple or the sepulchral shrine, and now supplemented by the force of the new state organization. There could be no room for sceptics or sectaries in the oldest cities.

These ten traits exhaust the factors common to the oldest cities that archaeology, at best helped out with fragmentary and often ambiguous written sources, can detect. No specific elements of town planning for example can be proved characteristic of all such cities; for on the one hand the Egyptian and Maya cities have not yet been excavated; on the other neolithic villages were often walled, an elaborate system of sewers drained the Orcadian hamlet of Skara Brae; two-storeyed houses were built in pre-Columbian *pueblos*, and so on.

The common factors are quite abstract. Concretely Egyptian, Sumerian, Indus and Maya civilizations were as different as the plans of their temples, the signs of their scripts and their artistic conventions. In view of this divergence and because there is so far no evidence for a temporal priority of one Old World center (for instance, Egypt) over the rest nor yet for contact between Central America and any other urban center, the four revolutions just considered may be regarded as mutually independent. On the contrary, all later civilizations in the Old World may in a sense be regarded as lineal descendents of those of Egypt, Mesopotamia, or the Indus.

But this was not a case of like producing like. The maritime civilizations of Bronze Age Crete or classical Greece for example, to say nothing of our own, differ more from their reputed ancestors than these did among themselves. But the urban revolutions that gave them birth did not start from scratch. They could and probably did draw upon the capital accumulated in the three allegedly primary centers. That is most obvious in the case of cultural capital. Even today we use the Egyptians' calendar and the Sumerians' divisions of the day and the hour. Our European ancestors did not have to invent for themselves these divisions of time nor repeat the observations on which they are based; they took over—and very slightly improved—systems elaborated 5,000 years ago! But the same is in a sense true of material capital as well. The Egyptians, the Sumerians and the Indus people had accumulated vast reserves of surplus food. At the same time they had to import from abroad necessary raw materials like metals and building timber as well as "luxuries." Communities controlling these natural resources could in exchange claim a slice of the urban surplus. They could use it as capital to support full-time specialists—craftsmen or rulers—until the latters' achievement in technique and organization had so enriched barbarian economies that they too could produce a substantial surplus in their turn.

2

RHOADS MURPHEY, Urbanization in Asia

Throughout most if not all of recorded history, there seems little question that there have been and still are more people living in cities, and more cities, in Asia than in any other continent. Until about 1750 or 1800, it seems likely that Asia (used throughout this paper to refer only to the area sometimes called "monsoon Asia," from Pakistan on the west to Indonesia and Japan on the east, but excluding Soviet Asia) contained more cities and more city-dwellers than the rest of the world combined, a position which it may have regained by the end of the present century if current rates of population growth and of urbanization continue. Indeed one of the primary reasons for distinguishing the area referred to as "monsoon Asia" from the Arab-Turkish-Persian world of the Middle East and from the areas now included in Soviet Asia is the density of its population and the importance of an urban-centered "great tradition," in Robert Redfield's phrase. Monsoon Asia has had so little common cultural ground with the rest of the Asian continent that it is both arbitrary and misleading to lump them together in almost any analysis of human institutions. This is so despite the fact that without much question the world's earliest true cities (as opposed to agricultural villages) arose in Asian Mesopotamia or in the Levantine uplands just west of it, and the probability that the rise of the first genuine cities in monsoon Asia owed something to direct or indirect contact with the earlier Mesopotamian model. But with the emergence of a civilized (literally, city-based) tradition in monsoon Asia, culture contact with the Middle East appears to have dwindled into relative insignificance (with the qualified exception of India) and the "great traditions" of south and east Asia matured and endured largely in isolation from the rest of the world. When external contact finally became of

Rhoads Murphey, "Urbanization in Asia," *Ekistics*, vol. 21, no. 122 (January 1966), pp. 8–17 Reprinted by permission. This paper was delivered during a conference on International and Comparative Urban Studies held at Rutgers—The State University in June 1965, under the auspices of the Rutgers Committee on International Education and the Urban Studies Center.

major importance, it was with the probings, colonialism, and traders of Europe and America, and it is this impact which has left the greatest marks on contemporary south and east Asia, most strikingly and perhaps most importantly in its cities.

Our knowledge of Asian urbanization is far from being proportional to its importance on the world scale. We cannot even measure with any precision what the total Asian urban population is, let alone delineate with assurance the factors responsible for its past and present growth or project its likely future shape. We are hampered both by inadequate data, reflecting imperfect census systems, and by a relative paucity of published studies. Present knowledge is, however, grossly uneven. Japan, with relatively complete and accurate data and with a history of detailed study by Japanese scholars, is in a class by itself in this as in so many other respects. Urbanization in India is more accurately measured and better analyzed and understood than in most other Asian countries apart from Japan. But China, which may currently contain more cities and more city-dwellers than any country in the world, is plagued by gross shortages of hard data of every kind, and has been given very little attention by students of urbanization. The same is true of Indonesia, the third most populous nation in Asia with a total population well over 100 million—how much over and how much of the total should be regarded as urban are not accurately known. China and Indonesia, in fact, illustrate particularly pointedly the data limitations which confront the student of Asian urbanization, especially by contrast with the relative wealth and reliability of census information in the West. It is not merely that precise population totals are often lacking, but that the wide spread and variety of demographic information provided for at least the past several decades by many Western censuses is simply not available for most of Asia.

Nevertheless, it seems reasonably clear that at least a third of the present world total of urban population is now in Asia (as defined above), no matter how "urban" may be defined, but that the *degree* of urbanization in Asia is still considerably lower than in Europe or North America, since well over half of the world's total population is Asian. In neither respect—the total number of urban dwellers or the degree or urbanization—is there a reasonable correlation, by Western standards, with the absolute amount or the proportional share of industrialization, or with per capita incomes. This suggests two apparently contradictory conclusions: that most of Asia is "overurbanized," and that urbanization in Asia is still in its early stages, with a much higher degree of urbanization clearly in prospect as industrialization and commercialization gather momentum and as the presently very high rates of urbanization continue. Indeed perhaps the most striking feature of Asian cities in the two decades since the end of World War II is their uniquely rapid growth, a phenomenon which has understandably led to both of the above conclusions. Their contradictory nature can, unfortunately, be rationalized only by assuming (as there are ample grounds for doing) that in most Asian cities living conditions will continue to deteriorate before they can improve. It may well be true that Asian urbanization has outrun its industrial-commercial base, which is the essence of the "overurbanization" argument, but this is not sufficient grounds for assuming either that this process will not continue, or that there is somehow a better viable alternative open to societies and economies which we fervently hope are already engaged in the inevitably painful process of economic growth and transformation. These and other general considerations will be discussed more fully below.

Apart from the simple shortage of reliable census figures in many Asian countries, the student or urbanization is also plagued by varying census definitions of "urban." This is of course a familiar problem even in the Western world, but it does grossly hamper comparability, and even within a single national unit may give rise to perplexing ambiguity. The varying definitions of "urban" are not however purely arbitrary, but reflect real and important differences. Probably the most important of these revolves around the nature of agricultural land use and settlement in Asia, which for the most part follow patterns distinct from any in the West. Many Asian settlements with populations well over 2,000 (the lower limit of the "urban" category in the United States census) are almost exclusively agricultural in function and include or perform little or none of the functions commonly regarded as urban. In recognition of this, the Indian census sets the lower limit of the "urban" category in population terms at 5,000, although it is recognized that some genuinely urban settlements may thereby be excluded. The Chinese census, on the other hand, in an attempt to adjust to a similar reality, stresses function as well as population size, setting a lower limit numerically at 2,000 but including as urban many smaller settlements whose functions are clearly urban in nature—transport or small mining or manufacturing centers, for example—while excluding larger places which are primarily agricultural villages. But no census system except the Japanese takes account of another factor which also helps to distinguish Asian cities—the inclusion within the urban area—whether empirically or arbitrarily defined—of significant amounts of agricultural land and of agricultural workers. Such intra-urban land is, of course, worked extremely intensively and population densities associated with it may be at an urban or near-urban level, but it is nevertheless probably misleading to lump population figures from such areas with those from the functionally separate city.

There is the further problem of defining the spatial limits of a city for census purposes. Traditional Asian cities were relatively sharply distinct from surrounding rural areas in spatial terms, and in probably the majority of the Asian cities of the present the rural-urban line is easier to draw than in almost any present Western city. But the tremendously high rate of urbanization characteristic of Asia especially during the past two decades, the beginnings of the kind of "transport revolution" which helped to transform Western cities, and the rise or further expansion of nearly thirty Asian cities in the million class have meant that "urban sprawl" is no longer a Western monopoly. It is at least as difficult now to make a neat census delineation of the largest Asian cities as it is for large Western cities. Tokyo and Calcutta represent the extremes; "greater Calcutta" and "greater Tokyo" are both in fact megalopolises, each including within a single contiguous urban area what were once several separate cities and making it really impossible to draw an unambiguous line around the spatial limits of either conurbation, or even around the limits of the "urban sprawl" at the peripheries, which tends increasingly to melt gradually into a rural-urban continuum along the Hooghly or around the shores of Tokyo Bay and the edges of the Tokyo basin. Such problems may be appropriate enough for Tokyo, as indisputably the world's largest city, or for Calcutta as an acknowledged urban giant, but they are beginning to be apparent or are already far advanced in many other Asian cities, notably Bombay, Karachi, Madras, Delhi, Singapore, Kuala Lumpur, Djakarta, Manila, and Osaka. In general, "urban" must be taken as what each national census says it is, while recognizing that this is not a uniform or necessarily accurate or reliable guide to reality.

One final difficulty which hampers the search for accurate and complete urban data in Asia is the very large and continuing role played by rural-urban migration. Almost every large Asian city has apparently owed half or more of its recent rapid growth to migration. But even so general a statement must be qualified, since the nature of migration makes accurate counting difficult and since in most Asian cities it is clear that many if not most migrants continue to maintain close ties with their rural origins and periodically return there; apart from this, there appears to be a significant though largely unmeasured amount of attrition which means that *net permanent* migration is less, to an undetermined extent, than gross migration as it might be revealed by a census or sample taken at any one time. As one illustration of the indeterminate or perhaps the qualified nature, both of rural-urban migration in Asia and of the completeness and validity of available data on it, one may cite the common Indian (and traditional Chinese) practice of giving one's ancestral village as place of origin or even of birth on the part of people who are unambiguously urban. At least in the Indian case, this is not entirely disingenuous since it is relatively common for urban women to go back to their villages to bear children and to return to the city domicile with their infants a few months after parturition. But uncertainties or ambiguities like these make it impossible to compile complete and accurate data on the role of migration in the growth of most Asian cities, and hence, given the admitted importance of that role, one is obliged to treat urban census figures with caution.

The reader should not, however, be left with the impression that there are no trustworthy data on Asian urbanization. Whatever their shortcomings, the data available afford students of urbanization ample opportunity to explore a field which Western scholars in particular have neglected in terms of its importance. The city has played an enormously significant role in both the traditional Asian societies of the past and in their current transformation, and any thorough understanding of the Asian half of the world must take full account of the urban factor. For students of urbanization per se, the Asian experience, past and present, offers an impressively wide and varied field which must be explored not merely for comparison with the Western experience but in order to understand the generic nature of cities. Through most of recorded history, Asia has bred more urbanism than the rest of the world. Its present rapid urbanization will not necessarily merely repeat the outlines of what has been called "the second urban revolution" in the West during the past two centuries; the urban revolution which now appears to be in progress in Asia is still in its early stages and will be shaped by Asian cultural and economic circumstances as well as by originally European innovations in manufacturing, trade, and transport.

The traditional Asian city was predominantly a political and cultural phenomenon rather than an economic one. The capitals and provincial administrative centers of the great Asian empires in China, India, Japan, and Southeast Asia functioned and were consciously intended as microcosms of the national policy—symbols of authority, legitimacy, and power, creators and molders of literate culture, seats of the dominant religious ideology, and resplendent thrones for the Great Tradition. Commercial and industrial functions were decidedly secondary, almost incidental, and were often in any case under varying degrees of control or manipulation by the state, whose chief monument was the city itself. Sites for such cities were chosen more with an eye to their administrative functions than to commercial advantage. Except for insular Japan (where productive and hence populous level land hugs the sea) and insular southeast Asia, traditional Asian cities were almost exclusively confined to inland locations from which they could best administer and control the territory of the state or best ensure its defense against incursion across what was regarded as the chief exposed frontier. Ch'ang An, Peking, and Delhi are classic examples of the former; Loyang, Nanking, Pataliputra, Ava, Ayuthia, Angkor, Polonnaruwa, and Jogjakarta of the latter. Cities were both sited and planned so as to ensure an appropriate symbolization of legitimate authority. In China and periodically in India the cities were walled (indeed the common Chinese word for *city* meant and still means also wall), not merely for protection but as a further mark of imperial or administrative sanction. City plans were in turn shaped by the great gates, one at each of the four cardinal points of the compass, from which major streets led to a center where some piece of monumental building—a drum tower, a temple, an array of government offices or troop barracks—further reinforced the symbol of authority. Commerce and manufacturing there certainly were, but although their absolute amounts were large, their relative importance rarely rivalled that of administration as the chief urban function, including the administration of trade; and commerce did not breed as in the West any significant group of independent entrepreneurs. In Japan, where cities were not walled, and in Southeast Asia where walling was at best inconsistent, the traditional city nevertheless functioned primarily as an administrative, ceremonial, and symbolic center rather than as a base for trade.

Cities of the sort described contrast forcibly with the urban type which has been dominant in the West for most of the past two or three millennia. At the beginning of the Western tradition, the cities of classical Greece were sea-oriented and trade-oriented, as were the city colonies which the Greeks established elsewhere on the shores of the Mediterranean. Even Rome, although it became the capital of a huge empire and thus came to play both a real and a symbolic role as a center of authority and administration, was at best a hybrid in that trade remained one of its important functions through its maritime link with the port of Ostia and its incorporation of the commerce-centered Greek Mediterranean. But the greatest cities of medieval Europe were not the cathedral towns or the seats of royal power but the centers of trade—Venice, Genoa, Florence, Hamburg, Bruges—and London and Paris as commercial foci rather than as political capitals. The distinction has been preserved to the present in the case of London, where "the City," until the eighteenth century a geographically separate entity, is at least symbolically still set off from the seat of political authority at Westminster farther up the Thames. With the Age of the Discoveries, the accelerated revival of trade, and the coming of technological revolutions in agriculture, transport, and manufacturing, the Western city became and remains predominantly an economic phenomenon and with overwhelmingly economic functions.

In Asia, what was clearly a Western kind of city, derived directly from Western experience, was in effect imported by the expanding Europeans who moved eastward in the immediate wake of the discoveries in search of trade. Their early accounts of what they observed in Asia, and of their dealings with Asian powers, have left us in fact with some of our most valuable material on the traditional Asian city, as well as on the early growth of the new kind of city which they, as entrepreneurs par excellence, began to construct on the maritime fringes of the Asian empires. They chose sites with an eye to commercial advantage in terms of overseas trade, sites which could best tap the parts of each country most productive of goods for export and which could at the same time be reached by ocean-going ships. They were interested, in other words, in the kind of access which had been of little or no concern to the builders of most traditional Asian cities; and from the nucleus of originally small trading factories, often with forts to protect them, there grew up on these sites the great majority of Asia's present large cities outside of Japan. Even in Japan, however, the growth and nature of Kobe and Yokohama link them generically to some degree with Bombay, Calcutta, Singapore, and the other foreign-founded or foreign-dominated port cities where almost all of Asia's urban growth has been concentrated during the past three centuries. Tokyo, Nagoya, and Osaka too, Japan's three urban giants, grew in considerable part along similar lines and for the same reasons: as booming centers of an expanding trade between Asia and the West, and increasingly as little urban islands of Europe-in-Asia. For it was in these port cities, from Karachi to Batavia to Dairen, that the basic institutions of post-Renaissance Europe were planted: the sanctity and freedom of private property, the virtues of free enterprise, the power and self-satisfaction of capital, and the battery of techniques which had burgeoned in Europe to carry on the business of the new urban-centered world—stock companies, agency houses, bills of exchange, banking and insurance facilities, legal safeguards and sanctions for the protection of enterprise and property, and the vastly improved means of transport which were necessary for the expanding trade which gave these cities life.

The functions which these cities performed, and the institutional structure on which they rested, were largely new to Asia, which had traditionally lacked both the economic and the institutional infrastructure for the kind of commercial enterprise which Europeans built. Physically and in their morphology the new port cities clearly revealed their Western and colonial origins. In most of them Westerners and Asians were spatially segregated for housing, with accompanying differences not only in street development and architecture but in levels of living and their spatial manifestations. Urban skylines came to be dominated by larger buildings in almost purely European or American style, and although the populations of all of them rapidly became and remained predominantly Asian, the look of at least the cities' centers was and remains unmistakably Western. The principal business of these new urban concentrations was overseas trade, and they were virtually all therefore port cities; but since they also needed to maximize access to their commercial hinterlands they often arose on or near the lower courses of navigable rivers. This in turn created increasing problems for many of them as the size of ocean-going vessels increased and as deltaic harbors became less and less adequate. But so long as ocean-going ships could reach them, with the help of assiduous dredging, the advantage of combined landward and seaward access and the commercial productivity of the areas which relatively easy access by water made tributary to each city were strong enough to offset the difficulties of their immediate sites. Only Bombay, Singapore, Manila, Hong Kong, Tsingtao, and Dairen, blessed with excellent natural harbors, escaped from such site problems, although in the cases of Bombay and Tsingtao at the sacrifice of easy access to their hinterlands. River valleys and their deltas are commonly productive places, in Asia as elsewhere, and the commercial opportunities which they presented were powerful attractions despite the navigational hazards.

There were of course important differences between the different port cities which arose as a result of the Western impact, and the list is extensive. But there is enough common ground between them to suggest that they do in fact belong to a single generic type. The largest cities in each Asian country now belong in varying degrees to this type in that they grew out of Western-founded ports and trading factories or in that they owe the bulk of their modern growth not merely to trade with the West but to the successful transplanting onto Asian urban soil of Western institutions and techniques, producing a city which was and is far more Western than traditional Asian. In most of the smaller Asian countries, the single dominant port became and remains not simply primate but the only genuine city in the national unit, in terms both of size and of what Westerners at least would regard as major urban functions. China, India, and Japan continue of course to support a number of large older cities, once the seats of the Great Tradition, including their national capitals. But in most cases, the nature of these older indigenous cities has been transformed to such an extent that the past has been overwhelmed. So the city of Tokyo, in form and in

function, has overwhelmed the old capital of Edo and its rather quaintly preserved castle in the middle of an exploding metropolis which is in many respects
the heir of the Western impact rather than of the traditional *bakufu*. In all of the
countries of Southeast Asia, sensitive new nationalism has still not prevented the
originally colonial or foreign-influenced port city from becoming the national
capital under independence. Not only was there no reasonable alternative, no
other genuine city in any of these smaller countries with situational advantages
and existing urban resources to rival those of the alien port, but the very origin
and growth of nationalism took place in these foreign-dominated cities, where the
Western model was planted for Asians to emulate.

There are now no Asian cities where the traditional form or function has
been preserved unscathed. Indeed perhaps the major significance of the Euro-
pean-dominated port cities since the sixteenth century has been their role as
centers of economic and institutional change which spread from them throughout
the rest of each country and which has penetrated and altered even the urban
citadels of the Great Tradition. Delhi and Peking are fully caught up in the
process of revolutionary economic change, having abandoned their role as administrative guardians of the status quo. Ava, Pegu, Ayuthia, Polonnaruwa, Ch'ang
An, and other inland capital cities of the past exist now only as archaeological
sites. "The Asian city" is now a hybrid, part Asian and part Western, not merely
in terms of its origins but in terms of its present functions, its physical character,
and its morphology. Distinct functional types may of course be discerned, as
among cities in the West, but just as Western cities have grown more and more
alike as economic and technological change [has] accelerated, so Asian cities
become more like one another and more like commercial-industrial cities everywhere else in the world. In general, then, the similarities between Asian and
Western cities have during the past century or two become more striking than
the differences. There are nevertheless some differences remaining, and some
which seem likely to endure.

Some of these have already been touched on at the beginning of this essay.
It is by no means clear, for example, that the West's experience with the process
of urbanization will be duplicated in Asia, nor even that it will necessarily go as
far, in terms of the proportion of the total population living in cities. If we take
a population figure of 20,000 as a safe urban minimum in any area, about 15
percent of the present Asian population is urban, as against about 45 percent in
the United States and about 40 percent in Europe. It is far from certain that most
Asian economies (again with the exception of Japan) can produce or can tolerate
the truly gargantuan urban population which would be represented by 40 percent
of population totals as they will be by the end of the present century. On the
other hand, there is also inadequate basis for assuming that urbanization in Asia
can or will continue only in the same proportion to industrialization and
commercialization as in the Western experience. It has already, in the view of
many, dangerously exceeded that proportion, and yet there are still no significant
signs of a major or permanent slowing of the urbanization rate. No one even

superficially familiar with living conditions in large Asian cities can wholly disregard the argument that most of Asia is already seriously "overurbanized." But this perhaps over-glib term has never been more than vaguely defined, much less proven. Even the present frighteningly crowded cities, lacking in the bare minimum of what is referred to as "social overhead"—housing, water supplies, sanitation, public services—let alone amenities, represent what are probably the most dynamic forces in the process of economic development and exert critically important productive and catalytic effects. Less urbanization would probably be worse than more, either as a symptom of lesser vigor in the economy or as a cause. It is, after all, in cities that economic growth concentrates, especially of the kind which Asia is currently seeking—industrialization. There are no cost-free solutions to the problem of economic development, and short-run misery for some may be an inevitable prelude to longer-run improvement for others, in Asia as in the past experience of the West. With some obvious exceptions, there are probably not more productive uses for capital or for labor in most Asian countries than in the cities, and investment there probably yields quicker returns and with a greater multiplying effect.

Even in the West, the rate and pattern of urbanization and its correlation with industrialization varied widely as between different countries and at different periods, and it is clearly doing so in Asia at present. Urbanization has been most rapid since 1945 in Japan, where Tokyo for example added an average of 300,000 to its population in each of the eleven years following the end of the war. (Tokyo Metropolitan Government, "Problems of an Excessively Growing City and the Development of a Capital Region," Tokyo, 1957, p. 2). This represented to some extent a recovery from the abnormal loss of urban population, especially from Tokyo, during the last years of the war, but more importantly it reflects an unprecedented rapid rate of economic growth, including industrialization. Japan as a whole has probably experienced the most rapid rate of urbanization in the history of the world, especially in the period since 1920. Hong Kong is obviously a special case which is hardly comparable with national units, but as a single city (including Kowloon and contiguous urban areas) its rate of increase in population since 1945 undoubtedly tops the list, and it also represents the peak of urban population density. Its growth, however, has rested on an equally high rate of industrialization. Malaya (including Singapore but excluding the rest of Malaysia) has also been characterized by very rapid urbanization, again in relation to a high rate of economic growth, and the same has been true of Taiwan. Urbanization rates since 1945 have been to varying degrees lower in Indonesia, the Philippines, South Korea, Vietnam, Thailand, Laos, Cambodia, Burma, Ceylon, India and Pakistan, at least in part as a reflection of lower rates of economic growth than in Japan, Malaya, Hong Kong, and Taiwan, although with the possible exceptions of Laos and Cambodia urbanization rates for these countries were nevertheless high by world standards and especially in the cases of India, Pakistan, Thailand, and the Philippines. It is difficult or impossible to measure overall urbanization rates in China since 1945 or since

1949 in the absence of complete or accurate census figures, especially for city populations, even in the one modern census which has been taken in 1953. Reports in the Chinese press do, however, make clear that there has been a phenomenal growth of many cities, some of them virtually new, as a result of the government's policy of concentrating new industrial investment in areas previously neglected. Lanchow, Paotou, and Urumchi, for example, have grown exceptionally rapidly, while Shanghai, still the largest Chinese city, has had its growth controlled by government restrictions on in-migration and by forced removals of what were regarded as excess numbers for return to the countryside or for reassignment to new areas or urban construction and industrialization in the northwest or in Sinkiang.

Except for its larger scale, there does not seem to be anything about this process in Asia which differs significantly from the Western experience, where cities also grew, especially in the earlier stages of modern industrialization and urbanization, more through migration than through natural increase and where there was serious overcrowding ("overurbanization") before employment, housing, and municipal services began to catch up with booming city populations. The difference in Asia, in large part as a result of the much greater scale involved, may be that it will take longer for urban life to reach minimum acceptable standards, or that they may never attain current, let alone future, Western urban standards. Population densities in most Asian cities have already reached enormously high levels, and this may indeed be the most significant single respect in which Asian urbanism differs from urbanism in the West. In India, for example, there are an average of about 150,000 people per square mile in Old Delhi as a whole, at least three times the figure for the most crowded sections of American cities. The worst or most crowded wards of Delhi, Bombay, or Calcutta show almost incredible densities ranging from 300,000 per square mile to over 450,000. Such fantastic crowding of often illiterate city dwellers under slum conditions further increases the difficulties of accurate census taking.

BIBLIOGRAPHY

The foregoing article has attempted to summarize in very general terms some of the salient features of Asian urbanization, the general status of present knowledge of it, and some of the outstanding problems which confront the student. In what follows, an attempt will be made to summarize more specifically the work which has been done on and in the separate regions of Asia, principally from the geographical point of view.

Japan

Japan has been a relatively highly urbanized country for at least the past two centuries. Studies of Japanese urbanization have also been made both more appropriate and more fruitful by the relative abundance of reliable urban data, as one reflection of the sophistication of economic, educational, and technological growth in Japan. Unfortunately from the Western point of view, a great deal of the published material on Japanese urbanism is in Japanese, but some is also available in English and the total amount is rich and varied.

The Association of Japanese Geographers established a Committee on Urban Studies in 1958, whose report titled *Research Materials on Urbanization* was published in 1959 (S. Yamaga, ed., *Toshika Kenyu Shiryo*, Tokyo, 1959). The report is primarily an inventory and bibliography, which has since been updated by S. Kiuchi, one of Japan's leading urban geographers, in an English-language article (S. Kiuchi, "Recent Developments in Japanese Urban Geography," *Annals*, Assoc. of Amer. Geographers, 1963, 93–102). All but a few of the studies mentioned in these two accounts are in Japanese. They include analyses of functional urban types, urbanization rates, rural-urban migration, "metropolitanization," economic base, land use, morphology, urban spread and absorption, urban influences on rural areas, inter-urban communications and flow, wage rates, and land prices. Considerable work has also been done in central place studies, the use of gravity models, densities and intensiveness, industrial location, historical studies of specific cities and city regions, and physical studies of urban sites. Some attention has also been paid by Japanese urban geographers to cross-culture comparison, and S. Kiuchi has in particular stressed the morphological differences between Japanese and Western cities (S. Kiuchi, "Problems of Comparative Urban Geography," in *Tsujimura Taro Sensei Koki Kinen, Chirigaku Rombunshu* ["Geographical Essays in Honor of Prof. Tsujimura's Seve11tieth Birthday"] Tokyo, 1961, pp. 557–73).

Urban planning has been increasingly emphasized in the literature on Japan, as a reflection of the virtual explosion of city populations and urbanized areas during the past two decades, and at least three Japanese journals are devoted to it: *Toshi Mondai*, *Toshi Mondai Kenkyu*, and *Shisei*. Most Japanese cities now have their own planning boards, many of which also carry out extensive studies of their own urban areas. (See for example the voluminous English-language report prepared for a U.N.T.A.B. mission to Japan titled *Basic Materials for the Comprehensive Development Plan of the Hanshin Metropolitan Region*, 2 vols., Osaka, 1960). The "castle-town" origins of many of Japan's cities have been examined in a great variety of published studies, some primarily historical, others which focus on current urban morphology and structure as they have been influenced by earlier forms. (See for example J. W. Hall, "The Castle Town and Japan's Modern Urbanization," *Far Eastern Quarterly*, 1955, 37–56 [English]; K. Tanabe, "The Development of Spatial Structure in Japanese Cities with Regard to Castle Towns," *Science Reports of Tohoku University*, VIIth Series, Geography, no. 8, 1959, pp. 88–105 [English]; T. Matsumoto, "The Structure of Modern Castle Towns," *Geog. Review of Japan*, 1962, 97–112 [articles in this journal are in Japanese, with short English summaries]. But the bulk of Japanese urban studies has been concentrated on contemporary problems, especially on what the Japanese literature refers to as "metropolitanization," the process of big-city expansion, suburbanization, regional concentration, changes in urban structure and morphology as a result of growth and of changes in transport and industrialization, and adjustments in the urban hierarchy. (For a recent review and some general conclusions, see T. Ishimizu, "The Present Status of Urbanization Studies among Japanese Academic Geographers," *Geog. Review of Japan*, 1962, 362–73. See also the forthcoming biographical essay by N. S. Ginsburg, "Urban Geography and Non-Western Areas," to appear in P. Hauser and L. Schnore, eds., *The Study of Urbanization*; I am indebted to Prof. Ginsburg for most of the inventory and bibliographical material presented here, especially on Japan, for which his forthcoming work gives much greater detail).

Western-language studies by geographers on Japanese urbanism are still discouragingly few, especially in proportion to the wealth of data and the impressive contributions of Japanese geographers. J. D. Eyre and J. H. Thompson have studied urban food supply problems and agricultural land use (J. D. Eyre, "Sources of Tokyo's Fresh Food Supply," *Geog. Review*, 1959, 455–76; J. H. Thompson, "Urban Agriculture in Southern Japan," *Economic Geography*, 1957, 224–37), and Eyre has also analyzed the sources of migrants to Tokyo, Osaka, and Nagoya in a series of revealing maps (Eyre, "Regional Variations in Japanese Internal Migration," *Papers of the Michigan Academy*, XLIX, 1964, 271–84). Older studies of urban origins, forms, and distribution by R. B. Hall and G. T. Trewartha are still valuable, (R. B. Hall, "The Cities of Japan; Notes on Distribution and Inherited Forms," *Annals*, Assoc. of Amer. Geographers, 1934, 175–200; G. T. Trewartha, "Japanese Cities: Distribution and Morphology," *Geographical Review*, 1934, 407–17), and P. Scholler has more recently examined modern metropolitan growth (P. Scholler, "Wachstum und Wandlung Japanischer Stadtregionen," *Die Erde*, 1962, 202–34). But of all of the areas of Asia, Japan offers the greatest opportunity to Western students of urbanization, and the least realized. The China field is proportionately much less extensively worked, but Japan is not only more highly urbanized but is equipped with a wide range of dependable data and an impressive body of knowledge as a result of the efforts of Japanese scholars over many years. Western sociologists and anthropologists have begun to make major contributions to our knowledge of Japanese urban life (see most notably R. P. Dore, *City Life in Japan*, Berkeley, 1958, O. Shunsuke, "The Urban Phenomenon in Japan," *Journal of Asian Studies*, 1964, 122–29, and his many references; also T. O. Wilkinson, "A Functional Classification of Japanese Cities, 1920–1955," *Demography*, Spring, 1964), but for other Western students of urbanization this is still largely an untilled and potentially richly rewarding field.

China

While it is true that any study of modern urbanization in China must confront what amounts almost to a vast statistical void, traditional or pre-modern China accumulated without question the most immense body of detailed data on virtually every aspect of human experience that has ever been preserved from any culture. Much of traditional Chinese culture, and especially its literate aspects, centered in the city so that a great deal of the materials which have been preserved deal with urban phenomena. Very little use has yet been made of these data, and especially of the thousands of county (*hsien*) gazeteers. Some indication of their value for urban studies is provided by two revealing studies by S. D. Chang, which focus on the functions and distribution of the *hsien* (county) capitals as administrative centers through two thousand years of Chinese history (S. D. Chang, "Some Aspects of the Urban Geography of the Chinese Hsien Capital," *Annals,* Assoc. of Amer. Geographers, 1961, 23–45; and "Historical Trends in Chinese Urbanization," *Ibid.,* 1963, 109–43). Some limited attention has also been paid to the capital cities and their symbolic role, particularly Peking but also Ch'ang An. (See for example A. Wright, "Symbolism and Function: Reflections on Ch'ang An and Other Great Capitals," forthcoming in *Journal of Asian Studies*, August 1965; ibid., "Ch'ang An, 583–904," in *Historic Ages of the Great Cities*, London, 1964.) The predominantly administrative consequences in institutional and locational terms are also considered and briefly contrasted with Western models, in an article by Murphey (R. Murphey, "The City as a Center of Change: Western Europe and China," *Annals,* Assoc. of Amer. Geographers, 1954, 349–62). In more general terms, the traditional Chinese city remains largely unstudied, as the representative of what was clearly the major urban tradition in the world until a century or two ago. (See however E. Balazs, "Les Villes Chinoises," *Receuils de la Soc. Jean Bodin*, vol. 6, 1954; W. Eberhard, "Data on the Structure of the Chinese City in the Preindustrial Period," *Ec. Dev. and Cultural Change,* April 1956.)

The treaty-ports have been given proportionately greater attention, but still relatively superficially, although for them as well there is a considerable body of data, principally in the records of the Maritime Customs, one of the oases in the statistical desert of modern China. Voluminous Western first-person and secondary accounts from the nineteenth and early twentieth centuries are also available. There is as yet only one book-length geographical or specifically urban study of any of the treaty-ports, although it does treat the largest and most important of them, Shanghai, and attempts to generalize from the Shanghai case (R. Murphey, *Shanghai: Key to Modern China*, Cambridge, Mass., 1953). Ginsburg, Spencer, and others have contributed smaller studies of other treaty-ports, including an example of those developed largely under the Japanese in Manchuria (N. S. Ginsburg, "Ch'ang Ch'un," *Economic Geography,* 1949, 290–307; N. S. Ginsburg, "Ch'ing Tao," *Economic Geography,* 1948, 181–200; J. E. Spencer, "Changing Chungking: The Rebuilding of an Old Chinese City," *Geographical Review,* 1939, 46–60; M. Hatch, "The Port of Tientsin," *Geographical Review,* 1935, 367–81; R. M. Hughes, "Hong Kong: An Urban Study," *Geogr. Journal,* 1951, 1–23; S. G. Davis, *Hong Kong in its Geographic Setting,* London, 1949). G. T. Trewartha's two articles on urban functions and distributions in pre-communist China are hampered by dependence on unreliable data and by superficial acquaintance with the Chinese setting (G. T. Trewartha, "Chinese Cities: Origins and Functions," *Annals,* Assoc. of Amer. Geographers, 1952, 69–93, and "Chinese Cities: Numbers and Distributions," *Ibid.,* 1951, 331–47).

The great acceleration of urban growth in China since 1949 has unfortunately not been accompanied by increased scholarly attention, primarily because of data shortages. On the basis of the incomplete data available, a few tentative analyses have been attempted. (The most useful of these is probably M. B. Ullman, "Cities ot Mainland China: 1953 and 1958," International Population Reports, Series P-95, Washington, 1961, which suggests a classification of cities according to both size and function. See also T. Shabad, "The Population of Chinese Cities," *Geogr. Review,* 1959, 32–42, which relies mainly on Russian sources: J. S. Aird, "The Size, Composition, and Growth of the Population of Mainland China," International Population Reports, Series P-90, Washington, 1961; and J. P. Emerson, "Manpower Absorption in the Non-Agricultural Branches of the Economy of Communist China," *China Quarterly,* 1961, 69–84). But even the gross outlines of Chinese urbanization during the past decade are still largely unknown. Material available in enormous volume from the Chinese periodical and scholarly press, in Chinese and in selected translation, is seldom directly helpful, in part because accurate statistical data are not available domestically either, although there are frequent generalized references to new or rapidly growing cities, to migration patterns, to urban living conditions, and to the urban-related aspects of planned industrial location.

Contemporary Chinese geography concentrates virtually exclusively on regional resource development and on physical geography, and its journals publish almost nothing directly concerned with urban analysis. The relatively small volume of Chinese geographical publication before 1949 includes a small number of primarily descriptive accounts of individual cities, but their usefulness to Western scholars is further limited by the language barrier. In summary, our knowledge of urbanism and urbanization in China is extraordinarily slight, and especially so by contrast with the size of the problem and with its great historical depth. It seems particularly regrettable that we are at least for the present unable to see how in this outstandingly important case modern urbanization, with a significant industrial component, is grafted onto or transforms a pre-existing administrative urban structure of some completeness, and how the original treaty-ports are also to be integrated in what is already clearly becoming an expanded hierarchy heavily influenced by political considerations.

Southeast Asia

The existing geographical literature on urbanism in Southeast Asia appropriately reflects the relatively recent origin of any extensive urbanization, most of which has occurred during the last century and a half at most, and directly as a result of the colonial and commercial activities of Westerners and/or Chinese. The origins and nature of these cities which now in every case dominate each country in Southeast Asia are examined in three parallel articles which nevertheless duplicate one another surprisingly little (D. W. Fryer, "The Million City in Southeast Asia," *Geogr. Review,* 1953, 474–94; N. S. Ginsburg, "The Great City in Southeast Asia," *Amer. Journ. of Sociology,* 1955, 455–62; and R. Murphey, "New Capitals of Asia," *Econ. Dev. and Cultural Change,* 1957, 216–43). More detailed work is seriously hampered by the shortage of adequate or reliable statistical data, especially for Indonesia, Thailand, Vietnam, and Burma. An account of these handicaps is given in an article by R. J. Neville (R. J. W. Neville, "An Urban Study of Pontian Kechil, Southwest Malaya," *Journ. of Tropical Geog.,* 1962, 32–56), which is however based mainly on work in Malaya where census and other relevant data are comparatively more abundant and dependable. As an understandable consequence, and also as a result of the presence of at least two major universities in Malaya (at Singapore and at Kuala Lumpur) with extensive research staffs and facilities, a disproportionate share of the published literature on urbanization in Southeast Asia deals with Malaya (E. H. G. Dobby, "Settlement Patterns in Malaya," *Geogr. Review,* 1942, 211–32; *ibid.,* "Singapore, Town and Country," *Geogr. Review,* 1940, 84–109; D. F. Allen, *The Major Ports of Malaya,* Kuala Lumpur, 1951, and *The Minor Ports of Malaya,* Singapore, 1953; E. Cooper, "Urbanization in Malaya," *Population Studies,* 1951, 117–31; H. Sendut, "Patterns of Urbanization in Malaya," *Journ. of Tropical Geog.,* 1962, 114–30; T. G. McGee, "The Cultural Role of Cities: A Case Study of Kuala Lumpur," *ibid.,* 1963, 178–96). Somewhat surprisingly, there has been relatively little attention paid by American geographers to urban phenomena in the Philippines, and in particular no adequate study of Manila, although one aspect of its commercial structure has been examined (W. E. McIntyre, "The Retail Pattern of Manila," *Geogr. Review,* 1955, 66-80). Two other Philippine studies attempt to establish a wider set of constructs. Ullman's examination of the urban hierarchy and of inter-island trade movements provides important comparative analysis with actual and theoretical hierarchies in other parts of the world (E. Ullman, "Trade Centers and Tributary Areas of the Philippines," *Geogr. Review*, 1960, 203–18), and Spencer attempts to supply a more reliable set of estimates for city sizes and for the structure of the urban hierarchy than the census figures alone suggest (J. E. Spencer, "The Cities of the Philippines," *Journ. of Geog.*, 1958, 288–94). Wernstedt has also examined the important Filipino commercial frame of inter-island trade in his study of Cebu (F. L. Wernstedt, "Cebu: Focus of Philippine Inter-Island Trade," *Econ. Geog.*, 1957, 336–46). One of the few geographical studies of urbanism in Indonesia is also concerned with city sizes, and with the rank-size rule, which the author finds does not appropriately fit his Indonesian data. The article attempts in addition to measure the proportions of non-Indonesian population (mainly Chinese) in each of the several cities considered, a matter which is of course especially relevant to all Southeast Asian cities (W. A. Withington, "The Kotapradja or 'King Cities' of Indonesia," *Pacific Viewpoint*, 1963, 87–91).

Urban structure and morphology are however probably the subjects of the largest single group of published studies on Southeast Asia, including the recent beginnings of a literature in the planning field, where attention has been focused in particular on Singapore (J. M. Frazer, "Town Planning and Housing in Singapore," *Town Planning Review*, 1953, 5–25; see also planning studies of Manila, Saigon, and Djakarta published in United Nations, *Public Administration Problems of New and Rapidly Growing Towns in Asia*, Bangkok, 1962). Earlier studies centering primarily on urban form include those by Spate and Trueblood on Rangoon (almost the only urban geographical study of Burma yet published in English), Dobby on Singapore (referred to above), and Withington on Medan (O. H. K. Spate and L. Trueblood, "Rangoon: A Study in Urban Geography," *Geog. Review*, 1942, 56–73; W. A. Withington, "Medan: Primary Regional Metropolis of Sumatra," *Journ. of Geog.*, 1962, 59–67).

The sociological/anthropoligical literature on the predominantly urban Chinese in Southeast Asia is relatively extensive, and a good deal of it deals directly with urbanism. (See for example G. W. Skinner, *Leadership and Power in the Chinese Community of Thailand*, Ithaca, 1958; Jacques Amyot, *The Chinese Community of Manila*, Chicago, 1960; D. Willmot, *The Chinese of Semarang*, Ithaca, 1960; Barrington Kaye, *Upper Nankin Street, Singapore*, Singapore, 1960.) Other perceptive analyses of the sociological aspects of urbanization in Southeast Asia include Geertz's recent study of the development of different forms of entrepreneurship in Javan towns, and Bruner's study of group identity (Clifford Geertz, *Peddlars and Princes: Social Development and Economic Change in Two Indonesian Towns*, Chicago, 1963; E. M. Bruner "Urbanization and Ethnic Identity in North Sumatra," *Amer. Anthropologist*, vol. 63, 508–21). The rapid mushrooming especially of Djakarta but also of Singapore, Kuala Lumpur, Manila, and Bangkok, accompanying urban sprawl, and the observable effects of local culture, national and political roles, and local economic realities on originally Western urban forms and functions have still to be examined in any detail.

India

Next to Japan, urbanization in India has received the greatest amount of research attention, but by both Indians and foreigners, and virtually all of the literature is in English. Probably its most important single theme is "overurbanization," in a variety of forms including the implications for economic planning and investment, schemes for urban development or re-development ("urban community development"), the dimensions and nature of rural-urban migration, surveys of living conditions in the cities, the debate over industrial "decentralization," and the problems of both urban and rural unemployment and underemployment. Discussions of Indian urbanization have also had to confront an essentially Gandhian anti-urban and pro-village sentiment which is still expressed, although it has had little or no apparent effect on the urbanization rate or in particular on the massive scale of rural-urban migration. The 1961 Census of India showed a slight slowing down of the rate of urbanization, as compared with the rate between 1941 and 1951, but this is not easy to account for beyond drawing attention to the possibility that living conditions and general economic opportunity in at least the larger cities may have been perceived by potential migrants from the rural areas as in balance slightly less favorable, a conclusion, which almost certainly does accord with reality. Not only are the larger cities increasingly and dangerously overcrowded but the beginning of some improvement in levels of living, and perhaps of employment, are apparent in parts of the countryside. Continued concentration of industrial investment and of population growth in the already crowded larger cities is however argued as rational, even though some new investment may also be allocated to other urban centers such as the new or expanded steel towns under the third five-year plan. The Bombay and Calcutta conurbations combined now contain about 40 percent of all Indian industrial plants, but such a degree of concentration is probably economic and does not necessarily distinguish India from industrial countries in the West. In any case, planning decisions for the regional allocation of urban investment should be governed by economic cost-benefit analysis rather than by sentiment or political considerations. The biggest cities will probably continue to grow relatively rapidly, and will continue to generate both more overcrowding and more urgent planning problems. The Calcutta conurbation alone may include eighty million people by the end of the present century.

The best single guide to Indian urbanization is the volume edited by Roy Turner which resulted from a 1960 seminar in Berkeley, California (Roy Turner, ed., *India's Urban Future*, Berkeley, 1962). Papers by Indians and Americans deal with urbanization rates and the role of migration, urban morphology and structure, sociological aspects of urban life, the economic implications of urbanization, the centralization-decentralization issue, and the role of the planner. A final paper by B. F. Hoselitz surveys the literature on urbanization in India and provides an excellent annotated bibliography. (An earlier version of the same paper appeared as "The Cities of India and Their Problems" in *Annals*, Assoc. of Amer. Geographers, 1959, 223–31.) As Hoselitz points out, there are a large number of socioeconomic studies of individual Indian cities, representing probably the largest single body of urban data, but fewer comprehensive analyses which succeed in providing an adequate spatial frame and which also consider urban structure and function, transport, hinterland relations, and planning problems. Outstanding among the latter are the two studies of R. L. Singh, on Banaras and Bangalore (R. L. Singh, *Banaras: A Study in Urban Geography*, Banaras, 1955, and *Bangalore: A Study in Urban Geography*, Banaras, 1964. See also J. M. Datta, "Urbanization in Bengal," *Geogr. Review of India*, 1956, 19–23; E. Ahmad, "Origins and Evolution of the Towns of Uttar Pradesh," *Geographical Outlook*, 1956, 38–58; O. H. K. Spate and E. Ahmad, "Five Cities of the Gangetic Plain," *Geogr. Review*, 1950, 260–78). John Brush has provided in his article in the Turner volume a good survey of Indian urban morphology, necessarily with considerable historical reference, an approach which also characterizes most of the many studies of urban form in Indian journals (John Brush, "The Morphology of Indian Cities," in Roy Turner, *op. cit.*, pp. 57–70; M. N. Nigam, "The Evolution of Lucknow," *Natl. Geographic Journ. of India*, 1960, 30–46; R. V. Joshi, "Urban Structure in Western India," *Geogr. Review of India*, 1956, 7–19; C. D. Deshpande, "Cities and Towns of Bombay Province: Aspects of Urban Geography," *Indian Geogr. Journal*, 1941, 284–97; P. P. Karan, "The Pattern of Indian Towns: A Study in Urban Morphology," *Journ. Amer. Inst. of Planners*, 1957, 70–75; V. R. Prabhu, "Dhawar: A Study in Indian Urban Landscapes," *Bombay Geogr. Magazine*, 1953, 56–63). The work of the geographer N. R. Kar is also notable for its comprehensive approach to the urban phenomenon especially of Calcutta, and for its use of statistical models, structural theory, and other recently developed analytic techniques as well as more traditional methods. His several studies are valuable not only because they help to illumine the nature and problems of India's largest city but also because they specifically delineate the differences and the similarities between Calcutta and Western cities, while at the same time stressing the controlling importance of the Western impact, in the case of Calcutta and of the Bengali and Indian urban hierarchy more generally (N. R. Kar, "Calcutta als Weltstadt," in J. M. Schultze, ed., *Zum Probleme der Weltstadt*, Berlin, 1959; *ibid.*, "Urban Characteristics of the City of Calcutta," *Indian Population Bulletin*, 1960, 34–67; *ibid.*, "Pattern of Urban Growth in Lower West Bengal," *Geogr. Review of India*, 1962, 42–59; *ibid.*, "Urban Hierarchy and Central Functions Around Calcutta, in Lower West Bengal, India, and Their Significance," in K. Norborg, ed., *Proceedings of the I.G.V. Symposium in Urban Geography, Lund, 1960*, Lund, 1962).

One of the few recent studies which also considers urban patterns before the British period is the paper by Robert Crane (R. I. Crane, "Urbanism in India," *Amer. Journ. of Sociology*, 1955, 107–14), but the British impact, especially on urban morphology, is treated in almost all of the analyses of contemporary city forms. The alien origins of the great port cities have been given relatively extensive historical treatment, but the geographic implications have been for the most part examined only incidentally. (For a specific geographic study of the Indian prototype of the treaty-ports, however, see R. Murphey, "The City in the Swamp: Aspects of the Site and Early Growth of Calcutta," *Geogr. Journal,* 1964, 241–56, which stresses the essentially Western nature of the city, the parallel with Bombay, Madras, and the port cities of Southeast Asia and China, and the role which Calcutta was the first to play in spreading economic change.) Bombay and Calcutta have been studied most extensively in the general urban literature, and especially in socioeconomic terms. Bombay has received particular attention as the chief center of the cotton textile industry, and a recent volume deals in great detail with the widespread implications of the recruitment of an urban industrial labor force (M. D. Morris, *The Emergence of an Industrial Labor Force in India: A Study of the Bombay Cotton Mills 1854–1947.* Berkeley, 1965). Socioeconomic work on Calcutta (see especially S. N. Sen, *The City of Calcutta: A Socio-Economic Survey,* Calcutta, 1960) has more recently been overshadowed by planning research on a very large scale as part of the project to produce a comprehensive metropolitan plan for Calcutta, still in its relatively early stages and for the most part not yet available in print. The similarly ambitious Delhi Planning Project is outlined at the pilot stage by B. Chatterjee, and dealt with in greater and more current detail by Clinard (B. Chatterjee, "Urban Community Development in India: The Delhi Pilot Project," in Roy Turner, *op. cit.,* pp. 71–93; M. B. Clinard, *Urban Community Development and Slums,* Glencoe, 1965—nine chapters of this work are devoted to the Delhi Project, and one to a similar but smaller project in Dacca, East Pakistan). The establishment in 1958 of an Indian journal devoted entirely to planning, *Urban and Rural Planning Thought* (Delhi), is a further indication of the rapid increase of planning research and activity in recent years.

Marketing systems and city hinterlands have been the subject of several smaller studies. (See for example Robert Mayfield, "The Range of a Good in the Indian Punjab," *Annals,* Assoc. of Amer. Geographers, 1963, 38–49; S. N. Reddy, "Vegetable Markets and Regional Relationships of Hyderabad City," *Geog. Review of India,* 1961, 24–40; W. C. Neale, H. Singh, and J. P. Singh, "Kurali Market: A Report on the Economic Geography of Marketing in Northern Punjab," *Ec. Dev. and Cultural Change,* 1965, 129–68; F. K. Khan and M. H. Khan, "Delimitation of Greater Dacca," *Oriental Geographer,* 1961, 95–120.) Functional classifications of cities, by employment, by size, and by population density have been attempted by Lal, Ahmad, and Learmonth (A. Lal, "Some Aspects of the Functional Classification of Cities and a Proposed Scheme for Classifying Indian Cities," *Natl. Geog. Journ. of India,* 1959, 12–24; N. Ahmad, "The Urban Pattern in East Pakistan," *Oriental Geographer,* 1957, 37–39; A. T. Learmonth *et al., Mysore State: An Atlas of Resources,* Calcutta, 1960, and *Mysore State: A Regional Synthesis,* Calcutta, 1962), and P. P. Karan has related industrial changes to urban growth (P. P. Karan, "Changes in Indian Industrial Location," *Annals,* Assoc. of Amer. Geographers, 1964, 336–54).

India may present the clearest or at least the best known Asian example of the mixing of Asian and Western urban forms and of the long-term operation of Western-derived and Western-managed economic forces on existing and developing urban systems and on individual cities. What may make Indian cities particularly distinctive is their rapid growth at a time when the economy as a whole has not achieved substantial and permanent net gains of a self-perpetuating sort which can leave sufficient margin for basic "social investment," hence the arguments centering around "overurbanization." How far into the future such a pattern may extend, and to what degree Indian cities will become more reflective of Indian cultural and economic conditions and less reflective of Western influences are fruitful subjects for speculation. For the present, the amount and quality of published research on Indian urbanism, and its unique availability to Western scholars, plus the recent boost given to urban studies by the major planning efforts in Delhi, Calcutta, and elsewhere leave our understanding at a more satisfactory level than anywhere else in Asia outside of Japan, and suggest that it will continue to increase rapidly as the process of urbanization enters what may be a more distinctively Indian stage.

Asia

It remains to mention, and to acknowledge, some general works which deal with urban problems in Asia as a whole. By far the most valuable of these for the present essay is the long chapter by Norton Ginsburg titled "Urban Geography and Non-Western Areas," forthcoming in *The Study of Urbanization* and edited by Philip Hauser and Leo Schnore. Most of Ginsburg's chapter deals in fact with Asia and provides an excellent critical summary of the published literature. An earlier volume edited by Philip Hauser, *Urbanization in Asia and the Far East*, the proceedings of a joint UN/UNESCO/ILO Seminar on Urbanization in the ECAFE region in 1956 and published by UNESCO in Calcutta in 1957, is still useful both for its individual papers on a variety of social and economic aspects of urbanism and for the general summary by Hauser. "The City in the Asian Polity," Hugh Tinker's inaugural lecture of 1963 as Professor of Government and Politics at the School of Oriental and African Studies, University of London, published in pamphlet form in 1964, provides a graceful and stimulating survey of the character and significance of the traditional Asian city and contrasts it with the basically different kind of city which arose as a result of the Western impact. Gideon Sjoberg's *The Preindustrial City, Past and Present* (Glencoe, 1960) is an unreliable guide to traditional Asian urbanism, but the long critical review of Sjoberg's book by Paul Wheatley (*Pacific Viewpoint*, 1963, 163–88) titled "What the Greatness of a City Is Said To Be" helps to set the record straight and adds much additional material on the great Asian cities of the past.

In general, however, the study of urbanization in Asia must be regarded as only just begun, both in terms of the past and present scale of the problem and of its likely future dimensions. If, as seems probable, Asia and most of the rest of the world are still in the early stages of a process which may in the foreseeable future make them as urban-centered as Europe and the United States, this is one of the most urgent fields of research for all students of human society.

3

HANS BLUMENFELD, The Urban Pattern

The Latin word *urbs* is related to *orbis*, the circle. Like the English "town" and the Slavic *gorod*, related to "yard" and "girdle," it denotes as the basic characteristic of the urban phenomenon the enclosure which separates it from the open country. This is the city as it has existed through recorded history: a static unit, confined and defined by its enclosing boundary, and with a definite pattern of its internal organization, in which each part has a stable and defined relation to the whole.

But this volume deals, not accidentally, with "urban development." The static concept of the city is no longer valid. It is constantly changing and growing, and, as it grows, it bursts its girdle and overflows into the countryside. The result is universally viewed with alarm as "urban sprawl," as being "neither city nor country."

In this fluctuating mass, the old static patterns dissolve. If any pattern can be discerned, it can only be the pattern of flux. This apparent chaos can no longer be grasped as formation but only as transformation, as historical process.

Hans Blumenfeld, "The Urban Pattern," *The Annals* of the American Academy of Political and Social Science, vol. 352 (March 1964), pp. 74–83. Reprinted by permission.

Emergence of the metropolis

For 5,000 years, two forms of human settlement predominated in all but the most scarcely populated areas of the globe: the city and the rural village. The vast majority lived in the latter, and most of the world's work was done there. The villages were largely self-sufficient, not only in agricultural products but also in such manufactured products and services as they required. The cities were the seat of the ruling elite—landowning, political, military, religious, commercial—and those who supplied them with goods and services; these constituted a small minority, hardly ever exceeding 20 percent of the population. The "services" which, in exchange for food and raw materials, they supplied to the countryside were limited to military protection, dispensation of justice, and religious guidance. Urban trade was trading with other cities and with such other seats of the ruling elite as castles, manors, and monasteries, most of which, in the course of time, either disappeared or became the nuclei of cities.

This pattern changed radically only with what we rather narrowly call the Industrial Revolution, meaning the application of scientific methods to the processes of production and distribution. This resulted in two closely related and interacting processes: increasing division of labor and increasing productivity. Increasing productivity set more and more labor free for the production of manufactured goods and of services, and more and more productive activities were specialized out of the village economy and transformed into urban industries.

Increasing division and specialization of labor required increasing interaction and cooperation, both within and between establishments. This interaction required proximity. The presence of specialized workers attracted industrial and commercial establishments, and these in turn attracted other establishments and more workers. The process fed on itself. The great country-to-city migration began and is still continuing everywhere.

This great process of concentration was made possible by the development of powerful means of long-distance transportation and communication, primarily the steamship, the railroad, and the electric telegraph, which, for the first time in history, made it possible to assemble at one point the food and raw materials required to support the life and work of millions of people.

Although technology had revolutionized long-distance transportation well before the middle of the nineteenth century, goods, persons, and messages within these huge agglomerations still moved almost exclusively by foot or by hoof. This limited their size to a radius of about one hour's walking time, or three miles. Within this narrow perimeter, houses, factories, docks, and railroad yards crowded together.

Almost half a century passed before new technology revolutionized internal transportation and communication: the bicycle, electric traction applied to streetcars and rapid-transit trains, the telephone, followed by the internal-combustion engine applied to passenger cars, trucks, and buses, and by radio and television. The city could expand. While the original inbound wave of the country-to-city migration continues in full force, it is now met by a new outbound city-to-suburb wave. This wave of expansion, which started about a century ago, is still gathering momentum. The result of the interaction of these two waves is a completely new form of human settlement which can no longer by understood in the traditional terms of town-and-country or of city-and-suburb. The concentrated nineteenth-century city with its separate suburbs was a short-lived transitional phenomenon. For the emerging new form of settlement we have as yet no word. For lack of a better term, I am calling it a metropolitan area or, for short, the metropolis.

The metropolis and its region

For the purpose of this discussion I am defining the metropolis as an area in which at least half a million people live within a distance not exceeding forty-five minutes travel time from its center by means available to the majority of the population. With current North American technology, this means a radius of about thirty miles.

The essence and reason for existence of the metropolis is, as for its predecessor, the city, mutual accessibility—primarily, though by means exclusively, mutual accessibility of place of residence and place of work. The metropolis extends as far as widespread daily commuting extends, and no farther.

However, its influence extends over a wider area which may be defined as the "metropolitan region," generally up to a time distance of about two hours from the center of the metropolis. Here the influence is twofold. Because the metropolis is easily accessible as a supplier of goods and of business and consumer services and also as a market for their products, establishments and households prefer to settle in towns within these regions rather than in those remote from metropolitan centers. While isolated towns are losing population relatively and often absolutely, each metropolis is typically surrounded by a number of active and growing "satellite" towns, based generally on manufacturing plants which are often branch plants of or migrants from the metropolis.

But the pattern of the region is determined not only by those functions which are served by the metropolis but also by those even more rapidly growing and wider ranging ones which serve the recreational needs of the metropolitan population: summer cottages, lodges, motels, camps, picnic grounds, parks, and facilities for a growing variety of land and water sports, with a host of services to their users. The Stockholm regional planners define a vast "summer Stockholm" surrounding the "winter" metropolis, and a similar "summer metropolis" can be identified everywhere in America.

A strange reversal is taking place. For thousands of years, the countryside

has been the main locus of production, while the city was largely a place of consumption. Now, all activities but the immediate cultivation of the soil—even the
raising and feeding of the new "animal" that draws the plow—have been specialized and transformed into "urban" activities. The same process, abetted by the
same transportation technology which at one pole transformed the city into the
giant metropolitan concentration, has, at the opposite pole, dissolved the village
into ever fewer and more widely dispersed farms. But, over wide areas, though
not everywhere, the dwindling farm population is being replaced by a different
group, those who "retire" to the countryside. The vast majority of these retire
only for short periods, weekends or a few weeks of vacation, but a growing
number are permanent residents. This is true not only of the insignificant numbers of gentlemen-farmers but of many people of modest means, living on
pensions, insurance, or other transfer payments, often supplemented by various
services to tourists. No systematic research has explored this phenomenon, but
casual observation indicates its growing significance. With increase in leisure time,
it may ultimately influence the pattern of the metropolis itself.

For the present we are dealing only with the latter, the area of regular daily
commuting, and only with its most frequent form, the "mononuclear" metropolis. There exist other metropolitan areas which are "polynuclear," resulting
from a process for which Patrick Geddes coined the term "conurbation," the
growing together of several important independent cities. This has occurred in
areas of old and dense urban developments which had already expanded rapidly
during the early phases of the Industrial Revolution. The English Midlands, the
"Randstad Holland," and the Rhine-Ruhr concentration are the three major
examples. In other areas of equally old and dense urban development which,
however, started their transformation only at a later stage of the Industrial
Revolution, one city increasingly assumes a dominant central role. Cases are
Stuttgart for Württemberg, Zurich for northwestern Switzerland, and Milan for
Lombardy. They become increasingly similar to the metropolitan areas in younger
countries which started out from a single big city such as Chicago or Melbourne.

Many observers believe that the process of conurbation is now repeating
itself on an enlarged scale in the United States, notably along the Atlantic sea-
board from Boston to Washington. However, analysis of available data shows that
daily commuting between the metropolitan centers located on this axis is quite
insignificant and that intervening areas show densities which are, on the average,
very low compared to those within the major metropolitan areas. The following
discussion will therefore deal only with the single monocentric commuting areas
as the "archetype" of the metropolis, recognizing, however, that its boundary
with the region is fluid and tends to expand.

Characteristics of the metropolis

The developing pattern of the transmutation of the traditional city into the
metropolis can be understood best by identifying their essential differences.

1. The metropolis combines with the traditional city function of central leadership the traditional function of the countryside to provide the bulk of material production.

2. As a result, as a country reaches the "developed" level, the majority of its population is now, or soon will be, living in metropolitan areas or, at least, in metropolitan regions. The population of the individual metropolis is much larger than that of the city. The biggest metropolis, New York, contains ten times the population of the biggest pre-industrial city, Imperial Rome.

3. This larger population is dispersed over a much larger territory. With a radius of thirty miles it comprises a hundred times more land than the area determined by the three-mile radius of even the biggest foot-and-hoof cities.

4. This vast territory contains not only "urban-developed" land but also extensive "open" areas, parks, golf courses, country clubs, institutional campuses, even farms and forests.

5. Places of work and places of residence are located in separate areas.

6. Residential areas are segregated according to class or income of their residents.

This last-named difference calls for some comment. At first sight, it seems paradoxical that democratic capitalism should have produced a pattern so contrary to democratic ideology. In preindustrial societies, a large part of the "lower" classes lived on the premises of their masters, as slaves or domestic servants. The alley dwellings of Washington and other southern cities still reflect this older pattern. Elsewhere, as in Chinese cities, ambulant craftsmen worked and often slept in the compounds of their wealthy clients. Almost everywhere in preindustrial cities hovels are found next to or behind palaces. This did not disturb the "upper" classes. Their status was secured by family, title, rank, speech, manner, and clothing. In contemporary American society, these no longer determine status. Only financial status remains and is documented by conspicuous consumption. The decisive status symbol is the residence in the "good neighborhood," legally protected by zoning and fiercely defended against any intrusion of nonconforming elements, structural or human.

7. Finally, and only fairly recently, there is another reversal of an historical trend. Previously, as manufacturing specialized out of the peasant village and proliferated, the old elite-service city had become the industrial city, with industrial workers forming the majority of its population. Now, the same process of increasing productivity and specialization leads to a proliferation of mass services, business services specializing out of production for the market and consumer services specializing out of households. Now, industrial workers are predominant and growing in number primarily in the satellite towns of the metropolitan regions. In the metropolis itself, manufacturing employment is decreasing relatively and sometimes absolutely. Generally, two-thirds or more of the labor force works in a great variety of tertiary or service industries.

Pattern of land uses

As a result of these transformations, four basic types of "land use" can be identified: central business, industrial, residential, and open areas.

The historical core of the metropolis, the original "city," tends to remain
its center. With the main lines of the transportation system oriented to it, this
center remains the point most accessible to all parts of the metropolis and therefore attracts all those functions which serve the entire area. Partly attracted by
these, partly for historical reasons, all those functions which require mutual contact also concentrate here, typically in office buildings. These two basic central
functions attract others which serve them, such as eating and drinking places and
parking facilities.

The resulting competition for space, both within the center and on the
transportation facilities leading to it, leads to a displacement from the center of
all those uses which require relatively much space and can also function elsewhere. These are primarily those dealing with goods, manufacturing, and ware-
houses, but also retail stores, consumer services, and residences.

As the metropolitan population grows and spreads out, outlying sectors
accommodate sufficient population and purchasing power to support "second-
order" services of their own, notably retail, but also most consumer and some
business services. With continuing growth, the quality of the "second order"
moves up, leaving a narrowing range of the "highest order" in the center. Similarly, second-order routine office functions also move out, leaving only the
highest-order contact functions in the center. However, with the overall growth
of the metropolis, both types of highest-order functions are growing and are being
augmented by others of still higher order which can only exist when the size of
the total market has reached a higher threshold.

Thus, the center is undergoing a process of continuous selective adaptation
to those functions for which it is uniquely suited. Surprisingly, this unending
change in quality seems to produce stability of quantity. The number of persons
entering the central areas of major American cities has remained constant over the
last thirty years. During the last twelve years, the same constancy has been observed in Toronto, a younger and smaller metropolis. Congestion acts as the
selective agent which maintains the balance. The center is always "choked" but
never "chokes itself to death."

From the center outward, density of population and of all activities de-
creases with amazing regularity. The curve, representing population density in
concentric circles, falls constantly toward the periphery. Over time, this curve
undergoes two typical modifications: it becomes flatter, and it becomes smoother.
The increasing smoothness seems to indicate that the center, despite its relative
decrease in quantity, increasingly dominates the entire area, superseding the
influence of other, preexisting centers. The flattening results from a slow de-

crease of density in the inner and a rapid increase in the outer zones, each of which, however, finally stabilizes at a lower density than the previous one.

Modification by transportation

Within this basic pattern, modifications are brought about by topography and by transportation. Whenever individual transportation predominates, time distances tend to be proportional to straight-line distances, and the overall form of the settlement tends to be circular. This was the case in the foot-and hoof city. The development of suburban railroads brought a change, because the trips made by their passengers were performed by two means of radically different speeds: a train at thirty miles an hour and walking at three miles per hour. As the technology of steam railroads dictated few and widely spaced stations, a pattern of small circular dots developed, strung out over a considerable length of railroad line, with a small commercial center at each station.

With the electric streetcar, stops were far more frequent, and the speed was only about three times walking speed. So the dots merged into solid and shorter lines, with commercial concentrations at their intersections.

When the automobile brought about a sudden and unpredictable reversal of the secular trend from individual to collective transportation, the use of one means of transportation for the entire trip and at fairly uniform speed reproduced, on a vastly larger scale, the circular form of the foot-and-hoof city. The structured pattern of developed and open land, which had begun to emerge in the railroad and streetcar areas, was submerged in universal sprawl. "Developments" were scattered all over the metropolitan area, cutting up the open space into smaller and oddly shaped remnants.

The developments are of two major types: industrial and residential. The former, used for manufacturing, warehousing, and transportation, select relatively large areas of level land with good access to transportation by water, air, rail, and road.

The residential pattern

Residential areas are practically unrestricted in their choice of location and cover much more extensive areas. They are patterned by two factors: family composition and income. Single adults and couples without children are more numerous in the inner zone, and families with children are more numerous in the outer zone. A recent survey of all nonsubsidized apartment houses in metropolitan Toronto showed that within each type—one-, two-, three-bedroom apartments—the percentage occupied by bachelors decreased and the percentage occupied by families with children increased from one concentric zone to the next one, from the center outward. This occurred despite the fact that, in the inner zones, the supply of one-bedroom apartments was higher and their vacancy rate lower than in the outer ones, and vice versa for the two and three bedroom apartments.

This is easy to understand: adults use the center city for work and many other purposes, but most of them have time and inclination for the use of open space only on weekends. Children hardly ever use the central city but use open space, private and public, at all hours of the day. The pattern of residential distribution by family type is entirely voluntary, deliberate, and rational. It is hard to find any sound reason for the fashionable outcry "to bring the middle-class family back into the city."

There are, of course, in the inner areas, families with children, many children indeed. But most of them live there not by choice but by economic compulsion, which, in part, limits their use of transportation but more generally and powerfully their choice of housing. Normally, a poor family has four choices: to build a shack, to double up with another family, to be subsidized, or to buy or rent secondhand—or twenty-secondhand—housing. The first choice has been completely barred and the second has been largely barred by the exercise of the police power. Subsidized housing, strictly limited-access, has, after a quarter century, accommodated barely one percent of American households. Only the last choice, constantly narrowed by slum clearance, remains.

At present, the pattern of segregation by income class is, in the United States, overlaid and obscured by race segregation. However, if and when colored citizens achieve full equality and the Negro middle class shares equally with the white middle class the right to segregate itself from the lower income groups, the pattern will stand out clearly. The lower income groups live exclusively in the inner zone, and most of the other income groups live in the outer zones.

Criteria

This is, in generalized terms, the "natural" pattern of the contemporary metropolis, as it develops without the benefit—or "malefit"—of planning. Is it "good"? In attempting to establish criteria of judgment, we have to resort to a series of pairs of contradictory desiderata.

1. *Minimize need and maximize opportunity for commuting to work.* As people come to the metropolis primarily "to make a living," it is important that they can find work close to their homes but also that they can avail themselves of the wide choice of jobs available in the metropolis. It is equally important to employers to be able to draw on the full range of skills available anywhere in the area.

2. *Access to center and to periphery.* As Ebenezer Howard put it, people are attracted by two magnets, "city" and "country." They want easy access both to central facilities and to open land.

3. *Separation and integration of functions.* Intermingling of different uses such as industry and housing tends to conflict. But complete isolation of different functions from each other threatens to narrow the horizon of the inhabitants of the metropolis and break it up into sterile and monotonous precincts.

4. *Identification with a part and identification with the whole.* People want to identify with and take part in the life of the community in which they live and which they can easily grasp and understand. But there is an equal if not greater need for understanding, interest, and pride in relation to the metropolis as a whole.

5. *Continuity and change.* Identification with any environment becomes impossible if it loses its identity. But change is the very nature of the metropolis and possibilities for change and growth must be kept open.

Finally, whatever demands may be derived from these or other criteria, they must be satisfied at the least possible cost.

Form of the metropolis

In the light of these criteria, we may try to evaluate the developing form of the metropolis and proposals for its modification.

The need for commuting can be minimized by providing employment in every part of the metropolitan area. This requires the reservation, by zoning or by creation of industrial "districts" or "estates," of land for industry. But, with a growing majority of the labor force employed in services, the location of these assumes even greater importance. Service employment outside the central business district is growing, but it is scattered. Much could be gained by concentrating into major subcenters or "secondary downtowns" consumer, public, professional, and retail services. Probably, manufacturing plants of those labor-intensive industries which can operate on small lots might be located in their proximity. Around and possibly also within these centers. housing at relatively high densities could be developed. The concentration would, in turn, make possible the establishment of higher-order services.

Such centers would also satisfy the criteria of variety and of integration of functions and would be identifiable focal points, continuous as to location and basic arrangements but changing in detail, of the districts which they serve. There is no certainty about the most desirable size of such districts. However, it is pertinent to note that the estimates of the minimum population required for a self-contained urban unit have been steadily going up. Ebenezer Howard thought of 20–30,000 for his "garden cities." The English "New Town" program started with a limit of 50–60,000 but subsequently has raised it to 100,000 and more. American planners now talk of a quarter million. It may be that the half-million, which we specified as the minimum population of a metropolis, is required to support a really vital and attractive secondary downtown.

The concentration of many potential trip destinations would reduce the number of trips and also make it possible to provide good public transportation. This is likely to result in substantial economies in transportation costs.

While such centers would also, to some extent, increase the choice of jobs, maximization of opportunity requires primarily a relative compactness of the entire metropolis which can be effectively served by an economical transportation system.

Compactness also facilitates access to the metropolitan center. However, complete compactness would make access to open country very difficult. At the same time, the frequently advocated proposal to isolate each urban unit by a "green belt" would increase the distances to the center as well as to other units and would increase the cost of transportation and of public utilities. Increasing distances would also result from a "linear" scheme, which would line up its urban units along one axis.

It seems preferable to line up such units along a greater number of shorter lines, which would radiate from the metropolitan center. This would result in a "stellar" or "finger" scheme, with easily accessible wedges of open country between the fingers. It would, by its orientation to the metropolitan center, facilitate identification with the metropolis as a whole, while the centers of the districts, out of which the fingers are composed, would encourage identification with the district. Growth would be possibly by adding new districts at the ends of the fingers, but it would be gradual, preserving continuity with the previous district.

Ends and means

It appears that some modification of the "natural" pattern of the metropolis could make it "better." However, such modifications are hardly possible without some fairly substantial institutional changes.

Deliberate modification of the pattern of the metropolis presupposes that its area is brought under one jurisdiction, by annexation, federation, or any other means—if there are others. Separate municipalities, each hard-pressed to balance its budget and with the real estate tax as the main source of income, must of necessity, like the private real estate owner, attempt to get those land uses which produce the highest revenue and require the least operating cost—industry, commerce, and wealthy residents, preferably without children. They can hardly be expected to provide open space for the recreation of their neighbors nor to house and educate workers to produce added value in the factories and spend their money in the stores of the next municipality.

A metropolitan government could, legally, implement a land-use pattern by zoning. But zoning transfers development rights from some property owners to others. If a strong secondary downtown is to be created, values from other sites which might be chosen by its occupiers would be transferred to its area. If an area is to be kept open, its development value is transferred to all sites in the development fingers. The blatant inequity of such a procedure makes it unfeasible. Substantial development rights can be shifted around only within the same ownership, which, in this case, means ownership by a metropolitan authority.

Such an authority could become the owner of all or most of the land within its boundaries only if it could tap the very substantial income generated within its boundaries far more effectively than our present three-level tax structure permits.

These three measures would make it possible to modify the general metropolitan pattern. They could not, however, deal with the most serious inadequacy of the present pattern, the exclusion of the low-income groups from the expanding outer zones of the metropolis. This could be accomplished only by assumption of public financial responsibility for standard housing. It is self-deception to talk of "socially balanced" new neighborhoods or "New Towns" when one-third of the population cannot possibly afford to live in them.

Metropolitan-wide governments with commensurate financial resources, public land ownership, housing financed, though not necessarily owned or managed, by and for the public, not token ghettos for the poor—these are all "radical" innovations in terms of current American thinking. However, in different forms and degrees, all of them have been adopted, singly or jointly, within the framework of democratic capitalism by the countries of northwestern Europe.

The American and Canadian people are faced with a dilemma. They want, and want badly, two things. They want to live in an efficient, convenient, healthy, and pleasant environment, and they want, as individuals and collectively as municipalities, to be able to make an honest dollar out of every piece of property they happen to own. The two are basically incompatible. Sooner or later they will have to decide which one is more important to them.

4

KENNETH E. BOULDING, The City as an Element in the International System

An international system may be defined as a set of social organizations or organized groups of people whose relations are governed mainly by threat and the perception of threat. Defined this broadly, the international system goes back a long way in human experience, and the primitive international systems of the paleolithic era may seem to have little resemblance to the complex international system of today. Nevertheless, in social evolution something like an international system has nearly always been present and can be thought of as a segment of the total ecological system of mankind that is at least moderately recognizable and has something of an evolutionary pattern of its own.

In spite of the observation that even very primitive peoples have organized groups, the relations among which are governed by some kind of threat system, a case can be made for the proposition that the international system as we would recognize it today emerges only with the development of cities and civilization—

Kenneth E. Boulding, "The City as an Element in the International System," *Daedalus*, vol. 97, no. 4 (Fall 1968), pp. 1111-1123. Reprinted by permission.

civilization, of course, being what goes on in cities. The threat relations among paleolithic people seem to be sporadic and very casual. In any case, before the invention of agriculture man was too near the margin of subsistence in most places to have any surplus left over, either for more elaborate organization or for organized fighting.

The domestication of plants and animals seems to have led at first to a degree of relative affluence in which productive activity paid off better than predatory, and hence the threat system seems to have been fairly well muted. A great many neolithic villages seem to have been undefended.

As long as population was sparse in relation to agricultural land, this idyllic Garden of Eden could persist. The rise of cities may well have been associated with population pressure that made simple expansion of the old way of life impossible. The first cities seem to have been created by internal threat systems. In the early days, this appears to have been mainly a spiritual threat. A charismatic priesthood somehow persuades the farmer to hand over some of his surplus food, and with this food the priests, the artisans, and the builders of temples, houses, and walls are fed, but not much comes back to the farmer.

The simplest model both of the city-state and of the international system would suppose each city to have a small agricultural hinterland around it, from which the surplus of food flows into the city and which receives from the city primarily spiritual goods or threats. At this stage at any rate, the city would have little in the way of products to export. The spiritual threat of the priest is usually succeeded by the more material threat of the king who uses the food that he extracts from the farmers to feed soldiers who can extract the surplus that feeds them by material threat. An international system develops out of this because of the fundamental principle that threat capability and credibility diminish with distance from the origin of the threat, since threat capability has a cost of transport. Consequently at a certain distance from the king or the city, its threat capability and credibility decline to the point where they can no longer control behavior. At this point, there is an opportunity for another king or city. Once the second city is established there comes to be a boundary of equal strength between the two cities, and we have an international system.

A model as simple as this, of course, could never have described a real situation, even in the earliest times. The system is always more complex than we have indicated. Even in the neolithic era, for instance, there seems to have been extensive trade covering thousands of miles. The development of metallurgy meant a quite early development, at least of specialized villages that exported metals in return for food. The development of pottery, jewelry, weaving, and crafts producing transportable articles led to the development of organized trade; and trading cities, such as Tyre, had economic structures very different from the simple exploitative city and also played a very different role in the international system. The threat capability of a trading city, for instance, may be used not so much simply for the extraction of commodities from unwilling producers, as for the monopolization of trade opportunities, as in the case of Venice.

The next stage of development of the city and the international system is empire, which begins when one city conquers another without destroying it. A system of city-states is only stable if what I have called the "loss of strength gradient"—that is, the decline in threat capability and (or credibility)[1] per mile of distance traveled away from its origin—is very high. Thus, for the system of city-states to be stable, the threat capability of the city must be exhausted once it has covered an area that is capable of feeding the city from its food surplus. One city, then, cannot conquer another, for as it expands its threats beyond its own territory, it becomes too weak, and the other city becomes too strong.

The cost of transport of threat capability however, for instance in the shape of organized armies, soon fell below the critical limit that would permit the city-state to be stable. This happened first along the great river valleys simply because water transportation of anything, including threats, is very cheap. It is not surprising, therefore, that we get empires along the Nile, along the Tigris and the Euphrates, along the Indus, and along the Hoang-Ho. One of the puzzling questions of human history, incidentally, is why the pattern in America was so different, where the great river valleys like the Mississippi did not produce any early civilizations, but the wild mountains of Mexico and Peru did. The answer may be that a river had to flow through at least a semi-arid region in order to support an empire due to the extraordinary difficulties of transportation through forests. Certainly the desert plays something of the role of the sea in transportation. Just as the Roman Empire was the product of the Mediterranean and of sea transport, so the empires of the nomads of Central Asia were a product of relatively unobstructed land transportation in semi-arid regions. Forests grow faster than man, with primitive tools, can cut them down. He can only conquer the forested regions once the techniques of clearing have gone beyond a certain point. Even the arid lands cannot support an empire without something like a horse, which is probably why the incipient city-states of the Southwest Pueblos in the United States never developed into empires, having neither navigable rivers nor horses.

In the empire, there is a sharp distinction between the capital city and the provincial cities. The capital city is more purely exploitative, though the empire as a system usually involves the collection of surplus food by the provincial cities, some of which is retained and some of which is passed on to the capital city. There is probably more incentive, however, for the provincial cities to become producers of specialized manufactures and to begin to exchange these with food producers for food. Here the exchange system slowly develops and spreads as an alternative to the threat system. Finally, with the advent of the so-called Industrial Revolution and the rise of science-based technology, we begin to get virtually apolitical cities like Birmingham (England) or Detroit, which grow up on a basis of pure production and exchange, usually outside the old political structures. These commercial and industrial cities play virtually no direct role in the international system though their indirect influence may be great in strengthening the power of the nation-state and the capital city to which they happen to be attached. Thus the rise of cities like Birmingham, Manchester, and Sheffield undoubtedly increased the power of Great Britain in the international system from the eighteenth century on. This increase in power, however, was largely accidental in the sense that it was not particularly planned by the central authorities and owed little to success or failure in war. What we had here was a quite independent dynamic of the exchange system that had a spillover effect on the international system.

The United States is an even more striking example of a country that has risen to power in the international system largely because of economic development through production and exchange. In the United States, the fact that the capital city of Washington was relatively insignificant over most of its history and even today is far from being the largest city symbolizes and illustrates the peculiar nature of this political organism. In the ideal type of national state, the capital city is the largest city in the country and dominates the life of the country, acting as a centralized focus for inputs of information and outputs of authority and, as the derivation of the word implies, as a "head" to the body of the rest of the country. One thinks of Paris, Rome, Madrid, Vienna, Warsaw, Copenhagen, Tokyo. The list could be extended. By contrast, Washington, Canberra, Ottawa, and, one should no doubt add, Brazilia play a different role in their respective countries. These might almost be called "economic" as opposed to "political" countries in which the major centers, such as New York, Montreal, Sydney, São Paulo are commercial and industrial cities rather than administrative and military centers. In this connection, it is interesting to note that even the state capitals of many American states are relatively minor cities like Lansing, Springfield, and Sacramento, and it is highly significant that the capital of West Germany is Bonn. One feels that it is almost a pity that the capital of France did not remain permanently at Vichy!

Another important aspect of the city in the international system is its role in creating security against threats and violence. In classical civilization, human life was frequently more secure against violence in the city than it was in the country. Adam Smith observes, for instance, that "order and good government, and along with them the liberty and security of individuals, were, in this manner, established in cities at a time when the occupiers of land in the country were exposed to every sort of violence."[2] Even today, one sees the contrast between the landscape of France and England where the greater authority of the central power permitted men to live in open farmsteads in the country without undue fear of violence and the landscape of Germany where farmers still huddle together in villages and the countryside between villages is empty of habitation. In earlier times the city wall was a symbol of the security of the city's inhabitants. Like all forms of security, this tended to break down in the long run, and virtually all walled cities have been destroyed at some time or another. Nevertheless, in what children call the "olden days," the inhabitant of the city did enjoy at least a temporary security frequently superior to that of his rural brother. Without this, indeed as Adam Smith again points out, the accumulation that went on in the cities, the increasing division of labor, and the improvement of technology would probably have been impossible, for unless the fruits of accumulation are reasonably secure, people will not accumulate.

With the advent of aerial warfare and especially the nuclear weapon, the position of the city is radically changed. The city and the civilian who lives in it have now become hostages, and the civilian's chances of survival in a major war are much less than that of his rural brother or even that of a member of the Armed Forces. In the modern world, both the city and the civilian are expendable to the lust of the national state. This has created a complete reversal of the traditional pattern. Whereas in the earlier period the national state fostered the growth of nonpolitical cities by creating relatively large areas free from the threat of serious violence, today the national state is one of the greatest threats to its cities. Hiroshima and Nagasaki, after all, were commercial not political cities and were sacrificed to the senseless ambition of the national state. It would be very surprising if in the next "X" years Boston, Cleveland, Seattle, and so on are not similarly sacrificed on the altar of the present national system. The cities have become helpless pawns in an international system that is developing rapidly toward a major breakdown.

I have argued to another occasion that there are many reasons why the classical city, clearly bounded in space and organized from within by a strong sense of community, is incompatible with modern technology and is likely to survive only in special cases as a kind of anomaly.[3] The ecological structure of the classical city depended on a high resources cost, both of transportation and communication. The city was clustered and bounded; spatially it tended to have a ring structure centered around a market square, a cathedral, or some other civic center. Its population density was high, and there was usually a fairly sharp boundary that separated it from the countryside.

Both the economic and the political structures of the modern world are dominated by the reduction in cost of transport of people, commodities, information, and violence. Clustering of any kind is a result of cost of transport of something. If cost of transport was zero, we would expect activity of all kinds to be uniformly spread over space. The lowering of cost of transport, therefore, inevitably reduces clustering and increases dispersion. We see this very clearly in what is happening to the cities. The central cities are decaying and disintegrating. The level of amenity in them has fallen, the level of violence has risen. The central cities may decay completely, and an urban structure may emerge that looks something like chicken wire; a network of ribbon development enclosing areas of country and rural settlement. The automobile, the telephone, the television, and the missile with a nuclear warhead—all move the ecological system in the same direction.

The critical question under these circumstances is what happens to the structure of community. Before the twentieth century, community was structured geographically in fairly well-defined ways. In his political role especially, a citizen belonged to a well-defined local community, whether village, town, or city, toward which he felt some attachment and some obligations. Beyond this were regional political organizations, such as counties and states, and beyond these again the national state. A great deal can be learned about the prevailing image of community by simply asking large numbers of people "Where do you live?" or "Where do you come from?" The answer, of course, depends somewhat on the context. If one is abroad, for instance, one would tend to respond by giving the name of one's national state. In the United States, one would be unlikely to respond by giving the name of one's county. A great many people probably do not even know it, for this is not a salient community. One suspects there might be almost an even chance of giving the name of a state or the name of a city. Some people would say "I come from Dedham," some might say "I come from Massachusetts." A person from Syracuse might even say "I come from upstate New York," thereby dissociating himself from the appendage at the lower end of the Hudson. On the other hand, a man may say "I come from Boston" when he actually lives in Concord, or "I come from New York" when he really lives in Scarsdale.

There can be little doubt that the impact of the modern world is to diminish allegiance to the local community and especially to the central city. The increase in mobility assures this. In the days when a man lived all his life in the place where he was born and where his forefathers had lived for generations, there was a strong tie to the local community. In the modern world, hardly anybody lives where he was born and a man changes his location many times during his life. Under these circumstances the sense of allegiance to the local community as something special declines, and if the local political community is to be run succesfully, it must rely less and less on allegiances and sentiment. It will have to rely on professionalization and the use of exchange in order to attract the kind of support necessary. Everybody recognizes that the great problem of the central city today is that the people who make the decisions about it do not live there and do not feel themselves to be part of its community. They may live in the suburbs or in another part of the world altogether. Hence the city as a decision-making unit is really disintegrating. From being a social organism, it has declined to being a chance aggregation without even the organizational structure that permits the decisions to be made that will affect the local community. One sees this, for instance, in the field of banking, finance, and corporate management where decisions may be made that profoundly affect the future of a particular community by people who have never even seen it. We see this even more dramatically in the international system where the decision of a man in the White House consigns the people of cities on the other side of the world to the flames. We have passed from the stage where the cities nurtured civilization to a world in which the city is simply a victim of forces far beyond its own control, a sacrificial lamb on the altar of corporate or national ambition. The great danger here is that the sense of local community will be wholly eroded by the sense of impotence on the part of local people and local decision-makers. This can create a situation in which the cities almost literally fall apart. The city is something that nobody loves, and what nobody loves will die.

It is not surprising, therefore, that in the modern world the city is in deep crisis. It is an aggregation of humanity that has lost its sense of community and cannot, therefore, provide a human identity. St. Paul was able to say with pride that he was a citizen of no mean city. Would the same be said by a resident of Harlem or of any of our central cities? The cities of today that are not mean, like Venice, Florence, Kyoto, and one might almost add Williamsburg, are the fossil relics of a departed age. There are a great many things in our own age and in our society in which we can take great pride—the pictures of Mars, the conquest of disease, the great universities, even let me say with some trepidation, the middle-class suburbs with pleasant lawns, solid comforts, and relaxed neighborliness. The city, however, is not on this list, perhaps because it is really a survival from a past age, and we have not yet made the adjustments that can transform it into something worthy of the rest of our accomplishments.

The crux of the problem is that we cannot have community unless we have an aggregate of people with some decision-making power. The impotence of the city, perhaps its very inappropriateness as a unit, is leading to its decay. Its impotence arises, as I have suggested earlier, because it is becoming a mere pawn in economic, political, and military decision-making. The outlying suburb is actually in better shape. It is easier for a relatively small unit to have some sense of community, and the suburb at least has a little more control over its own destiny. It is somewhat less likely to be destroyed in war. Its economic base tends to be diversified as its residents commute over a wide area; hence its fate is not in the hands of a single decision-maker. Its local government, its school board, and other community agencies often are able to gather a considerable amount of support and interest from the people they serve.

It is not wholly absurd to ask whether we should not abolish the city altogether as a political organization. Let us divide Chicago and Detroit into thirty suburbs, small enough so that they have some chance of achieving a sense of local community and local responsibility for things that can be done locally. Then, of course, we would need "functional federalism"—metropolitan water boards covering a wide area, air pollution agencies, educational finance institutions that would equalize local opportunities without destroying local initiative, police forces of different levels of size and function, and so on. Political scientists have often lamented about the multitude of political agencies in the United States, but the case against this may easily have arisen out of a prissy desire for tidiness. In terms of productivity, a multiplicity of agencies may be precisely what the times require. We seem quite incapable of expanding the central cities out into their suburban environments. Perhaps we should try reversing the recipe and move the suburbs into the city, building up around them a network of functional agencies.

The problem of integrating the city into the world community is much more difficult than the problem of reorganizing it locally. Nevertheless, the future of the city as an institution probably depends more on the future of the international system than it does on any other aspect of social life. More than any other aspect of the sociosphere, the international system is destroying the city, either physically by bombing or more critically by eroding its problem-solving capacity through the withdrawal of both intellectual and physical resources into the international system itself. The brain drain into the international system and the war industry is one of the principal reasons why the city receives so little attention and why what attention it has received in such efforts as urban renewal and public housing has been largely disastrous. The impact of urban renewal and of throughways on a city is physically not unlike that of a small nuclear weapon, but with less damage to bodies and perhaps more damage to minds. Both urban renewal and nuclear destruction come from the national state. They are both thunderbolts hurled at the city from afar without regard to the tender ecological structure of its life and community. The cities by themselves, of course, cannot solve the problem of the world community, though one would think they might exercise a little bargaining power on it. The difficulty here is twofold. In the first place, the cities seem to have astonishingly little bargaining power in general. This is a puzzling phenomenon. One looks, for instance, in the United States at the extraordinary bargaining power of the agricultural interest, even at a time when it has shrunk to an almost insignificant proportion of the total electorate. By comparison with the apparent impotence of the cities, one sees the even more astonishing bargaining power of the military, who both starve and threaten the cities and eat high off the hog at a time when the cities have to be content with scraps. The second difficulty is that the international system is not really salient to the people who live in cities, even though it affects them so profoundly. The decision-makers in the international system are few, they are remote, and it all seems a long way from the experience of the ordinary citizen. Hence he is inclined to "leave this to father" even when the great White House father is dangerously incompetent in these matters. It is not the importance of a problem that determines how much attention will be paid to it, but its salience. Unfortunately, importance and salience are very loosely related, sometimes even negatively related.

All these difficulties resolve themselves into a single structural deficiency. There are virtually no channels in society or in the world at large by which the city as such can exercise bargaining power. One wonders what would happen if the cities were represented directly, as states, not only in the United States Senate, but in the United Nations. Could we envisage a new Hanseatic League of cities against the national state and the military establishments that are threatening to destroy them? All these suggestions, alas, sound like brainstorming and pipe dreams.

Nevertheless, what we face here is perhaps the most important single example of a much larger problem of political and social organization. The conflict in the world today—underlying the cold war at the international level, civil rights and the Black Power movement in the United States, and the inability of so many tropical countries to resolve their internal conflicts to the point where economic development becomes possible—is a conflict of two political concepts. The names "individualism" and "collectivism" are quite inadequate to describe these concepts, but these are probably the best words we have. On the one hand, there is the political ideal of the individual acting as an individual and independent person in a larger community, exchanging his capacities with other individuals in a social contract and in a market economy, expressing his political activity primarily by voting in elections on the one-man, one-vote basis. In political organization, this leads to what we might call "atomistic parliamentarism." In economic organization, it leads to capitalism and the free market. In religious organization, it leads to Protestantism and sectarianism; in family life, to the free choice of partners. It goes along with the life style of mobility and rootlessness, entrepreneurship, achieved rather than ascribed status, and so on. On the other side, we have the collective ideal stressing the notion that the identity of the individual is so bound up with the community with which he identifies that he can only become an individual as part of a community. His political activity here is exercised by activity influencing the decisions and the bargaining power of a series of concentric communities, rather than as an individual among other individuals. This leads toward a consensus-oriented society, totalitarianism, socialism, catholicism, monasticism, associationism, such things as trade unions and professional associations, collective rather than individual bargaining, and the corporate rather than the parliamentary state. Each of these philosophies has its own virtues and vices, and almost any political system is some sort of uneasy compromise between the two. Some lean toward one side, and some toward the other. At the present moment in history, the crisis of the cities has arisen because in *no* political structure is the city adequately represented. At the level of individualistic democracy, the city has lost its sovereignty and independence. It has become a pawn in the sense that its local autonomy has been destroyed. At the level of collective organization, the city is not organized as a bargaining unit. It does not bargain with the other agencies of society, such as the national state or the corporation, as effectively, shall we say, as the labor unions bargain with the employers. The city, therefore, gets the worst of both worlds. Its citizens as such are effective neither as political individuals nor as members of a bargaining collectivity.

Much of the same problem is seen in the Negro or other minority groups. The rise of the Black Power movement is in a sense a breakdown of individualistic democracy at this level. On the other hand, the Black Power solution is also likely to fail, because black power is not very great and the movement is likely to raise expectations that will probably be disastrously disappointed. One sees the same problem in the demands for "student power," which are simply not constructive, though occasionally they can be destructive, as in Latin America and Japan. Nevertheless, the student is not satisfied to be a mere individual and feels the need of identifying himself with a collectivity.

The synthesis and reconciliation in both structure and philosophy of the two political "modes," as they might be called, of individualism and collectivism perhaps represent the greatest single long-run problem of the human race at its present state of development. The city, or at least the urban collectivity, is one of the principal arenas in which this problem is or is not being worked out, as the case may be. Almost the only consideration that leads to any hopefulness about the future is that communication and aggregation foster the process of human learning. In the age of civilization, the concentration of people in cities unquestionably contributed to the slow growth of knowledge, simply because of the facilitation of communication that this concentration implied. Rural isolation leads to rural backwardness and cloddishness. The implications of the words "civilized," "civil," "urbane," and even "civilian," as over against "rustic" and "bucolic," suggest the values that have arisen from easy urban communication. The country may be the depository of traditional virtue, but new ideas come out of the wicked city. The city, therefore, historically has been the main source of change, both in the international system and in all aspects of the social system, as it has produced new ideas, new ideologies, new philosophies, and new technologies. The towns, as Adam Smith observes, improve the country. The decay of the city today does not represent a return to rural virtue or to rural ignorance. It is a symptom, if anything, of the urbanization of the whole world. The communications revolution has created, in effect, a world city, and this is why the local cities are in decay. It is to be hoped, therefore, that we can look forward to new knowledge, new ideas, and even a transformation of the international system that will give us security, arising out of the knowledge process of the world.

The essential key to this process may be the development of self-consciousness in the city dweller that he is a member of a city and indeed of the world city. One suspects that the unexploited bargaining power of the city is great simply because the city, disorganized as it is, is inevitably a focus or nodal point of the world network of communication. Airports are the synapses of the world communications network; so in a sense are the television stations and the newspapers of the city. So are its universities. It is a pretty fair generalization in the theory of location to say that the synapses, the gaps, or the switches in the communications and transportation network produce the city in the first place. This is why, for instance, so many cities have arisen at ports, at heads of navigation, and at points of trans-shipment. In a world in which the transportation of communication is beginning to overshadow the transportation of commodities, the city—because of its position in the communications network—has real power that is as yet unexploited, mainly because it is not self-conscious. If I can take a leaf out of the book of Karl Marx, and this is one occasion where the leaf may be better than the book, we may urge the rise of self-consciousness in the cities, a rise of their joint self-consciousness of the community as a world city representing the constructive and developmental forces of humanity as against the essentially backward-looking or destructive tendencies of the country and the military. Our motto, therefore, perhaps should be "Cities of the world unite, you have nothing to lose but your slums, your poverty, and your military expendability." On this note of modest long-run optimism, I had better conclude for fear that the pessimism of the short run catches up with us first.

References

1. It is the credibility of the threat which really matters from the point of view of its ability to organize social systems. Credibility in very complex ways is related to capability. The relationship is closer in the case of material threat than in the case of spiritual threat where capability is hard to demonstrate, but where the threat often justifies itself: for example, the fear of Hell. Even in the case of material threat, credibility can remain long after capability has disappeared. Nevertheless, in the long run there must be a tendency for capability and credibility at least to run parallel.

2. Adam Smith, *The Wealth of Nations*, Book 3, Ch. 3.

3. Kenneth E. Boulding, "The Death of the City: A Frightened Look at Post-civilization," in *The Historian and the City*, eds. Oscar Handlin and John Burchard (Cambridge, 1963), pp. 133–45.

CHAPTER 3

CONTENTS

THE PROCESS OF URBANIZATION

The articles in this section provide a structuralist perspective on the scale and consequences of the process we call urbanization. The first piece, from the Population Division of the United Nations, sets forth several criteria for delimiting urban localities and on the basis of these standards indicates the magnitude of urbanization in worldwide, longitudinal terms. Given this depiction of "how much" of a phenomenon we have, the following articles deal with questions about "what kind" of a phenomenon it is.

In separate essays, Oscar Lewis and Philip Hauser critically examine the notion of a "rural-urban continuum" that might be associated with differences in the life experiences of people residing in more or less urbanized localities. Their general conclusion is that these concepts are very crude guides to an understanding of social change and require much more detailed analysis. Lewis provides one such analysis in the case of Mexico City, and Hauser suggests a large set of research questions. In the same spirit, Janet Abu-Lughod's analysis of migrant adjustment to life in Cairo provides an absorbing account of some of the variety that characterizes recent migrant populations. A unique feature of this volume is Professor Abu-Lughod's postscript written for this volume, in which she reflects on her argument of twelve years earlier and some of the changes that have occurred in Cairo in the ensuing years.

The next article, by Bert Hoselitz, raises certain larger structural questions about the economics of cities. Like the foregoing, this essay challenges conventional thinking, particularly the belief that cities invariably grow up as a response to economic necessity. Also in keeping with earlier themes, Hoselitz calls for a more discriminating analysis of alternative urban structures.

The final article in this chapter is by Raymond Mack and Dennis McElrath, an elegant theoretical statement of how resources are allocated—how the goodies are passed around in urban society. Their scheme of analysis based on occupational, ethnic-migrant, and life-style differentiation as the dimensions of resource allocation is highly suggestive. It appears useful, for example, to think comparatively about cities on these dimensions as a way of explaining who gets what proportion of the amenities of urban life.

In its general organization, Chapter 3 seeks to build logically from basic population processes to higher levels of generalization concerning the variety of ways urban life is experienced by different sections of the population. A general theme among the separate selections is the need to evaluate commonsense interpretations through more careful scrutiny of the data generated in comparative studies. Clearly, any one group of selections cannot tap all important dimensions, but the articles presented here do give a strong flavor of how critical thinking about the process of urbanization should proceed.

5

UNITED NATIONS POPULATION DIVISION, World Urbanization Trends, 1920–1960

A. PROBLEMS OF SUBSTANCE AND METHOD

Comparability and relevance

Internationally comparable statistics on urban population are not easily assembled. This in itself is an important observation. It compels us to recognize that urbanization is a process of both quantitative and qualitative change. In the process of growth, the characteristics and functions of localities, and particularly of towns and cities, are transformed, and this raises the question of the relevance of comparisons.

The two criteria which generally distinguish the urban element in a country's population are the quantitative in terms of population concentration, and the qualitative, such as the characteristics of the economy and modes of living which have "urban" rather than "rural" attributes. The correlations between these two criteria vary with time, location, and the "urban" features of the particular locality; hence the difficulty in determining criteria of general applicability. Many different census definitions are used among countries, and in addition it has been found necessary in recent censuses within countries to modify standards used earlier. There is also the great variation in urban and rural environments throughout the world to take into account.

United Nations Bureau of Social Affairs, Population Division, "World Urbanization Trends, 1920–1960 (An Interim Report on Work in Progress)." Inter-Regional Seminar on Development Policies and Planning in Relation to Urbanization, organized by the United Nations Bureau of Technical Assistance Operations and the Bureau of Social Affairs in cooperation with the Government of the United States of America, Working Paper Number 6 (University of Pittsburgh, Pittsburgh, Pennsylvania, USA, October 24-November 7, 1966).

Selection of criteria must therefore be made rather arbitrarily, frequently as a compromise between comparability, relevance, and the expediency of available statistics or methods of estimating them. An estimate of the world's urban population, at best, can so far only be derived from a patchwork of figures broadly selected, adjusted and interpolated.

The United Nations Population Division is now preparing a report on the growth of urban and rural population in the world.[1] The results so far are still preliminary in many respects and are undergoing revision. This paper presents a summary of the study to date, with many figures used tentatively and subject to further modification. Geographic settlement patterns are considered as a first step, leaving for examination at a later date their demographic, economic and social features.[2]

Methods of delimiting urban localities

It scarcely need be said that the transformation of settlements into towns and cities has been accomplished according to the influence of the particular historic period. During the last century, the pattern of growth of urban localities in areas of recent European overseas settlement differed from that of the cities of Europe, South and East Asia and Africa founded much earlier, but by identification with their size and function the new localities assumed similar distinctions of "towns" and "cities."[3]

In general throughout the world, where a fundamental change in settlement pattern related to the modern growth of commerce and industry took place, some towns of minor importance expanded rapidly, outgrowing original administrative boundaries. Where boundaries were inflexible, the localities were re-defined as "agglomerations." The simultaneous growth of several towns within a small radius often caused them to merge into a "conurbation." In some cases, *de facto* conurbations became incorporated under a new combined urban administration, such as the cities of Wuhan in China, or Wuppertal in Germany. In others, the growth of large cities or "metropolises" absorbed adjacent towns, villages, or smaller cities without affecting their political autonomy, although certain services such as water, police, etc., were supplied under the administration of the agglomeration. With the increase in the number of large cities, the concept of "agglomeration" has gained more generalized use as an alternative to that of "city proper" in the statistics of many countries.

The more inclusive classification of "metropolitan area," as for Greater London, Greater New York, Greater Paris or Greater Tokyo, has evolved where a network of road and rail transportation has further expanded the confines of the settlement pattern. This broader concept has not been restricted to the largest cities, however.[4]

In comparing urban data, problems arise in connection with the adjustment of municipal boundaries. Where boundaries are flexible, "city proper" data may provide a realistic comparison of urban growth. Where boundaries have proved relatively rigid, the "agglomeration" is more meaningful provided it is re-defined at each census, a practice not followed in all countries. Also, there have been instances of drastic urban boundary adjustment which distort time comparisons. In Japan, *shi* have been suddenly widened from very constricted limits, particularly in the period 1950-1955 when they were enlarged to include a multiple of the previous area. This has occurred more recently in Peking and possibly also in other important cities in China.

It has proved practical to include in the agglomerations of large cities some rural areas serving the growing city for suburban residence and urban facilities. The growth of motor transport has made it reasonable for some countries to define "metropolitan region" as including such rural or semi-rural territory.[5]

Entire belts or regions comprising cities, towns, their closely related rural areas, and connecting tracts with a mixture of features which cannot be described as either wholly "urban" or "rural," and having a recognizable pattern of inter-dependence, have thus emerged as a recent phenomenon.

Standards applied in this study

It is recognized that typical villages in some countries are considerably larger than typical towns in others; also, that in some dominantly rural and agrarian regions, villages are so close and settlement so highly concentrated that average population densities over large areas are greater than those found elsewhere in large portions of urbanized territory within metropolitan agglomerations. But the rural settlement pattern is not a subject for consideration in this report.

Modest size limits are implied in the official definitions of "urban" population in the censuses of most countries, but a common international measure is more readily found when the limit is set relatively high. For the purpose of this study, therefore, "urban" population is defined as that of localities with 20,000 or more inhabitants, while the population of smaller localities or the open countryside is referred to as the "rural and small-town population."[6]

Tradition also suggests a distinction for localities with at least 100,000 inhabitants. Earlier in the present century anyway, their functions seemed usually to differ sufficiently from those of smaller towns to justify their separate consideration.[7] The significance of the distinction at this level of size, however, has diminished where considerably bigger cities have become much more numerous, and also when the international scope of the study is widened. In this report, localities with 20,000-99,999 inhabitants will be referred to as "towns," larger localities as "cities."

The distinction of "urban" populations at the limits of 20,000 and 100,000 suggests the use of a multiplier of five to arrive at additional limits for a more detailed size classification.

Accordingly, the following combinations of "urban" population have been estimated for countries, regions, major areas, and the world:

20,000 and over:	"urban population";
100,000 and over:	"city population";
500,000 and over:	"big-city population";
2,500,000 and over:	"multi-million cities"; and
12,500,000 and over:	"metropolitan regions" (ie., those of New York and Tokyo at the present time)

Towns and cities of up to 500,000 residents are so numerous that for many large countries their exact number could not be ascertained for the particular dates. Often only the combined populations comprising the group 20,000-99,999 could be interpolated, and sometimes this had to be done also for the 100,000-499,999 group. Since each town could not be investigated individually, and censuses are tabulated more often in terms of administrative limits than the geographic extent of urbanized territory, the definition in this report for these two size groups is mainly that of "city proper," in the administrative sense.

The attempt to measure and estimate the populations included in agglomerations, as variously defined, was restricted to big cities and multi-millions cities only, i.e., all those of at least 500,000 inhabitants. Their number is not formidable,[8] and in the period 1920–1960 their emergence could be recognized and the growth of each estimated, in the main. Additional cities and towns included in the agglomerations are considered as absorbed in the major agglomeration, and hence not counted again among cities and towns of smaller size.

One consequence of the more generous definition of big cities, in contrast with smaller ones, is a partial discontinuity in size distribution. Some "cities proper" (i.e. when more narrowly defined) have, say, 300,000 or 400,000 inhabitants but when defined more liberally are parts of agglomerations in excess of 500,000. Acknowledging disparity in definitions used here, such localities are then counted among the big cities, and not among the smaller ones, leaving a gap in the "cities" group. This affects particularly the estimates for Northern America.

No attempt has been made to go beyond the concept of agglomeration, or metropolitan region. The world's two largest cities have been defined liberally, so that the metropolitan region of New York includes north-eastern New Jersey, and that of Tokyo comprises Yokohama. Consideration has not been given to the definition of even larger "megalopolitan" belts, whose demarcations would be indefinite in any event, though it is believed that their importance and relevance will become increasingly apparent in the future.

Types of data used

For the various parts of the world, the data differ in definition, period of coverage and number of observations, and recency; their approximation to accuracy and completeness is also unequal.[9] They have been dealt with in a number of ways, some still regarded as unsatisfactory from the standpoint of comparability. Most of the raw data are those of population censuses, variously interpolated to coincide with the selected dates, namely mid-year 1920, 1930, and so forth. A detailed account of the data and of the manner in which they have been used or adapted must be postponed until a more definitive report can be issued. Many of the provisional figures used in this report, and much of their comparison, are considerably affected by individual choices made in the use of data.

This makes it mandatory to draw the reader's attention to some of the principal decisions that were taken for the present purpose. For instance, in Northern America and Oceania the population of metropolitan regions has been estimated for past dates on an assumption that, with the early spread of networks of motor transportation, there had been a continuous geographic penetration of urban influence into the areas now recognized as metropolitan rings. No such assumptions have been made, on the other hand, in estimates for metropolitan regions in Europe or Latin America though there the networks of intensive transport have also widened conspicuously in recent years. It is evident that comparability cannot be established by such differing methods of estimation, and many of the estimating problems are still unresolved.

Figures are here presented for major areas and regions of the world as defined in a recent United Nations report on future world population,[10] with a few exceptions. These areas and regions are described in the Appendix to this report.

B. PROVISIONAL ASSESSMENT OF TRENDS

Worldwide urban and rural population growth

The severe shortcoming of the figures used in this provisional report have been pointed out. It must be emphasized that the estimates are neither accurate nor comparable, and that many will be revised before a more definitive report can be published.

According to approximate determinations in other studies of total population growth, the number of the world's inhabitants has risen from about 1,860 million in 1920 to 2,069 million in 1930, 2,297 million in 1940, 2,517 million in 1950, and 2,994 million in 1960[11] (see Table 1). The estimated increases in successive decades were by 209, 228, 220, and 477 million, respectively. This recent sharp upturn in population growth has affected both the urban and the rural populations.

Table 1. Distribution of world population by size of locality, 1920–1960 (rough estimates, in millions)

Size of locality (inhabitants)	1920	1930	1940	1950	1960
Total Population	1,860.2	2,069.3	2,296.9	2,516.8	2,994.4
Under 20,000	1,607.3	1,741.2	1,869.9	1,985.3	2,241.0
20,000 and over	252.9	328.1	427.0	531.5	753.4
100,000 and over	160.0	216.6	287.6	360.0	525.5
500,000 and over	94.9	133.6	175.8	224.4	351.6
2,500,000 and over	30.3	48.8	66.5	84.3	139.4
12,500,000 and over	. . .	. . .	. . .	. . .	27.7[a]
20,000–99,999	92.9	111.5	139.4	171.5	227.9
100,000–499,999	65.1	83.0	111.8	135.6	173.9
500,000–2,499,999	64.6	84.8	109.3	140.1	212.2
2,500,000–12,499,999	30.3	48.8	66.5	84.3	111.7
12,500,000 and over	. . .	. . .	. . .	. . .	27.7[a]

[a]Metropolitan regions of New York (including northeastern New Jersey) and Tokyo (including Yokohama).

In terms of the present tentative estimates, the world's urban population (localities of 20,000 and more inhabitants) has grown from 253 million in 1920 to 753 million in 1960, a three-fold growth in forty years, or a net addition of roughly 500 million urban residents.

By subtraction, it can be seen that the world's rural and small-town population has apparently increased from about 1,607 million in 1920 to 2,241 million in 1960, hence more than 600 million have been added to the localities which have remained rural or small towns. This is rather more than an increase by one-third.

Absolute increases in urban population, in the successive four decades, were by an estimated 75, 99, 105, and 221 million, respectively. Absolute increases in rural and small-town population, in the same decades, are here estimated as 134, 129, 115, and 256 million. In the 1920s, 1930s and 1940s, the absolute increments in urban population rose gradually, and those in rural population diminished gradually, while in the 1950s, both in the urban areas and in rural areas and small towns the population gain was of twice the magnitude of the gains made in the preceding decade. Of the world's total population gain, as estimated, the urban percentage in the successive decades was 36, 43, 48, and 46; the rural and small town 64, 57, 52 and 54.

In relative terms, the world's total population grew by 11 percent in the 1920s, 11 percent in the 1930s, 10 percent in the 1940s, and 19 percent in the 1950s. Urban population in each of these four decades increased by 30, 30, 25, and 42 percent; rural and small-town population by 8, 7, 6 and 13 percent. Both urban and rural localities shared in the fluctuation of the world's population growth, its slight slackening in the 1940s and sharp acceleration in the 1950s. The fluctuation was more emphatic in the growth of urban population, which slowed noticeably in the war-torn 1940s, and greatly accelerated thereafter. Acceleration in the growth of rural and small-town population in the 1950s was a striking reversal of a previously more stable trend.

In this report, no attempt is made to propose answers to the problems connected with urbanization. Its purpose is mainly to indicate with these tentative estimates the unprecedented magnitude and changing structure of the phenomenon and to mention certain repercussions resulting from similar growth trends in the two types of environments. A simple arithmetic exercise suffices to show that, with the accelerated growth in total population, rural population growth would have accelerated enormously if urban population had grown constantly at the 1920 rate throughout the period considered; similarly, had the growth in rural population continued merely at the rates of preceding decades, the number and size of towns and cities would have shown gains to an even greater degree.[12] In actual fact, both the urban and the rural areas shared in the accelerated population growth of the 1950s.

Of the world's total population, the percentage in urban localities rose from 14 in 1920 to 16 in 1930, 19 in 1940, 21 in 1950, and 25 in 1960. Another illustration of the large environmental change is found in the ratio of rural and small-town population to urban population: 6.4 to one in 1920, 5.3 in 1930, 4.4 in 1940, 3.7 in 1950 and 3.0 to one in 1960. To consider another aspect, produce of rural areas was diverted in increasing, though not always adequate, amounts to the rising proportion of urban consumers, in addition to supplying a growing rural population. The terms of trade for marketing the increased surplus were not always beneficial to the rural economy. These changing quantities and balances in population and production naturally have an impact on investment and other elements of the economic structure, with effects extending beyond national boundaries.

Among the figures for urban population shown in Table 1, perhaps those for total urban (20,000 and over) are more nearly trustworthy. Less confidence can be placed in rural population estimates, particularly for East Asia and Africa. For the larger localities, total estimates are susceptible to increase or decrease depending on the criteria by which agglomerations are defined, or re-defined while their physical limits expand. The larger the cities, the more uncertain are their boundaries drawn for purposes of comparison. All these problems affect the comparison of the population estimates for the separate size groups.

According to the tentative estimates of Table 1, the size distribution within the urban population has undergone much change. It is possible that no less important structural changes have occurred in the rural population, but data have not been assembled to illustrate changing proportions of inhabitants of the rural categories of localities. Structural changes in both rural and urban sectors can have profound implications for the needs and potentialities of economic and social development.

As these figures indicate, the urban population (20,000 and over) grew in the four successive decades by 30, 30, 25 and 42 percent; the city population (100,000 and over) increased by 35, 33, 25 and 46 percent; the successive increases in big-city population (500,000 and over) were by 41, 32, 28 and 57 percent; and those in multi-million cities (2,500,000 and over) by 61, 36, 27 and 65 percent. While the shifts in structure were less in the economically depressed 1930s or the war-ravaged 1940s than in the 1920s and 1950s, their momentum was not interrupted.

Increasing number of previously smaller towns and cities which grow into the size-classification of larger localities partly contribute to the higher rates of growth of the latter. Although a large number of small towns must also have crossed above the lower size limit of 20,000 during the same periods, the accrued population has not been sufficient to permit rates of increase of the magnitude of those in the larger localities. In fact, an increase in "top-heaviness" has been under way in the urban population, for the urban population (20,000 and over) tripled in forty years while the big-city population (500,000 and over) quadrupled.

Urbanization, 1920–1960, in eight major areas of the world

Urbanization varied considerably from one major world area to another. The provisional figures which are here being compared are shown in tables 2, 3, 4, 5 and 6. They differ from estimates which have appeared in other sources[13] and, as explained in the introductory chapter, they may still have to be revised considerably before they can be published in more definitive form.

In 1920, Europe (i.e. without the Soviet Union) had 41 percent of the entire world's urban population, but while urban population in Europe has grown from 104 million in 1920 to 174 million 1960, that is by two-thirds, Europe's share in the world's urban population has shrunk to an estimated 23 percent. By contrast, East Asia's urban population, grown four-fold from 39 million in

Table 2. Urban population (localities of 20,000 or more inhabitants) in major areas of the world, 1920–1960 (rough estimates, in millions)

Major area	1920	1930	1940	1950	1960
World Total	252.9	328.1	427.0	531.5	753.4
Europe (ex. USSR)	104.4	123.3	140.1	147.6	173.8
Northern America	43.5	58.0	64.3	83.2	112.5
East Asia	39.1	56.6	81.6	105.8	160.5
South Asia	27.0	34.6	50.5	77.0	116.1
Soviet Union	16.0	24.0	47.0	50.0	78.0
Latin America	12.9	18.1	25.2	40.6	67.8
Africa	6.9	9.7	13.8	21.5	36.4
Oceania	3.1	3.8	4.5	5.8	8.3

Table 3.   Population in rural areas and small towns (smaller than 20,000) in major areas of the world, 1920–1960 (rough estimates, in millions)

Major area	1920	1930	1940	1950	1960
World Total	1,607.3	1,741.2	1,869.9	1,985.3	2,241.0
Europe (ex. USSR)	220.1	230.5	238.7	244.1	250.7
Northern America	72.2	76.2	80.0	82.9	86.2
East Asia	514.3	534.6	553.9	578.9	633.6
South Asia	442.8	494.4	559.6	619.7	741.8
Soviet Union	139.3	155.0	148.0	130.0	136.4
Latin America	76.6	89.4	104.7	121.8	144.6
Africa	136.0	154.1	177.7	200.0	239.3
Oceania	6.0	7.0	7.3	7.9	8.4

Table 4.   Urban population (20,000 and over) as a percentage of total population in major areas of the world, 1920–1960 (rough estimates)

Major area	1920	1930	1940	1950	1960
World Total	14	16	19	21	25
Europe (ex. USSR)	32	35	37	38	41
Northern America	38	43	45	50	57
East Asia	7	10	13	15	20
South Asia	6	7	8	11	14
Soviet Union	10	13	24	28	36
Latin America	14	17	19	25	32
Africa	5	6	7	10	13
Oceania	34	35	38	42	50

Table 5.   Decennial increases in urban population (20,000 and over) in major areas of the world, 1920–1960 (rough estimates, percent)

Major area	1920-30	1930-40	1940-50	1950-60
World Total	30	30	25	42
Europe (ex. USSR)	18	14	5	18
Northern America	33	11	29	35
East Asia	45	44	30	52
South Asia	26	46	52	51
Soviet Union	50	96	6	56
Latin America	40	39	61	67
Africa	41	42	56	69
Oceania[a]	22	19	29	42

[a]Percentage computed with unrounded data.

Table 6. Decennial increases in rural and small-town population (localities smaller than 20,000) in major areas of the world, 1920–1960 (rough estimates, percent)

Major area	1920-30	1930-40	1940-50	1950-60
World Total	8	7	6	13
Europe (ex. USSR)	5	4	2	3
Northern America	6	5	4	4
East Asia	4	4	5	9
South Asia	12	13	11	20
Soviet Union	11	−5	−12	5
Latin America	17	17	16	19
Africa	13	15	13	20
Oceania[a]	15	5	5	8

[a]Percentage computed with unrounded data.

1920 to 160 million in 1960, now approaches that of Europe and, given its steep trend, may soon surpass it. It must be admitted, however, that the comparison is dubious because of varied definitions and characteristics applying to the respective urban populations in those two major areas.

The urban population of Northern America in 1920 was second to that of Europe in size, amounting to nearly 44 million. This has grown 2 ½-fold in forty years, to about 112 million by 1960. However, the urban population of South Asia, estimated as 27 million in 1920, and more than four times greater, namely 116 million, in 1960, now apparently surpasses it.

Approximately five-fold increases are estimated to have occurred between 1920 and 1960 in the urban populations of the Soviet Union, Latin America and Africa, while the smaller urban population of Oceania grew about 2 ½-fold, as did that of Northern America.

The largest relative increase of urban population in a single decade, as here estimated, occurred in the Soviet Union in the 1930s, when it nearly doubled within only ten years. Increases of the order of two-thirds in a decade are estimated for Latin America in the 1940s and 1950s, and for Africa in the most recent decade. Increases of urban population by at least one-half are also estimated in the 1920s for the Soviet Union, in the 1940s for South Asia and Africa, and in the 1950s for East Asia, South Asia, and the Soviet Union.

By contrast, in each of the four decades Europe's urban population is estimated to have gained by less than one-fifth, and in the 1930s the urban gains in Northern America and Oceania were similarly moderate. Because of the destruction and disorganization caused by the war, only small urban increases occurred in the 1940s in Europe and in the Soviet Union and also in East Asia. It must be admitted that the urban population estimates for the Soviet Union and East Asia in 1950, also those for East Asia in 1940, partly depend on rather tenuous extrapolations of either the preceding, or the subsequent, trends. It is probable that accelerated urban growth in Europe, East Asia and the Soviet

Union in the 1950s represents in part a compensation for the retardation of the 1940s. A different condition obtained in South Asia, where the fast growth of cities in the 1940s was followed by somewhat slower, though still very noticeable, growth in the 1950s; it is probable that the large refugee movements resulting from the partition of India and Pakistan reinforced the accelerated growth of cities particularly in the 1940s, but not so much in the 1950s.

Gains in estimated rural and small-town population were also diverse but did not fluctuate so much. Exceptions are the Soviet Union, where rural population diminished in the 1930s, and more substantially in the war years of the 1940s; and Oceania where the apparent gains in rural and small-town population of the 1920s have not recurred since then. In Europe and Northern America, perhaps also in Latin America, relative gains in rural and small-town population gradually slowed down between 1920 and 1950. In East Asia and Africa, they may have fluctuated without any decided trend, but the data are too uncertain to bear out such a contention. With the possible exception of Northern America, it is evident that rural and small-town population growth accelerated in all major areas in the 1950s; the acceleration was slight in Europe, Latin America and Oceania, but substantial in South Asia, Africa, and probably also in East Asia. Part of the resumed growth in rural and small-town population in the highly urbanized regions of Europe, Northern America, the Soviet Union and Oceania may be attributable to the spread of improved means of transportation, permitting residence in small towns by workers and families who gain their livelihood in nearby cities.

The greatly varied rates of growth in rural and small-town population have made for very uneven gains in such population among the world's major areas. In the entire world, this population is here estimated to have increased by 634 million from 1920 to 1960; of that increase, nearly 300 million accrued to South Asia, 120 million to East Asia, 100 million to Africa, and 70 million to Latin America. In Europe, the rural and small-town population gained only about 30 million in forty years, and in Northern America about 14 million, whereas in the Soviet Union it is estimated to have been smaller in 1960 than in 1920.

Northern America, Oceania and Europe have been, and have remained, the world's most urbanized major areas, in terms of the percentage of total population contained in localities of 20,000 or more, while Africa, South Asia and East Asia have been, and still are, the least urbanized. Urbanization progressed most conspicuously in the Soviet Union and Latin America from levels in 1920 that would now be regarded as low to levels in 1960 that would have ranked among the highest some forty years previously.

Growth of big cities and multi-million cities

Proportions in distribution and increase during 1920-1960 are altered when the comparison is confined to big cities, i.e. agglomerations or metropolitan areas of at least 500,000 inhabitants (see tables 7, 8 and 9). The validity of the compari-

Table 7. Big-city population (agglomerations of 500,000 and more inhabitants) in major areas of the world, 1920–1960 (rough estimates, in millions)

Major area	1920	1930	1940	1950	1960
World Total	94.9	133.6	175.8	224.4	351.6
Europe (ex. USSR)	43.9	54.6	60.7	62.2	72.7
Northern America	21.8	31.0	36.4	50.0	72.0
East Asia	14.7	23.2	34.4	44.2	86.4
South Asia	4.6	6.3	13.4	26.1	42.4
Soviet Union	1.9	6.2	13.8	13.3	26.9
Latin America	5.4	8.4	11.8	19.6	35.2
Africa	0.9	1.8	2.9	6.0	10.8
Oceania	1.7	2.1	2.4	3.0	5.2

Table 8. Big-city population (500,000 and over) as a percentage of urban population (20,000 and over) in major areas of the world, 1920–1960 (rough estimates)

Major area	1920	1930	1940	1950	1960
World Total	38	41	41	42	47
Europe (ex. USSR)	42	44	43	42	42
Northern America	50	53	57	60	64
East Asia	38	41	42	42	54
South Asia	17	18	27	34	37
Soviet Union	12	26	29	27	34
Latin America	42	46	47	48	52
Africa	13	19	21	28	30
Oceania[a]	54	55	54	51	62

[a]Percentage computed with unrounded data.

Table 9. Big-city population (500,000 and over) as a percentage of total population in major areas of the world, 1920–1960 (rough estimates)

Major Area	1920	1930	1940	1950	1960
World Total	5	6	8	9	12
Europe (ex. USSR)	14	15	16	16	17
Northern America	19	23	25	30	36
East Asia	3	4	5	6	11
South Asia	1	1	2	4	5
Soviet Union	1	3	7	7	13
Latin America	6	8	9	12	17
Africa	1	1	2	3	4
Oceania[a]	18	19	21	22	31

[a]Percentage computed with unrounded data.

son is limited by the numerous difficulties of definition which have been encountered. In particular, there is cause to question whether the growth of cities
in Europe and in Northern America has been traced comparably, and the reader
is advised to refer to the notes in the Appendix.

Accepting the tentative estimates at face value, we may note that almost
one-half the world's big-city population in 1920 was found in Europe, while in
1960 Europe had only one-fifth of the world's big-city residents. As compared
with big cities of Europe in 1920, those of Northern America had only one-half
as much population, and those of East Asia only one-third; in 1960, Northern
America's big-city population equalled that of Europe, and that of East Asia
surpassed it.

Except in 1940, Latin America's big cities at most dates had more inhabitants than did the big cities of the Soviet Union, though in the Soviet Union the
combined urban population (including smaller cities and towns) always exceeded
that of Latin America.[14] In Africa, only Cairo had more than 500,000 inhabitants in 1920, whereas by 1960 Africa's ten big cities comprised a population of
appreciable size (10.8 million).

Regions of varied economic development and varied population density

Some of the major areas discussed in the foregoing contain regions of varied
economic development. Thus, Japan, Temperate South America, and Australia
and New Zealand are economically more developed than other regions of East
Asia, Latin America and Oceania. It is of interest, therefore, to differentiate the
estimates of urban and rural population for the more developed regions and for
the less developed ones. In addition, regions of greater average population density have been distinguished from those of less density. Comparisons are presented
first for more developed and for less developed regions combined (types A and
B), followed by additional comparisons for four sub-types of regions, as distinguished both by economic development and average density (sub-types 1 and
2 of A and B). The regions are grouped in the following manner:[15]

Type A-1. More developed regions of high population density: All of Europe,
and Japan.

Type A-2. More developed regions of lower population density: Northern
America, the Soviet Union, Temperate South America, and Australia
and New Zealand.

Type B-1. Less developed regions of high population density: East Asia without Japan, Middle South Asia, Southeast Asia, and the Caribbean.

Type B-1. Less developed regions of lower population density: Southwest Asia,
Tropical South America, the Middle American Mainland, all of
Africa, and Oceania without Australia and New Zealand.

Table 10. Multi-million cities in major areas of the world, 1920–1960 (rough estimates, in thousands)

City	1920	1930	1940	1950	1960
World Total	30,294	48,660	66,364	84,923	141,156
Europe total	16,051	18,337	18,675	18,016	18,605
London	7,236	8,127	8,275	8,366	8,190
Paris	4,965	5,885	6,050	6,300	7,140
Berlin	3,850	4,325	4,350	3,350	3,275
Northern America total	10,075	13,300	17,300	26,950	33,875
New York	7,125	9,350	10,600	12,350	14,150
Los Angeles	(750)[a]	(1,800)[a]	2,500	4,025	6,525
Chicago	2,950	3,950	4,200	4,950	6,000
Philadelphia	(2,025)[a]	(2,350)[a]	(2,475)[a]	2,950	3,650
Detroit	(1,100)[a]	(1,825)[a]	(2,050)[a]	2,675	3,550
East Asia total	4,168	11,773	15,789	16,487	40,806
Tokyo	4,168	6,064	8,558	8,182	13,534
Shanghai	(2,000)[a]	3,100	3,750	5,250	8,500
Osaka	(1,889)[a]	2,609	3,481	3,055	5,158
Peking	(1,000)[a]	(1,350)[a]	(1,750)[a]	(2,100)[a]	5,000
Tientsin	(800)[a]	(1,000)[a]	(1,500)[a]	(1,900)[a]	3,500
Hong Kong	(550)[a]	(700)[a]	(1,500)[a]	(1,925)[a]	2,614
Shenyang	...[b]	(700)[a]	(1,150)[a]	(1,700)[a]	2,500
South Asia total	...	...	3,400	7,220	12,700
Calcutta	(1,820)[a]	(2,055)[a]	3,400	4,490	5,810
Bombay	(1,275)[a]	(1,300)[a]	(1,660)[a]	2,730	4,040
Djakarta	...[b]	(525)[a]	(1,000)[a]	(1,750)[a]	2,850
Soviet Union total	...	2,500	7,700	4,250	9,550
Moscow	(1,120)[a]	2,500	4,350	4,250	6,150
Leningrad	(740)[a]	(2,000)[a]	3,350	(2,250)[a]	3,400
Latin America total	...	2,750	3,500	12,000	22,300
Buenos Aires	(2,275)[a]	2,750	3,500	5,150	6,775
Mexico	(835)[a]	(1,435)[a]	(2,175)[a]	3,800	6,450
Rio de Janeiro	(1,325)[a]	(1,675)[a]	(2,150)[a]	3,050	4,700
Sao Paulo	(600)[a]	(900)[a]	(1,425)[a]	(2,450)[a]	4,375
Africa total	...	...	...	...	3,320
Cairo	(875)[a]	(1,150)[a]	(1,525)[a]	(2,350)[a]	3,320

(Slight discrepancies with figures shown elsewhere are the result of rounding.)

[a] Cities smaller than 2,500,000 are not included in totals.
[b] Smaller than 500,000.

As shown in Table 11, from 1920 to 1960 total population grew by about 300 million in the more developed regions, and more than 800 million in less developed regions.

In both groups of regions in the forty years, urban population was augmented by about 250 million. But the urban population of the more developed regions, initially larger, increased by about 2.3 times while in the less developed regions urban population grew in the same period by 4.7 times.

Between 1920 and 1960, the rural and small-town population of the more developed regions had a net growth of only about 60 million, an increase of less than one-eighth the 1920 size. In the less developed regions, meanwhile, the addition to rural and small-town population was nearly 580 million, which is more than one-half its size in 1920.

Table 11. Trends in total, rural, urban and big-city population in regions of different levels of economic development, 1920–1960 (rough estimates, in millions)

Group of regions	1920	1930	1940	1950	1960
			Total population		
World total	1,860.2	2,069.3	2,296.9	2,516.8	2,994.4
More developed regions	672.3	757.8	821.6	858.0	976.5
Less developed regions	1,187.9	1,311.5	1,475.3	1,658.8	2,017.9
			Rural and small-town population		
World total	1,607.3	1,741.2	1,869.9	1,985.3	2,241.0
More developed regions	487.5	523.6	529.7	527.8	543.8
Less developed regions	1,119.8	1,217.6	1,340.2	1,457.5	1,697.2
			Urban population (20,000 and over)		
World total	252.9	328.1	427.0	531.5	753.4
More developed regions	184.8	234.2	291.9	330.2	432.7
Less developed regions	68.1	93.9	135.1	201.3	320.7
			Big-city population (500,000 and over)		
World total	94.9	135.6	176.8	224.4	351.6
More developed regions	80.1	111.2	133.8	149.8	212.4
Less developed regions	14.8	24.4	43.0	74.6	139.2
			Urban population as a percentage of total population		
World total	14	16	19	21	25
More developed regions	27	31	36	38	44
Less developed regions	6	7	9	12	16
			Big-city population as a percentage of urban population		
World total	38	41	41	42	47
More developed regions	43	47	46	45	49
Less developed regions	22	26	32	37	43
			Big-city population as a percentage of total population		
World total	5	7	8	9	12
More developed regions	12	15	16	17	22
Less developed regions	1	2	3	5	7

(Slight discrepancies with figures shown elsewhere are the result of rounding.)

The growth in big-city population, from 1920 to 1960, is estimated as 130 million in the more developed regions, and almost as much also in the less developed regions. But in the first type of regions big-city population was already of substantial size in 1920, and in 1960 it came to about 2.7 times that size; in the less developed regions, by contrast, where big cities in 1920 were still rather few and not exceedingly large, the forty years' growth in big-city population was more than nine-fold as estimated here.

In the more developed regions, the level of urbanization (percentage of total population in localities of at least 20,000 inhabitants) rose from 27 in 1920 to 44 in 1960, exceeding the rise in the percentage of urban population in less developed regions, where it increased from 6 percent in 1920 to 16 percent in 1960. From a relative point of view, however, it is correct to say that urbanization advanced more rapidly in the less developed regions, for there the level was initially low. Also, in the developed regions there was a comparatively slower growth in total population.

The concentration of urban population in big cities advanced relatively little in the more developed regions, namely from 43 percent in 1920 to 49 percent in 1960. In less developed regions, by contrast, the share of big cities rose from 22 to 43 percent of the urban population during that time.

A further subdivision in introduced in Table 12, showing the changes in urban and rural population in the two regions of economic development for regions of high and low average population density. Until many geographic and other factors are weighed, these density measures are of undetermined significance, and their consideration is included in this provisional report as a matter of interest for further research.

From reference to Table 12 it can be seen that the 1960 percentage distributions of the world's population among the four categories have a somewhat similar pattern for both total and rural and small-town population, with about 50 percent in the less developed higher density region and the remainder fairly evenly divided among the other three regions. The distribution of the world's urban population appears to be in nearly equal numbers among both regions of higher density and the more developed lower density region, while the proportion in the less developed lower density region is about half that of any of them.

In the period 1920–1960, for both total and urban population within each economic region, greater growth occurred in the less densely inhabited areas. For total population, increases amounted to 57 percent for type A-2 region compared with 36 percent for A-1, and 108 percent for B-2 compared with 60 percent for B-1. Urban population doubled in the type A-1 and tripled in the A-2 region, increased by 4½ times in B-1 and by more than 5 times in B-2. The highest level of urbanization was registered in the A-2 region, technologically advanced and possessing natural resources in great supply, increasing from 23 percent in 1920 to 47 percent in 1960. For type A-1, B-1 and B-2 regions, urbanization advanced by similar percentage points, from 31 to 42, 5 to 15 and 8 to 19, respectively.

Total population growth rates are, of course, closely linked to fertility

Table 12. Total, rural, urban and big-city population in regions of varied development and density for the world, 1920-1960 (rough estimates)

Group of regions	Population (millions)					Percent of world total				
	1920	1930	1940	1950	1960	1920	1930	1940	1950	1960
Total population										
World total	1,860.2	2,069.3	2,296.9	2,516.8	2,994.4	100	100	100	100	100
A[a]-1[b]	379.9	417.7	451.3	474.9	517.9	20	20	20	19	17
A-2[c]	292.4	340.1	370.3	383.1	458.6	16	16	16	15	15
B[d]-1	948.8	1,036.5	1,149.5	1,269.7	1,519.8	51	51	50	50	51
B-2	239.1	275.0	325.8	389.1	498.1	13	13	14	16	17
Rural and small-town population										
World total	1,607.3	1,741.2	1,869.9	1,985.3	2,241.0	100	100	100	100	100
A-1	262.5	275.9	283.7	296.1	301.2	16	16	15	15	13
A-2	225.0	247.7	246.0	231.7	242.6	14	14	13	12	11
B-1	898.8	965.9	1,047.7	1,122.0	1,294.8	56	56	56	56	58
B-2	221.0	251.7	292.5	335.5	402.4	14	14	16	17	18
Urban population (20,000 and over)										
World total	252.9	328.1	427.0	531.5	753.4	100	100	100	100	100
A-1	117.4	141.8	167.6	178.8	216.7	46	43	39	34	29
A-2	67.4	92.4	124.3	151.4	216.0	27	28	29	28	29
B-1	50.0	70.6	101.8	147.7	225.0	20	22	24	28	29
B-2	18.1	23.3	33.3	53.6	95.7	7	7	8	10	13
Big-city population (500,000 and over)										
World total	94.9	135.6	176.8	224.4	351.6	100	100	100	100	100
A-1	51.9	65.9	76.1	76.3	97.2	54	49	43	34	28
A-2	28.2	45.3	57.7	73.5	115.2	30	33	33	33	33
B-1	10.3	18.1	33.4	56.2	102.3	11	13	19	25	29
B-2	4.5	6.3	9.6	18.4	36.9	5	5	5	8	10

(Slight discrepancies with figures shown elsewhere are the result of rounding.)

[a]A. More developed regions.
[b]B. Less developed regions.
[c]1. Regions of higher average population density.
[d]2. Regions of lower average population density.

levels, which are known to be higher in regions of lower population density.[16] The higher urban growth rates in these regions may in addition be related to the fact that urbanization occurred there more recently, advancing from a lower level in these regions as compared with Europe (see discussion in the following section).

Observations on regions grouped by recency of urbanization

Because world regions differ in pace of population growth as well as in levels, the element of time is here specifically examined in connection with the process

Table 13. Summary of changes in total, rural, urban and big-city populations in regions of the world classified by recency of urbanization, 1920-1940 and 1940-1960 (rough estimates, in millions)

Group of regions	1920	1940	1960	1940 per 100 in 1920	1960 per 100 in 1940
		Total population			
World total	1,860.2	2,296.9	2,994.4	123	130
Group I[a]	297.9	353.9	452.3	119	128
Group II[b]	503.9	648.0	813.6	129	126
Group III[c]	1,058.4	1,295.0	1,728.5	122	133
		Rural and small-town population			
World total	1,607.3	1,869.9	2,241.0	116	120
Group I	176.6	187.5	206.4	106	110
Group II	426.9	493.6	545.0	116	110
Group III	1,003.8	1,188.8	1,489.6	118	125
		Urban population (20,000 and over)			
World total	252.9	427.0	753.4	169	176
Group I	121.3	166.4	245.9	137	148
Group II	77.0	154.4	268.6	201	174
Group III	54.6	106.2	238.9	195	225
		Big-city population (500,000 and over)			
World total	94.9	175.8	351.6	186	200
Group I	57.6	83.4	135.0	144	162
Group II	26.0	60.1	115.6	231	192
Group III	11.3	32.3	101.0	286	313
		Urban population as a percentage of total population			
World total	14	19	25		
Group I	41	47	54		
Group II	15	24	33		
Group III	5	8	14		
		Big-city population as a percentage of urban population			
World total	38	41	47		
Group I	47	50	55		
Group II	34	39	43		
Group III	21	30	42		
		Big-city population as a percentage of total population			
World total	5	8	12		
Group I	19	24	30		
Group II	5	9	14		
Group III	1	2	6		

[a]Regions at least 25 percent urbanized by 1920.
[b]Regions at least 25 percent urbanized by 1960 but not by 1920.
[c]Regions not yet 25 percent urbanized by 1960.

of urbanization. Estimates for regions grouped according to attainment of 25 percent urban in total population by specified years are given in the Appendix tables and summarized in Table 13. The groups are as follows:

I. Regions at least 25 percent urbanized by 1920: Western Europe, Northern Europe, Northern America, Temperate South America, and Australia and New Zealand.

II. Regions at least 25 percent urbanized by 1960 but not by 1920: Southern Europe, Eastern Europe, Japan, Other East Asia, the Soviet Union, Tropical South America, the Middle American Mainland, Northern Africa, and Southern Africa.

III. Regions not yet 25 percent urbanized by 1960: Mainland East Asia, Middle South Asia, Southeast Asia, Southwest Asia, the Caribbean, Tropical Africa, and other Oceania.

Urbanization is shown in Table 13 to progress fastest at the intermediate level, group II, but not so fast where the level is still low, or where it is already high.

In 1960, total population in group II was nearly twice that of group I, and total population in group III approximately twice that of group II. On the other hand, total urban populations in the three groups were nearly equal. The distribution of the world's rural population, accordingly, was all the more uneven: 9 percent of the world's rural and small-town population, in 1960, was in group I, 24 percent in group II, and 67 percent in group III.

Increases in urban and rural population proceeded unequally among the three groups of regions. Between 1920 and 1960, total population increased 52 percent in group I, 61 percent in group II, and 63 percent in group III, comparatively slight differences in rates. During the same time, urban population doubled in group I, grew by 3½ times in group II, and 4½ times in group III; rural population grew by 17 percent in group I, 28 percent in group II, and 48 percent in group III. In short, similar rates of total population growth have produced varied rates of urban and rural growth according to the levels of urbanization: where the level of urbanization was already high, only moderate rates of growth in both the urban and the rural populations occurred, but where the level of urbanization was low, both the urban and the rural populations grew with greatest rapidity. Expressed in average annual rates, the phenomenon was as follows:

Type of regions	Average annual rate of population growth, 1920–60		
	Total	Urban	Rural and small-town
I. Early urbanized	1.0	1.8	0.4
II. Recently urbanized	1.2	3.2	0.6
III. Least urbanized	1.2	3.8	1.0

The recent acceleration of population growth in most of the world's regions, particularly the less developed ones, has merely intensified this phenomenon. Patterns are similar, but rates of growth in urban and rural populations diverged more widely.

The average annual rates for the 1950–1960 period are shown below.

Type of regions	Average annual rate of population growth, 1950–1960		
	Total	Urban	Rural and small-town
I. Early urbanized	1.3	2.3	0.3
II. Recently urbanized	1.7	4.0	0.8
III. Least urbanized	1.9	4.5	1.5

If this analysis can serve to illustrate the nature of the momentum of urbanization, and if the distinctions made are relevant, the following general conclusions are suggested:

(a) With a given rate of growth in total population, and a low level of urbanization, both the urban and the rural populations are apt to grow rapidly, and yet the level of urbanization can advance only gradually;

(b) With a similar rate of growth in total population, and an intermediate level of urbanization, urban population can grow rapidly, and the level of urbanization can advance rapidly, without necessarily any rapid growth in rural population; and

(c) With a similar rate of growth in total population, and a high level of urbanization, both urban and rural population can grow at relatively moderate rates, while the level of urbanization progresses also at a moderate pace.

These dynamic considerations—in terms of rates of growth—must also be coordinated with a consideration of the resulting balance in absolute numbers

Type of regions	Absolute increases in population (millions)		
	Total	Urban	Rural and small-town
	1920–1940		
I. Early urbanized	56	45	11
II. Recently urbanized	144	77	67
III. Least urbanized	237	52	185
	1950–1960		
I. Early urbanized	56	50	6
II. Recently urbanized	129	87	42
III. Least urbanized	294	86	208

and structural proportions. As compared with urban areas, the rural rates of growth are more moderate, but it should not be overlooked that those rates give large increases in numbers of rural inhabitants where the rural population is of large size. A comparison is made on the preceding page of absolute increases in total, urban and rural populations in the three types of regions for the twenty-year period from 1920 to 1940 and the ten-year period from 1950 to 1960. Both periods have been relatively undisturbed by war, and the world's total population has grown about as much in the recent decade as it did in the earlier two decades.

The momentum of urbanization
and of concentration in big cities

The analysis of changes in urban and rural population by each individual region and for each decade cannot yield or has not yet yielded much that is useful for purposes of broad generalization. First, the present estimates still suffer from many defects with respect to accuracy and comparability. Secondly, circumstances are differently combined in each region, causing an interaction of factors impenetrable to any quick analysis. Finally, events of particular decades, such as wars, economic depression, and periods of rehabilitation affected regions diversely. Much remains to be learned from intensive regional studies.

The fluctuations caused by short-term interferences with normal regional developments are partly disposed of when the analysis is confined to long periods. The peculiarities of circumstances in particular regions are partly compensated for when regions are grouped. Salient features can then be deduced from data such as those brought together in Table 16. Quite obviously, on a worldwide scale, and over long periods, urbanization is characterized by a powerful momentum of its own. Similarly, it can be shown that the tendency of urban population to become increasingly concentrated in big cities also appears possessed of an inherent trend.

Big cities can become numerous and increase in size only where the urban population is already large. Part of the increase in big-city population is drawn from the surpassing of size-limits and the absorption of previously smaller cities and towns. In addition, individual big cities tend to grow in rough proportion with the general increase in urban population. It seems possible to consider that some average relationship might persist between levels of urbanization, general growth in population, and the emergence and growth of big cities. The possibility of such a relationship is suggested in a comparison of a few summary figures, given on the following page.

As it happens—and no precise reason is known—in six of the eight sets of figures the percentages of urbanization and the percentages of total population gains accruing to big cities are within one point of each other. The two exceptions are found for 1940-1960: in regions of type III (not yet highly urbanized), big cities appear to have grown slightly faster than indicated by the level of urbanization; in regions of type I (early urbanized), they appear to have grown

Type of regions	1940	1960	1920–40	1940–60
	Total population		*Gain in total population*	
World total	2,296.9	2,994.4	436.7	697.5
I. Early urbanized	353.9	452.3	56.0	98.4
II. Recently urbanized	648.0	813.6	144.1	165.6
III. Least urbanized	1,295.0	1,728.5	236.6	433.5
	Urban population (20,000 and over)		*Gain in big-city population (cities of 500,000 and over)*	
World total	427.0	753.4	80.9	175.8
I. Early urbanized	166.4	245.9	25.8	51.6
II. Recently urbanized	154.4	268.6	34.1	55.5
III. Least urbanized	106.2	238.9	21.0	68.7
	Urban population as a percentage of total population		*Gain in big-city population as a percentage of gain in total population*	
World total	19	25	19	25
I. Early urbanized	47	54	46	52
II. Recently urbanized	24	33	24	34
III. Least urbanized	8	14	9	16

somewhat more slowly. But these deviations are easily within the range of errors of the estimates. For instance, the metropolitan area populations in Europe have for the most part been estimated within constant boundaries, though the limits of urbanized territory probably were smaller at earlier dates.

C.   A TENTATIVE LOOK AT THE FUTURE

A crude method of projection

The dynamics of trends in total population have been studied in terms of fertility, mortality, international migration, and composition by age groups. Although unforeseen factors may affect them, trends in total population nevertheless can be projected into the future with some degree of plausibility. Use is made here of a recent set of regional and world projections of total population.[17]

Only crude methods are indicated at this time for projections of urban population derived from those of total population. The worldwide conditions attending urbanization are not clearly understood, and the factors which can modify them at any time are numerous and complex. With the present information, it is unlikely that more refined methods can yield more trustworthy results. Based on the foregoing observations, two crude devices were used to obtain for the year 1980 estimates of urban (localities of 20,000 and over) and big-city (agglomerations of at least 500,000) population.

Comparing the magnitudes of increase in the percentages of urban population over the period 1920–1960, it can be seen from reference to Table 13 that the greatest increase accrued to the group intermediate in the scale of recency of urbanization, the least increase to the level of least urbanization, with the group of highest urbanization progressing at an intermediate rate. A logistic curve was fitted to the three series of group averages by assuming that together they may constitute a long time sequence, group II in 1920 being linked directly with group III in 1960, and being followed, after an interpolated time interval, by the sequence in group I. It was also assumed that urbanization would never exceed the level of 70 percent in any world region. With this logistic curve, which fitted the data tolerably well, it was possible to estimate from a given percentage level of urbanization what might be—in conformity with the average of observed past trends—the percentage level of urbanization to be expected twenty years later. Of course this is an exceedingly crude method.

The second device is based on the observation made in the preceding section. For reasons which are unclear, a near coincidence has been observed between the percentage level of urbanization at the end of a twenty-year period, and the percentage of the absolute increment in total population during the twenty-year period which is gained in the big cities. Big-city population can be tentatively projected on the crude assumption that this relationship will also hold true in the future.

The two crude assumptions, namely (a) a logistic curve for the extrapolation of the percentage of urban population, and (b) derivation from that percentage of estimates of growth in big-city population, have been applied, in rough calculations for a period up to 1980, to the estimates and projections of total population for each of the twenty-one regions. This was done indiscriminately, though it is unlikely that such crude assumptions can be applied with equal justification to regions where numerous other circumstances differ so much. Naturally, much study of the possible effects of various factors on urbanization is recommended as a basis for more realistic projections into the future, if these are to have any forecasting value.

The present projections should be regarded as not much more than a game in numbers, indicative perhaps of plausible orders of magnitude, but not as forecasts related to any detailed pertinent conditions. For whatever they may be worth, summary results of these calculations are shown in Table 14, together with estimates from 1920 onward, by twenty-year time intervals. The same calculations have also been used as the basis for the appended charts.

The projections suggest that, in the world as a whole, population may increase by as great an amount from 1960 to 1980 as it did in the forty years from 1920 to 1960. The 1960–1980 additions to the rural and small-town population may equal or slightly surpass those of the preceding forty-year period, and future increments to the urban population may be considerably larger than those of the selected past period. It is possible that the population in the world's big cities (500,000 and more) may double between 1960 and 1980. This may happen though the several 1960–1980 increments in Europe, Northern America and Oceania may be smaller than have been those of the 1920–1960 period, and the

Table 14. Crude tentative projections of total, rural, urban and big-city population in major world areas, 1960–1980, and estimates for 1920–1960 (millions)

Major areas and type of settlement	1920 (est.)	1940 (est.)	1960 (est.)	1980 (project.)	Absolute increment 1920–60	1960–80
World total						
Total population	1,860	2,298	2,994	4,269	1,134	1,275
Rural, small-town	1,607	1,871	2,242	2,909	635	667
Urban	253	427	752	1,360	499	608
(Big cities)	(96)	(175)	(351)	(725)	(255)	(374)
Europe (excluding USSR)						
Total population	324	379	425	479	101	54
Rural, small-town	220	239	251	244	31	−7
Urban	104	140	174	235	70	61
(Big cities)	(44)	(61)	(73)	(99)	(29)	(26)
Northern America						
Total population	116	144	198	262	82	64
Rural, small-town	72	80	86	101	14	15
Urban	44	64	112	161	68	49
(Big cities)	(22)	(36)	(72)	(111)	(50)	(39)
East Asia						
Total population	553	636	794	1,038	241	244
Rural, small-town	514	554	634	742	120	108
Urban	39	82	160	296	121	136
(Big cities)	(15)	(34)	(86)	(155)	(71)	(69)
South Asia						
Total population	470	610	858	1,366	388	508
Rural, small-town	443	560	742	1,079	299	337
Urban	27	50	116	287	89	171
(Big cities)	(5)	(13)	(42)	(149)	(37)	(107)
Soviet Union						
Total population	155	195	214	278	59	64
Rural, small-town	139	148	136	150	−3	14
Urban	16	47	78	128	62	50
(Big cities)	(2)	(14)	(27)	(56)	(25)	(29)
Latin America						
Total population	90	130	213	374	123	161
Rural, small-town	77	105	145	222	68	77
Urban	13	25	68	152	55	84
(Big cities)	(5)	(12)	(35)	(100)	(30)	(65)
Africa						
Total population	143	192	276	449	133	173
Rural, small-town	136	178	240	360	104	120
Urban	7	14	36	89	29	53
(Big cities)	(1)	(3)	(11)	(47)	(10)	(36)
Oceania						
Total population	9	12	16	23	7	7
Rural, small-town	6	7	8	11	2	3
Urban	3	5	8	11	5	3
(Big cities)	(2)	(2)	(5)	(8)	(3)	(3)

(Slight discrepancies with figures shown elsewhere are the result of rounding.)

Table 15. Crude tentative projections of total, rural, urban and big-city population in more developed, and less developed regions of the world, 1960–1980, and estimates for 1920–1960 (millions)

Type of settlement	1920 (est.)	1940 (est.)	1960 (est.)	1980 (project.)	Absolute increment 1920–60	Absolute increment 1960–80
			World total			
Total population	1,860	2,298	2,994	4,269	1,134	1,275
Rural, small-town	1,607	1,871	2,242	2,909	635	667
Urban	253	427	752	1,360	499	608
(Big cities)	(96)	(175)	(351)	(725)	(255)	(374)
		A. More developed regions				
Total population	672	821	977	1,189	305	212
Rural, small-town	487	530	544	566	57	22
Urban	185	291	433	623	248	190
(Big cities)	(80)	(134)	(212)	(327)	(132)	(115)
		B. Less developed regions				
Total population	1,188	1,476	2,017	3,080	829	1,063
Rural, small-town	1,120	1,341	1,698	2,343	578	645
Urban	68	135	319	737	251	418
(Big cities)	(16)	(41)	(139)	(398)	(123)	(259)
	Less developed regions as a percentage of world total					
Total population	64	64	67	72	73	83
Rural, small-town	70	72	76	81	91	97
Urban	27	32	42	54	50	69
(Big cities)	(16)	(24)	(40)	(55)	(48)	(69)

(Slight discrepancies with figures shown elsewhere are the result of rounding.)

1960–1980 increments in East Asia and the Soviet Union may not be significantly larger. The acceleration of increments in total, rural, urban and big-city population is likely to become most conspicuous in South Asia, Latin America and Africa. At the same time, there will also occur a further re-distribution in urban population among different parts of the world.

Possible implications

The estimates and tentative projections for each region can also be brought together so as to distinguish the group of more developed and that of presently less developed regions (i.e., regions of types A and B, as previously described), and this is done for comparative purposes in Table 15. The percentage shares of the less developed regions relative to world totals are particularly noteworthy.

Of the world's total population, 64 percent was that of less developed regions in 1920, 64 percent in 1940, 67 percent in 1960, and by 1980 it may be 72 percent. Of the world's population increase from 1920 to 1960, 73 percent accrued to the less developed regions, and of the increase projected from 1960 to 1980 the less developed regions may absorb 83 percent.

In terms of rural and small-town population, the share in the less developed regions has risen from 70 percent in 1920 to 72 percent in 1940 and 76 percent in 1960, and it may attain 81 percent in 1980. The remarkable observation can be made that of the world's increase in rural and small-town population in the past four decades 91 percent occurred in the less developed regions, and the tentative projections suggest that almost 97 percent of increments in the world's rural and small-town inhabitants may accrue there in the two decades to come.

Less developed regions have had a rapidly expanding share in the world's urban population, a trend that is likely to continue. Their share amounted to 27 percent in 1920, 32 percent in 1940, 42 percent in 1960, and may rise to 54 percent by 1980. One-half of the world's increase in urban population occurred there during 1920–1960, and more than two-thirds may occur there in 1960–1980. The less developed regions' share in the world's big-city population, initially low, has increased even more sharply.

Perhaps the following comparisons are most eloquent. In 1960, the more developed regions had a rural population of 544 million and an urban population of 433 million, of which 212 million [were] in big cities. As tentatively calculated here, in the presently less developed regions the net additions to the 1960 population may by 1980 amount to 645 million rural and 418 million urban inhabitants, of which 259 million [will be] in big cities. The *1960–1980 population increase in less developed regions,* therefore, can exceed the *1960 total population in the developed regions.* According to this projection, an excess would appear in the big-city and rural and small-town populations, while the urban population would be nearly the equivalent of the 1960 urban population in the more developed regions.

Whatever the errors of estimate in so crude a projection, it is certain that the trend of urbanization will include far-reaching implications, many foreseeable and many as yet obscure.

Some of the foreseeable consequences of the momentum of urbanization cause much concern. To mention a few of the problems, there are those related to food production and distribution adequate for the dietary needs of city-dwellers and the economic needs of agriculturists; the equitable flow of capital and terms of trade between diversely endowed regions; the mental and physical health of the society; planning for housing, transportation networks and other physical needs for localities of all sizes and for the modes of exchange and interaction between cities, towns and countryside, within and beyond country borders.

From another viewpoint, urban growth can be regarded as a powerhouse for development. Throughout history, towns and cities have been the crucible of a cultural, social and economic innovation and transformation permeating society. Urbanization, therefore, creates environments conducive to a quickened rate of progress. Certainly, the best possible use should be made of a process which, in any event, can hardly be circumvented.

It is also probable that further phases in the development process will affect the underlying population trends themselves and, by such "feedback" effects, cause them to differ from those that can be more directly projected. As pointed out at the beginning of this study, the observed environmental changes are simultaneously quantitative and qualitative. Not only do cities grow, but in the process they become something different from what they have been. The traditional dichotomy between urban and rural areas is becoming increasingly blurred and new types of environment have begun to emerge under diverse conditions which can no longer be fittingly described as either "urban" or "rural." The process of urbanization may come to surpass itself and give rise to geographic and social forms of human settlement to which the current vocabulary can no longer be validly applied. Complementarity and mutual benefits may be generated among areas where at present only a conflict of local interests is most in evidence.

APPENDIX

I.   Major areas and regions of the world.
II. Charts of big-city, other urban, and rural and small-town population in major areas of the world:
   A.   1920 (estimated)
   B.   1940 (estimated)
   C.   1960 (estimated)
   D.   1980 (projected)
III. Tables of estimated population in world regions grouped by recency of urbanization, 1920–1960:
   A.   Total population
   B.   Urban population
   C.   Rural and small-town population
   D.   Urban population as a percentage of total population

NOTES

1. An earlier United Nations document on this topic is entitled "World Survey of Urban and Rural Population Growth" (Preliminary Report by the Secretary-General to the Population Commission), E/CN.9/187, 8 March 1965.

2. Another approach is the study of interaction between changes in settlement pattern, viz. urbanization, and changes in economic and social circumstances, as affecting an entire population. That is the approach adopted in the companion paper at this Conference, "Urbanization and Economic and Social Change."

3. For a comprehensive discussion, see L. Mumford, *The City in History,* New York, 1961, and P. M. Hauser (ed.), "World Urbanism," a symposium, *American Journal of Sociology,* vol. 60, no. 5, March 1955.

4. The most systematic attempt to define such areas comparably is that of Kingsley Davis, *et al., The World's Metropolitan Areas,* International Urban Research, Berkeley and Los Angeles, 1959.

5. See a discussion by A. W. Gilmore, *Transportation and the Growth of Cities,* Glenmore (Ill.), 1953.

6. This definition has come into wide use in international research. It has at least the advantage that localities of a "rural," i.e., mainly agrarian, type, are thereby virtually ex-

cluded. True, it is also reported that many of the rural communes recently constituted in China comprise more than 20,000 persons, but there is little quantitative information concerning them, nor is it certain that the administrative arrangements have necessarily caused a coalescence in the settlement pattern of hitherto separate villages. An early use of 20,000 as a lower size limit in the study of urban population appears in Kingsley Davis and Hilda Hertz, "The World Distribution of Urbanization," *Bulletin of the International Statistical Institute,* vol. 33, part IV.

7. This distinction came into wide use especially in many German studies of urban population and geography. In those studies, localities with 100,000 and more inhabitants were generally referred to as "big cities" (Grosstaedte).

8. Cities estimated as 500,000 or larger numbered 75 in 1920, 98 in 1930, 125 in 1940, 159 in 1950 and 232 in 1960.

9. See also, on this problem, the United Nations document "World Survey of Urban and Rural Population Growth," *op. cit.*

10. *Provisional Report on World Population Prospects, as assessed in 1963.* United Nations, ST/SOA/Ser. R/7, 1965.

11. Some of these figures differ slightly from those published in other sources, and are subject to further revision.

12. Assuming urban population had grown by 30 percent in the 1950s (as it actually did in the 1920s and 1930s), the accelerated growth in the world's total population would have caused rural population to grow from 1,985 million in 1950 to 2,302 million in 1960, that is by 317 million, or by 16 percent. Assuming rural population had grown by 7 percent in the 1950s (as it actually did on the average of the decades from 1920 to 1950), the accelerated growth in the world's total population would have caused urban population to grow from 532 million in 1950 to 870 million in 1960, that is by 338 million, or by 64 percent.

13. E.g., K. Davis *et al., The World's Metropolitan Regions, op. cit.*; United Nations, "World Survey of Urban and Rural Population Growth," *op. cit.*; Homer Hoyt, *World Urbanization,* Urban Land Institute, Technical Bulletin No. 43; and numerous other sources.

14. It is of interest to note the difference in the "top-heaviness" of urbanization in these two areas. This may be largely attributable to two circumstances. First, many of Latin America's big cities are the seats of separate national governments, and these tend to grow large in a number of countries having few other sizable cities. Secondly, regional planning efforts in the Soviet Union have stimulated the growth of a number of widely distributed cities of considerable size, and thereby the tendency of urbanization to become concentrated in a small number of very large cities has been counter-balanced to a certain extent.

15. The same regional groupings were used also in the United Nations *Provisional Report on World Population Prospects, op. cit.*

16. See, in these respects, the United Nations *Provisional Report on World Population Prospects, . . . op. cit.,* and also the introductory chapter in *Population Bulletin of the United Nations, with special reference to conditions and trends of fertility in the world,* New York, 1965.

17. *Provisional Report on World Population Prospects, op. cit.* The projections are for the same major areas and regions as used in the present study and set forth in the Appendix.

6

OSCAR LEWIS, Further Observations on the Folk-Urban Continuum and Urbanization with Special Reference to Mexico City

My interest in studies of urbanism and the urbanization process in Mexico City has been a direct outgrowth of my earlier study of Tepoztlan. In that work I suggested that the folk-urban continuum was an inadequate theoretical model for the study of culture change and that it needed drastic revision.[1] Later, in my follow-up study of Tepoztecans who had migrated to Mexico City, I found evidence which strengthened this conviction, this time viewing the problem from the urban pole.[2]

Each of the terms folk, rural, and urban encompasses a wide range of phenomena with multiple variables which have to be carefully sorted out, ordered, dissected, and perhaps redefined if we are to establish meaningful, causal relationships among them. Each of these terms implies relatively high-level abstractions intended for the characterization of whole societies or large segments thereof. Although such characterizations are attractive because of their simplicity and may be useful in distinguishing gross stages or types in societal evolution, they confuse issues in the study of short-run changes, and their heuristic value as research tools has never been proven.

Hauser has put this criticism admirably. He writes,

> There is evidence, by no means conclusive as yet, that both parts of these dichotomies [i.e., folk-urban and rural-urban] represent confounded variables and, in fact, complex systems of variables which have yet to be unscrambled. The dichotomizations perhaps represent all too hasty efforts to synthesize and integrate what little knowledge has been acquired in empirical research. The widespread acceptance of these ideal-type constructs as generalizations, without benefit of adequate research, well illustrates the dangers of catchy neologisms which often get confused with knowledge.[3]

In his elaboration of the folk-urban continuum, Redfield sought to achieve greater sophistication than earlier societal typologies by utilizing traits or variables that were of a general, more abstract nature. For example, whereas Hobhouse, Wheeler, and Ginsburg distinguished among food-gathering, hunting and

Oscar Lewis, "The Folk-Urban Ideal Types: A. Further Observations on the Folk-Urban Continuum and Urbanization with Special Reference to Mexico City," in Philip M. Hauser and L. F. Schnore (eds.), *The Study of Urbanization* (New York: John Wiley & Sons, Inc., 1965), pp. 491–503. Reprinted by permission.

fishing, agricultural, and pastoral economies, and sought to establish their social and juridical correlates, Redfield's definition of the folk society as an ideal type never specified a type of technology or economy beyond stating that it was simple, subsistence motivated, without money, familial, and so on.

In his later work Redfield showed some important but subtle changes in his thinking which have not been given sufficient emphasis by his followers and disciples, many of whom suffer from fixation or culture lag. Here I should like to mention two such changes. First, he seemed to be less sanguine about the possibility of deriving sound general propositions concerning social and cultural change and gave more stress to descriptive integration, "understanding,"and the element of art in the social sciences. Compare, for example, his *Folk Culture of Yucatán* with *The Village That Chose Progress.* In the former, he was still optimistic about finding regularities in culture change. In the latter, he gave us a brilliant description of changes in Chan Kom but made no attempt to relate these changes to the theoretical framework of the folk-urban continuum.

A second change is to be seen in *The Primitive World and Its Transformations,* where he no longer conceives of the folk society exclusively as an ideal type. Rather, he treats it as a type of real society. In this book Redfield takes a frank neo-evolutionary stance, identifying the folk society with the preagricultural or preneolithic period and with the tribal (and I would add pretribal) level. In an effort to find common elements he paints with a big brush, lumping together all the peoples of the world prior to the neolithic, irrespective of whether they were food-gatherers, fishers, or hunters, whether they had rich or poor resources, whether they were starving or produced some surplus. In the very nature of the case, this approach glosses over the more refined archeological distinctions, between the Lower and Upper Paleolithic, each with subdivisions based upon new technologies and inventions.

True, we have little evidence about societal types for the prehistoric periods. However, a theoretical scheme must somehow take into account many levels and types of societal development prior to the rise of cities. Otherwise, there are unexplained and sudden breaks in the postulated evolutionary sequence from folk to urban. Indeed, if one had to choose between evolutionary schemes, there is still a good deal to be said in favor of Morgan's *Ancient Society* despite its many factual errors and crude technological determinism. Fortunately, we have other and more sophisticated alternatives, such as the multilinear evolution of Julian Steward and the recent work of Irving Goldman.[4]

The identification of the folk society with the preneolithic seems to me to invalidate or, at least, to raise serious questions about Redfield's work in *The Folk Cultures of Yucatán,* since all of the Yucatán communities were agricultural peasant societies, which, by his own definition, are part societies subject in varying degree to urban influences. Even his most "folk-like" community of Quintana Roo was producing hennequin for the world market!

Similarly, some of my own criticism of his Tepoztlan work, as well as Sol Tax's criticism based on the Guatemalan studies, would seem to be beside the point since both Tax and I were dealing with communities which had left the folk stage (if they were ever in it) for at least a few thousand years. To this extent, Ralph Beals's comment that Tepoztlan was not a crucial case for evaluating the transition from folk to peasant to urban has considerable merit, because Tepoztlan was already a well-advanced peasant society in pre-Hispanic days. But by the same token, I know of no other contemporary community study in Meso-America which would serve this purpose any better. Actually, Redfield had assumed a survival of folk, that is, paleolithic, elements in Tepoztlan, a period for which we have no evidence in that village.

The traditional contrast between societies based on kinship versus those based on nonkinship or contract is not only inaccurate but of so broad and general a nature as to be of little help in the analysis of the process of change. To say of a society that it is organized on a kinship basis does not tell us enough for purposes of comparative analysis. It may be a nuclear family system as among the Shoshone Indians, a lineage system as in Tikopia, or a clan system as among the Zuni Indians. We still have a lot to learn about the more modest problem of how and under what conditions in a given society, a simple nuclear, bilateral system turns into a unilateral clan system, and the social, economic, and psychological concomitants thereof. As a general proposition I would like to suggest that we may learn more about the processes of change by studying relatively short-run sequential modifications in particular aspects of institutions in both the so-called folk and urban societies, than by global comparisons between folk and urban.

Preurban and preindustrial societies have been capable of developing class stratification, elaborate priesthoods, status rivalry, and many other phenomena that are implicity and unilaterally attributed to the growth of cities, according to the folk-urban conception of social change. Tonga, the Maori, and native Hawaii are good examples of this. Even among a fishing and hunting people like the Kwakiutl Indians, we find class stratification, slavery, and war. The Kwakiutl case illustrates the importance of including natural resources as a significant variable in evolutionary schemes. I find no such variable in the folk-urban continuum.

In place of, or in addition to, the handy designations, folk society, peasant society, urban society, we need a large number of subtypes based on better defined variables and perhaps the addition of new ones.[5] Hauser's observations on the western ethnocentrism implicit in the folk-urban and rural-urban dichotomies is well taken. Redfield's firsthand research experience in Mexican communities, which were essentially endogamous, tended to confirm his preconception of the folk society as "inward-looking." The thinking of Simmel, Tönnies, Durkheim, and others, which influenced Redfield, was also based on experience with the endogamous peasant communities of Europe. Had these men done field work with the Nuer of Africa, with the Australian aborigines, or with the north Indian peasants, it is quite possible that Redfield's ideal-type model of the folk society might have been somewhat different.

Before turning to an examination of some of the assumptions of the

Simmel-Wirth-Redfield axis regarding urbanism, I would like to present in brief some of my own research findings in Mexico which can serve as a starting point for the discussion. The relevant findings of my first Mexico City study of 1951 can be summarized as follows: (1) Peasants in Mexico City adapted to city life with far greater ease than one would have expected judging from comparable studies in the United States and from folk-urban theory. (2) Family life remained quite stable and extended family ties increased rather than decreased. (3) Religious life became more Catholic and disciplined, indicating the reverse of the anticipated secularization process. (4) The system of *compadrazgo* continued to be strong, albeit with some modifications. (5) The use of village remedies and beliefs persisted.

In the light of these findings I wrote at the time, ". . . this study provides evidence that urbanization is not a single, unitary, universally similar process but assumes different forms and meanings, depending upon the prevailing historic, economic, social, and cultural conditions."[6]

Because of the unusual nature of my findings, I decided to test them in 1956–1957 against a much wider sample of non-Tepoztecan city families. I selected two lower-class housing settlements or *vecindades,* both located in the same neighborhood within a few blocks of the Tepito market and only a short walk from the central square of Mexico City. In contrast with the Tepoztecan city families who represented a wide range of socioeconomic levels and were scattered in twenty-two *colonias* throughout the city, my new sample was limited to two settlements whose residents came from twenty-four of the thirty-two states and territories of the Mexican nation.[7]

On the whole, my research findings tended to support those of the earlier study. The findings suggested that the lower-class residents of Mexico City showed much less of the personal anonymity and isolation of the individual which had been postulated by Wirth as characteristic of urbanism as a way of life. The *vecindad* and the neighborhood tended to break up the city into small communities that acted as cohesive and personalizing factors. I found that many people spent most of their lives within a single *colonia* or district, and even when there were frequent changes of residence, they were usually within a restricted geographical area determined by low rentals. Lifetime friendships and daily face-to-face relations with the same people were common, and resembled a village situation. Most marriages also occurred within the *colonia* or adjoining *colonias.* Again, I found that extended family ties were quite strong, as measured by visiting, especially in times of emergency, and that a relatively high proportion of the residents of the *vecindades* were related by kinship and *compadrazgo* ties.

In spite of the cult of *machismo* and the overall cultural emphasis upon male superiority and dominance, I found a strong tendency toward matricentered families, in which the mother played a crucial role in parent-child relations even after the children were married. In genealogical studies I found that most people recalled a much larger number of relatives on the mother's side than on the father's side.

I also found that the *vecindad* acted as a shock absorber for the rural migrants to the city because of the similarity between its culture and that of rural communities. Both shared many of the traits which I have elsewhere designated as "the culture of poverty." Indeed, I found no sharp differences in family structure, diet, dress, and belief systems of the *vecindad* tenants according to their rural-urban origins. The use of herbs for curing, the raising of animals, the belief in sorcery and spiritualism, the celebration of the Day of the Dead, illiteracy and low level of education, political apathy and cynicism about government, and the very limited membership and participation in both formal and informal associations, were just as common among persons who had been in the city for over thirty years as among recent arrivals. Indeed, I found that *vecindad* residents of peasant background who came from small landholding families showed more middle-class aspirations in their desire for a higher standard of living, home ownership, and education for their children than did city born residents of the lower-income group.

These findings suggest the need for a reexamination of some aspects of urban theory and for modifications which would help explain the findings from Mexico City and other cities in underdeveloped countries, as well as those from Chicago.

Wirth defines a city as "a relatively large, dense, and permanent settlement of socially heterogeneous individuals." By "socially heterogeneous" he had in mind primarily distinctive ethnic groups rather than class differences. Wirth defines urbanism as the mode of life of people who live in cities or who are subject to their influence. Because Wirth thinks of the city as a whole, as a community (and here, I believe, is one of his errors), he assumes that all people who live in cities are affected by this experience in profound and similar ways, namely, the weakening of kinship bonds, family life, and neighborliness, and the development of impersonality, superficiality, anonymity, and transitoriness in personal relations. For Wirth the process of urbanization is essentially a process of disorganization.[8]

This approach leads to some difficulties. For one thing, as Sjoberg has pointed out, ". . . their interpretations [i.e., those of Park, Wirth and Redfield] involving ecology have not articulated well with their efforts to explain social activities."[9] Wirth himself showed some of the contradictory aspects of city life without relating them to his theory of urbanism. He writes of the city as the historic center of progress, of learning, of higher standards of living, and all that is hopeful for the future of mankind, but he also points to the city as the locus of slums, poverty, crime, and disorganization. According to Wirth's theory both the carriers of knowledge and progress (the elite and the intellectuals) and the ignorant slum dwellers have a similar urban personality, since presumably they share in the postulated urban anonymity and so on.

It is in the evaluation of the personality of the urban dweller that urban theory has gone furthest afield. It leaps from the analysis of the social system to conjecture about individual personality; it is based not on solid psychological theory but on personal values, analogies, and outmoded physiopsychological concepts. Some of the description of the modern urbanite reads like another version of the fall of man. The delineation of the urbanite as blasé, indifferent, calculating, utilitarian, and rational (presumably as a defensive reaction to preserve his nervous system from the excessive shocks and stimuli of city life), suffering from anonymity and anomie, being more conscious and intellectual than his country brother yet feeling less deeply, remain mere statements of faith.[10]

Besides the lack of an adequate personality theory, it seems to me that some of the difficulty stems from the attempt to make individual psychological deductions from conditions prevailing in the city as a whole. The city is not the proper unit of comparison or discussion for the study of social life because the variables of number, density, and heterogeneity as used by Wirth are not the crucial determinants of social life or of personality.[11] There are many intervening variables. Social life is not a mass phenomenon. It occurs for the most part in small groups, within the family, within households, within neighborhoods, within the church, formal and informal groups, and so on.

Any generalizations about the nature of social life in the city must be based on careful studies of these smaller universes rather than on a priori statements about the city as a whole. Similarly, generalizations about urban personality must be based on careful personality studies. The delineation of social areas within cities and a careful analysis of their characteristics would take us a long way beyond the overgeneralized formulations of "urbanism as a way of life."

Basic to this Simmel-Wirth-Redfield approach are the supposed consequences of the predominance of primary relations in small rural communities versus the predominance of secondary relations in large cities. It seems to me that the psychological and social consequences of primary versus secondary relations have been misunderstood and exaggerated for both the country and the city. I know of no experimental or other good evidence to indicate that exposure to large numbers of people per se makes for anxiety and nervous strain or that the existence of secondary relations diminishes the strength and importance of primary ones. Primary group relations are just as important psychologically for city people as they are for country people, and sometimes they are more satisfying and of a more profound nature. And although the sheer number of secondary relations in the city is much greater than in the country, these relations can also be said to be secondary in the sense that their psychological consequences are minor.

The number of profound warm and understanding human relationships or attachments is probably limited in any society, rural or urban, modern or backward. Such attachments are not necessarily or exclusively a function of frequency of contact and fewness of numbers. They are influenced by cultural traditions which may demand reserve, a mind-your-own-business attitude, a distrust of neighbors, fear of sorcery and gossip, and the absence of a psychology of introspection.

George Foster's recent comparative analysis of the quality of interpersonal relations in small peasant societies, based on anthropological monographs, shows that they are characterized by distrust, suspicion, envy, violence, reserve, and withdrawal.[12] His paper confirms my earlier findings on Tepoztlan.

In some villages, peasants can live out their lives without any deep knowledge or understanding of the people whom they "know" in face-to-face relationships. By contrast, in modern Western cities, there may be more give and take about one's private, intimate life at a single "sophisticated" cocktail party than would occur in years in a peasant village. I suspect there are deeper, more mature human relationships among sympathetic, highly educated, cosmopolitan individuals who have chosen each other in friendship, than are possible among sorcery-ridden, superstitious, ignorant peasants, who are daily thrown together because of kinship or residential proximity.

It is a common assumption in social science literature that the process of urbanization for both tribal and peasant peoples is accompanied by a change in the structure of the family, from an extended to a nuclear family. It is assumed that the rural family is extended and the urban, nuclear. It must be pointed out that not even all primitive or preliterate people are characterized by a preponderance of the extended family as the residential unit. The Eskimo is a good example. Among peasantry, also, one finds a wide range of conditions in this regard. In most highland Mexican villages the nuclear family predominates as the residence unit. Very often and without any evidence, this fact is interpreted as a symptom of change from an earlier condition. In India, one finds a remarkable difference in family composition by castes within a single village. For example, in Rampur village in the state of Delhi, the Jats and Brahmans, both of whom own and work the land, have large, extended families, whereas the lower-caste Sweepers and Leatherworkers have small nuclear families.

I suggest that we must distinguish much more carefully between the existence of the extended family as a residence unit and as a social group. In Mexico the extended family is important as a social group in both rural and urban areas where the nuclear family predominates as the residence unit. In Mexico the persistence of extended family bonds seems compatible with urban life and increased industrialization. Moreover, the *compadre* system, with its extension of adoptive kinship ties, is operative, though in somewhat distinctive ways, on all class levels. I suspect that increased communication facilities in Mexico, especially the telephone and the car, may strengthen rather than weaken extended family ties.

One of the most distinctive characteristics of cities, whether in the industrial or preindustrial age, is that they provide, at least potentially, a wider range of alternatives for individuals in most aspects of living than is provided by the nonurban areas of the given nation or total society at a given time. Urbanism and urbanization involve the availability of a wide range of services and alternatives in terms of types of work, housing, food, clothing, educational facilities, medical facilities, modes of travel, voluntary organizations, types of people, and so on.

If we were to accept these criteria as definitive traits we could then develop indices of the degree of urbanization of different sectors of the population within cities. For example, if the population of any subsector of a city had fewer alternatives in types of clothing, foods, and so on, either because of traditional ethnic sanctions or lack of economic resources, we could designate this population sector as showing a lower degree of urbanization than some other sector. This does not apply to the city alone; the scale of urbanization can also be applied to villages, towns, and to their respective populations.

As I see it, therefore, there are two sides to the urbanization coin: one, the amount and variety of services and the like to be found in any city, and two, the extent to which different sectors of the city residents can partake of these services. From this distinction it follows that two cities may show the same urbanization index in terms of the number and variety of services per capita but may be very different in terms of the degree of urbanization (cosmopolitanism) of the various sectors of its inhabitants.

It also follows that there are many ways of life which coexist within a single city. This is particularly evident in the underdeveloped countries where class or caste differences are sharp. In Mexico City, for example, there are approximately a million and a half people who live in one-room *vecindades* or in primitive *jacales,* with little opportunity to partake of the great variety of housing facilities available for the tourists and the native bourgeoisie. Most of this large mass still have a low level of education and literacy, do not belong to labor unions, do not participate in the benefits of the social security system, make very little use of the city's museums, art galleries, banks, hospitals, department stores, concerts, airports, and so on. These people live in cities, indeed, a considerable portion were born in the city, but they are not highly urbanized. From this point of view, then, the poor in all cities of the world are less urbanized, that is, less cosmopolitan, than the wealthy.

The "culture of poverty" is a provincial, locally oriented culture, both in the city and in the country. In Mexico it is characterized by a relatively higher death rate, a higher proportion of the population in the younger age groups (less than 15 years), a higher proportion of gainfully employed in the total population, including child labor and working women. Some of these indices for poor *colonias* (districts) of Mexico City are much higher than for rural Mexico as a whole.

On another level the "culture of poverty" in Mexico, cutting across the rural and the urban, is characterized by the absence of food reserves in the home, the pattern of frequent buying of small quantities of food many times a day as the need occurs, borrowing money from money lenders at usurious interest rates, the pawning of goods, spontaneous informal credit devices among neighbors, the use of secondhand clothing and furniture, particularly in the city which has the largest secondhand market in Mexico, a higher incidence of free unions or consensual marriages, a strong present-time orientation, and a higher proportion of pre-Hispanic folk beliefs and practices.

In the preoccupation with the study of rural-urban differences, there has been a tendency to overlook or neglect basic similarities of people everywhere. In a recent paper Bruner[13] has illustrated this point for Indonesia where he found that the urban and rural Toba Batak are essentially part of a single social and economic ceremonial system.

Mexico-India contrasts also illustrate his point. In Mexico, Catholicism gives a similar stamp to many aspects of life in both rural and urban areas. The nucleated settlement pattern of most Mexican villages with the central church and plaza and the barrio-subdivisions, each in turn with its respective chapel, makes for a distinctive design which is in marked contrast to the north Indian villages where Hinduism and the caste system have made for a much more segmented and heterogeneously organized type of settlement pattern. It is my impression that a similar contrast is to be seen in some of the cities of these two countries and I believe this merits further study. Taking another example from India, we find that the way of life of the urban and rural lower castes, such as Washermen and Sweepers, have much more in common with each other than with the higher caste Brahmans in their respective urban and rural contexts.

Although I agree that number, density, permanence of settlement and heterogeneity of population is a workable definition of a city, I believe we need an additional, more elementary set of variables, with a narrower focus, to explain what goes on within cities. The sheer physical conditions of living have a considerable influence on social life, and I would include, among the variables, such factors as stability of residence, the settlement pattern, types of housing, the number of rooms to a family, and property concepts.

A type of housing settlement like the *vecindad,* which brings people into daily face-to-face contact, in which people do most of their work in a common patio, share a common toilet and a common washstand, encourages intensive interaction, not all of which is necessarily friendly. It makes little difference whether this housing and settlement pattern is in the city or the country, indeed whether it occurs among the tribal peoples of Borneo or the Iroquois Indians. In all cases it produces intense interaction, problems of privacy, quarrels among children, and among their parents.

Stability of residence too has many similar social consequences wherever it occurs. As I have already shown, in Mexico City the *vecindades* make for a kind of community life which has greater resemblance to our stereotyped notions of village life than to Wirth's description of urbanism. Stability of residence may result from a wide variety of factors, both in rural and urban areas. Nor can we assume that it is a necessary concomitant of nonurban societies; witness the nomadism of the Plains Indians or of agricultural workers in parts of the Caribbean.

Certain aspects of the division of labor stand up well as an elementary narrow-focus variable. When the family is the unit of production and the home and the work place are one, certain similar consequences follow for family life, both in the country and the city. I have in mind similarities in family life of small artisans in Mexico City and rural villages. In both, husband and wife spend most of the day together, children are early recruited into useful work, and there is much interaction among family members. Thus, in terms of the amount of time husbands spend away from home, there is much more similarity between a peasant and a factory worker than between either of these and an artisan.

What we need in comparative urban studies as well as in rural-urban comparisons, within a single culture and crossculturally, are carefully controlled, narrow-focus comparisons of subunits. Here I shall list what seem to me to be priorities in research, with special reference to the underdeveloped countries.

1. The delineation of distinctive regions within cities in terms of their demographic, ecological, economic, and social characteristics with the objective of developing measures of urbanization for distinctive population sectors as well as for the city as a whole.
2. Crosscultural studies of comparable population sectors within cities. For example, we might compare lower-class areas in cities of Japan, India, England, and Mexico, utilizing a common research methodology, so that we could check the role of distinctive cultural factors on comparable urban sectors.
3. Comparisons of the economic, social, and psychological aspects of an equal number of families with the same full-time nonagricultural occupations in a village and in the city within a single country. One objective would be to test the influence of the rural versus the urban milieu and the many theories associated with the presumed differences between them.
4. Studies of the socioeconomic and psychological consequences of the introduction of factories in villages and towns in predominantly peasant countries. A crucial methodological point in such studies would be to select communities prior to the introduction of the factory so that we could have a solid baseline against which changes can be measured. One of the weaknesses of practically all studies to date is that they have had to reconstruct the prefactory conditions of the community. For example, the otherwise excellent study of a Guatemalan community by Manning Nash had to reconstruct the village culture as it was seventy years before, when the factory was first introduced.
5. Most studies of the influence of factories have dealt with light industries such as textiles or rayons. It would be good to have studies on the effects of heavy industries such as steel or mining, or chemical plants which demand more skilled labor and continuous operation.
6. Intensive case studies of individuals and families who have moved from tribal communities to urban centers, focusing on the problems of adjustment and the process of acculturation. In terms of method, it would be important to select families from communities which have been carefully studied.
7. Similar studies should be done for peasants and plantation workers who move to the city. The objective of studying subjects from different backgrounds is to learn what differences, if any, this will have upon the urbanization process. I suspect that the greater disorganization reported by Joseph A. Kahl in his review of African materials as compared to Mexican data can be

explained by the fact that the African studies reported on tribal peoples moving to the city whereas in Mexico we are dealing with peasants. On purely theoretical grounds I would expect that culture shock would be greater for tribal peoples.

Notes

1. Oscar Lewis, *Life in a Mexican Village: Tepoztlan Restudied* (Urbana, Ill.: University of Illinois Press, 1951).
2. There has been a growing literature of criticism of the folk-urban and rural-urban dichotomies by urban sociologists. See, for example, Theodore Caplow, "The Social Ecology of Guatemala City," *Social Forces,* 28 (December 1949); Philip M. Hauser, "Observations on the Urban-Folk and Urban-Rural Dichotomies as Forms of Western Ethnocentrism," [Article 7] of this chapter; William L. Kolb, "The Social Structure and Function of Cities," *Economic Development and Culture Change* (October 1954); O. D. Duncan and Albert J. Reiss, Jr., *Social Characteristics of Urban and Rural Communities, 1950* (New York: Wiley, 1956), part 4; Gideon Sjoberg, "Comparative Urban Sociology," *Sociology Today* (New York: Basic Books, 1959), pp. 334–359. Horace Miner has attempted to defend the Redfield position in what seems to me to be a rather apologetic article. A careful reading will show that he accepts most of the criticism although he swallows hard. See his "The Folk-Urban Continuum" in Paul K. Hatt and Albert J. Reiss, Jr. (eds.), *Cities and Society* (Glencoe, Ill.: The Free Press, 1957), pp. 22–34.
3. Hauser, *op. cit.*, p. 514.
4. Julian H. Steward, *Theory of Culture Change* (Urbana, Ill.: University of Illinois Press, 1955); Irving Goldman, "Status Rivalry and Cultural Evolution in Polynesia," *American Anthropologist,* 57, No. 4 (August 1955), pp. 680–697; Irving Goldman, "Cultural Evolution in Polynesia: A Reply to Criticism," *Journal of the Polynesian Society,* 66, no. 2 (June 1957), pp. 156–164; Irving Goldman, "The Evolution of Status Systems in Polynesia," in A. F. C. Wallace (ed.), *Men and Cultures* (Philadelphia, 1960), pp. 255–260.
5. I have made this point in an earlier paper "Peasant Culture In India and Mexico," in McKim Marriott (ed.), *Village India, American Anthropologist,* vol. 57, no. 3, part 2. Memoir No. 83, June 1955: "For both applied and theoretical anthropology we need typologies of peasantry for the major culture areas of the world. . . . Moreover, within each area we need more refined subclassifications. Only after such studies are available will we be in a position to formulate broad generalizations about the dynamics of peasant culture as a whole." P. 165.
6. Oscar Lewis, "Urbanization Without Breakdown: A Case Study," in *The Scientific Monthly,* 75, no. 1 (July 1952). In this article I have suggested a number of specific Mexican conditions which might explain the special findings. More recently, Joseph A. Kahl has restated and elaborated upon some of these points in his article "Some Social Concomitants of Industrialization and Urbanization: A Research Review," *Human Organization,* 18 (Summer 1959), pp. 53–74.
7. Oscar Lewis, "The Culture of the Vecindad in Mexico City: Two Case Studies," *Actas del III Congreso Internacional de Americanistas,* tomo I, San Jose, Costa Rica, 1959, pp. 387–402.
8. Louis Wirth, "Urbanism as a Way of Life," *American Journal of Sociology,* 44 (July 1938), pp. 1–24.
9. Sjoberg, *op. cit.*, p. 340.
10. Wirth, "Urbanism as a Way of Life," in *Community Life and Social Policy* (Chicago: University of Chicago Press, 1956), pp. 119–120.
11. Sjoberg has correctly criticized the logic of comparison inherent in the writings of Redfield and Wirth on folk-urban theory on the ground that they were comparing a whole society with a part society. Here my criticism is that Wirth treated the city as a whole society for purposes of social relations and personality.
12. George Foster, "The Personality of the Peasant," paper read at the 58th Annual Meeting of the American Anthropological Association, Mexico City, 1959.

13. Edward M. Bruner, "Urbanization and Culture Change: Indonesia," paper read at the 58th Annual Meeting of the American Anthropological Association in Mexico City, December 28, 1959.

7

PHILIP M. HAUSER, Observations on the Urban-Rural Dichotomies as Forms of Western Ethnocentrism

That relatively permanently settled large-population agglomerations make a difference in the way of life has been recognized perhaps for as long as there have been large cities. In the Hebrew literature, for example, the prophets discussed the effects of urbanization, and they explained such phenomena as corruption, personal disorganization, and other evidences of social and personal pathology as products of the urban environment.[1] In much of the nineteenth-century literature, including material that may be regarded as prolegomena for the emergence of sociology, systematic efforts were made to explain the differences between urban and preurban behavior.[2] For example, in 1861, Maine in his *Ancient Society* differentiated between organization based on kinship in which position was fixed by "status" and that based on territory in which position was manifest in "contract." Tönnies, in his *Gemeinschaft und Gesellschaft,* published in 1887, set forth his well-known dichotomization of community and society with considerable elaboration of their differential characteristics. Durkheim, in his *Division of Labor* and other works, differentiated between the "mechanical" and "organic" society and discussed with great insight, in his consideration of "social morphology," the significance of "volume," "mass," and "density" in the social order.

In the more recent past Sumner in his discussion of folk society, Goldenweiser in his description of primitive societies, and Becker in his elaboration of the "sacred society" have added to the literature which focuses largely on the characteristics of "folk society."[3] Redfield brought much of the earlier observations to a head in a series of works highlighted by his article in "The Folk Society."[4]

Paralleling the literature focusing largely on the characteristics of the folk society, there were other series of writings that noted the difference between the "urban" and "rural" social orders in Western societies. This literature included,

Philip M. Hauser, "The Folk-Urban Ideal Types: B. Observations on the Urban-Folk and Urban-Rural Dichotomies as Forms of Western Ethnocentrism," in Philip M. Hauser and L. F. Schnore (eds.), *The Study of Urbanization* (New York: John Wiley & Sons, Inc., 1965), pp. 503–517. Reprinted by permission.

of course, a treatment of the urban-rural dichotomy by the United States Bureau of the Census, and such considerations as set forth by Williams in 1925, Park and Burgess in 1925 and 1926, and Ogburn in 1937.[5] Wirth perhaps provided the most systematic statement of the personal and social effects of the city in his now classical article "Urbanism as a Way of Life" published in 1938.[6]

Differentiation between the folk and urban society and the urban and rural social orders became so widely diffused in the literature of sociology and anthropology, in the literature of general education, and in the general lay literature, as well, that they were accepted as generalizations resulting from sociological and anthropological research. Yet the fact is that most of the scholars who contributed to the emergence of these concepts regarded them not as generalizations based on research but, rather, as "ideal-type constructs."

The wide acceptance of these constructs as products of research, however, together with the increasing recognition of students that there were many departures in reality from the ideal-type constructs, led to a literature of criticism especially during the past two decades. Among the critics were Tax in 1939 and 1941; Wirth in 1951; Oscar Lewis in 1951; William Kolb in 1954; Dudley Duncan and Albert Reiss in 1956; and with the rising choruses of voices this writer in 1955 and 1957.[7]

This chapter is an attempt to focus, more explicitly than has been done so far, on the details of the ideal-type constructs in relation to the characteristics of metropolitan areas in Asia. The analysis up to this point is based primarily, on the one hand, on a summary of the literature and, on the other, on impressions of the writer gleaned from residence in a number of cities in Asia over a period of about two years. The primary purpose of the paper is to call for more rigorous inquiry into the matter. Such research could lead among other things to a reformulation of these ideal-type constructs, which have been in the literature now for a number of decades.

The constructs

Redfield in his construction of the "folk" ideal type made quite explicit the method which he pursued and the purpose of the construct.

> The construction of the type depends indeed upon special knowledge of tribal and peasant groups. The ideal folk society could be defined through assembling in the imagination, the characters which are logically opposite those which are to be found in the modern city. . . . The complete procedure requires us to gain acquaintance with many folk societies in many parts of the world, and to set down in words general enough to describe most of them those characteristics which they have in common with each other and which the modern city does not have.[8]

The rationale behind the ideal-type construct was also explicitly stated by Redfield: "As the type is constructed real societies may be arranged in order of the degree of resemblance to it. The conception develops that any one real society is more or less folk."[9]

The characteristics of the folk society as set forth by Redfield may be listed as follows: small; isolated; nonliterate; homogeneous; strong sense of group solidarity; simple technology; simple division of labor; economically independent; possessing "culture," that is, an organization of conventional understandings; behavior strongly patterned on a conventional basis—traditional, spontaneous, uncritical; informal status; no systematic knowledge—no books; behavior is personal; society is familial; society is sacred; mentality is essentially personal and emotional (not abstract or categoric); animism and anthropomorphism manifest; no market, no money, no concept of "gain."

Redfield was quick to acknowledge that the ideal-type constructs are not to be found in the real world. He asserted, for example, that "the societies of the world do not arrange themselves in the same order with regard to the degree to which they realize all of the characteristics of the ideal folk society."[10] And he went on to say, "On the other hand there is so marked a tendency for some of these characteristics to occur together with others that the interrelations among them must be in no small part that of interdependent variables."[11]

The "urban" ideal type is the opposite of the "folk" ideal type. In his treatment of "urbanism as a way of life," Wirth not only stated the characteristics of the "urban" ideal-type construct but linked them with the characteristics of the urban society which he designated as: large population; density; heterogeneity; and permanence. According to Wirth,

> The central problem to the sociologist of the city is to discover the forms of social action and organization that typically emerge in relatively permanent, compact settlements of large numbers of heterogeneous individuals. We must also infer that urbanism will assume its most characteristic and extreme form in the measure in which the conditions with which it is congruent are present.[12]

The specific characteristics of the "urban" social order as elaborated by Wirth will be enumerated in detail later in relation to the presence or absence of such characteristics in the metropolis in the economically less developed areas, such as in Asia.

The criticism

In his discussion of Guatemala, Tax saw in that society a folk order that departed from the characteristics of the ideal-type construct. A stable society can be small, unsophisticated, homogeneous in beliefs and practices "with relationships impersonal, with formal institutions dictating the acts of individuals, and the family organization weak, with life secularized, and with individuals acting more from economic or other personal advantage than from any deep conviction or thought of the social good." Tax was quoted by Redfield in his article (p. 308). Redfield also took note of Tax's criticism: "A primitive world view, that is a disposition to treat nature personally, to regard attributes as entities, and to make 'symbolic' rather than causal connections coexists with a tendency for relations between man and man to be impersonal, commercial, and secular as they tend to be in the urban society."[13]

Wirth was quite explicit about the limitations of the ideal-type construct as empirical generalizations. In a fragment published posthumously in 1956, although first uttered in 1951, he stated:

> To set up ideal typical polar concepts as I have done, and many others before me have done, does not prove that city and country are fundamentally and necessarily different. It does not justify mistaking the hypothetical characteristics attributed to the urban and rural modes of life for established facts, as has so often been done. Rather it suggests certain hypotheses to be tested in the light of empirical evidence which we must assiduously gather. Unfortunately this evidence has not been accumulated in such a fashion as to test critically any major hypothesis that has been proposed.[14]

I submit that Wirth's observation in 1951 is as applicable today as it was then.

Without question the most detailed and documented criticism of the ideal-type folk-urban construct and its use is found in the works of Oscar Lewis. In his *Life in a Mexican Village,* in 1951, he first makes the following general basic methodological point:

> Still other differences, such as those summarized in the preceding pages, must be attributed to the most part to differences in theoretical orientation and methodology, which in turn influence the selection and coverage of facts and the way in which these facts were organized. In rereading Redfield's study in the light of my own work in the village, it seems to me that the concept of the folk-culture and folk-urban continuum was Redfield's organizing principle in the research. Perhaps this helps to explain his emphasis on the formal and ritualistic aspects of life rather than the every day life of the people and their problems, on evidence of homogeneity rather than heterogeneity and the range of custom, on the weight of tradition rather than deviation and innovation, on unity and integration rather than tensions and conflict.[15]

Lewis goes on to indicate that this is probably what led Beals in his review of Lewis to comment on what he regards as "the heretical suggestions" that "to insist that field studies must have a theoretical hypothesis is perhaps a dangerous procedure."[16] This observation might well be compared with Francis Bacon's injunction against "anticipating nature." Lewis also notes, however, that Beals in one sense comes to Redfield's defense in suggesting that due to proximity to urban centers Tepoztlan was not a good example of a folk society. Thus he shifts his criticism of Redfield in pointing to Redfield's failure to place Tepoztlan in any historical or geographic context, as a "control" in his construction of the folk ideal type.

Lewis in his analysis then proceeds with a presentation of six other criticisms of the folk-urban dichotomy. They consist of:

1. focus on the city as a source of change;
2. the notion that change can come from increasing heterogeneity of culture elements in a nonurban society;
3. the erroneous treatment of criteria of folk society as interdependent variables —that is, they might better be treated as independent (Tax's earlier observations are supported by Lewis's study);
4. the folk-urban typology obscures "one of the most significant findings of modern cultural anthropology," that is, the wide range of ways of life and value systems among primitive peoples; it also tends to obscure urban differences;
5. has serious limitations in guiding research because of "highly selective implications of categories and narrow focus";
6. value judgments underlie the dichotomy in Redfield. Redfield, like Rousseau, envisioned "noble savages," a point of view that is documented, says Lewis, in a number of Redfield's writings.

All in all, from a reading of Lewis on the dichotomy, there is implied in his work, if not a complete junking, a drastic revision of it.

William L. Kolb in "The Social Structure and Functions of Cities," attacks the urban end of the dichotomy to complement Lewis's attack on the folk end.[17] Kolb does so, however, through the vehicle of disagreements with ecologists, following the Firey line, and the use of the Parsonian pattern variable schema which adds little to the issue. Kolb states, "size and density of cities will not by themselves or assisted by heterogeneity create the primacy of secondary relations, isolation and loneliness. Only when there is extreme stress on universalism and achievement accompanied by other features of industrialization, can these demographic factors produce such social characteristics."[18]

Kolb in general and in somewhat extreme fashion argues that generalizations about the urban mostly derive from Park and his students' work on the Chicago of the 1920s. The ideal-type construct is not based on universal observation then; it tends more to be a unique description of a given city in a given time and place. In this respect he undoubtedly misreads Park, as Hughes indicates,[19] but there is something to his observation that generalizations based on the study of Chicago have not been subjected to the kind of test consistent with the imagery of science.

Duncan and Reiss in their *Social Characteristics of Urban and Rural Communities,* a monograph based on the 1950 Census, not only indicate that the urban-rural dichotomy might better have been stated as a continuum, but also that the continuum itself does not hold when reality is examined.[20] Various characteristics of populations ordered by city size from the very largest metropolises to the rural-farm population reveal quite a variety of patterns in relationship, that is, the relationship is not necessarily linear. The deviations from the dichotomization of the urban and rural documented in a volume such as Duncan and Reiss's may be regarded as evidence of the departure of reality from the ideal-type construct. Along with other evidence, it also points to the need for modification of the construct itself.

Finally, as a brief note prior to the elaboration of my own thinking on the matter, I should state that the folk-urban and urban-rural dichotomies, although they had troubled me earlier in connection with observations in the city in the United States itself, struck me as especially inadequate after my exposure to Asian cities and also to South American cities, especially since 1951. My personal observations convinced me that the dichotomizations in the literature in the form of the folk-urban and urban-rural ideal-type constructs were on the whole inapplicable to the metropolis of the less-developed area, and that more refined constructs were probably desirable for the furthering of research in this general field.

Although my major quarrel with the folk-urban and urban-rural dichotomies lies with the way in which they have seeped into the literature and have become accepted as generalizations based on research, rather than their utility as ideal-type constructs, I have come to feel that even in the latter role they perhaps may have outlived their usefulness. In view of this, it is perhaps a little sad that a tendency is evident to defend the constructs, as such. I regard this situation as sad because any ideal-type construct has its defense in its utility. If it fails to be as useful as it might be then the time has come for its modification.

Redfield in his article "The Folk Society" in 1947 recognized Tax's criticism, as I have already indicated. He acknowledges, "So it may appear that under certain conditions a literate and, indeed, at least partly urbanized society may be both highly commercial and sacred—as witness, also, the Jews—while under certain other conditions an otherwise folklike people may become individualistic, commercial and perhaps secular."[21] He does say, "It is, of course, the determination of the limiting conditions that is important,"[22] but he does not follow through, either with an indication of the limiting conditions or the modification of the dichotomy.

In a more recent article, "The Cultural Role of Cities" with Singer, the folk society and the city are further considered with no reference to the work of the critics. The folk society concept is presented as in the past as an "imagined combination of societal elements."[23] The city is visualized "as that community in which orthogenetic and heterogenetic transformations of the folk society have most fully occurred."

The former has brought about the Great Tradition and its special intellectual class, administrative officers and rule closely derived from the moral and religious life of the local culture, and advanced economic institutions, also obedient to these local cultural controls. The heterogenetic transformations have accomplished the freeing of the intellectual, esthetic, economic and political life from the local moral norms, and have developed on the one hand an individuated expediential motivation, and on the other, a revolutionary, nativistic, humanistic, or ecumenical viewpoint, now directed toward reform, progress and designed change.[24]

Cities are then classified by type as orthogenetic or heterogenetic. Without further pursuing the implications of these neologisms and the questions they raise, it may be noted, for the moment, that folk society is now differentiated from the two types of cities which are set up.

The "transformations of folk societies" is then considered in two forms—"primary" and "secondary" urbanization. Cities are more closely integrated with the country in the primary phase of urbanization, the city flowing from the Great Tradition. The Great Tradition and the Little Tradition, in primary urbanization, are held together as it were—for in primary urbanization literature the intelligentsia and the cosmopolitan are prominent. In secondary urbanization, in contrast, integration depends more on symbiotic relations, on the rate of technological development, and on the scope and intensity of contact with other cultures. The Redfield-Singer analysis builds on the folk-urban dichotomy and is in large measure, then, dependent on the folk ideal-type construct. To the extent that that construct does not correspond to reality, it follows that the additional edifices also are defective.

Redfield and Singer do note exceptions to the expected folk-urban dichotomy. "In societies where social change is slow, and there has developed an adjustment of mutual usefulness and peaceful residence side by side of groups culturally different but not too different, the culturally complex society may be relatively stable. But where urban development is great such conditions are apt to be unstable."[25] On the whole, however, the Redfield-Singer discussion presents an extension of the older dichotomizations rather than a modification based on continued research and commentaries of the critics.

Application of the ideal-type constructs to the metropolis in the economically less-advanced area

As a preliminary to the type of research and analysis by means of which the ideal-type constructs, both the folk-urban and the urban-rural dichotomizations, could be subjected to the test of empirical research, there follows a detailed listing of the characteristics of the urban social order as set forth by Wirth, in relation to the characteristics of the urban society, that is, size, density, and heterogeneity, respectively. For each of these items, a judgment is indicated in column 2 on whether the characteristic is, in fact, observable in the urban society in

Asian cities in which the writer has lived (primarily Rangoon, but including Bangkok, Djakarta, and Calcutta).

Urban condition	Expected characteristic	Actual characteristic (presence of characteristic in urban areas of less developed countries)
Size	1. Atomization (Simmel)	No
	2. Schizoid character	No
	3. Segmental roles	Some
	4. Secondary contacts	Some
	5. Superficiality	Some
	6. Anonymity	Some
	7. Sophistication	No
	8. Rationality	No
	9. Loses spontaneous self-expression	Mainly no
	10. Utilitarian contact	Some
	11. Pecuniary nexus	Some
	12. Interdependence–specialization	Some, but very limited
	13. Mass media of communication	Mainly no
Density	1. Differentiation and specialization	Mainly no
	2. Shift in media through which we orient ourselves to urban milieu and fellow man, that is the emphasis on vision world of artifacts, etc. (Simmel)	Very little
	3. Place of work separated from place of residence	Some, but limited
	4. Glaring contrasts Poverty and riches Squalor and splendor Ignorance and intelligence	Some
	5. Patterning of city ecologically—the Burgess hypothesis	Yes and no
	6. Secularization of life	No
	7. Competition, aggrandizement, and mutual exploitation	Yes and no
	8. Clock and traffic signals as symbols	No
	9. Loneliness	Yes and no
	10. Friction, irritation, frustration	Some
Heterogeneity	1. Breaks caste lines, complicating class structure	No
	2. Instability and insecurity of individual	Yes and no
	3. Sophistication and cosmopolitanism	Mainly no
	4. No single group has undivided allegiance	No
	5. Turnover in group membership rapid	Mainly no
	6. Personality segments corresponding to group memberships	Mainly no
	7. Place of residence, employment, income, interests fluctuate	Mainly no
	8. Not a home owner	No
	9. Mass behavior fluid and unpredictable	No
	10. Depersonalization	Yes and no
	11. Money economy	Yes and no
	12. Mass media communication operate as leveling influences	Mainly no

If we turn next to a consideration of the characteristics of folk society set forth by Redfield, and look for their presence or absence in the large urban area in the economically less-advanced areas in the world, a similar table may be prepared.

Expected characteristic	*Actual characteristic (presence in urban areas in less developed countries)*
Social unit is:	
1. Small	Yes
2. Isolated social world	Yes and no
3. Nonliterate order	Yes
4. Homogeneous groups	Yes
5. Strong group solidarity	Yes
6. Simple technology	Yes
7. Simple division of labor	Yes
8. Economically independent	Yes and no
9. "Culture"—the organization of conventional understanding	Yes
10. Behavior strongly patterned conventional	Yes and no
11. Status	Yes
12. No systematic knowledge	Yes
13. Behavior personal	Yes
14. Society familial	Yes and no
15. Society sacred	Yes
16. Mentality personal and emotional	Yes
17. No market	Yes and no

It is hardly necessary to reiterate that the responses indicating the "actual" in relation to the "expected" are not responses grounded in empirical research. *They are based largely on the limited experience and impressions of the writer.* They are not presented, therefore, as definitive answers to the questions raised, but rather as approximations or hypotheses that merit further investigation for their validation or rejection.

Concluding observation

The folk-urban and the urban-rural dichotomies may be regarded as ideal-type constructs which are the products of Western writers. These ideal-type constructs have not been used in accordance with Weber's injunctions on the use of ideal-type constructs.[26] Even in the literature of social science as well as that in general education, there has been a relatively blind acceptance of the ideal-type constructs as generalizations based on research rather than as tools to be utilized in research. Investigators have been more impressed with their findings of conformance than motivated to look for deviations from the constructs. Moreover, fundamental logical errors have been committed in the utilization of these constructs in the drawing of diachronic conclusion from synchronic observations. That is, the concepts have also been used in a neo-evolutionary way on the assumption that the "folk" and the "urban" actually represented different stages in the development of societies.[27]

There is evidence, by no means conclusive as yet, that both parts of these dichotomies represent confounded variables and, in fact, complex systems of variables which have yet to be unscrambled. The dichotomizations perhaps represent all too hasty efforts to synthesize and integrate what little knowledge has been acquired in empirical research. The widespread acceptance of these ideal-type constructs as generalizations, without benefit of adequate research, well illustrates the dangers of catchy neologisms which often get confused with knowledge. In some respects, these ideal-type constructs represent an admixture of nineteenth-century speculative efforts to achieve global generalization, and twentieth-century concern with the integration of knowledge for general education purposes, as a result of which integration is often achieved of that which is not yet known.

It is hoped that the materials which have been presented will help to highlight the need for next steps in the evaluation of these ideal-type constructs. Obviously, what is necessary are well-designed empirical researches in which deviations from the constructs are noted in greater detail and with greater precision than are now available. Such research would better illuminate the nature of diverse social orders and, in the process, perhaps lead to the construction of ideal typology more useful than that which is now available as prolegomena to empirically based generalizations.

Notes

1. Joyce O. Hertzler, *Social Thought of the Ancient Civilizations* (New York: McGraw-Hill, 1936), pp. 298ff.

2. Henry Maine, *Ancient Law* (London: J. Murray, 1961); Ferdinand Tönnies, *Gemeinschaft und Gesellschaft* (1st ed., 1887), trans. and ed. Charles P. Loomis as *Fundamental Concepts of Sociology* (New York: American Book Co., 1940); *Emile Durkheim on the Division of Labor in Society*, trans. George Simpson (New York: Macmillan, 1933).

3. William Graham Sumner, *Folkways* (Boston: Ginn, 1907); A. A. Goldenweiser, *Early Civilization* (New York: Knopf, 1922); Howard Becker and Harry Elmer Barnes, *Social Thought from Lore to Science* (Washington, D. C.: Harren Press, 1952), chap. 1.

4. Robert Redfield, *Tepoztlan, A Mexican Village* (Chicago: University of Chicago Press, 1930). See also his: "The Folk Society and Culture," Louis Wirth (ed.), *Eleven Twenty-Six* (Chicago: University of Chicago Press, 1940), pp. 39–50; *The Folk Culture of Yucatan* (Chicago: University of Chicago Press, 1941); "The Folk Society," *American Journal of Sociology*, 41 (January 1947), pp. 293–308; (with Milton Singer), "The Cultural Role of Cities," *Economic Development and Cultural Change*, 3 (October 1954), pp. 53–73; *The Primitive World and Its Transformations* (Ithaca, N. Y.: Cornell University Press, 1953).

5. James Mickel Williams, *Our Rural Heritage* (New York: Knopf, 1925); Robert E. Park, Ernest W. Burgess, and R. D. McKenzie, *The City* (Chicago: University of Chicago Press, 1925); Ernest W. Burgess (ed.), *The Urban Community* (Chicago: University of Chicago Press, 1926); William F. Ogburn, *Social Characteristics of Cities* (Chicago: The International City Managers Assn., 1937).

6. Reprinted in Wirth's posthumous *Community Life and Social Policy* (Chicago: University of Chicago Press, 1956), pp. 110–132.

7. Sol Tax, "Culture and Civilization in Guatemalan Societies," *Scientific Monthly*, 48 (May 1939). Also his "World View and Social Relations in Guatemala," *American An-*

thropologist, 43, no. 1 (January–March 1941), pp. 27–42. Louis Wirth, "Rural-Urban Differences," in *Community Life and Social Policy* (Chicago: University of Chicago Press, 1956). Oscar Lewis, *Life in a Mexican Village: Tepoztlan Restudied* (Urbana, Ill.: University of Illinois Press, 1951). William Kolb, "The Social Structure and Function of Cities," *Economic Development and Cultural Change,* 3, no. 1 (October 1954), pp. 30–46. O. D. Duncan and Albert J. Reiss, Jr., *Social Characteristics of Urban and Rural Communities, 1950* (New York: Wiley, 1956). This paper was originally written in 1955 for the Institute of Social Research at the University of Chicago. See also Philip M. Hauser (ed.), *Urbanization in Asia and the Far East* (Calcutta: UNESCO, 1957), p. 195.

　　8. Redfield, "The Folk Society," *op. cit.,* p. 294.

　　9. *Ibid.*

　　10. *Ibid.,* p. 306.

　　11. *Ibid.*

　　12. Wirth, *op. cit.,* p. 117.

　　13. Redfield, *op. cit.,* p. 308.

　　14. Wirth, *op. cit.,* pp. 173–174.

　　15. Lewis, *op. cit.,* pp. 431–432.

　　16. Ralph L. Beals, book review of Oscar Lewis, *Life in a Mexican Village: Tepoztlan Restudied* (Urbana, Ill.: University of Illinois Press, 1951), *American Sociological Review,* 16, no. 6 (December 1951), pp. 895–896.

　　17. Kolb, *op. cit.,* pp. 30ff.

　　18. *Ibid.,* p. 44.

　　19. Everett Hughes, "Robert E. Park's Views on Urban Society: A Comment on William L. Kolb's Paper," *Economic Development and Cultural Change,* 3 (October 1954), pp. 47–49.

　　20. Duncan and Reiss, *op. cit.,* chap. 2.

　　21. Redfield, "The Folk Society," *op. cit.,* p. 308.

　　22. *Ibid.*

　　23. Redfield and Singer, *op. cit.,* p. 58.

　　24. *Ibid.*

　　25. *Ibid.,* p. 69.

　　26. Max Weber, *The Theory of Social and Economic Organization,* trans. A. M. Henderson and Talcott Parsons (New York: Oxford University Press, 1947), pp. 11ff.

　　27. For example, Robert Redfield, in *The Primitive World . . . , op. cit.*

8

JANET ABU-LUGHOD, Migrant Adjustment to City Life: The Egyptian Case[1]

One of the most dramatic phenomena of recent decades has been the urbanization of large segments of the world's peasant folk, particularly in rapidly industrializing countries. In few places has this urban growth been as vigorous as in
Egypt—at first spasmodically in the 1940s stimulated by a war economy, then
more gradually in the 1950s in response to the indigenous demands of a developing economy[2]—until, at present, one out of every three Egyptians lives in an
urban place having 20,000 or more persons.

Migration from rural areas has been chiefly responsible for Egypt's soaring
rate of urbanization, even though natural increase, still as high in cities as in rural
areas, accounts for half the annual rate of urban growth. This migration has favored the very largest cities of the country, bypassing those of moderate and
small size. Therefore there has been a tendency for cities to conform to the
principle of allometric growth, with high growth rates correlated positively with
rank as to size.[3] Indeed, for the last three decades, cities of highest rank size
have sustained average rates of growth which are more than twice the rate of
natural increase, while smaller towns, of between 20,000 to 30,000, have failed
to keep pace with rates of natural increase, i.e., have actually experienced net
losses of population.

Migration, then, has had its prime impact on the largest cities, and the tow-
ering giant of Cairo, with a present population of close to three and one-half
million, has been the most important recipient of the newly urbanizing population. This paper, therefore, concentrates on the adjustment of Egyptian villagers
to life in Cairo, inquiring into its nature and exploring the elements which mediate
any dramatic transition between rural and urban life.

I. THE RURAL AND THE URBAN IN CAIRO

Sociologists studying the adjustment of rural migrants to city life have been
trapped in a dilemma of their own making. Even after the replacement of the
rural-urban dichotomy by the more reasonable continuum, the sequence and dynamics of adjustment have still been deduced as though the dichotomy were
valid; the unconscious assumptions have led many students to an oversimplified
image of a one-way adjustment of rural man to a "stable" urban culture, despite
lip service paid to feedback and mutual assimilation.

Janet Abu-Lughod, "Migrant Adjustment to City Life: The Egyptian Case," *The American
Journal of Sociology* (July 1961), pp. 22–32. Copyright © 1961 The University of Chicago.
Reprinted by permission.

This adjustment is assumed to be disorganizing in the extreme. Physically, it is envisioned as drastically altering the dwelling, changing the accoutrements within the home as well as the neighborhood surrounding it, transforming the appearance and dress of the migrant himself. Economically, the migrant is seen as adjusting to changed occupations and rhythms of work, to a new division of labor within the family, and to different relationships between work associates. Socially, it is hypothesized that the migrant weans himself from the intimacy of the village to the harsh superficial relationships inherent in urban life, adapts himself from the homogeneous peer group to the diversified reference groups of the city, and suffers a reduction in proximity-centered social life and neighboring. Culturally, he is assumed to undergo a revolution in motivation, values, and ideology. In short, according to the rural-urban dichotomy, a hypothetical villager is to be dropped, unarmed, into the heart of urban Cairo to assimilate or perish. He is to be granted no cushions to soften his fall.

It is our contention here that the dichotomy is as invalid in Egypt and in many other newly awakening nations as it is in Western nations, but for a somewhat different reason. In these cases the dichotomy has not yet sharpened due to the continual ruralization of the cities.[4]

Only one fact need be cited to support this allegation: More than one-third of the permanent residents of Cairo have been born outside the city, that is, one out of every three Cairenes is a migrant of one sort or another, and the overwhelming majority are from the rural hinterlands within Egypt.[5] To speak about one-way assimilation to a stable urban culture when so large a minority comes equipped with needs and customs of rural origin is folly. Numbers alone should alert us to the probability that migrants are shaping the culture of the city as much as they are adjusting to it.

These rural migrants are drawn from two extreme types which face basically different problems of adjustment. One type, qualitatively the cream but numerically the less significant, consists of bright youths who migrate in search of education or wider opportunities. These have both the drive and the facility for rapid assimilation into the culture of the city. This paper ignores their real but different problems. The second type, referred to here as the "non-selective" migrants, are drawn primarily from the have-nots of the village. Numerically dominant, they are as much driven from the village by dearth of land and opportunity as they are attracted to the city.[6] With a lower capacity for assimilation, they tend to build for themselves within the city a replica of the culture they left behind. They are the subject of this article.

A second circumstance which has kept Cairo more rural than would be expected is the continual incorporation into the built-up metropolitan region of pre-existing villages. While some of these villages go back into history, such as Mataria, the pharaonic town of On (Greek, Heliopolis), some are of fairly recent origin. It would take a keen observer indeed to distinguish between a village within Cairo and one located miles beyond its fringes. In fact, the city of Cairo contains within its boundaries an extensive rural-urban fringe which stands juxtaposed against modern villas on the west, intervenes on the alluvial flats between urban Misr Qadima and suburban Maadi on the south, dips deep into the very heart of the city from the north, and, in somewhat different fashion, encircles Medieval Cairo on its eastern border. As can be seen from Figure 1, there are vast quarters within the mosaic of Cairo where, physically and socially, the way of life and the characteristics of residents resemble rural Egypt.

While full proof of this contention lies outside the scope of this paper,[7] a few figures may illustrate this point. High literacy is associated in Egypt with urbanism. In the largest urban centers, literacy rates in 1947 ranged between 40 and 45 percent, while smaller towns and villages had literacy rates of under 25 percent. Yet, in one out of eight census tracts in Cairo, the literacy rate was less than 25 percent. As might be expected, the rural-urban fringe had the lowest literacy rates (5 and 7 percent), but, surprisingly enough, even some of the more inlying zones contained populations no more literate than the rural. Similar comparisons made for other urban variables, such as refined fertility rates, religious and ethnic homogeneity, and condition and type of building, reveal the same

Figure 1. City of Cairo

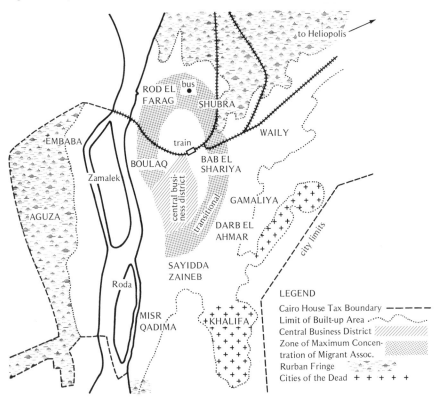

LEGEND

Cairo House Tax Boundary	— — — —
Limit of Built-up Area	········
Central Business District	/////////
Zone of Maximum Concentration of Migrant Assoc.	
Rurban Fringe	
Cities of the Dead	+ + + + +

inescapable fact that within the city of Cairo there exist numerous subareas whose physical and social characteristics closely approximate the villages of the countryside.

II. WHERE MIGRANTS SETTLE IN CAIRO

It is therefore possible for migrants to live in any of the large sections of the city which retain basic similarities to the village. To what extent do they actually select such areas as their ports of entry into the city's structure? Since our hypothesis is that one of the major cushions in the assimilation of rural migrants is the nature of the subcommunity to which they gravitate, our concern will be with the areas of first settlement of "non-selective" migrants.

Direct evidence of where migrants settle in the city is not available in the Cairo census.[8] In our attempt to approximate their ecological distribution, however, we are aided by several circumstances: First, small sample studies made in Egypt and other industrializing countries indicate that a fairly typical pattern of initial settlement is followed by many rural immigrants.[9] The typical migrant, here as elsewhere, is a young man whose first contact in the city is often with a friend or relative from his original village, with whom he may even spend the first few nights. Later, more permanent lodgings are found, usually within the same neighborhood. This process, in the aggregate, results in a concentration of migrants from particular villages within small subsections of the city, far beyond what would be expected by chance. Second, migration to Cairo has tended to occur in major spurts, the most important of recent times occurring in the early 1940s. Therefore, not only did the typical migrant gravitate to a small area of the city already containing persons from his home village, but he was not the only newcomer at the time of his arrival.

These two factors, operating together, resulted in the formation of small conclaves of ex-villagers sharing a common past in the village and a similar and often simultaneous history of adaptation to the city. A parallel between this and the ethnic ghettos of large American cities at the turn of the century readily suggests itself. While the congregations of villagers from Kafr Bagour and Garawan are smaller than were the Little Sicilies and although villagers are segregated (and segregate themselves) from the main stream of urban life by less powerful barriers than language and Old World customs, they also have developed the protective pattern of physical proximity and certain social institutions which help mitigate the difficulties of transition.

The formal associations founded for and developed by migrants are important, directly, in the dynamics of rural to urban adaptation, but are even more important indirectly, since their location and distribution in the city offer the *only* evidence as to where migrants settle in Cairo. Before analyzing the locational pattern of these institutions, however, some explanation of their nature is essential.

The *Directory of Social Agencies* in Cairo[10] lists more than 110 village benevolent associations. The Garawan Benevolent Society is typical. Garawan, a village of 8,000, is located in the heart of the Egyptian Delta some forty miles northwest of Cairo. Population pressure resulted first in the formation of several daughter villages, but eventually many of the men had to seek work in Cairo. (The village has a heavy excess of females.) The Garawan Benevolent Society was founded in 1944 to "extend aid to members" and to "provide burial facilities." Self-supporting, it sustains its activities through the dues contributed by "320 Egyptian Muslim adult males from Garawan," according to the directory's entry. Using a most conservative estimate of size of family (two dependents per adult male), one estimates that approximately 1,000 persons are to some extent involved in the core community of ex-Garawan residents.

One must make two basic assumptions if the locations of these societies are to be used as indirect evidence of migrant settlements. First, it must be assumed that migrants from specific villages are not distributed randomly throughout the city but that the processes described above result in aggregate settlements of persons from the same village.[11] Second, it must be assumed that the office of the migrant association is located in or near the subarea of the city which contains the maximum concentration of members. While this would not be true in every case, one might reasonably expect some relationship between office and clientele.

Even if these assumptions were absolutely beyond question (which they are not), an analysis of the locations of the associations would be irrelevant if they were scattered capriciously throughout the entire city. This, however, is fortunately not the case. When the addresses listed in the directory are located on a spot map, a definite, although not simple, pattern emerges which indicates in rough fashion the areas where rural migrants seem to be concentrated. Most associations fall within the elliptical belt around but never within the central business district. The arc contracts both east and west to a bare quarter of a mile from central business district and expands north and south to more than a mile from city center, thus conforming to the general contours of the city.

Northern settlement

One-third of the migrant associations cluster in the segment of the city which radiates northward from the central business district, circumscribed south and east by major rail lines, and bounded by the Nile to the west and an agricultural zone to the north. This section contains two subareas of densest concentration: the first in the vicinity of the Khazindar bus station; the other in Al Sharabiya, northeast of the main train terminal.

The Khazindar bus station has served since the twenties as the terminus of bus lines connecting Lower Egyptian provinces (the Delta) with Cairo. Within a radius of one-fourth of a mile of this station are eight village associations, all representing Delta villages; within half a mile are sixteen associations, ten actually concentrated in a four-by-six-block area just northeast of the station. This area has a strange mixture of urban and rural features. Behind the main street on which the station stands, narrow unpaved streets and alleys harbor prematurely aged, badly deteriorated, urban housing interspersed with the rural type of structure. The two- and three-story buildings contrast markedly with the six- to eight-story structures which dominate the main street. A cluster of black-garbed women squat to gossip; old men sit in doorways; a sheep bleats; children swarm in packs. When this area received its major influx of migrants, it was an outpost of urban settlement. As recently as 1940 there were farms just to the north. By now, however, the city has swept beyond it.

The second concentration of migrant associations is located in the tiny quarter of Al Sharabiya, where seven associations almost all from Delta villages are located within four blocks. Occupationally, many residents are bound to the rail yards that virtually surround it. Despite its geographically central location, this section presents a distinctly rural aspect and retains a close functional tie to the rural fringe, since farms bound it where rail lines do not. Lower buildings, some of mud brick, predominate. Commercial establishments are those of the large village or small town. Al Sharabiya and Khazindar areas contain most of the migrant associations of the city's northern quadrant. (The remainder are scattered within the belt shown on Fig. 1.)

Most of the associations in this quadrant represent Lower Egyptian villages. Hence many migrants have presumably settled close not only to their point of origin but, even more specifically, to their point of entry into the city, i.e., the bus terminal. Moreover, the migrants settling in this part of the city selected areas which were, at the time of settlement at least, on the outer edge of the built-up city.

Southern settlement

Another third of more of the migrant associations are clustered directly south of the central business district, quite distant from the southern rural-urban fringe. The densest concentration is found in the transitional business district—a curved interstitial belt buffering the Western-style commercial zone north and west of it from the native market and residential quarters to its south and east. Twenty-five associations are located in this zone, while the remainder are scattered farther south toward Old Cairo.

Most striking is the fact that the majority of these associations represent villages of Upper Egypt. Thus the principle of least effort seems to determine migrant distribution. Villagers coming from north of the city favor the northern quadrant of the city, while those coming from the south prefer location in the southern quadrant. But, whereas the former have their associations in family residential zones near the city's fringe, the latter have theirs in a marginal commercial district characterized by a heavy excess of unmarried males.[12] Further examination reveals that the latter are primarily in rented offices, whereas the former are frequently in the home of the association's president.

What accounts for the remarkable difference? One hypothesis can be offered here. Migrants from Delta villages follow a different pattern of migration and hence make a different type of adjustment to the city than do migrants from Upper Egyptian villages. First, migrants from the Delta move primarily in family groups, while those from the south either remain single or leave their wives and children in their home villages. In Cairo in 1947, of the 400,000 migrants from Lower Egypt, half were males and half females, but 200,000 out of the 250,000 migrants from Upper Egypt were males. Thus the sex ratio of Delta migrants was remarkably well balanced, while there were four men for every woman among Upper Egyptian migrants in Cairo.

Second, significant occupational differences between the two migrant groups affect both adjustment patterns and spatial distribution. Upper Egyptian migrants go primarily into domestic and other personal services or work in unskilled labor gangs, while the occupations followed by Lower Egyptian migrants are both more varied and less likely to include housing as a part of wages.[13]

In the light of this, the major differences between the location of migrant associations representing Upper and Lower Egyptian villages become more comprehensible. The associations of Upper Egyptians are located in an area which serves as a leisure-time focal point as well as a residential area catering to single men. This is both cause and effect of the character of Upper Egyptian migrants. The associations play a more active role in their lives, in part because their members are denied access to the alternative social unit, the family.

Central zone, east and west of the central business district

The remaining associations are divided between Boulaq, which forms the western quadrant of the ellipse, and Bab al-Shariya and Waily, the eastern portion of the belt. Ten associations are located within the former zone, while twenty have addresses in the latter. Just as the ecological position of these areas is midway between the northern concentration of Delta village associations and the southern concentration of Upper Egyptian associations, so, sociologically, they lie midway, containing associations from both regions of the country in roughly equal proportions. They share still other similarities. Both are close to the central business district; both rank low in socioeconomic status (below both Shubra and the transitional business zone); both are primarily family areas; and both contain the densest slums of the city: densities of up to 900,000 persons per square mile are recorded for small subsections of Boulaq, and the overall density of the community area of Bab al-Shariya is the highest in the city. Of the two, Boulaq is the older and hence the one retaining more rural qualities in its buildings and streets, but even Bab al-Shariya, despite its uniformly high apartment buildings looming above narrow access alleys, contains a population more rural than urban in its ways.

These, then, are the areas to which migrants have gravitated within the city. That they are relatively scarce in the highest rental zones of the city is attributable to their low socioeconomic status. Migrants are relatively absent, also, from the rural-urban fringe proper which would, as we have seen, provide them with the most familiar and protective environment. The lack of rental housing in these areas (privately owned farms with villages for laborers only), the dearth of public transportation, and their desire to live close to their new jobs are undoubtedly important reasons for their rejection of these areas. A second area surprisingly overlooked in the search for "near-the-fringe" living is Medieval Cairo, that rectangular belt of oldest structures toward the eastern edge of the city. The complete absence of new housing in these districts, coupled with a low turnover rate (the population works at traditional crafts and trades where production, selling, and living quarters are often in the same structure), have probably prevented mass invasions by new migrants.

III. HYPOTHESES CONCERNING MIGRANT ADJUSTMENT

Earlier, the hypotheses of migrant adjustment were broken down into four classes: physical, economic, social, and ideological. In light of the locational material presented above, plus observations of both rural and city life in Egypt,[14] these will be defined here in an attempt to describe the peculiarities of migrant adjustment in Egypt.

Physical

We have already suggested that many migrants gravitate to areas lying close to the rural-urban fringe, while others settle in areas which have at least a cultural resemblance to semirural areas. In these sections, interior streets and alleyways are seldom used for wheeled traffic, leaving undisturbed the rural functions of the street as pathway, meeting place, playground, and tethering area for animals.

Greater adjustments are required with respect to both the dwelling and the physical neighborhood. Housing occupied by the majority of migrants is more urban than rural in style. This results in functional overcrowding more severe than in the villages. The village home minimizes the number of inclosed rooms in order to maximize private open space (a ground-level interior courtyard or a protected roof courtyard in a more commodious two-story home). This cherished space is eliminated in the multifamily flats of the city. While many of the tasks assigned to the courtyard are no longer performed in the city (drying dung cakes, storing crops, tethering animals), other social uses such as cooking, eating, and just sitting are driven indoors or to the streets in the city.

Not only is the home more compressed due to the loss of outdoor "overspill" space, but the neighborhood is also more concentrated. While residential densities in Egyptian villages are surprisingly high, they nowhere approach the densities of Cairo's poorer districts. Many families using a common stairwell and public utilities means, paradoxically, more intensive contact with neighbors than in the village; and adjusting to the inadvertent intimacy may be extremely difficult for people new to the city, particularly for women.

Within the home itself are other changes, of which the loss of the ovenroom is perhaps the most important. In the rural home one full room is devoted to the massive flat-topped oven in which bread is baked daily and which, during the winter months, heats the adjacent areas and provides a snug bed for a blanketless family. That its loss is viewed with distress by at least some migrants is evidenced by the fact that some seek the top floor of an urban dwelling to construct a village oven and advise newcomers from their village to do the same.[15]

Other changes in the home are viewed more favorably, since they conform to the aspirations of villagers. Among the objects high in status found in the most prosperous rural homes are small kerosene burners instead of dung-cake fires for cooking, wardrobes and china closets to store a growing stock of consumption items and the high four-poster bed with its black wrought-iron frame embellished with gilt, which remains, in the city as in the village, the *most* important sign of status. These are items with which migrants tend to crowd their urban homes, as soon as they can afford them.

The dress of migrants changes little in the city. Only the selective migrants change completely from the *galabiya* (long loose robe) to pants and shirts; for non-selective migrants the change is rarely required to conform to the urban pattern, and it is occupation rather than status per se or place of birth which dictates appropriate attire. It is perhaps because of this that the change is more frequently attempted by Delta than by Upper Egyptian migrants.

Change in dress presents more difficult problems for the women. The universal dress of village women is a high-necked, long-sleeved printed gown which is then covered by a black one of similar cut. A kerchief and then a black mantilla completely cover the hair. While many village women retain this attire in the city (as do many old city residents), some of the younger of them first discard the black garment and later may adopt a modified urban version of the printed gown with cutout neckline and daring three-quarter-length sleeves.

The foregoing remarks apply best to Delta families making a relatively permanent adjustment to the city. They do not apply with equal force to upper Egyptian migrants working as domestic servants or in other occupations where housing is provided or to those who remain unmarried or leave their families in the village. Paradoxically, this group, exposed most intensively to a completely new physical environment, is least assimilated to Cairo. A lifetime spent in sections of the city which contrast sharply with the village environment affects a superficial sophistication unmatched by the manual laborer from the Delta living in a quasi-rural district. It seems, however, that the very lack of gradual transition and of the mediating influences of family and neighborhood has the reverse effect of prolonging the period when one is a stranger. This type of migrant often completely rejects urban life, confining his periodic social contacts to co-villagers often in his own profession and his "real" life to infrequent sojourns to his village family.

Economic

In their villages of origin, migrants were engaged almost exclusively in agriculture. Men worked long and hard during the three sowing and harvesting periods in the Delta and the two crop-change periods in Upper Egypt, these periods of intense activity being followed by slower seasons of maintenance and community sociability. The basic rhythm of rural life thus dictated large finite jobs alternating with lighter routine work. The length of the work day varied with the stage of the cycle.

Women's work was more evenly distributed, with child care, the preparation of food and bread, the making of dung cakes, and the tending of livestock performed daily. Work in the fields was done during the early morning hours, except during the busy seasons, when it absorbed a greater portion of the day. Labor was communal within the extended family home and, when outdoors, was usually performed in company. This often changes in the city.

Laundry is a case in point. In the village, washing is done in the canal or now, increasingly, at the communal water taps. It is never a solitary activity. Contrast this with how laundry is done in Al Sharabiya, a migrant area described above.[16] Water is also secured from communal taps, but a man guards the tap, effectively discouraging women from washing at the site. Women carry their water home to wash in solitude within their dwellings. Other functions are similarly driven indoors or eliminated altogether. Thus the ex-village woman experiences a reduction in her work load (except where outside employment is taken), but, at the same time, she experiences an even greater reduction in the social life which formerly attended her labors.

The experience of migrant men, on the other hand, is often the reverse. The work of a city manual laborer is probably more taxing, certainly more evenly distributed over time, and usually *less* solitary than rural work. Exceptions must be made for migrants working as itinerant peddlers, shoe-shiners, tea-makers, etc., and, of course, for those working as domestic servants. These occupations are both more independently regulated and somewhat more isolating from contacts of a primary nature.

To what extent do migrants working at steady jobs in the company of others come into contact with associates from different backgrounds? Social heterogeneity is one of the distinguishing characteristics of urbanism, but for this to create the mental counterpart—cultural relativity—heterogeneous persons must come into intimate contact with each other. While in large-scale factories the mixing of diverse people undoubtedly occurs, the overwhelming majority of commercial and industrial firms in Cairo employ only a few persons, often within the same family. Furthermore, migrants often depend upon their compatriots to guide them to their first jobs. Sometimes, migrants seek out well-known "successes" from their village to give them employment. Thus migrants cluster together not only residentially but also on the job as well. In the smaller firms of Cairo, then, a far greater homogeneity of the work force exists than would have been expected by chance. Far from isolating the migrant from his fellow villagers, his job may actually consolidate his village ties.

Social

The hypotheses presented by Louis Wirth in his logical statement[17] of the differences between the rural and urban ways of life have been misused, as if they were facts, and many of the concepts almost self-evident to sociologists studying American cities have proved less valid when applied to the growing body of data about non-Western and preindustrial cities. While isolated refutations have appeared,[18] as yet there has been no major reformulation of the theory.

Wirth hypothesized that the ecological determinants of a city (large numbers of heterogeneous people in dense, permanent settlement) would have certain social consequences, notably anonymity, dependence upon impersonal relations and sanctions, sophistication, and tolerance of change. To what extent do the social relationships in Cairo conform to these predicated types, and, further, how much does the rural migrant really have to adjust his personality to become a functioning member of urban society?

While these questions are too ambitious to be answered here, two propositions are suggested. First, the culture of Cairo fails to be characterized chiefly by anonymity, secondary contacts, and the other attributes of urban life. Second, migrants to Cairo are active creators of a variety of social institutions whose major function is to protect migrants from the shock of anomie.

Middle Eastern culture places a high value on personal relationships, even at a sacrifice of privacy and internal development. This, combined with a system of relationships based on the extended kinship group, serves to increase the number of primary ties far beyond what Western sociologists, reasoning from their own experience, dare to assume possible.[19] This network of personal associations enmeshes not hundreds but thousands of individuals.

Were Cairo merely an amorphous mass of individuals, this network, large as it is, might account for but a small fraction of the individual's contacts. However, Cairo is not one community but, rather, many separate social communities. Functional sections of each community may be geographically separated—residence in one section, business in another, recreation in still another. A member of one community may pass daily through the physical site of communities other than his own, neither "seeing" them nor admitting their relevance to his own life. But, within his own community, there is little if any anonymity.

It is within this context of "urbanism" that the Egyptian migrant is called upon to adjust. His adjustment is further facilitated by the formal and informal institutions he develops within his small community, one of which has already been mentioned—the village benevolent society. Through it many migrants receive moral support from their compatriots as well as insurance against the insecurities of urban life, that is, isolation in poverty, sickness, and death.[20] It is unlikely, however, that more than 100,000 migrants are involved in these associations, while it will be recalled that their number exceeded 600,000 in 1947. Thus, even if these associations are important to the persons they serve, they fall short of absorbing most migrants.

Other formal institutions play a relatively minor role in providing social groups for migrant identification. Labor unions (except for craft guilds), civic associations, charitable organizations, and political groups are all relatively undeveloped social institutions in Cairo. One must look, then, to the informal social institutions for a fuller understanding of patterns of adjustment. Unfortunately, documentation in this area is totally lacking. While a few may be singled out as playing important roles, no estimate of their magnitude can be offered.

First in importance is undoubtedly the coffee shop in which Middle Eastern males conduct their social and often their business lives. The comparable Western institution is probably the old style of British pub which, with its set of steady patrons and its intimate atmosphere, served as a social focus for the individual's life. Many an Egyptian coffee shop is run by a villager to serve men from that particular village. News of the village is exchanged, mutual assistance for employment is given, and the venture more resembles a closed club than a commercial enterprise.

For the women no such informal association is available. While within the village there are also no purely female informal associations, religious festivals, births, deaths, marriages, circumcisions, etc., are all village-wide events in which women have important roles to play. Within the city, however, these events become more private, and the role of women as full participants is probably reduced. Social life in the city is confined more and more to the immediate neighborhood.

It is this immediate neighborhood, however, which constitutes, after the family, the most important informal social institution for migrants in the city. The cohesiveness of the neighborhood is strengthened by the tendency of persons from the same village to settle together. Similar to the situation elsewhere, it is the women, children, and very old persons who are the most active participants in neighborhood-centered social life.

Motivations and ideology

The *Weltanschauung* of the city man is presumed to differ from the peasant's in several significant ways. First, relaxation of the heavy hand of personal social control in the village is assumed to give greater latitude for individual differentiation. Second, cities are assumed to foster a more secular, rational, and mechanistic ordering of activities. Third, cities are gateways to a more sophisticated knowledge of the outside world. Finally, cities have traditionally been the centers of movements of social change, from new religions to new political ideologies and transfers of power.

While these statements are valid premises, data on Cairo are lacking which would permit us to place rural migrants along the continuum from the sacred, conformist, isolated, and relatively static state of the ideal folk society to the extreme of urbanism outlined above. For one thing, the Egyptian village hardly conforms to the ideal prototype of a folk society. Where farmers raise cash crops tied to international markets (cotton and sugar), listen to radios, travel often to market towns, have relatives or friends in the cities, and send their children to schools following a national curriculum, the magic ring of isolation has already been broken. On the other hand, as already demonstrated, it is possible within Cairo to lead a fairly circumscribed existence outside the main stream of urban life. Therefore, while there may be a wide gap between the least-sophisticated villager and the most-sophisticated urbanite, there is certainly no indication that migrants necessarily pass from one pole to the other.

POSTSCRIPT

Twelve years have now elapsed since the above article was written. Seldom does one have the opportunity to reconsider ideas "inscribed on the record," and even less frequently to share later thoughts with readers. The editors of this volume, sympathetic to my anxieties about the calcification of sociological doctrine, have graciously allowed me to append some afterthoughts. These have arisen from two sources: the first, hindsight; the other, changing social reality.

In retrospect I believe that the article commits as gross an error as the one it sought to refute. The relationship between "city" and "hinterland" is a complex, changing and, indeed, a reciprocating or "tidal" one. At moments in history, urban centers surge ahead of their containing cultures, only gradually pulling the countryside with them. At times, the lag may be so great that it appears unbridgeable. However, the deeper symbiotic ties between city and country cannot for long remain strained, and the countryside often reengulfs the city temporarily, pulling it back to its roots, as it were. Nor are cities the sole sites of change; they are often merely the more visible arenas within which rural revolutions reverberate.

To a significant extent, "classical American urban theory" (its continental roots codified by Wirth) developed at one such truncated moment in the ongoing attraction-repulsion, lead-follow relationship between cities and their rural areas. It thus stressed unduly the gap between urban and rural life—a gap which we increasingly recognize to have been but a temporary phase which Western societies have now largely moved beyond (at least in *that* form). I used Egyptian data to illustrate an "exception," not recognizing that it was the staticism more than the content of the "theory" I wished to undermine. In so doing, I fear that I have merely engendered another static "myth," namely, that in "underdeveloped countries" cities are more rural than one would expect. I too had captured only one "still shot" in the moving process, since my truncated moment of history led me to stress the return to rural roots.

During the past decade the balance between urban and rural in Cairo, and between city and countryside in Egypt, has again shifted, which requires some updating of the findings. First, as predicted, the rural areas have undergone substantial "modernization," thus creating a somewhat better prepared rural migrant, one who now often bypasses traditional occupations and moves directly into the modern industrial sector of the urban economy. (Some of these observations are expanded upon in my article in *Middle Eastern Cities,* ed. by Lapidus, University of California Press, 1969; and even more in my "Migration and Politics in Egypt," in a forthcoming volume on *Social Change in the Middle East,* Indiana University Press.) Second, few rural-like settlement areas are left within easy access of the central city to which migrants wishing to maintain older patterns might gravitate. Cairo's population now exceeds five (or some say, even six) million. Given this dramatic increase in numbers, construction and urban development have been rapidly eroding the residual parts of the rural fringe; furthermore, the preferred locations for the expanding large-scale industrial establishments have been peripheral. This has had a double effect. On the one hand it has led to quite a bit of counter-commuting; on the other hand, it has permitted industrial workers to seek more decentralized residential locations, often tied not to "migrant ghettoes" but to the "company town." Third, the contrast between the characteristics of migrants from Upper Egypt and those from the Delta (Lower Egypt) has virtually disappeared, at least demographically and, one suspects, sociologically as well. The sex ratios for both groups are now remarkably well balanced, indicating that large numbers of Upper Egyptian and Nubian males who migrated singly have now been joined by their families and that today's migrant tends to move in the nuclear family unit at least. This usually means less indiscriminate dependence upon co-villagers and often indicates a stronger commitment to the move as permanent. Thus, while villagers still flock to Cairo, they are usually a bit more "urbane" when they arrive and much more interested in rapid assimilation once there. Finally, certain events which could not have been predicted have altered the migrant flow. With the bombardment of the canal zone cities in the 1967 war came a massive evacuation of a highly urbanized population, many of whom resettled in Cairo. As many as half a million urban-to-urban migrants may have arrived in Cairo within the past few years, infusing the city with another impulse toward "urbanization."

Paradoxically, this has meant rapid strides in "urbanity" in the cityscape which makes the gap between Cairo and the countryside appear to be growing again. In that symbiotic reciprocity between city and hinterland, Cairo has again forged ahead. Dress has changed only slightly in rural areas, but virtually all urban males have abandoned the *galabiyah* and now dress in Western pants and shirts. Outside of the ubiquitous transistor radio, manufactured consumer goods are still not widely diffused in the rural areas, but in the cities items once reserved for the aristocracy when they had to be imported, are now becoming part of the expected "market basket," now that they are locally produced. The growing "syndicalist" nature of modern Egyptian institutions is probably making work a more central determinant of life style and work associates an increasingly significant source of social sustenance. Hence, the dynamics of migrant adjustment now require new data and a revised appraisal.

Notes

1. This article is a revised summary version of a paper presented to a conference on "The Emerging Arab Metropolis" (Congress for Cultural Freedom and the Egyptian Society of Engineers, co-sponsors) in Cairo, December 1960.

2. Expulsion from supersaturated rural environment ranks as an equally important element in this growth.

3. See Charles Stewart, Jr., "Migration as a Function of Population and Distance," *American Sociological Review*, XXV (June 1960), 347–56; George Zipf, *Human Behavior and the Principle of the Least Effort* (Cambridge, Mass.: Addison-Wesley Press, 1949). Application of hypothesis to Egyptian data prepared by present writer.

4. It probably *never* will sharpen to the same extent as it did in the West because simultaneously with this ruralization of the cities is occurring an urbanization of rural areas (extension of roads, education, and social services). These processes were temporarily distinct in Western development.

5. The *1947 Census of the Governorate of Cairo* shows that, of a total population of little more than 2 million, only 1.3 million had been born within the city; 51,000 were born in other governorates (large cities); 59,000 were born outside Egypt. Thus more than 630,000 residents of Cairo came from more or less rural sections of Egypt.

6. See the unpublished findings of two American sociologists, Karen and Gene Petersen, who have made a sample study of 1,250 migrant families from five Delta villages.

7. It is presented in full detail in *The Cairo Fact Book,* prepared by the writer, published by the Social Research Center of the American University at Cairo.

8. A table showing place of birth by census tract of current residence has, unfortunately, never been included in any Cairo census.

9. See H. Saaty and G. Hirahayashi, *Industrialization in Alexandria* (Cairo: Social Research Center, 1959); "Demographic Aspects of Urbanization in the ECAFE Region," in *Urbanization in Asia and the Far East* (Calcutta: Research Center on the Social Implications of Industrialization in Southern Asia, 1957); a variety of papers in UNESCO, *Social Implications of Industrialization and Urbanization in Africa South of the Sahara* (Paris: United Nations, 1956), among others.

10. Prepared by Isis Istiphan and published by the Social Research Center, American University at Cairo, 1956.

11. Obviously, not all ex-residents would be found in the Cairo settlement of maximum concentration, since some, probably the most successful economically, may have already moved to other sections of the city, while others never did follow the typical pattern, for example, the selective migrants or those with intervening experiences, such as army service.

12. The sex ratio here is 129 in the ages most likely to be imbalanced by migration, 15 to 49; in the northern section it is only 104. Forty percent of males of marriageable age are unmarried here, while only 25 percent are unmarried in the northern section (computed from 1947 census).

13. The *Directory of Social Agencies* lists the dominant occupations of members of each association. Government and manual workers are listed most frequently for Lower Egyptian associations, while servants, porters, and messengers are the most frequently mentioned occupations for Upper Egyptian associations.

14. The author has spent more than three years in Egypt, one and a half at a UNESCO project in a village area and two years in Cairo studying the structure of that city. Many observations have been further authenticated by anthropologists and social workers with longer and more intimate experience in both areas, to whom the author expresses gratitude.

15. Reported by Hind Abu el Seoud, an anthropologist studying a small Delta village and its ex-residents in Cairo.

16. Account provided by Abdel Monem Shawky, former social worker in the district for fourteen years.

17. Louis Wirth, "Urbanism as a Way of Life," *American Journal of Sociology,* XLIV (July 1938), 1–24, which essentially reformulates the work of earlier German scholars, such as Max Weber, *The City,* ed. and trans. D. Martindale and G. Neuwirth (Glencoe, Ill.: Free Press, 1958); and Georg Simmel, "The Metropolis and Mental Life," in *The Sociology of Georg Simmel,* trans. Kurt Wolff (Glencoe, Ill.: Free Press, 1950), pp. 409–24.

18. See, e.g., Gideon Sjoberg, "The Preindustrial City," *American Journal of Sociology,* LX (March 1955), 438–45; Horace Miner, *The Primitive City of Timbuctoo* (Princeton, N. J.: Princeton University Press, 1953).

19. Weber himself rejected impersonal relations as a useful part of the city's definition, noting that "various cultural factors determine the size at which 'impersonality' tends to appear" (*op. cit.,* p. 65). See also Richard Dewey, "The Rural-Urban Continuum," *American Journal of Sociology,* LXVI (July 1960), 60–66.

20. Burial services, offered by almost all associations, parallel the burial-insurance organizations of Negro rural migrants to northern cities.

9

BERT F. HOSELITZ, Generative and Parasitic Cities

This paper has a threefold purpose. It is supposed to be a critical summing up of the preceding discussion; it should attempt to state a general theory of the relations between urbanization and economic growth and cultural change; and it should suggest some lines along which further fruitful research might be undertaken in order to obtain more precise knowledge about the interrelations of the processes of urban growth and development and those of economic progress and cultural change. This is a very ambitious task and one which, I fear, I am not able to fulfill satisfactorily. But I hope that my comments on these three topics might prove fruitful for further discussion.

There is agreement among the authors of the preceding papers that the growth and development of cities is a necessary condition of economic development. Lampard, in particular, points to the need for greater specialization of tasks which has been associated invariably with urban centers; Kolb stresses the need for a universalist-achievement-oriented value structure which is indispensable for a successful rationalization of production, and hence for industrialization, and finds also that the urban environment was a necessary condition for the evolution of such values; Davis and Hertz re-echo these views and show that the concentration of economic activities within the relatively narrow geographical space

Bert F. Hoselitz, "Generative and Parasitic Cities," *Economic Development and Cultural Change* (April 1955), pp. 278–294. Copyright © The University of Chicago. Reprinted by permission.

This essay summarizes the contributions of the Conference on the Role of Cities in Economic Development and Cultural Change published in the previous two numbers of *Economic Development and Cultural Change.*

of a city creates important savings which make possible a greater degree of specialization of production because of the closeness of complementary producers. This, in turn, is supported by Lampard's analysis of external economies to the firm and to the industry, which creates a situation of decreasing costs and stimulates further specialization. Supplementary to this process of progressive specialization is the development of new service industries, the growth of which is correlated with the size of cities on the one hand and the level of income on the other. The former is discussed by Vining and treated more exhaustively by the protagonists of the theory of urban hierarchy. In the table, which Vining cites from Brush's study of southwestern Wisconsin, the proliferation of specialized tertiary industries with increasing size of the central places is clearly shown. Yet this table includes only central places of the lowest three orders and it need hardly be pointed out that higher-order central places would exhibit not merely a larger population, but also a much greater variety of specialized service industries. The correlation between level of income and relative preponderance of service industries has been emphasized especially by Colin Clark,[1] but it is implicit in the discussion of Davis and Hertz, Lampard, and Vining. In terms of a theory embracing the concepts of urban hierarchy it can be stated by saying that higher-order central places are spaced more closely together in countries with higher incomes than in countries with lower incomes, and that the population of higher-order central places form a larger proportion of the total population in countries with higher incomes than in countries with lower incomes. This result is confirmed by the comparative data on the proportion of urban population to total population calculated by Davis and Hertz. Stated in very simple and commonplace terms, this may be expressed by saying that the richer a country, the more urbanized it is and the larger a city in any country the wealthier it is.

It would seem, therefore, cities have, on the whole, exercised a generative function on real income and that, in the light of the available evidence, it is wrong to speak of a "parasitism" of urban centers. But in spite of the apparently overwhelming evidence offered by the study of urban history and the worldwide comparative analysis of urban centers, it may be useful to open up the problem once more.

If we speak of "generative" and "parasitic" cities, we must first explain these concepts. A city may be considered generative of many things, some of them desirable and others undesirable. As has been shown by the authors of the preceding papers, cities have been important centers providing an impetus for economic growth and cultural change, but also a fertile soil has been found in cities for social disorganization, criminality, and other presumably undesirable forms of social behavior. Cities have generated economic progress and crime, they have been places where new forms of cultural adaptation were hammered out, but also where an old culture which had lost vigor and vitality found its last stronghold and refuge. In order to avoid confusion and uncertainty, it is therefore important to state explicitly from what viewpoint a city will be regarded as "generative" or as "parasitic." The answer to this question should be clear from the context in which this paper is written. A city will be designated as generative if its impact on economic growth is favorable, i.e., if its formation and continued existence and growth is one of the factors accountable for the economic development of the region or country in which it is located. A city will be considered as parasitic if it exerts an opposite impact. A parallel relation may be stipulated between the formation and continued existence of a city and cultural change. If we apply this definition to the classification of cities which Redfield and Singer present, we must conclude that cities of heterogenetic transformation tend to generate cultural change, whereas cities of orthogenetic transformation tend to limit, and in the extreme, may fully impede cultural change. But this does not mean that orthogenetic cities are necessarily parasitic with regard to economic growth. The process of primary urbanization, though leading to a reinforcement of existing cultural patterns, may be generative of economic growth, and, at the same time, it is thinkable that cities in certain stages of secondary urbanization may exert an unfavorable effect upon economic growth of the wider geographical unit of which they form a part.

In the view of Redfield and Singer the process of primary urbanization is characterized by the development of a Great Tradition. This is in its core an intellectual process which is viewed as leading to the development of a class of *literati,* the final redaction of "sacred texts" and the evolution of a hierarchy of social control which often also is interpreted as being based on some sacred order. But the development of a Great Tradition may often—though not necessarily always—be bound up with the release of forces which exert a beneficial effect on economic growth. This appears to be suggested by the very definition of the process of primary urbanization, as implying a certain alteration in the essentially rural small-scale folk society. Historically this process has been associated with the evolution of often large and powerful empires. I am not competent to discuss the cultural, intellectual and general social trends involved in the development of a great tradition among the Chinese, Indians, Maya, or several other peoples referred to by Redfield and Singer. But it is generally acknowledged that the formation of the great tradition in the ancient river valley civilizations of Egypt and Mesopotamia led not merely to the development of complex religious systems and governmental organizations, but also to scientific and technological innovations which played an important role in the more rational exploitation of agricultural resources and the increase in the total product. Similarly the process of primary urbanization which occurred in the early Middle Ages in towns which formed the seat of an ecclesiastical lord exerted often a favorable initial impact on the conditions of economic growth. In fact the ultimate rise in the late Middle Ages of many free cities, which originated as seats of a bishop or archbishop, was inaugurated by the "defection" of the bishop's *ministeriales* in the struggle between the merchants and artisans and their ecclesiastical overlords.[2]

Let us now take a look at the obverse situation, one in which a city is in the stage of secondary urbanization, i.e., undergoes culturally heterogenetic transformation, but at the same time exerts an unfavorable impact upon economic development of the wider geographical unit of which it forms a part. Redfield and Singer mention, among others, as typical examples of cities in the heterogenetic order, certain colonial administrative centers. Several of these cities may be regarded as forming exclaves of the countries in which they are located and as contributing to a stagnation—albeit often only a temporary stagnation—of the economic growth of their countries. Examples for this situation can be found more often in the past history of colonialism than in the present. The early urban settlements of the various European nations in the New World, but also in parts of South and Southeast Asia, appear to have been of that kind. It is granted that the new techniques introduced by the colonizing power, the increase of trade and commerce carried on by the Europeans, did result in economic growth within the city itself and its immediate environs. But the advantages accruing from this kind of urban growth to the wider region in which such a city was located were counterbalanced by an excessive depletion of natural resources, and the exploitation of peasants and other primary producers. This had the consequence that often stagnation and economic decline rather than economic growth of the region as a whole ensued.

We thus obtain four possible classes into which cities may be placed. They may foster both economic growth and cultural change; they may foster cultural change but exert an unfavorable impact upon the economic development of their hinterland; they may foster economic growth but resist cultural change; and they may induce economic stagnation and impede cultural change at the same time. It may be, of course, that one or more of these "boxes" will prove to be empty. It should also be stressed that any one city may be placed into more than one class in the course of its history. For example, it would appear *on first sight* that ancient Rome during its stages of primary urbanization tended to affect economic growth favorably, that it continued to do so during the early years of the Empire, although it had entered the stage of secondary urbanization, and that in the last two centuries of the Western Roman Empire it was a factor contributory to the economic decline and stagnation of Italy and other parts of the Roman West. Whether or not this impression can be verified would depend upon a careful and exhaustive analysis of the impact exercised by Rome upon the general level of economic activity of the empire of which it was the capital.

If we accept the distinction between an orthogenetic and a heterogenetic urbanization process, and if we admit that a city may at certain times of its history impede rather than react favorably upon economic growth, we are faced with two problems. (1) The period during which a city exerts a generative (or conversely a parasitic) impact may be of unequal duration. We may speak of a generative (or parasitic) impact in the short run or in the long run. The meaning of the concepts of short run and long run in this context is not quite identical with the usage of these terms by Redfield and Singer nor with the meaning attached to them in standard economic analysis. Short run relates to a period which may have some duration, but the end of which may be foreseen with a high degree of probability. Long run, on the other hand, designates a period which may be expected to continue indefinitely. This distinction may be expressed more precisely perhaps in the following terms. We will speak of a short-run generative (or parasitic) impact of a city if we can observe the presence or formation of factors which may be expected with a high degree of probability to change that impact. We will speak of a long-term impact, if such factors are not present or in formation.

Before I proceed it may perhaps be useful to make these distinctions clearer by one or two examples. I have mentioned earlier the impact of the establishment of colonial capitals. They initiated usually a culturally heterogenetic cycle of urbanization but at the same time exerted an unfavorable influence on the potentialities of economic growth of the surrounding country. The founding of Batavia is an instance of such a culturally generative but economically parasitic process of urbanization.[3] Many of the settlements of the British East India Company in India should be placed into the same class, and also Spanish colonial capitals in Mexico and elsewhere in Latin America. The processes unleashed in all these urban centers were similar. The old native ruling class was deprived of power; the desire on the part of the Europeans to attain a monopoly in the trade of the colony led to the destruction or debasement of the native merchant class; the country was exploited by the colonizing power with the sole view of yielding a maximum of profit to it.

But the divergent trends of economic development within these cities and outside them, in the wider countryside, had the effect of creating a situation which tended to counteract and eventually turn the parasitic impact of these cities into its opposite. The increasing difference in the average income which could be earned in the city as compared with the countryside tended to attract migrants, or at least discouraged many who had come to visit the city to return to their homes. The population of the city swelled; a labor force came into existence which served not merely the trading and domestic service needs of the foreigners, but which made the establishment of industry attractive. This in turn exerted a favorable influence upon the potentialities of economic development of the wider countryside in which the raw materials for the industries, which had developed in the cities, were produced. It also created increased demand for food, and in some instances, export crops. The net result was the gradual improvement of economic conditions in the countryside and the widening of economic development over an increasing area affecting a growing proportion of the population outside the city.

This process is described here in its most idealized and simple form. In some cases it has not yet gone very far and the masses of the people in many colonial and ex-colonial countries are still miserably poor. Moreover, in some of the most important underdeveloped countries in which colonial capitals and a few subsidiary administrative centers formed such parasitic exclaves the attainment of independence brought about a new process of urban growth which occurred in response partly to political insecurity and warfare in some parts of the country.

This wave of urbanization which can be witnessed in most nonindustrialized countries is a very recent development. It has been noted by Davis and Hertz, who present data for Africa south of the Sahara. Similar processes of rapid urban growth can be observed in most countries of South Asia, Latin America, and the Middle East. I shall return later to this phenomenon.

The parasitic impact of colonial capitals and other administrative centers may be regarded as having been a short-run impact in the sense in which this term is employed here. Although for a time the city tended to exert a clearly unfavorable influence on the potentialities of economic development of its hinterland, we saw that factors of change developed in and around the city which had the effect of turning the parasitic character of the city into a generative one.

It is not easy to discover actual instances in which the city has exerted a long-run parasitic influence on the economic development of the region which it dominated. I have referred earlier to the decline of ancient Rome in the fourth and fifth centuries, but I also pointed out that the determination of whether this is a conclusive case of long-run parasitism in the field of economic development could be verified only if the history of the impact of the city of Rome on Italy and the Western Empire were studied more extensively with this problem in mind. At the time of the decline of the Western Roman Empire, Rome was, of course, a city with clearly heterogenetic cultural orientation. Though one might be inclined to think that the historical development of Rome presents a somewhat unique situation and that one would encounter examples of long-run parasitism with regard to economic growth in cities which have become the strongholds of a Great Tradition and therefore resist the intrusion of culture elements from the outside, most actual examples of long-run parasitism that come to mind appear to have occurred in cultures dominated by cities in heterogenetic transformation. Apart from Rome of the third to the fifth centuries A.D., one might mention Constantinople from the middle of the twelfth to the middle of the fifteenth centuries, or the cities of the Iberian peninsula in the seventeenth and eighteenth centuries. In both civilizations the decline set in after contact with other cultures had been made and after the cities had become centers inhabited by a very mixed population.

On the basis of this reasoning we may draw a number of conclusions, which form a bridge to the second major problem, the general theory of urbanization in its relation to economic development and cultural change. The most important phase of the history of a city from the point of view of its impact on economic growth is its phase of cultural heterogeneity. In this phase, a city most often exerts a generative impact on the economic growth of the region it dominates. Concrete instances of this process have been cited by Lampard, Kolb, and Davis and Hertz, and they need not be repeated here. But in some cases a culturally heterogenetic city may exert a parasitic impact on economic growth, and this impact may either be of short or long duration. An important question to resolve is whether we can indicate the variables which determine whether a culturally heterogenetic city will have a generative or a parasitic impact.

A further point which results from the preceding discussion is that the generative or parasitic quality of a city must not be judged with reference to economic growth within the city and its immediate environs, but only with reference to the wider region which the city dominates. This implies that we assume the relation between a city and the region in which it is located to be one of urban dominance over the rural parts of the region. Whether or not such dominance exists, and which city among several tends to predominate above the others, may be ascertained by the application to concrete cases of the theories of urban hierarchy to which Vining refers. Although Vining, as well as the two urban geographers he cites, Walter Christaller and John E. Brush, are concerned primarily with economic dominance, cultural and political dominance by a city might be exerted along similar lines. Patterns of cultural and political dominance may differ from patterns of economic dominance. For example, in Renaissance Italy the cultural dominance of Florence was not matched by its political importance in relation to other Italian cities; similarly in the United States, Washington has supreme political dominance, but is not dominant from either the economic or cultural viewpoint; at the same time, Detroit and Chicago are economically dominant, but inferior in terms of cultural dominance to Boston and Los Angeles. On the other hand, there are countries in which a city at one and the same time has political, cultural, and economic dominance. Paris, Prague, Athens, Bangkok, Copenhagen, Oslo, Budapest, and many other cities are examples.

A city usually thus exerts dominance over a larger or smaller territory in which it is located, and dominance patterns vary depending upon whether we are concerned with economic, cultural, or political influence. The resultant of these partially overlapping and partially extrinsic fields of dominance appears to be a factor influencing the generative or parasitic impact exercised by a culturally heterogenetic urban center. In the case of colonial administrative centers, which we found to be often parasitic in the short run, the explanation of this outcome lies in the fact that the colonial capital is politically and sometimes culturally dominant within the colony, but economically subordinate to the metropolis. This is true not only of colonial capitals in the narrow sense of the term but often even of cities which have an analogous position to colonial capitals, but which are located in politically independent countries. Montevideo, Panama, or Caracas are politically dominant in the countries of which they are the capitals. But they are economically subordinate to the great centers of world trade of which they are the gateways to the hinterland which they dominate. This tends to produce parasitic features in these cities which at times may overbalance the generative features they normally would be expected to display.

This dichotomy between cultural-political dominance, on the one hand, and economic subordination to external centers, on the other, appears also to have been at the basis of the parasitic role of cities like late medieval Constantinople and seventeenth century Lisbon. Constantinople's economic subordination under Venice during the last three centuries of the Byzantine Empire is too well known to need repetition. Similarly Lisbon in the period after the loss of Portuguese independence came under the economic dominance first of Spain and later of Britain.

These cities occupy a Janus-faced position with regard to the regions within which they have cultural and political dominance, but whose economic subordination they represent at the same time. Further light on their parasitism is thrown by the presence at the same time of different social-structural variables in their economic and cultural-political relations. Kolb has shown that the formation of the western city, of which Chicago was chosen as the prototype, was associated with a transformation of a particularistic-ascriptive value orientation to an universalistic-achievement oriented one. He also argues that the process of urbanization in underdeveloped countries, in order to be successful, must follow a similar pattern. This argument is in agreement with views I expressed in a recent article on the social-structural change associated with a transition from economic underdevelopment to economic advancement. However, I confined my analysis there only to "those sets of action systems which pertain to a description of economically relevant behavior, i.e., behavior related to the production and distribution of goods and services."[4] Moreover, I included in the analysis not merely the ascription-achievement and the universalism-particularism dichotomies but also a consideration of the other three pairs of pattern variables stipulated by Parsons, particularly the specificity-diffuseness dichotomy. This last pair of variables is stressed by Lampard in his analysis of division of labor and increasing specialization. Its addition appears to me important because, in general, there exists a close functional correlation between ascription, particularism, and functional diffuseness on the one hand, and achievement, universalism, and functional specificity, on the other. But although such a close functional relation between each pair of pattern variables may be stipulated for a given area of social action, e.g., economic activity or political activity, it is not necessary that in the same society all fields of social action display the same structural variables. It is conceivable that economic relations, for example, are ruled by principles of achievement, universalism, and functional specificity, but that political relations display the principles of ascription, particularism, and functional diffuseness.

Differences such as these appear to account for the more or less permanent parasitism of certain cities. In its domestic environment, in the cultural-political order, the city is governed by principles of ascription and particularism; in its economic relations, which are dominated by strangers, achievement, universalism, and functional specificity dominate, or at least are in the ascendancy. The conflict between these two principles in different spheres of social life and action may produce incongruences which we describe as parasitism. The difference between long-run and short-run parasitism with regard to economic growth results from the preponderance of either the economic or the cultural-political relations in a given city. If there is reason to assume that the more "modern and rational," i.e., universalistic-achievement oriented tendencies of economic action are likely to prevail, the city's parasitism may be expected to change over into a state of generativeness. If, on the other hand, cultural-political resistances, the domination of vested interests, or the rigidity of a "great tradition" on the defensive, predominate, we may expect parasitism with regard to economic growth in the long run. In this situation only a revolutionary change in the political or cultural order of the city may end its parasitic role.

This discussion has led us already some distance into the field of a general theory of the relations between urbanization, economic growth and cultural change. It is not necessary to point out that we cannot boast of possessing a full theory, and that even those theoretical propositions which are summarized here, and which appear in the other papers submitted to this conference would require still a considerable amount of empirical support in order to be conclusively verified.

In this task one must distinguish three cases which are related to one another but may be analyzed separately: (1) the problem of economic growth and cultural change within a city; (2) the relation between a city's economic growth and cultural change and associated development in the region in which the city is dominant; and (3) the problem of economic development and cultural change of a country mediated through the development of a system of urban places, which come to form the urban hierarchy in the country in process of change. The papers of Lampard and Kolb as well as a substantial portion of the paper of Redfield and Singer are directed to the first problem. Similarly, the theoretical summary in the paper by Davis and Hertz centers on the first problem, although some comments of the second are included. Vining's paper deals primarily with the third problem, whereas some of the comments made in the preceding pages of this paper relate primarily to the second problem.

In summarizing the entire discussion it may perhaps be useful to state the agreements and disagreements in terms of these three cases. This may provide us with a rough guide of where there are still gaps and lacunae in our theoretical framework, and it may also point to those portions of our theory which need refinement, further verification, or revision.

As concerns the first problem, economic growth and cultural change within the confines of the city and its immediate environs, we may attain a fairly complete theory if we combine the propositions of Lampard and Davis and Hertz about economic change (spatial concentration of production; specialization of productive tasks; external economies due to geographical propinquity; availability of a trained labor force and of social overhead; favorable conditions for the development of tertiary industries) with those of Redfield and Singer about cultural change (cities of heterogenetic transformation, with special emphasis on the patterns of cultural change in "metropolis-cities of the worldwide managerial and entrepreneurial class"; rise of a consensus based on self-interest and pecuniary calculation, i.e., a consensus appropriate to the modern, Western technical order; evolution of sentiments of common cause attached to groups drawn from culturally heterogeneous backgrounds; emphasis on prospective rather than retrospective view of man in the universe) and with those of Kolb on changes in social structure (development of universalistic-achievement oriented values and all that implies). Social structure and economic activity may be related by clarifying the connections between an universalistic-achievement oriented society and a culture which places emphasis on a prospective rather than retrospective view of man and in which consensus appropriate to a rationalized technical-economic order is achieved.

This framework describes in the most general terms the relations between the process of economic development and cultural change and the growth and development of a city. There is, however, one caution which should be exercised. Redfield and Singer mention as a special case the "colonial" cities, and ask whether they can reverse from the heterogenetic to the orthogenetic transformation. They conclude that such a development is unlikely. Since these cities do not display a clearly dominant cultural pattern, we may ask further whether the "normal" development described in the preceding paragraph may be expected in them. Redfield and Singer have shown the typical (though not necessarily universal) process of cultural change associated with economic development to be from primary to secondary urbanization. But primary urbanization normally implies the development of a strong, dominant, integrated culture within a city, which then becomes modified in the process of heterogenetic cultural transformation. In general this heterogenetic transformation consists in an accommodation of new culture elements into the dominant culture. The development of the economy of the city is made possible without excessive degree of social disorganization because, and to the extent to which, the dominant culture of the city is flexible enough to permit a more or less gradual and "orderly" introduction of new culture elements. Kolb has shown how strong may be the forces making for social disorganization and how powerful must be the cultural restraints in order to prevent rapid economic development from creating social chaos and thus defeating itself, in the long run.

In many "colonial" cities a strong, dominant, integrated culture is absent. In addition, the recent process of urban growth in many of these cities has been characterized by the following characteristics: (1) It has been unusually rapid (as is shown, for example, by the data for Africa presented by Davis and Hertz). (2) It has, in many cases, reinforced the ethnic and cultural heterogeneity of the urban population. (3) It has occurred not in response to the availability of economic opportunities, especially employment opportunities, in the cities, but as a result of pushes and pulls created by political and military insecurity in the countryside and "psychic" attractions of city life. (4) It has been concentrated in a few central cities, sometimes at the expense of the growth of other smaller cities. The already existing imbalance in the distribution of urban centers in some colonial or "quasi-colonial" countries has been reinforced. The capitals of these countries have grown relatively faster than other cities and have become, in the words of Mark Jefferson, "primate" cities.[5] I shall return to this problem later in the discussion of the relationship between economic development and cultural change and the evolution of an entire urban hierarchy.

If we consider the first three of these factors, especially the second and third, we must conclude that we are facing a phenomenon of urban growth which is somewhat unique. It is, of course, true that some primate cities in Europe reached rather large size before the widespread introduction of industry. For example, Paris had some 750,000 inhabitants around the year 1700, and several other European capitals were not very much behind even though their degree of industrialization was of subordinate magnitude.[6] But the most rapid period of growth of European cities falls in the period of the industrialization of the various countries, and, as Lampard shows, there was an intimate connection between the economic demands for labor exerted by progressive accumulation of capital in urban industry and the growth of urban centers. This peculiar condition is absent in many of the primate cities of underdeveloped countries in Asia, Africa, and Latin America. Migration to cities takes place for a number of reasons. In part, it is caused by the destruction of the permanent basis for existence in the traditional surroundings of the migrants. In some cases population pressure in the farming regions may become so strong that emigration is necessary for mutual survival, and in other, more frequent cases, peasants are deprived of their traditional livelihood from tillage because of military insecurity, warfare, dacoity, banditry, and other forms of violence. In part the migration to cities is, however, due to pulls exerted by urban conditions. The relatively strong pull of superior consumption patterns has often been noted, and the very low living standards prevailing in most rural areas of underdeveloped countries, coupled with the drabness and the hardships of agricultural labor under conditions of backward technology, makes life in the city appear attractive. It is granted that there are compensations in rural regions, which counterbalance some of these relative disadvantages, but the loosening of cultural restraints as a consequence of inroads made by a more advanced economy, by warfare and political unrest, and a partial breakdown of the traditional kinship ties, create a climate facilitating geographical mobility of persons and their gradual congregation in the primate cities and a few other urban centers.

In spite of the development of intense nationalistic sentiments in some underdeveloped countries, the recent rapid growth of their capitals continues to exhibit culturally heterogenetic features. Migrants to the cities come from the various cultures indigenous to the underdeveloped country rather than from foreign countries. But the cultural heterogeneity of a city like Rangoon is not much diminished if instead of a mixture of Burmans, Indians, and Britishers, the mixture is one of Burmans, Karens, Shans, and Chins. Moreover, the agglomeration of the population occurs on the grounds of economically "irrational" motivations. It is provoked not by an increasing demand for labor in urban centers, but rather by considerations outside the sphere of resource allocation and use.

The combined impact of these factors is likely to prevent the smooth development of a universalist-achievement oriented value structure. To the extent to which tendencies for its development have been present in colonial and "quasi-colonial" capitals, they have been fostered by the dominant influence of

Europeans and have perhaps been reinforced by the characteristics of these cities as exclaves in their countries. To the extent to which the attainment of independence and the rise of nationalism tend to destroy or diminish this European influence, the main cultural group favoring the development of universalist-achievement oriented values becomes pushed into a subordinate position. At the same time, there is nothing to take its place, for the "impersonal forces of the market" which were a characteristic aspect of European capitalism and one of the main forces favoring the development of these values are operating only haltingly and imperfectly in the primate cities of underdeveloped countries. Their operation is, moreover, concentrated in those activities which are oriented towards the world markets rather than the domestic labor market, or even the domestic commodity markets.

The prospective socioeconomic development of the cities in underdeveloped countries may, therefore, not follow the pattern of development exhibited by cities in advanced Western countries. Kolb recognizes this when he suggests that an alternative pattern prevailing there may be based on universalistic-ascriptive orientations. In view of the development of cultural heterogeneity in these cities which is characterized not any more by a contrast of a dominant European to a submerged native culture, but rather by a diversity of value orientations based only in part on ethnic disparity and to an increasing degree on social differentiation, particularism, rather than universalism, may play an important role.

Let us take another look at Rangoon in order to clarify this statement. Before independence the characteristic mark impressed upon Rangoon was the dominance of Europeans. This dominance was exerted primarily by the fact that Rangoon's major function was that of a port through which the products of Burma passed into the world markets and through which, at the same time, the products of the world market entered Burma. Rangoon was, therefore, the main locus at which the culture of Burma became affected and modified by that of the West. Economically Westerners were dominant, and even in the second rank of economic dominance we find Indians (culturally more adjusted to the West than the native Burmese). Moreover, even among the Burmese preference was given to those who adopted certain Western cultural values, such as Christianity, for example. The cultural heterogeneity of Rangoon can be described as exhibiting the impact of Western culture on the native culture of Burma and the modifications occurring in this culture provoked by the economic dominance of Westerners. The greater economic "success" of the West was the means by which the cultural impact was primarily exerted. This preponderance of the economic factor (which has led, among others, to Boeke's well-known theory of the dual economy)[7] made Rangoon an exclave of Burma. It existed as one of the emporia of the world market rather than as a capital of a native, culturally distinct, population.

After independence this situation changed. Rangoon's economic position with regard to the world market became altered relatively little. But the internal relationship between the dominance of Rangoon's economic function and its cultural function as a center of a native culture became reversed. Although it remains the gate through which the foreign trade of Burma passes, this function is now subordinated to Rangoon's function as the capital of an independent country with its own culture. But Burmese society is not homogeneous. It is linguistically and culturally heterogeneous and the distinctions between Burmans, Karens, Shans, and Chins are not confined to culture but extend to the social-political level. Whereas a society with a "dual economy" exhibited fairly clearcut distinctions, and a relatively unambiguous pattern of dominance and subordination, the "plural society," which replaced it, is in many ways more complex and dominance patterns vary as between different areas of social action. Though the Burmans may hold a monopoly of political power, Karens exert greater economic power in some fields, and European and Indian influences are not eradicated in certain intellectual milieus. The Burman elite itself is not and cannot be culturally "pure." The consequence of this situation appears to be a reinforcement of particularistic values.[8] Hence the problem of the prospective development of cities in underdeveloped countries is not yet fully clear and it appears that here is an important further problem for research.

The development may lead toward a universalist-achievement oriented value structure and some cities in underdeveloped countries could be mentioned which apparently provide examples for this alternative. Sao Paulo, Caracas, and some other cities, especially in Latin America, belong in this group. The development may lead also to the predominance of particularistic-achievement oriented values, and some of the capitals of South Asian nations, Colombo, Rangoon, Jakarta, and others—as well as the cities in India, if Marriott's analysis is accepted —fall in this group. Finally, we may have the development of universalist-ascription oriented values, and these may be the patterns of urban growth in China. Some cities in underdeveloped countries may, moreover, exhibit several of these features simultaneously. This represents a transitional stage the general outcome of which is as yet uncertain.

I now wish to turn shortly to a discussion of the problem of the relation between economic growth and cultural change within the city and the associated development of the region in which the city is dominant. So far I have tacitly assumed that the impact is essentially a one-way process, that change occurs in the city and is transmitted to the surrounding countryside. This uniformity is questioned, and in my opinion, rightly so, by Redfield and Singer. The obvious exception which they cite is the process of primary urbanization. But apart from this instance, which we will disregard here because we are concentrating only on situations of cultural heterogeneity, they suggest that the process of mutual cultural interaction between the city and the country needs further exploration. Here is a problem which is, as yet, very little studied and which would require the formulation of some testable hypotheses. Most of the methods which have been developed to study the interrelations between city and country have been based on several implicit assumptions. One of these has been that of the cultural dominance of the city. This is exhibited by the very ingenious devices developed by urban geographers and social ecologists who analyzed the urban hierarchy or the sociology of urban centers.[9] Other characteristics of these methods are that they are essentially static, i.e., relate to the description of a situation at one point in time, rather than to a process, and that they concentrate almost exclusively upon the economic functions of the city. Both of these characteristics, as well as the assumption of urban dominance, are displayed also in Bogue's work on metropolitan communities.[10] In fact, as the subtitle of Bogue's work indicates, he is concerned essentially with the patterns of urban dominance, and, as his work shows, this pattern of dominance is exhibited particularly in the economic relations of cities. It is perhaps no accident that Bogue can discern patterns of urban dominance so clearly in the United States. This is the country with the most highly developed economy. It is sometimes said that in the United States urban culture has penetrated into the most remote spots of the countryside. But its high degree of economic development also implies a high degree of economic interdependence, and for this reason economic factors may be used with greater advantage than others as indicators of the closeness or remoteness of relations between population centers and surrounding areas. Bogue's scheme of dominance is, therefore, entirely based on the economic relations between cities and their less densely populated hinterlands. Although some of the other schema developed to describe patterns of urban hierarchy are not as rigidly tied to economic relations as Bogue's model, they rarely include any measures which clearly fall into the realm of cultural contacts. It is true that such measures as newspaper readership are sometimes added, or that—as is done, for example, by Christaller—certain political or administrative factors are included, but the most important variables which these models include are economic indicators. This means that even to the extent to which static models of the mutual impact between cities and their wider hinterland exist, only a partial set of factors relevant for this interdependence have so far been examined, and it would be desirable to develop methods which would take account of noneconomic factors. I have no doubt that this would be an extremely difficult procedure, and that it would be especially difficult to find variables which could be subjected to quantitative analysis as easily as can many economic variables. At the same time, it might be possible to obtain more light on this mutual interdependence in areas of noneconomic activity if such factors as linguistic and ethnic differences in cities and their hinterlands, perhaps membership in religious organizations and intensity of religious activities, length and purposes of seasonal migrations and travel, were studied. Which of these (or any other) factors should receive prominence would depend on the development of a theoretical framework of cultural dynamics and this is, alas, still lacking in most of its essential portions.

The fact that most existing models of the interrelations between cities and their hinterlands are static is of less concern. It is, of course, granted that what we are interested in chiefly is an analysis of the process of cultural change and economic growth. But this does not mean that this process can be studied only by applying dynamic models. As a first approximation the method of comparative statics may be used. In other words, the process of cultural change and related economic development and their interrelations with the process of urbanization may be adequately explored by attempting to find functional relationships between these variables and subvariables and by comparing static situations which are related to one another through time. Here the contribution of the historical study of urbanization may be most important. But in order to obtain results about the relationship of cities to their hinterlands, the historical study of cities must free itself from concentrating on urban history in the narrow sense and must expand into a study of the historical dimension of city-country interdependence and interrelations. Again I am ready to acknowledge that it is not easy to state in specific terms the concrete formulation of problems which may be expected to yield meaningful research results. But I hope that a recognition of this problem may lead to such formulation and to the discovery of appropriate methods by which answers to the kinds of questions posed here may be found.

The third problem area is the determination of relationships between economic growth and cultural change and the development not of one city but an entire net of cities which stand in some order of hierarchy to one another. This problem is treated explicitly by Vining though it is dealt with, by implication, also by the authors of all the other papers. The first comment which may be made here, and which follows from much of what has been said earlier in this paper, is that the "system of cities" as described by Vining, in which cities if ordered by rank and size are distributed in accordance with Pareto's law, seems to hold only for countries with a relatively high degree of industrialization. In the industrially less developed countries, the "law of primate cities" in its more extreme form appears to hold. In fact, in some underdeveloped countries this "law of the primate city" is so strong that apart from a capital which may have a million inhabitants or more, there are no other "large" cities, i.e., cities of more than 100,000 inhabitants. Perhaps the two most outstanding examples are Thailand and Peru.[11] In each the metropolitan city (with environs) has a population of around a million and the country lacks any other urban region exceeding 100,000 inhabitants. Yet Thailand has a population of more than 18 million and Peru of almost 10 million. In some other less developed countries the predominance of the capital is not so pronounced, but the overall disproportions between the largest, the small group of large, and the mass of small and minute cities is also sufficiently pronounced so as to make the rank-size rule inapplicable. This extreme degree of urban concentration in relatively few centers can be found not only in many underdeveloped countries, but also in many European countries before the industrial revolution. The preeminence of Paris at the time of Louis XIV has already been mentioned. It should be added, however, that at the time Paris had several hundred thousand inhabitants, there was no other French city which even reached 100,000. The same was true of Britain. At the time of the Glorious Revolution, London had around 700,000 inhabitants, and Bristol, the second city in Great Britain at that date, only around 50,000.[12]

If Vining is correct in his statement that a Pareto distribution holds in all "developed systems of cities," and that in the United States this size-rank distribution has "maintained a fairly stable form since 1790," we are faced with two problems: (1) The development of a system of cities in the United States—perhaps as a consequence of its rapid settlement—has been unusual and it is, therefore, perhaps not proper to draw inferences from its past development to what may happen in presently underdeveloped countries, especially those which are more densely populated now than the United States was before the middle of the nineteenth century. (2) The present system of cities in the United States is characteristic of a "developed" system of cities. If countries of reasonably sizeable population are found in which this relationship does not hold, can we infer that these countries have an "underdeveloped" system of cities? And if so, what are the characteristics of an "underdeveloped" system of cities? In France and Britain the relative preponderance of the capital is still very pronounced, in spite of the relatively high level of economic development which these two countries exhibit. In France, especially, the rank-size rule does not fit well. It would be approximated much better if the agglomeration of Paris were left out of the picture. But Paris cannot be left out of the picture—not only because without Paris France would not be France—but rather because France exhibits, in spite of industrialization and economic growth, the pattern of predominance of a primate city. This means that even granting the general applicability of the rank-size rule to a system of cities in an economically developed country, we are left with the problem to determine what distortions of this rule are caused by cultural and political factors, the differences between trends towards political centralization as against federalism, the historical patterns of settlement of a country, and, in the last resort, its entire demographic and economic history.

What I am trying to say is that the apparently neat and simple relationship that can be stipulated—in a rough way—for the system of cities of some countries, may become strongly modified if other, especially noneconomic, factors are introduced. Depending upon whether the factors accounting for the deviation of any actual distribution from the theoretically postulated one are all outside the realm of economic relations or not, it will become possible to predict with a somewhat higher degree of dependability how and in what ways economic growth and a rank-size distributed system of cities are related. I fear that some of the factors determining the deviations are economic, or at least demographic-historical factors, and hence any close correlation between the level of economic development and a particular pattern of distribution of urban centers may never be established.

Although some of these factors may be of importance with reference to the problem in which we are here primarily interested, the most important query that arises, if one considers the usefulness of such models for the study of economic development and cultural change, is the meaning of the function of the various central places in the model. The list of service functions in Wisconsin hamlets, villages and towns, which Vining cites from Brush, exhibit characteristic aspects of a highly developed economy. A similar list of hamlets, villages and towns in an underdeveloped country, say India, would show a very different set of typical functions of each central place of a given order. Whether a theory of central places can be applied to our problem depends, therefore, not so much on the presence or absence of regularities in locational patterns, but rather on whether we can compare meaningfully central places of different order in countries on different levels of economic development. Moreover, since cultural factors affect the functions of cities, differences in culture would add another element possibly still further limiting comparability. Yet, it is probable that an urban hierarchy analogous to that in southern Germany or Wisconsin exists in underdeveloped countries, especially those with many central places. The higher-order central places would probably be more similar in their service functions to one another in countries with different levels of economic development than central places of lower order. For example, a city like Bombay or Madras would differ less (in significant service functions) from Chicago or Milwaukee than some Indian small town of 10,000 inhabitants from Baraboo or Prairie du Chien, Wisconsin. At the same time, it is doubtful whether in Wisconsin, or the entire United States, central places could be found which correspond in function to Benares or Mecca.

Since the characteristics of central places of different order are derived primarily from economic functions, those central places in underdeveloped countries which in their economic structure most resemble corresponding central places in more developed countries would show the greatest functional similarities. This is true primarily of the large cities, especially those which in the colonial and ex-colonial countries form exclaves, i.e., in their primary function, are appendages of the system of world markets. But the cult places, as well as those central places in underdeveloped countries in which assimilation to Western culture has progressed the least, would show much greater functional differences with corresponding central places in Western countries. A comparative analysis of central places might show therefore the degree to which a rationalized Western system of economic organization and activity has penetrated a given country and might be a fairly good measure of the breadth on which the economic development of a country has taken place. Here again, cultural differences and historical traditions would blur the picture and introduce deviations which would have to be specially accounted for in each case.

All these procedures, however, only provide yardsticks for comparison, approximations of stages of economic development, and criteria for classification. They would have to be supplemented by a theory in which the development of a given system of cities is related to processes of economic growth. Such a theory is as yet nonexistent, but it is possible that further study and refinement of some of the relations studied by the protagonists of urban hierarchy or the theorists of systems of cities may lead to one. Here then is a field in which research has just begun and has therefore progressed very little. It presents perhaps a greater challenge and offers a wider scope for research than almost any problem area discussed so far.

It appears as if we had come a long way from our original problem, the distinction between generative and parasitic roles of cities, but in truth, the propositions discussed in the previous paragraphs are alternative statements of this problem, especially if we consider that the question of whether and under what circumstances cities exert a generative or a parasitic impact is an alternative way of asking what are the general relations between the processes of economic growth and cultural change on the one hand, and urbanization on the other. Depending upon whether we focus on these processes within a city, in the city's hinterland, or in an entire country undergoing a process of development accompanied by the formation of a net of urban centers, we encounter different subproblems and may come out with different evaluations of the generativeness or the parasitism of a given city or set of cities.

The overall process of development of a system of cities corresponding more or less to the functional and size distribution presented by Vining may be considered as the most general pattern of economic development in which urbanization plays a predominantly generative role. To the extent to which this development of a system of cities is impeded, or to the extent to which a topheavy system exhibiting the characteristics of primate-city domination cannot be overcome (and especially in those cases where the dominance of a primate city is reinforced in the process of urbanization), we may find a series of at least temporary parasitic influences exerted by the primate city. The particular form of this parasitism as well as the seriousness and duration of its impact will depend, as I believe to have shown, upon the particular constellation of economic and noneconomic (primarily cultural, political, and social-structural) factors. The determination of these factors, and of their interrelations, becomes then one of the primary research tasks in the study of the mutual interrelation between urbanization and economic development and cultural change.

Notes

1. Colin Clark, *The Conditions of Economic Progress,* 2nd ed. (London, 1951).
2. For a description of this process in Strassburg, for example, see Gustav Schmoller, *Strassburgs Blüte und die volkswirtschaftliche Revolution im XIII Jahrhundert,* Strassburg, 1875, pp. 11 ff.; the same development in thirteenth and early fourteenth century Geneva has been described by Francis de Crue, *La guerre féodale de Genève et l'etablissement de la commune (1285-1320),* Geneva, 1907.
3. See on the early history of Batavia and its impact, for example, J. J. Van Klaveren, *The Dutch Colonial System in the East Indies,* Rotterdam, 1953, pp. 40 ff.
4. Bert F. Hoselitz, "Social Structure and Economic Growth," *Economia Internazionale,* vol. VI, no. 3 (August 1953), p. 57.
5. Mark Jefferson, "The Law of the Primate City," *Geographical Review,* vol. XXIX, no. 2 (April 1939), pp. 226-232.
6. See Emile Levasseur, *La population française,* Paris, 1889, I, 213.
7. See J. H. Boeke, *The Structure of the Netherlands Indian Economy,* New York, 1942, ch. I.

8. McKim Marriott arrives at a similar conclusion by a somewhat different process of reasoning.

9. A good review of some of the most recent literature is presented by John E. Brush, "The Urban Hierarchy in Europe," *Geographical Review,* vol. XLIII, no. 3 (July 1953), pp. 414–416.

10. Don J. Bogue, *The Structure of the Metropolitan Community: A Study in Dominance and Subdominance,* Ann Arbor, 1950.

11. For further examples, see Jefferson, *op. cit.*

12. These data are based on the estimate of Sir William Petty, "Essays in Political Arithmetic," in *Tracts,* Dublin, 1759, pp. 182 ff.

10

RAYMOND W. MACK & DENNIS C. McELRATH, Urban Social Differentiation and the Allocation of Resources

Urbanization is the development of a social and spatial organization within which both the valued and the deplored products of a complex and elaborate society are allocated. The urban mode of distribution has been built upon a folk, peasant, feudal, and industrializing past. These backgrounds influence the present state of urbanization and the system of distribution in contemporary societies throughout the world. They are the foundation upon which this process of urbanization has developed.

URBANIZATION

Is it possible to look at this process in broad enough terms to specify its impact on the distribution of choice and constraint; of ideas and products wherever it occurs? We believe so: to do this we shall first sketch the process of urbanization and then link it to its corresponding mode of distribution.

Scale

Urbanization involves the transformation of a total society. Only in the past century and a half has the world approached truly urban *societies,* in which a high proportion of the total population live in cities. As recently as 1800, only 2.4 percent of the world's population lived in cities of 20,000 or more; today over one-fifth of the people live in such cities. Furthermore, the proportion of people living in large cities has risen even more dramatically. By 1950 the proportion of people in the world living in cities was higher than that in even the most urbanized country before modern times.

Raymond W. Mack and Dennis C. McElrath, "Urban Social Differentiation and the Allocation of Resources," *The Annals* of the American Academy of Political and Social Science, vol. 352 (March 1964), pp. 25–32. Reprinted by permission.

Between 1800 and 1850, the total population of the world increased only 29 percent, but the population living in cities of 5,000 or more grew by 175 percent, that in cities of 20,000 or more by 132 percent, and the population in cities of 100,000 or more increased by 76 percent. Then, from 1850 to 1900, the impact of scientific technology began to be felt in rapid industrialization. During this period, the total population of the world increased by 37 percent. But, in this span of time, cities of 5,000 or more increased by 192 percent, those of 20,000 or more by 194 percent, and those of 100,000 or more by 222 percent. During the next half century, from 1900 to 1950, cities expanded at an even more accelerated rate. While the population of the world increased by 49 percent, the three size categories of urban population grew, respectively, 228, 240, and 254 percent.

If this trend continues at its present rate, more than a fourth of the world's people will be living in cities of 100,000 or more by the year 2000, and more than half by 2050. If the present rate of urbanization continues to the year 2050, over 90 percent of the world's people will live in cities of 20,000 or more.

Today, we have whole societies which can be called "urbanized." Over four-fifths of the people in England live in urban places; nearly 40 percent of them live in cities of over 100,000. In societies such as our own, with radio, television, rapid transportation, and an industrial distribution system, what is a fad on Manhattan Island today is a fad in Manhattan, Kansas tomorrow.

Even if the present rate of urbanization should slow, the prospect is that the future will see an ever-increasing proportion of the world's people living in urbanized societies.

The most obvious change associated with urbanization is the development of a far-reaching network of interdependent activities. This network usually proceeds from the loose linking of peasant villagers to the city through tangential interdependence with urban commercial, religious, political, or military centers to the almost complete interdependence of an urbanized world. This change in the scale of society obviously affects the ways in which the products of civilization are allocated. For example, most of the world's population lives in little communities on the fringes of urban society where interdependence with distant urban centers is slight and limited in scope. Redfield has noted the special place of "hinge people" in these communities. These representatives of limited areas of interdependence—the schoolteacher, the village priest, the merchant-traders, or the representatives of distant political and military authority—have special access to the benefits of urban civilization. They act as filters or transmitters in the system of allocation centered in the city. Their power derives from limited interdependence between village and city. Their role is important today and likely to become increasingly so as interdependence increases.

This description of the process of urbanization leans heavily on the aggregation of people in cities. This aggregation is one important sociological change which defines the process of urbanization. But, in addition to this increase in scale, urbanization is characterized by the accretion of control and coordination activities in cities and by the development of a network of urban centers.

Coordination and control

Urbanization involves locating coordination and control functions in cities. Wide-ranging activities are originated in, funneled through, or transformed by the urban posts of command and coordination. This centralizing function is evidenced by the presence in all modern cities of a substantial tertiary labor force. It is a truism that the city is the home of workers whose major functions involve coordinating and controlling wide-ranging economic, political, military, and religious activities.

The urban mode of distribution, thus, always places the city dweller at the hub of the distribution system. Through his hands and mind pass the products of an urban society. His access to these products is built into a society where cities are the accumulators and distributors of the products of civilization.

Network of urban sites

Finally, the process of urbanization involves the development of a system of urban sites, a network of cities which jointly house a myriad of urban activities. This system varies widely in contemporary societies. Students have attempted to describe it in such terms as: primacy and a hierarchy of cities; functional specialization of cities; regional networks of dominant and subdominant centers; sheer relative aggregation of the population; cities vis-à-vis their hinterlands or vis-à-vis a peasant foreland. Clearly, this variety is crucial to the way in which the products of civilization are distributed. If, for example, a society contains a single, multifunctioned primary city with all other centers being much smaller, one would expect the flow of products and access to this flow to be quite different from those in societies with a lower level of primacy or a flattened hierarchy of cities. In the high primacy situation, the flow of ideas, beliefs, and products of civilization would be highly centralized in every institutional area. Control personnel and initiators of action within the major institutional arenas might well overlap. How different this is from the society where religious centers are separate from the economic and these from the political seats of power! Here, in a society with several large and specialized cities, one is likely to find centralization within each institutional area, but little overlapping and substantial insulation.

Increasing scale, centralizing control and coordination, and developing a network of urban sites—these describe the process of urbanization. Any society may be situated at a given scale, with a certain degree of coordination and control, and characterized by a particular system of urban locations. Each of these facets of the urbanization of that society influences the way in which products are, or could be, allocated.

DIFFERENTIATION AND ALLOCATION

The pattern of distribution which emerges in societies with relatively advanced levels of urbanization is characterized by three broad systems of distribution and deprivation: (1) occupational differentiation, (2) ethnic and migrant differentiation, and (3) life style or familial differentiation.

Occupational differentiation and class access

Until the past couple of centuries, there has been relatively little differentiation of the labor force beyond that based on age and sex. Only within the last 200 years, with the technological applications of the discoveries of scientists, have societies existed in which a large proportion of the population learned occupational roles differentiated from one another on other grounds.

Other consequences of the growth of science and technology are elaborate occupational specialization and an increase in the content of culture. Bushmen do not have much more to transmit than one Bushman can know. Americans have so much more shared, learned behavior to transmit than one American could know that the task of organizing a program of general education becomes staggering.

A complex division of labor through a whole society leads to what some sociologists have called "situses"—sets of related occupational specialties arranged hierarchically parallel to and separate from other sets of related roles, which also are arranged in hierarchies. Each situs, or family of related occupations, builds up a set of norms peculiar to it. These occupational subcultures insulate their participants from the members of another situs. Doctors and nurses hold values not shared by railroaders and truck drivers; the occupational norms of the longshoreman are not those of the laboratory worker.

Occupational specialization contributes a good share to what we call the impersonality of urban life. People in urban-industrial societies have segmentalized roles. One may be an assembly-line worker, a Methodist, a Grand Vizier at the lodge, a father, a member of the bowling team. No one of these bears the same necessary relationship to another that the roles filled by a tribesman in an unspecialized society do. In a society which has not felt the impact of technology, one need only know a man's clan membership to predict his occupation, his religion, his educational attainment. Among the segmentalized roles which a man plays in an urban-industrial society, occupation is crucial. It is more specialized than most of his roles; he has an enormous investment in it. An adult male in our labor force spends more of his waking hours at work than at home; his work is likely to be a powerful factor in shaping his view of the world.

Societies with elaborate occupational differentiation, therefore, while bound together by a common culture, are at the same time fragmented by occupational subcultures. People who share an occupational history develop norms, enforce an in-group ideology, and come to serve as a reference group for each other. We see this at its extreme when physicists from the Soviet Union and from the United States have more to talk about with each other than either group has with the farmers from its own country.

But let us remember that role segmentalization is not synonymous with a fragmented social structure. The stuff of occupational subcultures can serve as the specialized urban-industrial worker's social substitute for community. Occupational codes can contribute to what Durkheim called organic solidarity; they can help replace the mechanical solidarity of the rural village. Occupational groups, with their shared values, can contribute to the sense of purpose which formerly was a function of the small community.

Various occupations, incomes, and amounts of education lead people to share different norms and to behave differently. In other words, the existence of a class structure leads to the development of class subcultures. And, in time, the subcultures themselves become criteria of placement in the class structure. Not just one's income but the way he spends it, not just his occupational status but his attitude toward it—these become factors partially determining his class status.

The evidence of differences in access to and enjoyment of the products of civilization includes variations by class in family pattern, religious participation, and many other culture patterns. People in the lowest income strata spend nearly three-fourths of their total income for food, while those in the higher strata spend less than one-fourth of their income for food. Obviously, this leaves lower-class families with not only less money but a lower proportion of their total incomes available for education and other expenditures which might improve their class position. The smaller amount of money available for purposes other than groceries is reflected in the fact that a sample of lower-class people exceeded those in wealthier classes both in symptoms of illness and in the proportion of those symptoms which were not being treated by a physician. Lack of money is likely to be only one of the factors accounting for this situation; lower education levels would make it less likely that the lower-income classes would be aware of the need for treatment of some symptoms.

The basic variables of class structure reinforce each other through the medium of life chances. People who have high incomes and college educations are more likely than those who do not to be able to afford to send their children to college.

A person's occupation, with its concomitant income, education, and class status, affects greatly the likelihood that certain things will happen to him. An individual's position in the class structure alters everything from the chance to stay alive during the first year after birth to the chance to view fine art, the chance to remain healthy and grow tall, and, if sick, to get well again quickly, the chance to avoid becoming a juvenile delinquent—and, very crucially, the chance to complete an intermediary or higher educational grade. It is easy to dismiss many factors which are really life chances with the notion that the individual controls his own destiny: the statement, for instance, that class status influences one's chances to view fine art can be brushed aside with the retort that museums are free and that, if a person does not take advantage of them, it is his own fault. Such an attitude fails to take into account the power of subculture. A child reared in a slum area who does not even know about the existence of museums or who has been socialized to believe that painting is for "sissies" has different chances for art experience than one brought up in a wealthy home and taught that all respectable people know something about art.

The significance of class consciousness for social mobility lies in the fact that attitudes and values have consequences in behavior patterns. If one believes he can be mobile, he will try to be. One's level of aspiration depends on what he has been taught to believe about his present status and the changes and desirability of altering it. Research has shown that manual workers are aware that most of them are not going to rise to managerial positions and that, reconciled to the status in which they find themselves, they do not plan upward mobility for themselves but project their ambitions onto their children. But we also know that the ones most likely to be upwardly mobile are those who actively seek to achieve upward mobility. This being so, there is an element of the self-fulfilling prophecy in vertical mobility.

Thus, just as race can become an ascribed status through the social definition imposed by the culture, so can class subcultures make education and occupation, and hence income, tend to be ascribed.

Access to the products of civilization in an urban society is structured, then, largely by class position, and, for many, this position is likely to persist for generations. Underlying this system is occupational differentiation built upon the requirements of large-scale enterprise which has become the dominant pattern in each institutional area. Big government, big military, big business, big church, big medicine and welfare are the *leit motif* of a society characterized by wide-ranging interdependence and centralized coordination and control housed in a web of urban locations. As other societies move toward this kind of social organization and as peripheral societies become enmeshed in it, they, too, may be expected to generate similar patterns of occupational differentiation and a corresponding way of distributing the social products.

Ethnic and migrant differentiations

Building an urban society requires a massive movement of peoples; the process of urbanization involves a redistribution of the population in space. Since urban fertility rates are never as high as those in the hinterland, a growing *proportion* of the total population can be settled in cities only by a net migration balance from rural to urban areas. Further, as the scale of society increases, the concentration of population as well as other resources brings people into cities from an ever-widening geographic base. This means that the cities of large-scale societies not only are composed of a substantial proportion of migrants but of migrants from widely dispersed origins. Thus, both the *rate* and *level* of urbanization are reflected in the ethnic composition of city populations. Rates of urbanization affect the relative volume of migration, and levels are reflected in the dispersion of origins of migrants.

At a given rate and level of urbanization, cities are composed of a proportion of migrants from a particular web of recruitment bases. This compositional change, when compounded with the selective character of migration, provides a basis for ethnic and migrant differentiation in every urban society: the establishment of a socially defined ethnic and migrant pecking order.

Excellent studies of the "newcomers" have been carried out in New York, Yankee City, London, and from Durban to Dallas. They all point to differential allocation patterned along the dimensions of ethnicity and migrancy.

The fastest *rates* of urbanization now are occurring in societies with relatively low *levels* of urbanization. Under this condition, the cities of these developing nations will be composed of a high proportion of migrants, but these migrants are likely to be recruited from a fairly narrow hinterland. *Migrant* differentiation is important in these areas today. As they increase in scale and widen their recruitment base, *ethnic* differentiation is likely to become more important to the distribution of life chances. More advanced societies, on the other hand, with existing high levels of urbanization, are now experiencing declining rates of urbanization. Here, ethnic differences are likely to persist for some time while migrancy declines as a basis for differentiation and allocation.

Life-style differentiation

A third dimension along which variation in access to facilities and rewards occurs is emergent in the urban sectors of advanced societies. This dimension appeared first among fairly wealthy city dwellers. It is a variation in style of life which we often associate with suburban growth and the development of familistic orientation. Recent urban developments, including advances in transportation technology, decentralized production location, opportunities for women to work outside the household, and a widening array of housing opportunities, permit variations in life style. By now, in most American cities, all except the central-city ethnics and recent migrants have generally become distributed along a life-style continuum. At one end of this continuum lie the fertile, familistic plains of suburbia. At the other are the more centrally located, small family or aged apartment dwellers oriented to career or consumption.

Access to the benefits of advanced societies are distributed along this continuum as well. Benefits available to the familistic consumer are in some instances constrained and in other cases widened by the demands of his orientation and location. Opportunities for neighboring, local acquaintances and local area participation may be high. He may find a limited but intense local community. He has access to the patio or rumpus-room culture and the creative pursuits of a garage or basement workshop. For him, the benefits of civilization are likely to revolve around family, school, and the local area.

Much of this is not available to the career- and consumption-oriented urbanite, but just beyond his elevator lie all the resources of the old central city. All the variety, liveliness, and sophistication of modern society are stored at his stoop, and much of it available in a stroll or a short commute. These products are available not only because of location but also as a consequence of the way in which he may allocate his scarce time, resources, and social capital. He has neither the choices nor the constraints of familism.

Increasing concern has been expressed about the durability of this variation. In recent years, thoughtful critics have suggested that rampant familism and the apparent popular association of it with suburban location may lead to the destruction of the advantages of central-city urban life style. Jane Jacobs, for example, has deplored the systematic destruction of urban liveliness. Others have questioned the ability of the institutions in the core city to survive in the midst of growing sprawl.

The evidence seems to support the optimists, however. Variation in life style can and does persist even in the most sprawling metropolitan areas. Marked variations in orientation and consumption have been observed even within the white middle class in Los Angeles.

A close look at these newer cities and the fringes of the old preautomobile cities suggests that several changes are likely to occur in the near future. The first is that life style will become less bound to a locality. Familism can and probably will return to the central area, and urbanism may spread to the suburbs and ex-urbs. At the same time, many of the advantages of the old urban core will be made more available to a diffused populace. This view does not deny the fact that the central city is likely to contain self-imposed ghettos of lively urbanites for some time nor deny that the suburbs will generally hold the familistically oriented community. Rather, we suggest that the differences will be less dramatic and that a much finer gradation will occur along the life-style continuum.

CONCLUSION

Our thesis has been that the process of urbanization arrays a populace along three major dimensions. Most of the cultural resources of an urban society are allocated via occupational, ethnic and migrant, and life-style differentiation. These three dimensions of differentiation develop and become effective at different points in the urbanization process. The occurrence of and persistence of ethnic and migrant differentiation apparently are contingent upon the rate and level of urbanization. Life-style differentiation appears to develop fairly late in this process of urbanization, while occupational differentiation arises quite early in the process and persists to relatively advanced levels.

Urbanization thus initiates a variety of systems of allocation. Ever since David Reisman added "inner-directed" and "other-directed" to the American lexicon, we have been asking one another whether there is too much conformity in American life. We worry that there is not enough encouragement of individualism, that we are too much a herd. We have, of course, a tradition of concern for fear we are too much bounded by social expectations; it has found expression from Henry David Thoreau to Sinclair Lewis. Still, each new analysis of "the Organization Man" or of "mass culture" brings a fresh rash of sermons, seminars, and soul-searching.

It is, perhaps, a healthy sign that so many Americans worry about whether there is too much conformity in our society, but there is something wryly amusing about it, too. The people of the United States tolerate a range of behavior in their fellow citizens which the people of most societies throughout human history would have found simply incredible. Our society defines as acceptable a wide range of behavior and will tolerate an enormous amount of deviance in familial roles, educational policy, economic behavior, political participation, and religious beliefs.

Urbanization gives rise to a great heterogeneity in the population. Urban life leads to ethnic and migrant differentiation and allows people with a different skin color or language or religion to pass relatively unnoticed in a way that could never be possible in the primary organization of a folk community. In addition, the occupational specialties associated with the complex division of labor create differences in the population: variations in training, values, work hours, recreation patterns, and, ultimately, differentiation in style of life.

CHAPTER 4

CONTENTS

URbAN life STylES

Reactions to urbanism have tended, in scholarly circles, to take certain well defined paths. One significant viewpoint has centered on the "rural-urban continuum" discussed in the last chapter. In the nineteenth century, one of the first critiques of cities arose out of the German tradition characterized by a sense of totalities, or *Gestalten*. Writers like Tönnies and Spengler saw, in cities, evidence of the decline of man's communal nature, his sense of rootedness in the small face-to-face group, and the growth of alienation, unhappiness, social dislocation, and the like. This point of view has always been a part of American social science too and, in fact, has been deeply imbedded in the American consciousness. Thus, it is probably safe to say that Americans are not really an urban people, for their *ideal* culture—that is, those images to which they respond and which form their fantasies—have always been nonurban. We have gone so far as to create a fictive American past, a Currier-and-Ives sense of the good life on the farm, which has helped us cope with an essentially alien existence: the realities of life in big cities.

The first section of Chapter 4 states two points of view about urban man, not necessarily contradictory. Stanley Milgram begins by reviewing the "urbanism as alien to man" argument sketched above. He reasons that some link must be established between the conditions of urban life—crowds, secondary relations, speed—and individual reactions; he introduces the concept of "overload" and uses it to analyze urban man. The conclusion that is significant for a sociology of urbanism is the fact that norms arise that are geared to promote privacy and to deal with impersonality and distrust. Thus, life in Manhattan is a quite different experience than life in a small town, and the difference is not merely quantitative but qualitative as well.

In a sense, Scott Greer's discussion takes off at this point, but in an entirely different direction. Noting that it has become fashionable to characterize urban man as atomized, i.e., a separate unto himself and without apparent roots, Greer provides data and an analysis based upon a city that has become legendary for its rootless qualities: Los Angeles. Greer's findings should surprise you, for he notes that, by and large, most urban people are imbedded into networks of kinship and voluntary organizations which act as buffers between the isolated in-dividual and the mass society of modern industrial states. More specifically, cities consist of many different sub-parts, some of which resemble Milgram's charac-terization, but many do not. In areas of strong ethnic identification—as, for example, Italian, German, Jewish—individuals have many ties, are familistic, and (one would presume) are relatively happy. Certainly many of the elements of the American rural culture still survive in cities of today both in the form of a "rural ideal culture" (i.e., rural traditions are best), but also in the forms of social organization that Greer uncovered in his research. No longer can we simply char-acterize urban life with broad sweeping generalizations; we must pay attention to the considerable variance in life styles to be found in any modern city.

The next section, "Alienation: White and Black," concentrates on two urban subpopulations, each of which comprises a significant portion of central cities—and, in the case of whites, suburbs also. The concept of "alienation" has undergone some curious changes of meaning since Marx, but in the sense used here it refers to powerlessness, of being trapped in a system that has increasingly less meaning and offers fewer and fewer rewards. The Peter Schrag article deals with the middle "majority" of American urbanites, or Richard Nixon's "silent majority." These are the same familistic people Greer discussed, but now we see the other side of their character: frustration with high taxation, with neighbor-hood instability, with encroachments of the black man. For American central cities, the legal boundaries of the pre-automobile metropolis before significant suburbanization seem to belong predominantly to these two groups: the white working class and the black. But despite their frustrations and fears, the American Dream seems to be still viable among these white middle-Americans; indeed, their revolt, if one can call it that, is certainly done in the name of many of the values associated with Americanism. As Robert Coles shows us, for the black child grow-ing up in the rotting and rotten ghettos of American cities, belief in that dream is becomingly increasingly impossible. The only recourses exist in fantasy, tough coping behavior, or revolution; and the techniques for success in the demanding (or impossible) environment of the black ghetto cannot function to help the black boy get out. It is the impossibility of escape that strikes us most forcefully and makes the tortured sounds of the middle-American seem hollow, even if they are well meant and valid within their frame of reference.

The final section takes another tack, that of emphasizing social organization in cities. Gerald D. Suttles, for example, describes the extent of social organiza-tion in a slum on Chicago's West Side prior to urban renewal. There have been other works on this subject, notably White's *Street Corner Society* and Gans's *The Urban Villagers,* and in most cases we are forced to recognize that areas of cities which are *apparently* disorganized actually possess a very complex and sophisticated social structures formed by the people who live there—their family ties and ethnicity—and by the hard demands of slum life. The second selection, "The American Urban Family," carries the discussion of urban social organization down to the microsocial unit—the human family. It demonstrates that urbanization per se does not shatter the family or necessarily reduce it in the size of its meaningful network, for many urban residents must depend upon familial relations to survive with any comfort. The basic question raised by the authors is the one of *instrumentalism*: What can the family do for its members, under what conditions, and for how long? The emerging view is that urban familism is still strong, viable, and an important source of goods, services, and trust—especially when alternative sources are wholly or partially closed off.

11

STANLEY MILGRAM, The Experience of Living in Cities

When I first came to New York it seemed like a nightmare. As soon as I got off the train at Grand Central I was caught up in pushing, shoving crowds on 42nd Street. Sometimes people bumped into me without apology; what really frightened me was to see two people literally engaged in combat for possession of a cab. Why were they so rushed? Even drunks on the street were bypassed without a glance. People didn't seem to care about each other at all.

This statement represents a common reaction to a great city, but it does not tell the whole story. Obviously cities have great appeal because of their variety, eventfulness, possibility of choice, and the stimulation of an intense atmosphere that many individuals find a desirable background to their lives. Where face-to-face contacts are important, the city offers unparalleled possibilities. It has been calculated by the Regional Plan Association (1) that in Nassau County, a suburb of New York City, an individual can meet 11,000 others within a ten-minute radius of his office by foot or car. In Newark, a moderate-sized city, he can meet more than 20,000 persons within this radius. But in midtown Manhattan he can meet fully 220,000. So there is an order-of-magnitude increment in the communication possibilities offered by a great city. That is one of the bases of its appeal and, indeed, of its functional necessity. The city provides options that no other social arrangement permits. But there is a negative side also, as we shall see.

Granted that cities are indispensable in complex society, we may still ask what contribution psychology can make to understanding the experience of living in them. What theories are relevant? How can we extend our knowledge of the

Stanley Milgram, "The Experience of Living in Cities," *Science,* vol. 167 (March 13, 1970), pp. 1461–1468. Copyright © 1970 by the American Association for the Advancement of Science. Reprinted by permission.

This article is based on an address of September 2, 1969, to the 77th annual meeting of the American Psychological Association in Washington, D. C.

psychological aspects of life in cities through empirical inquiry? If empirical inquiry is possible, along what lines should it proceed? In short, where do we start in constructing urban theory and in laying out lines of research?

Observation is the indispensable starting point. Any observer in the streets of midtown Manhattan will see (i) large numbers of people, (ii) a high population density, and (iii) heterogeneity of population. These three factors need to be at the root of any sociopsychological theory of city life, for they condition all aspects of our experience in the metropolis. Louis Wirth (2), if not the first to point to these factors, is nonetheless the sociologist who relied most heavily on them in his analysis of the city. Yet, for a psychologist, there is something unsatisfactory about Wirth's theoretical variables. Numbers, density, and heterogeneity are demographic facts but they are not yet psychological facts. They are external to the individual. Psychology needs an idea that links the individual's *experience* to the demographic circumstances of urban life.

One link is provided by the concept of overload. This term, drawn from systems analysis, refers to a system's inability to process inputs from the environment because there are too many inputs for the system to cope with, or because successive inputs come so fast that input A cannot be processed when input B is presented. When overload is present, adaptations occur. The system must set priorities and make choices. A may be processed first while B is kept in abeyance, or one input may be sacrificed altogether. City life, as we experience it, constitutes a continuous set of encounters with overload, and of resultant adaptations. Overload characteristically deforms daily life on several levels, impinging on role performance, the evolution of social norms, cognitive functioning, and the use of facilities.

The concept has been implicit in several theories of urban experience. In 1903 Georg Simmel (3) pointed out that, since urban dwellers come into contact with vast numbers of people each day, they conserve psychic energy by becoming acquainted with a far smaller proportion of people than their rural counterparts do, and by maintaining more superficial relationships even with these acquaintances. Wirth (2) points specifically to "the superficiality, the anonymity, and the transitory character of urban social relations."

One adaptive response to overload, therefore, is the allocation of less time to each input. A second adaptive mechanism is disregard of low-priority inputs. Principles of selectivity are formulated such that investment of time and energy are reserved for carefully defined inputs (the urbanite disregards the drunk sick on the street as he purposefully navigates through the crowd). Third, boundaries are redrawn in certain social transactions so that the overloaded system can shift the burden to the other party in the exchange; thus, harried New York bus drivers once made change for customers, but now this responsibility has been shifted to the client, who must have the exact fare ready. Fourth, reception is blocked off prior to entrance into a system; city dwellers increasingly use unlisted telephone numbers to prevent individuals from calling them, and a small but growing number resort to keeping the telephone off the hook to prevent incoming

calls. More subtly, a city dweller blocks inputs by assuming an unfriendly coun-
tenance, which discourages others from initiating contact. Additionally, social
screening devices are interposed between the individual and environmental inputs
(in a town of 5000 anyone can drop in to chat with the mayor, but in the metropolis organizational screening devices deflect inputs to other destinations). Fifth,
the intensity of inputs is diminished by filtering devices, so that only weak and
relatively superficial forms of involvement with others are allowed. Sixth, specialized institutions are created to absorb inputs that would otherwise swamp the
individual (welfare departments handle the financial needs of a million individuals
in New York City, who would otherwise create an army of mendicants continuously importuning the pedestrian). The interposition of institutions between the
individual and the social world, a characteristic of all modern society, and most
notably of the large metropolis, has its negative side. It deprives the individual of
a sense of direct contact and spontaneous integration in the life around him. It
simultaneously protects and estranges the individual from his social environment.

Many of these adaptive mechanisms apply not only to individuals but to
institutional systems as well, as Meier (4) has so brilliantly shown in connection
with the library and the stock exchange.

In sum, the observed behavior of the urbanite in a wide range of situations
appears to be determined largely by a variety of adaptations to overload. I now
deal with several specific consequences of responses to overload, which make for
differences in the tone of city and town.

Social responsibility

The principal point of interest for a social psychology of the city is that moral
and social involvement with individuals is necessarily restricted. This is a direct
and necessary function of excess of input over capacity to process. Such restriction of involvement runs a broad spectrum from refusal to become involved in
the needs of another person, even when the person desperately needs assistance,
through refusal to do favors, to the simple withdrawal of courtesies (such as
offering a lady a seat, or saying "sorry" when a pedestrian collision occurs). In
any transaction more and more details need to be dropped as the total number
of units to be processed increases and assaults an instrument of limited processing
capacity.

The ultimate adaptation to an overloaded social environment is to totally
disregard the needs, interests, and demands of those whom one does not define as
relevant to the satisfaction of personal needs, and to develop highly efficient perceptual means of determining whether an individual falls into the category of
friend or stranger. The disparity in the treatment of friends and strangers ought to
be greater in cities than in towns; the time allotment and willingness to become
involved with those who have no personal claim on one's time is likely to be less
in cities than in towns.

Bystander intervention in crises. The most striking deficiencies in social responsibility in cities occur in crisis situations, such as the Genovese murder in Queens. In 1964, Catherine Genovese, coming home from a night job in the early hours of an April morning, was stabbed repeatedly, over an extended period of time. Thirty-eight residents of a respectable New York City neighborhood admit to having witnessed at least a part of the attack, but none went to her aid or called the police until after she was dead. Milgram and Hollander, writing in *The Nation* (5), analyzed the event in these terms.

> Urban friendships and associations are not primarily formed on the basis of physical proximity. A person with numerous close friends in different parts of the city may not know the occupant of an adjacent apartment. This does not mean that a city dweller has fewer friends than does a villager, or knows fewer persons who will come to his aid; however, it does mean that his allies are not constantly at hand. Miss Genovese required immediate aid from those physically present. There is no evidence that the city had deprived Miss Genovese of human associations, but the friends who might have rushed to her side were miles from the scene of her tragedy.
>
> Further, it is known that her cries for help were not directed to a specific person; they were general. But only individuals can act, and as the cries were not specifically directed, no particular person felt a special responsibility. The crime and the failure of community response seem absurd to us. At the time, it may well have seemed equally absurd to the Kew Gardens residents that not one of the neighbors would have called the police. A collective paralysis may have developed from the belief of each of the witnesses that someone else must surely have taken that obvious step.

Latané and Darley (6) have reported laboratory approaches to the study of bystander intervention and have established experimentally the following principle: the larger the number of bystanders, the less the likelihood that any one of them will intervene in an emergency. Gaertner and Bickman (7) of The City University of New York have extended the bystander studies to an examination of help across ethnic lines. Blacks and whites, with clearly identifiable accents, called strangers (through what the caller represented as an error in telephone dialing), gave them a plausible story of being stranded on an outlying highway without more dimes, and asked the stranger to call a garage. The experimenters found that the white callers had a significantly better chance of obtaining assistance than the black callers. This suggests that ethnic allegiance may well be another means of coping with overload: the city dweller can reduce excessive demands and screen out urban heterogeneity by responding along ethnic lines; overload is made more manageable by limiting the "span of sympathy."

In any quantitative characterization of the social texture of city life, a necessary first step is the application of such experimental methods as these to field situations in large cities and small towns. Theorists argue that the indifference shown in the Genovese case would not be found in a small town, but in the absence of solid experimental evidence the question remains an open one.

More than just callousness prevents bystanders from participating in altercations between people. A rule of urban life is respect for other people's emotional and social privacy, perhaps because physical privacy is so hard to achieve. And in situations for which the standards are heterogeneous, it is much harder to know whether taking an active role is unwarranted meddling or an appropriate response to a critical situation. If a husband and wife are quarreling in public, at what point should a bystander step in? On the one hand, the heterogeneity of the city produces substantially greater tolerance about behavior, dress, and codes of ethics than is generally found in the small town, but this diversity also encourages people to withhold aid for fear of antagonizing the participants or crossing an inappropriate and difficult-to-define line.

Moreover, the frequency of demands present in the city gives rise to norms of noninvolvement. There are practical limitations to the Samaritan impulse in a major city. If a citizen attended to every needy person, if he were sensitive to and acted on every altruistic impulse that was evoked in the city, he could scarcely keep his own affairs in order.

Willingness to trust and assist strangers. We now move away from crisis situations to less urgent examples of social responsibility. For it is not only in situations of dramatic need but in the ordinary, everyday willingness to lend a hand that the city dweller is said to be deficient relative to his small-town cousin. The comparative method must be used in any empirical examination of this question. A commonplace social situation is staged in an urban setting and in a small town—a situation to which a subject can respond by either extending help or withholding it. The responses in town and city are compared.

One factor in the purported unwillingness of urbanites to be helpful to strangers may well be their heightened sense of physical (and emotional) vulnerability—a feeling that is supported by urban crime statistics. A key test for distinguishing between city and town behavior, therefore, is determining how city dwellers compare with town dwellers in offering aid that increases their personal vulnerability and requires some trust of strangers. Altman, Levine, Nadien, and Villena (8) of The City University of New York devised a study to compare the behaviors of city and town dwellers in this respect. The criterion used in this study was the willingness of householders to allow strangers to enter their home to use the telephone. The student investigators individually rang doorbells, explained that they had misplaced the address of a friend nearby, and asked to use the phone. The investigators (two males and two females) made 100 requests for entry into homes in the city and 60 requests in the small towns. The results for middle-income housing developments in Manhattan were compared with data for several small towns (Stony Point, Spring Valley, Ramapo, Nyack, New City, and West Clarkstown) in Rockland County, outside of New York City. As Table 1 shows, in all cases there was a sharp increase in the proportion of entries achieved by an experimenter when he moved from the city to a small town. In the most extreme case the experimenter was five times as likely to gain admission to homes

Table 1. Percentage of entries achieved by investigators for city and town dwellings (see text).

Experimenter	Entries achieved (%)	
	City*	Small town†
Male		
No. 1	16	40
No. 2	12	60
Female		
No. 3	40	87
No. 4	40	100

*Number of requests for entry, 100.
†Number of requests for entry, 60.

in a small town as to homes in Manhattan. Although the female experimenters had notably greater success both in cities and towns than the male experimenters had, each of the four students did at least twice as well in towns as in cities. This suggests that the city-town distinction overrides even the predictably greater fear of male strangers than of female ones.

The lower level of helpfulness by city dwellers seems due in part to recognition of the dangers of living in Manhattan, rather than to mere indifference or coldness. It is significant that 75 percent of all the city respondents received and answered messages by shouting through closed doors and by peering out through peepholes; in the towns, by contrast, about 75 percent of the respondents opened the door.

Supporting the experimenters' quantitative results was their general observation that the town dwellers were noticeably more friendly and less suspicious than the city dwellers. In seeking to explain the reasons for the greater sense of psychological vulnerability city dwellers feel, above and beyond the differences in crime statistics, Villena (8) points out that, if a crime is committed in a village, a resident of a neighboring village may not perceive the crime as personally relevant, though the geographic distance may be small, whereas a criminal act committed anywhere in the city, though miles from the city-dweller's home, is still verbally located within the city; thus, Villena says, "the inhabitant of the city possesses a larger vulnerable space."

Civilities. Even at the most superficial level of involvement—the exercise of everyday civilities—urbanites are reputedly deficient. People bump into each other and often do not apologize. They knock over another person's packages and, as often as not, proceed on their way with a grumpy exclamation instead of an offer of assistance. Such behavior, which many visitors to great cities find distasteful, is less common, we are told, in smaller communities, where traditional courtesies are more likely to be observed.

In some instances it is not simply that, in the city, traditional courtesies are violated; rather, the cities develop new norms of noninvolvement. These are so well defined and so deeply a part of city life that *they* constitute the norms people are reluctant to violate. Men are actually embarrassed to give up a seat on the subway to an old woman; they mumble "I was getting off anyway," instead of making the gesture in a straightforward and gracious way. These norms develop because everyone realizes that, in situations of high population density, people cannot implicate themselves in each others' affairs, for to do so would create conditions of continual distraction which would frustrate purposeful action.

In discussing the effects of overload I do not imply that at every instant the city dweller is bombarded with an unmanageable number of inputs, and that his responses are determined by the excess of input at any given instant. Rather, adaptation occurs in the form of gradual evolution of norms of behavior. Norms are evolved in response to frequent discrete experiences of overload; they persist and become generalized modes of responding.

Overload on cognitive capacities: anonymity. That we respond differently toward those whom we know and those who are strangers to us is a truism. An eager patron aggressively cuts in front of someone in a long movie line to save time only to confront a friend; he then behaves sheepishly. A man is involved in an automobile accident caused by another driver, emerges from his car shouting in rage, then moderates his behavior on discovering a friend driving the other car. The city dweller, when walking through the midtown streets, is in a state of continual anonymity vis-à-vis the other pedestrians.

Anonymity is part of a continuous spectrum ranging from total anonymity to full acquaintance, and it may well be that measurement of the precise degrees of anonymity in cities and towns would help to explain important distinctions between the quality of life in each. Conditions of full acquaintance, for example, offer security and familiarity, but they may also be stifling, because the individual is caught in a web of established relationships. Conditions of complete anonymity, by contrast, provide freedom from routinized social ties, but they may also create feelings of alienation and detachment.

Empirically one could investigate the proportion of activities in which the city dweller or the town dweller is known by others at given times in his daily life, and the proportion of activities in the course of which he interacts with individuals who know him. At his job, for instance, the city dweller may be known to as many people as his rural counterpart. However, when he is not fulfilling his occupational role—say, when merely traveling about the city—the urbanite is doubtless more anonymous than his rural counterpart.

Limited empirical work on anonymity has begun. Zimbardo (9) has tested whether the social anonymity and impersonality of the big city encourage greater vandalism than do small towns. Zimbardo arranged for one automobile to be left for 64 hours near the Bronx campus of New York University and for a counterpart to be left for the same number of hours near Stanford University in Palo Alto. The license plates on the two cars were removed and the hoods were opened, to provide "releaser cues" for potential vandals. The New York car was stripped of all movable parts within the first 24 hours, and by the end of 3 days was only a hunk of metal rubble. Unexpectedly, however, most of the destruction occurred during daylight hours, usually under the scrutiny of observers, and the leaders in the vandalism were well-dressed, white adults. The Palo Alto car was left untouched.

Zimbardo attributes the difference in the treatment accorded the two cars to the "acquired feelings of social anonymity provided by life in a city like New York," and he supports his conclusions with several other anecdotes illustrating casual, wanton vandalism in the city. In any comparative study of the effects of anonymity in city and town, however, there must be satisfactory control for other confounding factors: the large number of drug addicts in a city like New York; the high proportion of slum-dwellers in the city; and so on.

Another direction for empirical study is investigation of the beneficial effects of anonymity. The impersonality of city life breeds its own tolerance for the private lives of the inhabitants. Individuality and even eccentricity, we may assume, can flourish more readily in the metropolis than in the small town. Stigmatized persons may find it easier to lead comfortable lives in the city, free of the constant scrutiny of neighbors. To what degree can this assumed difference between city and town be shown empirically? Judith Waters (10), at The City University of New York, hypothesized that avowed homosexuals would be more likely to be accepted as tenants in a large city than in small towns, and she dispatched letters from homosexuals and from normal individuals to real estate agents in cities and towns across the country. The results of her study were inconclusive. But the general idea of examining the protective benefits of city life to the stigmatized ought to be pursued.

Role behavior in cities and towns. Another product of urban overload is the adjustment in roles made by urbanites in daily interactions. As Wirth has said (2): "Urbanites meet one another in highly segmental roles. . . . They are less dependent upon particular persons, and their dependence upon others is confined to a highly fractionalized aspect of the other's round of activity." This tendency is particularly noticeable in transactions between customers and individuals offering professional or sales services. The owner of a country store has time to become well acquainted with his dozen-or-so daily customers, but the girl at the checkout counter of a busy A&P, serving hundreds of customers a day, barely has time to toss the green stamps into one customer's shopping bag before the next customer confronts her with his pile of groceries.

Meier, in his stimulating analysis of the city (4), discusses several adaptations a system may make when confronted by inputs that exceed its capacity to process them. Meier argues that, according to the principle of competition for scarce resources, the scope and time of the transaction shrink as customer volume and daily turnover rise. This, in fact, is what is meant by the "brusque" quality of city life. New standards have developed in cities concerning what levels of services are appropriate in business transactions (see Figure 1).

Figure 1. Changes in the demand for time for a given task when the overall transaction frequency increases in a social system. [Reprinted with permission from R. L. Meier, *A Communications Theory of Urban Growth,* 1962. Copyrighted by M.I.T. Press, 1962]

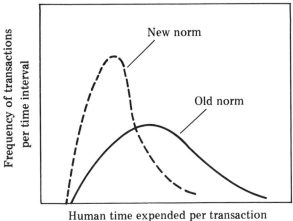

McKenna and Morgenthau (11), in a seminar at The City University of New York, devised a study (i) to compare the willingness of city dwellers and small-town dwellers to do favors for strangers that entailed expenditure of a small amount of time and slight inconvenience but no personal vulnerability, and (ii) to determine whether the more compartmentalized, transitory relationships of the city would make urban salesgirls less likely than small-town salesgirls to carry out, for strangers, tasks not related to their customary roles.

To test for differences between city dwellers and small-town dwellers, a simple experiment was devised in which persons from both settings were asked (by telephone) to perform increasingly onerous favors for anonymous strangers.

Within the cities (Chicago, New York, and Philadelphia), half the calls were to housewives and the other half to salesgirls in women's apparel shops; the division was the same for the 37 small towns of the study, which were in the same states as the cities. Each experimenter represented herself as a long-distance caller who had, through error, been connected with the respondent by the operator. The experimenter began by asking for simple information about the weather for purposes of travel. Next the experimenter excused herself on some pretext (asking the respondent to "please hold on"), put the phone down for almost a full minute, and then picked it up again and asked the respondent to provide the phone number of a hotel or motel in her vicinity at which the experimenter might stay during a forthcoming visit. Scores were assigned the subjects on the basis of how helpful they had been. McKenna summarizes her results in this manner:

People in the city, whether they are engaged in a specific job or not, are less helpful and informative than people in small towns; . . . People at home, regardless of where they live, are less helpful and informative than people working in shops.

However, the absolute level of cooperativeness for urban subjects was found to be quite high, and does not accord with the stereotype of the urbanite as aloof, self-centered, and unwilling to help strangers. The quantitative differences obtained by McKenna and Morgenthau are less great than one might have expected. This again points up the need for extensive empirical research in rural-urban differences, research that goes far beyond that provided in the few illustrative pilot studies presented here. At this point we have very limited objective evidence on differences in the quality of social encounters in city and small town.

But the research needs to be guided by unifying theoretical concepts. As I have tried to demonstrate, the concept of overload helps to explain a wide variety of contrasts between city behavior and town behavior: (i) the differences in role enactment (the tendency of urban dwellers to deal with one another in highly segmented, functional terms, and of urban sales personnel to devote limited time and attention to their customers); (ii) the evolution of urban norms quite different from traditional town values (such as the acceptance of noninvolvement, impersonality, and aloofness in urban life); (iii) the adaptation of the urban dweller's cognitive processes (his inability to identify most of the people he sees daily, his screening of sensory stimuli, his development of blasé attitudes toward deviant or bizarre behavior, and his selectivity in responding to human demands); and (iv) the competition for scarce facilities in the city (the subway rush; the fight for taxis; traffic jams; standing in line to await services). I suggest that contrasts between city and rural behavior probably reflect the responses of similar people to very different situations, rather than intrinsic differences in the personalities of rural and city dwellers. The city is a situation to which individuals respond adaptively.

Further aspects of urban experience

Some features of urban experience do not fit neatly into the system of analysis presented thus far. They are no less important for that reason. The issues raised next are difficult to treat in quantitative fashion. Yet I prefer discussing them in a loose way to excluding them because appropriate language and data have not yet been developed. My aim is to suggest how phenomena such as "urban atmosphere" can be pinned down through techniques of measurement.

The "atmosphere" of great cities. The contrast in the behavior of city and town dwellers has been a natural starting point for urban social scientists. But even among great cities there are marked differences in "atmosphere." The tone, pacing, and texture of social encounters are different in London and New York, and many persons willingly make financial sacrifices for the privilege of living within a specific urban atmosphere which they find pleasing or stimulating. A second perspective in the study of cities, therefore, is to define exactly what is meant by the atmosphere of a city and to pinpoint the factors that give rise to it. It may seem that urban atmosphere is too evanescent a quality to be reduced to a set of measurable variables, but I do not believe the matter can be judged before substantial effort has been made in this direction. It is obvious that any such approach must be comparative. It makes no sense at all to say that New York is "vibrant" and "frenetic" unless one has some specific city in mind as a basis of comparison.

In an undergraduate tutorial that I conducted at Harvard University some years ago, New York, London, and Paris were selected as reference points for attempts to measure urban atmosphere. We began with a simple question: Does any consensus exist about the qualities that typify given cities? To answer this question one could undertake a content analysis of travel-book, literary, and journalistic accounts of cities. A second approach, which we adopted, is to ask people to characterize (with descriptive terms and accounts of typical experiences) cities they have lived in or visited. In advertisements placed in the *New York Times* and the *Harvard Crimson* we asked people to give us accounts of specific incidents in London, Paris, or New York that best illuminated the character of that particular city. Questionnaires were then developed, and administered to persons who were familiar with at least two of the three cities.

Some distinctive patterns emerged (12). The distinguishing themes concerning New York, for example, dealt with its diversity, its great size, its pace and level of activity, its cultural and entertainment opportunities, and the heterogeneity and segmentation ("ghettoization") of its population. New York elicited more descriptions in terms of physical qualities, pace, and emotional impact than Paris or London did, a fact which suggests that these are particularly important aspects of New York's ambiance.

A contrasting profile emerges for London; in this case respondents placed far greater emphasis on their interactions with the inhabitants than on physical surroundings. There was near unanimity on certain themes: those dealing with the tolerance and courtesy of London's inhabitants. One respondent said:

> When I was 12, my grandfather took me to the British Museum . . . one day by tube and recited the *Aeneid* in Latin for my benefit. . . . He is rather deaf, speaks very loudly and it embarrassed the hell out of me, until I realized that nobody was paying any attention. Londoners are extremely worldly and tolerant.

In contrast, respondents who described New Yorkers as aloof, cold, and rude referred to such incidents as the following:

> I saw a boy of 19 passing out anti-war leaflets to passersby. When he stopped at a corner, a man dressed in a business suit walked by him at a brisk pace, hit the boy's arm, and scattered the leaflets all over the street. The man kept walking at the same pace down the block.

We need to obtain many more such descriptions of incidents, using careful methods of sampling. By the application of factor-analytic techniques, relevant dimensions for each city can be discerned.

The responses for Paris were about equally divided between responses concerning its inhabitants and those regarding its physical and sensory attributes. Cafes and parks were often mentioned as contributing to the sense that Paris is a city of amenities, but many respondents complained that Parisians were inhospitable, nasty, and cold.

We cannot be certain, of course, to what degree these statements reflect actual characteristics of the cities in question and to what degree they simply tap the respondents' knowledge of widely held preconceptions. Indeed, one may point to three factors, apart from the actual atmospheres of the cities, that determine the subjects' responses.

1. A person's impression of a given city depends on his implicit standard of comparison. A New Yorker who visits Paris may well describe that city as "leisurely," whereas a compatriot from Richmond, Virginia, may consider Paris too "hectic." Obtaining reciprocal judgment, in which New Yorkers judge Londoners, and Londoners judge New Yorkers, seems a useful way to take into account not only the city being judged but also the home city that serves as the visitor's base line.

2. Perceptions of a city are also affected by whether the observer is a tourist, a newcomer, or a longer-term resident. First, a tourist will be exposed to features of the city different from those familiar to a long-time resident. Second, a prerequisite for adapting to continuing life in a given city seems to be the filtering out of many observations about the city that the newcomer or tourist finds particularly arresting; this selective process seems to be part of the long-term resident's mechanism for coping with overload. In the interest of psychic economy, the resident simply learns to tune out many aspects of daily life. One method for studying the specific impact of adaptation on perception of the city is to ask several pairs of newcomers and old-timers (one newcomer and one old-timer to a pair) to walk down certain city blocks and then report separately what each has observed.

Additionally, many persons have noted that when travelers return to New York from an extended sojourn abroad they often feel themselves confronted with "brutal ugliness" (13) and a distinctive, frenetic atmosphere whose contributing details are, for a few hours or days, remarkably sharp and clear. This period of fresh perception should receive special attention in the study of city atmosphere. For, in a few days, details which are initially arresting become less easy to specify. They are assimilated into an increasingly familiar background atmosphere which, though important in setting the tone of things, is difficult to analyze. There is no better point at which to begin the study of city atmosphere than at the moment when a traveler returns from abroad.

3. The popular myths and expectations each visitor brings to the city will also affect the way in which he perceives it (see 14). Sometimes a person's pre-

conceptions about a city are relatively accurate distillations of its character, but preconceptions may also reinforce myths by filtering the visitor's perceptions to conform with his expectations. Preconceptions affect not only a person's perceptions of a city but what he reports about it.

The influence of a person's urban base line on his perceptions of a given city, the differences between the observations of the long-time inhabitant and those of the newcomer, and the filtering effect of personal expectations and stereotypes raise serious questions about the validity of travelers' reports. Moreover, no social psychologist wants to rely exclusively on verbal accounts if he is attempting to obtain an accurate and objective description of the cities' social texture, pace, and general atmosphere. What he needs to do is to devise means of embedding objective experimental measures in the daily flux of city life, measures that can accurately index the qualities of a given urban atmosphere.

Experimental comparisons of behavior

Roy Feldman (15) incorporated these principles in a comparative study of behavior toward compatriots and foreigners in Paris, Athens, and Boston. Feldman wanted to see (i) whether absolute levels and patterns of helpfulness varied significantly from city to city, and (ii) whether inhabitants in each city tended to treat compatriots differently from foreigners. He examined five concrete behavioral episodes, each carried out by a team of native experimenters and a team of American experimenters in the three cities. The episodes involved (i) asking natives of the city for street directions; (ii) asking natives to mail a letter for the experimenter; (iii) asking natives if they had just dropped a dollar bill (or the Greek or French equivalent) when the money actually belonged to the experimenter himself, (iv) deliberately overpaying for goods in a store to see if the cashier would correct the mistake and return the excess money; and (v) determining whether taxicab drivers overcharged strangers and whether they took the most direct route available.

Feldman's results suggest some interesting contrasts in the profiles of the three cities. In Paris, for instance, certain stereotypes were borne out. Parisian cab drivers overcharged foreigners significantly more often than they overcharged compatriots. But other aspects of the Parisians' behavior were not in accord with American preconceptions: in mailing a letter for a stranger, Parisians treated foreigners significantly better than Athenians or Bostonians did, and, when asked to mail letters that were already stamped, Parisians actually treated foreigners better than they treated compatriots. Similarly, Parisians were significantly more honest than Athenians or Bostonians in resisting the temptation to claim money that was not theirs, and Parisians were the only citizens who were more honest with foreigners than with compatriots in this experiment.

Feldman's studies not only begin to quantify some of the variables that give a city its distinctive texture but they also provide a methodological model for other comparative research. His most important contribution is his successful application of objective, experimental measures to everyday situations, a mode of study which provides conclusions about urban life that are more pertinent than those achieved through laboratory experiments.

Tempo and pace

Another important component of a city's atmosphere is its tempo or pace, an attribute frequently remarked on but less often studied. Does a city have a frenetic, hectic quality, or is it easygoing and leisurely? In any empirical treatment of this question, it is best to start in a very simple way. Walking speeds of pedestrians in different cities and in cities and towns should be measured and compared. William Berkowitz (16) of Lafayette College has undertaken an extensive series of studies of walking speeds in Philadelphia, New York, and Boston, as well as in small and moderate-sized towns. Berkowitz writes that "there does appear to be a significant linear relation between walking speed and size of municipality, but the absolute size of the difference varies by less than ten percent."

Perhaps the feeling of rapid tempo is due not so much to absolute pedestrian speeds as to the constant need to dodge others in a large city to avoid collisions with other pedestrians. (One basis for computing the adjustments needed to avoid collisions is to hypothesize a set of mechanical manikins sent walking along a city street and to calculate the number of collisions when no adjustments are made. Clearly, the higher the density of manikins the greater the number of collisions per unit of time, or, conversely, the greater the frequency of adjustments needed in higher population densities to avoid collisions.)

Patterns of automobile traffic contribute to a city's tempo. Driving an automobile provides a direct means of translating feelings about tempo into measurable acceleration, and a city's pace should be particularly evident in vehicular velocities, patterns of acceleration, and latency of response to traffic signals. The inexorable tempo of New York is expressed, further, in the manner in which pedestrians stand at busy intersections, impatiently awaiting a change in traffic light, making tentative excursions into the intersection, and frequently surging into the street even before the green light appears.

Visual components

Hall has remarked (17) that the physical layout of the city also affects its atmosphere. A gridiron pattern of streets gives the visitor a feeling of rationality, orderliness, and predictability but is sometimes monotonous. Winding lanes or streets branching off at strange angles, with many forks (as in Paris or Greenwich Village), create feelings of surprise and esthetic pleasure, while forcing greater decision-making in plotting one's course. Some would argue that the visual component is all-important—that the "look" of Paris or New York can almost be equated with its atmosphere. To investigate this hypothesis, we might conduct studies in which only blind, or at least blindfolded, respondents were used. We would no doubt discover that each city has a distinctive texture even when the visual component is eliminated.

Sources of ambiance

Thus far we have tried to pinpoint and measure some of the factors that contribute to the distinctive atmosphere of a great city. But we may also ask, Why do differences in urban atmosphere exist? How did they come about, and are they in any way related to the factors of density, large numbers, and heterogeneity discussed above?

First, there is the obvious factor that, even among great cities, populations and densities differ. The metropolitan areas of New York, London, and Paris, for example, contain 15 million, 12 million, and 8 million persons, respectively. London has average densities of 43 persons per acre, while Paris is more congested, with average densities of 114 persons per acre (18). Whatever characteristics are specifically attributable to density are more likely to be pronounced in Paris than in London.

A second factor affecting the atmosphere of cities is the source from which the populations are drawn (19). It is a characteristic of great cities that they do not reproduce their own populations, but that their numbers are constantly maintained and augmented by the influx of residents from other parts of the country. This can have a determining effect on the city's atmosphere. For example, Oslo is a city in which almost all of the residents are only one or two generations removed from a purely rural existence, and this contributes to its almost agricultural norms.

A third source of atmosphere is the general national culture. Paris combines adaptations to the demography of cities and certain values specific to French culture. New York is an admixture of American values and values that arise as a result of extraordinarily high density and large population.

Finally, one could speculate that the atmosphere of a great city is traceable to the specific historical conditions under which adaptations to urban overload occurred. For example, a city which acquired its mass and density during a period of commercial expansion will respond to new demographic conditions by adaptations designed to serve purely commercial needs. Thus, Chicago, which grew and became a great city under a purely commercial stimulus, adapted in a manner that emphasizes business needs. European capitals, on the other hand, incorporate many of the adaptations which were appropriate to the period of their increasing numbers and density. Because aristocratic values were prevalent at the time of the growth of these cities, the mechanisms developed for coping with overload were based on considerations other than pure efficiency. Thus, the manners, norms, and facilities of Paris and Vienna continue to reflect esthetic values and the idealization of leisure.

Cognitive maps of cities

When we speak of "behavioral comparisons" among cities, we must specify which parts of the city are most relevant for sampling purposes. In a sampling of "New Yorkers," should we include residents of Bay Ridge or Flatbush as well as inhabitants of Manhattan? And, if so, how should we weight our sample distribution? One approach to defining relevant boundaries in sampling is to determine which areas form the psychological or cognitive core of the city. We weight our samples most heavily in the areas considered by most people to represent the "essence" of the city.

The psychologist is less interested in the geographic layout of a city or in its political boundaries than in the cognitive representation of the city. Hans Blumenfeld (20) points out that the perceptual structure of a modern city can be expressed by the "silhouette" of the group of skyscrapers at its center and of smaller groups of office building at its "subcenters" but that urban areas can no longer, because of their vast extent, be experienced as fully articulated sets of streets, squares, and space.

In *The Image of the City* (21), Kevin Lynch created a cognitive map of Boston by interviewing Bostonians. Perhaps his most significant finding was that, while certain landmarks, such as Paul Revere's house and the Boston Common, as well as the paths linking them, are known to almost all Bostonians, vast areas of the city are simply unknown to its inhabitants.

Using Lynch's technique, Donald Hooper (22) created a psychological map of New York from the answers to the study questionnaire on Paris, London, and New York. Hooper's results were similar to those of Lynch: New York appears to have a dense core of well-known landmarks in midtown Manhattan, surrounded by the vast unknown reaches of Queens, Brooklyn, and the Bronx. Times Square, Rockefeller Center, and the Fifth Avenue department stores alone comprise half the places specifically cited by respondents as the haunts in which they spent most of their time. However, outside the midtown area, only scattered landmarks were recognized. Another interesting pattern is evident: even the best-known symbols of New York are relatively self-contained, and the pathways joining them appear to be insignificant on the map.

The psychological map can be used for more than just sampling techniques. Lynch (21) argues, for instance, that a good city is highly "imageable," having many known symbols joined by widely known pathways, whereas dull cities are gray and nondescript. We might test the relative "imagibility" of several cities by determining the proportion of residents who recognize sampled geographic points and their accompanying pathways.

If we wanted to be even more precise we could construct a cognitive map that would not only show the symbols of the city but would measure the precise degree of cognitive significance of any given point in the city relative to any other. By applying a pattern of points to a map of New York City, for example, and taking photographs from each point, we could determine what proportion of

Figure 2. To create a psychological map of Manhattan, geographic points are sampled, and, from photographs, the subjects attempt to identify the location of each point. To each point a numerical index is assigned indicating the proportion of persons able to identify its location.

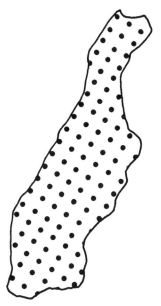

a sample of the city's inhabitants could identify the locale specified by each point (see Figure 2). We might even take the subjects blindfolded to a point represented on the map, then remove the blindfold and ask them to identify their location from the view around them.

One might also use psychological maps to gain insight into the differing perceptions of a given city that are held by members of its cultural subgroups, and into the manner in which their perceptions may change. In the earlier stages of life, whites and Negroes alike probably have only a limited view of the city, centering on the immediate neighborhood in which they are raised. In adolescence, however, the field of knowledge of the white teen-ager probably undergoes rapid enlargement; he learns of opportunities in midtown and outlying sections and comes to see himself as functioning in a larger urban field. But the process of ghettoization, to which the black teen-ager is subjected, may well hamper the expansion of his sense of the city. These are speculative notions, but they are readily subject to precise test.

Conclusion

I have tried to indicate some organizing theory that starts with the basic facts of city life: large numbers, density, and heterogeneity. These are external to the individual. He experiences these factors as overloads at the level of roles, norms, cognitive functions, and facilities. These overloads lead to adaptive mechanisms which create the distinctive tone and behaviors of city life. These notions, of course, need to be examined by objective comparative studies of cities and towns.

A second perspective concerns the differing atmospheres of great cities, such as Paris, London, and New York. Each has a distinctive flavor, offering a differentiable quality of experience. More precise knowledge of urban atmosphere seems attainable through application of the tools of experimental inquiry.

References and notes

1. *New York Times* (15 June 1969).
2. L. Wirth, *Amer. J. Soc.* 44, 1 (1938). Wirth's ideas have come under heavy criticism by contemporary city planners, who point out that the city is broken down into neighborhoods, which fulfill many of the functions of small towns. See, for example, H. J. Gans, *People and Plans: Essays on Urban Problems and Solutions* (Basic Books, New York, 1968); J. Jacobs, *The Death and Life of Great American Cities* (Random House, New York, 1961); G. D. Suttles, *The Social Order of the Slum* (Univ. of Chicago Press, Chicago, 1968).
3. G. Simmel, *The Sociology of Georg Simmel*, K. H. Wolff, Ed. (Macmillan, New York, 1950) [English translation of G. Simmel, *Die Grossstadte und das Geistesleben Die Grossstadt* (Jansch, Dresden, 1903)].
4. R. L. Meier, *A Communications Theory of Urban Growth* (M.I.T. Press, Cambridge, Mass., 1962).
5. S. Milgram and P. Hollander, *Nation* 25, 602 (1964).
6. B. Latané and J. Darley, *Amer. Sci.* 57, 244 (1969).
7. S. Gaertner and L. Bickman (Graduate Center, The City University of New York), unpublished research.
8. D. Altman, M. Levine, M. Nadien, J. Villena (Graduate Center, The City University of New York), unpublished research.
9. P. G. Zimbardo, paper presented at the Nebraska Symposium on Motivation (1969).
10. J. Waters (Graduate Center, The City University of New York), unpublished research.
11. W. McKenna and S. Morgenthau (Graduate Center, The City University of New York), unpublished research.
12. N. Abuza (Harvard University), "The Paris-London-New York Questionnaires," unpublished.
13. P. Abelson, *Science* 165, 853 (1969).
14. A. L. Strauss, ed., *The American City: A Sourcebook of Urban Imagery* (Aldine, Chicago, 1968).
15. R. E. Feldman, *J. Personality Soc. Psychol.* 10, 202 (1968).
16. W. Berkowitz, personal communication.
17. E. T. Hall, *The Hidden Dimension* (Doubleday, New York, 1966).
18. P. Hall, *The World Cities* (McGraw-Hill, New York, 1966).
19. R. E. Park, E. W. Burgess, R. D. McKenzie, *The City* (Univ. of Chicago Press, Chicago, 1967), pp. 1–45.
20. H. Blumenfeld, in *The Quality of Urban Life* (Sage, Beverly Hills, Calif., 1969).
21. K. Lynch, *The Image of the City* (M.I.T. and Harvard Univ. Press, Cambridge, Mass., 1960).
22. D. Hooper (Harvard University), unpublished.
23. Barbara Bengen worked closely with me in preparing the present version of this article. I thank Dr. Gary Winkel, editor of *Environment and Behavior*, for useful suggestions and advice.

12

SCOTT GREER, Urbanism Reconsidered: A Comparative Study of Local Areas in a Metropolis

The investigation of the internal differentiation of urban population has been concerned chiefly with economic rank and ethnic diversity, and with the differences which accompany variations in these factors. Such studies throw little light upon the broad, non-ethnic, cultural differences generated in the metropolitan environment, i.e., upon "urbanism as a way of life." While there has been much concern, theoretically, with the effects of the metropolitan ambit upon all social relationships, most of the empirical basis of urban theory has been the study of small "natural areas" or the study of gross regularities in census data, arranged spatially for analysis.

Perhaps the best evidence bearing upon this larger question of "urbanism" has been the study of urban neighborhoods. The work of Donald Foley, for example, indicates that in a sample of Rochester residents (1) the neighborhood pattern still exists to some degree, but, (2) many individuals do not neighbor and do not consider their local area to be a social community.[1] Such studies approach the propositions that urban society is functionally rather than spatially organized and that urbanites are mobile, anonymous, and lacking in identification with their local area.

To gauge the generality of Foley's conclusions, however, one needs to know where the neighborhoods he studied fit in an array of neighborhoods. Because wide variation exists, the relation between the area studied and others is crucial for the hypothesis tested; most of Rochester may be much more neighborhood oriented, or much less so, than the area studied.

The Shevky-Bell typology of urban subareas is useful in this connection, for it allows any census tract to be located in three different arrays by means of three indices constructed from census data.[2] It is hypothesized that these represent three dimensions within urban social space, each statistically unidimensional and independent of the others. The dimensions are social rank, segregation, and urbanization.[3] The last largely measures differences in family structure, and, it is assumed, indicates corollary differences in behavior. Thus, when social rank and segregation are controlled, differences in the index of urbanization for specific

Scott Greer, "Urbanism Reconsidered: A Comparative Study of Local Areas in a Metropolis," *American Sociological Review*, vol. 21 (February 1956), pp. 19–25, Reprinted by permission.
Revised version of paper read at the annual meeting of the American Sociological Society, September 1954. The study was carried out by the Laboratory in Urban Culture, a research facility of Occidental College, with the support of the John Randolph Haynes and Dora Haynes Foundation. I wish to express gratitude to Ella Kube, Research Associate, for assistance in the computation and analysis upon which the report is based.

tract populations should indicate consistent variations in social behavior. One purpose of the present research was to determine the nature of such corollary differences, and particularly differences in social participation.

This report is based upon a pilot study of differences in social participation between sample populations in two Los Angeles areas (census tracts 35 and 63).[4] The two tract populations are nearly identical with respect to two of the indices (social rank and segregation) and differ on the third, urbanization. For simplicity in presentation the tract with the higher urbanization index score (tract 63) will hereafter be called the high-urban tract, the other (tract 35) the low-urban tract.

The two sample tracts compare as follows. *History:* The low-urban tract is in an area that thirty years ago was separately incorporated for a brief time; the high-urban tract has always been a part of Los Angeles proper. *Location:* the low-urban tract is approximately fifteen minutes from the city center by auto; the high-urban tract is about half as far. (The low-urban tract is adjacent to the competing centers of Glendale and Pasadena.) *Social rank:* both tracts fall within the large middle range, being slightly above the median for the County. The social rank index for the low-urban tract is 68, for the high-urban tract, 66, as of the 1950 census of population, based upon the standard scores developed by Shevky with 1940 census data. *Ethnicity:* in neither tract does the foreign-born and non-white population amount to more than 5 percent. *Urbanization:* the two tracts represent the extremes of the middle range of the urbanization index, within which a majority of the Los Angeles County census tracts lie. The low-urban tract had an urbanization index of 41, the high-urban tract, 57. There are much more highly urban tracts at middle rank, and much lower ones, in the County. The sample is weighted against the instrument, so that if striking and consistent variations appear in this middle range, they probably indicate more extreme variations at the poles.

Field procedure and the sample

The field study included scheduled interviews on the participation of adult members of households in formal organizations, neighboring, cultural events, visiting, domestic activities, the mass media, the kin group, and other social structures.

Visiting was measured by questions concerning friends or relatives who were visited regularly at least once a month. The respondent was asked to give the address of the residence visited, both as a control over the accuracy of the information, and as a clue to social space position in the Shevky-Bell typology. Neighboring was measured by Wallin's "Neighborliness Scale," which was developed for a similar population in Palo Alto, California.[5] The scale assumes that neighborliness is unidimensional and can be measured by a small battery of questions referring to the degree of interaction with neighbors. The reproducibility for the present sample has not yet been determined. Cultural events were recorded and categorized in the manner devised by Queen, in his studies of social participation in St. Louis.[6] Individuals were asked about their attendance in the past month at movies, classes and study groups, athletic contests, lectures and speeches, museums and exhibits, musical events, and stage shows. They were also asked the location of the event and who accompanied them. Special schedules of questions were developed for the purpose of describing participation in formal organizations of various sorts, definitions of the local area, domestic participation, neighborhood play of children, and other aspects of participation which will not be reported here.

An area random sample was interviewed in each tract, with 161 respondents in the low-urban tract, 150 in the high-urban tract. These households represented approximately 7 percent of the populations of the two census tracts chosen. The housewife was the respondent, and the response rate was over 85 percent, being higher in the low-urban area. Interviewers were advanced and graduate students at Occidental College, and the average interview time was approximately one hour.

The two samples of households compare as follows:

Income: 20 percent of the households in each area had less than $3,000 annually; 37 percent in the low-urban area and 31 percent in the high-urban area had annual incomes between $3,000 and $5,000; 35 percent in the low-urban area and 38 percent in the high-urban area had over $5,000 annually. Those who did not know or declined to state were 8 percent in the low-urban area, 11 percent in the high-urban area. The chief difference was a preponderance of middle income households in the low-urban area, with somewhat more heterogeneity in the high-urban area. *Occupation:* using the blue collar-white collar break, the samples were identical. In both areas, 72 percent of the employed respondents were white-collar. Seventy-two percent of the husbands in each area were in clerical jobs or higher.

Education: if education is divided into three classes, elementary or less, some high school or completed high school, and some college or more, the low-urban sample is slightly more homogeneous. Both respondents and husbands are 60 percent high-school educated, with approximately 15 percent below and 25 percent above this class. In the high-urban sample the middle category accounted for only 50 percent, with approximately 25 percent below and 25 percent above this class.

Such differences are not great but seem to indicate a consistent tendency towards somewhat more heterogeneity in the high-urban sample. It includes a slightly higher proportion of low-income, low-education persons, and also a slightly higher proportion of high-income, high-education persons. The high-urban sample is also more heterogeneous with respect to ethnicity. Although the percentage of non-white and foreign-born is similar in the two samples (9 for the low-urban sample, 11 for the high-urban) differences in religious affiliation indicate more ethnic diversity in the high-urban sample.

The low-urban area sample is much more homogeneous and Protestant in affiliation and preference. The high-urban sample, however, includes sizeable representations of the minority American religious beliefs: Jewish and Roman Catholics are, together, only 20 percent of the low-urban sample; they are 37 percent of the high-urban sample. This heterogeneous and non-Protestant population in the high-urban sample is probably, to a large degree, made up of second and later generation ethnic individuals. Since the census tracts with high indexes of segregation in middle economic ranks are usually found in the more highly urbanized areas of the Shevsky-Bell grid, it is likely that "later generation ethnics" (not identified in census data) are also concentrated in the more highly urbanized tracts of the middle social rank.

Such a correlation between second and later generation ethnic populations and urbanization, however, does not allow the reduction of the urbanization dimension to the ethnic component. In truth, many of these individuals are in process of leaving their ethnic status behind. Instead, it may be said that one of the attributes indicated by the urbanization index is apt to be the presence of second and later generation ethnics in the midst of acculturation. Such heterogeneity between faiths and within faiths is one of the conditions that give highly urbanized populations their particular characteristics.

Empirical findings

Table 1 gives differences in participation between two areas with respect to the localization of community. The low-urban sample differed sharply and consistently in the direction of more participation in the local community. Their neighboring score was higher, they were more apt to have friends in the local area, and these constituted a larger proportion of all close friends, i.e., those visited at least once a month. They were more apt to go to cultural events such as movies, athletic contests, stage shows, and study groups, in the local area, and they were more apt to use local commercial facilities of certain types.

The low-urban sample had a higher rate of membership and participation in formal organizations other than church, and, more important, a larger proportion of their organizations were local in nature. A large majority of the respondents' organizations held meetings in the local area, and although the husbands' organizations usually met outside the area, still a much larger proportion met locally than did in the high-urban sample. Furthermore, the members of formal organizations to which the low-urban sample belonged were more apt to live in the immediate local community. In the high-urban sample other members were most apt to be scattered over the metropolis as a whole.

Further indication of the differential importance the local based organization had for these two samples is the greater familiarity of the low-urban sample with local community leaders. (See Table 2.)

While the samples were equally able (and unable) to name Los Angeles leaders, there was a significantly higher proportion who could name local leaders in the low-urban area sample. This probably indicates a uniform engagement of middle-rank populations in the affairs of the metropolis as a

Table 1. Local community participation in two urban areas

Type of social participation	Low urban*	High urban*
Percent of respondents with high neighboring scores		
(Scale types 2 through 5)	67†	56†
N of respondents	(162)	(150)
Percent of respondents with friends in the local area	50	29
N of respondents	(162)	(150)
Percent of all respondents' friends who live in local area	41	25
N of all friends	(441)	(316)
Percent of respondents attending cultural events in local		
area, of those attending any cultural events	45	18
N attending any events	(101)	(92)
Percent of respondents' formal organizations which meet in:		
Local area	62	26
Other areas	35	71
No response	3	3
N of organizations	(126)	(67)
Percent of respondents' formal organizations with the		
majority of members residing in:		
Local area	57	33
Other area	18	18
Scattered over the city	23	45
No response	2	4
N of organizations	(126)	(67)
Percent of husbands' formal organizations (as reported		
by respondent) which meet in:		
Local area	21‡	5‡
Other areas	73	86
No response	6	9
N of husbands' organizations	(104)	(57)
Percent of husbands' formal organizations (as reported by		
respondent) with the majority of members residing in:		
Local area	25	10
Other area	23	12
Scattered over the city	45	77
No response	7	1
N of husbands' organizations	(104)	(57)

*P (x^2) <.01, with exceptions noted below.
†P (x^2) slightly above .05 level: x^2 = 3.77.
‡P (x^2) between .01 and .02 levels.

whole, but definite variations in their interest and involvement with respect to local affairs.

It is sometimes stated, almost as an axiom, that the urban milieu results in the extreme attrition of kin relations. The present study indicates this to be questionable. The most important single kind of social relationship for both samples is kinship visiting. A large majority of both samples visit their kin at least once a month, and *half of each sample visit their kin at least once a week.* These data,

Table 2.   Respondents' ability to name leaders of the local area and of Los Angeles

	Low urban	High urban
Percent of respondents who could name at least one local leader	32*	21*
N of respondents	(162)	(150)
Percent of respondents who could name at least one Los Angeles leader	38†	37†
N of respondents	(162)	(150)

*P (x^2) between .02 and .05 levels.
†Difference not significant.

reported in Table 3, are consistent with the findings of Bell in his comparable study of social areas in the San Francisco Bay Region.[7]

Both samples indicated complacency with their neighborhood and said they were satisfied with it as a home, but in giving their reasons for liking it, they tended to differ. The low-urban sample described their area as a "little community," like a "small town," where "people are friendly and neighborly." The high-urban sample, on the other hand, most frequently mentioned the "convenience to downtown and everything," and spoke often of the "nice people" who "leave you alone and mind their own business." The high-urban sample seemed less committed to remaining in their present area—a higher proportion stating that there were other neighborhoods in the city in which they would rather live.

A tendency toward differential association with populations at a similar level of urbanization is indicated in the visiting patterns of the two samples outside their local areas. The residences of close friends and the meeting places of social circles are almost mutually exclusive for the two samples. Furthermore, when the census tracts in which are located the homes of the friends they visit are categorized by urbanization scores, clear differences appear. The low-urban sample is more apt to have friends in other low-urban areas, while the high-urban sample is apt to visit in other high-urban areas. (See Table 4.)

When it is recalled that these two samples are almost identical with respect to social rank and segregation, the importance of the urbanization dimension is underlined. These visiting patterns refer to well structured friendship relations of probable importance. Such differential association may result from proximity, as well as selective visiting by levels of urbanization. The relative importance of proximity will be measured through the use of the intervening opportunities model. However, even if such differential association is to a large degree a function of spatial proximity, its significance in certain respects would remain. For, if populations at given levels of urbanization interact more intensely within those

Table 3. Kin visiting in two urban areas

Percent visiting kin	Low urban*	High urban*
Once a week or more often	49	55
At least once a month, but less than once a week	24	21
A few times a year, but less than once a month	11	8
Never	5	9
No kin in Los Angeles	11	7
N of respondents	(162)	(150)

*No significant difference between low and high urban area samples.

Table 4. Residence of friends visited, outside of the local area, by urbanization index score*

	Low urban†	High urban†
Percent of friends living in tracts with urbanization index score of		
1–20	13	12
21–40	35	25
41–60	41	33
61–80	8	19
81–100	3	11
N of friends visited	(180)	(162)

*Friends' addresses which could not be coded (80 in the low-urban area, 65 in the high-urban) are excluded.
†P $(x^2) < .001$.

levels than with other populations, such interactions should result in fairly stable networks of informal communication and influence. The content of such communication should vary with urbanization.

Summary and interpretation

In order to investigate empirically the complex of notions surrounding the nature of urban social behavior, the Shevky-Bell typology, applied to sub-areas in Los Angeles County, was used to select two neighborhoods which differed clearly on the index of urbanization. Social rank was not used as the chief factor accounting for differential social participation, as was the case in the studies of Komarovsky, Goldhamer, and others.[8] Instead, rank was controlled, and the urbanization dimension was tested for broad differences in social participation.

It should be noted that this study investigates the effects of urbanization at a *particular* level of rank and segregation; at other levels, the effects of urbanization remain problematical. It is hoped that future studies will clarify, for example, the effects of differential urbanization at higher and lower social ranks, as well as in segregated populations. The Shevky-Bell typology, based upon a three dimensional attribute-space model of urban society, calls attention not only to three separate factors, but also to the possibility that the particular effects of one may be transformed as either or both of the others vary.

However, the urbanization dimension was the focus of the present study. It was not identified with the other notion of urbanism which implies that all city populations are changing in the direction of atomistic, mass society.[9] Instead, it was assumed that there is a continuum of alternative life-styles at the same economic level and that these are concentrated in different urban sub-areas. In this framework, the low-urban areas are just as characteristic of modern urban society as are the high-urban areas. Both types continue to be alternatives in the urban complex. In this view, the Shevky-Bell index of urbanization is a putative means of identifying such variations in "ways of life." Instead of concentrating on urbanism as *a* way of life, the present study was focused upon the variations possible.

Two social aggregates, inhabiting tracts with similar economic rank and ethnicity but varying with respect to the urbanization index, were sampled. The sample populations were then studied by means of reported social participation.

The findings are consistent with the hypothesis that, where rank and ethnicity are equal, differences in the urbanization index will indicate differences in social behavior. Had the index identified populations not significantly different, doubt would have been cast upon its utility at the level of individual social behavior, for the urbanization dimension of modern society, as conceived by Shevky in his theoretical structure, implies such differences in social behavior.[10] However, the present study indicates that the index, constructed primarily with items related to family structure, does identify differences in social participation which are associated with variations in family structure but not derived solely from them. The general validity of the hypothesis must rest upon further studies in Los Angeles and other urban complexes. Although this study and that of Bell indicate the urbanization dimension does affect social participation to an impressive degree, the regularity with which these differences form a continuum at this intersection of social rank and segregation, and the nature of the hypothesized continuum, remain to be spelled out. Still, in the interpretation of the findings here reported, the following implications come to mind:

1. The local area in the contemporary American metropolis may be viewed as attracting population, not only by the economic rank and ethnic composition of the population already in the area, but also by the degree of urbanization characteristic of the area—the way of life common to the older inhabitants.

2. Such areas may attract populations on at least two different functional bases: (1) the demographic and the cultural characteristics of the older settlers, who give the area its "tone," may attract people, as seems true in the

low-urban sample, or, (2) the area as a socially neutral, but convenient, base of operations for various segmental interests, may attract people as in the high-urban sample. Such different principles of attraction would tend to produce greater homogeneity of background and interest in low-urban areas, and from this similarity a higher degree of community-type behavior and of conformity would be expected.

3. A continuum is hypothesized for non-segregated, middle-rank areas. At one pole lie the local areas which select a predominantly "old American" population with similar jobs, aspirations, incomes, who wish to raise children, neighbor, participate in local community groups, and, in brief, carry on a life in many ways similar to that of the small towns described by Warner and his associates.[11] At the other pole lie those areas of the city which are more heterogeneous, with fewer children and little interest in the local area as a social arena. Such areas may approach, in many ways, the ideal type of urban environment hypothesized by Wirth.[12]

4. In this perspective, the local area is important as a framework for interaction, as a "social fact," just where it is least representative of the total urban society. The small community, as studied by Warner and others, is a very poor example of the urban complex, since it will include the fewest elements of urban society as a whole. At the same time, the high-urban tract as a sample of urban society is only slightly less biased, for in it the local area as a social fact disappears altogether. Thus it is not possible to use either the model of a small, spatially enclosed community or the stereotype of the continually more atomistic mass society in describing social participation in the contemporary metropolis.

There are, however, certain common structural threads running through the fabric of modern society. As Paul Hatt noted, the indices developed by Warner and others to measure social status may be generalized to the total society, since the various methods correlate highly with one universal attribute—occupation.[13] The present approach is, then, to ask: How does this attribute become defined and organized, how does it influence participation, in different sub-areas of the metropolis?

A tentative answer is that the individual's social position is defined differently and his social participation is patterned differently as the focus shifts from the low-urban populations to the high-urban populations. One may envisage the low-urban areas as somewhere between the small town and the conventional picture of metropolitan living. Where the local area is a social fact, where common interests and associations obtain, generalizations derived from small community studies may have validity. For here the individual's status will result, in part, from participation in a known and used local organizational structure and from family ties that are publicly understood.

When, however, high-urban populations are considered, social participation is organized around position in other organizational contexts, as for example, the corporation, politics, the labor union, or perhaps, as Riesman has suggested, categories derived from the popular culture of the mass media.[14] Here also are many individuals whose life, aside from work, is ordered by participation in small informal groups, and informal groups only, floating within the vast culture world of the market and the mass media. In such populations the locally defined community is largely irrelevant to status and participation. Associations are spread geographically, but ordered and concentrated in terms of selected interests. Family, in this context, is still important. It is slightly more important in the high-urban sample described. But it is probably much more private in its reference. In fact, kin relations may be seen as growing in importance just because of the diminished reliance placed upon neighborhood and local community.

What has been sketched above is a tentative model which will allow the use of contributions from earlier research, (studies of small cities, natural areas, the apartment house family, the suburban fringe) within a framework which integrates and orders them in relation to one another. Such a frame of reference also relates, eventually, to the increasing importance of large-scale organizations in a society which allows many alternative life patterns for individuals at the same functional and economic level.

Notes

1. Donald L. Foley, "Neighbors or Urbanites? The Study of a Rochester District," *The University of Rochester's Studies of Metropolitan Rochester,* Rochester, New York, 1952.
2. Eshref Shevky and Wendell Bell, *Social Area Analysis,* Stanford, California: Stanford University Press, 1955. See also, Eshref Shevky and Marilyn Williams, *The Social Areas of Los Angeles,* Berkeley and Los Angeles: The University of California Press, 1948.
3. For a description of the statistical analysis and testing of the typology, see Wendell Bell, "Economic, Family, and Ethnic Status," *American Sociological Review,* 20 (February 1955), pp. 45-52.
4. The extension of the study to include two additional sample tracts will be reported later; results are generally consistent with the findings reported here. Rank and segregation are the same in the added tract samples, but the new tracts extend to the extremes of the urbanization index within middle economic rank.
5. Paul Wallin, "A Guttman Scale for Measuring Women's Neighborliness," *American Journal of Sociology,* 49 (November 1953), pp. 243-246.
6. Stuart A. Queen, "Social Participation in Relation to Social Disorganization," *American Sociological Review,* 14 (April 1949), pp. 251-256.
7. Wendell Bell (with the assistance of Maryanne Force and Marion Boat), "People of the City," (processed) Stanford University Survey Research Facility, Stanford, California, 1954.
8. Mirra Komarovsky, "The Voluntary Associations of Urban Dwellers," *American Sociological Review,* 11 (December 1946), pp. 868-896; Herbert Goldhamer, "Voluntary Associations in the United States," unpublished Ph.D. thesis, University of Chicago, 1942.
9. See Louis Wirth, "Urbanism as a Way of Life," *The American Journal of Sociology,* 44 (July 1938), pp. 1-24.
10. Shevky and Bell, *op. cit.,* especially Chapter II.
11. See, for example, W. Lloyd Warner and associates, *Democracy in Jonesville,* New York: Harper and Brothers, 1949.
12. Wirth, *op. cit.*
13. Paul K. Hatt, "Stratification in the Mass Society," *American Sociological Review,* 15 (April, 1950), pp. 216-222.

14. David Riesman, in collaboration with Reuel Denny and Nathan Glazer, *The Lonely Crowd, A Study of the Changing American Character,* New Haven: Yale University Press, 1950, especially Chs. X, XI, XII.

13

PETER SCHRAG, The Forgotten American

There is hardly a language to describe him, or even a set of social statistics. Just names: racist-bigot-redneck-ethnic-Irish-Italian-Pole-Hunkie-Yahoo. The lower middle class. A blank. The man under whose hat lies the great American desert. Who watches the tube, plays the horses, and keeps the niggers out of his union and his neighborhood. Who might vote for Wallace (but didn't). Who cheers when the cops beat up on demonstrators. Who is free, white and twenty-one, has a job, a home, a family, and is up to his eyeballs in credit. In the guise of the working class—or the American yeoman or John Smith—he was once the hero of the civics book, the man that Andrew Jackson called "the bone and sinew of the country." Now he is "the forgotten man," perhaps the most alienated person in America.

Nothing quite fits, except perhaps omission and semi-visibility. America is supposed to be divided between affluence and poverty, between slums and suburbs. John Kenneth Galbraith begins the foreword to *The Affluent Society* with the phrase, "Since I sailed for Switzerland in the early summer of 1955 to begin work on this book . . ." But *between* slums and suburbs, between Scarsdale and Harlem, between Wellesley and Roxbury, between Shaker Heights and Hough, there are some eighty million people (depending on how you count them) who didn't sail for Switzerland in the summer of 1955, or at any other time, and who never expect to. Between slums and suburbs: South Boston and South San Francisco, Bell and Parma, Astoria and Bay Ridge, Newark, Cicero, Downey, Daly City, Charlestown, Flatbush. Union halls, American Legion posts, neighborhood bars and bowling leagues, the Ukrainian Club and the Holy Name. Main Street. To try to describe all this is like trying to describe America itself. If you look for it, you find it everywhere: the rows of frame houses overlooking the belching steel mills in Bethlehem, Pennsylvania, two-family brick houses in Canarsie (where the most common slogan, even in the middle of a political campaign, is "curb your dog"); the Fords and Chevies with a decal American flag on the rear window (usually a cut-out from the *Reader's Digest,* and displayed in counter-protest against peaceniks and "those bastards who carry Vietcong flags in demonstrations"); the bunting on the porch rail with the inscription, "Welcome Home, Pete." The gold star in the window.

When he was Under Secretary of Housing and Urban Development, Robert C. Wood tried a definition. It is not good, but it's the best we have:

> He is a white employed male . . . earning between $5,000 and $10,000. He works regularly, steadily, dependably, wearing a blue collar or white collar. Yet the frontiers of his career expectations have been fixed since he reached the age of thirty-five, when he found that he had too many obligations, too much family, and too few skills to match opportunities with aspirations.
>
> This definition of the "working American" involves almost 23 million American families.
>
> The working American lives in the gray area fringes of a central city or in a close-in or very far-out cheaper suburban subdivision of a large metropolitan area. He is likely to own a home and a car, especially as his income begins to rise. Of those earning between $6,000 and $7,500, 70 percent own their own homes and 94 percent drive their own cars.
>
> 94 percent have no education beyond high school and 43 percent have only completed the eighth grade.

He does all the right things, obeys the law, goes to church and insists— usually—that his kids get a better education than he had. But the right things don't seem to be paying off. While he is making more than he ever made— perhaps more than he'd ever dreamed—he's still struggling while a lot of others— "them" (on welfare, in demonstrations, in the ghettos) are getting most of the attention. "I'm working my ass off," a guy tells you on a stoop in South Boston. "My kids don't have a place to swim, my parks are full of glass, and I'm supposed to bleed for a bunch of people on relief." In New York a man who drives a Post Office trailer truck at night (4:00 p.m. to midnight) and a cab during the day (7:00 a.m. to 2:00 p.m.), and who hustles radios for his Post Office buddies on the side, is ready, as he says, to "knock somebody's ass." "The colored guys work when they feel like it. Sometimes they show up and sometimes they don't. One guy tore up all the time cards. I'd like to see a white guy do that and get away with it."

What counts

Nobody knows how many people in America moonlight (half of the eighteen million families in the $5,000 to $10,000 bracket have two or more wage earners) or how many have to hustle on the side. "I don't think anybody has a single job anymore," said Nicholas Kisburg, the research director for a Teamsters Union Council in New York. "All the cops are moonlighting, and the teachers; and there's a million guys who are hustling, guys with phony social-security numbers who are hiding part of what they make so they don't get kicked out of a housing project, or guys who work as guards at sports events and get free meals that they don't want to pay taxes on. Every one of them is cheating. They are underground people—*Untermenschen*. . . . We really have no systematic data on any of this. We have no ideas of the attitudes of the white worker. (We've been too busy studying the black worker.) And yet he's the source of most of the reaction in this country."

The reaction is directed at almost every visible target: at integration and welfare, taxes and sex education, at the rich and the poor, the foundations and students, at the "smart people in the suburbs." In New York State the legislature cut the welfare budget; in Los Angeles, the voters reelect Yorty after a whispered racial campaign against the Negro favorite. In Minneapolis a police detective named Charles Stenvig, promising "to take the handcuffs off the police," wins by a margin stunning even to his supporters: in Massachusetts the voters mail tea bags to their representatives in protest against new taxes, and in state after state legislatures are passing bills to punish student demonstrators. ("We keep talking about permissiveness in training kids," said a Los Angeles labor official, "but we forget that these are our kids.")

And yet all these things are side manifestations of a malaise that lacks a language. Whatever law and order means, for example, to a man who feels his wife is unsafe on the street after dark or in the park at any time, or whose kids get shaken down in the school yard, it also means something like normality—the demand that everybody play it by the book, that cultural and social standards be somehow restored to their civics-book simplicity, that things shouldn't be as they are but as they were supposed to be. If there is a revolution in this country—a revolt in manners, standards of dress and obscenity, and, more importantly, in our official sense of what America is—there is also a counter-revolt. Sometimes it is inarticulate, and sometimes (perhaps most of the time) people are either too confused or apathetic—or simply too polite and too decent—to declare themselves. In Astoria, Queens, a white working-class district of New York, people who make $7,000 or $8,000 a year (sometimes in two jobs) call themselves affluent, even though the Bureau of Labor Statistics regards an income of less than $9,500 in New York inadequate to a moderate standard of living. And in a similar neighborhood in Brooklyn a truck driver who earns $151 a week tells you he's doing well, living in a two-story frame house separated by a narrow driveway from similar houses, thousands of them in block after block. This year, for the first time, he will go on a cruise—he and his wife and two other couples— two weeks in the Caribbean. He went to work after World War II ($57 a week) and he has lived in the same house for twenty years, accumulating two television sets, wall-to-wall carpeting in a small living room, and a basement that he recently remodeled into a recreation room with the help of two moonlighting firemen. "We get fairly good salaries, and this is a good neighborhood, one of the few good ones left. We have no smoked Irishmen around."

Stability is what counts, stability in job and home and neighborhood, stability in the church and in friends. At night you watch television and sometimes on a weekend you go to a nice place—maybe a downtown hotel—for dinner with another couple. (Or maybe your sister, or maybe bowling, or maybe, if you're defeated, a night at the track.) The wife has the necessary appliances, often still being paid off, and the money you save goes for your daughter's orthodontist, and later for her wedding. The smoked Irishmen—the colored (no one says black; few even say Negro)—represent change and instability, kids who cause trouble in school, who get treatment that your kids never got, that you never got. ("Those fucking kids," they tell you in South Boston, "raising hell, and not one of 'em paying his own way. Their fucking mothers are all on welfare.") The black kids mean a change in the rules, a double standard in grades and discipline, and—vaguely—a challenge to all you believed right. Law and order is the stability and predictability of established ways. Law and order is equal treatment—in school, in jobs, in the courts—even if you're cheating a little yourself. The Forgotten Man is Jackson's man. He is the vestigial American democrat of 1840: "They all know that their success depends upon their own industry and economy and that they must not expect to become suddenly rich by the fruits of their toil." He is also Franklin Roosevelt's man—the man whose vote (or whose father's vote) sustained the New Deal.

There are other considerations, other styles, other problems. A postman in a Charlestown (Boston) housing project: eight children and a ninth on the way. Last year, by working overtime, his income went over $7,000. This year, because he reported it, the Housing Authority is raising his rent from $78 to $106 a month, a catastrophe for a family that pays $2.20 a day for milk, has never had a vacation, and for which an excursion is "going out for ice cream." "You try and save for something better; we hope to get out of here to someplace where the kids can play, where there's no broken glass, and then something always comes along that knocks you right back. It's like being at the bottom of the well waiting for a guy to throw you a rope." The description becomes almost Chaplinesque. Life is humble but not simple; the terrors of insolent bureaucracies and contemptuous officials produce a demonology that loses little of its horror for being partly misunderstood. You want to get a sink fixed but don't want to offend the manager; want to get an eye operation that may (or may not) have been necessitated by a military injury five years earlier, "but the Veterans Administration says I signed away my benefits"; want to complain to someone about the teenagers who run around breaking windows and harassing women but get no response either from the management or the police. "You're afraid to complain because if they don't get you during the day they'll get you at night." Automobiles, windows, children, all become hostages to the vague terrors of everyday life; everything is vulnerable. Liabilities that began long ago cannot possibly be liquidated: "I never learned anything in that school except how to fight. I got tired of being caned by the teachers so at sixteen I quit and joined the Marines. I still don't know anything."

At the bottom of the well

American culture? Wealth is visible, and so, now, is poverty. Both have become intimidating clichés. But the rest? A vast, complex, and disregarded world that was once—in belief, and in fact—the American middle: Greyhound and Trailways bus terminals in little cities at midnight, each of them with its neon lights and its cardboard hamburgers; acres of tar-paper beach bungalows in places like Revere and Rockaway; the hair curlers in the supermarket on Saturday, and the little girls in the communion dresses the next morning; pinball machines and the *Daily News,* the *Reader's Digest* and Ed Sullivan; houses with tiny front lawns (or even large ones) adorned with statues of the Virgin or of Sambo welcomin' de folks home; Clint Eastwood or Julie Andrews at the Palace; the trotting tracks and the dog tracks—Aurora Downs, Connaught Park, Roosevelt, Yonkers, Rockingham, and forty others—where gray men come not for sport and beauty, but to read numbers, to study and dope. (If you win you have figured something, have in a small way controlled your world, have surmounted your impotence. If you lose, bad luck, shit. "I'll break his goddamned head.") Baseball is not the national pastime; racing is. For every man who goes to a major-league baseball game there are four who go to the track and probably four more who go to the candy store or the barbershop to make their bets. (Total track attendance in 1965: 62 million plus another 10 million who went to the dogs.)

There are places, and styles, and attitudes. If there are neighborhoods of aspiration, suburban enclaves for the mobile young executive and the aspiring worker, there are also places of limited expectation and dead-end districts where mobility is finished. But even there you can often find, however vestigial, a sense of place, the roots of old ethnic loyalties, and a passionate, if often futile, battle against intrusion and change. "Everybody around here," you are told, "pays his own way." In this world the problems are not the ABM or air pollution (have they heard of Biafra?) or the international population crisis; the problem is to get your street cleaned, your garbage collected, to get your husband home from Vietnam alive; to negotiate installment payments and to keep the schools orderly. Ask anyone in Scarsdale or Winnetka about the schools and they'll tell you about new programs, or about how many are getting into Harvard, or about the teachers; ask in Oakland or the North Side of Chicago, and they'll tell you that they have (or haven't) had trouble. Somewhere in his gut the man in those communities knows that mobility and choice in this society are limited. He cannot imagine any major change for the better; but he can imagine change for the worse. And yet for a decade he is the one who has been asked to carry the burden of social reform, to integrate his schools and his neighborhood, has been asked by comfortable people to pay the social debts due to the poor and the black. In Boston, in San Francisco, in Chicago (not to mention Newark or Oakland) he has been telling the reformers to go to hell. The Jewish schoolteachers of New York and the Irish parents of Dorchester have asked the same question: "What the hell did Lindsay (or the Beacon Hill Establishment) ever do for us?"

The ambiguities and changes in American life that occupy discussions in university seminars and policy debates in Washington, and that form the backbone of contemporary popular sociology, become increasingly the conditions of trauma and frustration in the middle. Although the New Frontier and Great Society contained some programs for those not already on the rolls of social pathology—federal aid for higher education, for example—the public priorities and the rhetoric contained little. The emphasis, properly, was on the poor, on the inner cities (e.g., Negroes) and the unemployed. But in Chicago a widow with three children who earns $7,000 a year can't get them college loans because she makes too much; the money is reserved for people on relief. New schools are built in the ghetto but not in the white working-class neighborhoods where they are just as dilapidated. In Newark the head of a white vigilante group (now a city councilman) runs, among other things, on a platform opposing pro-Negro discrimination. "When pools are being built in the Central Ward—don't they think white kids have got frustration? The white can't get a job; we have to hire Negroes first." The middle class, said Congressman Roman Pucinski of Illinois, who represents a lot of it, "is in revolt. Everyone has been generous in supporting anti-poverty. Now the middle-class American is disqualified from most of the programs."

"Somebody has to say no . . ."

The frustrated middle. The liberal wisdom about welfare, ghettos, student revolt, and Vietnam has only a marginal place, if any, for the values and life of the working man. It flies in the face of most of what he was taught to cherish and respect: hard work, order, authority, self-reliance. He fought, either alone or through labor organizations, to establish the precincts he now considers his own. Union seniority, the civil-service bureaucracy, and the petty professionalism established by the merit system in the public schools become sinecures of particular ethnic groups or of those who have learned to negotiate and master the system. A man who worked all his life to accumulate the points and grades and paraphernalia to become an assistant school principal (no matter how silly the requirements) is not likely to relinquish his position with equanimity. Nor is a dock worker whose only estate is his longshoreman's card. The job, the points, the credits become property:

> Some men leave their sons money [wrote a union member to the *New York Times*], some large investments, some business connections, and some a profession. I have only one worthwhile thing to give: my trade. I hope to follow a centuries-old tradition and sponsor my sons for an apprenticeship. For this simple father's wish it is said that I discriminate against Negroes. Don't all of us discriminate? Which of us . . . will not choose a son over all others?

Suddenly the rules are changing—all the rules. If you protect your job for your own you may be called a bigot. At the same time it's perfectly acceptable to shout black power and to endorse it. What does it take to be a good American? *Give the black man a position because he is black, not because he necessarily works harder or does the job better.* What does it take to be a good American? Dress nicely, hold a job, be clean-cut, don't judge a man by the color of his skin or the country of his origin. What about the demands of Negroes, the long hair of the students, the dirty movies, the people who burn draft cards and American flags? Do you have to go out in the street with picket signs, do you have to burn the place down to get what you want? What does it take to be a good American? *This is a sick society, a racist society, we are fighting an immoral war.* ("I'm against the Vietnam war, too," says the truck driver in Brooklyn. "I see a good kid come home with half an arm and a leg in a brace up to here, and what's it all for? I was glad to see *my kid* flunk the Army physical. Still, somebody has to say no to these demonstrators and enforce the law.") What does it take to be a good American?

The conditions of trauma and frustration in the middle. What does it take to be a good American? Suddenly there are demands for Italian power and Polish power and Ukrainian power. In Cleveland the Poles demand a seat on the school board, and get it, and in Pittsburgh John Pankuch, the seventy-three-year-old president of the National Slovak Society demands "action, plenty of it to make up for lost time." Black power is supposed to be nothing but emulation of the ways in which other ethnic groups made it. But have they made it? In Reardon's Bar on East Eighth Street in South Boston, where the workmen come for their fish-chowder lunch and for their rye and ginger, they still identify themselves as Galway men and Kilkenny men; in the newsstand in Astoria you can buy *Il Progresso, El Tiempo,* the *Staats-Zeitung,* the *Irish World,* plus papers in Greek, Hungarian, and Polish. At the parish of Our Lady of Mount Carmel the priests hear confession in English, Italian, and Spanish and, nearby, the biggest attraction is not the stickball game, but the *bocce* court. Some of the poorest people in America are white, native, and have lived all of their lives in the same place as their fathers and grandfathers. The problems that were presumably solved in some distant past, in that prehistoric era before the textbooks were written— problems of assimilation, of upward mobility—now turn out to be very much unsolved. The melting pot and all: millions made it, millions moved to the affluent suburbs; several million—no one knows how many—did not. The median income in Irish South Boston is $5,100 a year but the community-action workers have a hard time convincing the local citizens that any white man who is not stupid or irresponsible can be poor. Pride still keeps them from applying for income supplements or Medicaid, but it does not keep them from resenting those who do. In Pittsburgh, where the members of Polish-American organizations earn an estimated $5,000 to $6,000 (and some fall below the poverty line), the Poverty Programs are nonetheless directed primarily to Negroes, and almost everywhere the thing called urban backlash associates itself in some fashion with ethnic groups whose members have themselves only a precarious hold on the security of affluence. Almost everywhere in the old cities, tribal neighborhoods and their styles are under assault by masscult. The Italian grocery gives way to the supermarket, the ma-and-pa store and the walk-up are attacked by urban renewal. And almost everywhere, that assault tends to depersonalize and to alienate. It has always been this way, but with time the brave new world that replaces old patterns becomes increasingly bureaucratized, distant, and hard to control.

Yet beyond the problems of ethnic identity, beyond the problems of Poles and Irishmen left behind, there are others more pervasive and more dangerous. For every Greek or Hungarian there are a dozen American-Americans who are past ethnic consciousness and who are as alienated, as confused, and as angry as the rest. The obvious manifestations are the same everywhere—race, taxes, welfare, students—but the threat seems invariably more cultural and psychological than economic or social. What upset the police at the Chicago convention most was not so much the politics of the demonstrators as their manners and their hair. (The barbershops in their neighborhoods don't advertise Beatle Cuts but the Flat Top and the Chicago Box.) The affront comes from middle-class people—and their children—who had been cast in the role of social exemplars (and from those cast as unfortunates worthy of public charity) who offend all the things on which working class identity is built: "hippies [said a San Francisco longshoreman] who fart around the streets and don't work"; welfare recipients who strike and march for better treatment; "all those [said a California labor official] who challenge the precepts that these people live on." If ethnic groups are beginning to organize to get theirs, so are others: police and firemen ("The cop is the new nigger"); schoolteachers; lower-middle-class housewives fighting sex education and busing; small property owners who have no ethnic communion but a passionate interest in lower taxes, more policemen, and stiffer penalties for criminals. In San Francisco the Teamsters, who had never been known for such interests before, recently demonstrated in support of the police and law enforcement and, on another occasion, joined a group called Mothers Support Neighborhood Schools at a school-board meeting to oppose—with their presence and later, apparently, with their fists—a proposal to integrate the schools through busing. ("These people," someone said at the meeting, "do not look like mothers.")

Which is not to say that all is frustration and anger, that anybody is ready "to burn the country down." They are not even ready to elect standard model demagogues. "A lot of labor people who thought of voting for Wallace were ashamed of themselves when they realized what they were about to do," said Morris Iushewitz, an officer of New York's Central Labor Council. Because of a massive last-minute union campaign, and perhaps for other reasons, the blue-collar vote for Wallace fell far below the figures predicted by the early polls last fall. Any number of people, moreover, who are not doing well by any set of official statistics, who are earning well below the national mean ($8,000 a year), or who hold two jobs to stay above it, think of themselves as affluent, and often use that word. It is almost as if not to be affluent is to be un-American.

People who can't use the word tend to be angry; people who come too close to those who can't become frightened. The definition of affluence is generally pinned to what comes in, not to the qualify of life as it's lived. The $8,000 son of a man who never earned more than $4,500 may, for that reason alone, believe that he's "doing all right." If life is not all right, if he can't get his curbs fixed, or his streets patrolled, if the highways are crowded and the beaches polluted, if the schools are ineffectual he is still able to call himself affluent, feels, perhaps, a social compulsion to do so. His anger, if he is angry, is not that of the wage earner, resenting management—and certainly not that of the socialist ideologue asking for redistribution of wealth—but that of the consumer, the taxpayer, and the family man. (Inflation and taxes are wiping out most of the wage gains made in labor contracts signed during the past three years.) Thus he will vote for a Louise Day Hicks in Boston who promises to hold the color line in the schools or for a Charles Stenvig calling for law enforcement in Minneapolis but reject a George Wallace who seems to threaten his pocketbook. The danger is that he will identify with the politics of the Birchers and other middle-class reactionaries (who often pretend to speak for him) even though his income and style of life are far removed from theirs; that taxes, for example, will be identified with welfare rather than war, and that he will blame his limited means on the small slice of the poor rather than the fat slice of the rich.

If you sit and talk to people like Marjorie Lemlow, who heads Mothers Support Neighborhood Schools in San Francisco, or Joe Owens, a house painter who is president of a community-action organization in Boston, you quickly discover that the roots of reaction and the roots of reform are often identical, and that the response to particular situations is more often contingent on the politics of the politicians and leaders who appear to care than on the conditions of life or the ideology of the victims. Mrs. Lemlow wants to return the schools to some virtuous past; she worries about disintegration of the family and she speaks vaguely about something that she can't bring herself to call a conspiracy against Americanism. She has been accused of leading a bunch of Birchers, and she sometimes talks Birch language. But whatever the form, her sense of things comes from a small-town vision of national virtues, and her unhappiness from the assaults of urban sophistication. It just so happens that a lot of reactionaries now sing that tune, and that the liberals are indifferent.

Joe Owens—probably because of his experience as a Head Start parent, and because of his association with an effective community-action program—talks a different language. He knows, somehow, that no simple past can be restored. In his world the villains are not conspirators but bureaucrats and politicians, and he is beginning to discover that in a struggle with officials the black man in the ghetto and the working man (black or white) have the same problems. "Every time you ask for something from the politicians they treat you like a beggar, like you ought to be grateful for what you have. They try to make you feel ashamed."

When hope becomes a threat

The imponderables are youth and tradition and change. The civics book and the institution it celebrates—however passé—still hold the world together. The revolt is in their name, not against them. And there is simple decency, the language and practice of the folksy cliché, the small town, the Boy Scout virtues, the neighborhood charity, the obligation to support the church, the rhetoric of open opportunity: "They can keep Wallace and they can keep Alabama. We didn't fight a dictator for four years so we could elect one over here." What happens when all that becomes Mickey Mouse? Is there an urban ethic to replace the values of the small town? Is there a coherent public philosophy, a consistent set of beliefs to replace family, home, and hard work? What happens when the hang-ups of upper-middle-class kids are in fashion and those of blue-collar kids are not? What happens when Doing Your Own Thing becomes not the slogan of the solitary deviant but the norm? Is it possible that as the institutions and beliefs of tradition are fashionably denigrated a blue-collar generation gap will open to the Right as well as to the Left? (There is statistical evidence, for example, that Wallace's greatest support within the unions came from people who are between twenty-one and twenty-nine, those, that is, who have the most tenuous association with the liberalism of labor.) Most are politically silent; although SDS has been trying to organize blue-collar high-school students, there are no Mario Savios or Mark Rudds—either of the Right or the Left—among them. At the same time the union leaders, some of them old hands from the Thirties, aren't sure that the kids are following them either. Who speaks for the son of the longshoreman or the Detroit auto worker? What happens if he doesn't get to college? What, indeed, happens when he does?

Vaguely but unmistakably the hopes that a youth-worshiping nation historically invested in its young are becoming threats. We have never been unequivocal about the symbolic patricide of Americanization and upward mobility, but if at one time mobility meant rejection of older (or European) styles it was, at least, done in the name of America. Now the labels are blurred and the objectives indistinct. Just at the moment when a tradition-bound Italian father is persuaded that he should send his sons to college—that education is the only future—the college blows up. At the moment when a parsimonious taxpayer begins to shell out for what he considers an extravagant state university system the students go on strike. Marijuana, sexual liberation, dress styles, draft resistance, even the rhetoric of change become monsters and demons in a world that appears to turn old virtues upside down. The paranoia that fastened on Communism twenty years ago (and sometimes still does) is increasingly directed to vague conspiracies undermining the schools, the family, order and discipline. "They're feeding the kids this generation-gap business," says a Chicago housewife who grinds out a campaign against sex education on a duplicating machine in her living room. "The kids are told to make their own decisions. They're all mixed up by situation ethics and open-ended questions. They're alienating children from their own parents." They? The churches, the schools, even the YMCA and the Girl Scouts, are implicated. But a major share of the villainy is now also attributed to "the social science centers," to the apostles of sensitivity training, and to what one California lady, with some embarrassment, called "nude therapy." "People with sane minds are being altered by psychological methods." The current major campaign of the John Birch Society is not directed against Communists in government or the Supreme Court, but against sex education.

(There is, of course, also sympathy with the young, especially in poorer areas where kids have no place to play. "Everybody's got to have a hobby," a South Boston adolescent told a youth worker. "Ours is throwing rocks." If people will join reactionary organizations to protect their children, they will also support others: community-action agencies which help kids get jobs; Head Start parent groups, Boys Clubs. "Getting this place cleaned up" sometimes refers to a fear of young hoods; sometimes it points to the day when there is a park or a playground or when the existing park can be used. "I want to see them grow up to have a little fun.")

Can the common man come back?

Beneath it all there is a more fundamental ambivalence, not only about the young, but about institutions—the schools, the churches, the Establishment—and about the future itself. In the major cities of the East (though perhaps not in the West) there is a sense that time is against you, that one is living "in one of the few decent neighborhoods left," that "if I can get $125 a week upstate (or downstate) I'll move." The institutions that were supposed to mediate social change and which, more than ever, are becoming priesthoods of information and conglomerates of social engineers, are increasingly suspect. To attack the Ford Foundation (as Wright Patman has done) is not only to fan the embers of historic populism against wealth and power, but also to arouse those who feel that they are trapped by an alliance of upper-class Wasps and lower-class Negroes. If the foundations have done anything for the blue-collar worker he doesn't seem to be aware of it. At the same time the distrust of professional educators that characterizes the black militants is becoming increasingly prevalent among a minority of lower-middle-class whites who are beginning to discover that the schools aren't working for them either. ("Are all those new programs just a cover-up for failure?") And if the Catholic Church is under attack from its liberal members (on birth control, for example) it is also alienating the traditionalists who liked their minor saints (even if they didn't actually exist) and were perfectly content with the Latin Mass. For the alienated Catholic liberal there are other places to go; for the lower-middle-class parishioner in Chicago or Boston there are none.

Perhaps, in some measure, it has always been this way. Perhaps none of this is new. And perhaps it is also true that the American lower middle has never had it so good. And yet surely there is a difference, and that is that the common man has lost his visibility and, somehow, his claim on public attention. There are old liberals and socialists—men like Michael Harrington—who believe that a new alliance can be forged for progressive social action:

> From Marx to Mills, the Left has regarded the middle class as a stratum of hypocritical, vacillating rear-guarders. There was often sound reason for this contempt. But is it not possible that a new class is coming into being? It is not the old middle class of small property owners and entrepreneurs, nor the new middle class of managers. It is composed of scientists, technicians, teachers, and professionals in the public sector of the society. By education and work experience it is predisposed toward planning. It could be an ally of the poor and the organized workers—or their sophisticated enemy. In other words, an unprecedented social and political variable seems to be taking shape in America.
>
> The American worker, even when he waits on a table or holds open a door, is not servile; he does not carry himself like an inferior. The openness, frankness, and democratic manner which Tocqueville described in the last century persists to this very day. They have been a source of rudeness, contemptuous ignorance, violence—and of a creative self-confidence among great masses of people. It was in this latter spirit that the CIO was organized and the black freedom movement marched.

There are recent indications that the white lower middle class is coming back on the roster of public priorities. Pucinski tells you that liberals in Congress are privately discussing the pressure from the middle class. There are proposals now to increase personal income-tax exemptions from $600 to $1,000 (or $1,200) for each dependent, to protect all Americans with a national insurance system covering catastrophic medical expenses, and to put a floor under all incomes. Yet these things by themselves are insufficient. Nothing is sufficient without a national sense of restoration. What Pucinski means by the middle class has, in some measure, always been represented. A physician earning $75,000 a year is also a working man but he is hardly a victim of the welfare system. Nor, by and large, are the stockholders of the Standard Oil Company or U. S. Steel. The fact that American ideals have often been corrupted in the cause of self-aggrandizement does not make them any less important for the cause of social reform and justice. "As a movement with the conviction that there is more to people than greed and fear," Harrington said, "the Left must . . . also speak in the name of the historic idealism of the United States."

The issue, finally, is not *the program* but the vision, the angle of view. A huge constituency may be coming up for grabs, and there is considerable evidence that its political mobility is more sensitive than anyone can imagine, that all the sociological determinants are not as significant as the simple facts of concern and leadership. When Robert Kennedy was killed last year, thousands of working-class people who had expected to vote for him—if not hundreds of thousands—shifted their loyalties to Wallace. A man who can change from a progressive democrat into a bigot overnight deserves attention.

14

ROBERT COLES, Like It Is in the Alley

"In the alley it's mostly dark, even if the sun is out. But if you look around, you can find things. I know how to get into every building, except that it's like night once you're inside them, because they don't have lights. So, I stay here. You're better off. It's no good on the street. You can get hurt all the time, one way or the other. And in buildings, like I told you, it's bad in them, too. But here it's o.k. You can find your own corner, and if someone tries to move in you fight him off. We meet here all the time, and figure out what we'll do next. It might be a game, or over for some pool, or a coke or something. You need to have a place to start our from, and that's like it is in the alley; you can always know your buddy will be there, provided it's the right time. So you go there, and you're on your way, man."

Like all children of nine, Peter is always on his way—to a person, a place, a "thing" he wants to do. *"There's this here thing we thought we'd try tomorrow,"* he'll say; and eventually I'll find out that he means there's to be a race. He and his friends will compete with another gang to see who can wash a car faster and better. The cars belong to four youths who make their money taking bets, and selling liquor that I don't believe was ever purchased, and pushing a few of those pills that *"go classy with beer."* I am not completely sure, but I think they also have something to do with other drugs; and again, I can't quite be sure what their connection is with a "residence" I've seen not too far from the alley Peter describes so possessively. The women come and go—from that residence and along the street Peter's alley leaves.

Peter lives in the heart of what we in contemporary America have chosen (ironically, so far as history goes) to call an "urban ghetto." The area was a slum before it became a ghetto, and there still are some very poor white people on its edges and increasing numbers of Puerto Ricans in several of its blocks. Peter was not born in the ghetto, nor was his family told to go there. They are Americans and have been here *"since way back before anyone can remember."* That is the way Peter's mother talks about Alabama, about the length of time she and her ancestors have lived there. She and Peter's father came north *"for freedom."* They did not seek out a ghetto, an old quarter of Boston where they were expected to live and where they would be confined, yet at least some of the time solidly at rest, with kin, and reasonably safe.

No, they sought freedom. Americans, they moved on when the going got *"real bad,"* and Americans, they expected something better someplace, some

Robert Coles, "Like It Is in the Alley," *Daedalus,* vol. 97, no. 4 (Fall 1968), pp. 1315–1330. Reprinted by permission.

other place. They left Alabama on impulse. They found Peter's alley by accident. And they do not fear pogroms. They are Americans, and in Peter's words: *"There's likely to be another riot here soon. That's what I heard today. You hear it a lot, but one day you know it'll happen."*

Peter's mother fears riots too—among other things. The Jews of Eastern Europe huddled together in their ghettos, afraid of the barbarians, afraid of the *Goyim,* but always sure of one thing, their God-given destiny. Peter's mother has no such faith. She believes that *"something will work out one of these days."* She believes that *"you have to keep on going, and things can get better, but don't ask me how."* She believes that *"God wants us to have a bad spell here, and so maybe it'll get better the next time—you know in Heaven, and I hope that's where we'll be going."* Peter's mother, in other words, is a pragmatist, an optimist, and a Christian. Above all she is American: *"Yes, I hear them talk about Africa, but it don't mean anything to us. All I know is Alabama and now it's in Massachusetts that we are. It was a long trip coming up here, and sometimes I wish we were back there, and sometimes I'd just as soon be here, for all that's no good about it. But I'm not going to take any more trips, no sir. And like Peter said, this is the only country we've got. If you come from a country, you come from it, and we're from it, I'd say, and there isn't much we can do but try to live as best we can. I mean, live here."*

What is "life" like for her over there, where she lives, in the neighborhood she refers to as "here"? A question like that cannot be answered by the likes of me, and even her answer provides only the beginning of a reply: *"Well, we does o.k., I guess. Peter here, he has it better than I did, or his daddy. I can say that. I tell myself that a lot. He can turn on the faucet over there, and a lot of the time, he just gets the water, right away. And when I tell him what it was like for us, to go fetch that water—we'd walk three miles, yes sir, and we'd be lucky it wasn't ten—well, Peter, it doesn't register on him. He thinks I'm trying to fool him, and the more serious I get, the more he laughs, so I've stopped.*

"Of course it's not all so good, I have to admit. We're still where we were, so far as knowing where your next meal is coming from. When I go to bed at night I tell myself I've done good, to stay alive and keep the kids alive, and if they'll just wake up in the morning, and me too, well then, we can worry about that, all the rest, come tomorrow. So there you go. We do our best, and that's all you can do."

She may sound fatalistic, but she appears to be a nervous, hard-working, even hard-driven woman—thin, short, constantly on the move. I may not know what she "really" thinks and believes, because like the rest of us she has her contradictions and her mixed feelings. I think it is fair to say that there are some things that she can't say to me—or to herself. She is a Negro, and I am white. She is poor, and I am fairly well off. She is very near to illiterate, and I put in a lot of time worrying about how to say things. But she and I are both human beings, and we both have trouble—to use that word—"communicating," not only with each other, but with ourselves. Sometimes she doesn't tell me something she really wants me to know. She has forgotten, pure and simple. More is on her mind than information I might want. And sometimes I forget too: *"Remember you asked the other day about Peter, if he was ever real sick. And I told you he was a weak child, and I feared for his life, and I've lost five children, three that was born and two that wasn't. Well, I forgot to tell you that he got real sick up here, just after we came. He was three, and I didn't know what to do. You see, I didn't have my mother to help out. She always knew what to do. She could hold a child and get him to stop crying, no matter how sick he was, and no matter how much he wanted food, and we didn't have it. But she was gone—and that's when we left to come up here, and I never would have left her, not for anything in the world. But suddenly she took a seizure of something and went in a half hour, I'd say. And Peter, he was so hot and sick, I thought he had the same thing his grandmother did and he was going to die. I thought maybe she's calling him. She always liked Peter. She helped him be born, she and my cousin, they did."*

Actually, Peter's mother remembers quite a lot of things. She remembers the "old days" back South, sometimes with a shudder, but sometimes with the same nostalgia that the region is famous for generating in its white exiles. She also notices a lot of things. She notices, and from time to time will remark upon, the various changes in her life. She has moved from the country to the city. Her father was a sharecropper and her son wants to be a pilot (sometimes), a policeman (sometimes), a racing-car driver (sometimes), and a baseball player (most of the time). Her husband is not alive. He died one year after they all came to Boston. He woke up vomiting in the middle of the night—vomiting blood. He bled and bled and vomited and vomited and then he died. The doctor does not have to press very hard for "the facts." Whatever is known gets spoken vividly and (still) emotionally: *"I didn't know what to do. I was beside myself. I prayed and I prayed, and in between I held his head and wiped his forehead. It was the middle of the night. I woke up my oldest girl and I told her to go knocking on the doors. But no one would answer. They must have been scared, or have suspected something bad. I thought if only he'd be able to last into the morning, then we could get some help. I was caught between things. I couldn't leave him to go get a policeman. And my girl, she was afraid to go out. And besides, there was no one outside, and I thought we'd just stay at his side, and somehow he'd be o.k., because he was a strong man, you know. His muscles, they were big all his life. Even with the blood coming up, he looked too big and strong to die, I thought. But I knew he was sick. He was real bad sick. There wasn't anything else, no sir, to do. We didn't have no phone and even if there was a car, I never could have used it. Nor my daughter. And then he took a big breath and that was his last one."*

When I first met Peter and his mother, I wanted to know how they lived, what they did with their time, what they liked to do or disliked doing, what they believed. In the back of my mind were large subjects like "the connection between a person's moods and the environment in which he lives." Once I was told I was studying "the psychology of the ghetto," and another time the subject of "urban poverty and mental health." It is hoped that at some point large issues like those submit themselves to lives; and when that is done, when particular but not unrepresentative or unusual human beings are called in witness, their concrete medical history becomes extremely revealing. I cannot think of a better way to begin knowing what life is like for Peter and his mother than to hear the following and hear it again and think about its implications: *"No sir, Peter has never been to a doctor, not unless you count the one at school, and she's a nurse I believe. He was his sickest back home before we came here, and you know there was no doctor for us in the county. In Alabama you have to pay a white doctor first, before he'll go near you. And we don't have but a few colored ones. (I've never seen a one.) There was this woman we'd go to, and she had gotten some nursing education in Mobile. (No, I don't know if she was a nurse or not, or a helper to the nurses, maybe.) Well, she would come to help us. With the convulsions, she'd show you how to hold the child, and make sure he doesn't hurt himself. They can bite their tongues, real, real bad.*

"Here, I don't know what to do. There's the city hospital, but it's no good for us. I went there with my husband, no sooner than a month or so after we came up here. We waited and waited, and finally the day was almost over. We left the kids with a neighbor, and we barely knew her. I said it would take the morning, but I never thought we'd get home near suppertime. And they wanted us to come back and come back, because it was something they couldn't do all at once—though for most of the time we just sat there and did nothing. And my husband, he said his stomach was the worse for going there, and he'd take care of himself from now on, rather than go there.

"Maybe they could have saved him. But they're far away, and I didn't have money to get a cab, even if there was one around here, and I thought to myself it'll make him worse, to take him there.

"My kids, they get sick. The welfare worker, she sends a nurse here, and she tells me we should be on vitamins and the kids need all kinds of check-ups. Once she took my daughter and told her she had to have her teeth looked at, and the same with Peter. So, I went with my daughter, and they didn't see me that day, but said they could in a couple of weeks. And I had to pay the woman next door to mind the little ones, and there was the carfare, and we sat and sat, like before. So, I figured, it would take more than we've got to see that dentist. And when the nurse told us we'd have to come back a few times—that's how many, a few—I thought that no one ever looked at my teeth, and they're not good, I'll admit, but you can't have everything, that's what I say, and that's what my kids have to know, I guess."

What *does* she have? And what belongs to Peter? For one thing, there is the apartment, three rooms for six people, a mother and five children. Peter is a middle child with two older girls on one side and a younger sister and still younger brother on the other side. The smallest child was born in Boston: *"It's the only time I ever spent in a hospital. He's the only one to be born there. My neighbor got the police. I was in the hall, crying I guess. We almost didn't make it. They told me I had bad blood pressure, and I should have been on pills, and I should come back, but I didn't. It was the worst time I've ever had, because I was alone. My husband had to stay with the kids, and no one was there to visit me."*

Peter sleeps with his brother in one bedroom. The three girls sleep in the living room, which is a bedroom. And, of course, there is a small kitchen. There is not very much furniture about. The kitchen has a table with four chairs, only two of which are sturdy. The girls sleep in one big bed. Peter shares his bed with his brother. The mother sleeps on a couch. There is one more chair and a table in the living room. Jesus looks down from the living room wall, and an undertaker's calendar hangs on the kitchen wall. The apartment has no books, no records. There is a television set in the living room, and I have never seen it off.

Peter in many respects is his father's successor. His mother talks things over with him. She even defers to him at times. She will say something; he will disagree; she will nod and let him have the last word. He knows the city. She still feels a stranger to the city. *"If you want to know about anything around here, just ask Peter,"* she once said to me. That was three years ago, when Peter was six. Peter continues to do very poorly at school, but I find him a very good teacher. He notices a lot, makes a lot of sense when he talks, and has a shrewd eye for the ironic detail. He is very intelligent, for all the trouble he gives his teachers. He recently summed up a lot of American history for me: *"I wasn't made for that school, and that school wasn't made for me."* It is an old school, filled with memories. The name of the school evokes Boston's Puritan past. Pictures and statues adorn the corridors—reminders of the soldiers and statesmen and writers who made New England so influential in the nineteenth century. And naturally one finds slogans on the walls, about freedom and democracy and the rights of the people. Peter can be surly and cynical when he points all that out to the visitor. If he is asked what kind of school he would *like*, he laughs incredulously. *"Are you kidding? No school would be my first choice. They should leave us alone, and let us help out at home, and maybe let some of our own people teach us. The other day the teacher admitted she was no good. She said maybe a Negro should come in and give us the discipline, because she was scared. She said all she wanted from us was that we keep quiet and stop wearing her nerves down, and she'd be grateful, because she would retire soon. She said we were becoming too much for her, and she didn't understand why. But when one kid wanted to say something, tell her why, she told us to keep still, and write something. You know what? She whipped out a book and told us to copy a whole page from it, so we'd learn it. A stupid waste of time. I didn't even try; and she didn't care. She just wanted an excuse not to talk with us. They're all alike."*

Actually, they're all *not* alike, and Peter knows it. He has met up with two fine teachers, and in mellow moments he can say so: *"They're trying hard, but me and my friends, I don't think we're cut out for school. To tell the truth, that's what I think. My mother says we should try, anyway, but it doesn't seem to help, trying. The teacher can't understand a lot of us, but he does all these new things, and you can see he's excited. Some kids are really with him, and I am, too. But I can't take all his stuff very serious. He's a nice man, and he says he wants to come and visit every one of our homes; but my mother says no, she wouldn't know what to do with him, when he came here. We'd just stand and have nothing to talk about. So she said tell him not to come; and I don't think he will, anyway. I think he's getting to know."*

What is that teacher getting to know? What *is* there to know about Peter and all the others like him in our American cities? Of course Peter and his friends who play in the alley need better schools, schools they can feel to be theirs, and better teachers, like the ones they *have* in fact met on occasion. But I do not feel that a reasonably good teacher in the finest school building in America would reach and affect Peter in quite the way, I suppose, people like me would expect and desire. At nine Peter is both young and quite old. At nine he is much wiser about many things than my sons will be at nine, and maybe nineteen. Peter has in fact taught me a lot about his neighborhood, about life on the streets, about survival: *"I get up when I get up, no special time. My mother has Alabama in her. She gets up with the sun, and she wants to go to bed when it gets dark. I try to tell her that up here things just get started in the night. But she gets mad. She wakes me up. If it weren't for her shaking me, I might sleep until noon. Sometimes we have a good breakfast, when the check comes. Later on, though, before it comes, it might just be some coffee and a slice of bread. She worries about food. She says we should eat what she gives us, but sometimes I'd rather go hungry. I was sick a long time ago, my stomach or something—maybe like my father, she says. So I don't like all the potatoes she pushes on us and cereal, all the time cereal. We're supposed to be lucky, because we get some food every day. Down South they can't be sure. That's what she says, and I guess she's right.*

"Then I go to school. I eat what I can, and leave. I have two changes of clothes, one for everyday and one for Sunday. I wait on my friend Billy, and we're off by 8:15. He's from around here, and he's a year older. He knows everything. He can tell you if a woman is high on some stuff, or if she's been drinking, or she's off her mind about something. He knows. His brother has a convertible, a Buick. He pays off the police, but Billy won't say no more than that.

"In school we waste time until it's over. I do what I have to. I don't like the place. I feel like falling off all day, just putting my head down and saying good-bye to everyone until three. We're out then, and we sure wake up. I don't have to stop home first, not now. I go with Billy. We'll be in the alley, or we'll go to see them play pool. Then you know when it's time to go home. You hear someone say six o'clock, and you go in. I eat and I watch television. It must be around ten or eleven I'm in bed."

Peter sees rats all the time. He has been bitten by them. He has a big stick by his bed to use against them. They also claim the alley, even in the daytime. They are not large enough to be compared with cats, as some observers have insisted; they are simply large, confident, well-fed, unafraid rats. The garbage is theirs; the tenement is theirs; human flesh is theirs. When I first started visiting Peter's family, I wondered why they didn't do something to rid themselves of those rats, and the cockroaches, and the mosquitoes, and the flies, and the maggots, and the ants, and especially the garbage in the alley which attracts so much of all that "lower life." Eventually I began to see some of the reasons why. A large apartment building with many families has exactly two barrels in its basement. The halls of the building go unlighted. Many windows have no screens, and some windows are broken and boarded up. The stairs are dangerous; some of them have missing timber. (*"We just jump over them,"* says Peter cheerfully.) And the landowner is no one in particular. Rent is collected by an agent, in the name of a "realty trust." Somewhere in City Hall there is a bureaucrat who unquestionably might be persuaded to prod someone in the "trust"; and one day I went with three of the tenants, including Peter's mother, to try that "approach." We waited and waited at City Hall. (I drove us there, clear across town, naturally.) Finally we met up with a man, a not very encouraging or inspiring or generous or friendly man. He told us we would have to try yet another department and swear out a complaint; and that the "case" would have to be "studied," and that we would then be "notified of a decision." We went to the department down the hall, and waited some more, another hour and ten minutes. By then it was three o'clock, and the mothers wanted to go home. They weren't thinking of rats anymore, or poorly heated apartments, or garbage that had nowhere to go and often went uncollected for two weeks, not one. They were thinking of their children, who would be home from school and, in the case of two women, their husbands who would also soon be home. *"Maybe we should come back some other day,"* Peter's mother said. I noted she didn't say *tomorrow*, and I realized that I had read someplace that people like her aren't precisely "future-oriented."

Actually, both Peter and his mother have a very clear idea of what is ahead. For the mother it is *"more of the same."* One evening she was tired but unusually talkative, perhaps because a daughter of hers was sick: *"I'm glad to be speaking about all these things tonight. My little girl has a bad fever. I've been trying to cool her off all day. Maybe if there was a place near here, that we could go to, maybe I would have gone. But like it is, I have to do the best I can and pray she'll be o.k."*

I asked whether she thought her children would find things different, and that's when she said it would be *"more of the same"* for them. Then she added a long afterthought: *"Maybe it'll be a little better for them. A mother has to have hope for her children, I guess. But I'm not too sure, I'll admit. Up here you know there's a lot more jobs around than in Alabama. We don't get them, but you know they're someplace near, and they tell you that if you go train for them, then you'll be eligible. So maybe Peter might someday have some real good steady work, and that would be something, yes sir it would. I keep telling him he should pay more attention to school, and put more of himself into the lessons they give there. But he says no, it's no good; it's a waste of time; they don't care what happens there, only if the kids don't keep quiet and mind themselves. Well, Peter has got to learn to mind himself, and not be fresh. He speaks back to me, these days. There'll be a time he won't even speak to me at all, I suppose. I used to blame it all on the city up here, city living. Back home we were always together, and there wasn't no place you could go, unless to Birmingham, and you couldn't do much for yourself there, we all knew. Of course, my momma, she knew how to make us behave. But I was thinking the other night, it wasn't so good back there either. Colored people, they'd beat on one another, and we had lot of people that liquor was eating away at them; they'd use wine by the gallon. All they'd do was work on the land, and then go back and kill themselves with wine. And then there'd be the next day—until they'd one evening go to sleep and never wake up. And we'd get the Bossman and he'd see to it they got buried.*

"*Up here I think it's better, but don't ask me to tell you why. There's the welfare, that's for sure. And we get our water and if there isn't good heat, at least there's some. Yes, it's cold up here, but we had cold down there, too, only then we didn't have any heat, and we'd just die, some of us would, every winter with one of those freezing spells.*

"*And I do believe things are changing. On the television they talk to you, the colored man and all the others who aren't doing so good. My boy Peter, he says they're putting you on. That's all he sees, people "putting on" other people. But I think they all mean it, the white people. I never see them, except on television, when they say the white man wants good for the colored people. I think Peter could go and do better for himself later on, when he gets older, except for the fact that he just doesn't* believe. *He don't believe what they say, the teacher, or the man who says it's getting better for us—on television. I guess it's my fault. I never taught my children, any of them, to believe that kind of thing; because I never thought we'd ever have it any different, not in this life. So maybe I've failed Peter. I told him the other day, he should work hard, because of all the 'opportunity' they say is coming for us, and he said I was talking good, but where was my proof. So I went next door with him, to my neighbor's, and we asked her husband, and you know he sided with Peter. He said they were taking in a few here and a few there, and putting them in the front windows of all the big companies, but that all you have to do is look around at our block and you'd see all the young men, and they just haven't got a thing to do. Nothing.*"

Her son also looks to the future. Sometimes he talks—in his own words—"big." He'll one day be a bombadier or "*something like that.*" At other times he is less sure of things: "*I don't know what I'll be. Maybe nothing. I see the men sitting around, hiding from the welfare lady. They fool her. Maybe I'll fool her, too. I don't know what you can do. The teacher the other day said that if just one of us turned out o.k. she'd congratulate herself and call herself lucky.*"

A while back a riot excited Peter and his mother, excited them and frightened them. The spectacle of the police being fought, of white-owned property being assaulted, stirred the boy a great deal: "*I figured the whole world might get changed around. I figured people would treat us better from now on. Only I don't think they will,"* As for his mother, she was less hopeful, but even more apocalyptic: *"I told Peter we were going to pay for this good. I told him they wouldn't let us get away with it, not later on."* And in the midst of the trouble she was frightened as she had never before been: *"I saw them running around on the streets, the men and women, and they were talking about burning things down, and how there'd be nothing left when they got through. I sat there with my children and I thought we might die the way things are going, die right here. I didn't know what to do: if I should leave, in case they burn down the building, or if I should stay, so that the police don't arrest us, or we get mixed up with the crowd of people. I've never seen so many people, going in so many different directions. They were running and shouting and they didn't know what to do. They were so excited. My neighbor, she said they'd burn us all up, and then the white man would have himself one less of a headache. The colored man is a worse enemy to himself than the white. I mean, it's hard to know which is the worst."*

I find it as hard as she does to sort things out. When I think of her and the mothers like her I have worked with for years, when I think of Peter and his friends, I find myself caught between the contradictory observations I have made. Peter already seems a grim and unhappy child. He trusts no one white, not his white teacher, not the white policeman he sees, not the white welfare worker, not the white storekeeper, and not, I might add, me. There we are, the five of us from the 180,000,000 Americans who surround him and of course 20,000,000 others. Yet, Peter doesn't really trust his friends and neighbors, either. At nine he has learned to be careful, wary, guarded, doubtful, and calculating. His teacher may not know it, but Peter is a good sociologist, and a good political scientist, a good student of urban affairs. With devastating accuracy he can reveal how much of the "score" he knows; yes, and how fearful and sad and angry he is: *"This here city isn't for us. It's for the people downtown. We're here because, like my mother said, we had to come. If they could lock us up or sweep us away, they would. That's why I figure the only way you can stay ahead is get some kind of deal for yourself. If I had a choice I'd live someplace else, but I don't know where. It would be a place where they treated you right, and they didn't think you were some nuisance. But the only thing you can do is be careful of yourself; if not, you'll get killed somehow, like it happened to my father."*

His father died prematurely, and most probably, unnecessarily. Among the poor of our cities the grim medical statistics we all know about become terrible daily experiences. Among the black and white families I work with—in nearby but separate slums—disease and the pain that goes with it are taken for granted. When my children complain of an earache or demonstrate a skin rash I rush them to the doctor. When I have a headache, I take an aspirin; and if the headache is persistent, I can always get a medical check-up. Not so with Peter's mother and Peter; they have learned to live with sores and infections and poorly mended fractures and bad teeth and eyes that need but don't have the help of glasses. Yes, they can go to a city hospital and get free care; but again and again they don't. They come to the city without any previous experience as patients.

They have never had the money to purchase a doctor's time. They have never had free medical care available. (I am speaking now of Appalachian whites as well as southern blacks.) It may comfort me to know that every American city provides some free medical services for its "indigent," but Peter's mother and thousands like her have quite a different view of things: *"I said to you the other time, I've tried there. It's like at City Hall, you wait and wait, and they pushes you and shove you and call your name, only to tell you to wait some more, and if you tell them you can't stay there all day, they'll say 'lady, go home, then.' You get sick just trying to get there. You have to give your children over to people or take them all with you; and the carfare is expensive. Why if we had a doctor around here, I could almost pay him with the carfare it takes to get there and back for all of us. And you know, they keep on having you come back and back, and they don't know what each other says. Each time they starts from scratch."*

It so happens that recently I took Peter to a children's hospital and arranged for a series of evaluations which led to the following: a pair of glasses; a prolonged bout of dental work; antibiotic treatment for skin lesions; a thorough cardiac work-up, with the subsequent diagnosis of rheumatic heart disease, a conference between Peter's mother and a nutritionist, because the boy has been on a high-starch, low-protein, and low-vitamin diet all his life. He suffers from one attack of sinus trouble after another, from a succession of sore throats and earaches, from cold upon cold, even in the summer. A running nose is unsurprising to him—and so is chest pain and shortness of breath, due to a heart ailment, we now know.

At the same time Peter is tough. I have to emphasize again *how* tough and, yes, how "politic, cautious and meticulous," not in Prufrock's way, but in another way and for other reasons. Peter has learned to be wary as well as angry; tentative as well as extravagant; at times controlled and only under certain circumstances defiant: *"Most of the time, I think you have to watch your step. That's what I think. That's the difference between up here and down in the South. That's what my mother says, and she's right. I don't remember it down there, but I know she must be right. Here, you measure the next guy first and then make your move when you think it's a good time to."*

He was talking about *"how you get along"* when you leave school and go *"mix with the guys"* and start *"getting your deal."* He was telling me what an outrageous and unsafe world he has inherited and how very carefully he has made his appraisal of the future. Were I afflicted with some of his physical complaints, I would be fretful, annoyed, petulant, angry—and moved to do something, see someone, get a remedy, a pill, a promise of help. He has made his "adjustment" to the body's pain, and he has also learned to contend with the alley and the neighborhood and *us*, the world beyond: *"The cops come by here all the time. They drive up and down the street. They want to make sure everything is o.k. to look at. They don't bother you, so long as you don't get in their way."*

So, it is live and let live—except that families like Peter's have a tough time living, and of late have been troubling those cops, among others. Our cities have become not only battlegrounds, but places where all sorts of American problems and historical ironies have converged. Ailing, poorly fed, and proud Appalachian families have reluctantly left the hollows of eastern Kentucky and West Virginia for Chicago and Dayton and Cincinnati and Cleveland and Detroit, and even, I have found, Boston. They stick close together in all-white neighborhoods—or enclaves or sections or slums or ghettos or whatever. They wish to go home but can't, unless they are willing to be idle and hungry all the time. They confuse social workers and public officials of all kinds because they want and reject the city. Black families have also sought out cities and learned to feel frightened and disappointed.

I am a physician, and over the past ten years I have been asking myself how people like Peter and his mother survive in mind and body and spirit. And I have wanted to know what a twentieth-century American city "means" to them or "does" to them. People cannot be handed questionnaires and asked to answer such questions. They cannot be "interviewed" a few times and told to come across with a statement, a reply. But inside Peter and his brother and his sisters and his mother, and inside a number of Appalachian mothers and fathers and children I know, are feelings and thoughts and ideas—which, in my experience, come out casually or suddenly, by accident almost. After a year or two of talking, after experiences such as I have briefly described in a city hall, in a children's hospital, a lifetime of pent-up tensions and observation comes to blunt expression: *"Down in Alabama we had to be careful about ourselves with the white man, but we had plenty of things we could do by ourselves. There was our side of town, and you could walk and run all over, and we had a garden you know. Up here they have you in a cage. There's no place to go, and all I do is stay in the building all day long and the night, too. I don't use my legs no more, hardly at all. I never see those trees, and my oldest girl, she misses planting time. It was bad down there. We had to leave. But it's no good here, too, I'll tell you. Once I woke up and I thought all the buildings on the block were falling down on me. And I was trying to climb out, but I couldn't. And then the next thing I knew, we were all back South, and I was standing near some sunflowers—you know, the tall ones that can shade you if you sit down.*

"No, I don't dream much. I fall into a heavy sleep as soon as I touch the bed. The next thing I know I'm stirring myself to start in all over in the morning. It used to be the sun would wake me up, but now it's up in my head, I guess. I know I've got to get the house going and off to school."

Her wistful, conscientious, law-abiding, devoutly Christian spirit hasn't completely escaped the notice of Peter, for all his hard-headed, cynical protestations: *"If I had a chance, I'd like to get enough money to bring us all back to Alabama for a visit. Then I could prove it that it may be good down there, a little bit, even if it's no good, either. Like she says, we had to get out of there or we'd be dead by now. I hear say we all may get killed soon, it's so bad here; but I think we did right to get up here, and if we make them listen to us, the white man, maybe he will."*

To which Peter's mother adds: *"We've carried a lot of trouble in us, from way back in the beginning. I have these pains, and so does everyone around here. But you can't just die until you're ready to. And I do believe something is happening. I do believe I see that."*

To which Peter adds: *"Maybe it won't be that we'll win, but if we get killed, everyone will hear about it. Like the minister said, before we used to die real quiet, and no one stopped to pay notice."*

Two years before Peter spoke those words he drew a picture for me, one of many he has done. When he was younger, and when I didn't know him so well as I think I do now, it was easier for us to have something tangible to do and then talk about. I used to visit the alley with him, as I still do, and one day I asked him to draw the alley. That was a good idea, he thought. (Not all of my suggestions were, however.) He started in, then stopped, and finally worked rather longer and harder than usual at the job. I busied myself with my own sketches, which from the start he insisted I do. Suddenly from across the table I heard him say he was through. Ordinarily he would slowly turn the drawing around for me to see; and I would get up and walk over to his side of the table, to see even better. But he didn't move his paper, and I didn't move myself. I saw what he had drawn, and he saw me looking. I was surprised and a bit stunned and more than a bit upset, and surely he saw my face and heard my utter silence. Often I would break the awkward moments when neither of us seemed to have anything to say, but this time it was his turn to do so: *"You know what it is?"* He knew that I liked us to talk about our work. I said no, I didn't—though in fact the vivid power of his black crayon had come right across to me. *"It's that hole we dug in the alley. I made it bigger here. If you fall into it, you can't get out. You die."*

He had drawn circles within circles, all of them black, and then a center, also black. He had imposed an X on the center. Nearby, strewn across the circles, were fragments of the human body—two faces, an arm, five legs. And after I had taken the scene in, I could only think to myself that I had been shown *"like it is in the alley"*—by an intelligent boy who knew what he saw around him, could give it expression, and, I am convinced, would respond to a different city, a city that is alive and breathing, one that is not for many of its citizens a virtual morgue.

15

GERALD D. SUTTLES, Anatomy of a Chicago Slum

Methodology: Gerald D. Suttles spent three years in the Near West Side of Chicago making a study of a multiethnic community that includes Italians, Mexicans, Negroes and Puerto Ricans. He took up residence in the area in the summer of 1963 and did not leave until almost three years later. It took him a year or more to acquire friends and enter the private worlds of families, social-athletic clubs and other groups. The findings of his study are published in The Social Order of the Slum *from which* Trans-action *has taken excerpts—chiefly from materials on the Italian population. The book in its entirety shows that there are broad structural similarities between all the ethnic groups—Italian, Mexican, Negro and Puerto Rican, although this structure is more clearly developed among the Italians. The excerpts draw on some of Suttles's more general observations rather than his detailed empirical findings.*

In its heyday, the Near West Side of Chicago was the stronghold of such men as Al (Scarface) Capone and Frank (The Enforcer) Nitti, and served as the kindergarten for several figures still active in the underworld. For convenience, I will call this part of Chicago the Addams area—after Jane Addams, who founded Hull House there. The name is artificial, since it is never used by the local residents.

The Addams area is one of the oldest slums in Chicago, and researchers have invaded it almost as often as new minority groups have. Like most slums, it remains something of a mystery. In some ways it is easiest to describe the neighborhood by describing how its residents deviate from the public standards of the wider community. The area has, for example, a high delinquency rate, numerous unwed mothers, and several adolescent "gangs." It is tempting to think that the residents are simply people suffering from cultural deprivation, unemployment, and a number of other urban ills. And if the residents insist upon the irrelevance of the standards of the wider community and the primacy of their own, this can be dismissed as sour grapes or an attempt to make of necessity a virtue.

Seen from the inside, however, Addams area residents require discipline and self-restraint in the same way as the wider community does. Conventional norms are not rejected but emphasized differently, or suspended for established reasons. The vast majority of the residents are quite conventional people. At the

Gerald D. Suttles, "Anatomy of a Chicago Slum," *Trans-action,* February 1969, pp. 16–25. Copyright © February 1969 by Transaction, Inc., New Brunswick, New Jersey. Reprinted by permission.

His article is an excerpt from his recent book, *The Social Order of the Slum: Ethnicity and Territoriality in the Inner City,* © 1968, all rights reserved by the University of Chicago Press.

same time, those who remain in good standing are often exceptionally tolerant of and even encouraging to those who are "deviant."

Certainly the social practices of the residents are not just an inversion of those of the wider society, and the inhabitants would be outraged to hear as much. Nor is the neighborhood a cultural island with its own distinct and imported traditions. The area's internal structure features such commonplace distinctions as age, sex, territoriality, ethnicity, and personal identity. Taken out of context, many of the social arrangements of the Addams area may seem an illusory denial of the beliefs and values of the wider society. But actually the residents are bent on ordering local relations because the beliefs and evaluations of the wider society do not provide adequate guidelines for conduct.

In anthropology, territorial grouping has been a subject of continued interest. Most anthropological studies begin by focusing upon social groupings that can be defined by their areal distribution. In turn, many of the social units singled out for particular attention—the domestic unit, the homestead, the tribe, and so forth—frequently have locality as one of their principles of organization. And where locality and structural forms do not coincide, anthropologists have regarded this discrepancy as a distinct problem that raises a number of theoretical and methodological issues.

The most obvious reason for focusing on locality groups is that their members cannot simply ignore one another. People who routinely occupy the same place must either develop a moral order that includes all those present or fall into conflict. And because almost all societies create a public morality that exceeds the capabilities of some of its members, territorial groups are always faced with the prospect of people whose public character does not warrant trust. In the United States a very large percentage of our population fails to meet the public standards we set for measuring someone's merit, trustworthiness, and respectability.

Many groups have avoided compromising these ideals of public morality by territorial segregation. More exactly, they have simply retreated and left valuable portions of the inner city to those they distrust. Obviously, this practice has its limits—it tends to aggregate those who are poor, unsuccessful, and disreputable in the same slum neighborhoods. These people must compromise the ideals of public morality or remain permanently estranged from one another.

In slum neighborhoods, territorial aggregation usually comes before any common social framework for assuring orderly relations. After all, ethnic invasion, the encroachment of industry, and economic conditions constantly reshuffle slum residents and relocate them around new neighbors. Since the residents lack obvious grounds for assuming mutual trust, a combination of alternatives seems to offer the most promising course:

- Social relations can be restricted to only the safest ones. Families can withdraw to their households, where they see only close relatives. Segregation by age, sex, and ethnicity are maneuvers that will prevent at least the most unfair and most likely forms of conflict and exploitation. Remaining close to the household cuts down on the range of anonymity and reduces the number of social relations. The general pattern, then, should be a fan-shaped spatial arrangement, with women and children remaining close by the house while males move progressively outwards, depending on their age.

- Slum residents can assuage at least some of their apprehensions by a close inquiry into one another's personal character and past history. Communication, then, should be of an intimate character and aimed toward producing personal rather than formal relations. In turn, social relations will represent a sort of private compact in which particular loyalties replace impersonal standards of worth.

Neither of these patterns will immediately produce a comprehensive framework within which a large number of slum residents can safely negotiate with one another. The segregation by age, sex, and territorial groups, however, does provide a starting point from which face-to-face relations can grow and reach beyond each small territorial aggregation. The development of personal relations furnishes both a moral formula and a structural bridge between groups. Within each small, localized peer group, continuing face-to-face relations can eventually provide a personalistic order. Once these groups are established, a single personal relation between them can extend the range of such an order. Thus, with the acceptance of age-grading and territorial segregation, it becomes possible for slum neighborhoods to work out a moral order that includes most of their residents.

The Addams area actually consists of four different sections, each occupied predominantly by Negroes, Italians, Puerto Ricans, and Mexicans. And each of these sections falls into a somewhat different stage in its development of a provincial order.

Despite this difference and others, all four ethnic sections share many characteristics and seem headed along the same social progression. The overall pattern is one in which age, sex, ethnic, and territorial units are fitted together like building blocks to create a larger structure. I have termed this pattern "ordered segmentation" to indicate two related features: (1) the orderly relationship between groups; and (2) the order in which groups combine in instances of conflict and opposition. This ordered segmentation is not equally developed in all ethnic sections but, in skeletal outline, it is the common framework within which groups are being formed and social relations are being cultivated.

My own experiences within the Addams area and the presentation of this volume are heavily influenced by the ordered segmentation of the neighborhood. I took up residence in the area in the summer of 1963 and left a little fewer than three years later.

As I acquired friends and close informants, my own ethnicity became a serious problem. A few people worked over my genealogy trying to find some trace that would allot me to a known ethnic group. After close inquiry, one old

Italian lady announced with peals of laughter, "Geraldo, you're just an American." She did not mean it as a compliment, and I remember being depressed. In the Addams area, being without ethnicity means there is no one you can appeal to or claim as your own.

Only after a year or more in the Addams area was I able to penetrate the private world of its families, street-corner groups, and insular establishments. These are the groupings within which Addams area residents are least cautious and most likely to expose themselves. In large part my experience with these groups is limited to many adolescent male street-corner groups and my own adult friends, who formed a group of this type.

By far the most striking contrast is between the Negro and the Italian sections. For instance, almost all the Negroes live in public housing; the Italians usually control both their households and commercial establishments. The Negroes have very similar incomes and almost no political power; among the Italians, there *is* some internal differentiation of income and political power. Such differences draw the Italians and Negroes apart and generate radically different styles of life.

In most ways, the Puerto Rican section is the least complex of those in the Addams area. There are no more than 1100 Puerto Ricans in the section and, within broad age ranges, most of them know one another. Until 1965, no named groups had emerged among the Puerto Ricans.

The Mexicans are more numerous, and several named groups have developed among the teenagers. Unlike the Italians, however, the Mexican groups have not survived into adulthood. The Mexicans seem to have much in common with the Italians, and frequently their relationships are congenial. What gives the Mexicans pause is the occasional necessity to divide their loyalties between the Italians and the Negroes.

Although one must not overemphasize the extent of differences between all these ethnic sections, such differences as do occur loom large in the Addams area. The residents are actively looking for differences among themselves. The ethnic sections in the area constitute basic guidelines from which the residents of each section can expect certain forms of reciprocity, and anticipate the dangers that may be in store elsewhere.

The portion of the Addams area now controlled by the Italians is only a residue from the encroachments of the three other ethnic groups. But in total land space, it is the largest of any controlled by a single ethnic group. In population, it is not exceptionally big, though, and throughout the section an unusually high percentage of Mexicans have been accepted by the Italians as neighbors.

What the Italians lack in numbers, they often make up for by their reputation for using sheer force and for easy access to "influence" or "connections." It is said, for example, that many of the Italians are "Outfit people," and that many more could rely on mobsters if they needed help. Also, it is the general view that the Italians control both the vice and patronage of the

First Ward, a political unit that includes the spoils of the Loop—downtown Chicago.

There are some very famous Italians in the Addams area, and they frequently get a spread in the city newspapers. There are many others not nearly so prominent but whose personal histories are still known in the neighborhood. At least five Italian policemen live in the area, and a few more who grew up there are assigned to the local district. The other ethnic groups have not a single resident or ex-resident policeman among them. Most of the precinct captains are also Italian; and, outside the projects, the Italians dominate those jobs provided by public funds. There are a number of Italian businessmen, each of whom controls a few jobs. It is also widely believed that they can "sponsor" a person into many of the industries of the city—the newsstands in the Loop, the city parks, the beauty-culture industry, a large printing company, and a number of clothing firms.

While there is some substance to this belief in Italian power and influence, it is actually quite exaggerated. Many of the Italian political figures seem to have little more than the privilege of announcing decisions that have been made by others. In most of the recent political actions that have affected the area, they have remained mute and docile. When the Medical Center was built and then extended, they said nothing. The Congress and the Dan Ryan Expressways were constructed with the local politicians hardly taking notice. Finally, when the University of Illinois was located at Congress Circle, the politicians, mobsters, and—indeed—all the male residents accepted it without even a show of resistance. In fact, only a group of Italian and Mexican housewives took up arms and sought to save some remnant of the neighborhood.

The Italians' notoriety for being in the rackets and having recourse to strong-arm methods is also a considerable exaggeration, or at least a misinterpretation. The majority of the local Italians are perfectly respectable people and gain nothing from organized crime. Yet, many of the common family names of the area have been sullied by some flagrant past episode by a relative. And in the area, family histories remain a basis for judging individual members and are extended to include all persons who share the same name. In another neighborhood, this information might be lost or ignored as improper; in the Addams area, it is almost impossible to keep family secrets, and they are kept alive in the constant round of rumor and gossip.

The local Italians themselves contribute to their reputation—because on many occasions they find it advantageous to intimate that they have connections with the Outfit. For example, outsiders are often flattered to think that they are in the confidence of someone who knows the underworld. Also, it is far more prestigious to have other people believe that one's background is buried in crime and violence than in public welfare. In America, organized crime has always received a certain respect, even when this respect had to be coerced. A recipient of public welfare is simply dismissed as unimportant. And during the Depression many of the Italians went on welfare.

"Right people" can protect them

In addition, some of the Italians feel that a reputation of being in with the "right people" can in some circumstances ensure them against victimization. They often hint about their connections with the Outfit when facing the members of another ethnic group under uncertain odds, or when in an argument among themselves. Yet with friends and relatives, the Italians often complain bitterly of how they are maligned by the press and by their neighbors.

Ironically, the Italians are cautious in their dealings with one another; more than any other group, they are intimidated by the half-myth that is partly of their own creation. And indirectly this myth gives them considerable cohesion, and a certain freedom from the judgments and actions of the wider society. It is almost impossible to persuade one of them to make a complaint to the police, for instance, because of their fear of the Outfit; indeed, they shun all public sources of social control. They handle grievances, contracts, and exchanges in a very informal manner, usually limited to the immediate parties. If in need, they exact aid in the form of favors and generally ignore sources available to the general public. As a result, the Italians have been able to sustain among themselves the image of an independent, powerful, and self-confident people.

Behind the scenes bargaining

Yet the cohesion and solidarity of the Italians are very limited. They are based primarily on the suspicion that social arrangements are best made by private settlements. This suspicion, in turn, is based on the assumption that recourse to public means can do little more than excite retaliation and vengeance. These same suspicions and doubts undermine the possibilities of a unified and explicit stance by the Italians toward the wider community and political organization. First, very few of them believe that the others will cooperate in joint efforts unless it is to their personal advantage or they are under some dire threat. Second, the Italians simply fear that a united public stand will elicit a similar posture on the part of their adversaries and eliminate the opportunity for private negotiations. Accordingly, the Italians either shun public confrontations or slowly draw away, once so engaged. In retrospect, the spirit of *omerta* seems ineffectual when it confronts the explicit efforts of the wider community.(Literally, *omerta* means a conspiracy between thieves. The Italians use it to mean any private agreement that cannot be safely broached before the general public.)

The inability of the Italians to accept or engage in public appeals leaves them somewhat bewildered by the Negroes' civil-rights movement. By the Italians' standards, the Negroes are "making a federal case" out of something that should be handled by private agreement. Indeed, even those who accept the justice of the Negroes' cause remain perplexed by the Negroes' failure to approach *them* in some informal manner. Throughout the summer of 1964, when demonstrators were most active, the Italians always seemed aggrieved and surprised that the Negroes would "pull such a trick" without warning. The Negroes took this view as a "sham" and felt that the Italians had ample reason to anticipate their demands. To the Italians this was not the point. Of course, they knew that the Negroes had many long-standing demands and desires. What struck the Italians as unfair about the Negroes' demonstrations was their tactics: sudden public confrontations, without any chance for either side to retreat or compromise with grace.

Ultimately, both the Italians and Negroes did take their differences behind closed doors, and each settled for something less than their public demands. The main bone of contention was a local swimming pool dominated by the Italians and their Mexican guests.

In the background, of course, was the oppressive belief that the benefits of social life make up a fixed quantity and are already being used to the maximum. Thus, even the most liberal Italians assume that any gain to the Negroes must be their loss. On their own part, the Negroes make the same assumption and see no reason why the Italians should give way without a fight. Thus, whatever good intentions exist on either side are overruled by the seeming impracticality or lack of realism.

The Italians' career in the Addams area has been shaped by a traditional world view that relies heavily on a belief in "natural man." For example, it is felt to be "natural" for men to be sexual predators; for mothers to love their children, regardless of what their children do; for girls to connive at marriage; for boys to hate school; for a businessman to cheat strangers; and for anyone to choose pleasure in preference to discipline and duty. Implicit in the concept of natural man is the conviction that moral restraints have little real power in a situation in which they contradict man's natural impulses. Civilization is a mere gloss to hide man's true nature.

Often, although not always, man's natural impulses are at odds with his moral standards. Indeed, otherwise there would be no need for the church, the police, the government, and all other bodies of social control. But it is not always possible for these external bodies of social control to keep track of what people are doing. Inevitably, then, there will be occasions when people are free to choose between acting naturally and acting morally. For their own part, the Italians may have considerable conviction of their personal preferences for morality. In their dealings with other people, however they have little faith in this thin thread of individual morality. Correspondingly, to them their own personal morality becomes utterly impractical and must be replaced by whatever amoral expedient seems necessary for self-defense.

The general outcome seems to be an overwhelming distrust of impersonal or "voluntary" relationships. The other side of the coin is an equally strong tendency to fall back on those relationships and identities where one's own welfare is guaranteed by "natural inclinations." For the most part these are kin relations, close friendship, common regional origins (*paesani*), joint residential unity, and sacred pledges like marriage, God, parenthood, etc. Thus, the Italians in the

Addams area have tended to turn in upon themselves and become a provincial moral world.

Actually, many of the Italians are quite "Americanized." Frequently, though, these people lead something of a double life. During the daytime they leave the neighborhood and do their work without much thought of their ethnicity. When they come home in the evening, they are obliged to reassume their old world identity. This need not be so much a matter of taste as necessity. Other people are likely to already know their ethnicity, and evasions are likely to be interpreted as acts of snobbery or attempts at deception. Moreover, members of the other three ethnic groups refuse to accept such a person's Americanization, no matter how much it is stressed. To others, an attempt to minimize one's ethnicity is only a sly maneuver to escape responsibility for past wrongs or to gain admission into their confidence. Finally, there are still many old-timers in the neighborhood, and it would be very ill-mannered to parade one's Americanism before them. Thus, within the bounds of the local neighborhood, an Italian who plays at being an "American" runs the risk of being taken as a snob, phony, opportunist, coward, or fink.

Among the Italians themselves, notions of ethnicity are particularly well-elaborated. For the most part, these internal subdivisions are based on regional origins in Italy. By contrast, the other ethnic groups have very little internal differentiation. The Negroes make only a vague distinction between those raised in the South and those raised in the North. Among the former, Mississippians are sometimes singled out for special contempt. However, none of these divisions lead to cohesive social unities. But among the Italians their *paesani* (regional origins) take on great importance, and it remains the first perimeter beyond the family within which they look for aid or feel themselves in safe hands. Most *paesani* continue to hold their annual summer picnics and winter dance. Some have grown into full-scale organizations with elected officers, insurance plans, burial funds, and regular poker sessions.

Of all the ethnic groups in the Addams area, the Italians still have the richest ceremonial life. Aside from the annual *paesani* dances and picnics, there are parades, *feste*, and several other occasions. In the summer, their church holds a carnival that duplicates much of the Italian *feste*. On Columbus Day there is a great parade in the Loop, exceeded in grandeur only by the one held by the Irish on St. Patrick's Day. During Lent there are several special religious events and afterwards a round of dances, parties, and feasts. Throughout the summer a local brass band periodically marches through the streets playing arias from Puccini and Verdi. Sidewalk vendors sell Italian lemonade, sausages, and beef sandwiches. Horsedrawn carts go about selling grapes during the fall winemaking season, tomatoes when they are ready to be turned to paste, and fruit and vegetables at almost any time of the year.

Communal ceremonies and festivities

Even weddings, communions, funerals, and wakes maintain some of their communal nature. Weddings are usually known of beforehand and often attract a number of onlookers as well as those invited. Afterwards the couple and their friends drive around the neighborhood in decorated cars, honking their horns at one another and whomever they recognize on the streets. Parochial-school children usually receive first communion as a group and attract a good deal of attention. Wakes are also open to almost anyone, and funeral processions often tour a portion of the neighborhood. On this sort of occasion, the Mexicans follow much the same practice, although they lack full control of a local church where they can carry out these affairs to the same extent as the Italians. Among the Negroes and Puerto Ricans, weddings, funerals, and religious events tend to be quite private affairs, open through invitation alone.

The Italians are also favored by the relatively long period over which many of them have been able to know one another and to decide upon whom they can or cannot trust. Over time, a considerable amount of information has been accumulated on many people, and this circulates in such a way as to be available to even a fairly recent resident. Moreover, the intertwining of social relations has become so extensive that contact with one person often opens passage to many others. In this sense, "getting acquainted" is almost unavoidable for a new resident.

The forms of social organization in the Italian section are far more extensive and complicated than those of the other ethnic groups. At the top are two groups, the "West Side Bloc" and the "Outfit," which share membership and whose participants are not all from the Addams area. The West Side Bloc is a group of Italian politicians whose constituency is much larger than the Addams area but which includes a definite wing in the area. Generally its members are assumed to belong to or to have connections with the Outfit. A good deal of power is attributed to them within the local neighborhood, city, state, and nation. The Outfit, more widely known as the Syndicate, includes many more people, but it is also assumed to reach beyond the Addams area. Locally, it is usually taken to include almost anyone who runs a tavern or a liquor store, or who relies on state licensing or city employment. A few other businessmen and local toughs are accredited with membership because of their notorious immunity to law enforcement or their reputed control of "favors."

Indirectly, the Outfit extends to a number of adult social-athletic clubs (s.a.c.'s). These clubs invariably have a storefront where the members spend their time in casual conversation or drink, or play cards. A few of their members belong to the Outfit, and a couple of these clubs are said to have a "regular game" for big stakes. Each group is fairly homogeneous in age, but collectively the groups range between the late 20s up to the late 60s.

Below these adult s.a.c.'s are a number of other s.a.c.'s that also have a clubhouse, but whose members are much younger. As a rule, they are somewhat beyond school age, but only a few are married, and practically none have children. To some degree, they are still involved in the extra-familial life that occupies teenagers. Occasionally they have dances, socials, and impromptu parties. On weekends they still roam around together, attending "socials" sponsored by other groups, looking for girls or for some kind of "action." Within each young man's s.a.c., the members' ages cover a narrow range. Together, all the groups range between about 19 and the late 20s. They form a distinct and well-recognized age grade in the neighborhood because of their continuing involvement in those cross-sexual and recreational activities open to unmarried males.

Nevertheless, these young men's s.a.c.'s are somewhat outside the full round of activities that throw teenagers together. A good portion of their time is spent inside their clubhouse out of sight of their rivals or most bodies of social control. Most members are in their 20s and are able to openly enjoy routine forms of entertainment or excitement that the wider community provides and accepts. When they have a dance or party, it is usually restricted to those whom they invite. Being out of school, they are not forced each day to confront persons from beyond their neighborhood. Since many of them have cars, they need not trespass too much on someone else's domain.

These s.a.c.'s are not assumed to have any active role in the Outfit. At most, it is expected that they might be able to gain a few exemptions from law enforcement and an occasional "favor," e.g., a job, a chance to run an illegal errand, a small loan, someone to sign for their clubhouse charter (required by law), and the purchase of stolen goods or of anything else the boys happen to have on hand. It is assumed that they could solicit help from the Outfit if they got into trouble with another group, but very rarely are they drawn into this type of conflict. Almost invariably the opponent is a much younger "street group" that has encroached on what the s.a.c. considers its "rights"—e.g., tried to crash one of their parties, insulted them on the streets, made noise nearby, or marked up their clubhouse. Even at these times, their actions seem designed to do little more than rid themselves of a temporary nuisance. Once rid of their tormentors, they usually do not pursue the issue further, and for good reason. To charter such a club requires three cosigners, and these people may withdraw their support if the group becomes too rowdy. Also, they have a landlord to contend with, and he can throw them out for the same reason. Finally, they cannot afford to make too many enemies; they have a piece of property, and it would be only too easy for their adversaries to get back at them. Unlike all the groups described in the other three sections, they have a stake in maintaining something like law and order.

All the remaining Italian groups include members who are of high-school age. While they too call themselves s.a.c.'s, none of them have a storefront. All of them do have an established "hangout," and they correspond to the usual image of a street-corner group.

While the street groups in this section of the area often express admiration for the adult s.a.c.'s, they seldom develop in an unbroken sequence into a full-fledged adult s.a.c. Usually when they grow old enough to rent a storefront they change their name, acquire new members from groups that have been their rivals, and lose a few of their long-term members. Some groups disband entirely, and their members are redistributed among the newly formed s.a.c.'s. Of the twelve young men's and adult s.a.c.'s, only one is said to have maintained the same name from the time it was a street-corner group. Even in this case some members have been added and others lost. Together, then, the Italian street-corner groups make up the population from which future young men's s.a.c.'s are drawn, but only a few street-corner groups form the nucleus of a s.a.c.

Conceptually, the Italian street groups and the older s.a.c.'s form a single unity. In the eyes of the boys, they are somewhat like the steps between grammar school and college. While there may be dropouts, breaks, and amalgamations, they still make up a series of steps through which one can advance with increasing age. Thus, each street group tends to see the adult s.a.c.'s as essentially an older and more perfect version of itself. What may be just as important is their equally strong sense of history. Locally, many of the members in the street groups can trace their group's genealogy back through the Taylor Dukes, the 40 game, the Genna Brothers, and the Capone mob. Actually, there is no clear idea of the exact order of this descent line; some people include groups that others leave out. Moreover, there is no widespread agreement on which specific group is the current successor to this lineage. Nonetheless, there is agreement that the groups on Taylor Street have illustrious progenitors. On some occasions this heritage may be something of a burden, and on others a source of pride. In any case, it is unavoidable, and usually the Italian street group preface its own name with the term "Taylor." Among the younger groups this is omitted only when their name is an amalgam made up from a specific street corner or block. Only the adult s.a.c.'s regularly fail to acknowledge in their name the immediate territory within which they are situated.

Direct line of succession from the Outfit

Since they see themselves in a direct line of succession to groups reputed to be associated with the Outfit, these street-corner groups might be expected to have a strong criminal orientation. In the Addams area, however, the Italian groups are best known for their fighting prowess, and their official police records show no concentration on the more utilitarian forms of crime. The fact is that, like the other adolescent groups in the area, the Italian boys are not really free to choose their own goals and identities. Territorial arrangements juxtapose them against similar groups manned by Negro and Mexican boys. If the Italian street-corner groups fail to define themselves as fighting groups, their peers in the other ethnic groups are certainly going to assume as much.

There is also considerable rivalry between Italian street-corner groups of roughly the same age. Commonly they suspect each other of using force to establish their precedence. In turn, each group seems to think it must at least put on a tough exterior to avoid being "pushed around." Privately there is a great deal of talk among them about the Outfit and about criminal activities, but it is academic in the sense that there is no strong evidence that their behavior follows suit.

It is interesting that the adult s.a.c.'s that actually have members in the rackets avoid any conspicuous claims about their criminal activities or fighting abilities. Their names, for example, are quite tame, while those of the street groups tend to be rather menacing. And their dances, leisure-time activities, and interrelationships are quite private and unpretentious. Unlike the street groups, they never wear clothing that identifies their group membership. The older men in the s.a.c.'s make no apparent attempt to establish a publicly-known hierarchy among themselves. Other people occasionally attribute more respect to one than another of them, but there seems to be little consensus on this. On their own part, the older groups seem to pay little attention to their relative standing and to be on fairly good terms. During my three years in the area, I never heard of them fighting among themselves.

Unlike the Negro and Mexican ethnic sections, there are no female counterparts to the named Italian street-corner groups. A very few Italian girls belong to two Mexican girls' groups that "hung" in the Mexican section. This, in itself, was exceptional; almost always the minority members in a street group are from a lower-ranking ethnic group. The Italian girls, however, are under certain constraints that may be lacking for those in the other ethnic groups. Naturally, their parents disapprove of such a blatant display of feminine unity. The Italian parents may gain stature by their power and precedence in comparison to the Negro and Mexican adults. Yet what seems far more significant is the general form that boy-girl relationships take among the Italians. On either side, the slightest hint of interest in the other sex is likely to be taken in the most serious way; as either a rank insult or a final commitment. Thus, any explicit alliance between a boys' and girls' group can be interpreted in only one of two ways: (1) all the girls are "laying" for the boys, or (2) they are seriously attached to each other. Neither side seems quite willing to betray so much and, thus, they avoid such explicit alliances.

This dilemma was quite evident on many occasions while I was observing the Italian boys and girls. The girls seemed extraordinarily coy when they were in a "safe" position—with their parents, in church, etc. When alone and on their own they became equally cautious and noncommittal. On public occasions, the boys seemed almost to ignore the girls and even to snub them. On Taylor Street, for instance, an Italian boys' group and an Italian girls' group used to hang about 10 feet from each other. Almost invariably they would stand with their backs to each other, although there were many furtive glances back and forth. During almost two years of observation, I never saw them talk. Later, I was surprised to learn that everyone in each group was quite well-known to the other. For either of them to have acknowledged the other's presence openly, however, would have been too forward. The boys are quite aware of this dilemma and complain that the girls are not free enough to be convenient companions. This, they say, is one reason why they have to go elsewhere to date someone. At the same time, they perpetuate the old system by automatically assuming that the slightest sign of interest by a girl makes her fair game. Out of self-defense, the girls are compelled to keep their distance. On private occasions, of course, there are many Italian boys and girls who sneak off to enjoy what others might consider an entirely conventional boy-girl relationship (petting, necking). In public, though, they studiously ignore each other. Throughout my time in the area I never saw a young Italian couple hold hands or walk together on the sidewalk.

The Barracudas were the first Mexican street-corner group to emerge in the Italian section. They first became a named group in the spring of 1964, and all members were Mexican.

Once established, the Barracudas installed themselves in the northwest corner of Sheridan Park. Virtually every Italian street group in the area makes use of this park, and several have their hangouts there. Other people in turn refer to the Italian groups collectively as "the guys from the Park." The park itself is partitioned into a finely graduated series of more or less private enclosures, with the most private hangout going to the reigning group and the least private to the weakest group. The northwest corner of the park is the most exposed of any portion, and this is where the Barracudas installed themselves. Even in this lowly spot, they were much resented by the other groups. To the Italians the Park was almost a sacred charge, and the Mexicans' intrusion was a ritual pollution. The Barracudas were harassed, ridiculed, and insulted. On their own part, they became belligerent and vaunted all sorts of outrageous claims about themselves. Soon the situation deteriorated and the Italian groups became extremely harsh with the Barracudas. Since the Barracudas were no match for even some of the younger Italian groups, they removed themselves to one member's house.

Their new hangout placed them in an anomalous position. Ethnically they were identified as a Mexican group. Yet they were located in a part of the area that had been conceded to the Puerto Ricans. And individually most of them continued to reside in the Italian section. The general result seems to have been that the Barracudas were isolated from any of the other group hierarchies and placed in opposition to every group in the area. Within a year every white group was their enemy, and the Negroes were not their friends. The Barracudas responded in kind and became even more truculent and boastful. More than any group in the area, they openly embraced the stance of a fighting group. They wrote their name all over the neighborhood and even on some of the other groups' hangouts. In the meantime, they made a clubhouse out of a lean-to adjacent to a building on Harrison Street. Inside they installed a shield on which they wrote "hate," "kill," and other violent words. Carrying a weapon became almost routine with them, and eventually they collected a small arsenal. In time they had several small-scale fights with both the Italians from the Park and the Mexicans around Polk and Laflin. In due course, they acquired so many enemies that they could hardly risk leaving the immediate area of their hangout. At the same time, some of them began to go to Eighteenth Street, where they had "connections"—relatives. This only brought them into conflict with other groups in this neighborhood. By the summer of 1965, the Barracudas were as isolated and resentful as ever.

"Incognitos" and the "Pica People"

There are two other groups in the Italian section, the Pica People and the Incognitos. The groups' names are themselves an expression of their isolation. The Incognitos self-consciously avoided comparison with the other groups: They did not hang in the Park, hold socials, or become involved in any of the local sidewalk confrontations. About the same age as the Contenders, the Incognitos were notably different in their exclusion from the local round of praise and recriminations.

"Pica People" is a derisive name meant as an insult for five young men about 19 to 25 years of age. Although these five individuals associate regularly, they claim no group identity and become angry when called the Pica People. Unlike the Incognitos, the Pica People are well-known and often accused of some predatory display. They do not fight for group honor, but there is friction between them and all the other street-corner groups in the Addams area.

It was impossible to determine how these two groups came into existence. (I talked only twice with the Incognitos, who simply said they "grew up together." Local people started calling the Pica People by that name after a movie in which the "Pica People" were sub-humans. I knew some of the members of this group, but they became so angry at any mention of the name that I could not discuss it with them.) What is known of their composition may throw some light on why they were excluded from the structure of the other groups. All informants described the Incognitos as "good guys," still in school and no trouble to anyone. They were not considered college boys but, if asked, most informants said they thought some of them might go to college. Local youth agencies made no attempt to work with them, and the entire neighborhood seemed to feel they were not dangerous. Other street-corner groups in the Italian section did not look down on them, but they did exempt them from the ambitions that brought other groups into opposition.

The Pica People were just the opposite. All members were boastful of their alleged Outfit connections and their ability to intimidate other people. But the Pica People possessed so many personal flaws that they were rather useless to the Outfit. One member was slightly claustrophobic. Another was so weak that even much younger boys pushed him around. A third had an exceedingly unfortunate appearance. Under the circumstances, their pretensions became laughable.

Extremes of street corner groups

The Incognitos and the Pica People seem to represent the extremes of a range in which the street-corner group is considered the normal adolescent gathering.

Modest and well-behaved youngsters are excluded as exceptions, as are crimi-nally inclined but unsuccessful young men. Both of these groups fell outside the range considered normal by the local residents and were thereby dissociated from the total group hierarchy.

The social context of the Italian street groups is somewhat different from that of the street groups in the other three ethnic sections. Among the Italians, the major share of coercive power still remains in adult hands. The wider com-munity may not be very pleased with the form *their* power takes, but it is the only case where the corporate power of the adolescents is tempered by that of the adults. Also, since many of the same adults have an active role in distributing some of the benefits that are held in store by the wider community, their power is augmented. Perhaps the most obvious result of the adults' ascendency is that the adolescents do not simply dismiss them or adulthood as unimportant. A more immediate consequence is to give many of the adults the prerogative of exacting considerable obedience from the local adolescents. It is not all uncommon to see an Italian adult upbraid and humble one of the local youths. Not all adults have this privilege; but many do, and their example provides a distinct contrast to the other ethnic groups where similar efforts would be futile.

In the long run, the effectiveness of these coercive controls among the Ital-ians may do little more than confirm their convictions that, outside of natural tendencies, there is no guarantee to moral conduct except economic and numeri-cal strength. Within their own little world, however, such coercive measures constitute a fairly effective system of social control. Personal privacy and anonym-ity are almost impossible. In turn, each person's known or assumed connections dampen most chances at exploitation because of the fear of unknown conse-quences. Thus, the opportunities for immorality presented by transient relations and "fair game" are fairly rare. Within these limits, such an authoritarian system of social control will work. Outside their own section, of course, these condi-tions do not hold; and the Italian boys find themselves free to seize whatever advantages or opportunities present themself. Among themselves, they are usually only a rowdy and boisterous crowd. With strangers or in other parts of the Addams area, they become particularly arrogant and unscrupulous.

With these qualifications, it appears that well-established adolescent street-corner groups are quite compatible with strong adult authority and influence. In fact, judging from the Italian section, these adolescent street-corner groups seem to be the building blocks out of which the older and more powerful groups have originated. The younger groups continue to replenish the older ones and help maintain the structure within which adults are shown deference.

Moreover, the total age-graded structure of groups in the Italian section relates youngsters to the wider society both instrumentally and conceptually. The Italian street groups see themselves as replacements in an age structure that becomes progressively less provincial. At the upper age level, groups even stop prefacing their name with the term "Taylor"; and a few of their members have a place in the wider society through the Outfit and West Side Bloc. The relationship between these age grades also provides a ladder down which favors and opportunities are distributed. The wider community may hesitate at accepting the legitimacy of these transactions, but they are mostly of a conventional form. The "Outfit" and the "West Side Bloc" have a strong interest in maintaining a degree of social order, and the sorts of wanton violence associated with gangs do not at all fit their taste.

In conclusion

The Addams area is probably a more orderly slum than many others, and it departs sharply from the common image of an atomized and unruly urban rabble. For all its historical uniqueness, the neighborhood does establish the possibility of a moral order within its population. The recurrence of the circumstances that led to its organization is as uncertain as the future of the Addams area itself. In spite of all these uncertainties, the Addams area shows that slum residents are intent upon finding a moral order and are sometimes successful in doing so.

16

DONALD E. CARNS, SHELDON GOLDENBERG & SCOTT GREER, Some Neglected Considerations on the American Urban Family

This brief essay focuses on the familial institution for a number of reasons. First, the family is the basic microsocial unit of all societies and indeed, in many societies, is the highest form of authority and social organization known (Blumberg, Carns, and Winch, 1970). Second, the family in its many forms and functions reflects man's attempt to solve certain constant problems of survival—procreation, hereditary maintenance of privilege, creation and concentration of wealth, status conference—as well as other less obvious needs, such as maintenance of trust relationships, the legal and social basis for territorial integrity (as in the household), a haven where ascription and not performance presumably is the foundation of personal acceptance and affection, and so forth.

And yet a third reason exists. All social institutions have been radically transformed as societies have urbanized; the family is no exception. The effects of urbanization on the family are generally characterized in terms of a "loss of functions," an argument which takes explicit account of the process of institutional specialization in urban/industrial milieus. But this is only part of the story, and a sociology of the urban family must take into account specific patterns of population concentration, cultural history, and economic relations.

Before proceeding, we should like to define the terms *family, household,* and *marriage,* since the impacts of urbanization and industrialization may affect each differently. Briefly, *household* is used here as a place with a definite spatial referent. It denotes a closed space with given interactional relations within. *Marriage,* on the other hand, involves a complex set of conditions including legal, familial, spatial, and cultural constraints; and in our society it generally refers to the legal mating of two persons of different genders who cohabit. Also in our cultural usage, *family* is used to denote a legal marriage plus offspring, but of course it frequently includes both lineal and lateral kinfolk whether they live in the same household or not. The size of this unit among various subpopulations shall be one of the themes of this essay.

INDUSTRIALIZATION AND URBANIZATION

Living in the western world as we do, we tend to associate certain pairs of concepts because we usually do not visualize their elements independently. In homespun terms, we know of cherry pie and ice cream, ham and eggs, and the like. We have come to equate long hair with the young and lying with politicians, but these may well be fairly transitory linkages. On a quite permanent historical basis, however, we tend to utter the words industrialization and urbanization in the same breath. We expect them to coexist, or more precisely to vary together, and if asked to describe that covariance, we are likely to propose elaborate models of variable interaction such that either of the two processes must be viewed as both antecedent to and a consequence of the other (Breese, 1969). As noted, the last five hundred years of Western history provide ample evidence in support of this generalization, but as with all modal cases, it does not adequately describe the non-Western experience, nor does it provide for the richness of deviant cases in our own society.

Most formulations of family change have not explicitly recognized the phenomenon of urbanization without (or with lagging) industrialization; put differently, they have implicitly dealt with the two phenomena as inseparable, thus paying little attention to large groups of people who have achieved urban status without being integrated into the system of industrialization prevailing at the time.

Urbanization without industrialization

Thus, we know of the *impulse* to urbanize in the so-called Third World, a process that is the product of compound pressures—small land yields and rural overpopulation, the residue of colonial centralization and administration, the prestige of urban residence and appeal of urbanity, the influence of kinsmen or townsmen who have already migrated (Breese, 1969). We know something of the end product of urbanization without attendant or supportive industrialization: poverty, crowding, disease, despair, the proliferation of tiny-scale shopkeeping and vending businesses (Mangin, 1967). In many ways the same processes have taken place in the United States, partly for the same reasons, but partly due to systematic or predictable patterns of discrimination, which have produced large urbanized populations only imperfectly integrated into the industrial system. Integration into the industrial system is indicated by sharing the values, goals, and means of the industrial work force of the society. Among recent migrant groups to cities, blacks, Spanish-Americans, and Appalachian whites are obvious examples of imperfectly integrated groups; the Jews provide another, earlier case of urbanization with limited industrialization (Goldstein and Goldscheider, 1968; and Winch, Greer, and Blumberg, 1967). The location of different groups on this scale of integration into the Western industrial system and the consequences of this location will be discussed more fully later on.

Industrialization and family in the West: a little history

The earliest Western cities contained entrepreneurs who, in one fashion or another, utilized their families as organizations of finance, labor, and trust. This proto-capitalist phase led quite directly into "high" capitalism: the organization of production in a centralized place that was surrounded by tenements for the laborers, and that was under the direction and control of the owner. If more than one owner existed, in many cases they were related by blood. The image of Victorian England gleaned from Dickens or Engels provides examples of this form of socioeconomic organization; the career of the Rothschild family in Europe provides another.

Since production and capital accumulation could, in all likelihood, be a family affair, the internal dynamics of the family were likely closer to the agricultural prototype than to the industrial one. Women held a second class status in a broader sense, but since the bulk of living (economic, social, and religious) centered in the family, this difference in power between men and women was likely quite cohesive. It related to a well understood pattern of intrafamilial duties and obligations. Thus the woman's power, and she certainly possessed a great deal, had an outlet in this small milieu.

As the older capitalists retired, and their frequently inept or uninterested sons or grandsons tried to run the businesses, pressures of population growth, scientific discovery, technological application, and increasing specialization necessitated both business expansion and corporate organization. The separation of managerial control from family ownership resulted in maintaining the male's relationship to industrial enterprise; it gave him status and personal freedom outside the family. But women either remained at home or attempted to work. If a woman did the former, she had little status beyond that conferred upon her by her husband; if she chose to, or was forced to, work she found that high prestige (and high paying) jobs went to men virtually without exception.

As its role in economic enterprise was reduced by twentieth-century industrial organization, the size of the family decreased. A large family was no longer so useful for the production of economic goods. The median size of a household was 5.4 persons in 1790 in the United States, 4.2 in 1900, and 3.3 in 1940 and 1967 (Census Bureau, 1968). While household size is not synonymous with family size, there is a great deal of overlap. The decline in household size can be attributed primarily to a sharp decline in the birth rate. As Winch notes, "toward the end of the eighteenth century the average fertile married woman was bearing eight children; the current figure seems to be a bit under three" (Winch, 1970).

Changes have also taken place in the death rate and the age at marriage. People live longer today and marry a little earlier. "For men in 1789 the expectation of life at birth was only 34.5 years. By 1966 it had risen to 70 for the population as a whole" (Winch, 1970). As a result of all these trends, a new stage of family life has emerged—an "empty nest" phase never before experienced. In 1890, the average marriage was broken by the death of a spouse before the last child married. Now the average family experiences fifteen years of marriage after the departure of the last child (Glick, 1957).

As all these processes took place, families came to resemble more closely the stereotype WASP family of today: a married couple and 2.5 children, relatively independent in every way of kin, being not often proximate, having lower rates of interaction and mutual aid, and somewhat less likely to find kin duty very important.

It is apparent that intrafamilial relations, at least in cases of the shrinking family, are increasingly characterized by an egalitarian role ideology (Goode, 1963). But in extrafamilial terms, the opposite has been the case; the woman has been expected to conform herself, and particularly her demands on the marriage and her family, to the needs of the corporation. Her major role-commitment has not changed; it is still rooted in the family. But the family is changed, and thus outlets for female self-expression have become fewer; and the family constitutes a relatively expendable unit in the economic system. If the decade of the 1950s was the highest period of industrial *social* organization in America, then Whyte (1957) is its historian, and Park Forest is a burlesque of the family's subservience to the behemoth corporation. Thus the concept of marriage and the family as a career for women and occupation in industrial enterprise for men have both been importantly shaped by the needs of the corporation.

The industrial nuclear family and beyond

As Bert Adams (1970) has indicated, sociologists "discovered" this industrial family sometime in the 1930s or 1940s, and by the next decade scores of essays and books had commented on the shrunken family and how it got that way. Since functionalism was in the forefront of sociological analysis at the time, most commentators felt the family had "lost its functions" in modern society and, consequently, broader kinship relations were not to be found in any meaningful sense. Man and wife and their offspring were the "new" family, and affection was the bond that held them together (Blood and Wolfe, 1960). These commentators were reacting to the kind of statistics we have just presented. In their eagerness to generalize about "universal" and "necessary" trends—consequences of urbanization and industrialization—they failed to detail the links in the argument. The fact is, this family form is neither new (Greenfield, 1961) nor, if divorce rates are any indication, very affectionate.

There was a virulent reaction to the "shrunken family" generalization, especially to something Parsons once said. He argued, for a variety of logical and plausible reasons, that the new family form was of the "isolated nuclear" variety. He felt a modern industrial economy required high mobility of the working population. It seemed obvious that frequent, often long-distance, moves would be disruptive of family ties. In a society in which children would often move into a higher social class than that of their parents, relations between parents and children would naturally be strained. How much more so for the grandchildren, who shared few of the values and goals of their grandparents! Parsons's argument (1943) was so plausible it was not challenged until the mid-1950s. By misreading and overreacting to Parsons, while correctly interpreting the spirit of his scholarship, many investigators set out to prove that the larger family form was not dead but alive and well and all around us (Adams, 1970). Thus, the general intent of family research in the 1950s and 1960s was to describe existing familial and kin systems, which were shown to be highly salient to most urban residents (Bell and Boat, 1957; Greer, 1956; Sussman, 1955; Young and Wilmott, 1957; Firth, 1956; Sussman and Burchinal, 1962; Litwak, 1960a and 1960b). Many urbanites spend a good deal of time with their close relatives, a finding that led one family researcher to conclude that "the isolated nuclear family is dead." The scholarly battle raged, each side claiming vindication and victory. By the mid-1960s such descriptive studies ". . . gave way first to summaries of the 'isolated nuclear family' debate, and subsequently to more complex research attempts aimed at *specification, interrelation,* and *comparison"* (Adams, 1970: 576, emphasis in original).

Thus, many articles recently written deal with the consequences of geographical and occupational mobility, treating the earlier assumption of the disruptive effects of mobility as a hypothesis to be tested. It seems, though the evidence is far from conclusive, that the relation of kinship ties to mobility is far more complex than earlier believed (Litwak, 1960; Stuckert, 1963; Aiken and Goldberg, 1969). Mobility certainly does not necessarily lead to disruption of kin ties any more than mere physical presence guarantees their utilization. Further, the *direction* of vertical social mobility undoubtedly has differential consequences. Along these lines, one variable that has received insufficient attention is the parents' attitude toward their children's social or geographical mobility. Different groups, obviously, differ in their degree of support or antipathy towards occupational mobility. At a minimum, it seems likely that spatial mobility (which frequently occurs with vertical movement) does necessitate a change in the form of contacts among kin. And, as a final note, one should keep in mind that it is precisely during the most geographically mobile phase of the family life-cycle, namely newlyweds, ages 20 to 26, that contact with kin is at its peak, partly for reasons discussed below.

It seems to us that Parsons and other systems-level functionalists were incorrect in two ways: *descriptively* of American society at mid-century and *predictively* of the immediate future of this country. In 1953, Parsons still characterized American society as "having a value system very close to the universalistic-achievement or performance ideal type." This has never been an especially accurate description of America as a whole, and most certainly does not anticipate the "repluralization" tendencies of the past decade. Further, Parsons wrote about the same time that Bell was signaling the "end of ideology" in politics, and popular writers, sociologists, and academicians were heralding the emergence of a new middle class that would incorporate all Americans in an orgy of consumer affluence, societal stability, and cultural homogeneity. Parsons's "pattern variable" analysis (1951) suggested that the United States, and the West in general, had moved inexorably from ascription to achievement, and from particularism to universalism. But America, and to a certain degree all complex societies, is a mixture of all these things. After all, groups—from families to large institutions—which gained an economic or political edge have always attempted not only to retain such power, but to do so through intergenerational transmittal, restrictive elitism, or other means.

We feel that the linear change assumptions inherent in Parsons's pattern variable scheme were not descriptively true of the postwar period when he wrote it, nor did they accurately predict the present period. Rather, we suggest that a more dialectical view, that newer forms of particularism are following hard on the heels of the universalistic society of the 1950s. Thus, trends in kinship, family, and marriage should reflect these "lags" or newer "adaptations," and should not completely conform to the industrial society model of a more or less isolated nuclear family.

Parsons's formulation has been criticized historically and logically by Greenfield (1961), Bennett and Depres (1960), and most thoroughly by Litwak (1960). Still, there is no general agreement that Parsons was clearly wrong (Smelser, 1966). Insofar as Parsons's assumptions are based on the functional interrelations between families and their societal milieus, we shall attempt to specify the nature of such interrelations in different urban subpopulations in order to arrive at a more coherent and descriptive view of urban family relations.

Functionality and kinship

It is first necessary to distinguish at least three analytical types of "functionality" of kin contact. In *instrumental* functionality, families or groups involved gain something tangible or useful in the course of an interaction. Examples include giving and receiving advice and financial aid, exchanges of help in doing housework, and aid in caring for the young and the ill. The second type of functionality we call *expressive*. It is exemplified in the exchange of psychological support among kinsmen, for example, family visiting and the exchange of greeting cards. A third basis for interaction with kin, a purely symbolic and nonfunctional act, is based on *duty*. This is not necessarily in the direct interest of the person initiating the contact, although it may well be, and such contacts certainly function to prop up the system as a whole. In any situation, these three relationships undoubtedly coexist and would be indistinguishable in the minds of the participants.

It seems to us that contact with kin and, in a sense, family size depend on the degree of instrumental functionality to be gained by such contact; and in a secondary sense, kinship networks may be influenced by expressively functional relations and "duty." As long as kinfolk are useful to one another, they will seek to interact and will maintain "networks" (Adams, 1968). At a basic level of reasoning, such a proposition is quite consistent with Parsons. To the degree the United States is truly a universalistic-achievement society, where everyone has access to the means of success, kin contact would have very little instrumental functionality, no reason for being. Cox (1965) has given us a portrait of new urban man in this light: he is middle to upper-middle class, well educated, and chooses his friends from a broad range of vocational and avocational interests, not on the basis of neighborhood or kinship.

But many groups in our society do not meet these criteria; they are situated at different points along the ascription-achievement continuum. Of these subpopulations, blacks, women, Jews, and recent immigrants come immediately to mind. All these people, in one fashion or another, have been systematically excluded from the broad range of opportunity structures, particularly in the higher echelons of industry. The location of these groups in an opportunity structure that defines success in a universal way accounts for much of the strength of kinship ties among these people.

Women are diminished as whole beings and forced, in most instances, to conform to a traditional image when they venture into industrial-bureaucratic situations. The marital career concept has remained for women the predominant mode of expression.

The case of American blacks is well known; they are usually allowed access only to those positions having both a high risk of failure and the probability of small gains, as in *petit* capitalism, which, in many ways, is the opposite problem a woman faces—she cannot get into a position to take risks, especially in bureaucracies.

In the case of Jews and other predominantly entrepreneurial ethnic categories, it was frequently only from kin that they could amass the necessary venture capital required to begin a new business.

If one considers "capital" in a broader sense, the Irish have used family and ethnicity to build up political capital, especially in urban politics, especially in certain eastern and mid-western cities (Greer, 1971).

Such differences of location in the opportunity structure are a function of time of arrival, already migrated kinsmen and townsmen (the latter especially relevant to white Southern migration to northern cities), skills obtained in the premigratory system, the nature of the opportunity structure (extensive-limited, open-closed, generalized-specialized). On these points see Greer (1971). Jews arrived with skills suitable to an urban society, or at least an established "achievement orientation," but they were excluded from participation in many phases of the industrial-bureaucratic system. They prospered by marshalling their resources in entrepreneurial and, later, professional pursuits (when American medical schools, for example, decided to admit significant numbers of Jews). Blacks have no traditional urban background in terms of either skills or attitudes, and they face even more exclusions in relation to opportunities in the industrial system. Where Jews could revert to the family for risk capital, trust, and labor, the black must use his family for sheer survival.[1] There is virtually no surplus for a black to invest. Were there such a surplus, it is unlikely that proper skills or attitudes would exist in the kinship network to exploit the opportunity (Nixon's "black capitalism" notwithstanding). As Liebow (1967) has noted, it is not that blacks cannot be future-oriented; it is that such activities have little real payoff.

Family life cycle and use of kin

We have also observed that both instrumentally functional and expressive relations change in direction and intensity over the family life cycle. "Expressive relations" refers to stages through which all families pass, like post-marriage; pre-children, young children, post-children, old age (Glick, 1957). The discussion which follows is taken from Goldenberg, Carns, and Greer (1971).

At certain times, kin prove to be very useful, notably in establishing a family and then its dissolution through aging. The middle phases of the family life cycle do not reveal nearly as frequent mutual aid relationships in parent-child relations as do the extremes. To the extent that kinship interaction levels remain relatively high during this middle phase (which we shall call the "independent" stage for obvious reasons), they do so as a function of expressive relations or kin duty (or "kin culture"), following strictly from the propositions mentioned above. Naturally, too, in middle-class urban families, this independent stage is characterized by continuing geographical mobility, thus spatial separation and reduced kin presence; all other things being equal, it is barely possible that someone would choose between two cities *because* they had kinfolk in one place. However, this does not automatically imply reduced functionality or a lack of long-distance interaction via telephone or letter as was earlier thought to

[1]We are not implying in any sense that black *marriages* are necessarily viable or intact. In fact, as with poor people of every race and region, black women and their offspring tend to be the significant nuclear family form, although not necessarily the majority one. With economic deprivation the role of husband-father tends to become untenable, especially in the face of policies which encourage his absence from the home. Thus, the family-as-marriage shrinks in size beyond that of the WASP pattern already discussed, and many negative consequences probably result. But this does not mean that blacks cannot and do not rely on blood relations, especially the wife to her mother, or on fictive lateral kin relations as in the case of the frequently detached and unemployed male (Liebow, 1967).

be the case (see Litwak, 1960a and 1960b). Such relations appear to be intimately related to *need*, not convenience or duty.

To summarize, we have suggested similar patterns for two levels of analysis:

1. At the macro-level, viewing the family along a time dimension leads to a consideration of the skills an immigrant possesses, recency of immigration, the economic market for his skills, his ability to adapt skills to the market, and the sociocultural constraints independent (or somewhat independent) of the market, such as prejudice. As noted earlier, when high-risk opportunities are open and safe routes are closed, the family can be highly functional as a locus for the concentration and use of economic capital, trusted labor, and high-risk credit. The basis for these processes is ascriptive in the very important initial phases: blood kin are eligible, indeed required, to participate. In later phases, performance and interest may be more important criteria in a highly competitive market; but even when this is the case, it is the performance of particular individuals—kin—that is required.

2. At the micro-level, analogies to the above point exist when an individual family is viewed along a temporal dimension defined by its own life cycle. The fledgling family lacks access to alternative institutional arrangements in much the same way new immigrants do: they have difficulty getting credit, they rarely accumulate capital, and their consumption "drain-off" is high, especially with young children. They also lack knowledge through inexperience. In such circumstances the kin network, or at least the parents, may be quite functional in an instrumental way. But as the younger nuclear family succeeds in linking itself with alternative institutions, such as banks and other services, the kinship network automatically becomes less instrumentally functional. However, it may remain expressively functional. As noted before, kin interaction will dip during the independent phase of the family life cycle, picking up again later.

Husbands, wives, and kin usage

We noted earlier that the "woman as nigger" concept appears to have some utility although, of course, important differences exist between women and blacks. Women will use kin (instrumentally and, in all likelihood, expressively) more than men. And family sociologists have long argued that kinship is fundamentally a female business, not only in pre-urban settings but also in urban-industrial societies. Thus, for example, mothers and daughters have particularly close ties, and widowed parents move in with married daughters more often than with married sons (Sweetser, 1963; Adams, 1964).

In some ways this emphasis on the female side of relations among kinsmen is really an overemphasis. *Any* group which cannot use the facilities of the broader society will likely turn to kin, and the same could be argued of expressive functionality. Considering only the matter of trust, there is a tendency among blue-collar people, who possess a broad range of skills, to exchange aid among kinsmen. Thus Uncle Harry knows how to fix your refrigerator, and you help him build an addition to his back porch. Aside from the pooled skills, this pattern could be caused both by the breakdown and high cost of services in what has been billed as a "post-industrial, service society." Among middle-class suburbanites who lack a kin pool of handyman skills, a neighbor might be a functional alternative. Bar this, the white-collar family must rely on an increasingly erratic, expensive, and whimsical system of services.

Turning to a group that lack actual kin and cannot utilize the institutions of modern urban society, it is significant that many blacks tend to rename close friends as kinsmen, creating a special status of trust for them. Even though technically fictive, "going for cousins" was one way a close relationship could be established in the hostile and unyielding environment around *Tally's Corner* (Liebow, 1967).

As further support for our point about the husband's side of household, we should note in passing that most financial aid received by a fledgling family, particularly if middle class, comes from the husband's parents, not the wife's. Indeed, data from the Detroit Area Study (1955) suggest that the husband's kin are generally more functional to a family over the entire family life cycle than are the wife's kin, even though there may well be more frequent interaction with the wife's kin. This is discussed at more length in Goldenberg, Carns, and Greer (1971). It is further supported in work done in Toronto by Wellman, *et al.* (p. 23). This appears to be sufficient reason to seriously question the overemphasis of kinship as primarily a female activity. But to reiterate, the use of kin is based on *need*. Thus males and females alike, faced with closed or untrustworthy routes, will turn to kin, kin substitutes, or possibly neighbors. The progressive spiraling of trust and response down to the microsocial, ascribed group appears to be pervasive phenomenon in American society.

SUMMARY

In a sense, much of what we have said about the urban family has been in the nature of a "deviant case analysis." That is, the modal pattern of the isolated nuclear family was described, discussed, and criticized early in this paper. Assuming, as the functionalists do, that family size (i.e., kin presence, interaction frequency, and functionality) is a product of societal complexity, with smaller families to be expected in a more urban-industrial society, we have been forced to move back along the abscissa of industrialization *within cities* in order to find substantial pockets of extended familism, kin utilization, and the like. (On a cross-cultural level, these ideas have been extensively treated by Winch and Blumberg, 1971). Such a position seems to synthesize, in a fruitful and very suggestive manner, the Parsonian arguments of the 1940s and the descriptive findings of the 1950s and 1960s. At its most general, our view is that some groups are imperfectly integrated into those very "complexity" phenomena with which we predict the shrinking of the family. And we conclude, incidentally, that greater numbers of people will be in disjunction with bureaucratic industrialization as urbanization increases worldwide, as automation proceeds, as systematic discrimination remains a highly significant fact of urban life, and as trust and confidence erode with the inefficiencies of the "service society." To be sure, in form at least, the White-Anglo-Saxon-Protestant, middle-class, suburban family is widespread in the United States; it is certainly the plurality if not the majority.

References

Adams, Bert N. 1964. "Structural Factors Affecting Parental Aid to Unmarried Children." *Journal of Marriage and the Family* 26: 327–331.
——. 1968. *Kinship in an Urban Setting*. Chicago: Markham Publishing Co.
——. 1970. "Isolation, Function, and Beyond: American Kinship in the 1960's." *Journal of Marriage and the Family* 32: 575–597.
Aiken, Michael, and D. Goldberg. 1969. "Social Mobility and Kinship: A Reexamination of the Hypothesis." *American Anthropologist* 71: 261–269.
Bell, Wendell, and M. Boat. 1957. "Urban Neighborhoods and Informal Social Relations." *American Journal of Sociology* 63: 391–398.
Bennett, John, and Leo Depres. 1960. "Kinship and Instrumental Activities." *American Anthropologist* 62: 254–267.
Blood, Robert O., and D. Wolfe. 1960. *Husbands and Wives*. Glencoe, Illinois: The Free Press.
Blumberg, Rae L., Donald E. Carns, and Robert F. Winch. 1970. "High Gods, Virgin Brides, and Societal Complexity." Unpublished paper read before the American Sociological Association.
Breese, Gerald. 1969. *The City in Newly Developing Countries*. Englewood Cliffs: Prentice-Hall, Inc.
Census, U.S. Bureau of the. 1968. *Statistical Abstract of the United States*. Washington, D.C.: U.S. Government Printing Office, Table 40.
Cox, Harvey. 1965. *The Secular City*. New York: The Macmillan Company.
Firth, Raymond. 1956. *Two Studies of Kinship in London*. London: Athlone Press.
Glick, Paul. 1957. *American Families*. New York: John Wiley & Sons, Inc.
Goldenberg, Sheldon, Donald E. Carns, and Scott Greer. 1971. "Family Life Cycle, Instrumental Functionality, and Kin Interaction." Unpublished paper read before the American Sociological Association.
Goldstein, Sidney, and Calvin Goldscheider. 1968. *Jewish Americans: Three Generations in a Jewish Community*. Englewood Cliffs: Prentice-Hall, Inc.
Goode, William. 1963. *World Revolution and Family Patterns*. New York: The Free Press.
Greenfield, Sidney. 1961. "Industrialization and the Family in Sociological Theory." *American Journal of Sociology* 67: 312–322.
Greer, Scott A. 1956. "Urbanism Reconsidered: A Comparative Study of Local Areas in a Metropolis." *American Sociological Review* 21: 19–25.
——. 1971. "On Ethnicity and Kin." Unpublished paper, Northwestern University.
Liebow, Elliot. 1967. *Tally's Corner*. Boston: Little, Brown and Company.
Litwak, Eugene. 1960a. "Occupational Mobility and Extended Family Cohesion." *American Sociological Review* 25: 9–21.
——. 1960b. "Geographical Mobility and Extended Family Cohesion." *American Sociological Review* 25: 385–394.
Mangin, William. 1967. "Squatter Settlements." *Scientific American* 217: 21–29.
Merton, Robert K. 1957. *Social Theory and Social Structure*. New York: The Free Press.
Parsons, Talcott. 1943. "The Kinship System of the Contemporary United States." *American Anthropologist* 45: 22–38.
——. 1951. *The Social System*. Glencoe, Illinois: The Free Press.

——. 1953. "A Revised Analytical Approach to the Theory of Social Stratification." In R. Bendix and S. M. Lipset (eds.), *Class, Status, and Power*. Glencoe, Illinois: The Free Press.

Smelser, Neil. 1966. "The Modernization of Social Relations." In Myron Weiner (ed.), *Modernization: The Dynamics of Growth*. New York: Basic Books, Inc.

Stuckert, Robert. 1963. "Occupational Mobility and Family Relationships." *Social Forces* 41: 301–307.

Sussman, Marvin. 1955. "The Help Pattern in the Middle Class Family." *American Sociological Review* 18: 22–28.

——. 1962. "Kin Family Network: Unheralded Structure in Current Conceptualizations of Family Functioning." *Marriage and Family Living* 24: 231–240.

Sweetser, Dorrian A. 1963. "Asymmetry in Intergenerational Family Relationships." *Social Forces* 41: 346–352.

Wellman, Barry, *et al.* 1971. "The Uses of Community: Community Ties and Support Systems." Unpublished paper, University of Toronto and Center for Urban and Community Studies.

Whyte, William F. 1957. *The Organization Man*. Garden City: Doubleday & Company, Inc.

Winch, Robert F. 1970. "Permanence and Change in the History of the American Family and Some Speculations as to Its Future." *Journal of Marriage and the Family* 32: 6–15.

Winch, Robert F., and Rae Lesser Blumberg. 1971. "First Steps Toward a Model of Familial Organization." Unpublished paper read before the American Sociological Association.

Winch, Robert F., and L. W. Goodman. 1968. *Selected Studies in Marriage and the Family*. Third edition. New York: Holt, Rinehart & Winston, Inc.

Winch, Robert F., Scott Greer, and Rae Lesser Blumberg. 1967. "Ethnicity and Extended Familism in an Upper-Middle-Class Suburb." *American Sociological Review* 32: 265–272.

Young, Michael, and Peter Wilmott. 1957. *Family and Kinship in East London*. Glencoe, Illinois: The Free Press.

CHAPTER 5

CONTENTS

EMERGiNG life STylES

The last chapter presented two general views of the urban condition. One dealt with societal response, in the form of social norms, to overload experienced in the urban environment. People in Manhattan are guarded, suspicious, and frightened. Greer's urban man, who may be evolving into a public actor but is still withdrawn and largely uninvolved, represents another side of the picture. In fact, one of the most significant byproducts of Greer's work is his stress on the similarity of styles between non-urban and urban peoples, as well as the resistance to change found in areas of cities which frequently contain persons of similar social rank, ethnicity, or familism, or some combination of the three.

The first theme in Chapter 5 is "the city as tolerance and freedom," a theme quite current in social science thinking. A few years ago, the theologian Harvey Cox in *The Secular City* suggested that the city represents freedom but also, *ipso facto*, responsibilities. He painted a picture of emerging urban man—secular, profane, pragmatic—whose city took shape not in physically delimited areas but in networks of interdependence and interest. But the essence of urban civility is another matter. Howard S. Becker and Irving L. Horowitz discuss San Franciscans' tolerance of an incredible range of life styles—beat, hippie, communal, pornographic; indeed, such styles give the city much of its distinctive flavor. Other American cities may follow suit to a lesser degree; but the reader should attempt to figure out what is unique about San Francisco—climate, occupational structure, leadership, history, ethnic composition—which puts it into the forefront of urban civility.

We next deal with urban population density and the creation of personal living space. You will recall that Milgram also pointed out the need for privacy in overload situations, and Greer mentioned privatization in this regard. The article by Starr and Carns in this chapter also relates to this point. In John Zeisel's article, however, we see an attempt to wed sociological thinking to realities of architectural design, in this case at a housing project in Harlem. Pay particular attention to the residents' cultural needs and the ways planners tried to design housing which provides personal space as well as functionally separate areas, all within the confines of a relatively small apartment. And the broader point of Zeisel's piece is that housing arrangements may provide the only significant escape from urban density, confusion, and overload by creating a haven or nest; but the way housing projects are usually built, especially for the poor, makes them function more as prisons than havens of tranquility, and consequent levels of frustration and anger have their effects in crime and disorder.

The next part, "coping with the city," is simply a sampling of two emerging urban styles, styles that show unique adaptive patterns to given demands in the urban milieu. In the case of the Blackstone Rangers, James McPherson shows how a turf-based street gang extended its power, how politicians attempted to buy them off with federal funds, and how these funds were siphoned off to the gang and its members. If one regards this as neutrally as possible, the whole sequence of events represents a highly successful effort of "streetsmanship" combined with a certain bureaucratic finesse. The article on "Singles and the City" deals with coping behavior in a different population: young, unmarried, educated residents of the central city. The authors stress the importance of friendship networks that stem largely from work situations, directly or indirectly. Other themes include work dissatisfaction, reasons for choosing particular housing locations, and the bar scene (dating and mating).

The final section takes up the appeals of "green grass" and reintroduces themes discussed before: that future growth of cities will be on the fringes and outward, that central cities are losing population, becoming black, and also losing their industrial, and thus tax, base. As noted earlier, this impulse to suburbanize probably has many causes, among them the shrinking ratio of space to time due to trucks and automobiles, the seeking of community, and American distrust of cities and rural ideal. At any rate, Herbert Gans demonstrates that the suburbanization trend is not only large but increasing. More recent data in *Time* in spring 1971, based on work done by pollster Louis Harris, showed the same thing: suburban growth. In fact, closer-in suburbs are being bypassed by young married people in favor of farther-out exurbs which were farmland only a few years ago. This is necessitated by economic conditions in the new household, but the trend is facilitated by the fact that a majority of suburbanites now do not work in central cities but are employed in or near the suburb where they live. And all this is aided by the development of "ring" expressways around metropolitan areas.

The James McIntosh article fits in here by discussing residents of the far fringes of metropolitan Philadelphia and New York who are characterized as "urban voyeurs." That is, they enjoy the green grass, rural style, small farming on occasion, hunting, fishing, and the like, but via television they can deal vicariously with the mounting problems of the big cities. Their fringe area benefits from the far-reaching impact of the cities, but exurbans do not have to pay many of the costs of city life. In many respects, McIntosh's respondents represent nonurban America as a whole, for electronic voyeurism has no spatial limits.

17

HOWARD S. BECKER & IRVING LOUIS HOROWITZ, The Culture of Civility: San Francisco

Deviance and democracy in "The City"

Deviants of many kinds live well in San Francisco—natives and tourists alike make that observation. The city's apparently casual and easygoing response to "sex, dope and cheap thrills" (to crib the suppressed full title of Janis Joplin's famous album—itself a San Francisco product) astounds visitors from other parts of the country who can scarcely credit either what they see happening or the way natives stroll by those same events unconcerned.

- Walking in the Tenderloin on a summer evening, a block from the Hilton, you hear a black whore cursing at a policeman: "I wasn't either blocking the sidewalk! Why don't you motherfucking fuzz mind your own goddamn business!" The visiting New Yorker expects to see her arrested, if not shot, but the cop smiles good-naturedly and moves on, having got her back into the doorway where she is supposed to be.
- You enter one of the famous rock ballrooms and, as you stand getting used to the noise and lights, someone puts a lit joint of marijuana in your hand. The tourist looks for someplace to hide, not wishing to be caught in the mass arrest he expects to follow. No need to worry. The police will not come in, knowing that if they do they will have to arrest people and create disorder.
- Candidates for the city's Board of Supervisors make their pitch for the homosexual vote, estimated by some at 90,000. They will not be run out of town; the candidates' remarks are dutifully reported in the daily paper, as are the evaluations of them by representatives of SIR, the Society for Individual Rights.
- The media report (tongue in cheek) the annual Halloween Drag Ball, for which hundreds of homosexuals turn out at one of the city's major hotels in full regalia, unharassed by police.
- One sees long-haired, bearded hippies all over the city, not just in a few preserves set aside for them. Straight citizens do not remark their presence, either by gawking, hostility or flight.
- Nudie movies, frank enough to satisfy anyone's curiosity, are exhibited in what must be the largest number of speciality movie houses per capita in the country. Periodic police attempts to close them down (one of the few occasions when repression has been attempted) fail.

The items can be multiplied indefinitely, and their multiplicity demands explanation. Most cities in the United States refuse to let deviants indulge themselves publicly, let alone tolerate candidates who seek their bloc votes. Quite the contrary. Other cities, New York and Chicago being good examples, would see events like these as signs of serious trouble, omens of a real breakdown in law enforcement and deviance control, the forerunner of saturnalia and barbarian take-over. Because its politicians and police allow and can live with activities that would freak out their opposite numbers elsewhere, San Francisco is a natural experiment in the consequences of tolerating deviance. We can see from its example what results when we ignore the warnings of the custodians of conventional morality. We can see too what lessons can be learned about the conditions under which problems that perhaps lie deeper than matters of morals or life style can be solved to the satisfaction of all the parties to them.

A culture of civility

We can summarize this low-key approach to deviance in the phrase "a culture of civility." What are its components, and how does it maintain itself?

San Francisco prides itself on its sophistication, on being the most European of American cities, on its picturesque cosmopolitanism. The picturesque quality, indeed the quaintness, rests in part on physical beauty. As the filling of the Bay and the destruction of the skyline by high-rise buildings proceeds to destroy that beauty, the city has come to depend even more on the presence of undigested ethnic minorities. It is as though San Francisco did not wish its Italians, Chinese or Russians to assimilate and become standard Americans, preferring instead to maintain a panoply of ethnic differences: religious, cultural and culinary (especially culinary). A sophisticated, livable city, on this view, contains people, colonies and societies of all kinds. Their differences create a mosaic of life styles, the very difference of whose sight and smell give pleasure.

Like ethnic minorities, deviant minorities create enclaves whose differences add to the pleasure of city life. Natives enjoy the presence of hippies and take tourists to see their areas, just as they take them to see the gay area of Polk Street. Deviance, like difference, is a civic resource, enjoyed by tourist and resident alike.

To enjoy deviance instead of fearing it requires a surrender of some commonsense notions about the world. Most people assume, when they see someone engaging in proscribed activity, that there is worse to come. "Anyone who would do that [take dope, dress in women's clothes, sell his body or whatever] would do anything" is the major premise of the syllogism. "If you break one law or convention, who knows where you'll stop." Common sense ignores the contrary cases around us everywhere: professional criminals often flourish a legionnaire's patriotism; housewives who are in every other respect conventional sometimes shoplift; homosexuals may be good family providers; some people, who habitually use the rings from poptop cans to work the parking meter, would not dream of taking dope, and vice versa. "Deviance," like conforming behavior, is highly selective. San Francisco's culture of civility, accepting that premise, assumes that if I know that you steal or take dope or peddle your ass, that is all I *know.* There may be more to know; then again, there may be nothing. The deviant may be perfectly decent in every other respect. We are often enjoined, in a generalization of therapeutic doctrine, to treat other people as individuals; that prescription comes nearer to being filled in San Francisco than in most places in the United States.

Because of that tolerance, deviants find it possible to live somewhat more openly in San Francisco than elsewhere. People do not try so hard to catch them at their deviant activities and are less likely to punish them when caught. Because they live more openly, what they do is more visible to straight members of the community. An established canon of social psychology tells us that we find it harder to maintain negative stereotypes when our personal experience belies them. We see more clearly and believe more deeply that hippies or homosexuals are not dangerous when we confront them on the street day after day or live alongside them and realize that beard plus long hair does not equal a drug-crazed maniac, that limp wrist plus lisp does not equal child-molester.

When such notions become embodied in a culture of civility, the citizenry begins to sense that "everyone" feels that way. We cannot say at what critical point a population senses that sophistication about deviance is the norm, rather than a liberal fad. But San Francisco clearly has that critical mass. To come on as an anti-deviant, in a way that would probably win friends and influence voters in more parochial areas, risks being greeted by laughter and ridicule in San Francisco. Conservatives who believe in law and order are thus inclined to keep their beliefs to themselves. The more people keep moralistic notions to themselves, the more everyone believes that tolerance is widespread. The culture maintains itself by convincing the populace that it is indeed the culture.

It gets help from public pronouncements of civic officials, who enunciate what will be taken as the collective sentiment of the city. San Francisco officials occasionally angle for the conservative vote that disapproves licentiousness. But they more frequently take the side of liberty, if not license. When the police, several years ago, felt compelled to close the first of the "topless joints," the judge threw the case out. He reasoned that Supreme Court decisions required him to take into account contemporary community standards. In his judgment San Francisco was not a prudish community; the case was dismissed. The city's major paper, the *Chronicle,* approved. Few protested.

Similarly, when California's leading Yahoo, Superintendent of Public Instruction Max Rafferty, threatened to revoke the teaching credentials of any San Francisco teacher who used the obscene materials listed in the standard high school curriculum (Eldridge Cleaver's *Soul on Ice* and LeRoi Jones' *Dutchman*), the City did not remove the offending books from its curriculum. Instead, it successfully sued to have Rafferty enjoined from interfering in its operation.

In short, San Franciscans know that they are supposed to be sophisticated and let that knowledge guide their public actions, whatever their private feelings.

According to another well-known law of social psychology, their private feelings often come to resemble their public actions, and they learn to delight in what frightens citizens of less civil cities.

We do not suggest that all kinds of deviation are tolerated endlessly. The police try, in San Francisco as elsewhere, to stamp out some vices and keep a ceiling on others. Some deviance frightens San Franciscans too, because it seems to portend worse to come (most recently, users and purveyors of methedrine— "speed merchants" and "speed freaks"—whose drug use is popularly thought to result in violence and crime). But the line is drawn much farther over on the side of "toleration" in San Francisco than elsewhere. A vastly wider range of activities is publicly acceptable. Despite the wide range of visible freakiness, the citizenry takes it all in stride, without the fear and madness that permeates the conventional sectors of cities like Detroit, Chicago, New York, Washington, D.C. and similar centers of undaunted virtue.

Madames and unionists

How does a culture of civility arise? Here we can only speculate, and then fragmentarily, since so few cities in the United States have one that we cannot make the comparisons that might uncover the crucial conditions. San Francisco's history suggests a number of possibilities.

It has, for one thing, a Latin heritage. Always a major seaport, it has long tolerated the vice that caters to sailors typical of such ports. It grew at the time of the gold rush in an explosive way that burst through conventional social controls. It ceded to its ethnic minorities, particularly the Chinese, the right to engage in prostitution, gambling and other activities. Wickedness and high living form part of the prized past every "tourist" city constructs for itself; some minor downtown streets in San Francisco, for instance, are named for famous madames of the gold rush era.

Perhaps more important, a major potential source of repressive action—the working class—is in San Francisco more libertarian and politically sophisticated than one might expect. Harry Bridges' longshoremen act as bellwethers. It should be remembered that San Francisco is one of the few major American cities ever to experience a general strike. The event still reverberates, and working people who might support repression of others know by personal experience that the policeman may not be their friend. Trade unionism has a left-wing, honest base which gives the city a working-class democracy and even eccentricity, rather than the customary pattern of authoritarianism.

Finally, San Francisco is a town of single people. Whatever actual proportion of the adult population is married, the city's culture is oriented toward and organized for single people. As a consequence, citizens worry less about what public deviance will do to their children, for they don't have any and don't intend to, or they move from the city when they do. (Since there are, of course, plenty of families in the city, it may be more accurate to say that there are fewer white middle-class families, that being the stratum that would, if family-based, provide the greatest number of complaints about deviance. Black, chicano and oriental populations ordinarily have enough to worry about without becoming guardians of public morality.)

The place to live

San Francisco is known across the country as a haven for deviants. Good homosexuals hope to go to San Francisco to stay when they die, if not before. Indeed, one of the problems of deviant communities in San Francisco is coping with the periodic influx of a new generation of bohemians who have heard that it is the place to be: the beatnik migration of the late fifties and the hippie hordes of 1967. But those problems should not obscure what is more important: that there are stable communities of some size there to be disrupted. It is the stable homosexual community that promises politicians 90,000 votes and the stable bohemian communities of several vintages that provide both personnel and customers for some important local industries (developing, recording and distributing rock music is now a business of sizeable proportions).

Stable communities are stable because their members have found enough of what they want to stay where they are for a while. If where they were proved totally unsatisfying, they presumably would move elsewhere, unless restrained. But no one forces deviants to live in San Francisco. They stay there because it offers them, via the culture of civility, a place to live where they are not shunned as fearsome or disgusting, where agents of control (police and others) do not regard them as unfortunate excrescences to be excised at the first opportunity. Because they have a place to stay that does not harass them, they sink roots like more conventional citizens: find jobs, buy houses, make friends, vote and take part in political activities and all the other things that solid citizens do.

Sinking roots stabilizes deviants' lives, as it does the lives of conventional citizens. They find less need to act in the erratic ways deviants often behave elsewhere, less need to fulfill the prophecy that because they are deviant in one respect they will be deviant in other, more dangerous ways. San Francisco employers know that homosexuals make good employees. Why not? They are not likely to be blackmailed by enterprising hustlers. The police seldom haul them off to jail for little reason or beat them because they feel like pushing some "queers" around. Homosexuals fear none of this in San Francisco, or fear it much less than in most places, and so are less given to the overcompensatory "camping" that gets their fellows into trouble elsewhere.

Police and others do not harass deviants because they have found, though they may deny it for public relations purposes, that looking the other way is sometimes a good policy. It is easier, when a Be-In is going on, to turn your back on the sight of open marijuana smoking than it is to charge into the crowd and try to arrest people who will destroy the evidence before you get there, give you a hard time, make a fool of you and earn you a bad press—and have no conviction to show for it. At the same time, when you turn your back, nothing worse is likely to happen: no muggings, no thefts, no rapes, no riots. Police, more calculating than they seem, often choose to reach just this kind of accommodation with stable deviant communities.

The accommodation works in circular fashion. When deviants can live decent lives, they find it possible to behave decently. Furthermore, they acquire the kind of stake they are often denied elsewhere in the present and future structure of the community. That stake constrains them to behave in ways that will not outrage nondeviants, for they do not want to lose what they have. They thus curb their activities according to what they think the community will stand for.

The community in turn, and especially the police, will put up with more than they might otherwise, because they understand that nothing else is forthcoming, and because they find that what they are confronted with is not so bad after all. If homosexuals have a Halloween Drag Ball, the community discovers it can treat it as a good-natured joke; those who are offended discover that they needn't go near the Hilton while it is happening.

No doubt neither party to such a bargain gets quite what he would like. Straight members of the community presumably would prefer not to have whores walking the downtown streets, would prefer not to have gay bars operating openly. Deviants of all kinds presumably would prefer not to have to make any concessions to straight sensibilities. Each gives up something and gets something, and to that degree the arrangement becomes stable, the stability itself something both prize.

Deviance and democracy

What we have just described verges on the idyllic, Peace and Harmony in Camelot forever. Such a dream of perfection does not exist in San Francisco, though more deviants there have more of the advantages of such a bargain, perhaps, than in any other city in the United States. Nor is it clear that the system we described, even in its perfect form, would be such an idyll.

In San Francisco, as everywhere, the forces of decency and respectability draw the line somewhere and can be every bit as forceful and ruthless the other side of that line as the forces of decency and respectability anywhere else. When the Haight-Ashbury got "out of hand" with the overcrowded transiency of 1967, the city moved in the police Tactical Squad, the City Health Department and all the other bureaucratic weapons usually used to roust deviants. They did it again with the growth of violence in that area associated with the use and sale of methedrine. In general, the city has responded with great toughness to those deviants it believes will not be satisfied with something "reasonable." In particular, political dissent has sometimes been met with force, though San Francisco police have never indulged themselves on any large scale such as that which made Chicago police internationally detested.

The system has beauty only for those deviants who do not mind giving up some portion of their liberty, and then only if the portion they are willing to give up is the same as what the community wants given up. This no doubt is the reason an accommodative system works well with those whose deviant desires are narrowly circumscribed, and may have less utility with those whose wants can be accommodated only at the expense of others who will not easily give up their privileges. In fact, current political difficulties clearly result from the breakdown of accommodation.

These considerations indicate the more general importance of San Francisco's experiment in tolerating and accommodating to the minor forms of deviance encompassed in sex, dope and cheap thrills. How can a complex and differentiated society deal with variety and dissent and simultaneously with its own urges for centralized control? An accommodative relationship to difference, in which it is allowed to persist while it pays some minimal dues to the whole, is what San Francisco recommends to us, suggesting that the amount of the dues and the breadth of the license be set where both parties will, for the time being, stand still for it. The resulting working arrangement will be at least temporarily stable and provide for all concerned a tranquility that permits one to go about his business unharmed that many will find attractive.

But is this no more than a clever trick, a way of buying off deviant populations with minor freedoms while still keeping them enslaved? Beneath the rhetoric, the analysis is the same. The more radical statement adds only that the people who accept such a bargain ought not to, presumably because they have, if they only knew it, deeper and more important interests and desires which remain unsatisfied in the accommodative arrangements. So, of course, do those who hold them in check. Perhaps that is the ultimate lesson of San Francisco: the price of civilization, civility and living together peacefully is not getting everything you want.

Limits of accommodation

It is tempting to think that an accommodation based on civility and mutual interest provides a model for settling the conflicts now wracking our urban areas. Our analysis suggests that this is a possibility, but no more than that. Peace can occur through accommodation, the example of the potheads and pimps tells us, only under certain not so easily attained conditions. Those conditions may not be present in the ethnic and political problems our major cities, San Francisco among them, are now experiencing.

Accommodation requires, as a first condition, that the parties involved prize peace and stability enough to give up some of what they want so that others may have their desires satisfied as well. But people take that point of view only when the accommodation leaves them enough of a share to want no more. Some urban groups no longer believe that they are getting that necessary minimum, either because they have learned to interpret their situation in a new light or because they have lost some advantages they once had.

Members of black communities may be no worse off than ever, but they are considerably worse off than whites and know it. For a variety of historical reasons, and as a matter of simple justice, some of them no longer regard the little they have as sufficient reason to keep the peace. All the discussion about how many blacks feel this way (is it 10 percent or 50 percent?) and how strongly they feel it (are they willing to fight?) is irrelevant to the main point: enough feel strongly enough to make a lot of trouble for the white community, thus changing the balance of costs to the whites and insisting on a new division of rights as the price of stability.

Some members of white communities probably are objectively worse off and may resent it sufficiently to give up peace and stability in an effort to raise the costs to others and thus minimize their losses. Many whites in civil service positions, in the skilled trades and in similar protected occupational positions have lost or are in danger of losing competitive job advantages as governments act to do something about the injustice that afflicts black communities. Without a general expansion of the economy, which is *not* what blacks demand, injustices inflicted on blacks can be remedied only by taking something away from more favorably situated whites. It may be possible to improve the education of poor black children, for instance, only by taking away some of the privileges of white teachers. It may be possible to give black youths a chance at apprenticeships in skilled trades only by removing the privileged access to those positions of the sons of present white union members. When whites lose those privileges, they may feel strongly enough to fracture the consensus of civility.

The deviant communities of San Francisco show us cases in which the parties involved agree in a way that leaves each enough. But that may only be possible when the interests to be accommodated involve morals and life styles. When those interests include substantial economic prizes, major forms of privilege and real political power, it may be that nothing less than a real-life assessment of relative intensities of desire and ability to inflict costs on others will suffice. That assessment takes place in the marketplace of conflict.

This suggests a second, more procedural condition for the achievement of urban peace through accommodation and civility. Mechanisms and procedures must exist by which the conflicting desires and resources for bargaining can be brought together to produce a temporarily stable working arrangement. The accommodations of enforcement officials and deviants typically occur in a host of minor bargaining situations. Hassles are settled by the people immediately involved, and settled "on their own merits"—which is to say, in a way that respects the strength of everyone's feelings and the amount of trouble each is prepared to make to have his way. The culture of civility works well because the myriad of separate local bargains respect and reflect what most of the involved parties want or are willing to settle for.

We do not allow ourselves this extreme degree of decentralized decision-making with respect to many important problems (though many critics have suggested we should). Instead, we allow federal, state or city bureaucracies to make general policies that inhibit local accommodation. While government might well intervene when circumstances make bargaining positions unequal, we know now that it is not ordinarily well equipped to reach accommodative agreements that will work at the grass roots. Unable to know what the people who inhabit local will want and settle for, officials turn to technocrats for solutions.

Thus, when we confront the problem of slums and urban renewal, we send for the planner and the bulldozer. But the lives of urban residents are not determined by the number or newness of buildings. The character of their relationships with one another and with the outside world does that. Planners and technocrats typically ignore those relationships, and their influence in shaping what people want, in constructing solutions. They define "slums" impersonally, using such impersonal criteria as density or deterioration, and fail to see how awakened group consciousness can turn a "slum" into a "ghetto," and a rise in moral repute turn a "ghetto" into a "neighborhood."

Too often, the search for "model cities" implies not so much a model as an ideology—a rationalistic vision of human interaction that implies a people whose consistency of behavior can nowhere be found. We already have "model cities": Brasilia at the bureaucratic end and Levittown at the residential end. And in both instances, the force of human impulses had to break through the web of formal models to make these places inhabitable. In Brasilia the rise of shantytown dwellings outside the federal buildings make the place "a city," whereas the Levittowners had to break the middle-class mode and pass through a generation of conformity before they could produce a decent living arrangement. To design a city in conformity to "community standards"—which turn out to be little more than the prejudices of building inspectors, housing designers and absentee landlords—only reinforces patterns of frustration, violence and antagonism that now characterize so many of America's large cities. To think that the dismal failure of larger housing projects will be resolved by their dismal replacement of small housing projects is nonsense. Minibuildings are no more of a solution than maxibuildings are the problem.

In any event, centralized planning operating in this way does not produce a mechanism through which the mutual desires, claims and threats of interested groups can sort themselves out and allow a *modus vivendi,* if one exists, to uncover itself. The centralized body makes bargains for everyone under its influence, without knowing their circumstances or wants, and so makes it impossible for the people involved to reach a stable accommodation. But centralized planning still remains a major solution proffered for urban problems of every kind.

Accommodations reached through the mechanism of old-fashioned city political machines work little better, for contemporary machines typically fail to encompass all the people whose interests are at stake. Richard Daley demonstrated that when the Chicago ghetto, supposedly solidly under his control, exploded and revealed some people his famed consensus had not included. Lyndon Johnson made the same discovery with respect to opponents of the Vietnam War. Insofar as centralized decision-making does not work, and interested parties are not allowed to make bargains at the local level, accommodative stability cannot occur.

So the example of San Francisco's handling of moral deviance may not provide the blueprint one would like for settling urban problems generally. Its requirements include a day-to-day working agreement among parties on the value of compromise and a procedure by which their immediate interests can be openly communicated and effectively adjusted. Those requirements are difficult to meet. Yet it may be that they are capable of being met in more places than we think, that even some of the knottier racial and political problems contain possibilities of accommodation, no more visible to us than the casual tolerance of deviance in San Francisco was thinkable to some of our prudish forebearers.

18

JOHN ZEISEL, Symbolic Meaning of Space and the Physical Dimension of Social Relations

An often articulated criticism of new housing in urban slums is that it is socially inadequate. Lack of money, antiquated zoning laws and an unresponsive political system are all blamed. Architects and planners have been unaware of how sociological data can increase the social adequacy of their designs. Sociologists have been slow to realize their potential contribution to an understanding of the relationship between social and physical environment.

The most obvious reason that mass housing fails to satisfy the needs of its residents is that their needs are often unknown to the architect. Originally an architect built houses for people with the same living habits and social relationships as himself. The form of the building, its design and its relationship to other houses nearby were dictated by tradition. When architects began to build houses for people they did not know well, they dealt mainly with one person: the client who paid for and lived in the building. Today, we often find architects with one set of social and cultural characteristics planning housing for people with quite a different set. The role of the traditional client has now been divided into two parts—the paying-client and the resident-client. The paying-client is the one with whom the architect deals. But the resident-client is the one who will live in the ultimate building.

PROVIDING THE ARCHITECT WITH SOCIOLOGICAL INFORMATION

Last summer I carried out a case study to find out what social information is relevant to design and what methods can best be used to gather the data. In cooperation with Brent Brolin, a New York architect, and the Real Great Society (RGS), a community group in East Harlem, we designed housing for the Puerto Rican residents of two tenement buildings on 110th Street in Manhattan.

RGS is made up of young Puerto Ricans and blacks who decided to organize for an improved community in the Lower East Side and in East Harlem. After setting up an educational exchange called the University of the Street, the group received a grant from the Astor Foundation to buy two brownstones and convert them into classrooms and offices for a school. Not wanting to add to the already oppressive housing shortage in New York City, they decided to combine the two buildings and renovate the apartments on the upper floors so that tenants already in the buildings could remain.

We carried out the research over a period of two weeks by talking and spending time with each of the dozen or so families in the building. One of the staff members of RGS participated in the research to help us gain access to the tenants, to translate if need be, to learn the research method, and finally to help analyze the findings.

The architect, the staff member, and I first explained the general purpose of the study to each family: "To find out what they, as the future residents, wanted and needed in the new design of the apartments." We talked with them about what they would like in new apartments, about what they did in the apartments, and about how they spent their day. We also showed them schematic diagrams of different apartment layouts and asked them to choose one and explain why.

At the same time we noted where people were when we came in, what they did while we were there, and who else came in. We noted the physical attributes of the apartments: furniture placement, wall decorations, and any changes the tenants made in their apartments. We looked for physical cues of use, misuse, changing of apartments, non-use, and of what a room or a space meant to the tenant.

Data and analysis

The many observations were grouped according to the general pattern they seemed to display. In some cases physical cues indicated a pattern:

Observations: On the walls of most of the livingrooms there are religious icons and pictures of John F. Kennedy. Statues of saints are predominantly displayed. The television set and all the best furniture are always in the living room. Plastic covers are on all the furniture and sometimes on the television set and the statues. (The respondents were often shocked by the idea of eating in the livingroom and entering directly into it with dirty shoes).

General pattern: Livingroom used as sacred space.

Observations: In almost every case, although respondents had a door which entered into the livingroom from the hall, that door was blocked by furniture or by odds and ends, or had curtains hanging in front of it.

Figure 1. Original tenement plan

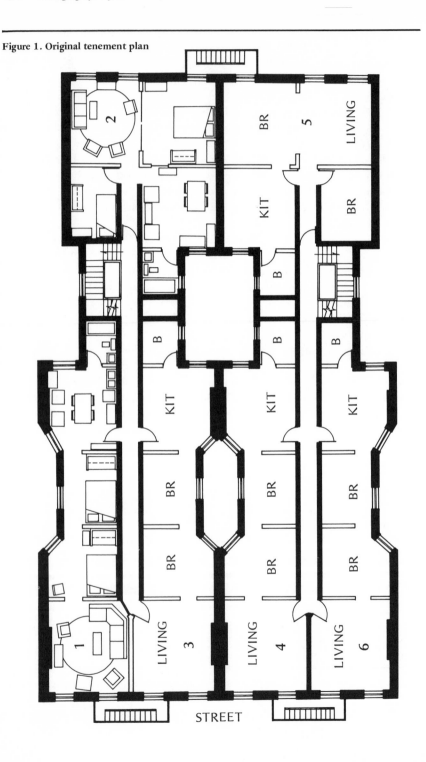

General pattern: Non-use of alternative entrance into apartment through living-room. (Related to keeping dirt out of sacred space.)

In other cases the patterns represented mainly behavioral observations:

Observations: When there are more than two generations in an apartment, the youngest generation usually stays in a different room from the older generation. Often, the middle generation takes care of the children while listening with half an ear to the older people's conversation. When the men are gathering in one room, the women usually stay in another.

General pattern: Separation of simultaneous activities by age and sex.

The general patterns were formulated in terms of requirements which the design of the apartments would have to meet so that the physical construction would not disrupt the patterns. Finally, the architect designed a plan which met the requirements.

Table 1 lists the general patterns, the specific form requirements derived from each, and the decisions made by the architect in designing his plan. Often one decision incorporates several requirements. By reading across the columns from left to right, one can see the transition from sociological findings to physical design. Following the list is the plan [Figure 2] for the new apartments incorporating all the design decisions.

Table 1

General patterns	*Form requirements*	*Design decisions*
1. Livingroom used as sacred space 1'. Kitchen used to eat in 2. Livingroom used for more formal activities 2'. Kitchen used for informal gatherings 3. Livingroom used as place to relax away from work areas, from kitchen 4. Separation of simultaneous activities by sex and age	1. Separate sacred space from profane activity area, from dirt, from eating, etc. 2. Separate formal from informal activity area 3. Separate livingroom from work area 4. Need for two separate areas of approximately equal size	Ia. Make living area and kitchen area approximately equal in size Ib. Separate the two areas from one another by at least a physical wall
5. Constant visual and/or aural surveillance, overseeing, of apartment	5. Some visual and aural connection between the two activity areas	II. Design apartments and construct walls between two activity areas so that some visual and aural communication between the two is possible

Table 1 (cont.)

General Patterns	*Form requirements*	*Design decisions*
6. Non-use of alternative entrance into apartment through livingroom (related to keeping dirt out of sacred space)	6. Entrance not into livingroom	III. Design apartment so that person in the kitchen is first to see who enters and last to see who leaves the apartment
7. Selection by respondents of diagram with entrance not in kitchen	7. Entrance not into kitchen	
8. Kitchen serves as turnstile and as lock for people going in and out of apartment—person in kitchen is controller	8. Entrance near or passing by area where most time is spent by the women of the home and near the informal guest area	
9. Windows used as posts for observation of and communication with street activity	9. Connect frequently used apartment areas and street	IVa. Locate livingroom and kitchens so that as many as possible face onto either the street or the adjacent park
		IVb. Maximize number of windows from livingrooms and kitchens to street and park
10. Privacy of bedroom is maximized	10. Separate bedrooms from interior of apartment and from street	Va. Construct walls so that bedrooms whenever possible have at most one window (minimum housing code requirement)
		Vb. Design apartment so that as few bedrooms as possible face onto the street or the adjacent park
11. Dissatisfaction with existing apartment layout—bathroom connected to kitchen	11. Separate bathroom entrance from kitchen	VI. Design apartment so that bathroom is not entered from kitchen
12. Much informal dropping-in among neighbors	12. Provide easy access between apartments	VII. Locate apartment entrances onto a common hallway and as close as possible to the stairway
13. Much verbal communication between apartments via hallway	13. Provide the possibility of verbal communication between apartments	VIII. Install an intercom system with phones in the kitchens so that apartments can contact each other without cost (a non-design solution)

Table 1 (cont.)

General patterns	*Form requirements*	*Design decisions*
14. Family size varies from two persons to seven persons	14. Need for different sized apartments	IX. Provide apartments with number of bedrooms ranging from one to three

A comparison: non-research-based design

Alternative designs, also based on the research findings, could have fulfilled the form requirements just as well. The following plan [Figure 3] designed for the same residents, but without specific social criteria in mind, unwittingly conflicts with many of the requirements. The architect, although familiar with the tenants, followed only one set of standards: what he, himself—a middle-class white American—would like, given the income limitation.

The livingroom—diningroom area in this plan is one large undifferentiated space. The possibility of the family splitting into two groups as our study showed was needed, would be practically impossible. In the two three-bedroom apartments, one passes by all the bedrooms before coming to the kitchen. The kitchen could not serve as a lock or turnstile—another requirement. None of the kitchens have windows facing onto the street. Communication would be impossible. In the two-bedroom apartments, the entrance is directly into the livingroom, and one must walk through the middle of the room to get anywhere in the apartment. There is no sacred space.

Although the layout of the apartments might seem compatible to many, it conflicts with the majority of the requirements found during our study of low-income Puerto Ricans in East Harlem.

Social information relevant to design

In providing information about future residents to those who are designing, planning and building houses, it is incumbent upon the sociologist first to provide sociological information relevant to physical planning, and then to demonstrate how each piece of data can be incorporated into the physical design.

Table 2 summarizes the five basic types of social information relevant to design, and the method or methods best suited to gather each type.

The problem of user wants

Our study underlines that knowledge of opinions of prospective residents is insufficient for the architect to design housing which meets their needs. Although this information is most often collected, it is difficult to incorporate into designs for several reasons:

Figure 2. Revised plans

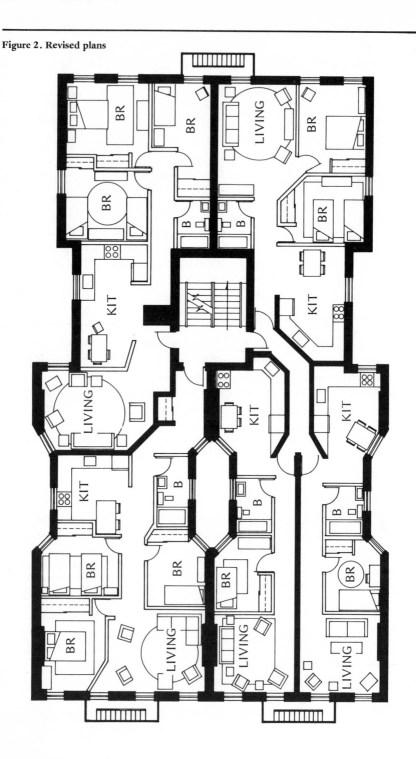

Table 2

Types of social information relevant to design	*Methods for gathering information*
1. OPINIONS about space and facilities a) general attitudes b) specific desires	1. SURVEY—ask about existing spaces and facilities and offer alternatives to choose from
2. SOCIAL RELATIONS and their physical dimension	2. NATURAL OBSERVATION (recording physical relationship of participants to one another as well as their age, sex and other status characteristics)
3. SYMBOLIC MEANING attributed by residents to given objects and spaces a) nonverbal vocabulary b) territoriality	3. NATURAL OBSERVATION, NATURAL EXPERIMENTS (introducing an artificial stimulus in a natural situation) and CATALOGUE OF PHYSICAL CUES (unobtrusive measures)
4. CONSCIOUS RULES about the use of space and facilities	4. SURVEY—talk with both the person making the rules and the person subject to them
5. USE of existing facilities and space	5. SURVEY OF USERS AND COUNTING OF USERS at natural site

1. People's opinions about housing—both general attitudes and specific desires—depend to a great extent on their housing experience: their residential situation and history. As Alvin Schorr points out, people who have just moved to slightly better quarters are more likely to be satisfied with what they have than those who have not moved for a long time.[1] Those living in better housing want more than those living in inferior housing. Low-income dwellers in particular have had such a degrading housing history that their responses will often be distorted.

2. Desires are often determined by familiarity with specific alternatives. Totally new alternatives are seldom expressed by a respondent unfamiliar with three-dimensional conceptualization. If offered a choice for a new physical environment, the layman is unlikely to be able to project an abstract physical design into an actual experience. For this reason, potential public housing residents, such as were our respondents, often refer to the layout and the physical relationships in a housing project as ideals, as inappropriate to their needs as these may be. Research of this sort can only reenforce the mistakes of the past.

3. Aspirations are also reflected in wants. Because rich people have terraces, slum dwellers may also want them—even if they have to sacrifice an extra bedroom or space in the kitchen to get them.

4. Finally, in articulating desires, people often overlook the most obvious necessities. They take them so much for granted that it is inconceivable for the architect—outsider though he may be—not to supply them. Often this is not the case. In our study almost no one mentioned the need to have a communi-

Figure 3. Non-research-based plan

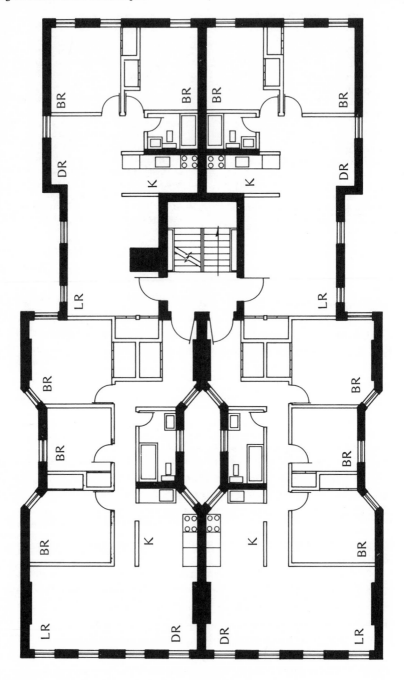

cation link with the street. I am sure, however, that they would have been surprised had this not been provided.

It is important to know what those who are going to live in a building or play in a recreation area want to have, and what they generally think about their environment. But the architect can no more accept these directives at face value than he can accept the demands of a client who is paying the bill directly. He is being paid to have imagination and insight: to combine what people say they want with his own understanding of their unexpressed needs. In our study, most of the respondents did not have strong attitudes about their apartments. Some of the attitudes they held—wanting bathroom entrance outside the kitchen, and wanting more privacy in the bedrooms—were incorporated into the final plans because in one case it was more sanitary and in the second, other observations reenforced the general pattern of bedroom privacy. Although residents preferred an entrance in the livingroom rather than in the kitchen—since this is how it is in the projects—all other indications pointed to the fact that such an entrance would be highly inappropriate. This demand was incorporated by keeping the entrance out of both areas.

To be able to interpret the opinions surveyed, and, more important, to help the architect identify needs as well as wants, the other methods of information-gathering must be employed.

Determining user needs

The most important information for us in East Harlem was the symbolic meaning of space and the physical dimension of social relations. Designers have never systematically gathered these types of information as a basis for planning. Instead, architects usually outline a program: a list of user needs to be satisfied by the physical environment. These needs are primarily biological—sleeping, eating, defecating—and physical—protection from the elements, sufficient light and air. Sometimes psychological needs are included, such as the need for a feeling of freedom or restfulness. These needs are incorporated into the design in terms of minimum space requirements.

Social needs are taken into account by describing formal and semiformal social activity areas—playrooms, community rooms, sitting areas, playgrounds, entertaining areas.

Architects define spaces and objects in terms of the manifest function each serves: bedrooms are for sleeping; diningrooms for eating; kitchens for cooking; windows for letting in light and air; livingrooms for entertaining, entrances for coming into and going out of the apartment; playgrounds for playing; parking lots for storing cars; sitting areas for people to rest.

1. Physical dimension of social relations. They seldom take into account either the latent function of the objects and spaces or the latent function of the behavior of the residents for whom they are planning.

Windows, as we found in East Harlem, are used not only for air and light, but also as observation posts and communication links with the street. The street, as a result, is more likely to be used as a place for showing off. Kitchens are not only places to cook and eat in, but are also places to which older people can go when younger ones are in the livingroom and for groups of men or women to chat among themselves. This separation of peer groups is integral to the social stability of several economic and cultural groups. A latent function of this separation is to reinforce the hierarchical age and sex structure necessary to maintain the social stability of these groups.

By putting no wall between the kitchen and living areas of an apartment, the architect of the nonresearched plan did not allow for this type of social separation.

To supply this kind of data to the architect, the social scientist must repeatedly observe specific social relations in a natural setting. By recording not only the activity, but also the physical relationship of the participants—be they connected to it as onlookers, or separated from it as those in another room—the observer begins to record the physical dimension of social relationships. When the status characteristics of participants—age, sex, social position—are also recorded, general patterns begin to emerge. In our study, many of the requirements reflect this approach.[2]

2. Symbolic meaning of space. To every individual, as Edward T. Hall has pointed out, space and objects have culturally and sub-culturally determined symbolic meanings.[3] These are evident in (a) his nonverbal vocabulary and (b) the one or more overlapping concepts of territory he holds. An architect or planner unaware of the particular meaning of space and of objects to the people for whom he is planning uses symbols familiar to himself to convey meaning, and runs the risk of being misunderstood.

a. Nonverbal vocabulary. In our study, we found that by cataloguing the John F. Kennedy wall hangings, the statues of saints and the plastic covers, a pattern emerged: the livingroom is a special, almost sacred place. The residents showed their allegiance to political, religious, and economic gods. By understanding this, we realized that we had to keep this area separate from more profane activities like eating—separate livingroom from kitchen—and walking in off the street—entrance not directly into the livingroom. The cordiality and hospitality expressed by having the entrance directly into the livingrooms of apartments for high-income groups would not be understood as such by the Puerto Ricans in East Harlem.

Another example of this symbolism is the kitchen. The kitchen is a place where the woman of the house demonstrates what a good wife she is by the food she prepares, the amount of time she spends there, the cleanliness of the room, and the number of appliances. The size and location of the kitchen in the apartment must therefore allow the woman to show off her womanly prowess. Among other groups (and this probably includes the groups from which most trained architects come) the kitchen is a utilitarian space. A woman communicates her proficiency by the amount of time she spends out of the kitchen and in the livingroom with her husband and guests. To provide a woman who spends most of her time in the kitchen with a small utilitarian space is once again to confuse the spatial vocabulary. It is essential, then, for sociologists to help architects by documenting the spatial vocabulary of the residents.

b. Territory. In East Harlem we found that, although the men and women and older and younger persons often stayed apart, it was not rare for one or the other to stand in the doorway to listen or pass by frequently to have a look. The entire apartment was visual and aural territory for all grown-ups. Children, on the other hand, were often slapped or shooed away when they came into a room occupied by adults. Their territory did not overlap that of the grown-ups.

By looking at and listening to the sanctions visited against violators of territory, the sociologist can determine what its boundaries are. As Robert Sommer points out, the observer can also violate a space himself and watch what happens. "The best way to learn the location of invisible boundaries is to keep walking until somebody complains."[4] This is a form of natural experimentation.

Territory, of course, exists at many scales: A child's territory is defined by how far a child can go from his mother; sexual territory is described by the separation or overlap of men's and women's activities; community territory is the distance from home which an individual considers his realm or turf; informal territory might be characterized as the area an individual feels he can walk around unshaven or in his T-shirt.

A knowledge of territoriality also benefits the planner. For example, a factor in the uproar over Columbia University's building a gymnasium in Morningside Park was the feeling among many Harlem residents that the park was theirs and was part of their turf. Although the park was seldom used, it apparently held symbolic meaning for Harlemites. Had research been carried out to determine the symbolic meaning of the park—by having respondents describe the "boundaries" of Harlem or by indicating these boundaries on a map or by asking people where they felt comfortable taking a walk—the potential violent opposition to Columbia's gym might have been foreseen.

We all realize that a way must be found to avoid socially harmful physical environments. Our case study suggests a modest beginning toward establishing a methodology to do this. Sociologists can provide physical guidelines to designers who, in turn, can design socially adequate environments.

Footnotes

1. Alvin L. Schorr, *Slums and Social Insecurity*, Washington, D.C.: U. S. Government Printing Office, 1963.
2. For further clarification of this approach, see Brent C. Brolin and John Zeisel, "Mass Housing: Social Research and Design," *The Architectural Forum*, July/August 1968.
3. Edward T. Hall, *The Hidden Dimension*, Garden City: Doubleday & Co., 1966; and Edward T. Hall, *The Silent Language*, Garden City, Doubleday & Co., 1959.
4. Robert Sommer, *Personal Space*, Englewood Cliffs: Prentice-Hall, Inc., 1969.

19

JAMES ALAN McPHERSON, Inside the Blackstone Rangers

Sometime between 1961 and 1963, according to evidence presented to a Senate subcommittee chaired by John McClellan of Arkansas last July, an unknown number of black young men, who lived in the general area of Sixty-sixth Place and Blackstone Avenue in the Woodlawn area of Chicago's South Side ghetto, organized a street gang. Like most street gangs, it was formed to protect its members from intimidation by other gangs in the South Side area. The most formidable enemy of this new group was a gang called the Devil's Disciples, which claimed part of the neighboring Kenwood area. In the years which followed, the Disciples became the traditional enemies of the Woodlawn youths, who called themselves Blackstone Rangers.

At first the Rangers were interested only in protecting their territory and their membership from attacks and retaliations by the Disciples, but by 1965 there were an estimated 200 of them in the group, and they were breaking with traditional gang patterns. They were organizing in Woodlawn. And this organization caused some public concern, and even fear, because it began during a period of violent rivalry between the Rangers and the Disciples. During these formative stages the Blackstone Rangers seemed to have placed the running feud between the Disciples and themselves secondary to their primary goal: organization. Soon their influence in Woodlawn caused minor, less influential, less powerful gangs to join them. And they came from all over the South Side: the Maniacs, the Four Corners, the Lovers, the V.I.P.'s, the Pythons, the Warlocks, the F.B.I., the Conservatives, the Pharaohs. At present there are anywhere from 3500 to 8000 boys and men who identify with the Blackstone Rangers and who have affixed the Ranger name to the names of their own gangs. Such is the organizational structure and size of the Blackstone Rangers today that they call themselves a Nation. The Ranger Nation is headed by a group of young men called the Main 21. Until 1968 the president of the organization was Eugene "Bull" Hairston, the vice president was Jeff Fort (also called "Angel" and "Black Prince"), and the warlord was George Rose (also called "Watusi" and "Mad Dog"). The Rangers' spiritual leader was Paul "The Preacher" Martin, and the rest of the Main 21 was made up of leaders of the minor gangs who had joined with the Rangers. Each individual gang, it seems, maintained its own organizational structure with its own officers; but collectively all of the gangs made up the Blackstone Nation, which is presently incorporated to do business under the laws of Illinois.

James Alan McPherson, "Inside the Blackstone Rangers, Part I," *The Atlantic Monthly*, vol. 223 (May 1969), pp. 74–84. Copyright © 1969, by The Atlantic Monthly Company, Boston, Mass. Reprinted with permission.

Since the emergence of the Ranger Nation, individual members have been charged with murder, robbery, rape, knifings, extortion of South Side merchants, traffic in narcotics, extortion and intimidation of young children, forced gang membership, and a general history of outright violence, especially against the Disciples who never joined the Rangers. On the other hand, the Ranger Nation has been credited with keeping the South Side of Chicago "cool" during the summer of 1967 and the spring of 1968, following the assassination of Dr. Martin Luther King. It has been said that they have kept drugs, alcoholics, prostitutes, and whites hunting for prostitutes out of their neighborhoods. They have also been credited with making genuine attempts to form lasting peace treaties between themselves and the Disciples in order to decrease the level of gang fighting on the South Side. They have been alternately praised and condemned by the national press, their community, the United States Senate, the local police, and Chicago youth organizations to such an extent that, if one depends on the news media for information, it is almost impossible to maintain a consistent opinion of the Blackstone Rangers.

Some of the Chicago papers have been quick to report any charges of violent activity against a Ranger. In newspaper accounts, the name of the gang takes precedence over the individual arrested and charged with crimes. Many of the charges are accurate; many of the young men who identify with the Rangers are guilty of various crimes. But much of the information passed on to the press is shown to have no substance upon thorough investigation. Still, the adverse publicity serves to keep the Chicago communities, both black and white, in a state of apprehension over the Blackstone Ranger organization, as opposed to the individuals in it.

There has been, and presently still is, a cry for a massive police crackdown on the Rangers. To accomplish this, the Chicago Police Department, following a general order issued by former Chicago Superintendent of Police O. W. Wilson, formed the Gang Intelligence Unit in March of 1967 to learn more about the Rangers and to decrease forcibly the level of gang violence in all areas of Chicago generally, and in the South Side area in particular. The stated purpose of the Unit was to eliminate "the antisocial and criminal activities of groups of minors and young adults in the various communities within the city."

In early June of 1967, The Woodlawn Organization (T.W.O.), a grass roots community association made up of one hundred or so block clubs, and civic, religious, and business organizations in the Woodlawn area of the South Side, received a $957,000 grant from the Office of Economic Opportunity to set up a special kind of youth project in the Woodlawn area. The purpose of the program was to utilize the existing gang structures—the Blackstone Rangers and the Devil's Disciples—as a means of encouraging youth in the gangs as well as non-gang youth to become involved in a pre-employment orientation, motivational project. The project was to include eight hundred out-of-school unemployed youths. And the entire program was to operate through four job-training centers which were to be set up in the home territories of the Rangers and Disciples. Reverend

Arthur Brazier, president of The Woodlawn Organization, was responsible for bringing the interest of OEO to the proposed program, which was admitted to be a "high-risk venture."

The money from OEO went directly to The Woodlawn Organization. It did not go through city agencies, although one of the conditions of the grant was that the mayor was to be "invited" to concur in the selection of a project director for the program. There is some opinion that the mayor's office was not pleased with this. In fact, the full operation of the program was delayed over two months because of the inability of the T.W.O. people and Mayor Richard J. Daley to come to an agreement on a director for the program. By the time the program officially began in September, a project director had not been hired, and the Rangers and Disciples had, apparently, lost much of their enthusiasm for the program.

In September of 1967, The Woodlawn Organization opened four training centers in the Woodlawn area: two for the Blackstone Rangers and two for the Devil's Disciples. One of the Ranger Centers was located in the First Presbyterian Church, a church in the Woodlawn area headed by Reverend John Fry, a white Presbyterian clergyman. The Xerox Corporation was hired to formulate the curriculum; the Chicago Urban League was hired to do job development; and Arthur Andersen & Company was hired to give T.W.O. monthly reviews. In addition, a Monitoring Unit with the Chicago police was set up to have two meetings a month with T.W.O. people and representatives from the two gangs, which had attempted to de-escalate the level of their violent rivalry since the new program had been announced.

The trainees were paid $45 a week to take five hours of instruction a day for five days a week, in addition to travel expenses. The instructors in the program, or Center Chiefs, were not professionals but gang leaders who were supposed to be under the supervision of professionals because, as Reverend Brazier stated before the McClellan Committee "many of these youth do not relate to professionals because the professionals with middle-class attitudes do not relate to them." Eugene Hairston, president of the Rangers, was hired as an assistant project director at a salary of $6500 a year. Jeff Fort, Ranger vice president, became a Center Chief and received $6000 a year. And many of the other members of the Main 21 occupied, at one time or another, salaried positions in the project. Apparently, there was not much public opposition to the hiring of gang leaders by the program. Rather, there seems to have been a reversal in public attitude toward the Rangers because of their performance in the year before the program began.

One of the activities which helped their public image was the production of a musical review called *Opportunity Please Knock*, which was sponsored by Oscar Brown, Jr., the jazz pianist, and performed by groups of Rangers and students from the Hyde Park High School. The show, which was eventually taken over by the Rangers, ran for six weeks in May and June of 1967. An estimated eight thousand people went to the First Presbyterian Church during the first weeks of its performance, and it received very favorable nationwide publicity.

Subsequent performances were given in various suburban communities around Chicago, and parts of the show traveled to Watts to perform. Some members of the troupe appeared on the Smothers Brothers show, and *Ebony* featured a large color story of the production in its August 1967 issue.

A second instance of positive Ranger activity, which also gained them favorable publicity, was their willingness to be bused out of town on August 12, Bud Billiken Day (named for a mythical folk hero created by the Chicago *Daily Defender,* a black newspaper). All past major conflicts between the Rangers and the Disciples had taken place during the Bud Billiken Day Parade and picnic in the South Side's Washington Park. In 1966 the city of Chicago had financed an out-of-town picnic for the Rangers through the Boys' Club, although there is some evidence that it considered the picnic idea a kind of blackmail exacted by the Rangers. In 1967, however, The Woodlawn Organization requested from OEO permission to use $5000 of its funds to take six hundred Rangers to an out-of-town picnic at Valparaiso University. The Rangers made the decision to leave town, it is said, because of rumors of a brewing riot and the public expectation that they would cause or at least participate in it.

The Ranger vice president, Jeff Fort, and been jailed on July 30 on murder charges and was still in jail on Bud Billiken Day. There are conflicting statements about whether or not Fort threatened to start a riot. Policemen have testified that he stated that if he were arrested, "the city would burn," while other sources reported that he cautioned the Rangers, after his arrest, not to riot. In any case, he remained in jail until early September of 1967, and there was no riot. The Rangers attended their picnic, and there were few incidents during the day. Whether or not the Rangers and Disciples actively contributed to the calm remains an open question. But a safe assumption can be made that when the T.W.O. project began in September, the Blackstone Rangers were enjoying a good deal of favorable press coverage and community support.

A final incident in the fall of 1967 helped their image in the city. In the Kenwood district, which adjoins Woodlawn, the police dispersed a black-power rally on September 15. The crowd then moved to a local high school, where bottles were thrown and two shots were fired by a sniper. The situation seemed to have been too tense for the police, when Herbert Stevens, leader of the Four Corners Rangers and a member of the Main 21 (known as "Thunder"), was said to have stood before the crowd and said, "All you who are willing to die, step up now. Otherwise, let's go home." And as he turned to leave he said, "When I come back, I don't want to see anybody on the streets. I want these streets cleared." When he returned in five minutes, the story goes, the crowd had broken up.

The Blackstone Rangers wanted to play a major role in determining how the OEO-Woodlawn project should be run, and there were meetings throughout the summer of 1967 between the gang leaders and representatives of T.W.O. to determine the extent of their voice in the project. These meetings were kept under surveillance by detectives from the Gang Intelligence Unit.

The public favor enjoyed by the Rangers during the summer of 1967 dropped off severely when the president and vice president were arrested in late September of 1967 for soliciting three juveniles—Marvin Martin, fifteen, Sanders Martin, fourteen, and Dennis Jackson, also fourteen—to murder a narcotics dealer named Leo McClure. McClure was in fact one of three men who were shot. Though he was not, it emerged, the prime target, he was the only one of the three who died. Dennis Jackson was alleged to have done the actual shooting. Hairston, the Ranger president, was kept in jail without bond, and the newspapers printed so many stories about a Teen-Age Murder, Inc., and so many details of the case against Hairston, that the first courtroom case ended in a mistrial.

During the same period the activities of Reverend John Fry and the First Presbyterian Church, which served as one of the T.W.O. training centers, were called into question. The church was said to be an arsenal for the Rangers to store their guns and a place where they sold and smoked marijuana, had sexual activity, and held their secret gang meetings. Then Jeff Fort was arrested in October and charged with murdering a Disciple. Both his arrest and the earlier arrest of Hairston encouraged the press to give extensive adverse publicity to The Woodlawn Organization because of their employment by the project. Soon afterward, three of the Main leaders, also members of the T.W.O. staff, were indicted for rape. The detectives of the G.I.U. made extensive visits to the training centers and found, according to their reports, no actual training taking place, the falsification of time sheets, gambling, and evidence that marijuana was being smoked on the premises. Finally, a Disciple was shot in one of the two Disciple Centers with a shotgun. The shooting was said to have been an accident, but the G.I.U. detectives who investigated the shooting found evidence that "light narcotics" (Robitussin) were being used at the Disciple Center. It was about this time that Senator McClellan's Permanent Subcommittee on Investigations of the Committee on Government Operations began to gather evidence in its planned investigation of The Woodlawn Organization's "high-risk" project.

The investigation began on June 28, 1968, in Washington. There was nationwide television coverage as all those who had connections with the project, official or otherwise, testified before Senators Jacob Javits, Carl Curtis, Fred Harris, Edmund Muskie, Karl Mundt, and of course Chairman John McClellan, who asked most of the questions.

Reverend Arthur Brazier made a desperate attempt to defend his project, explaining how participation of gang members was necessary for its success and charging that harassment from the Gang Intelligence Unit and explosively adverse news publicity had made it almost impossible for the project to develop as anticipated. Members of the Gang Intelligence Unit testified that they had made extensive visits to the training centers during the period of their operation and had found very little, if any, instruction going on. They also testified to the long list of crimes said to have been committed by gang members while under the sponsorship of T.W.O., especially the murder which was said to have been solicited by Eugene Hairston and Jeff Fort.

Perhaps the most damaging testimony against the program, if not against the Rangers themselves, came from George Rose, a former warlord of the Rangers who had defected from the organization, and a Mrs. Annabelle Martin, a black mother of ten who claimed to have had a very close relationship with the gang. The two Martin boys allegedly solicited by Hairston to commit the murder of Leo McClure were her sons.

Rose testified that the Rangers were involved in the sale of narcotics; that trainees in the program were forced to kick back to the organization from $5 to $25 each week; that the Rangers, from the start, had no interest in job training and that the program was used only to increase the gang's membership and its treasury; and that the First Presbyterian Church and its people—Reverend John Fry, Charles Lapaglia, and Anne Schwalbach, all white—were attempting to control and direct the gang through influence over Jeff Fort.

According to Rose's testimony, Reverend Fry had actually written the proposal for the OEO grant and had turned it over to Reverend Brazier; the church was used for the sale of narcotics, the storage of guns, and a convenient place for the Rangers to engage in sexual activity. He also told the Committee that Lapaglia had taken some of the Main 21 leaders on a trip to Michigan to purchase guns and on another trip to Philadelphia to attend a black-power conference where the murders of certain nonmilitant civil rights leaders were plotted. He said that the Rangers had made it known to Reverend Brazier that they considered the OEO money theirs and would not let outsiders—school dropouts who were not Rangers—into the program. And, according to his testimony, Brazier consented to this without informing OEO officials. Rose told the Committee that many of the gang leaders who had been hired as instructors or Center Chiefs had fifth- or sixth-grade educations and that Jeff Fort, who served as a Center Chief, could not read or write. Finally, he stated that students from regular schools were forced to drop out in order to join the program and the gang, and that those who refused were beaten, shot in the arms, forced to keep off the streets, or killed. In this way, he said, the Rangers induced "a couple hundred" students to leave public schools and join the program, and that it was a practice of the Rangers to solicit juveniles to commit murder because they received a lighter sentence if they were caught.

Of special interest was his testimony that the Rangers had offered to help the police, and, in fact, did outfit themselves in black uniforms, called themselves the police of the Blackstone Ranger Nation, policed their neighborhoods, and turned over to the police several non-Rangers in order to clear the name of their organization. He stated that the police accepted them at first, but then, "after we turned a couple of guys in and made it known that they weren't our guys, the police still started cracking our young fellows' heads, just because of the uniforms. They called us storm troopers because we had black jump boots, black pants tucked into the top of the boots. . . . They didn't like this at all. They called it mob action."

Rose also testified that after the Rangers were rejected by the police,

Reverend John Fry advised them to begin extorting merchants. "Since we were being accused of it," he said, "there wasn't anything we could lose by doing it." Rose said that the Rangers got from $5000 to $8000 a week from tavern owners and various sums from shoe stores, clothing stores, food stores, and drugstores through threats of future violence against them.

Robert L. Pierson of the Chicago State's Attorney's Office told the Committee that the Rangers "are the beginning of a Black Mafia." He testified that the Rangers were, in fact, extorting merchants but that the merchants would not complain because of fear of retaliation from the gang. During the April days following the murder of Martin Luther King when the Rangers distributed signs to be displayed in the windows of neighborhood merchants, he said, they charged $50 for their protection.

Jeff Fort, who had assumed leadership of the gang after Hairston was convicted in May of 1968, was subpoenaed to testify before the Committee. He was sworn in but never sat down before Senator McClellan. Marshall Patner, Fort's lawyer, submitted a request that the Committee allow Fort to confront and cross-examine the witnesses who had testified against him. The request was refused by Senator McClellan under authority of the Committee Rules. After a heated exchange between Patner and Senator McClellan during which both the lawyer and Fort were reminded of the possibility of contempt charges if Fort refused to accept protection from the Fifth Amendment and proceed with his testimony, Marshall Patner turned to Fort, still standing beside him, and said: "We really must go." Then they walked out.

The Woodlawn, Kenwood, and parts of the Hyde Park areas of the South Side of Chicago are said to be Ranger territories. While the Rangers' presence in Hyde Park, especially in the area around the University of Chicago, is not very obvious to the casual observer, the walls of buildings in Woodlawn and Kenwood advertise their existence. It is impossible to pass a single block in Woodlawn without seeing the signs. Many of the buildings are being torn down, but most of the signs look fresh and bold and new; "Black P. Stone," "Stone Run It," "Almighty Black P. Stone Nation," "Don't Vote! B.P.S." they read. The wind blows bits of dirt and plaster into the faces of the children who play among the bricks and rubbish in the lots where houses once stood.

Blackstone Rangers are shy these days. They do not talk to most strangers. Whenever Jeff Fort is arrested, and he has been arrested many times since the McClellan Committee hearings, the story is picked up by almost every major newspaper in the country. Perhaps it is because of determined harassment from the Gang Intelligence Unit that the Rangers have grown tight and uncommunicative. Whatever the cause, they are suspicious of strangers, and their meetings are held in secret. They no longer make much use of the First Presbyterian Church; they may meet there from time to time, but not regularly. Possibly their only facility open to the public is the Black P. Stone Youth Center on the corner of Sixty-seventh and Blackstone, in the heart of the Woodlawn community. The building was once a Chinese laundry, and at another time it was a poolroom. Now it seems to serve as the central point for most Ranger activities. The building is windowless, and it is painted black. Few non-Rangers go into the building uninvited; only those who have dealings with the Nation seem to feel free to enter. And perhaps this is because of the large black-and-red "Almighty Black P. Stone" diamond-shaped symbol painted on the Blackstone Street side of the building. During the days adults hurry past the teen-age boys and men who may be standing outside the door. There is a bar a few doors away from the Center, and many of the older people who pass the building go in there to escape the wind, or into the barbecue house next to the bar, or else continue about whatever business they may have further down Sixty-seventh Street. The latch is broken, and the door is never really shut. Anyone can walk in, but for the most part only the children do.

Jeff Fort is the "Black Prince," the president, the "Chief" of the entire Blackstone operation. One cannot think of learning about the Nation without assuming that Jeff Fort is the key, the source of all information. To see Jeff, it is necessary to go to the Black P. Stone Youth Center and wait. It is necessary to wait a long time. Jeff Fort is extremely busy. Besides leading the Rangers, he is fighting a contempt of Congress conviction for walking out of the McClellan hearings last July (he was found guilty in November); awaiting certain cases pending against him in the Cook County courts; and, until he resigned in early December, working as a community organizer for the Kenwood-Oakland Community Organization (KOCO).

But waiting for Jeff Fort to come to the Center gives one the opportunity to observe some of the Rangers as they wander in and out of the smaller, first room of the place, which serves as an office. The room is painted black. There are two desks, a telephone, ancient magazines, a water cooler with no water, and a bulletin board. Tacked on the board are job announcements, pictures of Rangers who participated in *Opportunity Please Knock*, messages, and cartoons—including one by Jules Feiffer. It is not an impressive office, but the door never stops opening as the children come in. There is little in the office to suggest why they come, but sitting in the one big ragged chair in a dark corner of the office, one is able to observe a steady flow of children, boys and girls, ranging in age from seven to fourteen, walking in and out of the office as if in search of something.

Lamar Bell, the coordinator of the Black P. Stone Youth Center, does not mind my waiting. "The Chief is due here in a few hours," he always says. And he says it again, much later in the evening. It is obvious that he does not trust me. Finally he asks why I want to see the Chief. "I want to do a story on the Nation," I tell him. "I want to see how the Nation relates to the community and the police." Bell turns off completely. "Put *that* in your story!" he says, pushing a pink mimeographed sheet close to my face. "The trouble with Black Police in our community," it reads, "is not police brutality to blacks, it is that these men and women are afraid of the power structure. So they join it to save themselves from the misery of being Black and powerless. The only way they can prove themselves, to their Brother's and Sister's, your Mother and Father and my Mother and Father, and our children. If they weren't police they would be in the same shape as any other oppressed Black man, Woman, or Child. God help them," it went on, "for they know not what they do. To them, it's a job for money; to us it's our lives, home and children."

"This is just what I want to write about," I tell him.

Lamar Bell walks to the door between the office and the back room, which has been off limits to me during my past visits to the Center, and says, "You'll have to talk it over with the Chief. He'll be here in a couple of hours."

Every evening for at least three hours Lamar Bell and Carl Banks, one of the Center's teachers, conduct a percussion class for some of the younger boys who come there. Banks has been a Ranger for two years. He is twenty-one, and came to Chicago from New York two years ago. He wants to become a professional drummer and earns money from infrequent band engagements. The rest of his time he spends in the Center, teaching a percussion class for neighborhood children. He is friendly and talkative. "The kids are really interested in expressing themselves," he told me. "A lot of these kids are misunderstood. Drumming gives them a way to express themselves. If I had money for the course, I would get more equipment and books, take the kids to see other drummers perform. Try to work out a little drum and bugle corps."

From the chair where I sat in the office during my first visits to the Center, I could hear the music they made with their drums in the mysterious back room.

One Saturday night Bell informed me that there was an extra bongo drum and invited me to sit in on the session. He allowed me to enter the back room, a kind of auditorium with a small stage, and the three of us played drums, without speaking, for several hours. While we played, some of the older Rangers came in and watched us. They looked at me, and then at Bell, then at me again. It was obvious that I was not a Stone.

"You didn't give off the right vibrations," Art Richardson, the director of the Black P. Stone Youth Center, told me later that night. "That's why I was watching you. But you *could* be a Stone because you came into the Center and participated on *our* level. That's what Stone is all about."

Art Richardson believes in vibrations as a method of determining the sincerity of people. Although he grew up on the South Side of Chicago, he has been a Ranger for only two years. He is not a member of the Main 21, but because he is articulate and extremely intelligent, he has been made a "head" and director of the Black P. Stone Youth Center. He is twenty-eight, married, and has served in the Army. He was given an Undesirable Discharge in 1965 because, he says, "I was just exposed to prejudice and reacted to it in the only way I knew." He has a police record. He also has a way with people. He would rather ride a bus than a cab because, he says, "You can't get vibrations from peoples in a cab." He never says people; the word always comes out peoples, with enough warmth and emphasis to suggest sincerity.

The Englewood Urban Progress Center, located at 839 West Sixty-fourth Street in an area which is said to be Disciple territory, houses a concentration of community service agencies. The building itself is a Masonic Temple which has been converted into offices. Only the ground floor is used for official purposes; the upper floors are essentially unused, although the second floor has a fairly large auditorium with a stage and good seating capacity, and there are many other, smaller rooms, all quiet and waiting to be put into use. In one of the larger rooms on the second floor, the one with the stage, Darlene Blackburn, an accomplished black dancer of considerable reputation in Chicago, gives creative dance lessons to girls from the community. Waiting for her in the semilighted room are children, boys and girls, who come to participate in the class or to watch her dance. Art Richardson and I wait with them. Art wants to ask her to dance at a Thanksgiving show he is organizing for the Black P. Stone Youth Center. While they wait, the children play at jumping off the stage and onto the floor, a distance of some three or four feet. Sometimes they fall on their faces, but they always laugh, and climb back onto the stage to jump again. It is a game.

"Look at that," Art told me.

A boy was dropping onto the stage from a trapdoor four or five feet above. He landed on his knees, unhurt, and climbed up to jump again.

"That's energy," Art said. "*We* can't do that anymore."

I agreed.

Art walked over to the stage and watched the boy jump again. This time he landed on his feet. "You know," he told me, coming back to where I was sitting, "the young brothers represent a form of energy just like any other energetic force in nature, just like the atom. If it could be channeled, if it could be turned to constructive directions just like the atom . . ." He began to walk about the room. "If I had a bigger place, if I had a place like this, I could bring more of the little brothers in and get that energy."

"What would you do with it?" I asked.

He looked up at the old Mason paintings on the walls and ceilings, half-hidden in the darkness. "I'd like to have job-training programs, arts and crafts workshops, adult workshops sort of like the P.T.A. to assemble adults just to get them to talk and maybe close the generation gap. Help them influence the kids in the necessary direction." He paused. "As a matter of fact, I would do exactly what the other organizations are trying to do. But only *I'd* do it. Most of the other organizations can't reach the kids. We can. We can give them something to relate to as theirs."

"What?" I asked him.

Art lowered his voice so that the children could not hear him. "Stone," he said softly. Most of Englewood, and whatever energy there is in it, still belongs to the Disciples.

No one really knows how many Rangers there now are in the South Side area. The Gang Intelligence Unit estimates that they claim a membership of from 1500 to 3000, while the Rangers themselves claim a membership of from 5000 to 8000. Perhaps the difficulty in estimating their number lies in the fact that the gang, if it can presently be called that, is not well organized. Aside from the Main 21, there seems to be very little perceptible formal organization or control by leaders over individual gang members. If anything, the Rangers seem to represent a certain spirit in their community, a spirit which is adopted by young people. But whether this adoption is voluntary or forced upon young people is one of the major controversial questions that concern the Woodlawn, Kenwood, Oakland, and Hyde Park communities.

During the McClellan hearings there was a good deal of testimony that small children were being forced to join the Rangers and pay protection money. There is some evidence, some opinion, that the Rangers are still recruiting. But few black people in the areas in which most of the intimidation is supposed to be going on seem willing to talk about it, especially to a black like myself who is not known to them. At the hearings, charges were also made that the Rangers were using The Woodlawn Organization's federal funds to line their own pockets. Few private black citizens have much to say about this either.

In the proposal for the Black P. Stone Youth Center the Rangers state that "above all things or ideas of personal materialistic gain, we intend to cultivate our people spiritually, mentally, physically, and economically. To construct and develop our ideal of a new method of existence and behavior." The proposed program is a plea for community support. At present, few adults come to the Center. "Our P.," the statement of intentions goes on, "stands for people, progress, and prosperity." There is no mention of power in the statement.

"We're only interested in trying to develop our community services," Art Richardson told me, "so that it becomes obvious to the peoples that we only have the community's interest at heart and the development of ourselves. We're interested in all peoples as long as they are interested in our philosophy."

The Rangers have scheduled weekly Saturday night meetings at the Center for adults. Some adults do come out, but they are few in number; and those who come wait around nervously for other adults to show and attempt to make conversation with the older Rangers. For the Rangers have a community relations problem. They lack the vocal support of the majority of adults in the areas in which they have an obvious influence over young people. Perhaps it is because many of the adults are unwilling to recognize the Rangers as a legitimate force in a community crowded with "letter-name" organizations, all claiming a certain rapport with the grass roots.

Al Garrison, for example, is a twenty-five-year-old machinist. He is black, and he lives in the Woodlawn area. He grew up in Chicago, is divorced, and has two children. He is not so much concerned about the Rangers as he is about the present state of affairs in this country. He is afraid that his children will not live to reach his age. He believes that the country will not survive much longer, and he wonders why he continues to work every day. He believes that the Chicago police are corrupt beyond control. And he believes that the Mafia controls many members of the police force and the Blackstone Rangers.

"A friend of mine who used to be pretty big in the Rangers told me that white men run the gang," Garrison confides. "He said that they give the guys a new kind of dope that makes them want to kill people. They just go crazy when they take it," he says. "The whites are just using those boys."

Garrison is not bitter nor militant. In fact, he cannot understand militancy at this late stage in what he believes to be the decline of America from causes still unclear to him.

The Rangers do not appear to be militant either, at least not in the contemporary sense of the word. They have refused to make a coalition with the Black Panthers. They do not seem to have any political philosophy. If anything, they believe only in themselves and in their motto: "Stone Run It!" But they are waiting too. Whether it is for more federal funds or for their presence and power to be recognized by the black community through their influence over ghetto youth, they are waiting. And their energy is at work.

"Just don't *do* it, put some *soul* into it! *I* got more soul than International Shoe Company!" the man says. His name is just "Buzz." He is a highly skillful pool player: he has beaten the great Minnesota Fats. But he is also a Blackstone Ranger, and for three hours every Monday afternoon, from 3 p.m. until 6 p.m., he is a disc jockey for a music program called *Stone Thang,* sponsored by the University of Chicago's student-run WHPK–FM radio station and the Black P. Stone Nation. Buzz takes his work seriously: he keeps time with his fingers, he sings along with the records, he makes spontaneous, soulful comments, he sweats and smokes, and he enjoys himself. The Rangers take the program seriously too: at least three of them assist him, tight-lipped and silent, in the little studio on the second floor of the university's student activities building. "If you got any soul at all," he announces to his FM audience, "give old brother Buzz a call." And the telephone keeps ringing for three hours, and Buzz keeps talking.

The station's program director, Tom Jacobson, is a senior at the university. He observed that since *Stone Thang* began in October, there has been an increase in the station's audience, and, he believes, some improvements in communications between the Ranger community and the University of Chicago-Hyde Park white community. The station, however, is a low-power operation, and only reaches FM sets in the Woodlawn, Hyde Park, and South Side areas. The students hope to expand the station's operations to AM sets in order to reach more people, but, Jacobson said, present expansion is doubtful because of lack of funds.

"We've been trying to do this type of show for months," Jacobson commented. "Finally we got Chuck Lapaglia from the First Presbyterian Church and Jeff Fort to help us set it up. The object of the show is to make the Black P. Stone Nation a part of the community."

Buzz and the Rangers who assist him are volunteers. Their only visible compensation lies in the plentiful opportunities Buzz has to say, "This is a *Stone Thang* presented by the All Mighty Black P. Stone Nation!" The other Rangers in the studio look solemn whenever he says this.

"The kids dig Stone," Carl Banks told me. "But the older people aren't sincere enough to come down and give help. We'd like to get to older people through their kids. In a sense, we're babysitting here because a lot of parents aren't interested in their kids and a lot of them don't trust the Stones. That's why we passed out a list of our intentions—to let them know that it's a peaceful thing. Some people in the area are skeptical because of the past, but they ought to come in and see us now."

The Rangers want money. They want to expand the range of activities presently offered in their Center and set up other Centers in the South Side area. They believe that they have the people, or at least the younger people, with them. Now they want money to put their programs into operation. Lamar "Bob" Bell, a former member of the Main 21, estimates that the Nation needs about $259,000 a year to put its present plans into operation. While his estimate may be far from conservative, it is obvious that for whatever cultural programs the Rangers may have in mind, the Sixty-seventh Street Center will not provide adequate accommodations. At present they have three rooms: the outer room, which serves as an office; the back room, with a small stage; and a sort of kitchen area, with a small bathroom. All of these rooms are in poor repair. For equipment they have a percussion set, two bongo drums, a ping-pong table, and about twenty-four metal chairs.

The Rangers are attempting certain ventures in business. The newly formed Kenwood-Oakland Community Organization, funded by a $100,000 grant from the Community Renewal Society of Chicago and headed by Reverend Curtis Burrell, has loaned the Rangers $3000 to open a restaurant on South Woodlawn Avenue. But there is a feeling, an old one, going back to the days of the OEO grant and the sponsorship of the Rangers by The Woodlawn Organization and Reverend Arthur Brazier, that a supposedly legitimate organization is subsidizing gang activities and allowing an already uncontrollable force to grow even larger and more powerful.

In 1968 there were two incidents which increased public interest and, perhaps, concern for the Blackstone Rangers. The first was their attempt to control the violence on the South Side of Chicago in the uncertain days in April after the assassination of Dr. Martin Luther King by passing out to neighborhood merchants hand-painted signs which read: "Do Not Touch . . . Black P. Stone . . . Jeff." They are said to have also set up a riot-control center in the First Presbyterian Church, where they received calls from troubled areas and directed Ranger leaders to the scenes of potential riotous activity. Finally, the Rangers and the Disciples called a truce on the Sunday following the assassination, during which some 1500 Rangers and 400 Disciples marched through the Woodlawn area and met in a park near the University of Chicago to negotiate the end of violence, or at least the immediate hostility, between the traditionally enemy groups. The march was covered by the local press, and the Rangers were given credit for preventing a riot on the South Side.

And in August, while the police and hippies rioted in the hotel area and in

Lincoln Park, the South Side remained calm. Whether or not the Rangers were responsible for the calm remains an open question. There is some evidence that the F.B.I. had investigated certain threats, some of them alleged to have been made by Reverend John Fry, that the Rangers were planning to riot in the Loop, disrupt the Convention, and assassinate Eugene McCarthy and Hubert Humphrey.

Captain Edward Buckney, head of the Chicago Police Department's Gang Intelligence Unit and the ninth black police captain in the history of the Chicago Police Department, does not believe that the Rangers were responsible for keeping their neighborhoods cool during the April riots. "Fry will tell you that they were responsible for keeping things cool last April," he says, "but in our opinion that's a lot of hogwash. We just don't believe that's so. We believe that idea was a brand of hysteria created by the group to get credit for something they didn't do."

As an example of the hysteria, Buckney related that in August of 1968, just after Jeff Fort was jailed for probation violation and before the Democratic Convention, Reverend Brazier and other community people requested a meeting with the superintendent of police. "Their basic pitch was 'We can't guarantee what will happen with Jeff in jail.' They were pressuring the police to release him on the implication of the possibility of future violence. To me it's a means of bartering or dickering with the community for their own betterment," Buckney said. "There were no disturbances on the South Side, and the reason was basically because the black community did not want to become involved. If the Rangers claim credit for it, that's some more hogwash."

"In April," he said, "there were about 5000 United States troops, policemen, and many other agencies in the Kenwood-Woodlawn area. Historically, in Chicago there have never been riots on the South Side; they have always been on the West Side. The closest one was in April, and most of the damage there was done in Ranger-Disciple territory. Also, you have to consider the fact that over in the Ranger end there is little else to destroy because they have already destroyed most of it."

Buckney was promoted to captain last November, just after the election. He senses that his police position has made him unpopular in certain areas of the black community. But he believes that his role as a policeman is clearly defined. "Our approach is the hard-line police approach," he says. "We're not concerned with sociological approaches. As long as they don't violate the law, we don't concern ourselves with them." And as a policeman Buckney is in fact determined to break up the gang. He believes that this can be accomplished if most of the older members, possibly those who exert a bad influence over the younger members, are taken out of the area. He believes that 95 percent of the young people in the gang are there because they have no choice in the matter. "No one likes to be continually shot at because he's not a member of the gang," he said. "If we could divorce those who religiously believe in it from the community, the others would have a chance to get out. If the courts deal severely with a considerable number of them, if the courts deal severely in the cases pending against Jeff Fort and some of the other Main leaders, I think the Rangers could be broken up."

Like many other public officials in Chicago, Captain Buckney blames over-zealous clergymen for the rapid growth of major gangs over the past two years. During the McClellan investigation, and later, in the Chicago papers and on television, he criticized Reverend John Fry and Reverend Brazier for supporting the activities of the Rangers and the Disciples. He was especially critical of Burrell's subsequent hiring of Jeff Fort as a community organizer. "From what we have seen already," he stated, "we can tell what kind of organizing he was doing. He used intimidation and fear to get young people to join the gang." He blames Reverend Fry's First Presbyterian Church for luring these youths away from the Boys' Clubs and into the church. Under Fry's guidance, according to Captain Buckney, the gang enjoyed a tremendous growth. He estimates the present membership of the Rangers to be between 1500 and 3000 youths, but indicates that Reverend Fry's estimation is closer to 4000. "But I doubt if you could find any more than 300 hard-core Rangers," he remarked.

The captain believes that the most notable achievement of the Rangers was the formation of an entertainment troupe, a major part of which was the "Black-stone Singers." "But you have to look at that with a jaundiced eye too," he cautioned me. "Most of them were high school kids, not hard-core Rangers." He feels that too much attention is being given the gang members to the exclusion of all the other poor children in the Woodlawn community. "If people keep pushing the bad things under the rug, at the rate they're going now they soon will become untouchable because they've already done almost everything attributable to organized crime.

"I believe in giving credit where credit is due," he says of the Rangers, "but they don't do anything constructive. All they're interested in is money in their pockets. If you have any dealings with them, the question always is what can *you* do for *them*. You won't get much out of them for nothing."

Buckney has been criticized for what some Chicagoans call his persecution of the Rangers. He is aware of this, and seems to be able to live with the constant criticism from community-minded whites as well as from some of his fellow blacks. "I'm often accused of persecuting the black community," he admitted. "But when I look at these homicides"—he picked up a pile of papers from his desk and dropped them before continuing—"when I look at these and see a minimum of 95 percent to 97 percent of them coming out of the black community—well, I believe you have to concentrate your men where the problem is." In 1968, the captain disclosed, there have been more than ten killings in Woodlawn.

"If they were so sincere about doing something constructive for the community and if they have knowledge of crime, why don't they turn it over to the police?" the captain asked. "There've been other gangs who have turned members over to the police for doing some wrong. But the Rangers have rarely if ever cooperated with the police and probably never will. If one of them is locked up, they'll try anything possible to spring him—bribing witnesses, even intimidation. They have a complete disdain for the law. They won't even show up for court appearances."

This sort of suspicion is reciprocated: the chief witnesses against the T.W.O. project and the Rangers before the McClellan Committee, George Rose and Annabelle Martin, are rumored to have been bribed by the police to testify as they did. Rose had been arrested for a narcotics violation, but charges were never brought; and the two sons of Annabelle Martin had been previously arrested for the murder of Leo McClure and were the principal witnesses in the case against Eugene Hairston. The charges against both the boys were dropped. Both Mrs. Martin and George Rose moved out of Chicago. Captain Buckney denies the bribery allegations: "Bribery is, point-blank, not true. In the case of George Rose, we got word that the Rangers wanted him killed. We got to him first. All we wanted was inside information on the Rangers. Mrs. Martin certainly wasn't bribed. She was merely asked by the senators if she wanted to go to Washington, and she agreed. We just arranged for her transportation out of the city."

Since its formation in March of 1967, the Gang Intelligence Unit has grown in power and importance in the Chicago Police Department. In 1968 there were only thirty-eight policemen, mostly black, assigned to the Unit; but since the first part of November, plans have been made to increase its strength to two hundred men. "We're striving for 100 percent integration of the Unit," Captain Buckney told me. It is highly probable that members of the Unit have infiltrated the gang; Captain Buckney seems well informed on Ranger activities. But it is also just as probable that the Rangers know a good deal about the activities of the Unit.

Some non-G.I.U. policemen, like Field Commander William B. Griffin, have attempted to work with the Ranger organization rather than against it. "Griffin's problems are different from mine," Buckney says. "He may have to do what is best for the community, while I, if I were in his place, might do something different. But the general consensus in the police department is the hard-line police approach."

20

JOYCE R. STARR & DONALD E. CARNS, Singles and the City: Notes on Urban Adaptation

In the early part of this century, about the time of the first World War, the University of Chicago was establishing its preeminence in the field of sociology (not that it had much competition). Probably the major thrust of that effort concerned the sociology department's approach to the city, specifically to the city of Chicago. Beginning with Robert E. Park's seminal article in 1916, its later version, and the work of Thomas and Znaniecki, Burgess, Shaw, Wirth, and others, the school of "human ecology" attempted to consider the city as an analog to the ecology of all living things, i.e., the relationship between organisms, their physical and social environments, and their functionally interrelated network of associations. In large measure they were successful in focusing our attention on *processes* of social life in relation to areas of the city; that is, they conceptualized the city in terms of *both* turf and function and dealt with it in such dynamic categories as assimilation, accommodation, conflict, and the like.

At least three kinds of urban studies stemmed from this school of thought. Some analyzed Chicago and other cities in a comparative way, seeking to establish universal descriptions of land use in terms of an ecological model, i.e., the interrelationships between areas of the city. Building on this work, still others correlated incidence and prevalence of various social patterns (including social "pathologies") with areas of the city, attempting to demonstrate that aspects of land use—density, debilitation, familism or isolation, and so forth—play a major role in causing individual deviance, group deviant adaptations, physical and mental illness, family dissolution, or whatever. Still a third group paid close attention to the byproducts of industrialization: functional interdependence, identity and life style as reflecting the work role, the process of migration and urban acculturation, all of which Park had delineated as primary foci for an urban sociology. These researchers went into the city, studied its life styles, talked to its people, and frequently let them speak for themselves. They provided for us a portrait of both the underbelly of urban life and its higher orders—peculiar adaptations to the urban milieu and some of the personal and social costs and benefits which accrued. From *The Polish Peasant* through *The Jackroller, The Gold Coast and the Slum,* and *Brothers in Crime* to (among others) Becker's work on marijuana use and jazz musicians, a tradition of hitting the streets and talking to people has continued in American sociology.

In many important ways, Chicago and other cities have changed since those early days, but in certain fundamental aspects they are the same. Early Chicago was a city of rapid growth through immigration, especially by peoples from eastern and southern Europe. In more recent years, blacks, Southern whites,

Spanish-Americans, and others have replicated this migration pattern to the city. Chicago is still segregated; there is still great competition for space and resources; and the processes of invasion and succession which produce neighborhood change continue unabated. Whether race and ethnicity as expressed in spatial use or socioeconomic position expressed in networks of interrelations is the criterion, nevertheless Chicago is still polyglot. It is on one particular social category that we wish to focus our attention in this essay: the educated, unmarried, urban young.

As much as in 1920, cities are still magnets today, for they maintain a virtual monopoly over access to the products and byproducts of an industrialized, mass-culture society. Even though colleges and universities are widely reputed to be marriage markets, channeling most students into legal marriages at or soon after graduation and thus ultimately into the suburbs, nevertheless large numbers of young college graduates migrate to the city each year, unmarried, more or less committed to a career, all sharing a fairly similar upbringing (in socioeconomic terms) and a virtually identical college experience. They do vary by gender and by sexual object preference (that is, most are straight but some are gay), by degree of career commitment, and by urbanity, to a certain extent.

This particular population is theoretically significant on a number of levels. In the first place, young, educated, single people constitute the focus of a considerable effort by advertisers and the media to create a "swinging" scene, whether it exists or not, or in what form it flourishes. In this sense, these singles are fully *au courant* as the "now" generation, the referent of much of our cultural fantasies about the good life: free and unrestricted, highly sexual and sensual, in short, *fun*. It is, of course, an empirical question: To what degree does the reality of urban single life approximate this media-generated fantasy? The question is significant in the same way any challenge to a stereotype is socially significant, whether it relates to blacks, women, students, communists, or whatever.

On a second level, young, educated, urban singles constitute the product of our advanced educational system, at least that segment which avoided marriage immediately after college. Although it shall not be a major focus of this paper, the degree that pre-urban socialization in school or at home prepared these people for the realities of urban living, or for its image, is a crucial question. It is crucial, of course, for it provides a partial test of the efficacy of these institutions, and it bears strongly on the adjustments these people make. Are they fulfilled, hopeful, nostalgic, sad, lonely, or what? These and other questions are being explored at length in other analyses currently under way.

And finally, this population will, in twenty years or so, be the married, middle-class suburbanites so well known to us all. To what degree do men and women anticipate this probable future state? What are their attitudes toward marriage? Monogamy? Security? Responsibility?

Our general strategy in this paper shall involve a discussion of three major task areas, each of which must be solved in order for a successful adjustment to urban life to take place: finding and maintaining a place to live; finding, keeping, or changing jobs; and meeting friends, dates, and potential mates (whether legal or consensual).

THE SETTING

In rough descriptive terms, Chicago's North Side singles' community extends approximately eight miles north of the Loop, two and one-half miles to the West—depending upon how far north, and is bounded on the east by Lake Michigan. More accurately, however, this general area encompasses four fairly distinct subareas, each of which is home to a wide range of life styles. Closest to the Loop lies the Near North, a city planner's horror of twenty-story high-rise apartments seeded between renovated brownstones providing a backdrop for a patchwork of stand-up style singles bars. Moving north, we find Chicago's Old Town, a subarea similarly characterized by aged brownstones, occasional duplexes, a few high-rises (being built at a feverish pace, therefore fundamentally altering the character of the neighborhoods), and Wells Street, a potpourri of fun houses, ice cream palaces, "headshops," and strip joints to which tourists and teenyboppers gravitate and which singles by and large avoid. Old Town merges into the Mid-North, a dense concentration of back-to-back high-rises and four-plus-ones (four-story apartment buildings, cheaply built, which took advantage of a loop-hole in Chicago's otherwise stringent building code; they are now illegal). In this area, there is only a smattering of night spots and other retail establishments. At some point, debated, the Mid-North ends and New Town begins. This latter area managed without a specific name until the commercial boom began to move north along Broadway and Clark streets, giving rise to a profusion of easy-entry stores: boutiques, antiques, waterbeds, ethnic cuisine, sit-down bars ("that give you a change to talk"), and a small sprinkling of Chicago's own "off-Broadway" and out-of-the-Loop theaters. It is also an area of mixed housing types: four-plus-ones, brownstones, occasional high-rises nearer to Lake Michigan; and it contains "homo-heights," which is exactly what the name implies.

The proportion of young college graduates is by no means equally distributed in these areas but tends to increase moving northward to the Mid-North and New Town neighborhoods as rents generally decrease. Moreover, despite the coverage the singles scene has received from feature sections of newspapers and from national magazines, other kinds of people living in these areas undoubtedly outnumber the young unattached graduates. Older persons, particularly widows, comprise a significant proportion of this less newsworthy population. There is a migration pattern back to the city on the part of suburban couples, with or without children, and there are large numbers of young married people unwilling to leave the city. Other residents include divorcees, bachelors over thirty, and students. The common link between these groups is neither age nor life style but rather an eye to convenience: proximity to the central business district.

THE DATA

The discussion which follows is based on approximately seventy face-to-face interviews, structured but essentially open-ended, conducted with never-married college graduates of both sexes in their early to mid-twenties, who have not done graduate work but have opted to come to or remain in Chicago and work. Interviewing was done during 1970 and the first half of 1971 and, in fact, is still under way. No systematic sampling method was considered feasible. Rather, a "snowball" technique of contacts plus attention to variability in occupations, living arrangements and locations, and other aspects of life style was used to recruit respondents.

Housing

Despite the media's attention to the singles scene, the typical graduate arriving in Chicago has minimal or nonexistent awareness of Chicago's singles panorama, much less the purposeful objective of peer segregation and subculture participation. Similarly, the actual decision to move to Chicago after finishing college is rarely a function of *informed* expectations concerning social life in the city. Rather, for the majority of those who were themselves raised in Chicago or its outlying areas, return is usually the result of a choice no more considered than "it seemed like the natural thing to do." On the part of other in-migrant graduates, the decision appears based on even more haphazard criteria: "I wanted to get away from home and Chicago is the nearest big city"; "A few of my close friends from college were coming here, and I had no place else to go so. . ."; "My boy friend had decided to move here"; "I figured the job market would be better here than New York or San Francisco"; "The job I was offered just happened to be based in this city." Female graduates typically offer one of the first three responses, while males are more likely to respond with one of the last two. Thus since the male's decision to come to a particular city is work-related, while his female counterpart's motive is more social, it is frequently the case that a male will move to a city where he has neither family nor friends while a female moves to one only where friends and/or family may serve whatever needs she has. It follows from this that an in-migrant male to Chicago is more likely to live alone when he first comes into the city, while the out-of-town female establishes living arrangements with one or two friends from college. Also contributing to this pattern, of course, is the fact that male graduates earn higher salaries, thus are better able to afford to live alone.

The data suggest that the typical in-migrant female does not have a car at her disposal, and thus the first criterion she employs in looking for a place to live is that it be close to transportation and within a reasonably short traveling distance from her place of work. A second major concern is safety, both in terms of household integrity and area of residence. Thus many females often restrict their apartment hunt to buildings equipped with doormen or buzzer systems and consequently are more likely than males to move initially into a high-rise or four-plus-one. By contrast, the typical male graduate moving to Chicago is largely unconcerned with safety and usually has a car as well. With entertainment expenses and automobile payments (not to mention astronomical urban insurance costs) in mind, he typically prefers to do his economizing on rental costs and is therefore more likely to seek an older building. Moreover, because of these different considerations, males frequently seek apartments in blue-collar and migrant neighborhoods which border the area on the west.

Both men and women, however, soon encounter the inescapable fact that desirable apartments are at a premium. With seldom more than a weekend's time to complete their search, for most out-of-town graduates the decisive criterion in their choice of a building, and consequently a neighborhood, often turns out to be that "the apartment was available." In Chicago, at least, this is further confounded by the tradition of May to October leasing periods, which means that relatively fewer apartments are available at other times of the year. Furthermore, a significant proportion of in-migrant graduates never go through the apartment hunting process; they either move in with a friend, or a friend of a friend, who already has an apartment, or they let their roommate-to-be do the hunting and deciding.

Unlike California and some other states, there are few, if any, "singles only" buildings or complexes in Chicago, and none on the North Side in the area we are discussing. Chicago's North Side area does contain one mega-complex which rose from the rubble of a decaying area under the rubric and financing of "middle-income housing," but which has not served that population in any significant way. It houses about 6,000 people and bears a reputation as a miniature "swingle's city," but in actuality, the majority of its residents are neither under twenty-five nor single. More to the point, the data suggest that the majority of graduates, males in particular, prefer *not* to live in a building that fabricates and formalizes the meeting and dating process. To be sure, they have fond recollections of the communal-like living arrangements of their college years: "I knew 90 percent of the people living in my building; here I don't even know my next-door neighbor." But the key terms, and the kind of living situations these graduates seek, are exemplified by "spontaneous," "casual," and "not forced." The majority of those interviewed expressed discomfort if not disdain for any type of living arrangement that highlights and exploits their single status. After all, the city is supposed to permit freedom. It is probable, however, that where the climate permits year-round outdoor facilities, such as swimming pools and tennis courts, such housing complexes may in fact be more acceptable as "natural" settings to this population. This is in distinct contrast ot "party rooms," "mixing lounges," and so forth that abound in cold-climate buildings bent on attracting single populations. This climate variable and all it entails is clearly a matter for future research.

It should be kept in mind that college students spend the bulk of their working day in classes or studying by themselves, alone. In classrooms, even surrounded by peers, the student is not actually interacting with anyone in an active and meaningful sense. Nor does performance in college depend upon such interactions even when they do occur. Although unlikely, it is quite possible to complete four years of college successfully and earn a bachelor's degree without ever speaking to a fellow student or, sad to say, a professor. This is very rarely the case in the world of work, where a great premium is placed on interpersonal skills no matter how high the level of technical proficiency. Graduates discover this fact of life very quickly. Ironically, when asked how, if at all, college prepared them for the experience of working, the typical response is "it taught me how to get along with people." It is not production as such, but rather the skills of performance that are essential in the work role, speaking of the modal case. And because the average working graduate in this sample finds himself or herself interacting with others eight or more hours per day, in pressure situations which could hardly be characterized as pure sociability, a great need for privacy results. The model graduate laments the cold and unfriendly nature of the city, the lack of neighboring, and recalls his school days with considerable nostalgia. But the majority admit with some embarrassment that in fact they have put forth little effort to alter the situation, rarely making an overture and/or failing to act upon overtures made by others. Clearly one's house is a haven of privacy in an environment of functional and personal interaction.

Despite this, the fact remains that there is a strong concentration of homogeneous social types in these neighborhoods. From what the data indicate, this fact coupled with the home-as-haven concept leads us to seriously question whether concentrations of people with similar ages and educational backgrounds is a sufficient condition for meaningful social interaction. Focusing on the establishment of friendships and dating relationships, the data would suggest that neighborhood and housing based interactions are not significant access routes for the modal graduate in this sample.

When asked about this lack of neighborhood-based interaction, reasons vary. Some place the blame on themselves, but with little remorse. "I just never think about it"; "I know enough people." Others maintain it is due more to a lack of time than a lack of interest. But the majority attribute this infrequency of neighboring to the hostile and secondary nature of the big city milieu where "everyone is in a hurry," or is "concerned with making it," and is "so self-centered." Many decry Chicago's long dreary winters as a significant contributor to both their own unfriendliness in neighborhoods as well as the ill-tempered moods of others.

It follows that spring and summer seem to sweep in a moratorium on distrust and aloofness (and, ironically, along with it higher incidences of forcible rape, breaking and entering, and other acts also encouraged by warm weather). People emerge from indoors to bicycle through Chicago's extensive lakefront park system, meander through shops, take in the sun at the beach, go to outdoor concerts. Not only do the seasons have a bearing on actual behavior; they are very much a part of the consciousness of these graduates. Warm weather will be a time "when I'll find out who my neighbors are." Nonetheless, on the whole the data indicate that despite this dramatic seasonal shift in casual street behavior— from stares and averted eyes to smiles—it is still the rare encounter that develops beyond a quick "hi." Only one male respondent followed up a street meeting by asking the girl out, and in this instance both persons recognized each other as tenants of the same building. The few relationships that had evolved from casual neighborhood meetings in shops or laundromats or through a street encounter were viewed as eventful because they were so atypical. Quite unlike the college community, where it is implicitly taken for granted that socioeconomic background and social motives converge, in the city one has only the *appearance* of youth as a common bond, and even that may be highly suspect.

Making a living

With reference to males, and in general cultural terms the concept of work, the preparations necessary for a lifetime work role and the behaviors essential for a successful performance in the occupational sphere are apparently well understood. These same things, however, are far more problematical for the educated woman. From data gathered from this sample, females may be placed in three categories, with some overlap: (1) the girl with a career orientation, one who has aspirations of developing her work role into a career, regardless of whether or not her particular college training was oriented to that end; (2) the female who views working as an "experience," who wants to gain satisfaction from her work and feel responsible, but who does not view this role as an end in itself or a lifetime career—likely to consider it as either temporary, until she marries, or as a definite secondary commitment to her primary future role as wife and mother (on the other hand, the career-committed girl tends to view the two roles as either comparable or complementary); (3) the girl who begrudges her work role, who would prefer not to have to work, either because she envisions herself as a wife and mother and not a worker, or simply because at this time in her life—and possibly for her entire lifetime—she is not ready to settle down to the responsibility of a job. In this category are girls who have not yet decided what they want to do with their lives. They may seek jobs that provide an extension to the moratorium on decision-making which characterized their college years; they may be, for example, waitresses or receptionists, working only to keep the body together.

Despite our claim that the work role for males is more culturally understood and accepted, nevertheless the males in this sample could also be placed into three categories with regard to their work orientation: (1) the conventional career-oriented male who seeks his successes within the corporate world or at least views success in traditional terms of prestige and financial gain; (2) the man who consciously rejects traditional work options and values and who works at temporary jobs—as a cab driver, in construction—with a concern primarily for minimal necessities, resembling, at this point, female type (3) above (also in this category are young men who attempt to gain satisfaction in non-middle class work situations, especially craftsmanship); (3) the male who straddles both worlds but belongs to neither. Typically craving material success, he lacks either talent or skill, or else his motivation to work—to conform to the exigencies of the corporate world—is low. Of the three types, this young graduate is most likely to find his work experiences highly frustrating, since it is unlikely that the type of job he is able to land or fulfill will, at the same time, satisfy his material cravings.

In a very real sense, however, the "straddler's" plight is shared, although to a lesser degree, by the typical graduate in the city, whether male or female. Some may be more, others less, concerned with the freedom only money can buy; but quite soon after graduation the majority confront what is perhaps one of this country's best-kept institutional secrets: a bachelor's degree is at best an admissions card to, not a guarantee of, upward mobility.

In *The Great Training Robbery*, Berger documents what the typical graduate objectively and subjectively experiences: the lack of fit between the proportion of educated persons in the United States and the number of jobs that call for such a background. It is not that certification in the form of a degree is without value but, that the elements of the certification process—socialization that encourages "creativity" and "responsibility" and unfolds within a relatively free and unstructured environment—do not in any significant way prepare the individual graduate for a work world in which creative and responsible positions are the exception rather than the rule, and where routinization prevails. While this reality both challenges and threatens the ego of the cream, it reveals above all the mediocrity of the crop. "Going to college" had previously been adequate testimony of personal worth; but simply "going to work" can soon provide evidence of abject failure.

Thus the typical graduate soon discovers that his or her job offers significantly less in the way of satisfaction or challenge than had been hoped for and, to a large extent, expected. In much the same way that personal associations have been documented as the major job satisfaction gained by blue-collar workers, so it is with these young urban graduates. And for the majority of the "contented-discontented," the status of young single and thus the necessary involvement in the meeting-mating process becomes an important compensating factor, both as a measure of self-worth and as a competition for time and attention.

Friends and dates

More than any other institution in the urban setting, the singles bar has received a disproportionate share of attention from the media. One has the image that young unmarried graduates rely almost solely upon the bar scene to establish the highly transitory relationships which seemingly form the underpinnings for the "sexual revolution:" casual one-night stands in which females are sexually liberated to the point that their sexuality is that of the traditional male's. In Chicago, such bars flourish in the Rush Street area in the first of the four residential areas discussed above.

From the data available, it appears that the typical graduate goes to singles bars only one or two nights a week, if then. These bars are, by and large, noisy; sitting is actively discouraged by an arrangement of narrow counters and a lack of seats; interaction is essentially nonverbal, especially at the point of attracting and initially establishing contact. But even this minimal contact with the stand-up bars would establish them as important settings in the singles panorama were it not for the fact that attendance at such places varies inversely with amount of time of residence in the city, and by the sixth month or so it is a fairly unusual woman who continues to frequent these places and establish her social contacts in this way. Certainly, by the time she is approaching the upper age point in this sample, twenty-five, the typical female has little use for this scene. Males may continue to go to swinging bars for a longer time. To understand this, it is merely necessary to differentiate between male and female sexual patterns and ignore the rhetoric of the sexual revolution. Males seek physical sex, or at least an environment which feeds their psychological fantasies, and since many high school educated females, e.g., secretaries, do frequent the swingers' bars, the age-old male pattern of having sex downward but marrying laterally or upward in the social spectrum is again played out in the urban setting. Using this same reasoning, male gay bars should and indeed do represent significant settings for meeting partners in the city, since a fair amount of the emphasis there is on the sexual side. There are a few lesbian-oriented bars in Chicago, but apparently far fewer than the number which cater to the male homosexual community. In summary, swinging bars are useful in the long run only if everyone is committed to swinging; or, in the case of upward-mobile women, they think that a certain proportion of sexual relationships which begin casually may well have a more permanent payoff.

Sit-down style bars, which abound in the more northerly parts of Chicago's North Side singles' area, get more of the long-term action, but it is a kind of action rarely mentioned in popular accounts of the single life style. In this sample, it is common to find women who frequent one or more of these bars, but they tend to define the crowd in terms of friends rather than potential dates. Thus, desiring conversation as they do, it is not uncommon to find young graduates in groups, with a date, or with a person of the same sex that they are interested in talking to.

One could argue that both styles of bars offer a nostalgic recreation of the college years in a peer-concentrated setting, but the payoff is more in terms of a feeling of security rather than actual dating relationships. In the case of the Rush Street bars, the security is apt to be hollow, since the scene tends to turn off these graduates with its contrived artificiality, the forced nature of the interaction patterns, and the highly strained and false conviviality so prevalent at most of them. Each bar has its following and thus its in-group which acts, for all intents and purposes, like a heterosexual fraternity. Since many of the regulars consist of persons with odd working hours—stewardesses, bartenders, waiters predominate—they are able to maintain this cliqueness in other settings, as, for example, having "their" section of Lake Michigan's Oak Street Beach for sunbathing during the week. However, most of the night-time regulars do not see each other outside of the bar setting. Most graduates, though, continuously refer to this scene as a "meat market" and the bar clientele as "plastic." For most persons are not aggressively or cosmetically suited for the kinds of interaction possible at these bars. Used to the informality of the college atmosphere, where "making it" just happened or involved only minimal effort, most graduates find the requirements for survival and success in the bar setting all the more repugnant.

If young urban graduates cannot establish dating relationships in the bars to any significant degree, where do they go? We have already discounted housing as a primary meeting-dating nexus. For a working person who spends his or her day at the office, interaction at home is likely to be restricted to the elevator or laundry room, the latter being the only facility in many buildings which could lend itself to this activity. But as one female graduate put it, recognizing that doing laundry is not one of the world's more delightful ways of spending an afternoon or evening, "I could go down there with all the beautiful people, but I like to get my laundry done in a hurry; I want to get it over with." Further, singles are a transient population and this fact reduces the probability of establishing lasting relationships in a building. But most significantly, a majority of graduates consider *home* as something private and inviolate. They do not like intrusions into their privacy; they do not wish to make the boundaries of their nest overly permeable. Thus many respondents reported that intrabuilding dating was "too close to home," that discontinued relationships could be awkward in such a setting. It was much more likely that graduates in this sample developed friends, rather than made dates, at or near their home bases.

Similarly, organizations do not appear to be significant sources of dating relationships in this sample. Other data indicate that persons in this age group are not volunteers to any great degree. Even those who were active in college find themselves unmotivated when it comes to seeking out organizations in the city. Comments such as "never get around to it" and "always seem to be busy" are common. Many do not perceive any great reward value from such associations, especially when compared to the payoffs from college associational involvement such as fraternities, student government, and the like. Comments indicating a kind of powerless alienation were also common; many felt they could have no significant effect on life through organizational activity in the city, whereas they had felt more intimately a part of the college community. More important, in college there was immediate recognition from peers that derived from such activities. In the city, where friends have scattered interests, there is no immediate and approving audience. Finally, formal voluntary organizations in a city like Chicago—for example, politics, antipollution groups, and those interested in the arts—tend to have a mixed membership including large numbers of married people. In short, they are not ideal ways to make dates and meet prospective mates.

But as places to meet dates, organizations fall short of the American ideal in the same way that buildings and bars do, for this ideal seems to stress *spontaneity* above all other values. The excitement which accompanies the American meeting-dating encounter seems to be centered on its accidental character. For the first twenty-one years of their lives, these graduates have been surrounded by their age peers and have rarely been forced to seek companionship. To do so now would involve a suspension of those values, and many are simply not prepared to take that step.

In passing, we should mention that parties are seldom cited by this sample as a vehicle for meeting dates. Partly this is because it takes time to establish enough contacts to guarantee invitations. Despite that, a majority of the graduates, even after having lived in the city for a period of time, either do not go to parties or find that they know most of the people at the parties they do attend. A number of comments to the effect that Chicago is a very clique-oriented city simply underscore the patterned nature of urban social interaction.

After eliminating most of the possible ways to meet dates, we are left with only one major alternative: the work situation. Among these respondents, work was the most frequently cited institutional setting for making friends and, indirectly, meeting persons of the opposite sex. And this should not be surprising, since it is at work that the average person spends most of his waking day; and due to the real requirements of the work role which were discussed previously, it is also the setting most likely to facilitate familiarity and emotional intimacy. By no means, however, does work automatically guarantee that a graduate will meet people. A necessary condition seems to be that the type of work bring the graduate into contact with persons who are not only close to him in age but also share his single status. Where the modal graduate finds himself in the exclusive company of fellow employees who are older or married, he is seldom able to develop close friendships. This fact, coupled with their odd working hours, may help explain the use of bars by many stewardesses (and thus contributes to our understanding of their sexualized image in popular culture).

The relationship between work and dating is frequently a two-stage process. It is on the job that most graduates form friendships, much in line with the view of the city as a pattern of functionally, not spatially, interrelated people. They do not, by and large, date persons from the office for a number of reasons, among them, a lack of eligibles and the tendency to avoid social intimacy with persons one must face each day whether the relationship succeeded or failed. But through office friends, dates are arranged. It is, in short, a friend-of-a-friend pattern that provides the raw material out of which dating relationships are formed by the typical graduate in this sample.

Summary

Two predominant themes have emerged from this discussion of young, single college graduates in the city.

First, popular imagery, formed and reinforced by the media, is simply inaccurate in this case. There is little in the bars to attract these people, especially women. They are not leading (in most instances) a wildly free and sensual existence. Their apartment buildings are not re-creations of coeducational dormitories without housemothers. The graduates are people coping with the same problems we all face: finding a place to live, trying to get some satisfaction from a job, and seeking friends, dates, and ultimately mates in an environment for which they have been ill-prepared and which does not easily lend itself to stable human relationships. That they are coping is significant; that they are doing it as well as they are indicates a resiliency in the face of considerable odds. In short, our imagery should be reversed: these people are among those on the front-line of urban existence, combining as they do the usual goals of middle-class America —materialism, mating, and the like—without many of the usual institutional supports for their activities.

Second, we should reinforce something which has been a theme of urban studies for over a half-century but which has not captured its share of the literature or, especially, the methodology of urban studies: Turf, or place, or the housing environment is not a useful concept in understanding the life styles of this large and growing urban subpopulation. To be sure, the retribalization or "new" pluralism used to describe urban minority actions during the past decade suggests that turf is still a viable concept, especially insofar as large and homogeneous urban subpopulations are residentially segregated and possess a similar consciousness. But the other side of Park, and of Durkheim and Simmel and many other urban students, should receive equal emphasis. For it is the way young graduates relate to the world of work, and the ways they form and dissolve friendships and establish associations out of work contexts, that does much to provide their stable anchors in the urban milieu. Perhaps Harvey Cox was being a bit hopeful when he proposed his two metaphors for the shape of *The Secular City:* "man at the giant switchboard" and "man at the cloverleaf"; but his basic point seems valid nonetheless. Emerging urban man must be studied as much in terms of his networks as his spaces. For these young graduates, at least, it is the former that provide his significant connections and form his sense of self and well-being, while the latter are becoming increasingly meaningless.

References

Becker, Howard S. *Outsiders*. New York: The Free Press, 1963.
Park, Robert. "The City: Suggestions for the Investigation of Human Behavior in the Urban Environment." *American Journal of Sociology* 32 (1926).
Park, Robert, Ernest W. Burgess, et al. *The City*. Chicago: University of Chicago Press, 1925.
Thomas, William I., and Florian Znaneicki. *The Polish Peasant in Europe and America*. Five volumes. Chicago: University of Chicago Press, 1918–1920.

Wirth, Louis. "Urbanism as a Way of Life." *American Journal of Sociology* 44 (1938).
Zorbaugh, Harvey W. *The Gold Coast and the Slum*. Chicago: University of Chicago Press, 1929.

21

HERBERT J. GANS, The White Exodus to Suburbia Steps Up

In this unpredictable world, nothing can be predicted quite so easily as the continued proliferation of suburbia. Not only have American cities stopped growing for more than a generation, while the metropolitan areas of which they are a part were continuing to expand lustily, but there is incontrovertible evidence that another huge wave of suburban home building can be expected in the coming decade.

Between 1947 and about 1960, the country experienced the greatest baby boom ever, ending the slowdown in marriages and childbirths created first by the Depression and then by World War II. Today, the earliest arrivals of that baby boom are themselves old enough to marry, and many are now setting up housekeeping in urban or suburban apartments. In a few years, however, when their first child is two to three years old, and the second is about to appear, many young parents will decide to buy suburban homes. Only simple addition is necessary to see that by the mid-seventies they will be fashioning another massive suburban building boom, provided, of course, that the country is affluent and not engaged in World War III.

The new suburbia may not look much different from the old; there will, however, be an increase in the class and racial polarization that has been developing between the suburbs and the cities for several generations now. The suburbs will be home for an ever larger proportion of working-class, middle-class and upper-class whites; the cities, for an ever larger proportion of poor and nonwhite people. The continuation of this trend means that, by the 1970s, a greater number of cities will be 40 to 50 percent nonwhite in population, with more and larger ghettos and greater municipal poverty on the one hand, and stronger suburban opposition to open housing and related policies to solve the city's problems on the other hand. The urban crisis will worsen, and although there is no shortage of rational solutions, nothing much will be done about the crisis unless white America permits a radical change of public policy and undergoes a miraculous change of attitude toward its cities and their populations.

Another wave of suburban building would develop even if there had been no post-World War II baby boom, for American cities have always grown at the edges, like trees, adding new rings of residential development every generation as the beneficiaries of affluence and young families sought more modern housing and "better" neighborhoods. At first, the new rings were added inside the city limits, but ever since the last half of the nineteenth century, they have more often sprung up in the suburbs.

Although these trends may not be so apparent to New Yorkers, who live in a world capital rather than in a typical American city, both urban and suburban growth have almost always taken the form of single family houses, first on large lots and later, as less affluent city dwellers could afford to move out, on smaller lots. Even inside most American cities—again, other than New York and a few others—the majority of people live in single-family homes.

Moreover, studies of housing preferences indicate that the majority of Americans, including those now living in the city, want a suburban, single-family house once they have children, and want to remain in that house when their children have grown up. This urge for suburban life is not limited to the middle class or just to America; the poor would leave the city as well if they could afford to go, and so would many Europeans.

The only people who clearly do not want to live in the suburbs are the single and some of the childless couples, and that handful of urban middle-class professionals and intellectuals living in New York and a few other cosmopolitan cities. For everyone else, suburbia means more housing space at less cost, a backyard and an up-to-date community—all of which make raising children significantly easier for the mother, more compatible neighbors, cleaner air, a chance to leave the dirt and congestion behind and, in recent years, a chance also to escape the expansion of Negro and poor neighborhoods. Even some of the dedicated urbanites move to the suburbs when their children are young, although they—but only they—miss the cultural facilities of the big city and are often unhappy in suburbia.

Obviously, the popular antisuburban literature, which falsely accuses the suburbs of causing conformity, matriarchy, adultery, divorce, alcoholism and other standard American pathologies, has not kept anyone from moving to the suburbs, and even the current predictions of land shortages, longer commuting and urban congestion in the suburbs will not discourage the next generation of home buyers. Most, if not all, metropolitan areas still have plenty of rural land available for suburban housing. Moreover, with industry and offices now moving to the suburbs, new areas previously outside commuting range become ripe for residential development to house their employees. Thus, for several years now, more than half the suburbanites of Nassau County have been commuting to jobs inside Nassau County; in the next decade, they will probably be joined by new commuters living in Suffolk County. Of course, all this leads to increasing suburban congestion, but most suburbanites do not mind it. They do not leave the city for a rural existence, as the folklore has it; they want a half acre or more of land and all their favorite urban facilities within a short driving distance from the house.

In some metropolitan areas, or in parts of them, land may indeed be too scarce and thus too expensive to permit another round of old-style suburbanization. There, people will move into "townhouses" and semidetached houses, which have less privacy than single family houses, but still provide private yards and a feeling of separateness from the next-door neighbors. The recent failure of Reston, Virginia, the much praised new town near Washington, D.C., suggests, however, that the exquisitely designed communal recreational areas cannot substitute for private space. Most home buyers do not seem to want that much togetherness, and Reston's townhouses, which lacked front or backyards, sold too slowly.

It goes without saying that almost all the new suburbanites—and the developments built for them—will be white and middle-income, for, barring miracles in the housing industry and in federal subsidies, the subdivisions of the seventies will be too expensive for any family earning less than about $7,500 (in 1967 dollars). Thus, even if suburbia were to be racially integrated, cost alone would exclude most nonwhites. Today, less than 5 percent of New York State's suburban inhabitants are nonwhite, and many of them live in ghettos and slums in the small towns around which suburbia has developed.

Nevertheless, the minuscule proportion of nonwhite suburbanites will increase somewhat in the future, for, if the current affluence continues, it will benefit a small percentage of Negroes and Puerto Ricans. Some of them will be able to move into integrated suburban communities, but the majority will probably wind up in existing and new middle-class ghettos.

If urban employment is available, or if the ongoing industrialization of the South pushes more people off the land, poverty-stricken Negroes will continue to come to the cities, overcrowding and eventually enlarging the inner-city ghettos. Some of the better-off residents of these areas will move to "outer-city" ghettos, which can now be found in most American cities; for example, in Queens. And older suburbs like Yonkers and Mount Vernon will continue to lose some of the present residents and attract less affluent newcomers, as their housing, schools and other facilities age. As a result of this process, which affects suburbs as inevitably as city neighborhoods, some of their new inhabitants may be almost as poor as inner-city ghetto residents, so that more and more of the older suburbs will face problems of poverty and social pathology now thought to be distinctive to the city.

That further suburban growth is practically inevitable does not mean it is necessarily desirable, however. Many objections have been raised, some to suburbia itself, others to its consequences for the city. For example, ever since the rise of the postwar suburbs, critics have charged that suburban life is culturally and psychologically harmful for its residents, although many sociological studies, including my own, have shown that most suburbanites are happier and emotionally healthier than when they lived in the city. In addition, the critics have charged that suburbia desecrates valuable farm and recreation land, and that it results in "suburban" sprawl.

Suburbia undoubtedly reduces the supply of farm acreage, but America has long suffered from an oversupply of farmland, and I have never understood why allowing people to raise children where other people once raised potatoes or tomatoes desecrates the land. Usually, the criticism is directed to "ugly, mass-produced, look-alike little boxes," adding a class bias to the charges, as if people who can only afford mass-produced housing are not entitled to live where they please, or should stay in the city.

Suburban developments sometimes also rise on recreational land, although state and federal funds are now available to save such land for public leisure-time use. Even so, I find it difficult to believe that child-raising and the at-home recreation that goes on in a suburban house is a less worthy use of land than parks, which people only visit during part of the year. Furthermore, there is no reason why we cannot have both suburbia and parks, the latter built farther out, with high-speed expressways and mass transit to bring them closer to visitors.

Suburban sprawl scatters residential developments over large areas because single-family houses take up so much more acreage than multiple dwellings. As a result, highways, transit systems, utility lines and sewers must be longer and, therefore, more expensive. These added costs are not a steep price for affluent suburbanites; they want low-density housing more than economy, and they do not care that sprawl looks ugly to the trained eye of the architect. There may even be somewhat less sprawl in the future, partly because of townhouse developments, partly because high land costs at the far edges of the suburbs may induce builders to fill up vacant land left in the existing suburban rings during earlier periods of residential construction. Moreover, the next wave of suburbia may finally generate sufficient political support for the building of high-speed mass transit systems, now languishing on the planners' drawing boards, to connect the parts of the sprawling area.

The harmful effects of suburbia on the city are a more important criticism. One charge, made ever since the beginning of suburbanization in the nineteenth century, is that the suburbs rob the city of its tax-paying, civic-minded and culture-loving middle class. Actually, however, middle-class families are often a tax liability for the city; they demand and receive more services, particularly more schools, than their taxes pay for. Nor is there any evidence that they are more civic-minded than their non-middle-class neighbors; they may be more enthusiastic joiners of civic organizations, but these tend to defend middle-class interests and not necessarily the public interest. Moreover, many people who live in the suburbs still exert considerable political influence in the city because of their work or their property holdings and see to it that urban power structures still put middle-class interests first, as slum organizations, whose demands for more antipoverty funds or public housing are regularly turned down by city hall, can testify.

The alleged effect of the suburbs on urban culture is belied by the vast cultural revival in the city which occurred at the same time the suburban exodus was in full swing. Actually, most suburbanites rarely used the city's cultural facilities even when they lived in the city, and the minority which did, continues to do so, commuting in without difficulty. Indeed, I suspect that over half the ticket buyers for plays, art movies, concerts and museums, particularly outside New York, are—and have long been—suburbanites. Besides, there is no reason why cultural institutions cannot, like banks, build branches in the suburbs, as they are beginning to do now. Culture is no less culture by being outside the city.

A much more valid criticism of suburbanization is its effect on class and racial segregation for the fact that the suburbs have effectively zoned out the poor and the nonwhites is resulting in an ever-increasing class and racial polarization of city and suburbs. In one sense, however, the familiar data about the increasing polarization are slightly misleading. In years past, when urban census statistics showed Negros and whites living side by side, they were actually quite polarized socially. On New York's Upper West Side, for example, the big apartment buildings are *de facto* segregated for whites, while the rotting brownstones between them are inhabited by Negroes and Puerto Ricans. These blocks are integrated statistically or geographically, but not socially, particularly if white parents send their children to private schools.

Nor is suburbanization the sole cause of class and racial polarization; it is itself an effect of trends that have gone on inside the city as well, and not only in America. When people become more affluent and can choose where they want to live, they choose to live with people like themselves. What has happened in the last generation or two is that the opportunity of home buyers to live among compatible neighbors, an opportunity previously available only to people in the middle- and lower-middle-income brackets. This fact does not justify either class or racial segregation, but it does suggest that the polarization resulting from affluence would have occurred even without suburbanization.

Class and racial polarization are harmful because they restrict freedom of housing choice to many people, but also because of the financial consequences for the city. For one thing, affluent suburbia exploits the financially bankrupt city; even when payroll taxes are levied, suburbanites do not pay their fair share of the city's cost in providing them with places of work, shopping areas and cultural facilities and with streets and utilities, maintenance, garbage removal and police protection for these facilities.

More important, suburbanites live in vest-pocket principalities where they can, in effect, vote to keep out the poor and the nonwhites and even the not very affluent whites.

As a result, the cities are in a traumatic financial squeeze. Their ever more numerous low-income residents pay fewer taxes but need costly municipal services, yet cities are taking in less in property taxes all the time, particularly as the firms that employ suburbanites and the shops that cater to them also move to the suburbs. Consequently, city costs rise at the same time as city income declines. To compound the injustice, state and federal politicians from suburban areas often vote against antipoverty efforts and other federal funding activities that would relieve the city's financial troubles, and they also vote to prevent residential integration.

These trends are not likely to change in the years to come. In fact, if the present white affluence continues, the economic gap between the urban have-nots and the suburban haves will only increase, resulting on the one hand in greater suburban opposition to integration and to solving the city's problems, and on the other hand to greater discontent and more ghetto rebellions in the city. This in turn could result in a new white exodus from the city, which, unlike the earlier exodus, will be based almost entirely on racial fear, making suburban-ites out of the middle-aged and older middle-class families who are normally re-luctant to change communities at this age and working-class whites who cannot really afford a suburban house. Many of them will, however, stay put and oppose all efforts toward desegregation, as indicated even now by their violent reaction to integration marches in Milwaukee and Chicago, and to scattered-site public housing schemes which would locate projects in middle-income areas in New York and elsewhere.

Ultimately, these trends could create a vicious spiral, with more ghetto pro-test leading to more white demands, urban and suburban, for repression, resulting in yet more intense ghetto protests, and culminating eventually in a massive exodus of urban whites. If this spiral were allowed to escalate, it might well hasten the coming of the predominantly Negro city.

Today, the predominantly Negro city is still far off in the future, and the all-Negro city is unlikely. Although Washington, D.C.'s population is already about 60 percent Negro, and several other cities, including Newark, Gary and Richmond, hover around the 50 percent mark, recent estimates by the Center for Research in Marketing suggest that only five of the country's 25 largest cities and 10 of the 130 cities with over 100,000 population will be 40 percent or more Negro by 1970. (New York's Negro population was estimated at 18 percent in 1964, although in Manhattan, the proportion of Negroes was 27 percent and of Negroes and Puerto Ricans, 39 percent.)

Moreover, these statistics only count the nighttime residential population, but who lives in the city is, economically and politically, a less relevant statistic than who works there, and the daytime working population of most cities is to-day, and will long remain, heavily and even predominantly white.

Still, to a suburbanite who may someday have to work in a downtown sur-rounded by a black city, the future may seem threatening. A century ago, native-born WASPs must have felt similarly, when a majority of the urban popu-lation consisted of foreign-born Catholics and Jews, to whom they attributed the same pejorative racial characteristics now attributed to Negroes. The city and the WASPs survived, of course, as the immigrants were incorporated into the American economy and suburban whites would also survive.

Today's nonwhite poor play a more marginal role in the urban economy, however, raising the possibility that if the city became predominantly Negro, many private firms and institutions, which hire relatively few Negroes, would leave to build a new downtown elsewhere, a phenomenon already developing on a small scale in Arlington Va., just outside Washington, D.C., and in Clayton, Mo., just outside St. Louis. If this trend became widespread, someday in the distant future only public agencies and low-wage industries, which boast integrated work forces, would remain in the present downtown area.

Many white suburbanites might welcome this development, for it would cut their remaining ties to the city altogether. Some Negroes might also prefer a predominantly black city, partly because they would be able to move into the good housing left by whites, and partly because they would take over political control of the city, thus promising the rank-and-file ghetto resident more sympathetic, if not necessarily better, treatment than he now gets from the white incumbents of city hall.

Nevertheless, the predominantly black city is undesirable, not only because it would create apartheid on a metropolitan scale, but because it would be a yet poorer city, less able to provide the needed public services to its low-income population and less likely to get the funds it would need from a predominantly white federal government.

Unfortunately, present governmental policies, local, state and federal, are doing little to reverse the mounting class and racial polarization of city and suburb. Admittedly, the strong economic and cultural forces that send the middle classes into the suburbs and bring poor nonwhite people from the rural areas into the city in ever larger numbers are difficult to reverse even by the wisest government action.

Still, governmental policies have not been especially wise. The major efforts to slow down class and racial polarization have been these: legislation to achieve racial integration; programs to woo the white middle class back to the city; plans to establish unified metropolitan governments, encompassing both urban and suburban governmental units. All three have failed. None of the open housing and other integration laws now on the books have been enforced sufficiently to permit more than a handful of Negroes to live in the suburbs, and the more recent attempt to prevent the coming of the predominantly black city by enticing the white middle class back has not worked either.

The main technique used for this last purpose has been urban renewal, but there is no evidence—and, in fact, there have been no studies—to show that it has brought back a significant number of middle-class people. Most likely, it has only helped confirmed urbanites find better housing in the city. The attractions of suburbia are simply too persuasive for urban renewal or any other governmental program to succeed in bringing the middle class back to the city.

Even most older couples, whose children have left the suburban house empty, will not return; they have just paid off the mortgage and are not likely to give up a cheap and familiar house for an expensive city apartment, not to mention their gardens, or the friends they have made in the suburbs. At best, some may move to suburban apartments, but most American cities other than New

York have too few downtown attractions to lure a sizable number of people back to the center.

Metropolitan government is, in theory, a good solution, for it would require the suburbs to contribute to solving the city's problems, but it has long been opposed by the suburbs for just this reason. They have felt that the improvements and economies in public services that could be obtained by organizing them on a metropolitan basis would be offset by what suburbanites saw as major disadvantages, principally the reduction of political autonomy and the loss of power to keep out the poor and the nonwhites.

The cities, which have in the past advocated metropolitan government, may become less enthusiastic as Negroes obtain political power. Since the metropolitan area is so predominantly white, urban Negroes would be outvoted every time in any kind of metropolitan government. Some metropolitanization may nevertheless be brought about by federal planning requirements, for as Frances Piven and Richard Cloward point out in a recent *New Republic* article, several federal grant programs, particularly for housing and community facilities, now require a metropolitan plan as a prerequisite for funding. Piven and Cloward suggest that these requirements could disfranchise the urban Negro, and it is, of course, always possible that a white urban-suburban coalition in favor of metropolitan government could be put together deliberately for precisely this purpose. Under such conditions, however, metropolitan governments would only increase racial conflict and polarization.

What, then, can be done to eliminate this polarization? One partial solution is to reduce the dependence of both urban and suburban governments on the property tax, which reduces city income as the population becomes poorer, and forces suburbs to exclude low-income residents because their housing does not bring in enough tax money. If urban and suburban governments could obtain more funds from other sources, including perhaps the federal income tax, parts of the proceeds of which would be returned to them by Washington, urban property owners would bear a smaller burden in supporting the city and might be less opposed to higher spending. Suburbanites would also worry less about their tax rate, and might not feel so impelled to bar less affluent newcomers, or to object to paying their share of the cost of using city services.

Class polarization can be reduced by rent- or price-supplement programs which would enable less affluent urbanites to pay the price of suburban living and would reduce the building and financing cost of housing. But such measures would not persuade the suburbs to let in Negroes; ultimately, the only solution is still across-the-board residential integration.

The outlook for early and enforceable legislation toward this end, however, is dim. Although election results have shown time and again that Northern white majorities will not vote for segregation, they will not vote for integration either. I cannot imagine many political bodies, federal or otherwise, passing or enforcing laws that would result in significant amounts of suburban integration; they would be punished summarily at the next election.

For example, proposals have often been made that state and federal governments should withdraw all subsidies to suburban communities and builders practicing *de facto* segregation, thus depriving the former of at least half their school operating funds, and the latter of Federal Housing Authority (F.H.A.) insurance on which their building plans depend. However desirable such legislation is, the chance that it would be passed is almost nil. One can also argue that Washington should offer grants-in-aid to suburban governments which admit low-income residents, but these grants would often be turned down. Many suburban municipalities would rather starve their public services instead, and the voters would support them all the way.

The best hope now is for judicial action. The New Jersey Supreme Court ruled some years back that builders relying on F.H.A. insurance had to sell to Negroes, and many suburban subdivisions in that state now have some Negro residents. The United States Supreme Court has just decided that it will rule on whether racial discrimination by large suburban developers is unconstitutional. If the answer turns out to be yes, the long, slow process of implementing the Court's decisions can at least begin.

In the meantime, solutions that need not be tested at the ballot box must be advanced. One possibility is new towns, built for integrated populations with federal support, or even by the federal government alone, on land now vacant. Although hope springs eternal in American society that the problems of old towns can be avoided by starting from scratch, these problems seep easily across the borders of the new community. Even if rural governments can be persuaded to accept new towns in their bailiwicks, and white residents could be attracted, such towns would be viable only if federal grants and powers were used to obtain industries—and of a kind that would hire and train poorly skilled workers.

Greater emphasis should be placed on eliminating job discrimination in suburban work places, particularly in industries which are crying for workers, so that unions are less impelled to keep out nonwhite applicants. Mass transit systems should be built to enable city dwellers, black and white, to obtain suburban jobs without necessarily living in the suburbs.

Another and equally important solution is more school integration—for example, through urban-suburban educational parks that will build up integrated student enrollment by providing high-quality schooling to attract suburban whites, and through expansion of the busing programs that send ghetto children into suburban schools. Although white suburban parents have strenuously opposed busing their children into the city, several suburban communities have accepted Negro students who are bused in from the ghetto; for example, in the Boston area and in Westchester County.

And while the Supreme Court is deliberating, it would be worthwhile to persuade frightened suburbanites that, as all the studies so far have indicated, open housing would not mean a massive invasion of slum dwellers, but only the gradual arrival of a relatively small number of Negroes, most of them as middle-class as the whitest suburbanite. A massive suburban invasion by slum dwellers of any color is sheer fantasy. Economic studies have shown the sad fact that only a tiny proportion of ghetto residents can even afford to live in the suburbs. Moreover, as long as Negro workers lack substantial job security, they need to live near the center of the urban transportation system so that they can travel to jobs all over the city.

In addition, there are probably many ghetto residents who do not even want suburban integration now; they want the same freedom of housing choice as whites, but they do not want to be "dispersed" to the suburbs involuntarily. Unfortunately, no reliable studies exist to tell us where ghetto residents do want to live, but should they have freedom of choice, I suspect many would leave the slums for better housing and better neighborhoods outside the present ghetto. Not many would now choose predominantly white areas, however, at least not until living among whites is psychologically and socially less taxing, and until integration means more than just assimilation to white middle-class ways.

Because of the meager success of past integration efforts, many civil-rights leaders have given up on integration and are now demanding the rebuilding of the ghetto. They argue persuasively that residential integration has so far and will in the future benefit only a small number of affluent Negroes, and that if the poverty-stricken ghetto residents are to be helped soon, that help must be located in the ghetto. The advocates of integration are strongly opposed. They demand that all future housing must be built outside the ghetto, for anything else would just perpetuate segregation. In recent months, the debate between the two positions has become bitter, each side claiming only its solution has merit.

Actually there is partial truth on both sides. The integrationists are correct about the long-term dangers of rebuilding the ghetto; the ghetto rebuilders (or separatists) are correct about the short-term failure of integration. But if there is little likelihood that the integrationists' demands will be carried out soon, their high idealism in effect sentences ghetto residents to remaining in slum poverty.

Moreover, there is no need to choose between integration and rebuilding, for both policies can be carried out simultaneously. The struggle for integration must continue, but if the immediate prospects for success on a large scale are dim, the ghetto must be rebuilt in the meantime.

The primary aim of rebuilding, however, should not be to rehabilitate houses or clear slums, but to raise the standard of living of ghetto residents. The highest priority must be a massive antipoverty program which will, through the creation of jobs, more effective job-training schemes, the negative income tax, children's allowances and other measures, raise ghetto families to the middle-income level, using outside resources from government and private enterprise and inside participation in the planning and decision-making. Also needed are a concerted effort at quality compensatory education for children who cannot attend integrated schools; federally funded efforts to improve the quality of ghetto housing, as well as public services; some municipal decentralization to give ghetto residents the ability to plan their own communities and their own lives, and political power so that the ghetto can exert more influence in behalf of its demands.

If such programs could extend the middle-income standard of living to the ghetto in the years to come, residential integration might well be achieved in subsequent generations. Much of the white opposition to integration is based on stereotypes of Negro behavior—some true, some false—that stem from poverty rather than from color, and many of the fears about Negro neighbors reflect the traditional American belief that poor people will not live up to middle-class standards. Moreover, even lack of enthusiasm for integration among ghetto residents is a result of poverty; they feel, rightly or not, that they must solve their economic problems before they can even think about integration.

If ghetto poverty were eliminated, the white fears—and the Negro ones—would begin to disappear, as did the pejorative stereotypes which earlier Americans held about the "inferior races"—a favorite nineteenth-century term for the European immigrants—until they achieved affluence. Because attitudes based on color differences are harder to overcome than those based on cultural differences, the disappearance of anti-Negro stereotypes will be slower than that of anti-immigrant stereotypes. Still, once color is no longer an index of poverty and lower-class status, it will cease to arouse white fears, so that open-housing laws can be enforced more easily and eventually may even be unnecessary. White suburbanites will not exclude Negroes to protect their status or their property values, and many, although not necessarily all, Negroes will choose to leave the ghetto.

Morally speaking, any solution that does not promise immediate integration is repugnant, but moral dicta will neither persuade suburbanites to admit low-income Negroes into their communities, nor entice urbane suburbanites to live near low-income Negroes in the city. Instead of seeking to increase their middle-income population by importing suburban whites, cities must instead make their poor residents middle-income. The practical solution, then, is to continue to press for residential integration, but also to eliminate ghetto poverty immediately, in order to achieve integration in the future, substituting government antipoverty programs for the private economy which once created the jobs and incomes that helped poorer groups escape the slums in past generations. Such a policy will not only reduce many of the problems of the city, which are ultimately caused by the poverty of its inhabitants, but it will assure the ultimate disappearance of the class and racial polarization of cities and suburbs.

There is only one hitch: This policy is not likely to be adopted. Although white voters and their elected officials are probably more favorable to ghetto rebuilding than to integration, they are, at the moment, not inclined or impelled to support even the former. They lack inclination to rebuild the ghetto because they do not want to pay the taxes that would raise ghetto incomes; they are not so impelled because neither the problems of the ghetto nor even its rebellions touch their lives directly and intimately. So far, most of them still experience the ghetto only on television. Until many white Americans are directly affected by what goes on in the ghetto, they will probably support nothing more than a minuscule antipoverty program and a token effort toward racial integration.

22

JAMES R. McINTOSH, The Urban Fringe: Social Life, Social Change, and the Urban Voyeur[1]

A popular weekly news magazine began a recent article with this eye-catching query: "Will the U.S. be one vast city with no rural population?" The occasion was the reporting of urban demographic data from the 1970 census.[2] The article went on to suggest that the trend is in the direction of creating a nation of cities. It reported that 73.5 percent of the population was concentrated in urban areas, compared to 69.9 percent a decade ago. Yet, the article also reflected the subtleties in the urbanizing trend. While the population in the urban areas of the country was increasing, in cities it was decreasing. The percentage of population living in the fifty largest cities in the nation decreased nearly 2 percent since 1960. Twenty-two of these cities lost citizens during the last decade.

It is suburbanization that accounts for the increase in population of the urban areas and a decrease in the cities. People are living near cities, not in them. People flee the city to the suburban area. Others move toward cities but not in them. There are both flight and flirtation, attractions and repulsions. It is the "almost urban" area that is appealing.

The demographic figures represent only one dimension of the urbanizing trend. The communication system, particularly television, has reduced the distances in our world. One does not have to live in center city to experience an urban riot. Network newscasts will bring the phenomenon into the livingroom. One need not be in Saigon to sense the devastation of rocket attacks. Marshall McLuhan speaks of the Vietnam war as being the first TV war, with every phase and main actions of the war being fought in American homes.[3] The urban world has electronically expanded as traffic tie-ups, race rebellions, strikes, financial crisis, pollution, crime and unsafe streets and all the other urban ills of this decade are experienced by all. With 95 percent of all households in the country containing at least one television set, few people are not participants in the electronic expansion of urban life.[4] The prospect is not a nation of cities, but a national urban society. The urban trend is an extension of urban life and not simply greater population concentration, though that occurs.

The demographic and electronic extensions are not occurring in empty

This article is original to this volume.

wastelands. The movement to the suburban areas places a heavy strain on existing land and institutions. As the pressures of this suburban concentration increase, spillage occurs. The urban fringe is breached. It is this loosely defined area that has been the source of much urban expansion.[5] It is peripheral to suburban communities. It is an area characterized by small settlements and an occasional town. Land usage patterns of the fringe vary intermittently with agricultural, commercial, and industrial activities competing for space. The most prominent land feature is likely to be vacant acres, the major attraction for the swollen urban areas. It is on these empty lands that housing subdivisions and developments are constructed, ultimately changing a fringe territory to a suburban community.

Despite the obvious importance of the urban fringe, data are scarce from this outpost. Reasons for this are many. Fringe areas are sparsely populated. The problems of the residents are not as dramatized as the problem of center city dwellers. Equally as important are the difficulties of conducting research in these areas. Economic factors and topographic and other logistic problems tend to deter research. Yet, it is this territory that provides the setting for contact between the expanding urban society and the rural living patterns of the fringe. It becomes crucial that something becomes known about urban fringe society. What forms of life styles are found there? What are the satisfactions, concerns, and worries of fringe residents? How do they prepare for the inevitable urban glacier creeping toward their home territory? While demographic encroachment may move slowly, the electronic incursion is accomplished swiftly and usually with the abetment of the fringe resident. Cable television or highpowered antennas instantly bring the electronic Trojan horse of center city to fringe livingroom. What is the effect on the resident located serenely on the periphery? This report is an attempt to indicate the direction answers to these questions take. As a pilot study of one urban fringe area, it has obvious limitations. Still, it is a beginning toward the accumulation of knowledge of life along the urban fringe.

THE FRINGE AREA AND THE SAMPLE

Monroe County is located in the northeast corner of Pennsylvania. It covers an area of 611 square miles and has a population of a little over 40,000. Stroudsburg, the county seat, has a population of approximately 14,000. New York City to the east and Philadelphia to the south are less than 100 miles away. Major east-west federal highways are almost completed, and a north-south highway is scheduled for completion in 1974. The county is a part of the Tocks Island Region that includes counties in New Jersey and New York as well as Pennsylvania. The area has long been a major recreational source for residents of Megalopolis, as it includes most of the Pocono and Catskill resort areas. In addition, a national park with a large lake is planned for the area that includes part of Monroe County. The continued growth of the New York-Philadelphia areas, the new highways and expanded playground facilities will ensure major changes in the area.

The sample for this pilot study was drawn from Ward One of Stroudsburg and near-by Jackson Township. For purposes not related to this report, the sample was deliberately biased in the direction of nonagrarian rural poor. These two areas appeared to have concentrations of lower-income people. Interviews with local officials familiar with the target sites confirmed the subjective judgments based on the deteriorating exteriors of houses of the areas. Scattered throughout both areas was an occasional home that was either new or in superior condition. These homes were included in the sample, but the majority of respondents fell into lower-income brackets.

In all, 117 interviews were completed, 66 in Jackson and 51 in Stroudsburg. Student interviewers were instructed to obtain an interview with either the male household head or the female household head. In all but four homes, they were successful at this. In the four exceptions, two interviewees were the oldest offspring while the other two persons declined to identify their household positions. The total sample represents 49 men and 68 women. The representation of more women than men is not surprising. Most of the interviews took place during weekday hours and on some weekends during daylight hours. While some evening contact took place, this was generally discouraged. Most of the students were not familiar with the area, particularly the backroads of Jackson Township. Also, evening interviews in these areas are difficult to obtain due to fear of strangers in out-the-way areas. A lack of sufficient street lighting making it difficult to arrive at the right home and making identification difficult played a role as well.

Vital statistics profile

In general, the sample consists of older people; that is, those born in the 1920s and 1930s or even earlier. While close to one-third of the population sample falls into an age range of 22 to 40 years of age, nearly two-thirds of the sample are over the age of 40. Of this older group, forty-five of the respondents are over the age of 50. One-fifth of the total sample falls into the 66 years of age or over category. On a nationwide basis, the 1960 census figures places only a little over 9 percent in this category. This skewing of the age distribution toward the over 40 group undoubtedly plays a major role in shaping the data on life styles and attitudes towards change to be presented below.

The age factor was further represented in terms of the number of children found in the household. In fifty-three homes, respondents reported no children residing with them. One child was reported in fourteen homes and in another fourteen homes there were three children. The modal category of those with children was two. Respondents in twenty-seven homes reported this number. Only 7.7 percent of the respondents reported having as many as four or five children. No larger families were found in the sample. Of the 151 children living with families in the sample households, 122 were under the age of 18. Nearly 60 percent of these potentially school-age children lived in Stroudsburg.

Home ownership was a common characteristic among the people in the sample. Approximately 64 percent of all respondents lived in their own homes.

The fact that nearly one-half of these homes were constructed prior to World War II was not surprising. Most of the houses were selected for the sample because of their deteriorating conditions. Fifty-eight sample homes were over 30 years old and another thirty-seven were between 11 and 30 years old. Only seventeen houses were built in the last ten years. Five respondents were unable to supply any age for their homes. The age factor apparently had little effect on the satisfaction of the respondents with their homes. Less than one-half replied positively to a question concerning their interest in home improvement projects, i.e., adding a new room, putting in a new heating system, etc. Finally, only five of the houses of the respondents lacked a complete indoor bathroom.

The educational characteristics of the respondents were only moderately reflective of achievement. Over one-half of the 234 respondents and their spouses reported less than a high school education. Nearly three-quarters of those without high school degrees failed to go beyond the ninth grade. A high school diploma was earned by sixty-seven respondents and spouses. Five people completed college training, and another thirteen had some college experience but failed to finish. These figures suggest considerably less schooling than that completed by the rest of the nation. The median number of school years completed for persons in this country 25 years or older was 12.1 in 1969.[6]

The traits of the potential work force of 234 men and women reflected the level of educational accomplishment. Out of this potential, 139 were involved in some form of employment. Of this group, 101 fell into one of the four following occupational categories: craftsmen, foremen, and kindred workers; operatives and kindred workers; laborers excluding farms and mines; service workers. Highway construction, subdivision building and factory employment were major occupational areas for the respondents. The service workers were usually associated with the resort industry in the area. The composition of the labor force by major occupational group for this sample approximated the findings of the 1960 census for rural nonfarm residence.

The incomes of the respondents had a wide range, but as intended, was skewed toward the lower levels. Approximately 56 percent of the sample earned less than an annual income of $7,000. At the lower end of the scale, nearly 21 percent of the respondents reported an income of less than $3,000. Those families reporting over $10,000 a year income comprised a little over 15 percent of the group responding to the income question. Eleven people refused to answer. When the Jackson-Stroudsburg data were separated, it was clear that the Jackson residents were financially better off. Almost 23 percent of the Jackson respondents were in the $10,000-or-more bracket, as compared to only 6 percent in Stroudsburg. In the $4,999 and downwards category, a little over 39 percent of the Stroudsburg respondents were found, whereas 24 percent of the Jackson people were located in this income bracket. The middle-income range of $5,000 to $9,000 represented no great difference between Jackson and Stroudsburg. It was only at the extremes of this wide range that there were notable differences between the two places.

Table 1.

Occupational Group	Combined occupations of respondents and spouses, 1960		Composition of the employed male labor force by major occupational group and urban and rural residence, 1960*		
	Sample%	*U.S.%*	*Urban%*	*Rural Nonfarm%*	*Rural Farm%*
Professional technical, and kindred workers	6.4	10.3	12.0	7.8	1.7
Farmers and farm managers	2.1	5.5	.4	3.5	53.0
Managers, officials, and proprietors	11.5	10.7	11.9	9.7	2.7
Clerical and kindred workers	2.8	6.9	8.3	4.6	1.6
Sales workers	2.1	6.9	8.0	5.1	1.6
Craftsmen, foremen, and kindred workers	26.6	19.5	20.2	22.3	7.0
Operatives and kindred workers	25.1	19.9	19.7	24.5	10.1
Private household workers	2.1	.1	.1	.2	.1
Farm laborers and foremen	0	2.8	.6	5.1	15.1
Laborers except farm and mine	8.6	6.9	6.6	9.2	3.9

*Source: Alvin Boskoff, *The Sociology of Urban Regions,* 2nd ed. (New York: Appleton-Century-Crofts, 1970), p. 59.

Table 2. Total family income as reported by respondents

	Total sample		Stroudsburg		Jackson	
	No.	*%*	*No.*	*%*	*No.*	*%*
Less than $2,000	12	10.3	7	13.7	5	7.6
$2,000–$2,999	12	10.3	6	11.8	6	9.1
$3,000–$4,999	12	10.3	7	13.7	5	7.6
$5,000–$6,999	29	24.8	11	21.6	18	27.3
$7,000–$9,999	23	19.7	11	21.6	12	18.2
$10,000 or more	18	15.4	3	5.9	15	22.7
No answer	11	9.4	6	11.8	5	7.6
	117	100.0	51	100.0	66	100.0

In terms of race and religion, the sample was mostly white and Protestant. There were fourteen blacks, all residing in Ward One. The sample contained a smattering of Catholics, 18 percent, and nobody of Jewish faith. The ethnicity of the area was predominantly German and, by the respondents' own definition, Pennsylvania Dutch. A little over 45 percent of the sample identified themselves as such, with the next most popular ethnicities being Anglo-Saxon and Irish. With the exception of the blacks, similar race, ethnicities, and religious preferences were found in Jackson and Stroudsburg.

The picture that became clear was that the expected characteristics of rural nonfarm residents were found in this sample of low-income Monroe County residents. In terms of income, race, ethnicity, religion, and occupational groupings, the findings were not unusual. Census Bureau data suggest that rural, nonfarm people are predominantly white, Protestant, and are heavily represented in such occupational categories as operatives and kindred workers, craftsmen, foremen and kindred workers.[7] This pilot study tends to confirm these characteristics.

Social life and socializing

The popular stereotype of a typical Monroe County resident derived from conversations with local officials was that of the last pioneer. The portrait that was drawn was that of a rugged individual, an outdoorsman who fished, trapped, and hunted as often as possible. The typical person was supposedly heavily involved in extended kin relationships providing the basic social structure for the locale. Such an image was not supported by the data. Instead a varied picture was established that weakened the imagery held of a typical resident.

When respondents were asked to name their favorite outdoor activity, a little over 23 percent reported that they had none. Only 26.5 percent replied by citing hunting, fishing, and trapping as their favorite. Outdoor work around the yard or garden was reported by 23 percent as the activity they liked to do most. Another 15 percent or so said that water activity such as boating or swimming, when available, was their favorite outdoor pleasure.

There were some marked differences between Jackson residents and Stroudsburg residents. Only 15 percent of the Jackson people denied any interest in outdoor activity while one-third of the Stroudsburg residents fell into this category. Also, in terms of percentages, twice as many Jackson respondents selected hunting and fishing as their favorite outdoor pursuit when compared to the Stroudsburg residents. Of the group that responded by identifying some outdoor activity, 85 percent reported engaging in their pastime at least once a month or more often. The outdoor type may not be as numerous as expected, but the resident is a regular participant.

Kinship-related social activities were by no means the dominant feature of social life in this sample. In fact, neighbors were as likely to be entertained as relatives. This does not mean that kinfolk were ignored. Nearly 48 percent of the respondents invite relatives over to their homes once a month or more often. However, 25 percent reported never getting together with any members of their family or seeing them only once a year. Jackson residents were more likely to entertain their relatives than the Stroudsburg people. Forty-four percent of those living in Jackson reported spending two or three evenings a month with their kin. Only 23 percent of the respondents in Ward One will see their relatives that often. Six percent of the Jackson respondents reported never having their kin visit them, while 18 percent of the Stroudsburg sample fall into this category.

As suggested, neighbors were nearly as important as relatives in the social life of the respondents. Approximately 46 percent of the sample report inviting neighbors to their homes once a month or more. Jackson residents were more neighborly than people in Ward One, with 53 percent reporting such activity.

In Stroudsburg, 37.3 percent indicated that neighbors came over for a social gathering once a month or more often. However, over one-third of all respondents reported never inviting neighbors into their homes or only extending invitations once a year. This was more likely to be the case for Ward One respondents than it was for people from Jackson.

Out-of-the-house entertainment is notable for its infrequency. Movies were seldom attended, with 72 percent reporting either that they never go or attend only once a year. In Stroudsburg, there was a hard core of 10 percent who saw a movie once a week. However, there was little else differentiating the two areas. While 45 percent of the respondents reported going out to eat at a restaurant once a month, a little over half of the respondents never went to bars or clubs for a drink. Drinking at a bar two or three times a month or more was done by only 22 percent of the population. A small group of regulars, 15 percent, reported going to their neighborhood tavern at least once a week. Interest in spectator sports was practically nil. Three-fifths of the sample said they only attend sporting events once a year or that they never went.

While one-quarter of the sample belonged to one voluntary association, a little over half belonged to no organizations or clubs. Most of the organizations people belonged to were sport or social clubs. Attendance at club events was rather weak. The highest frequency of attendance was once a month, with 21 percent reporting this. Just over half of the Stroudsburg respondents belonged to some club, while just under a half of the Jackson residents were members of some association.

Newspaper-reading and television-watching appeared to be popular activities. Almost nine out of ten respondents said that they read a daily or weekly newspaper. The local newspaper was cited by over three-quarters of the group as the paper they read most often. Television was ubiquitous, with 109 respondents reporting having at least one set. Over three-fifths of the sample received seven television stations or more. Nearly one-half of the respondents reported someone watching their set four or more hours after 6:00 each evening. Two-thirds of the homes had somebody viewing television at least three hours every night.

The overall picture of the life style found in Jackson and Stroudsburg is one that stresses primary groups and home entertainment. Having the neighbors and relatives in one's home is a major source of social activity. Going out to more formally organized activities are eschewed in favor of the intimacy and ease of such primary groups. Television is always available, and with cable television and powerful antennas a wide variety of programs are received from nearby metropolitan areas. For those respondents that enjoy the outdoors, there is much to do and they take advantage of this. While three-fifths of the respondents reported shopping in metropolitan areas several times a year, life is anchored in Monroe County. The people in this sample stay close to home, and social activities are not complicated. Their life styles are conditioned by their socio-economic status, their ages and the pace of the rural setting.

RESISTANCE TO SOCIAL CHANGE:
THE URBAN VOYEUR

In trying to assess the resistance to social change, respondents were asked whether they favored the eventuality of possible future events either affecting themselves or all of Monroe County. In general, the residents resisted changes directly involved in their lives. They were not interested in a major uprooting of their current life styles. The respondents were selective in their attitudes toward future events affecting Monroe County as a whole.

Four of the statements about future events that affected the respondent were negatively received and one was supported. The latter concerned having their children go to college and the former dealt with jobs and homes. The respondents were not interested in obtaining higher paying jobs outside of the county nor accepting an increase in pay on a new job within the county if it involved more responsibility. Few respondents were interested in owning new homes that had more room. Finally, only a little over a quarter of the respondents were interested in a second home in warmer climates.

Questions about future happenings concerning all of Monroe County dealt with improved services, new industry, increased tourism, and more people moving into Monroe County. The pattern of answers that was received is of interest because it appears to support social change. Better medical facilities, more concern with air and water pollution, a major shopping center in the area, and improved roads in the county drew enthusiastic support from the respondents. The occurrence of these events would alarm few of the people. Even increasing the number of jobs available and bringing in new industry received much support from the people. But then again, these are "good" happenings by definition. Who would oppose better health service? Who can be against new jobs and industry as long as they remained only vaguely defined? These "good" events deal with the image of growth and not the spectre of change. While growth and change cannot be logically separated, they are in everyday parlance. Politicians and

Table 3. Attitude towards possible changes affecting respondents

Respondent would like to:	Agree		Disagree		Don't know		No answer	
	No.	%	No.	%	No.	%	No.	%
Have a new job that pays more but has more responsibility	34	29.1	70	59.8	8	6.8	5	4.3
Move from Monroe County for a better paying job	15	12.8	89	76.1	8	6.8	5	4.3
Have a new home with more room	36	30.8	78	66.7	2	1.7	1	.9
Own a second home in a warmer climate	31	26.5	82	70.1	3	2.6	1	.9
Have children go to college	96	82.1	7	6.0	8	6.8	6	5.1

Table 4. Attitude towards possible changes affecting Monroe County

Respondent would like to see:	Agree		Disagree		Don't know		No answer	
	No.	%	No.	%	No.	%	No.	%
Building of new highways	72	61.5	37	31.6	7	6.0	1	.9
More concern about air and water pollution	100	85.5	9	7.7	7	6.0	1	.9
An increase in number of available jobs	98	83.8	13	11.1	4	3.4	2	1.7
More motels and resorts	34	29.1	70	59.8	12	10.3	1	.9
Improved medical facilities	110	94.0	3	2.6	3	2.6	1	.9
Development of new industry	98	83.8	10	8.5	8	6.8	1	.9
More people moving into the area	56	47.9	51	43.6	8	6.8	2	1.7
Development of a major shopping center	88	75.7	21	17.9	7	6.0	1	.9

opinion-makers can preach growth and development without mentioning change. As long as the talk remains nonspecific, it is not threatening. New jobs and industry are rarely dealt with except in the generalities.

When the respondents were asked about specific events that are the closest to the reality of the future, they were ambivalent or resistant. When asked if they would like to see an increase in motels and resorts in the area, nearly three-fifths were opposed to this happening. No clear attitude toward having an increase of population in the area existed. While there were a few people who could not make up their minds on this issue, 47.9 percent were in favor of it and 43.6 percent were opposed to new residents. Clearly, these two things are quite likely to happen in the next decade or so. The national park will be the catalyst for the additional resorts and motels. Urban expansion will bring more people into the area. It is in this harsh area of reality that unsure and resistant attitudes are likely to surface.

This reluctance or ambivalence by Monroe residents toward the future is to be expected. The natural beauty of the area with its lakes and mountains is appealing. The pace of life is built around the home that is secure, stable, and satisfying. Yet, the respondents are not living a quiet life of rural isolation. The surrounding tranquility is technologically interrupted. With the wide variety of television programming available from center city studios, the Monroe County resident has a window on the urban fringe. This fringe location makes the Monroe County resident an urban voyeur, an outsider looking in. He has access to the film clips of urban difficulties from network news telecasts as well as from the affiliated local newcasts. From the relative serenity of his locus he observes urban life, albeit through the selective focus of electronic journalism. His observation post allows the resident to weigh the simplicity of his routine against the complexities of the megalopolis that he views nightly. Watching the spectacles offered by the media confirms the belief that life in the country may have some problems but certainly not as serious as those of the city. Crime in the streets, strikes, race riots, and pollution form the litany of the urban voyeur. His electronic window permits the viewing of an urban life style, one radically alien from his own and one of which he wants no part.

The highly selective information from the media operates as a reference point for the rural resident. He can compare himself to the urban dweller and, adding up his perceptual advantages, comes out with a higher sum than that of his urban counterpart. He may not have all he desires, but he does have the uncluttered environment, security and an easy pace. From this perspective, the Monroe County resident regards encroachments upon his life style as threatening. Social change will alter his way of life and while he is familiar with its shortcomings, he has been offered nothing better. Sensory data support his resistance.

The future lumpenproletariat?

The electronic invasion of Monroe County by the media of center city is accomplished. It serves the purpose of sounding the alarm. The resistance of the locals to the portent of urbanization is hardened. It would accomplish little to argue that the urban voyeur sees only a highly selective glimpse of urban life. The voyeur sees what is available and that is his experience. There is little that the urban voyeur views that is appealing.

The demographic encroachment will soon follow the media into Monroe County. As the expansion of the New York and Philadelphia metropolitan areas continues, their surrounding fringes will soon be their suburbs. People seeking relief from the now crowded suburbs will inch further away from center city. The highways in the area will ensure this. Land developers, speculators, and real estate interests will see to the rest. The increased recreational facilities will be an attraction leading to more tourism. The chain motels and resort companies will expand their interests in the area.

All of this means that for the next decade or so, the area will be one of growth and development. The local resident will enjoy a short-term boom. Increased building and construction labor will be needed, and such work is what the local resident has been doing. During this period, the rural people are likely to grumble about many developments in the area, but ready employment will calm discontent.

The long-run forecast is bleak. The limited financial resources of the residents will mean they will not be able to invest in the area's growth. The limited occupational skills of the local people will preclude anything but limited opportunity. When the construction and building boom levels off, the local residents will be laid off. The outside financial interest and the new residents streaming out of the city and suburb will be the major beneficiaries of the development of this urban fringe. The exurban voyeur will soon find himself a participant in his own metropolitan telecast of urban ills.

Notes

1. Some of the materials in this article were originally published in *Life Styles and Attitudes Just Beyond the Urban Fringe*. Tocks Island Regional Advisory Council, 612 Monroe Street, Stroudsburg, Pennsylvania 18360. I also want to thank Donald Carns and Eric Ottervik for their helpful suggestions and Molly Reynolds who persevered while typing several drafts of this article.

2. *U.S. News and World Report,* February 22, 1971, p. 37.

3. Marshall McLuhan, *War and Peace in the Global Village* (New York: Bantam Books, 1968), p. 134.

4. U.S. Bureau of Census, *Statistical Abstract of the United States: 1970* (91st Edition) Washington, D.C.: U.S. Government Printing Office, 1970, p. 496.

5. Alvin Boskoff, *The Sociology of Urban Regions,* 2nd edition (New York: Appleton-Century-Crofts, 1970), pp. 121–122.

6. U.S. Bureau of Census, *op. cit.,* p. 109.

7. Boskoff, *op. cit.,* chapter 4.

chapter 6

CONTENTS

poliTics ANd CONTROL

If, as some political scientists suggest, politics is the study of power, this section reflects four definitive perspectives from which power phenomena can be viewed. The articles in the first subsection treat questions concerning who has the power in urban society and how are decisions made. John Walton's original essay reviews the literature on this topic from its inception, the classic work of Floyd Hunter, *Community Power Structure.* Walton's point is that this is a widely developed research tradition which may have an important bearing on the role of social science in public policy-making. Frank Munger, with Roscoe Martin and others, provide a detailed analysis of public issues and policy-making processes in one American city. The value of their study is to provide a reasonable and well-researched alternative to the conclusions of Floyd Hunter and others who interpret the actions of urban decision-makers from an elitist perspective. Munger and his colleagues conclude that in Syracuse the data suggest a more democratic process. The article by Michael Aiken and Robert Alford is the best illustration of recent developments in this field, particularly the interest in comparative analyses of a large number of cities concerning the practical outcomes, in this case urban renewal, of different structural arrangements. Of special interest is their review and assessment of a variety of theoretical arguments and their subsequent proposal of a new explanation of policy effectiveness—innovation—based on local organizational structure.

A second approach to urban politics and policy-making is the "political culture" school. In some senses, this is a more fundamental approach than the analysis of power. Exponents of this view argue that cities, like countries, have unique cultures or styles of doing things. Analyses of these styles, rather than of particular policy-makers, is therefore a more definitive way of accounting for what gets done in the policy arena. Clearly there is no conflict between these two approaches, and they can be combined in a single study. James Q. Wilson's sparkling account of the political culture of Southern California is both good social science and good reading. Essentially, he argues that to understand the often bizarre and unpredictable political behavior of this segment of the country, one must appreciate its ecological and social interaction patterns.

The theme is continued in the articles in the third subsection on participation, where the articles deal with concrete cases of citizen participation in public issues. They also provide an interesting contrast, William Kornhauser showing some negative consequences of broad participation, while Jon and Sally Van Til indicate some failures of elites to allow effective citizen participation.

Once again, there is transitional link between the Van Tils' emphasis and the final two articles, dealing with groups excluded from power. Robert Blauner analyzes judiciously the parallel between disenfranchised colonized peoples and the problems of American ghetto communities. Finally, Harvey Molotch shows that the poor and disenfranchised may not be the only victims of powerful special interests. His article documents how a middle-class antipollution movement was frustrated in its efforts to prevent practices engaged in by large corporations with high level political support.

The general theme of Chapter 6 is an analysis of the process and consequences of urban decision-making as viewed from several perspectives. Certainly the conclusions to be drawn from these selections vary. They reflect, for example, cases of more and less competitive power structures, more and less effective participation in decision-making, and so forth. Nevertheless, the selections are representative of the literature on urban politics which, indeed, is highly diversified and not yet susceptible to easy generalization.

23

JOHN WALTON, The Bearing of Social Science Research on Public Issues: Floyd Hunter and the Study of Power

An issue of increasing importance in social science concerns the interrelationship of research and public policy. Although the issue is not entirely of recent origin, it has become particularly salient in the last few years as a result of the expanding scope of research endeavors and the advent of new opportunities for social scientists to examine, if not advise on, policy-related problems. As one observer has forcefully put it, "At long last, social science has come on center stage in American society."[1]

This change has been looked upon with mixed feelings. Optimistic appraisals view it as an opportunity to enlighten and rationalize public policy, while pessimistic assessments fear cooption by or the disingenuous use of research for the benefit of special political interests. Certain hardbitten "realists" seem to feel that both of these positions are naïve and that social research does not make a hell of a lot of difference one way or the other. The normative and empirical problems presented by these developments are extremely complex, and so far, our experience may be too limited to yield any generalizations. Thus, any discussion of the topic is well advised to limit its scope and deal with problems about which there is some relatively unambiguous information.[2]

The general topic of the interrelationship between research and public policy can be approached in three ways. The first concerns the question of how social science might influence policy: whether it can have some useful effect, how much effect, under what circumstances, and with what perils. A second, and perhaps more manageable approach, is how public policy influences social science: from a sociology of knowledge standpoint, how policies affecting research grants or the availability of information help shape the content and orientation of social science. A third approach is to focus more specifically on the methods social scientists have actually used to examine public issues. Although less inclusive than the first-named approaches, this tack does allow one to get down to cases and assess the utility of current methods for generating some understanding of public issues.

The third approach is adopted in the present essay. One reason for that choice is that the questions it raises logically precede some of the other issues. That is, the question of how social science might influence policy must await an answer to the prior question, "Is social science ready?"[3] Is it, in specific areas, capable of generating understandings which the responsible social scientist would be willing to stand by as policy directives? It is one thing to decry willy-nilly policy-making that is uninformed by evidence concerning likely outcomes; it is quite another to presume that contemporary social science has a large stockpile of such evidence ready to deliver to any nonperverse policy-maker. In short, our first concern should be an assessment of specific research areas to determine whether the accumulated evidence suggests directives that bear on policy issues. Here it is reasonable to assume we shall encounter a good deal of variation. For example, we probably now possess more policy-related evidence on racial prejudice than on the consequences of rapid urbanization.

A second reason for adopting the present approach rests on substantive rather than logical considerations. Fortunately, there exists an extensive research literature devoted to the study of community power and decision-making.[4] An assessment of this field, particularly the cumulative contribution of a great many studies since 1953, when Floyd Hunter began this kind of work, will provide a unique and direct illustration of the bearing of social research on public issues.[5]

Floyd Hunter's contribution

In 1953, Floyd Hunter published his classic work, *Community Power Structure: A Study of Decision Makers.*[6] A minimal yet interesting criterion of why this book can be called a classic is that it was Hunter who coined the term "power structure" which has now so thoroughly infused the vocabularies of social scientists and political activists.

There are, however, more compelling reasons for placing this work among a small handful of modern sociological classics, reasons which were never properly understood or which became obscured in the controversies that followed from Hunter's study. In the first place, it was a pioneering work, an original item. As Bonjean and Olson observe, "Prior to 1953 and the publication of Floyd Hunter's *Community Power Structure,* the question "Who governs?" was answered in much the same manner by both social scientists and the lay public."[7] With a true craftsman's skill, Hunter independently fashioned a set of research techniques that represented the first systematic approach to the study of power and that continued to undergird contemporary research designs.[8]

In its time, *Community Power Structure* was also a unique example of macrosociological research. Rather than focusing on a gang, a factory, or a prison, Hunter took on a major American city of half a million people.

The principal purpose of the book was also bold. Hunter's opening paragraph makes this clear:[9]

> It has been evident to the writer for some years that policies on vital matters affecting community life seem to appear suddenly. They are acted upon; but with no precise knowledge on the part of the majority of citizens as to how these policies originated or by whom they are really sponsored. Much is done, but much is left undone. Some of the things done appear to be manipulated to the advantage of relatively few.

The purpose of the study, then, was to identify the leaders and patterns of power (i.e., leadership groupings and methods of exercising power) that would explain how the policies just mentioned were decided upon and implemented.

Hunter's study of Atlanta, Georgia, answers these questions in several fundamental themes. Because these findings have been so widely misunderstood or misinterpreted by subsequent critics, they will be succinctly put forth here.

1. Hunter employed a variety of specific techniques for identifying leaders and policy-making processes. The first involved questioning a panel of expert or knowledgeable community residents from a variety of institutional areas about who were the most important people in town when it came to getting things done. On the basis of these nominations, and for practical reasons, Hunter first arbitrarily took the top forty persons as policy-making leaders and examined their occupations, positions, and organizational affiliations. These leaders represented the following occupational categories: eleven commerce; seven banking, finance, or insurance; six professional (five were lawyers); five manufacturing and industry; five leisure (social leaders); four government; two labor. Six of the forty were women, concentrated mainly in leisure. Thus, as a first approximation of local leadership structure, Hunter concluded that business

interests were most frequently represented; twenty-three of forty or, if lawyers are included, twenty-eight of forty, were from the business community. It is important to note at this stage that the judges making these selections were not themselves from business but represented a broad range of local organizations.

2. The next step in Hunter's method was to interview twenty-seven of the top forty leaders to determine their selections.[10] Answers to the simple question "Who is the biggest man in town?" and the request to rank the ten most important persons produced a rank-order of influence. The result was a high degree of consensus between procedures (1) and (2).

3. A third distinctive technique sought to determine whether those persons listed actually constituted social groups. To answer the question, Hunter employed three separate sociometric measures. First, leaders were asked, "Who might best decide on a project?" This produced a clustering of mutual choices or "sociometric nets." The second index asked leaders how well they knew other leaders. Third, a more objective measure of interaction was employed that ranked leaders on interlocking club memberships. The conclusion Hunter drew from these separate measures was that the leaders did, indeed, form social groups, they knew and interacted with one another and, further, they also formed among themselves smaller cliques or "crowds." Finally, and most important, these data showed that the leaders were organized into "higher and lower limits groups" that played distinctive roles in the policy-making process, the higher groups more responsible for policy formulation and the lower for policy execution.

4. Rather than accepting these measures as definitive, however, Hunter pressed further for information on the policy-making process. In a chapter entitled "Projects, Issues and Policy," he examined five specific issues to determine patterns of decision-making (the city's Plan of Development, traffic control, the sales tax question, the Voter's Plan, and the Negro question). This distinctive method is often overlooked, perhaps because it appears after he had discussed the general structure of power. Nevertheless, it is clear that his study of actual issues informed that earlier discussion. For example, specific reference is made earlier to the Plan of Development as a prototypical policy decision.

5. From the use of these complementary methods and a process of "triangulation," Hunter reached his major substantive conclusions. The leadership process is carried out by groups with differential power playing different roles. A relatively small group of top policy-makers, drawn largely from the business community, tend to formulate policy, while a much larger group of "understructure personnel" are charged with policy implementation. Across issues there is more "overlap" (multiple-issue participation) by top leaders than by understructure personnel, who tend to be specialists confined to single-issue areas. Later, the same kinds of distinctions are made using four levels of influence. Of fundamental importance, however, is the fact that the *same set* of leaders *do not* make policy decisions in all areas; they simply exhibit a greater

degree of multiple-issue participation than lesser influentials. Hunter was most explicit about this when he talked of *multiple pyramids* of power with changing constituencies across issues. For example, he clearly states:[11]

> ... I doubt seriously that power forms a single pyramid with any nicety in a community the size of Regional City. There are *pyramids* of power in this community which seem more important to the present discussion than *a* pyramid.

and later:[12]

> In the above illustration of structural action, the "men of independent decision" are a relatively small group. The "executors of policy" may run into the hundreds. This pattern of a relatively small decision-making group working through a larger under-structure is a reality, and if data were available, the total personnel involved in a major community project might possibly form a pyramid of power, but the constituency of the pyramid would change according to the project being acted upon.

As though to make the point incapable of misinterpretation Hunter goes on to provide several diagrams of how these constituencies and their leadership shift with issues.

6. In a final summary of the argument, Hunter endeavors to clarify the point that his leadership group is not to be confused with the entire business community or the upper classes:[13]

> Each man mentioned as belonging to a crowd also belongs to a major business enterprise within the community—at least the clique leader does. His position within the bureaucratic structure of his business almost automatically makes him a community leader, if he wishes to become one. The test for admission to this circle of decision-makers is almost wholly a man's position in the business community in Regional City ... Society prestige and deference to wealth are not among the primary criteria for admission to the upper ranks of the decision-makers according to the study of Regional City.

In short, the power of the leaders derives from their business organizational position, *not* from wealth or prestige, and leaders are those top business position occupants who *choose* to become involved in local decision-making.

7. In addition to these central themes, *Community Power Structure* uniquely explored several other areas. Given again that the study was conducted in the early 1950s, two of these were particularly prophetic: the study of the black subcommunity, and the state and national impact on local politics. These cannot be discussed in detail, but suffice it to say that a final virtue of Hunter's method was that it reached out upward and downward to identify constraints on

and consequences of urban decision-making. In the case of the "Negro sub-community," Hunter found that its top leaders knew and interacted with only second echelon decision-makers. He also saw this situation as changing:

The traditional methods of suppression and coercion are failing.[14]

The Negro citizenry is becoming increasingly organized, however, and the politicians are paying more attention to the demands of this group.[15]

In this instance policy formerly settled is being challenged by a group which is organized to a point where its voice must be heard, and the older methods of intimidation and coercion against this group are no longer effective. Many of the Negro leaders are relatively secure financially, and their own positions of leadership are threatened within their community if they remain subservient to the dominant group.[16]

Having produced this analysis prior to the emergence of Martin Luther King's organizational efforts in Atlanta, Hunter demonstrated perceptive and prophetic insights that are exceeding rare in social science. Once again, for this alone Floyd Hunter's work is classic.

Development of the field

Perhaps the most relevant criterion for judging the importance of a contribution to social science is the amount of subsequent research it stimulates. In this respect Hunter's legacy is impressive. In the twenty years since *Community Power Structure* appeared, more than 500 books and articles have been written on the topic, some critical in commentary and some original studies of one or several communities; and the literature continues to grow.[17] One would be hard pressed to cite comparable instances of research stimulation by a single work.

In the years immediately following Hunter's work, studies by Robert Agger, Delbert Miller, William D'Antonio, William Form, and others sought to replicate the Hunter technique in other cities and try out comparative designs. Frequently, these studies also involved certain methodological innovations. Generally, they found that by contrast to Atlanta, their cities exhibited less centralized and cohesive power arrangements. Often these differences were accounted for by reference to the characteristics of the cities, the special methods employed or the issues examined.

A major challenge to the Hunter approach was mounted by a group of Yale political scientists in the late 1950s led by Robert Dahl. Both the merits and the polemics of this challenge produced one of the most high-spirited debates in the recent history of American social science.[18] Essentially, Dahl and the "pluralists" argued that Hunter and the "elitists" had produced a biased and wrongheaded interpretation of American urban politics. Much of the fault, it was claimed, lay in the Hunter "reputational" method of analysis which biased the results in favor of finding power elites as opposed to some alternative, more democratic arrangement. Specifically, the critics alleged that the method relied exclusively on reputations for influence rather than on actual influence, that it assumed an elite structure, and that it failed to deal with the actual decision-making process. The pluralists recommended a "decisional" or "event analysis" method that would reconstruct decision-making events to determine who actually participated and who influenced outcomes. The belief was, of course, that such a procedure would lead to a largely different interpretation of power and decision-making at the urban level.

In his study of New Haven, *Who Governs? Democracy and Power in an American City,*[19] Dahl systematically advanced several new techniques, particularly historical analysis of the changing economic and ethnic backgrounds of city government officials and the analysis of three major issues: urban renewal, public education, and political campaigns. Case study analyses indicated the large pools of issue participants in each. Next, Dahl developed lists of "social and economic notables," or the socially prominent and economically influential persons in New Haven. The *coup de grâce* of the analysis was to show, first, that a large number of varied individuals participated in these issues; and, second, that a rather small number of these participants were social or economic notables. Therefore, by implication, the Hunter thesis was to be rejected, for New Haven at least.

Unquestionably, Dahl produced a valuable book, and it is probably also true that the vigorous and protracted debate over elitism vs. pluralism had some beneficial consequences in the clarification of methods, assumptions and concepts. What is clearly incorrect, however, is the notion that Dahl's study tests Hunter's thesis or that Hunter committed the errors laid on his doorstep by the pluralists. On the first point, Dahl's test of the "elite dominance" notion through the use of lists of social and economic notables completely misses Hunter's point about the constituency of the top policy-making group.[20] As we saw in the quotation from Hunter, "society prestige and deference to wealth" were not the criteria that determined leadership status, rather it was business organizational position plus the choice to become involved. Second, as to the claim that Hunter did not study actual issues and issue participation, a careful reading of his book shows this to be a blatant oversight.

Just as Hunter attracted a group of followers, so did Dahl and the pluralists. Although the two camps appeared to differ markedly in their ideologies, their substantive results were often quite similar. Indeed, the only published comment by Floyd Hunter on the elitist-pluralist debate that raged for years around him was a generally supportive review of *Who Governs?* in which he noted:[21]

> When he states, for example, that he finds little or no connection between economic dominance and processes of decision and reasons his way to a

position of "political control" of affairs, whatever that is, I tend to fall off the cart. But I get back on when he finds connections between the mayor's official roles and his business roles. I have no trouble in understanding that "democratic pluralism" is at work in the upper reaches of the one-half of 1 percent of the policy-making array of New Haven. The fact that Dahl finds no connection between this narrow band of civic democrats and the large body politic does not, as suggested, surprise anyone.

More important than a contrast between Dahl and Hunter is a broad review of the many studies that follow generally in this tradition. A paper of my own indicates specific propositions drawn from this literature about which there is more and less agreement.[22]

Robert Alford, a relatively objective student of the field, has indicated a series of points on which different studies agree. His analysis is quoted in detail because the general points are important to the subsequent discussion.[23]

Yet, the substantive findings of the community power studies are in remarkable agreement. The ideological disputes over method and terminology are due to a failure of both sides to recognize that the reputationalists are not concerned with the contemporary role of business leaders, but rather with the long-range impact of economic and political activity of various status groups, and that the pluralists are not analyzing the nature of deeply embedded institutions, but rather the situational impact of many different factors affecting current decisions. Most studies share the following conclusions.

1. Public decision-making at any specific time occurs within a relatively narrow "agenda of alternatives" determined by constraints of political and economic structure and culture, deriving from the history of the nation, state, and local community.

2. The middle and upper classes provide most community leadership.

3. When working-class groups are organized into politically active unions, a base of opposition to the middle class is created which allows the raising of a variety of issues not usual when only the middle class is active.

4. In particular public decision-making situations, a variety of groups is likely to be active and the same persons are not likely to be found in all issue areas, except for certain public leaders like the mayor or the city manager.

5. At any specific point in time, distinctions concerning the proper boundaries between private and public actions establish the legitimacy of actions by government and public leaders.

6. As a corollary, many major decisions are made autonomously by private economic leaders and are not subject to public control.

While the pluralists bent on repudiating Hunter committed their own errors, particularly in failing to analyze the community as a social structure rather than as a collection of autonomous individuals, they did contribute healthily to the expanding literature by developing alternative methods (e.g., issue analysis) and theoretical insights about democratic politics (e.g., Dahl's model of "dispersed inequalities," power resources and "slack systems"). That is, to some extent, a critical balance was struck. But once more some of the appearance of balance in the pluralists' writing stems from their misleading characterization of Hunter, who was just as concerned with issue analysis and democracy and power as was Dahl. Hunter begins and ends his book on these themes:

> The line of communication between the leaders and the people needs to be broadened and strengthened—and by more than a series of public relations and propaganda campaigns—else our concept of democracy is in danger of losing vitality in dealing with problems that affect all in common.[24]

> The task of social reconstruction may never be finished once and for all. It is a recurring task confronting each generation, which somehow manages to find courage to meet social issues as they arise. In spite of the limitations that confront the individual in relation to community participation on the level of policy decision, there is still room for him in this area. He may not find himself at the top; but, with proper attention given to structural arrangements of power in the community, he may find ways of having a voice in determining who should be at the top.[25]

Summarizing the development of this unique field since Hunter's initial study, two conclusions appear justified. First, despite differences in method and interpretation, there is a good deal of continuity in a large number of studies over a twenty-year period. Indeed, different researchers arrive at many common conclusions. In short, it is one distinct and relatively well-developed research tradition. Second, researchers of various persuasions share a common interest in the question of participation and policy-making.

Contemporary significance of the field and its bearing on public issues

This essay began with the observation that the role of social science in public policy is an issue of increasing importance. Having gone some distance in characterizing a specific field where the study of policy-making is of central concern, we can now inquire into its bearing on the issue.

As was mentioned, the literature on community power runs to many hundreds of titles. Among these can be counted an impressive array of studies dealing with power and decision-making analyses of the following policy areas:

1. Urban renewal[26]
2. Social welfare[27]
3. General community or civic welfare[28]
4. Health and hospital services[29]
5. Community conflict[30]

6. Race relations[31]
7. Education[32]
8. Poverty programs[33]
9. Housing[34]
10. Ghetto violence[35]
11. Economic development[36]
12. Metropolitan government[37]
13. Absentee-owned corporations[38]
14. International border relations[39]

Within the scope of the present essay it would be impossible to generalize the particular results of these studies dealing in different ways with such disparate issues. Several of the studies do attempt their own theoretical explanation of differential success at policy implementation and are recommended as starting points for comparative generalizations.[40] What can be accomplished here is an interpretive synthesis of the principal themes in these studies and some suggestions for future applications.

Five general points appear to summarize the literature on power and public policy. First, these studies agree that the way power is distributed among leaders, participants, and the general population does make a difference in what gets done and what doesn't in a city. This is not to say that the power structure variable is the only or even the consistently most important factor in explaining community policy action. For example, the most progressive urban leadership groups may be frustrated in policy implementation due to legal and financial limitations or public indifference. To illustrate, progressive urban environmentalist groups may lack jurisdiction over nearby corporate polluters. Studies of fluoridation referenda indicate that the greater the voting turnout, the *less* likely are such beneficial, leadership-sponsored measures to be passed.[41] Conversely, even the most retrograde group of local leaders cannot stave off certain policy changes imposed from without. For example, public housing built with federal money must meet certain standards of integration, as must employment in federally sponsored construction, defense projects, and so forth. Within these limits, however, the structure and style of local decision-making is generally found to be one of the important factors in explanations of urban action or inaction.

No easy generalization is now possible concerning what specific power arrangements are likely to be associated with given policy outcomes or action vs. inaction. Several studies suggest that more decentralized power structures are associated with policy action although this plausible hypothesis needs greater specification and documentation.[42]

The second point of general agreement is that leadership structures can be reliably and validly identified through a combination of the techniques discussed earlier. It also appears that successive replications tend to converge on the generalization that American urban leadership structures represent a very small numerical proportion of the communities they serve and usually involve an alignment of top political and business positions; other interests may be represented in varying degrees, but this appears to be the baseline. This is not to infer that such power arrangements are necessarily close-knit or elitist; again we can expect variation there. What it does suggest is that the modal case reflects the disproportionate representation of political and economic interests of the middle and upper classes. Some studies suggest that this may be changing in the direction of more competitive arrangements as a result of increasing interdependence between urban and national institutions.[43]

A third suggestion, limited to more recent literature, is that the key variable in explaining power arrangements and policy outcomes may be the organizational structure of the city. Organizations, particularly public agencies, corporations, civic associations, civil rights and action groups, and the like, are to be understood as power resources and their interlinkages as "resource networks."[44] The greater the number of such resource networks (or what Mott[45] has suggestively termed "organizational interfaces"), the more likely is policy action. It should be noted that these power networks are not an automatic consequence of city size, but depend on historical factors and the nature of the organizations themselves.[46] Recent studies support the proposition and suggest intriguing possibilities for future studies of substantially greater explanatory significance.[47]

The fourth common theme represents somewhat of a paradox. Most of the literature concludes that numerous possibilities exist for intervention, organization, and policy-oriented social action, given an understanding of the power and decision-making process. Indeed, this was the larger point of Hunter's initial study and is eloquently elaborated in his concluding chapter when he discusses the differences between his approach and that of Saul Alinsky's community organization movement. Alinsky's point in *Reveille for Radicals*[48] was that conventional community action programs have been ineffective because of their piecemeal and nonstructural interpretation of the causes of local problems. This led him to the belief, which he acted upon, that effective change must rely on "people's organizations." While Hunter shares the same sympathies for needed change, he felt the Alinsky approach to be "politically utopian" and that more effective change could come from, first, a knowledge of the location of community (establishment) power and, second, more intensive participation in existing, functional organizations that are more likely of getting mass support. Nevertheless, Hunter was not unmindful of the paradoxical problem involved. In another prophetic passage, he noted,[49]

> The leaders in the policy-making realm are not going to open the doors of participation with charitable graciousness. It has been noted that they may even use police power and the power of governmental machinery to keep back criticism and threatening political elements.

Yet he concludes more optimistically,[50]

> Such tactics eventually will not win out if dissident groups are in earnest concerning a voice in the affairs of government or economic operations.

In short Hunter is arguing a tactical question which we may not have the evidence for deciding. More likely is the possibility that he and Alinsky are both right, depending upon the issue at hand and the nature of existing organizations. The significance of the point in the present context is that power and decision-making research is generally in agreement with Hunter's cautious optimism and provides evidence of more and less successful policy-oriented action that may suggest some explanations. One such tentative explanation is that community action is more effective when it relies on power resources external to the community than when it relies on local grassroots resources.

A final theme about which there appears to be some agreement is that broader effective political participation on policy questions is by no means a romantic, unrealistic, or "disfunctional" prospect. This is particularly true of recent critiques of "elite pluralism" or "democratic elitism"—belief that elites are inevitable and good for you.[51] Some evidence is available, and more appears forthcoming, that broader participation in policy-making is both possible and beneficial.[52] Although the point may sound platitudinous, many "functionalist" social scientists have justified nonparticipation for its efficient and stabilizing consequences.

Reflecting on these summary points, it could be argued that they are not especially definitive and, therefore, no source of encouragement concerning the prospects of a public policy-oriented social science. This, of course, is largely a matter of interpretation; dim light is better than no light, but not terribly handy if you can't see where you are going. In this specific case, however, the summary points do suggest some directives as well as a large set of questions for more discriminating future research. This is no mean accomplishment, given the complexity of the problem. Clearly, we need more concrete and detailed analyses of problems like minority economic opportunities, welfare organization, health care, and alternative styles of urban living. Yet the social science heritage, from Floyd Hunter to the burgeoning contemporary concern with public policy and social action, indicates that social science is "ready" in the sense of possessing interest and experience to draw from. This is not to suggest that social scientists will make better policy-makers, an ambition of one of the founding fathers of sociology, August Comte, which (fortunately) was never taken seriously. What it does suggest is that in the hands of well-informed and unpretentious researchers, the tools and experience of social science can lead to more informed judgments on policy issues. The constraints on and consequences of such research are largely open questions.

Footnotes

1. Peter H. Rossi, "No Good Idea Goes Unpublished: Moynihan's Misunderstandings and the Proper Role of Social Science in Policy Making," *Social Science Quarterly,* 53 (December 1969), 469–479.

2. For some recent sources of such information, see a special issue of the *Social Science Quarterly,* 53 (December 1969), on planned social intervention, and Dean Schooler, Jr., *Science, Scientists and Public Policy* (New York: The Free Press, 1971).

3. Cf. Joseph J. Spengler, "Is Social Science Ready?" *Social Science Quarterly,* 53 (December 1969), 449–468.

4. This literature is conveniently summarized in several sources that include extensive bibliographies: cf. Michael Aiken and Paul E. Mott (eds.), *The Structure of Community Power* (New York: Random House, 1970); Charles M. Bonjean, Terry N. Clark, and Robert Lineberry (eds.), *Community Politics: A Behavioral Approach* (New York: The Free Press, 1971); Frederick Wirt and Willis Hawley, *The Search for Community Power* (Englewood Cliffs: Prentice-Hall, Inc., 1968).

5. It should be recognized that we are treating here a unique topic in policy relevance. Many sociological interests (e.g., drug usage, racial prejudice, juvenile delinquency, etc.) have policy implications. Here we are dealing with research on policy making itself.

6. Floyd Hunter, *Community Power Structure: A Study of Decision Makers* (Chapel Hill: University of North Carolina Press, 1953).

7. Charles M. Bonjean and David M. Olson, "Community Leadership: Directions of Research," *Administrative Science Quarterly,* 3 (December 1964), 278–300.

8. Compare, for example, the methodological similarities between Hunter's work and such recent, important books as Robert E. Agger, Daniel Goldrich and Bert E. Swanson, *The Rulers and the Ruled* (New York: John Wiley & Sons, 1964); or Robert Presthus, *Men at the Top* (New York: Oxford University Press, 1964).

9. Hunter, *Community Power Structure, op. cit.,* p. 1.

10. Though he doesn't say so, it is presumed that the other thirteen leaders were not available for interviews.

11. Hunter, *op. cit.,* p. 62.

12. *Ibid.,* p. 66.

13. *Ibid.,* pp. 78–79.

14. *Ibid.,* p. 149.

15. *Ibid.,* p. 250.

16. *Ibid.,* p. 217

17. See note 4 above.

18. The debate and its protagonists, positions are described in the works mentioned in note 4 and in Terry N. Clark (ed.), *Community Structure and Decision Making: Comparative Analyses* (San Francisco: Chandler Publishing Co., 1968).

19. Robert Dahl, *Who Governs? Democracy and Power in an American City* (New Haven: Yale University Press, 1963).

20. On this error is predicated portions of Nelson W. Polsby's book, *Community Power and Political Theory* (New Haven: Yale University Press, 1963). Other portions of the book report further on the New Haven study in which Polsby and Raymond Wolfinger assisted Dahl.

21. Floyd Hunter, review of *Who Governs?* in *Administrative Science Quarterly,* 6 (March 1962), p. 518.

22. John Walton, "A Systematic Survey of Community Power Research," in Aiken and Mott, *The Structure of Community Power, op. cit.,* pp. 443–464.

23. Robert R. Alford, *Bureaucracy and Participation: Political Cultures in Four Wisconsin Cities* (Chicago: Rand McNally & Co., 1969), p. 194.

24. Hunter, *op. cit.,* p. 1.

25. *Ibid.,* p. 253.

26. Amos Hawley, "Community Power and Urban Renewal Success," *American Journal of Sociology,* 68 (January 1963), 422–431; Terry N. Clark, "Community Structure, Decision-Making, Budget Expenditures, and Urban Renewal in 51 American Communities," *American Sociological Review,* 33 (August 1968), 576–593; Michael Aiken and Robert R.

Alford, "Community Structure and Innovation: The Case of Urban Renewal," *American Sociological Review*, 35 (August 1970), 650–665 [see pp. 369–388 of this book].

27. Floyd Hunter, Ruth C. Schaffer, and Cecil G. Sheps, *Community Organization: Action and Inaction* (Chapel Hill: University of North Carolina Press, 1956).

28. C. Wright Mills and Melville J. Ulmer, "Small Business and Civic Welfare," reprinted in Aiken and Mott, *The Structure of Community Power, op. cit.*, 154–162; Irving A. Fowler, *Local Industrial Structures, Economic Power and Community Welfare: Thirty Small New York State Cities 1930–1950* (Totowa, New Jersey: Bedminister Press, 1964); William Kornhauser, "Power and Participation in the Local Community," *Health Education Monographs*, 6 (1959), 28–37.

29. Presthus, *op. cit.*; Ivan Belknap and John Steinle, *The Community and Its Hospitals* (Syracuse: Syracuse University Press, 1963).

30. James S. Coleman, *Community Conflict* (New York: The Free Press, 1957); William A. Gamson, "Rancorous Conflict in Community Politics," *American Sociological Review*, 31 (February 1966), 71–81; Herbert Danzger, "A Quantified Description of Community Conflict," *American Behavioral Scientist*, 12 (November–December 1968), 9–14.

31. Hunter, *op. cit.*; Danzger, *ibid.*; James McKee, "Community Power and Strategies in Race Relations," *Social Problems*, 6 (Winter 1958–1959), 41–51.

32. Dahl, *op. cit.*; Warner Bloomberg and Morris Sunshine, *Suburban Power Structures and Public Education: A Study of Values, Influence and Tax Effort* (Syracuse: Syracuse University Press, 1963); Ralph B. Kimbrough, *Political Power and Educational Decision Making* (Chicago: Rand McNally & Co., 1964).

33. Clark, *op. cit.*; Michael Aiken, "The Distribution of Community Power: Structural Bases and Social Consequences," in Aiken and Mott, *The Structure of Community Power, op. cit.*; Michael Aiken and Robert R. Alford, "Community Structure and The War on Poverty: Theoretical and Methodological Considerations," in Mattei Dogan (ed.), *Studies in Political Ecology* (in press).

34. Aiken, "The Distribution of Power," *op. cit.*; Floyd Hunter, *Housing Discrimination in Oakland, California*, A study prepared for the Mayor's Committee on Full Opportunity and the Council of Social Planning of Alameda County, 1964; Michael Aiken and Robert R. Alford, "Community Structure and Innovation: The Case of Public Housing," *American Political Science Review*, 64 (September 1970), 843–864.

35. Peter H. Rossi and Richard A. Berk, "Local Political Leadership and Popular Discontent in the Ghetto," *The Annals* of the American Academy of Political and Social Science, 391 (September 1970), 111–127.

36. Presthus, *op. cit.*; John Walton, "Development Decision Making: A Comparative Study in Latin America," *American Journal of Sociology*, 75 (March 1970), 828–851.

37. Edward Sofen, "Problems of Metropolitan Leadership: The Miami Experience," *Midwest Journal of Political Science*, 5 (February 1961), 18–38; Edward Sofen, *The Miami Metropolitan Experiment* (Garden City: Doubleday—Anchor Books, 1966).

38. Roland J. Pellegrin and Charles H. Coates, "Absentee Owned Corporations and Community Power Structure," *American Journal of Sociology*, 61 (March 1956), 413–419; Robert O. Schulze, "The Bifurcation of Power in a Satellite City," in Morris Janowitz (ed.), *Community Political Systems* (Glencoe, Illinois: The Free Press, 1961).

39. William V. D'Antonio and William H. Form, *Influentials in Two Border Cities: A Study in Community Decision Making* (South Bend: University of Notre Dame, 1964).

40. Cf. Presthus, *op. cit.*; Aiken, "The Distribution of Power," *op. cit.*; Aiken and Alford, "The Case of Urban Renewal," *op. cit.*; Walton, "Development Decision Making," *op. cit.*

41. Kornhauser, *op. cit.*; William A. Gamson, "Community Issues and Their Outcome: How To Lose a Fluoridation Referendum," in Alvin W. Gouldner and S.M. Miller (eds.), *Applied Sociology: Opportunities and Problems* (New York: The Free Press, 1965).

42. Aiken, "The Distribution of Power," *op. cit.*; Clark, *op. cit.*

43. John Walton, "Differential Patterns of Community Power Structure: An Explanation Based on Interdependence," in Terry N. Clark (ed.), *Community Structure, op. cit.*

44. Cf. Robert Perrucci and Marc Pilisuk, "Leaders and Ruling Elites: The Interorganizational Bases of Community Power," *American Sociological Review*, 35 (December 1970), 1040–1057.

45. Paul E. Mott, "Configurations of Power," in Aiken and Mott, *The Structure of Community Power, op. cit.,* 85–100.

46. Aiken, "The Distribution of Power," *op. cit.;* Walton, "Development Decision Making," *op. cit.*

47. Aiken and Alford, see the several articles cited above.

48. Saul Alinsky, *Reveille for Radicals* (Chicago: The University of Chicago Press, 1946).

49. I cannot resist the parenthetical comment that Hunter appears in this passage to be talking about the 1968 Democratic Party Convention, the Nixon Administration's policies toward the Black Panther Party, or publication of documents on U. S. involvement in Vietnam. It is a mark of the man's perceptivity and honesty that he dealt with these issues in a time when most sociology was banal and irrelevant to policy issues.

50. Hunter, *Community Power Structure,* 251–252.

51. Peter Bachrach, *The Theory of Democratic Elitism: A Critique* (Boston: Little, Brown and Company, 1967).

52. Carole Pateman, *Participation and Democracy* (New York: Oxford University Press, 1970).

24

FRANK J. MUNGER, Community Power and Metropolitan Decision-Making

In these accounts of decision-making in the Syracuse metropolitan area we have reviewed some twenty-two cases or points of decision or action. Obviously they are not equal as regards breadth, depth, time span, importance of the participants, or significance of the issues; on the contrary, they vary greatly when appraised by these and other relevant criteria. They vary, too, in their pertinence to the subject and their contribution to achievement of the announced purpose of the study. Yet because of their common environment and subject-matter focus all contain suggestions for useful hypotheses. These may be examined under the dual headings of community power and metropolitan decision-making.

COMMUNITY POWER

The mythology of community power in Syracuse today is very clear. Any number of observers, including many knowledgeable in local affairs, will assert that a single man stands at the top (or, some might say, behind the top) of community affairs and runs things. This is Stewart F. Hancock, lawyer, banker, gentleman, spokesman for the old-line aristocracy, without whose consent, tacit or explicit, nothing of importance can be done. One writer refers to Hancock as

From Roscoe C. Martin, *et al., Decisions in Syracuse* (Bloomington: Indiana University Press, 1961), chapter 14, pp. 317–347. Reprinted by permission. This chapter of Martin, *et al.,* was prepared by Frank J. Munger.

"Mr. Syracuse."[1] Harking back to the categories advanced in Chapter I [of *Decisions in Syracuse*], Syracuse is commonly believed to have a slack, monolithic, pyramidal power structure with a businessman-attorney as its dominant figure. Many who hold this view concede that Hancock's power is now declining. The time spanned by this study, however, covers the period of his greatest reputed power, and the cases examined should demonstrate his leadership if in fact it possessed substance.

These analyses of actual decisions taken with respect to public problems in the Syracuse metropolitan area do not support an interpretation based on the concept of monolithic power. What is clear from the cases is that the pattern of decision-making in Syracuse has changed markedly over the last thirty years. The cases suggest that at one time the current myth had a solid foundation in fact, for earlier there was a high concentration of community authority in the hands of a single man, simultaneously a political leader and a public official. Expanding the already substantial powers vested in his predecessor as Republican county chairman, Rolland Marvin consolidated those powers with his authority as mayor to wield an unprecedented influence over public decisions. Moreover, he exercised his control with a minimum of public oversight. His ultimate rejection resulted partly from reaction against his autocratic methods, but more from the bitter opposition of Governor Thomas Dewey, still smarting over Marvin's support of Wendell Willkie at the 1940 Republican national convention.

After Marvin's defeat, a disintegration of political power took place. It was during this period that Stewart Hancock maximized his influence, and community leadership passed from a combined political boss and elective public official to a lawyer-businessman with no pronounced inclination for public notice. In the process, a change occurred in the process of leadership itself. Partly in reaction to the tight control exercised by Marvin, partly perhaps as a result of the example set by the Post-War Planning Council, the circle of participants in community affairs broadened. Such a change was no doubt inevitable in any case in view of the steady growth in the size of the metropolitan community and the complexity of its interests; nevertheless it accompanied, perhaps as both cause and effect, a significant change in the pattern of leadership. Since more persons were involved in community affairs and more individuals therefore had to be consulted, no successor's influence could be as unequivocally dominant as that of Marvin. Indeed, in the cases examined here Hancock appears only as one among several leaders.[2] A notable consequence of Marvin's fall was the collapse of central control over the Republican party organization. Lacking this essential part of Marvin's arsenal, subsequent community figures have never been able to force through measures over town opposition with Marvin's abandon. Whether the power system can at present be regarded as polylithic or whether it is in transition to monolithic control by some new individual leader is clearly an open question, although the fact that the change in the type of community leadership has accompanied changes in social forces would seem to suggest the former.

Even during the period of monolithic control, the case studies demonstrate the point that broad areas of public policy were left undirected by the dominant leaders of the community. That fact does not necessarily destroy the monolithic concept. As noted before, some distinction between major and minor policy must necessarily be made. So long as the top leaders continued to exercise tight control over such focal concerns as city and county budgets, they might properly be considered to be dominant even though they failed to assert control at all points of decision-making. The establishment of a children's court, for example, might be offered to interested citizens' groups as a minor concession which would not affect substantially the central financial concerns of local government.

Although this abdication of control over certain areas of policy-making may be accommodated to a monolithic interpretation of the exercise of community power, it nevertheless has important consequences which are particularly evident within the real estate field. Chapters XI through XIII [of *Decisions in Syracuse*] make clear that in this area especially many lesser decisions are continually being made without reference to the power structure at its top levels. These decisions may be minimized as affecting only minor policy, but the fact remains that their cumulative impact has tremendous effect in shaping the course of development of the metropolitan area. The only recognized tool that might give the community leaders effective control over the accumulation of these decisions would be area-wide planning of land use, and either through tradition or through their own laissez-faire inclinations the leaders have been slow to grasp this weapon.

With respect to local-state relations, the cases clearly reveal the legislative advantages enjoyed by Syracuse and Onondaga County. By reason of their Republican affiliation both city and county are accorded a friendly reception in the perennially Republican legislature. When they ask for a special law, the legislature is quick to oblige. The only law sought from the state that provided any difficulty involved passage of the Alternative County Government law, a statute of general application. Two measures were indeed blocked, but both by gubernatorial vetoes.

The cases also demonstrate the difficulty of obtaining popular approval of a proposal for governmental reorganization. Three referenda were held on variations of this proposal. The first, supported by Democrats and opposed by Republicans, failed in both city and towns. The next, supported by neither party but opposed by neither, suffered a like fate. And even the third proposal (the county director plan), which was supported by both newspapers, a banner list of city leaders, and numerous party officials, failed to receive a county majority though carrying the city. The uniform lack of success of these efforts attests the conservatism of the electorate, the influence of the county bureaucracy, and the strong opposition of the towns (and more particularly their supervisors) to change.

Of the twenty-two cases examined, fourteen are found on examination to have involved decisions at the county level. Isolating these fourteen in order to obtain greater comparability through greater uniformity, it is possible to make an analysis of the effectiveness of exercise of power from an examination of the decisions reached. Robert Dahl has suggested a possible formula for such a calculation in his definition of a community leader in terms of ability to (1) initiate proposals and carry them through, (2) override substantial opposition on behalf of a proposal, and (3) veto a proposal initiated by others. Making some rather arbitrary groupings of the interests involved in the cases at hand, the power demonstrated in these terms assumes the following pattern:

	Won	Lost	Did not participate
Republican Party	5	2	7
Democratic Party	1	3	10
Manufacturers Association	2	0	12
Chamber of Commerce–Governmental Research Bureau	2	2	10
CIO	0	1	13
Real estate interests	3	0	11
League of Women Voters	2	5	7
Community Chest/Council of Social Agencies/Onondaga County Health Association	2	2	10
Town government officials	5	2	7
Post-Standard	3	2	9
Herald-Journal	2	4	8
Village weekly newspapers	3	0	11

Such a listing, while of course not conclusive, nevertheless has high suggestive value. It demonstrates clearly that, in terms of community decision-making, the Democratic Party is not very important in Onondaga County; the lone Democratic victory represents the party's success in persuading Governor Lehman (Democrat) to veto a Republican county reorganization measure. The tabulation likewise shows that the League of Women Voters concerns itself with many problems, but is not very effective in winning acceptance for its proposals. The League's chief value obviously lies in the service it performs in calling problems up for consideration. The list also instances the ineffectiveness of organized labor in local decision-making. It indicates that labor does not lose; it simply fails to participate. Likewise less effective than might have been expected are the daily newspapers, which together lost oftener than they won.

The group with what appears to be the best record of effective action is the Republican Party. In only two cases, however, can the party be said to have initiated the action it supported, and both of those involved Rolland Marvin as leader. The party organization therefore was rather a vehicle through which other interests sought to attain their goals. Success in obtaining party support usually guaranteed victory; but the party's own role was passive or instrumental, consisting in most cases of embracing decisions made elsewhere and seeing that the county government carried them out. The town officials were equally successful with, perhaps because often indistinguishable from, the Republican Party. The industrialists and the realtors had a low rate of participation, but were uniformly successful where they elected to commit their resources.

The most striking feature of the tabulation is the low level of participation in the decision-making process. No group tested its strength in a majority of the decisions, and most were involved in only a few cases. This warrants the conclusion that separate clusters of decision areas exist, each with its own distinct group of participants.[3] It effectively eliminates the notion of an all-sovereign wielder of community power, and it attacks (though it does not necessarily destroy) the concept of a monolithic power structure as applied to Syracuse. Under such circumstances it is meaningless to say that group A is more powerful than group B when A and B have never tested their strength against each other and because of their differing interests are not likely to.

The tabulation provides no clue concerning the problem of differential commitment, which as observed earlier is central to an appraisal of power and its exercise. The Chamber of Commerce, to illustrate, may take a mild interest in one measure and satisfy itself with a simple endorsement; in another case more tangibly related to the economic interest of its members, it may throw all its resources into a life-and-death struggle. It is manifestly unrealistic to regard the two commitments as being in any wise equal, for neither the rates nor the efficiencies of use of influence are comparable.

In summary, the decisions analyzed in this study afford no basis for easy generalizations about the structure and exercise of community power in the Syracuse metropolitan area. Only three overall conclusions seem warranted by the materials examined. First, the myth that significant decisions in Syracuse emanate from one source does not stand up under close scrutiny. Second, there tend to be as many decision centers as there are important decision areas, which means that the decision-making power is fragmented among the institutions, agencies, and individuals which cluster about these areas. Third, in reality there appear to be many kinds of community power, with one kind differing from another in so many fundamental ways as to make virtually impossible a meaningful comparison.

COMMUNITY POWER ROLES

The cases clearly indicate that a full model of the decision-making process would have to take into account the fact that decisions do not eventuate from single, individual choices but from a flow of choices. Who raised the issue and brought it to public attention? Who formulated the alternatives and marshaled the facts employed by the decision-makers in reaching their conclusions? To what extent were the decision-makers free to choose among these alternatives? A series of acts are involved in a decision to take or not to take a particular public action. It will prove useful to examine the process briefly. This may be done by identifying the roles involved in the exercise of community power.

The initiators

Innumerable problems calling for remedial action can be identified within a metropolitan area, for urban life is never perfect. Of these, however, only a limited number are—or in normal circumstances can be—brought forward for consideration. At times the process by which action is initiated may be almost automatic. Thus when an event occurs which sharply changes existing conditions to the detriment of a vocal group, a demand for action can be confidently expected. When the Big Sister and Big Brother programs were closed, the way was opened for creation of a county children's court. When a legislative act cut off child guidance funds to Onondaga County, establishment of a mental health board followed. The city's fiscal crisis of the late 1930s produced the county welfare consolidation. And so on.

More difficult to explain is the process by which action is initiated to remedy long-existent evils. Onondaga County's government structure is notoriously outdated; it has undergone no important change, much less anything approaching basic reorganization, for more than a century. As county agencies and functions have multiplied, the resulting problems have become steadily more severe. Only within comparatively recent years, however, did the League of Women Voters pick up the problem and make it an issue. What defines the point past which men (and women, too) are no longer disposed to endure?

The exercise of leadership by which action is initiated has come most frequently from the professional members of the governmental agencies. State Health Department officials initiated consideration of a county health department; Richard Greene of the city probation office launched action looking toward a children's court; Sergei Grimm, director of the City Planning Commission, inspired the Post-War Planning Council; the psychiatry department of the State College of Medicine proposed the creation of the mental health clinic.

This fact in itself may not appear surprising; for a widely popular belief holds that governmental agencies continually seek to expand their powers and budgets, and this might appear to be evidence substantiating that view. But contrary evidence appears in the fact that the county, whose agencies were to be expanded, has most frequently resisted growth. County supervisors have shown little desire to engage in empire-building. They personify the town governments, and they prefer to keep county taxes low. An example is provided by the County Public Works Commission, which accepted only reluctantly operating responsibility for the metropolitan sewage treatment plant. State and city governmental officials have served as initiators of county action, but seldom have county spokesmen done so.

This undoubtedly is one factor in the difficulty of effecting a reorganization of the county government. If there were a county manager or other executive he might be expected to attempt to strengthen his own powers, much as the strong mayor seeks to grow stronger in the city. With no county executive to make a beginning, however, there is no place at which to begin; and leadership of the county reorganization movement therefore falls to such groups as the League of Women Voters.

The experts

Providing an idea concerning something that needs to be done is, however, only the beginning. An idea may be sufficient to start the ball rolling, but sooner or later the central idea must be fleshed out into a plan for action. If the need is for county reorganization, a proposal in detail must be offered. If it is for sewage treatment, the response must be a carefully conceived scheme for meeting it. If the need is complex, so also will be the plan. This means that a need for technicians arises early and insistently in the decision-making process.

The most obvious source for expert assistance is the reservoir of local government employees. In practice this means the professional people in the various functional fields.[4] On occasion they may be the initiators of action themselves, but in any event they are likely soon to be consulted. Their availability is undoubtedly one reason why unifunctional changes are easier to accomplish than general reorganizations, a phenomenon often noted. In Onondaga County the most commonly employed source of expert assistance is quasi-governmental. The engineering firm of O'Brien and Gere provides professional advice on virtually every major public works project in the county.

There are limits, however, to the opportunities for utilizing governmental experts. If the public employees are inert, incompetent, or suspected of seeking opportunity to feather their own nests, an alternative source of expertise must be found. It is this dilemma that was responsible for the creation of the Governmental Research Bureau. In effect the business and industrial interests hired themselves a rival set of experts in whom they felt greater confidence.

Not all groups concerned with government problems can afford to hire their own experts. In this more normal situation several possibilities exist, any or all of which may be utilized. One alternative source of knowledge lies in the state administrative departments, which may find options that have been missed locally. In one sense this is what the state legislature attempts to accomplish in such a measure as the alternative government law. Options by themselves are not enough, however, and experts are needed to point out and facilitate their local applications. This function is performed by the state Health Department and the state Education Department, among others.

An additional source of professional assistance resides in Syracuse University and, to a lesser extent, LeMoyne College. The significance of the role played by the Syracuse University faculty lies particularly in the technical support it provides for programs outside the area of economic interest of the business and industrial communities, and in the assistance it gives to minority interests in the formulation of policy alternatives. In such fields as mental health, education, youth development, county planning, urban renewal, and, quite recently, metropolitan matters, university personnel are active participants. The agitation for county reorganization in the late 1930s was sparked by a Syracuse University faculty professor, and other faculty members have rendered expert assistance on all manner of community issues called up for public decision.

The publicists

It is not enough, however, to have an idea—even an expertly prepared one—in order to have an issue. As the 1934 Bar Association plan for county reorganization demonstrated, a proposal must be known to the public to become an issue. This is peculiarly the province of the newspapers. In an objective measurement of community power the two Syracuse dailies would not rank particularly high; more often than not, as we have observed, the measures they support are defeated. But they are capable of forcing consideration of an issue. By reports of events, feature stories, and editorials they are able to push the decision-makers into hard choices on matters they might prefer to ignore. In other language, they can compel items to be placed on the community's public-action agenda. Television likewise plays an increasingly important role in this respect.

There are limits to the newspapers' freedom of choice, for certain groups and individuals by their position or prestige can force newspaper copy. High public officials, the Chamber of Commerce, the Medical Society can command newspaper coverage. Even here, however, the choice of the newspaper to report minimally or to "play up" a news event may make a good deal of difference. And newspaper publicity is likely to prove indispensable to the success of lesser causes.

The only serious rival to the newspapers in this respect is, curiously enough, the Democratic Party. Rarely does that party sit in the seat of power, and when it does nothing much may happen: the only Democratic mayor in three decades was ineffectual as a party spokesman. But the Democratic Party can force issues on the attention of the community. Ordinarily the party does not initiate issues, but rather chooses among those initiated by others. By offering resolutions and debating them within the Common Council and the Board of Supervisors, the Democrats command newspaper space since party conflict is good copy. Beyond this, through campaigns for office Democratic candidates mobilize other means of communication—television and radio time, advertising, rallies, word of mouth, etc.—to make issues of the matters chosen for discussion.

The influentials

The nominal target of this publicity is the general public, which may indeed be the real target if an election for office or a referendum is at stake. More frequently, however, the proponents of a program address the public in order to attract the attention of a limited number of persons believed to hold the power of decision. The purpose is to convince them that something that affects them is at stake, and so to enlist their support. Key public officials are an obvious target of such a campaign. So also are the major economic groups with stakes in the community. Gathered together in the Chamber of Commerce and the Manufacturers Association, they are important individually as well—Niagara Mohawk, General Electric, Carrier, the banks, etc.

Depending on the issue, the target also includes the major institutionalized social welfare and professional groups, such as the Community Chest, the Council of Social Agencies, and the Medical Society. Members of such groups may be drawn from the same social class as the leaders of the economic organizations, and indeed may sometimes be the same individuals; but their interest in social welfare, plus the effect of professional contacts, influences their behavior in different directions and makes them useful for different causes.

The struggle to win acceptance for a proposal may revolve largely around the effort to gain support among such groups without much attention to the formal governmental process, and a defeat here may end the tale. This was the case with the postwar version of the county health department plan. When it failed to command the support of the Medical Society the proposal was dropped by the supervisors, who were only too glad to be relieved of the responsibility for making a decision.

The brokers

As has been suggested, the core of the influentials consists of the economic groups with the most substantial stake in the community. This does not mean, however, that the heads of the corporations are themselves involved in the decision-making process. Normally they are hidden behind an intervening curtain of community representatives. These may be public relations men, or in the more recent jargon of General Electric, a "community relations team." But most frequently they are drawn from local law firms.

It is customary for a major corporation, though employing national legal advisors, to retain local counsel to represent it within the community. Similarly, if a real estate developer wants to rearrange or facilitate his relations with government, he goes to one of the principal law firms. And if a town government wants something, it too is likely to turn to a lawyer. In the cases examined in the previous chapters, the names of two law firms recurred frequently: Melvin and Melvin, and Bond, Schoeneck, and King. At least two others might be added, but, in so far as these cases reveal, they are not especially active in the negotiation of metropolitan decisions.

Community conflicts—and those involving economic interests in particular—are rarely fought out between the principals, but are handled by their legal representatives. And since it is the legal counsel who tells the principal what is possible and what is not, the latter's vision of political reality is shaped accordingly. In the process the lawyers, though brokers of power, wield substantial power themselves. And because the hostilities are conducted through intermediaries, community conflicts rarely erupt as open warfare but simmer along as protracted negotiations. Accommodation and compromise are emphasized in place of the all-or-nothing rewards of outright victory or complete defeat.

Less well-financed interests (that is, those of a noneconomic character) usually must serve the representative function themselves. As a result they may stumble, or suffer costly delays. As another result the decisions they seek are far more likely to be made in public, and to be couched in the extreme terms the skilled broker is able to avoid through negotiation and compromise.

The transmitters of power

Just as the true leaders of the economic interests are masked in the process of community decision-making by their representatives, so too are the final decision-makers, the governmental officials, concealed by a cover. Instead of dealing directly with, for example, the Board of Supervisors or its members, the representative of an economic group seeking action from the government is likely to go to the Republican party leader. And since both representative and leader are usually lawyers, the task may be no more complex than talking the matter over with his law partner. Under some circumstances, the representative may find himself as party leader. The New Process Gear case provides an illustration of the manner of operation of—and the results achieved by—the transmitters of power.

Republican party leaders ordinarily do not initiate action: in the cases presented above only Rolland Marvin could be said to have done so. But by possessing the capacity to issue orders to subordinates that will be obeyed, they enormously simplify the task of political contact for those with access to the party leadership. The clearest evidence of the effort and time they save is provided by the difficulties attending those groups—the League of Women Voters, for example—which have dealt with supervisors and the like on an individual basis, winning their support one by one.

The authority of government

Only the final step in the process of decision-making is the act of government itself, the approval or rejection of the proposal by the officials formally vested with the authority of office. Because the individual members of the Common Council or the Board of Supervisors are rarely persons of prominence in the community—customarily they consist of young men making their reputations and older men of long experience in the limited world of party affairs—it is conventional to minimize their role. When the time arrived for official action, Clarence King secured the votes he needed from them. With less persuasion and more power, Rolland Marvin did the same.

It is possible, however, to understate the role of the Common Council or the Board of Supervisors as well as to overstate it. The approval of the supervisors is essential since, for better or worse, they are the government of the county. Some supervisors, especially those from the rural towns, show a substantial capacity for independent action. Their resistance to change can be seen in the recurrent city-town struggles described in the cases above. Stubborn supervisors have at times delayed board approval for long periods, and when their own positions seem to them to be at stake, as in the case of a proposal for county governmental reorganization, they may exercise an effective veto over action. The role of the supervisors in decision-making is negative, but negative power may be as effective in its way as positive. Substantially the same may be said of the Common Council and its members.

Interrelationships among the roles

The traditional approach to the study of community power has been to emphasize the role of the community influentials. Under the concept of power as a process, however, other roles become important. It is the argument of this analysis that isolation of the possessors of power from the participants in the flow and process of decision-making has little meaning. Power has value and substance only as it is used for something. The "powerful" community leader without idea men to suggest possibilities to him, or experts to package his program, or publicists to put wheels under it, or brokers to facilitate its consideration, or transmitters to bring it before the nominal decision-makers, can do little with his power. Community power is a network of action, not a locus of residence.

It is meaningless to try to measure these strands of community power against one another, to argue that the lawyer is more influential than the corporation executive, who in turn is more influential than the consulting engineer. Their power roles are not competitive, but complementary; they are links in a chain. When none of the partners to the process is expendable, none can truthfully be described as the inferior of any of the others.

The environment and freedom of choice

One final aspect of the power process in relation to local decision-making remains to be considered: the degree of choice exercised within the community. The earliest studies of community power structure assumed a high measure of freedom for the individual community to choose its own course of action. A more recent line of inquiry, however, has opened the question of the degree to which decisions attributed to the local community are in fact determined by the unavoidable impact of such environmental factors as the population of the community, its resources, its taxable property, its ongoing commitments, its position *vis-à-vis* the state, etc. A striking part of Robert Wood's recent study of the governments in the New York City metropolitan area was an attempt to determine the extent to which local governmental expenditures in New Jersey are fixed by such factors, and to delimit the residual, unexplained variations in expenditures that might be attributed to the actual decisions of local governments. A similar study, concerned with expenditures for education, is now under way at Syracuse University.

In so far as these cases may be held to provide a guide, the realistic choices available to the Syracuse metropolitan community appear to be substantial. The size, growth pattern, and composition of the population would seem to offer no special problem. There is considerable unused or underused space within the city, with land to accommodate great growth outside; moreover, there are no physical barriers to expansion, either residential or industrial. The multiplicity of local governmental units serves as a complicating factor, but this is a normal obstacle to metropolitan action. The community's reserve resources are substantial, for while there are constitutional limits on both taxes and public debt, these have not usually proved to be a serious damper on government spending.[5] The state has embraced certain policies which have the effect of limiting local choice, but for the most part these have not been pursued rigorously. The most serious trammel is found in the native conservatism of the people, and even that yields before the blandishment (or the bludgeoning) of the Republican Party. In short, there are few environmental limitations on decision-making in the Syracuse metropolitan area which cannot be overridden where there is a combination of need and will.

In another sense, however, it is necessary to indicate a limit upon the conception of a decision as a free choice among alternatives by a determinate set of decision-makers. This concerns what might be called the "inadvertence" of decisions. The cases make clear that many decisions are made partly by accident, that chance factors may play an important role, that sometimes a decision is the inevitable end product of past decisions that were made without anticipation of their consequences. Particularly in the real estate field this inadvertence of decision-making is evident. The Industrial Park was made possible by a confluence of seemingly unrelated past decisions—the forehanded accumulation of land, the provision of sewage facilities, the convenient location of a Thruway interchange, the laying of railroad trackage, etc. It might be argued that some of these decisions—as that of the Public Works Commission to provide sewerage—were taken in anticipation of some future industrial development, if not in fore-knowledge of the Eagan project. This cannot be said, however, of Franklin's decision in the 1920s to obtain title to the lands involved. Yet without his action it is unlikely that an industrial park would have been created in this particular form or at this place. Industrial Park, then, was made possible by a series of individual actions taken over a period of thirty years without contemplation of any such eventuation as ultimately occurred. The cases examined here warrant the hypothesis that is characteristic of community decision-making in general.

METROPOLITAN COOPERATION
AND ITS COMPONENTS

So far the analysis has been concerned with community power and the process of decision-making generally; it is now necessary to relate the subject to the metropolitan context of multiple governments. For many types of public decision within a metropolitan area it is necessary to secure favorable action from two or more governments, each subject to its own particular and peculiar combination of pressures. The schematic representation offered in Figure 1 will illustrate the point. There a hypothetical proposal that requires the support of three governments is presented, along with certain assumed combinations of pressures that admit of various courses of action. From the drawing, it is possible to identify three types of situations in which cooperative action becomes possible.

Parallel action

The first and simplest of these is portrayed in diagrams A and B of Figure 1. A particular interest group seeks action from the three governments. So far as Government A is concerned, it may find that competing or conflicting interests are pushing in other directions, some favorable to action but of a modified character, others opposed to the program sought. Government B may present a somewhat different situation, with a new combination of interests playing upon the government officials and influencing their behavior, while Government C may

Figure 1. Metropolitan decision-making: a schematic representation

A. Parallel Action: Success

B. Parallel Action: Failure

C. Action by Compromise

D. Action by Intermediary

KEY
→ Pressure on Government
⇒ Action by Government

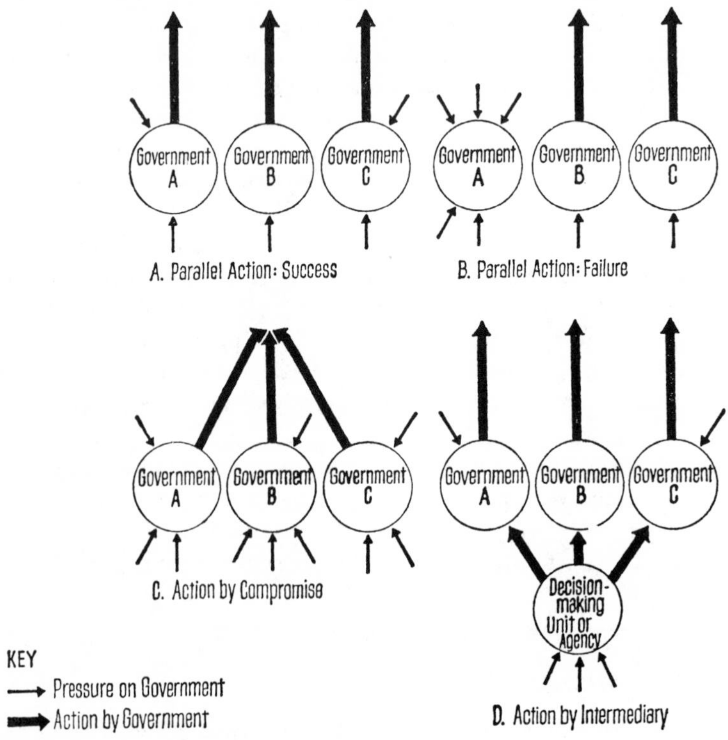

involve a still different pattern. In diagram A the assumption is made that the interest group favoring action is sufficiently influential within each governmental jurisdiction to produce identical decisions among the three governments. In this instance metropolitan action is secured through the ability of a single interest (or coalition of interests) to bring pressure on each of the separate governments adequate to procure parallel action. Diagram B shows how a similar situation may produce contrary results. Although Governments B and C are responsive to the pressure from the group seeking action, the weight of the influences brought to bear upon Government A is such that it refuses to co-operate. Since the cooperation of all three is assumed to be necessary to adoption of the proposal, failure ensues.

All this may seem obvious, but the nature of the forces affecting the application of community power to governmental decision-making in a metropolitan context is ignored with astonishing frequency. When numerous governments exist within a metropolitan area, it is not realistic to assume that the same constellation of interests will exist or will exert equal weight in each. Consequently, when the cooperation of two or more governments is required differences are more to be expected than agreement, and deadlocks of the variety depicted in diagram B may easily develop. In this context it is wholly natural to expect that the influence of a particular community interest will vary with the nature and organization of the governmental unit called upon to act. The structure of government within the metropolitan area thus becomes a dynamic factor in the analysis of community power.

Situations requiring parallel action are particularly common in the field of real estate development. Ordinarily action or at least approval by several governments and governmental agencies is required in advance of development. Frequently, however, there is no particular opposition to the proposal in any of the governmental units. A developer who lacks the necessary personal contacts may find it necessary to hire a representative to make the arrangements for him—most probably, as observed above, a legal firm with prior experience in this type of work—but once this is done the project is likely to proceed smoothly.

There are exceptions, of course. A shopping center, like that proposed in Fayetteville, may be adequately endowed with water supplies and sewerage and yet fail to win the necessary rezoning from a local government dominated by hostile interests. Faced by such an obstacle, the entrepreneur must choose between the alternatives of abandoning his project or modifying it and trying again. And this is equally true whether the promotion is a real estate development or a new inter-town park or other metropolitan cooperative program.

The hostile forces that block action may originate with rival interests possessing superior influence or with the local government officials themselves. It would be a mistake to forget that governmental units—in the sense of their personnel—have lives of their own and are not always easily pushed about by the pressures brought to bear on them. Equally, of course, positive leadership in a cooperative undertaking may be provided by the public official, either because of his conviction that action is needed or because the bold and imaginative exercise of leadership is at times an effective political gambit. The argument has been advanced above that cooperative programs are often the result of the desires of public officials to head off pressures for governmental reorganization and consolidation. This is simply to restate the point made in Chapter I, that public officials and governmental bureaucracies must themselves be regarded as participants in the contest over governmental decision-making.

Action by compromise

A second type of situation also may produce cooperative action at the metropolitan level. This situation is portrayed in Figure 1-C. Again parallel action by three governments is regarded as essential to the success of the proposal. Again it is assumed that the influences brought to bear upon the three governments differ; these pressures, however, are so distributed as to produce a desire for action in each of the three governments, though action in differing forms. By negotiation and compromise an agreement is reached and parallel action is thus finally secured.

This type of cooperation seems to be relatively rare in the metropolitan area, and the reasons why this should be so are important to understanding the dynamics of the metropolitan power structure. It will already have become evident that this analysis of the means by which several governments can be brought into harmony on a common program is not necessarily peculiar to the metropolitan area. The same type of analysis can be applied to cooperation among the officials of a particular government. Each member of a city council is likely to be subject to different pressures: if a measure is to pass the council, it is necessary that agreement be reached among its members. The city council and the mayor in turn are subject to different pressures, and they must be brought into agreement. The same could be said of the president and the two houses of Congress on the national level.

There is, however, a difference. Cooperative action in the city and in Washington is continuous; the negotiating and bargaining never stop, and a concession on one issue can be balanced upon the next. But metropolitan bargaining involves the negotiation of agreement between two or more governments that have perhaps never cooperated before and may not again for years. Sayre and Kaufman have pointed out the sporadic and *ad hoc* character of both cooperative and competitive interrelationships between New York City and its neighbors.[6] It is clear from the case studies that the same can be said of relationships among the multiple governments of the Syracuse metropolitan area. In the absence of either a tradition of negotiation or diplomatic skills in bargaining, it is hardly surprising that agreements are reached but slowly and that insoluble deadlocks frequently block any action.

Action by intermediary

In the absence of effective procedures for negotiated compromises, recourse must be had to some other device when powerful pressures for metropolitan action are blocked by one or more obstinate local governments. The third type of arrangement may be labeled action by intermediary. It may take the form of an appeal to some higher level of government, as the county or the state, for intercession when cooperation among towns, villages, and cities has failed. Or it may be found in an appeal to an extra-governmental organization capable of exercising control over the several local governments involved, as when the power of the political party is used to compel acquiescence in a decision. The common factor in both cases is that the issue is taken to some single, superior forum where the pressures for and against action can be assessed and a decision reached without the risk of veto within each of a series of local governments. A schematic representation of the direction of the pressures involved is suggested in Figure 1-D. Instances of both kinds of cooperative action by intermediary can be found in the cases above. Particularly interesting are the decisions in which the political party has been employed as a device to secure cooperation from governmental units that showed reluctance to act.

Within the Syracuse metropolitan area the Republican Party might be described as a kind of superstructure for decision-making which is called into action only on certain occasions. These include action on (1) issues that involve the party interest as such, e.g., nominations for office (not explored in this study), governmental reorganizations, etc.; and (2) issues that concern individuals in a position to ask the party's help. Such individuals include the top industrial leaders who, it seems plausible to say, can secure party help when they need it regardless of the magnitude of the issue as measured, say, in dollars and cents. Presumably some relationship exists between the fact of access and campaign contributions to the party. Reversing this, it does not appear that the party leadership intervenes in an issue because it is big in thousands of dollars, but because it is big to persons who are important to the party.

Thus the Republican Party organization became the basic mechanism by which those interested in the relocation of the New Process Gear plant secured the cooperation of the local governmental officials. In an earlier quite similar case, not related in detail in this study, the Republican Party leadership intervened to prevent Solvay Process from moving when a zoning regulation by the Town of Camillus blocked the use of property for dumping sludge that the corporation considered essential for that purpose. In this case, which was remarkably similar to the New Process Gear incident, the initiative for action came from the Chamber of Commerce, whose leaders, working through party officials, arranged the complex intergovernmental trades necessary to persuade Camillus to rescind its zoning ordinance. On the other hand the establishment of the mental health board, involving very large expenditures, was determined without apparent intervention by the top political party leaders.

This last illustration is, of course, different in that it involved action by the Board of Supervisors rather than by several individual local governments. In an important sense, however, action by that body on intergovernmental issues may be regarded as metropolitan action, and has been so treated here. The members of the board actually are the heads of the significant local governments outside the City of Syracuse, the towns, and a major decision by the Board of Supervisors is therefore suggestive of group action by the towns. It is true that the institutional structure creates a somewhat different situation, since the rule of unanimity is replaced by one of majority vote; but in practice this has little effective meaning since all decisions are reached first in caucus and the Republican supervisors, who represent all or almost all of the towns, vote as a block.

This suggests that all actions of the Board of Supervisors might be termed action by intermediary, since all are taken through the Republican caucus. In a sense this is true, but there is an important distinction between two types of issues taken to caucus. Some groups with sufficient access to the top party leadership will take their case directly to these leaders, who will then convey orders through the caucus to the individual supervisors. Others will take their plea directly to the individual members of the government. They may do this because (1) they do not know any better; (2) they consider it more democratic to "contact everyone" (and boast that they do); or (3) they are unable to gain access to the superstructure. Ordinarily their requests will necessitate party action too, since the party caucus is dominant in decision-making; but the caucus in the latter case will play the role of a decision-making unit rather than a vehicle to convey orders from the top.

Emphasis on the role of the political party as an intermediary in reaching metropolitan decisions should not becloud recognition of the fact that the state government often performs the same role. A common thread running through the cases is the ease with which problems of local cooperation within Onondaga County have been resolved when necessary by special legislation. Time and again when the provisions of the General County Government Law do not fit the perceived needs of the county, or when a local agency (e.g., the Public Works Commission) is to be created, or whatever the need may be, the legislature has smoothed the way by a special act.

This role played by the legislature is not, however, unrelated to the political party considerations treated above. Both phenomena result from the same cause: that Onondaga County differs from the usual image of a metropolitan area in that the central city, its surrounding suburbs, the county, and the state legislature all are Republican. It is highly significant that this identity of partisan affiliation exists in a state in which party names are not nominal (as they might be in the South with reversed party labels), but in which instead party organizations are relatively tightly structured and capable of exercising discipline over their members. It is this concurrence of party membership that makes it possible for a Republican mayor of Syracuse, who is also Republican county chairman, to integrate welfare functions in the county, as Marvin did in the 1930s, and it is this concurrence further that makes the Republican legislative leadership so readily responsive to the wishes of Onondaga County. It is not meant to suggest that such coincidence uniformly makes for metropolitan action, for legislative responsiveness may be to a negative as well as to a positive stimulus.

The reverse of this proposition also is valid. A report for Utica (in Oneida County) suggests that the absence of partisan identity between the central city administration and the county board—a far more frequent occurrence than in Syracuse, since Utica is more often Democratic than not—has produced conflicts that have sometimes acted as barriers to metropolitan cooperation.[7] That partisan differences between the central city and the surrounding areas, as well as between the city and the legislature, hamper the resolution of problems in the New York City metropolitan area is so evident as hardly to require documentation.[8]

The conclusion seems inescapable therefore that one of the potent forces encouraging and facilitating metropolitan action in the Syracuse metropolitan area has been the existence of a universal and disciplined party allegiance that has united central city, suburban governments, county government, and state legislature in common cause.

METROPOLITAN DECISION-MAKING AND INSTITUTIONAL CHANGE

In Chapter I [of *Decisions in Syracuse*] a model of metropolitan decision-making was presented; one ingredient was missing from that model, however, which is included in the pattern of decision-making described by Sayre and Kaufman. In their model the contest over the control of governmental action occurs within an institutional framework characterized as the "rules of the game." These consist partly of rules laid down by law determining the structures and jurisdictions of governments, partly of rules emanating from social consensus. The rules of the game are not unvarying, but are subject to change.

Study of metropolitan governmental reorganization consists in essence of an examination of the circumstances under which the rules of the game in the metropolitan contest over decision-making actually do change. In general two kinds of circumstances can be identified under which changes are made in that part of the rules of the game consisting of formal governmental institutions. In the first place, an institutional change may occur as the result of an effort by one of the contestants in the decision-making struggle to secure an advantage for himself. An individual or group may seek advantage by tinkering with the governmental institutions, by using control over some of the powers of government to introduce changes in order to make easier control over other parts of the government. This sort of maneuver occurs constantly in government, particularly with respect to the rules affecting the selection of government personnel. Election laws are altered, election dates changed, electoral districts reapportioned, changes made in terms of administrative officials, etc.

"Reform" movements of this sort are likely initially to possess only a narrow basis of support; if they were strong, they would not need to seek such advantages. The permanence of such a change, therefore, is likely to depend upon its effectiveness. If the strategy succeeds in securing a monopolistic power position for the contestant who profits by it, then the change will be retained. On the other hand, there may be circumstances in which the change has unexpected consequences and groups that feared they would be injured come to approve it. Sayre and Kaufman suggest that the creation of the City of Greater New York in the 1890s occurred somewhat in this fashion. One of the prime movers in the consolidation of the cities of Brooklyn and New York, the greatest metropolitan governmental reorganization in American history, was Thomas C. Platt, Republican leader in New York State, who anticipated that the position of the regular Republicans in the combined municipality would be improved. He was wrong, but the new system proved sufficiently flexible to accommodate itself to the interests of other groups who, initially opposed, ultimately came to support it.

The rules of the game can be changed for a second reason also, namely that the contestants agree generally that the existing institutions are incapable of producing solutions to the problems of society. Explanation of what is meant will require consideration of a model different from that which views decision-making as a contest. For while governmental policy-making may legitimately be regarded as a contest, government at the same time must be recognized as a social institution with a social purpose. Its purpose is the solving of problems of conflict among groups within the society, and its efficacy in accomplishing that purpose depends in considerable part upon its internal organization. If the institutions of government are hopelessly disorganized, they may fail completely in the solving of problems. In the language of the contest previously used as a model, no major group will find it possible to achieve a significant innovation in governmental policy, and as new problems arise the failure to find solutions will produce a steady accumulation of tensions. This is the precise charge leveled against the government of the Fourth Republic in France, which was generally characterized by the term *immobilisme*. *Immobilisme* is not, however, a national disease that can be suffered only by Frenchmen; it can also affect other governments, including those of metropolitan areas within the United States.

Such a formulation suggests the existence of three variables which determine the likelihood of substantial governmental reorganization: (1) the number of problems facing the society; (2) the expectations of its members as to how many of their problems should be resolved through the instrumentality of government; and (3) the capacity of the governmental institutions to resolve problems. Variation in any one of the three factors or any combination of the three may generate demands for reorganization. A movement for reform may therefore result from: (1) new problems introduced by technological developments; (2) demands by substantial parts of the population for higher levels of governmental service; (3) a relative decline in the efficiency of government (for whatever reason); or (4) some combination of these factors. Reform movements of this kind are distinguished from those aimed at creating advantages for one of the parties to the contest both by the generality of the support they receive and by the greater durability of any changes they may bring about.[9]

It is commonplace to cite the role of crisis in encouraging experimentation with governmental institutions. A flood that leads to creation of a flood control district is an obvious illustration. Or the crisis may be felt secondhand: John Gaus has called attention to the effects of the disastrous Cocoanut Grove fire in Boston in tightening fire regulations generally across the country. The fatal school fire in Chicago in the late 1950s had something of the same effect, at least so far as school buildings were concerned. In the present context, a crisis may be defined as a rapid multiplication of the problems faced by government. Although a slow accumulation of problems of similar magnitude eventually may produce much the same overloading of the problem-solving capacity of the governmental institutions, it appears that a rapid decline in governmental ability to meet public expectations produces a greater psychological readiness to make changes in the institutions themselves.

This analysis has relevance to the Syracuse metropolitan area. If Onondaga County faced crisis, more incentive for change might be found; but the metropolitan area has not experienced a real disaster and there is no reason to expect that it will. A breakdown in government could provide the occasion for drastic reorganization, but no such event has occurred. If the governments of Syracuse and Onondaga County are not spectacularly good, neither are they dramatically bad; and there has been no public evidence of gross mismanagement or other emergency to provoke significant structural change. The physical environment has been the source of only minor annoyances. Onondaga Creek, which runs through the heart of the city's central business district, overflowed its banks for a century but the largest flood of record caused damage of no more than $100,000. This is not the stuff of which governmental reorganizations are made. Rather the floods led to a succession of minor ameliorative measures—the straightening and deepening of the channel in 1868, extensions of the improved channel from time to time—and finally to a federally financed $4,252,200 flood control project in 1950. The only stringency that might have forced any sort of governmental reorganization was the cost of the 1950 project, and the assumption of responsibility by the federal government eliminated even that mild compulsion.[10]

Today the disaster most likely to precipitate substantial governmental action would be a major exodus of industry. Both exodus and drastic action, however, seem highly unlikely eventualities. Individual industries have moved or threatened to move from the city, but public reaction to such threats has been for the most part sporadic and piecemeal. As individual problems, such as sewage or water, have emerged, they have been dealt with on an *ad hoc* basis. Little enthusiasm has been shown for the creation of new governmental institutions to deal on an area-wide basis with the multiplicity of metropolitan problems.

In this Syracuse deviates little from the national norm, for it is universally observed that multi-functional reform, that is, general governmental reorganization, is far more difficult to secure than a redistribution of individual functions among existing governments. Probably the most significant reason for this lies in the character of the different interest groups involved. Elevation of a single program to the metropolitan level is ordinarily sought by an economic interest group which finds a new governmental service necessary to its economic well-being. In the standard situation, this means that local industry has been brought face to face with the problem of a shortage of water, an oversupply of pollution, an undersupply of transportation, or whatever, and demands—successfully—that government take a hand in the matter. Although economic interests may be alleged to be at stake in government reorganizations (which are often sold as moves to save money by eliminating "waste"), the monetary gains involved are more diffuse, less certain, and often suspect. The industrialist or businessman may fear that a rejuvenated government, even if more efficient in its use of tax moneys, might seek to justify itself by embarking on new and more expensive programs. The cause of metropolitan reorganization is therefore likely to be supported only by individuals attracted by its rational simplicity, but without either an established position of influence within the community or the kind of economic commitment that will produce vigorous action.

An additional factor which encourages the piecemeal approach to metropolitan problems in the Syracuse area is the coincidence of the county boundary with what has long been regarded as the metropolitan area. On the positive side this has facilitated the handling of metropolitan problems by their transfer to the county government, a procedure frequently employed. Solution of individual problems in this way, however, relieves the pressure for a more general reorganization. On a limited scale this phenomenon was encountered in the proposal for a county health department. Because the most serious of the rural health needs have been met by state programs, private action, the county mental health program, etc., insufficient incentive has been found to support a drastic change. In words appropriate to a formula proposed above it may be said that, although both the number of problems and the expectations of what government should do about them have been increasing in the Syracuse metropolitan area, the existence of a county with a metropolitan jurisdiction has made possible a problem-solving process effective enough to head off serious metropolitan governmental proposals.

The build-up of functions at the county level has in turn created a further problem by making more serious the consequences of the failure to reorganize the county government. There seems little reason to doubt that Onondaga County will follow the other metropolitan counties of the state within the next few years and reorganize.[11] If we are to learn from history this will entail the creation of a county executive, who will immediately become the center of a move for expanding the county government's powers. County reorganization thus will result in a growth in county authority, and in the relaxation and ultimate abandonment of the tradition of minimal local government.

In the long run, the most effective practical argument for the transfer of urban governmental functions to the county is likely to emphasize not the increase in the problem-solving capacity of government but the preservation of party advantage. Syracuse has long been a citadel of Republicanism. It seems improbable, however, that the Republican Party can do more than delay the partisan realignment likely to occur within the city as a result of population change. In local elections in the past the Republicans have succeeded in maintaining their hold on the Negro vote. By national standards such a situation is unnatural, and the vote of the rapidly increasing Negro population may be expected eventually to tip the balance within the city to the Democratic Party. Another prospective development pointing in that direction is the growth in the political strength of labor. The approach of equality and the threat of superiority in the city by the Democrats is likely to encourage a rapid transfer of functions to the county by the Republican leaders, secure in the conviction the county government constitutes a stronghold from which they cannot easily be routed. If such a transfer does not take place, indeed, it is logical to anticipate a steady accumulation of metropolitan conflicts as the unifying force of Republicanism relaxes its grip. In such a twilight of the *Pax Republicana,* the resulting tensions would erupt in violent party warfare. He would be rash who would prophesy the outcome in terms of possible solutions to metropolitan problems.

Notes

1. Wayne Hodges, *Company and Community: Case Studies in Industry-City Relationships* (New York: Harper and Brothers, 1958).

2. It is worth reiteration that the cases studied center on governmental decision-making. It is quite possible that an examination of decisions taken in the private sector, as in private charity or cultural affairs, would provide convincing evidence of Stewart Hancock's power in those areas. Similarly, an analysis of day-to-day decision-making—action on zoning variances, the choice of government personnel, the letting of contracts, etc.—might produce different conclusions from those recorded here.

3. This conclusion corroborates the findings of another contemporary study of community leadership in Syracuse. See Linton C. Freeman and others, *Local Community Leadership* (Syracuse: University College of Syracuse University, 1960).

4. The creation in recent years of the Department of Research and Development and the Regional Planning Board suggests that the county is conscious of the need for developing sources of its own for general staff assistance.

5. A recent report states that the unused borrowing capacity of the local governments in Onondaga County (including city and county) totals $143,500,000. Metropolitan Development Association, *A Profile of Onondaga County*, pp. 16–18.

6. Wallace S. Sayre and Herbert Kaufman, *Governing New York City* (New York: Russell Sage Foundation, 1960), p. 562.

7. State of New York, Special Legislative Committee on Revision and Simplification of the Constitution, *Staff Report on Metropolitan Utica-Rome* (Report 6, May 1958). The report specifically makes this point.

8. See Sayre and Kaufman, *op. cit.*, p. 562.

9. The author is indebted to Coleman Woodbury for suggesting this line of reasoning. The concept of ineffective problem-solving may provide a substitute for the normative framework ordinarily used to justify metropolitan reorganization, which in effect simply states that a metropolitan government would be more sensible. To the extent that the

reports pleading for the creation of new metropolitan governments written within this normative framework are effective, it would seem probable that they produce their impact by changing the expectations of the population as to what government service levels should be. It seems plausible that they might be still more effective if they were aimed deliberately at that objective.

    10. Jonathan B. Pollard, "The Effects of the 1950 Flood Control Project upon Utilization of the Onondaga Valley Flood Plain, New York" (unpublished M.A. thesis, Syracuse University, July, 1960).

    11. Some see hope for early and perhaps significant action in the work of the county charter commission appointed late in 1960. See Chapter IX for a brief comment on recent developments respecting county reorganization.

25

JAMES Q. WILSON, A Guide to Reagan Country: The Political Culture of Southern California

A person like myself, who grew up in Southern California, finds it increasingly difficult to understand people who say they understand California. "Explaining California," especially Southern California, has always been a favorite pastime for New Yorkers and Bostonians who have changed planes in Los Angeles, or made a two-day trip to the RAND Corporation, or just speculated on what kind of state could be responsible for Hollywood. Nor need one be an Eastern to play the game; living in San Francisco carries with it a permanent license not only to explain but to explain away (*far away*) Los Angeles.

    This game might have been regarded as an amusing (though to me, irritating) diversion so long as what was being explained or "understood" was Hollywood and Vine, or orange-juice stands shaped like oranges, or Aimee Semple McPherson, or the Great I Am, or traffic on the Los Angeles freeways. It became a little less amusing when the same "explanations" thought appropriate for Aimee and the poor orange-juice vendors (most of whom, by the way, have disappeared) were applied to the John Birch Society and other manifestations of the Far Right. Anybody crazy enough to buy orange juice at such places or to drive on those freeways must be crazy enough to be a Bircher. Let two Birchite loudmouths pop off anywhere else in the country and we rush to our sociology texts to see whether it is alienation or the decline of the small entrepreneur that is the cause; let two of them say the same thing in Los Angeles, and we just smile knowingly and murmur, "It figures."

    Even this systematic application of the double standard was harmless enough before Ronald Reagan. Now a striking conservative personality has become

James Q. Wilson, "A Guide to Reagan Country: The Political Culture of Southern California," *Commentary*, vol. 43 (May 1967), pp. 37–45. Reprinted from *Commentary*, by permission; Copyright © 1967 by the American Jewish Committee.

governor of the largest state in the union by an election plurality of over a million votes, most of which he picked up in Southern California. This Hollywood-actor-turned-politician ("it figures") has, to the amazement of many, made a rather considerable impression, not only on the voters of his state but on Republicans around the country including, apparently, a group of presumably toughminded fellow governors. From now at least through the 1968 convention we have to take Reagan quite seriously, and even if he fails to go the distance we must, I think, take Reaganism seriously. It will be with us for a long time under one guise or another. We will not take it seriously by trying to explain it away as if it were something sold at one of those orange-juice stands or preached from the pulpit at some cultist church.

I grew up in Reagan country—not Hollywood, but the lower-middle-class suburbs of Los Angeles. It was a distinctive way of life. I think I could still recognize another person who grew up there no matter where I should meet him, just as surely as an Italian can spot a person from his village or region even though they are both now in Queens. I am under no illusion that anyone has the slightest interest in my boyhood (I have next to no interest in it myself), but I do suspect that it may be useful to try to explain what it was like at least in general terms, and how what it was like is relevant to what is happening there today. Though I grew up and went to school there, I left a long time ago in order to acquire some expensive Eastern postgraduate degrees and a political outlook that would now make me vote against Reagan if I had the chance. I do not intend here to write an apology for Reagan; even if I thought like that, which I don't, I would never write it down anywhere my colleagues at Harvard might read it.

I

The important thing to know about Southern California is that the people who live there, who grew up there, love it. Not just the way one has an attachment to a hometown, any hometown, but the way people love the realization that they have found the right mode of life. People who live in Southern California are not richer or better educated than those who live in New York; the significant point about them is that they don't live in New York, and don't want to. If they did, they—the average Los Angeleno (my family, for example)—would have lived most of their lives in a walkup flat in, say, the Yorkville section of Manhattan or not far off Flatbush Avenue in Brooklyn. Given their income in 1930, life would have been crowded, noisy, cold, threatening—in short, *urban.* In Long Beach or Inglewood or Huntington Park or Bellflower, by contrast, life was carried on in a detached house with a lawn in front and a car in the garage, part of a quiet neighborhood, with no crime (except kids racing noisy cars), no cold, no smells, no congestion. The monthly payments on that bungalow—one or two bedrooms, one bath, a minuscule dining room, and never enough closets—would have been no more than the rent on the walkup flat in Brooklyn or Yorkville. In 1940, with the Depression still in force, *over half the population* of Los Angeles lived in single-family homes. Only about half of these were owner-occupied, but even to rent a house was such a vast improvement over renting an apartment that nobody looked back; they only looked ahead to the time they could pick up their own mortgage. San Francisco in the same year was another matter. Only a third of the population lived in single-family homes there, the reason being that there were almost no *houses* to rent; if you wanted a house, you had to buy it, and not many people in 1940 could afford to buy.

There has been a good deal of loose talk about "radical" politics (which I suppose means anything to the Right of Earl Warren) developing out of a rootless, highly mobile population with no sense of *place,* of continuity, of stability. That may explain radical politics somewhere, but not in Los Angeles. The people who voted for Reagan have lived for years, in many cases decades, in Southern California. And they have lived in houses, not anonymous, impersonal apartment buildings.

Indeed, it was during the period of Los Angeles's greatest population growth that it voted, over and over again, for Earl Warren—the very embodiment (then) of moderation. The explanation, I believe, is quite simple: truly rootless, mobile people are more likely to vote the way established institutions—newspapers, churches, labor unions, business firms—tell them to vote. Revolutions are never made by the last man to get off the train; they are made by those who got off a long time ago and, having put down roots and formed their own assessment of matters, have the confidence, the long-nurtured discontent, and the knowledge of how to get things done sufficient to support independent political action. (Radical politics, I suspect, follows the same pattern as Negro riots: contrary to what the McCone Commission asserted but did not prove, the Negroes who rioted in Watts—or at least those who rioted violently enough to get themselves arrested—were Negroes who had been in Watts for a long time. Over half the teenage Negroes arrested had been *born* in California; over three-fourths had lived there for more than five years.)

In any case, it is a mistake to try to explain a particular election by underlying social trends. Elections, after all, are choices, and how they come out depends on who the voters have to choose between. That Reagan won last year does not mean that *last year* some ineluctable social force finally surfaced and carried the day. A vote for Reaganism was always possible in Southern California (and had revealed itself in countless congressional and local elections). The point I wish to make is that there has for a long time been a "Reagan point of view" in the Southern California electorate, that this point of view was powerfully shaped by the kinds of people who went to California and the conditions of life there.

The people who in 1940 lived in those hundreds of thousands of detached and semi-detached homes came from all over the country, but primarily they came from the Midwest, the border states, and the "near South." Almost none came from Europe: about 6 percent, to be exact, had been born in Italy, Ireland, Germany, France, Sweden, or Russia; another 2½ percent had been born in

Mexico. (In San Francisco, the proportion of foreign born was twice as large.) But 28 percent had been born in the American heartland—the dustbowl states (Texas, Oklahoma, Arkansas, Louisiana, Kansas, Nebraska), or the border states (Indiana, Missouri, Tennessee, Kentucky) and the upper plains (Iowa, Wisconsin, Minnesota, the Dakotas). If you add in the nearby mountain and Southwestern states (Colorado, Utah, Arizona, New Mexico, Nevada), the total proportion rises to over a third. And if you add in the persons whose parents had been born in these states, the proportion no doubt (there are no figures) exceeds a half. Again, San Francisco is a contrast—only about a tenth of its people in 1940 were from the heartland states. Between 1920 and 1940, during the Depression, over 400,000 persons born in the heartland moved to Los Angeles. *Less than a tenth* as many moved to San Francisco.

Except for Arkansas, Louisiana, and Texas, no Southern states are included in these migration figures. This is important to bear in mind—such conservatism as Southern California displays was not imported from the Deep South. In fact, even those who came from Southern states were likely to be from places like West Texas, where Confederate sentiment was never very strong.

These migrants were rural and small-town people. And here, of course, another popular explanation of Southern California politics takes the stage. These voters are supposed to yearn for the simpler life and the small-town virtues that they left behind. They are reactionary, it is claimed, in the precise sense: seeking to turn back the clock to a day when life was easier, virtues less complicated, and the Ten Commandments a sufficient guide. Perhaps so—there is no doubt some truth in this. But it flies in the face of the fact that these are people who *left* small-town and rural America (millions more stayed behind, after all)—and left it for jobs in big defense plants and large office buildings. I was never aware of any effort to re-create small-town America in Southern California, unless you put in that category the Victory Gardens people planted to raise vegetables during the war. On the contrary, they adopted rather quickly a suburban style of life, with its attendant devotion to the growing of a decent lawn (how many farms have you ever seen with a good lawn?). Furthermore, it is not the migrants themselves who on the whole have voted for Reaganism, but their children. The migrants voted for Roosevelt and Upton Sinclair and looked on disapprovingly as their children began to adopt the hedonistic mores of Southern California teenage life. There was as much intergenerational conflict among the Okies and Arkies in California as among the Italians and the Irish in Boston or New York. And yet it was these youngsters who grew up, married, moved out to Orange County or to Lakewood, and voted for Reagan and castigated Pat Brown, the last of the New Deal-Fair Deal Democrats. (To be completely accurate, a lot of the older people voted for Reagan, too, but they, I imagine, found it much harder to let go of their traditional attachment to Franklin Roosevelt and Earl Warren; the young people had no trouble at all.)

This is not to say that the migrants brought nothing with them. On the contrary, they brought an essential ingredient of Southern California life—

fundamentalist Protestant individualism. We like to think of the store-front church as being a Negro invention; not so. I remember scores of white store-front churches—mostly of small Pentecostal and Adventist sects—lining the main streets of Long Beach. Most people, of course, went to established churches, but these were only bigger and slightly more orthodox versions of the same thing—Baptists, Methodists, Mormons, Brethren, Church of God, and so on. Church was a very important part of life, but hardly any two people belonged to the same one. We were Catholics, and we had to drive out into the dairy farming country (I will never forget the way Sunday morning smelled—incense and cow manure, in equal portions) where there were enough Mexican farm-hands and Dutch Catholic dairymen to make up a parish. All my friends sang hymns and listened to "preachin'." And the preaching was evangelical, funda-mentalist, and preoccupied with the obligation of the *individual* to find and enter into a right relationship with God, with no sacraments, rituals, covenants, or grace to make it easy.

The religious character of San Francisco was strikingly different. In 1936 (the last time the government took a census of church organizations), 70 percent of the reported church membership of San Francisco, but only 40 percent of that in Los Angeles, was Catholic. And of the claimed members of Protestant sects, 40 percent in San Francisco, but only 26 percent in Los Angeles, belonged to the high-status, non-fundamentalist churches—Congregational, Episcopalian, Unitarian, and Universalist. Both cities had about the same proportion of Jews, but, as will be argued in a moment, the leadership, at least, of the two Jewish communities was rather different. Los Angeles, and even more its middle-class suburbs, was Protestant and fundamentalist Protestant at that.

The social structure did nothing to change the individualistic orientation of life. People had no identities except their personal identities, no obvious group affiliations to make possible any reference to them by collective nouns. I never heard the phrase "ethnic group" until I was in graduate school. I never knew there were Irishmen (I was amazed many years later to learn that, at least on my mother's side, I had been one all along) or Italians (except funny organ grinders in the movies, all of whom looked like Chico Marx). We knew there were Negroes (but none within miles of where we lived) and Jews (they ran Hollywood and New York, we knew, but not many of us had ever met one). Nobody ever even pointed out to me that I was a Catholic (except once, when a friend explained that that was probably the reason I wouldn't join the Order of De Molay, a young people's Masonic group).

The absence of such group identities and of neighborhoods associated with those identities may be one reason for the enormous emphasis on "personality." Teenagers everywhere, of course, place great stock in this, mostly, I suppose, because they feel such an urgent need to establish an identity and to be liked by others. But in Southern California, it went far beyond that—there was a cult of personality that dominated every aspect of life. Everybody was compared in terms of his or her personality; contests for student-body office were based on it. To be "popular" and "sincere" was vital. In a New York high school, by contrast, personality would have to share importance in such contests with a certain amount of bloc voting among the Irish, Italians, and Jews, or between "project" people and brownstone people, or even between leftists and far leftists.

Perhaps because of the absence of ethnic and religious blocs which in turn are associated with certain political positions, perhaps because Southern California (then) was very remote from those urban centers where "The Future of Socialism" was being earnestly debated, student life in and around Los Angeles was remarkably apolitical. Most people were vaguely for Roosevelt, though there was a substantial (and growing) group that announced defiantly that while their parents had voted for FDR in '32, and perhaps even in '36, they weren't going to do *that* anymore. Registered Democrats who voted Republican were commonplace, but after noting that fact there wasn't, politically, much left to be said. (It was different in downtown Los Angeles where the Jews lived; L.A. High, and later Los Angeles State College, were very political. A considerable Wallace movement flourished in 1948. Many of those people are now in the Democratic club movement.)

Politics for these people came to mean, in later years, expressing directly one's individual political preferences and expecting them to be added up by a kind of political algebra into a general statement of the public interest. "Bloc voting" and group preferences were unheard of and, when heard of, unthinkable. And the idea that political parties ought to do anything besides help add up preferences was most heterodox—the worst thing that could be said about it was that it was "Eastern." The well-known institutional features of California's political system—weak parties, the extensive use of the referendum to decide policy issues, nonpartisanship—were perfectly matched to the political mentality that was nurtured in Southern California.

That nurturing was distinctive but hard to describe. Rural Anglo-Saxon Protestants have lived in lots of states, but they haven't produced the Southern California style of politics anywhere else. One reason is to be found in what it was like, and to a considerable extent is still like, to grow up in Southern California. Everybody, as I have already noted, lived in a single-family house. There was no public transportation to speak of, so that the movement of people within the city followed no set corridors. People moved about freely and in so doing saw how everybody lived. That movement was institutionalized in the Sunday Afternoon Drive—not to the beach or an amusement park, but just "around" to look at homes, call on friends, or visit distant relatives. A house was, as a Catholic might put it, the outward and visible sign of inward grace. There was no anonymity provided by apartment buildings or tenements or projects. Each family had a house; there it was, for all to see and inspect. With a practiced glance, one could tell how much it cost, how well it was cared for, how good a lawn had been coaxed into uncertain life, and how tastefully plants and shrubs had been set out.

A strong, socially reinforced commitment to property was thus developed, evident in how people treat those homes today. An enormous amount of energy and money is devoted to repairing, improving, remodeling, extending, and land-scaping. Even in areas with fairly low incomes, such as those where the elderly and the retired live, houses are not on the whole allowed to deteriorate. A family might buy a house for six or seven thousand dollars with, for the period, a big mortgage, and then spend several times that over a generation or two in home improvements. Those who could not afford it substituted labor for capital. People were practicing do-it-yourself in Southern California long before anybody in the advertising business thought to give it a name. Year-round warm weather made year-round outdoor labor possible—and, of course, year-round outdoor inspection by one's critical neighbors.

Much of this labor was cooperative. The Southern California equivalent of the Eastern uncle who could "get it for you wholesale" was the Los Angeles brother-in-law who would help you put on a new roof, or paint the garage, or lend you (and show you how to use) his power saw. A vast, informally organized labor exchange permeated the region, with occasional trades of great complexity running through several intermediaries—the friend who would ask his brother, the plumber, to help you if you would ask your uncle with the mixer to lay the concrete in front of somebody's sister's home. Saturday saw people driving all over the county carrying out these assignments.

Driving. Driving everywhere, over great distances, with scarcely any thought to the enormous mileages they were logging. A car was the absolutely essential piece of social overhead capital. With it, you could get a job, meet a girl, hang around with the boys, go to a drive-in, see football games away from home, take in the beach parties at Laguna or Corona del Mar, or go to the Palladium ballroom in Hollywood. To have a car meant being somebody; to have to borrow a car meant knowing somebody; to have no car at all, owned or borrowed, was to be left out—way out.

Those cars led parents and professional moralists to speak of "teenagers and their jalopies." They were not jalopies—not to us, anyway. The oldest, most careworn Ford Model A was a thing of beauty. To be sure, the beauty often had to be coaxed out; yet what was life for but to do the coaxing and take credit for the beauty? Beauty, of course, meant different things to different boys. For some, it was speed and power; and so they would drop a V-8 block into the "A" chassis and then carefully, lovingly, bore it out, stroke it, port it, and put two barrels or four barrels on it. For others, beauty was in the body, not the engine, and their energies would go into customizing the car—dropping the rear end, chopping down the top, leading in the fenders, stripping off the chrome (it took Detroit decades to recognize the merits of these changes and then to mass-produce them), and above all painting, sanding, rubbing, painting, sanding, rubbing—for ten or fifteen or twenty coats, usually of metallic paint. Again, warm weather made it easier—you could work outside year round and if you ran out of money before the job was finished (which was most of the time), you could drive around in the unfinished product with no top, primed but not painted, and no hood over the engine. Of late, Mr. Tom Wolfe of *New York* magazine has discovered car customizing and decided it is a folk art. It wasn't folk art in the '40s; it was life.

The sense of property developed by this activity has never been measured and perhaps never can be; I am convinced it was enormous and fundamental. After marriage, devoting energy to the improvement of a house was simply a grown-up extension of what, as a juvenile, one had done with cars. There is, of course, a paradox here: the car was used in great part to get girls. It was a hand-polished, custom-made rolling bedroom, or so its creators hoped. (In this they were as often disappointed as a Harvard man taking a Radcliffe girl into his house rooms during parietal hours; every girl likes to be *seen* in such places, but a distressingly small proportion are inclined to *do* anything there.) But the hedonistic purposes to which the car might be put did not detract from its power to create and sustain a very conventional and bourgeois sense of property and responsibility, for in the last analysis the car was not a means to an end but an end in itself. Shocked parents never got that point: they saw the excess that the car permitted, they did not see the intensely middle-class values that it instilled.

Low-density, single-family homes, a lack of public transportation, the absence of ethnic neighborhoods, and the use of cars combined to prevent the formation of streetcorner gangs, except in very central portions of Los Angeles and one or two older cities. The principal afterschool occupation of a teenage Eastern boy from a working-class family is to "hang out" at the corner candy-store, the ice-cream parlor, or in front of the drugstore with class and ethnic compatriots. Having a "corner" of your own—or having "turf," in the case of the ambitious and imperialistic—would have made no sense to an equivalent group of young men in Southern California. The Eastern life-style produced a feeling of *territory*, the Western life-style a feeling of *property*. Teenagers in Southern California hung out together, to be sure, but not in any fixed spot, and where they did hang out tended to be a place reached by a car, with lots of free parking for other cars. The drive-in restaurant was the premier institution catering to this need. But it was also a very democratic institution, since it was not (and because of its location some distance from one's home, could not become) the "turf" of any particular gang. Rich and poor, Protestant and Catholic, anybody with a car could get there and, barring a losing fight over a girl, stay there. There were rivalries, but like modern warfare they tended to be between large, heterogeneous, and impersonal rivals—one high school against another, not one ethnic group against another.

Can all this explain why Southern California is so different, politically, from Northern California—why it, so much more than the Bay Area, supported Goldwater and Reagan? Perhaps not entirely. And yet I believe the kind of people living there and their life-styles are very important, much more important than, say, the presumed influence of the conservative Los Angeles *Times*. The Oakland *Tribune* is even more conservative, but the East Bay region it serves is more "liberal" in its voting than L.A. And the very liberal McClatchey newspapers in the Central Valley do not seem to have turned back the Reagan tide. On the other hand, San Francisco has Southern-California-style suburbs as well, with bungalows and cars and the like, and the people there are not as conservative as their counterparts in the South. But as we have seen, the people who migrated to San Francisco in the '30s and '40s were different from those who settled in Los Angeles. And once the different life-styles of the two cities became apparent, non-Californians must have begun deciding to move to the Bay Area or to Los Angeles on the basis, in part, of what they had heard about those styles. A small but visible difference in the beginning thus became a very large difference in the end.

II

The political institutions and economic character of Southern California reinforced the life style and gave it expression. Politics, as I have said, was nonpartisan, free-swinging, slightly populistic—a direct appeal to the people was to be made on all issues. The major parties for decades were virtually moribund and therefore never performed their customary (and to my thinking, desirable) task of aggregating interests, blurring issues, strengthening party loyalties, and finding moderate candidates. Not that the people wanted immoderate candidates. So long, at least, as the issues were not very grave—before civil rights, and welfare, and Berkeley, and crime—they wanted honest, competent administrators who favored change but in an orderly manner. In Earl Warren they got such a man and he made sure the regular Republican party, whose fat cats were on the whole considerably to his Right, would not have a chance to replace him. He built a personal following outside the regular, and cumbersome, party apparatus. Like most personal followings, however, it made no provision for a transfer of power. The obvious Warren protégé—Thomas Kuchel—was in the Senate, Warren's personal following in the state could not be handed to another man, and the party was in no shape to find a candidate of its own. Any man with money and a good smile could take a crack at capturing the nomination on his own, and many did.

Such organization as existed tended to be in the North, rather than the South. San Francisco and Alameda County across the bay had more in the way of party machinery, financed on a steady basis, than the South had, at least until the emergence of the California Democratic clubs. A little organization goes a long way in an organizational vacuum, and the North exercised a disproportionate influence in California politics for some time. The Northern Democrats had some old families—many Jewish—who helped pay the party's bills during the long, lean years.

The South had few such persons—or more accurately, it had some very rich, self-made men from the oil business and from the vast agricultural enterprises of the Imperial Valley who were conservative Democrats in the (by now) well-documented tradition of the American Southwest. They may be more visible in Texas today, but twenty years ago they were more influential in California.

Why? There were Jews in Southern California, tens of thousands of them in and around Los Angeles. (Yet looking back on my high-school days, I can think of only one Jew I was personally acquainted with, and he went to another high school across town. Jews were Hollywood, we all knew.) Many of them were in the movie industry and in command of wealth and great resources for publicity. Why didn't they help to finance and lead the Southern California Democratic party? Some did—or tried—at least for a while. A high point of that influence was the 1950 senatorial campaign of the liberal Helen Gahagan Douglas, the movie actress. It wasn't George Murphy or Ronald Reagan who put Hollywood into politics, it was Mrs. Douglas, who lost to Richard Nixon. Two years before, many of her supporters had turned, in frustration, to third-party politics and become important figures in the 1948 campaign of Henry Wallace. It was a disaster. Bolting the party nationally was a far more serious thing than bolting it locally, where it could hardly be said to exist. The Truman Democrats took control in California and, when Communist party influence in the Wallace movement became too obvious to be denied (Wallace himself was to admit it later), they were in a position to treat the Douglas and Wallace Democrats as thoroughly discredited in the eyes of the voters. Shortly thereafter, the era of McCarthyism descended upon the country, and in Hollywood involvement in politics was for the time being finished. What Mrs. Douglas had begun, Henry Wallace and Joe McCarthy succeeded in ending.

But it was not only that Hollywood Jews had lost power, it was also that Hollywood Jews were different from those in other urban centers. The social and economic heights of Hollywood were commanded, not by German Jews, but by East Europeans; not by old families but by immigrants; not by Wall Street smoothness but by *nouveau riche* entrepreneurship. Such Hollywood money as went into politics was used much as money was then used in the movie industry—impulsively, by dictatorial men used to having their own way, and on behalf of "stars." If the star system worked on the movie lots, why couldn't it work in politics? Thus, a glamorous figure, a big name and occasionally a conspicuous nut could get *personal* backing for a campaign, but there was little or no money for organization, for routine affairs, or for professional (and necessarily bureaucratic) leadership.

Anyway, the voter wasn't much interested in liberalism even if it could be financed. Los Angeles was prosperous, and even greater prosperity seemed just around the corner. The aircraft plants and shipyards had taken tens of thousands of families and given every member, including the mother, a job, thereby putting them, in four years' time, in a wholly different and higher economic bracket. A generation of slow gain was compressed into a few years; progress wasn't around the corner, or something you hoped for for your kids, it was right here and now. War prosperity affected the whole country, but it had a special effect on Southern California—there was more of it, because there was more war industry located there, and it benefited people who only a few years before had been fighting for survival on a dust-swept farm in the Texas panhandle. John

Steinbeck has told us how those farmers and sharecroppers saw California as the Promised Land. But they had only been promised relief checks from the Farm Security Administration; instead, they found overtime checks from Lockheed.

Next to the kind of people who live there, the rate of economic growth of Southern California—and today, of the whole Southwest—is the main key to its political life. Visiting scholars make much of the business domination of Dallas, or the presumed influence of the Los Angeles *Times* in Southern California, or the "Chamber of Commerce mentality" of San Diego. The important thing to understand is that these have not been alien influences imposed from above on the populace—they are merely the more obvious indicators of the fact that business values are widely shared. (Not business *control*; voters are as quick to resent that, when it is pointed out to them, in Los Angeles as anywhere. Sam Yorty became mayor by running against the *Times* and other "downtown interests," and he is still very popular in his city, however much ridicule he may take from Robert Kennedy in Washington.) Business values are here meant in the widest sense—a desire for expansion and growth, a high rate of increase in property values, finding and developing mass markets, and keeping capital moving and labor productive.

No one was immune from this psychology. How could he be? Everyone was buying, or intended to buy, his own home. Many factory workers and salesmen speculated in real estate on the side. A favorite topic of conversation at our dinner table, and I am sure at thousands of dinner tables just like it, was the latest story about the fantastic price a certain parcel had just been sold for and what a shame it was that we passed up the chance to buy it two years ago for peanuts. (We never seemed to have enough peanuts around at the right time.) The purpose of government was to facilitate this growth—open up new land, bring in water, make credit easy, keep the defense plants rolling. Government was not there to keep painfully-acquired positions secure by paying out benefits or legislating new regulations. Government was there to help bring in the future, not protect the past.

Not everyone felt this way, of course. Elderly people who came to California to retire had a different view. They wanted pensions, benefits, regulations. They were numerous and visible, but though they come quickly to mind when one thinks back on the shuffleboard and croquet courts at Lincoln Park in Long Beach or on the soapbox orators and bench-sitters in Pershing Square in Los Angeles, they were never representative of the local political ethos. They were the butt of countless jokes and the target for much political criticism: they wanted to hold back tomorrow (it was believed), cash their relief checks, and lie in the sun. That was *wrong,* most working families thought. The Negro, who today is the victim of the anti-welfare sentiment, was actually the second victim; the first was the old folks. They were attacked for moving to California "just to get a pension," told to "go back where they came from," and fought against in countless welfare issues. (About the only thing they were spared were allegations that they constituted a sexual threat. I cannot recall my father, no paragon of tolerance, ever trying to clinch an argument against a liberal by asking him how he would like it if his daughter grew up and married an old man.)

The old folks fought back, but in California it was a *protest* movement. George McLain organized the old folks (nobody ever called them "senior citizens"; they didn't even call themselves that) and made them a potent force in state politics, but it was a force directed *against* the two major parties and their candidates. He won concessions for his followers and now they may be so secure as to be accepted as a political fact of life; what they wanted, however, was never accepted.

Southern California's political culture, including but not limited to what might be called Reaganism, is one which I suspect is characteristic of areas experiencing rapid economic growth and general prosperity, especially if there are few institutions—political parties, churches, labor unions—to frame the issues and blunt popular instincts. People there are concerned about the growth in the size of the economic pie, not (except for the elderly) in preserving the size of their present slice. The attributes in a person to be admired are those which indicate his ability to enhance his position and expand his resources, not conserve his position and maintain his resources. If I had to cite only one way in which Southwestern politics differ from Northeastern politics, it would be this: the former region is developmental, future-oriented, and growth-conscious; the latter is conserving, past- or present-oriented, and security-conscious. Note that I say "conserving," not conservative; there is a difference. The Northeast by some measures is less "conservative" than the Southwest, though it is easy to exaggerate the difference. A conserv*ative* is usually thought of as a person who favors limited government, minimized administrative involvement in private affairs, maximum free choice. A conserv*er*, on the other hand, needs *more* government in order to protect present stakes from change, from threats posed by other groups, and from competition.

Before we get carried away with the difference, some qualifications are in order. There are conserving forces at work in Southern California. One is the elderly. Another is the slowly emerging labor movement. For years Los Angeles was a tough city in which to be a trade unionist. There are still people who remember with horror the bombing of the Los Angeles *Times*. But unions are making headway. One is the Retail Clerks, which is organizing in the supermarkets and dime stores; another is the Machinists, active in aircraft and auto assembly plants. And the region's economic growth has not unleashed anything like the hysteria of the Florida land boom.

Even more important as a challenge to the general political culture of the region, with its concern for property, propriety, individual responsibility, economic growth, and limited government, is ideological liberalism. By the time McCarthyism was ending and the blacklists were beginning to lose their grip on Hollywood (perhaps because faced with the competition from television and European producers, Hollywood could no longer afford the luxury of a blacklist), Adlai Stevenson was making his appearance as a force in the Democratic party. The enormous outpouring of support for him in Southern California has been oft remarked upon, as has the vigorous club movement that grew up in the aftermath of his 1952 and 1956 Presidential campaigns. The movement activated a wholly new generation of political enthusiasts and provided a new base of operations for some of the leftovers from older forms of liberal and radical politics.

These clubs did not recruit the people I have been describing in earlier pages, nor have they taken hold in the areas in which these people live. The clubs grew up on the northern and eastern periphery of the region—the Hollywood hills, Santa Monica, Beverly Hills, Pacific Palisades, and out into the college towns, such as Pomona, in the interior. Young Jews, young intellectuals, persons transplanted to Los Angeles from the East (by 1940, about 10 percent of the population had been born in New England, New Jersey, or Pennsylvania), and older California radicals flocked into the clubs. But the clubs never really took root among the working-class and middle-class bungalows of Long Beach, Inglewood, or Redondo Beach, to say nothing of Orange County to the Southeast. The Democratic clubs initially had little interest in Southern California; they were interested in national and international issues. (The civil-rights movement has changed that; the clubs are now deeply involved in such matters locally.) They had, at the outset, no real program for California (though they had one for just about everything else), and thus there was no necessary conflict between what they wanted and what those who later voted for Reagan wanted—no necessary conflict, perhaps, but conflict nonetheless. And the most intense kind of conflict, for what was at stake were large and symbolic issues—Red China, capital punishment, world peace, and civil liberties. The Southern California electorate quickly became deeply polarized.

The polarization is not immediately evident in voting statistics. In the aggregate, Southern California elects a mixture of liberals and conservatives much like any other region, and on many of its famous referenda votes for and against public expenditures about like other areas. But these aggregate figures conceal the real symptoms of polarization—several Democrats (not all) are as far to the Left of their party as is possible; several Republicans (not all) are as far to the Right of their party as possible. And on referenda issues—especially those involving such matters as open occupancy in housing—the returns and the polls suggest that Southern California has both the most intense proponents and the most intense opponents (the latter outnumbering the former: the region as a whole was against fair housing by a considerable margin; in San Francisco, the vote was both less lopsided and, I suspect, based on less intensely polarized views). This is *not* the same thing as saying that Southern California is more "bigoted" than the Bay Area. Because of the way the issue was framed, people were asked to vote *for* the *right* to sell their property to whomever they chose. In Southern California, property rights are vital and freedom in their exercise staunchly defended. There have been, I would guess, fewer attacks on Negro families seeking homes in white neighborhoods in Southern California than in say, Pennsylvania, Ohio, or Illinois. The housing issue was fought out at a more general level—not over whether one was for or against Negroes, but over alternative conceptions of what freedom requires. And the polarization of opinion on this issue, as on most, was most intense among persons of higher status. The educated, affluent Easterners and intellectuals (who work in law firms or the communications media or the universities) are more inclined than their less well-off fellows to support the Democratic clubs and liberalism; the educated, affluent sons and daughters of the Midwestern migrants (who now work as engineers and accountants in aerospace and petroleum industries) are more inclined than their less well-off fellows to support Goldwater and Reagan.

III

Is Southern California's political culture unique? Not really—it is but the earliest, most publicized, and most heavily populated example of a pattern now to be found throughout much of the Southwest. It appeared first in Southern California because more people went there and because California's political institutions gave almost immediate expression to it. In other states, the party structure constrained its free expression for a time; the ambitions of rival politicians and factions in Texas and Arizona made the ideology less evident, at least for a while. Goldwater's easy victory at the 1964 Republican convention indicates how widespread are certain aspects of that culture—in fact, it overstates it, because Goldwater himself overstated many features of that culture. The Southern Californians about whom I have written want limited government, personal responsibility, "basic" education, a resurgence of patriotism, an end to "chiseling," and a more restrained Supreme Court. They are not quite so certain that they want an adventurous foreign policy or a high-risk international confrontation with Communism. No doubt the militant Goldwater enthusiasts wanted such a policy, but they must have mistaken what the rank-and-file would support. Reagan has not yet made the same mistake—he took Goldwater's views, stripped away the foreign policy (except for very general statements) and references to turning back the clock on Social Security (after all, he wanted a coalition between the elderly and the young).

But Goldwater, however badly-managed his campaign, won the convention and won it by methods and with supporters which, in whatever state they were found, could very easily have been found in Southern California. Amateur political clubs, impassioned volunteers, appeals to highly moral and symbolic issues—the Republican party professionals had, to their profound irritation, to put up with all of it, just as party professionals in California, Democrats and Republicans alike, have been putting up with it since the early 1950s.

The Southern California political style is spreading; it seems to be, at least in the Western part of the United States, the concomitant of the American success story. There, millions of people are realizing their ambitions. They are not "rootless" or yearning for "small-town simplicity" or profoundly irritated by all the hustle and bustle; they are acquiring security, education, living space, and a life style that is based in its day-to-day routine on gentility, courtesy, hospitality, virtue. Why then, are they so discontent? It is not with their lot that they are discontent, it is with the lot of the nation. *The very virtues they have and practice are, in their eyes, conspicuously absent from society as a whole.* Politics is corrupt—not in the petty sense, though there is that—but in the large sense; to these people, it consists of "deals," of the catering to selfish interests, of cynical manipulation and doubletalk. The universities are corrupt—children don't act as if they appreciate what is being given them, they don't work hard, and they are lectured to by devious and wrongheaded professors. And above all, everywhere they look, somebody is trying to get "something for nothing," and succeeding.

These views may not be confined only to the political culture in which they are now articulated. Surveys I have taken, and others I have read, indicate that the single most widespread concern of middle-class Americans is over the "decay of values"—evidenced by "crime in the streets," juvenile delinquency, public lewdness, and the like, but going much beyond these manifestations to include everything that suggests that people no longer act in accordance with decent values and right reason. In many places, especially in the Northeast, our political institutions (happily) do not allow such views to play much part in elections. Parties, led by professionals, instinctively shun such issues, feeling somehow that public debate over virtue is irrelevant (what can government do about it?) and dangerous (nobody can agree on what virtue is or that your party has more of it). Powerful nonpolitical institutions tend, also, to keep such issues out of politics or to insist that they be matters of private conscience. For one, the Catholic Church, which draws the religious and moral interests of its followers inward, toward the sacraments and the educational and religious facilities of the Church which must be maintained and served. For another, large labor unions which have never mistaken a "stamp out smut" campaign for a fifty-cent increase in the minimum wage. And a self-conscious intelligentsia with common ties to prestigious centers of liberal-arts education has, in many regions, especially the East and the Bay Area, an important role to play among local elites. They use their access to the mass media and to officialdom to make certain that other, non-moral issues predominate—after all, the major function of the schools they went to was to induce them to rebel against the "middle-class morality" which, in the modern parlance, is a hangup.

Regional differences will never disappear entirely, and thus the political culture of Southern California will never be *the* political culture of our society. But the strength of all those institutions which resist it is waning, and thus we are likely to have more of it in more places in the future. I happen to think that morality is important and that those concerned about it are decent people (after all, I'm related to a sizable number of them). But I fear for the time when politics is seized with the issue. Our system of government cannot handle matters of that sort (can any democratic system?) and it may be torn apart by the effort.

26

MICHAEL AIKEN & ROBERT R. ALFORD, Community Structure and Innovation: The Case of Urban Renewal

The search for determinants of public policy innovation in American cities has received little attention from social scientists. The controversy over "community power structure" focused almost entirely upon case studies of "who governs" in particular cities and barely at all upon the policy consequences of different configurations of power in the local community (Jacob and Lipsky, 1968; Alford, 1969; Aiken, 1970). However, a number of comparative studies have appeared recently focusing upon such policy outputs as urban renewal, fluoridation, and desegregation. The data used in these studies, often rather crudely, indicate the concepts they allegedly represent. Such slippage between available data and theoretical constructs has resulted in the proliferation of diffuse explanations of public policy innovations and identical or even contradictory empirical indicators.

In this paper we shall review a number of theories of community policy innovation, examine some empirical findings about innovation in urban renewal, and conclude by suggesting an alternative theory which conceives of the community as an interorganizational system. Parallel papers to this one analyze innovation in public housing and in poverty programs (Aiken and Alford, 1970 a, b).

The nature of community innovation

Little attention has been given to innovation in communities, although they are continually introducing new ideas, activities, processes, and services. In the comparative perspective utilized here, we are interested not only in knowing those structures and processes in communities that are associated with the

Michael Aiken and Robert R. Alford, "Community Structure and Innovation: The Case of Urban Renewal," *American Sociological Review*, vol. 35 (August 1967), pp. 650–664. Reprinted by permission.

This research was supported in part by funds granted to the Institute for Research on Poverty at the University of Wisconsin by the Office of Economic Opportunity pursuant to the provisions of the Economic Opportunity Act of 1964. The conclusions are the sole responsibility of the authors. We are indebted to Terry N. Clark, Robert L. Crain, and Paul E. Mott for their detailed and helpful comments. We are grateful to the Institute for its research and administrative support, and to Elizabeth Balcer, Janet Jensen, and Ann Wallace for their competent and vital research assistance.

adoption of an innovation, but also with the *speed* of the innovation and the *level of output* or performance of the innovative activity. In particular, we are interested in identifying the underlying structural properties and community processes that explain why some communities moved quickly to enter the urban renewal program while others were either slow to innovate or have never participated at all in this federal program. At least five theories of innovation which are relevant to this question can be found in the recent social science literature. Nowhere have these various explanations of community innovation been brought together. In part this lack of theoretical integration is due to the diverse concepts used; what we consider to be innovation has also been called community decision-making, community decision outcomes, and policy outputs.

Some theories of community innovation

The five general hypotheses of community innovation are as follows:

1. *Political culture:* Cities with majorities holding "public-regarding" values are more innovative with respect to policies benefiting the community as a whole than cities dominated by groups with "private-regarding" values (Wolfinger and Field, 1966; cf. Wilson, 1966).
2. *Centralization of formal political structure:* Cities with centralized administrative arrangements and a strong mayor, that is, cities with city manager or partisan mayor-council governmental structures, are more innovative (Crain *et al.,* 1969; Greenstone and Peterson, 1968).
3. *Concentration or diffusion of community power:* There are two aspects to this argument: concentration of systemic power (Hawley, 1963) and diffusion of power through mass citizen participation (Crain and Rosenthal, 1967). In both cases the hypothesis is the same: the greater the concentration of power, the greater the degree of innovation.
4. *Community differentiation and continuity:* Older and larger cities are more bureaucratic and consequently less receptive to policy innovations than younger and smaller cities (Dye, 1968).
5. *Community integration:* Cities in which community integration breaks down or is extremely low have a lower probability of innovation or other collective actions. Consequently innovation should be highest in integrated communities (Coleman, 1957; Pinard, 1963).

We have presented these five explanations separately because it is possible to conceive of them as five independent factors. However, one or more of these factors may be either spurious or intervening variables for the operation of another more fundamental factor, such as the sheer need for a program. Also, as we shall see, the indicators of the theoretical variables have been quite diverse, overlapping, and are sometimes used for quite different concepts. This diversity in the use of the same empirical indicators is partly a result of the great "distance" of the easily available quantitative indicators from the theoretical variables of greatest concern to most scholars.

Most of the data we use are no better, but we have the advantage of bringing together most of the various indicators used in the previous literature, as well as adding several measures which have the merit of being considerably closer to the theoretical variables to which they refer, although they have defects of their own.

Data and methods

Urban renewal programs have been the most frequently studied aspect of public policy making in American cities in recent years. In the scholarly literature, the aspects studied have been diverse, including whether or not a program had reached a planning or execution stage in a given city, urban renewal expenditures, and the number of years a city took to enter the program. The problems which have led to its study include community power structure, the political ethos of the city, and the capacity of shrewd political leaders to generate support. (There seems to be little doubt that the main effect of the program has been to reduce the stock of low-cost housing, since the original legislation explicitly forbade local governments to use income from the sale of land to build new low-rent housing, and relatively few cities have built public housing with other funds, whether federal or nonfederal.)

The findings of this study are based on the universe of 582 American cities in 1960 with the following characteristics: (1) incorporated urban places of size 25,000 population or more, (2) location in states that had state enabling legislation prior to 1958 permitting cities to enter the urban renewal program, and (3) cities in existence in 1950. Of the 676 incorporated urban places of size 25,000 population or more in 1960, 74 are omitted because they were located in eleven states which did not get enabling legislation until 1958 or later (Idaho, Montana, New Mexico, Utah, and Wyoming), or which had highly restrictive enabling legislation, reversals of decision, or no enabling legislation at all as of June 30, 1966, or had a combination of these (Florida, Louisiana, Maryland, Mississippi, Oklahoma, and South Carolina). Another twenty cities that did not exist in 1950 are also omitted.

Since the cities that are included in this study constitute the population of all eligible cities of 25,000 or more, one may question the appropriateness of using statistical tests of significance. The use of statistical tests of significance when the data do not meet the assumptions of those tests (as in the case here) has been a continual problem for sociologists (cf. Gold, 1969; Morrison and Henkel, 1969; Winch and Campbell, 1969). Even though we have exhausted all the units in the universe, there is still the possibility that the observations were produced by errors of measurement. In addition, because we have no other criteria, we utilize significance tests to distinguish between negligible and appreciable correlations, although we recognize that this test, strictly speaking, is not one of statistical significance, nor does it provide assurance of substantive significance (cf. Gold, 1969).

The various measures of community structure were taken from the *Municipal Year Books* of 1963 and 1964, the 1950 Census of Housing and the 1960 Census of Population. Information about the innovation measure, i.e., participation in the urban renewal program, was taken from the *Urban Renewal Directory: June 30, 1966,* Department of Housing and Urban Development, U.S. Government, Washington, D.C., 1966.

We shall ignore in this paper changes in federal urban renewal legislation from 1949 on, although such changes may alter the incentives of different cities to obtain such resources. The original 1949 act required that 55 percent, or more, of the project area be residential either before or after renewal in order to qualify for federal assistance. This requirement was gradually eased by subsequent legislation. Undoubtedly the incentives of local industrialists, real estate investors, and local groups of residents to initiate, support, or oppose urban renewal were altered by these changes, and therefore the probabilities of a given program being carried through, but we do not have the data to investigate this possibility (Ventre, 1966).

We measure the presence or absence of innovation by whether or not a community has ever participated in the urban renewal program. Of the 582 cities in the analysis here, 372 (or 64 percent) had innovated an urban renewal program, although thirty-two of these later dropped out of the program. Among the remaining 340 cities, 187 had completed at least one urban renewal program as of June 30, 1966; 130 others had reached the execution stage of the program; and the other twenty-three were still in planning. There were 210 communities that had never innovated an urban renewal program.

The speed of community innovation is measured by the number of years after 1949 before the city entered the urban renewal program. This is similar to a measure developed by Straits (1965) in his critique of Hawley's (1963) work, although Straits used 1951 to calculate the speed with which a community entered the urban renewal program. The distribution of this variable was slightly skewed toward the lower end of the distribution, but skewness was not of sufficient magnitude to warrant a transformation of this variable.

Since some cities were located in states that did not enact enabling legislation until after 1949, another measure of speed in innovation was constructed: the number of years it took the city to enter the program after state enabling legislation was enacted.

The level of output measure is the number of urban renewal dollars reserved per capita as of June 30, 1966. This measure is similar to those used by Wolfinger and Field (1966) and Clark (1968b), although not strictly comparable. The measure used here was computed by determining the total number of dollars reserved for all urban renewal projects as of June 30, 1966, and then standardizing this figure by the population size, thus yielding a dollar amount reserved per capita for all urban renewal projects. This distribution was highly skewed toward the upper end of the scale so that a natural logarithm transformation of this variable (which was approximately normally distributed) was used in the computation of correlation coefficients.

The relationships among these measures of innovation are quite high, as shown in Table 1, although not so high as to make them equivalent measures. Nor are they logically the same.

Findings

A preliminary test of the several different theories of community innovation is found in Table 2. We have classified each indicator under only one theoretical concept, although it may have been used to measure more than one concept.

First, *political culture*. There is some question about the authorship of this theory. Wilson (1966) has written that he and Banfield (Banfield and Wilson, 1963; Wilson and Banfield, 1964) never developed the theory that Wolfinger and Field (1966) attributed to them. In spite of the question of exactly whose theory this is, we still include it here as an alternative theory of community innovation. According to this theory, a low proportion of foreign born in the city's population, a small proportion of Catholics, and a high proportion of the population that is middle class have been regarded as indicators of a likelihood that a community is composed of a majority of individuals and

Table 1. Relationships among indicators of community innovation

	Presence of innovation/ Presence of urban renewal program	Speed of innovation		Level of output/ Number of dollars reserved per capita (natural log)
		Number of years after 1949 before entering the urban renewal program	Number of years it took after state enabling legislation was present	
Presence of participation in the urban renewal program		−.69***	−.62***	.86***
Number of years after 1949 before the community entered the urban renewal program			.88***	−.80***
Number of years it took after state enabling legislation was present				−.71***
Number of urban renewal dollars reserved per capita (natural logarithm)				

*** $p < .001$.

Note: The number of cases is 582 except for the proportion of registrants voting, which was 370. The presence of urban renewal programs of one or another form of political structure was treated as a "dummy" (binary) variable for purposes of correlations and regressions in subsequent analysis. The natural logarithm of four highly skewed variables was used for correlation analysis, in order to produce an approximately normal distribution.

Table 2. Relationships between indicators of innovation, speed, and outputs and various measures of community structure and culture

Theoretical categories and empirical indicators	Presence of innovation/ Presence of urban renewal program	Speed of innovation — Number of years after 1949 before entering the urban renewal program	Number of years it took after state enabling legislation was present	Level of output/ Number of dollars reserved per capita (natural log)
Political Culture				
Percent of native population of foreign or mixed parentage[a]	−.01	−.04	.10*	.02
Percent of elementary school children in private schools[a]	.06	−.08*	.05	.08*
Median family income[a]	−.33***	.26***	.37***	−.29***
Percent voting Democratic, 1964[b]	.09*	−.13***	−.10*	.08*
Political Structure				
Presence of a city-manager form of government[c]	−.16***	.14***	.05	−.14***
Presence of nonpartisan elections[c]	−.14***	.14***	.04	−.18***
Percent of city council elected at large[c]	−.04	−.04	−.10*	−.02
Number of members of the city council[c]	.16***	−.13***	−.04	.14***
Centralization of Community Power				
MPO ratio[a]	−.30***	.29***	.21***	−.32***
Citizen Participation				
Percent of adult population with four years of high school education[a]	−.38***	.36***	.32***	−.38***
Percent of registrants voting[d]	.18***	−.20***	−.10*	.18***
Community Differentiation and Continuity				
Age of the city (census year city reached 10,000 population)[a]	−.48***	.54***	.46***	−.48***
Size of the city (natural logarithm)	.33***	−.49***	−.49***	.33***
Community Integration				
Percent unemployed[a]	.23***	−.25***	−.24***	.25***
Percent migrant[a]	−.23***	.25***	.12***	−.24***
Poverty				
Percent of housing dilapidated, 1950[a]	.20***	−.14***	−.28***	.13***
Percent of families with less than $3,000 income per year, 1959[a]	.26***	−.22***	−.34***	.21***
Percent adults with less than five years education (natural logarithm)	.36***	−.36***	−.40***	.34***
Percent 14–17 year olds in school[a]	−.33***	.29***	.35***	−.30***
Percent of population that is non-white (natural logarithm)	.37***	−.44***	−.46***	.39***

* p <.05.
** p <.01.
*** p <.001.

groups holding "public-regarding" values. The consequence should be a high level of performance on policies which do not directly benefit the persons voting. While it can be argued that urban renewal directly benefits downtown businessmen rather than the poor, at least one study has tentatively accepted the appropriateness of measuring the consequence of public-regarding values by urban renewal outputs (Wolfinger and Field, 1966).

In addition, we have added the percent voting for the Democratic candidate for president in 1964 as an additional indicator of the presence of a population holding private-regarding values. Cities that are heavily Democratic (as measured by the Democratic vote in 1964) are likely to be highly ethnic ($r = .32$), have many Catholics (as measured by the proportion of school children in private schools, $r = .23$), and have many working-class persons ($r = .22$). This is surely a more direct political measure than any of these demographic characteristics. Thus, if the political culture theory works, we should find that Democratic communities are less likely to have urban renewal.

Table 2 shows that of the sixteen relationships between the four indicators of political culture and four indicators of community innovativeness, only one is in the expected direction. Most of the relationships between percent in private schools, median family income, and percent voting Democratic in 1964 are in the opposite of the predicted direction. In the case of percent of foreign stock, one of the indicators of speed of innovation is significant and in the predicted direction, but the others have no relationship with this measure of political culture. The political culture theory is thus (with one exception) not supported by any of the indicators and is contradicted by an additional one—percent voting Democratic in 1964.

Second, *centralization of formal political structure*. This argument has two aspects, one based on centralization of formal power, the second related to the political culture argument. In the first place, the thesis in the literature is that the more centralized the formal political structure, the more innovative it should be and the more capable it is of policy outputs (Crain *et al.,* 1969). There is some disagreement on what the indicators of centralization should be, since the usual conception of "reform" government is that its structural devices—the

---

Sources of the data are as follows:

[a]U.S. Census of Population, 1960.

[b]*County and City Data Book,* 1967. The county Democratic vote in 1960 was coded as follows: 60% or more Republican, 55–59% Republican, 50–54% Republican, 50–52% Democratic, 53–58% Democratic, 59% or more Democratic, to create six nearly equal groups. The two cities for which data were not available (Washington, D.C., and New York) were assigned to the mean category.

[c]*The Municipal Year Book,* 1963 (International City Managers' Association, 1963). Four or five cities with missing data on one or more of the measures of political structure were assigned to the mean category. The categories for the number of members of the city council were collapsed as follows: 3–4, 5, 6, 7, 8, 9, 10–19, 20–29, 30–50.

[d]Data are from a survey taken by Eugene C. Lee, Director, Institute of Governmental Studies, University of California at Berkeley. For further details and analysis of the voting data, see Alford and Lee (1968).

city manager form, nonpartisan elections, at-large elections, small city councils—were intended to centralize power in the hands of a small executive and a professional manager at the same time that potential power in the hands of citizen groups was fragmented and dispersed by removing the instruments of the political party and the ward organization. On the other hand, some have argued that strong political parties were the most effective device for centralizing power. But in either case there was agreement that administrative or political centralization should lead to a greater capability for innovation and greater policy outputs, regardless of the institutional form which centralization took.

The second aspect of political structure is related to the political culture argument, because it has been argued that reform political institutions were part of the array of policies favored by groups with public-regarding values, and presumably the instruments of such values should produce consequences similar to that of sheer demographic composition.

In most respects, the predictions of innovation which would be made by either the administrative centralization or political cultural interpretation of the indicators of political structure would be the same. The prediction is ambiguous only in the case of the form of election. If nonpartisan elections are regarded as decentralized, then, according to this line of reasoning, they should be associated with less innovation. But if they are regarded as instruments of groups with public-regarding values, then nonpartisan elections should be associated with more innovation.

Table 2 shows that the relationships of urban renewal innovation and output with political structure contradict the centralization of formal political structure hypothesis completely. Manager, nonpartisan, at large, small council cities are with one exception either *less* likely to innovate, or there is no relationship. The relationship between at large elections and the modified speed of innovation measure is in the predicted direction, but this is the only one. The centralization argument is also contradicted, unless one wishes to accept the argument that partisan elections lead to administrative centralization, and therefore greater innovation. The data support the latter proposition.

Third, *concentration or diffusion of community power.* We refer here to two related explanations of community structure and consequences for the distribution of power: the ecological or systemic theory which sees power as a property of dominant institutions, and a mass participation theory which argues that those structural features which reduce mass participation will, as a consequence, concentrate power. We cannot test with our data a third, an "elite-participation" hypothesis, which argues that the smaller the number of elite participants and the more homogeneous their interests, the more centralized the power structure and the greater the policy outputs (cf. Clark, 1968b). While these theories differ in the feature of community organization which they single out as the critical measure or cause of concentration of power, they share the general assumption that the fewer the actors, whether mass or elite, and the more those actors represent dominant institutions, the more concentrated the power. The further inference that concentrated power leads to greater innovation is not always explicitly stated, but we believe that it is a justified extension of the theories.

In his study of urban renewal, Hawley (1963) argued that communities with a greater concentration of power will have a high probability of success in any collective action affecting the welfare of the whole. Hawley used participation in urban renewal programs as his measure of a successful collective action, and he used the MPO ratio (the proportion of the employed civilian labor force that are managers, proprietors, or officials) as his measure of the degree of concentration of community power. He reasoned that system power is exercised through managerial functions, and that those functions can be more readily coordinated if there are few positions performing those functions relative to the number of all other positions.

The data in Table 2 support Hawley's empirical prediction: cities with high MPO ratios are less likely to innovate in all respects that we have measured than cities with low MPO ratios.

Other data drawn from case studies raise questions about the meaning of the MPO ratio, however. Aiken (1970) classified thirty-one case studies of community power on a four-point scale of concentration of power ranging from "monolithic" to "pyramidal" to "pluralistic" to "dispersed power" arrangements, using qualitative judgments of the number of groups involved in major issues in the community as the measure of degree of dispersion of power. The results show a tendency for less centralized communities to have higher levels of innovation and outputs, and for cities having high MPO ratios to have higher concentrations of power than cities with low MPO ratios. Another study of fifty-one cities (Clark, 1968b) found that the greater the decentralization of persons involved in decision-making in four issues (urban renewal, air pollution, poverty programs, and the selection of the mayor), the greater the number of urban renewal dollars per capita secured from the federal government.

Thus, cities with high MPO ratios are found to have little urban renewal, as Hawley predicted, but few active power centers, which finding appears to be inconsistent with his thesis. But since centralization for Hawley referred to the distribution of systemic power while the meaning of centralization here refers to elite participation, this does not mean that Hawley's thesis is necessarily wrong. Systemic power may be highly dispersed, yet few actors or power centers may be active. Still, such an inconsistency does raise interesting questions about the meaning of centralization and about an adequate explanation for this inconsistency.

The second aspect of the concentration of power theory refers to citizen participation. Crain and Rosenthal (1967) argued that the higher the level of education in a community, the higher the political participation, which in turn leads to higher conflict, then stalemate, and consequently less innovation in urban renewal. Their hypothesis links a high level of educational attainment with a low degree of community innovation and output, and posits an intervening process of heightened political participation and consequent community conflict and blockage. The relationship between the percent of adults with a high school education and the four measures of innovation supports this hypothesis (Table 2).

While the empirical relationships between these variables are clear, the meaning of this educational variable and the intervening process may be questioned. Does a high level of educational attainment in a community reflect the presence of many well-educated, relatively affluent persons? Or does it reflect merely the absence of a poor population and less urban decay? Do cities with many well-educated persons have greater citizen participation and consequently more stalemate and inaction, or do they simply have less of an apparent need for urban renewal? Among cities over 25,000 population, the correlations between median education and the upper extremes—percent of adults who have completed college and percent of families with incomes of $10,000 or more per year—are .62 and .63 respectively. But cities with high median education also have fewer adults with less than five years of education (r = −.77), fewer families with incomes of less than $3,000 per year (r = −.53), less housing built before 1929 (r = −.48), and less dilapidated housing (r = −.39). The interpretation of educational level clearly depends on which end of the stratification scale one wants to emphasize, the degree of poverty, low educational attainment and poor housing stock, or the degree to which an articulate middle class is present.

In the analysis of thirty-one case studies of community power (Aiken, 1970), it was found that there were fewer power centers active in cities with high educational levels than in those with low educational levels, although the relationship was not a strong one. Similarly, Clark (1968b) found a positive relationship between the median educational level of a city and the degree of centralization (i.e., fewer elites participating in the four decision areas he examined). If centralization refers to the degree of elite participation, middle-class cities appear to be more centralized than working-class cities. Even if this is true, it is still possible that citizen participation is greater in highly educated cities, thus accounting for less innovation in urban renewal. They, like we, lack direct data on the key intervening variable of participation. Unfortunately, adequate data on political participation do not exist for a large sample of cities. If voting turnout can be regarded as a crude indicator, a recent study (Alford and Lee, 1968) has shown that better-educated cities have *lower* voting turnout than less well educated cities. We find among the 381 cities in our study for which data on voting turnout are available that *higher* voting turnout is associated with greater innovation, although the relationship is not a strong one (see Table 2).

Our empirical relationships between level of education and innovation in urban renewal are quite consistent with the findings of Crain and Rosenthal, although empirical indicators vary slightly. Middle class cities have less urban renewal, but they also apparently have *less* elite participation. If centralization means elite participation, then we find that there is less urban renewal in centralized cities. If centralization means citizen participation (as measured by educational levels) or dispersed systemic power (as measured by the MPO ratio), then we find that there is less urban renewal in decentralized systems. We do not mean to suggest that the well-reasoned theories of Hawley and Crain and Rosenthal are incorrect; we don't have the evidence to demonstrate that. But we do wish to point out the various usages of the term centralization in the literature on comparative community decision-making and to call attention to an inconsistency in conclusions about the relationship between centralization of power and innovation. Clearly, greater conceptual refinement and additional research using more direct measures of mass participation and distribution of systemic power will be necessary to unravel the meaning of an inconsistency such as this.

Fourth, *community differentiation and continuity.* As noted at the outset, the few articles that have used the variables of age and size of cities have disagreed about their interpretation, arguing on the one hand that older and larger cities would be more rigid, more set in their ways, more complex and, therefore, more incapable of action, and, on the other hand, that such cities should be more adaptable, more experienced, more flexible (Dye, 1968; Mohr, 1969).

The data of Table 2 show that older and larger cities are in fact more likely than younger and smaller cities to have innovation in urban renewal. The correlation coefficients of these two characteristics with the various innovation measures are the largest of any in Table 2. Whether or not age and size are merely a reflection of a high level of structural degradation of the housing and building stock, and hence only a reflection of need for urban redevelopment, is a question which will be addressed later.

Fifth, *community integration.* The argument here is that more highly integrated communities, i.e., those with highly developed networks of communication and contact among social groups, should suffer less from paralyzing conflict in the case of a new issue requiring decision, because, on the one hand, channels of communication to work out compromises exist and, on the other hand, isolated factions standing fast on their own positions would not be present (Pinard, 1963). The indicators used for community integration are quite diverse, and include several already mentioned under other headings, but two additional variables—the unemployment level in the community and the amount of migration—are also included in this argument. Pinard's thesis is that high unemployment levels will produce disintegration of community life by reducing attachments to community institutions resulting in high conflict levels and low innovation capabilities. High levels of city growth and in-migration reduce integration because they disrupt long-standing networks of communication and interchange between the organizations comprising the community. He also argues that racial and ethnic diversity and large city size indicate low community integration and that high political participation indicates the bringing into the political system of those least attached to the community, therefore those most likely to oppose innovation.

Table 2 shows that in the case of urban renewal these theoretical expectations, with one exception, are not supported. As already seen, highly ethnic and large cities are *more* likely to innovate, as are cities with high voting turnout. And cities with high unemployment are more likely to have urban renewal, contradicting the hypothesis. Cities with high levels of in-migration have less urban renewal, in accordance with the hypothesis.

Few of the hypothesized relationships drawn from the literature are borne out completely; in the case of those that were supported, we have noted some inconsistencies in the meaning of the concept of centralization. Our main empirical findings are that older and larger cities and those with low levels of

Table 3. Partial correlations between community characteristics and speed of innovation (after enabling legislation) and level of output, controlling for size of community and percent of housing dilapidated in 1950

	Speed of innovation (after enabling legislation)	Log N urban renewal dollars per capita
Political Culture		
Percent of native population of foreign or mixed parentage	−.04	.09*
Percent of elementary school children in private schools	−.02	.11**
Median family income	.23***	−.24**
Percent in the county voting Democratic, 1964	−.03	.02
Political Structure		
Presence of a city-manager form of government	.01	−.12**
Presence of nonpartisan elections	.04	−.18***
Percent of city council elected at large	−.10*	−.03
Number of members of the city council	.09*	.06
Concentration and Diffusion of Community Power		
MPO ratio	.14***	−.28**
Percent of adult population with four years' high school education	.21***	−.34***
Community Continuity		
Age of city (year city reached 10,000 population [log n])	.26***	−.38***
Community Integration		
Percent unemployed	−.14**	.21***
Percent migrant	.08*	−.21***
Poverty and Need		
Percent of families with less than $3,000 income per year	−.19***	.18***
Percent of adults with less than five years' education (log n)	−.24***	.28***
Percent 14–17 year olds in school	.17***	−.22***
Percent population that is nonwhite (log n)	−.25***	.29***

* $p < .05$.
** $p < .01$.
*** $p < .001$.

education and income, high unemployment, fewer managers and officials, and low levels of in-migration and growth are more innovative.

The first question which these results raises is whether or not a community's innovation in urban renewal is simply a function of the poor quality of the housing stock, the deterioration of the central business district, and the generally lower levels of economic growth in older cities. To answer this question, we have included some additional measures of poverty and housing conditions in Table 2. Cities with more dilapidated housing in 1950, more poor families, fewer well-educated families, and more nonwhites were far more likely to have entered the urban renewal program, entered it faster, and have higher levels of participation in the program.

Given the strong and consistent relationships between city size and these need measures and innovation in urban renewal, we may pose the question whether or not many of the previously discussed relationships, regardless of the concepts they were alleged to represent, are not simply functions of a high degree of community need for urban renewal. To answer this question, we computed a series of partial correlations between two measures of innovation and most of the variables in Table 2, controlling for city size and level of dilapidated housing. As shown in Table 3, the relationships between the variables that were strongly related to the innovation measures in Table 2 are still relatively strong when city size and the amount of dilapidated housing are partialed out.

Stepwise, regression analyses which introduced the five "need" measures were first performed, and showed that approximately 18 percent of the variance was accounted for by those measures. Additional variables, each accounting

Table 4. Means of indicators of innovation in urban renewal within region

Region[a]	Number of cities	Presence of urban renewal program	Number of years after 1949 before community entered urban renewal program	Number of years it took after state enabling legislation was present	Number of dollars reserved per capita (natural log)
Northeast	164	82%	9.1	8.9	7.25
South	191	62%	11.5	8.0	5.18
Midwest	219	48%	13.5	12.7	3.86
Far West	102	36%	13.9	13.0	3.10
All Cities	676	58%	11.9	10.6	4.97

[a]The states included in each region are as follows:
Northeast: Maine, New Hampshire, Vermont, Massachusetts, Connecticut, Rhode Island, New York, New Jersey, Pennsylvania, Maryland, Delaware, and District of Columbia.
South: Texas, Oklahoma, Kansas, Missouri, Arkansas, Louisiana, Alabama, Mississippi, Florida, Georgia, North Carolina, South Carolina, Virginia, West Virginia, Kentucky, and Tennessee.
Midwest: Ohio, Indiana, Illinois, Michigan, Wisconsin, Minnesota, Iowa, North Dakota, South Dakota, Nebraska, Montana, Idaho, Colorado, Utah, Wyoming, Arizona, and New Mexico.
Far West: California, Oregon, Washington, Nevada, Alaska, and Hawaii.

for at least 1 percent of the variance, were age of city, city size, percent migrant, percent foreign stock, and median family income (listed in order of selection).

A few words are necessary on the relationships between both the independent and dependent variables and the regional location of a city. Cities in the Northeast are most likely to have urban renewal, followed in order by cities in the South, the Midwest, and the Far West, as shown in Table 4. Similarly, Northeastern cities were faster in applying for and more successful in obtaining money for urban renewal. But these cities are also likely to be older, poorer, and have higher levels of ethnicity and out-migration. The question can be raised whether all of these relationships are accounted for by regional location of a city.

Although we cannot present the data in detail, the major findings hold up when they are examined within the four regions. Age and size of city are closely related to all four measures of innovation in all four regions, as are education, income, MPO ratio, and nonwhite composition, with only a few exceptions. Almost all of the original relationships that were low remain low in all four regions, except for a few cells for which we have only *ad hoc* explanations. Political structure, Democratic vote, and voting turnout are significantly associated with innovation only in the Far West, for example. Our general conclusion, however, is that the findings previously discussed are, with some exceptions, also true even within regions in spite of strong regional variations in innovation rates (see Aiken and Alford, 1970a).

We have also examined the correlation coefficients between the various independent variables and the speed and output measures among the 372 cities that had ever entered the urban renewal program. This is a very conservative procedure since it excludes cities that never innovated in urban renewal. We would expect the correlations between the various independent variables and the speed and output measures of innovation to be attenuated. While the size of the correlations among this subset of 372 cities that have ever innovated is indeed reduced, the major findings remain intact. Age, size, nonwhite composition, low income and low education are still related in the same direction to the speed and output measures. Evidently the same factors that contribute to innovation in the first place also affect the speed with which innovating cities enter the urban renewal program and their level of outputs in the program.

But even if we know which are the best predictors or that our results are not simply a function of the size and level of need, regional variations, or results produced by including noninnovating cities in our study, we still do not know why and how some communities enter the urban renewal program and others do not. The mind is not set at rest by such findings. In the first place the relationships are not strong. In the second place the condition of housing or the age of a city does not tell us anything about the intervening processes which enabled some cities to displace its blacks for new businesses or expensive apartments while others did not use urban renewal in this way.

Structural differentiation and community innovation

Let us start negatively by reviewing the rejected explanations. Global properties of the political ethos of majorities and integration seemed to fare most poorly. While the zero-order predictions of Hawley and Crain and Rosenthal were as predicted, we have shown that even these relationships can be removed by partialing procedures. That is, hypotheses referring to properties of the city as a whole rather than properties of groups or organizations making up that city seemed (1) to use concepts most distant from the available data and (2) to be supported most weakly by the data. If anything, the data point in the opposite direction. Cities that appear to be heterogeneous, differentiated, and fragmented—as indicated by ethnicity, a large working class, nonwhite composition, size, and the qualitative data on centralization (elite participation) in the works of Clark (1968b) and Aiken (1970)—are most likely to have innovated in urban renewal. The same studies show that the more groups and actors participating in current decisions, the higher is the level of innovation and outputs.

Additional and more directly relevant data support the proposition that the more differentiated the organizational structure of a city, the more innovative it will be. A more direct measure of organizational complexity than simply city size would be a count of the number of organizations of various types which play some role in community life. We have data on three such types of organizations—manufacturing firms, banks, and trade unions—although only for a subsample of cities in each case. Unfortunately, we lack data on other more crucial types of organizations such as political parties, voluntary associations or the local government.

Not only the sheer number of organizations may be important, but also the number having sufficient resources to affect critically the course of community innovation. For this reason we have chosen the number of manufacturing establishments with 100 or more employees and the number of independent banks with assets of at least fifty million dollars as our measures of organizational complexity and differentiation. Unfortunately, the unionization data cannot be treated in exactly the same way. But because larger firms are more likely to be unionized and because the data include all establishments in which a majority of the plant workers are unionized, we believe that this measure is an appropriate indicator of the organizational complexity of a community.

These data relating structural differentiation and community innovation are presented in Table 5. Because the level and character of unionization can be presumed to be different in the North and the South, the data for that variable are presented by region. The results are consistent with our expectations. The more manufacturing establishments, the more independent banks, and the more unionized plants that a city has, the more innovative it is.

These measures of structural differentiation can be regarded as ways of spelling out more precisely what it means to be a large city as far as capacity to

Table 5.   Differentiation of economic structure and innovation in urban renewal in American cities[a]

	Manufacturing/ Number of establishments of size 100 or more	Banking/ Number of independent banks with assets of $50 million or more	Unionization/ Percent of plant workers unionized among all industries	
			North	South
Innovation				
Presence of urban renewal	.27***	.33***	.22*	.33**
Speed of Innovation				
Number of years after 1949 it took the city to enter the urban renewal program	−.42***	−.46***	−.15	−.48***
Number of years it took after state enabling legislation was present	−.33***	−.37***	−.03	−.03
Outputs				
Log N urban renewal dollars reserved per capita	.32***	.36***	.24**	.40**
	N = (217)	(217)	(77)	(35)

[a]Source: Manufacturing and banking data are available for the 217 nonsuburban cities in the size range 25,000 to 250,000 population which had 20% or more of their labor force in manufacturing in 1960. The unionization of manufacturing establishments is available for 84 metropolitan areas, which provide an estimate of unionization in 112 cities within them. See Michael Aiken, "Economic Concentration and Community Innovation," unpublished manuscript, 1969, for details on the construction of the measures. The banking data were taken from *Polk's Bank Directory* (Nashville: R. L. Polk and Co., March, 1966). The data on unions are drawn from Bulletin No. 1465-86, Bureau of Labor Statistics, U.S. Department of Labor, Washington, D.C., October 1966, titled *Wages and Related Benefits: Part I, 84 Metropolitan Areas, 1965−66*. The measure is the approximate percent of all plant workers employed in establishments in which a union contract covered a majority of workers during the period July 1964 to June 1966. We have assigned the degree of unionization in the SMSA to the urban place as the best estimate we have on the unionization of the city itself.
* $p < .05$.
** $p < .01$.
*** $p < .001$.

innovate is concerned. Large cities have a greater diversity of social organizations, and they also have greater innovation.

An alternative explanation

Because we find none of the previously discussed theories completely satisfactory, we here propose one approach that seems to be more consistent with the previous findings. Our alternative explanation of the findings can be only a suggestion since we do not have the empirical data to test directly our ideas. Therefore, we shall only suggest here some of the concepts that appear to us at this time to be most relevant in explaining innovation in such decision-areas as urban renewal, public housing, and the war on poverty.

Our tentative alternative explanation is that such innovations are a product of the nature and state of interorganizational networks in communities (cf. Turk, 1970). Such networks are properties of community systems that have developed historically through the interaction of organizational units and their leaders. If the population of a community is relatively stable, these interorganizational networks are not likely to be disrupted by the continuous influx of new citizens and organizations, and thus greater potential exists for increasing their capacity for coordination over time.

The degree of historical continuity in a community structure—especially as it affects interorganizational networks—may also influence innovation. Presumably older cities have had a longer time for existing organizations to work out patterns of interactions, alliances, factions, or coalitions. In such communities the state of knowledge in the community system about the orientations, needs, and probable reactions to varying proposals for community action is likely to be quite high, thus increasing the probability of developing a sufficiently high level of coordination in order to implement successfully a community innovation.

The degree of structural differentiation and complexity of a community may also influence innovation for two reasons. First, larger cities are likely to have more organizations devoted to specific kinds of decision-areas—i.e., more likely to have a redevelopment agency, a housing agency, a community action agency, a city development agency for Model Cities, welfare councils, and other community decision organizations. Such organizations are likely to have larger, more specialized, and more professional staffs to provide the technical, administrative, and political knowledge required to innovate successfully, not only within their organizations, but also in the activation of interorganizational relationships and establishment of critical coalitions (cf. Mohr, 1969). Secondly, it is precisely in the larger, more structurally differentiated communities that coalitions that can implement an innovation will be easiest to establish. If we assume that only a limited number of organizational units need to be mobilized to bring about a successful innovation, then it follows that in large, highly differentiated communities a lower proportion of the available organizations will participate in such decisions, and that there will be wider latitude in selecting organizations for these critical coalitions. In other words, the "issue arena" involved in the innovation will require the participation of only a few of the organizations that exist in the community system. In one sense, this proposition is simply a spelling out of what is meant by "structural differentiation" or "functional specialization." The more highly differentiated or specialized a community system, the higher the proportion of decisions that are likely to be made by subsystems and the less likely the entire system will be activated on most issues.

The extent to which the interorganizational field is "turbulent" may also influence innovation (cf. Terreberry, 1968). Where many people are moving out of the city, the existing historically developed network of organizational relationships may be relatively undisturbed, except insofar as out-migration indicates an economic or perhaps political crisis which existing institutions cannot handle. Conversely, where many people are moving in, bringing with them different ideas about the appropriate functions of local government, and perhaps creating demands for new services, newly established organizations may be severely limited since they are less likely to be in an organizational network which can aid in achieving an adequate level of coordination for a proposed community innovation.

We thus suggest that three properties—structural differentiation, the accumulation of experience and information, and the stability and extensiveness of interorganizational networks—may contribute to the capacity of a community to innovate. Let us turn to more concrete concepts and hypotheses that might be consistent with this particular approach.

Community systems can be conceived of as interorganizational fields in which the basic interacting units are *centers of power.* A center of power can be defined as an organization which possesses a high degree of autonomy, resources, and cohesion. The linking mechanisms among centers of power in a community system we call *interfaces* (see Mott, 1970). Interfaces are not only the current set of interorganizational relationships in the community, but more importantly include the historical accumulation of knowledge and experience among various centers of power. An *issue arena* is the organization set (Evan, 1966) of centers of power which must be activated on a given issue in order to effectuate a decision.

We hypothesize that the greater the number of centers of power in a community and the more pervasive and encompassing the interfaces, the higher the probability of innovation in a given issue arena. In other words, the more choice among acting units in the system—centers of power—and the greater the state of information about organizational actors, the higher the probability that a minimum coalition can be formed. For many issues this will mean the creation of an organization whose specific task is the implementation of the decision to innovate. Warren (1967a, b) refers to these as "community decision organizations," and he cites community action agencies, housing authorities, welfare councils, health departments as examples. The community decision organization is a special type of center of power whose mission is to supervise the planning, coordination, and delivery of the innovated activity. The professional staffs of such organizations are likely to generate further innovations.

The structural conditions in the community that lead to the introduction of an innovation in a given activity—organizational differentiation and historical continuity—may not be the factors that are most conducive to high levels of performance by community decision organizations. Once the innovation has been introduced, the community decision organization may seek to develop relatively tightly controlled relationships with cooperating organizations in their issue arena and thus gain legitimacy for an exclusive mandate from other community decision organizations. If so, communities with high levels of performance in various community action activities may well be those in which relatively autonomous issue arenas have emerged. It may be that the structures of relationships within such subsystems are indeed "centralized" in the sense of a given organization having strong control over units within that issue arena. If this is true, it would suggest that Hawley's thesis may be appropriate if a community subsystem is taken as the unit of analysis.

It is possible, however, that this model is only applicable to decisions for which the major actors are organizations. To the extent that private citizens are mobilized on a given decision—such as in the case of fluoridation—this model may not be appropriate, or at least it may be incomplete.

What we have suggested is a two-stage process in which the overall state of a community system may be most important for understanding the community's propensity for innovation across a wide spectrum of issues, but that the appropriate analytic unit for understanding specific innovations, as well as performance in such innovations, is a subsystem of a community in which the central actor is the community decision organization. Our data do not permit us to test the validity of assertions such as these; that would require a completely different type of comparative study. But this particular approach appears to us to be as consistent with the data presented in this paper as any of the theories we have examined, if not more so.

References

Aiken, Michael. 1970. "The distribution of community power: Structural bases and social consequences." In Michael Aiken and Paul E. Mott (eds.), *The Structure of Community Power: An Anthology.* New York: Random House.

Aiken, Michael, and Robert R. Alford. 1970a. "Community structure and innovation: The case of public housing." *American Political Science Review* 64, September.

———. 1970b. "Community structure and the war on poverty: Theoretical and methodological considerations." In Mattei Dogan (ed.), *Studies in Political Ecology.* Paris.

Alford, Robert R., with the collaboration of Harry M. Scoble. 1969. *Bureaucracy and Participation: Political Cultures in Four Wisconsin Cities.* Chicago: Rand McNally.

Alford, Robert R., and Eugene C. Lee. 1968. "Voting turnout in American cities." *American Political Science Review* 62 (September): 796–813.

Banfield, Edward C., and James Q. Wilson. 1963. *City Politics.* Cambridge: Harvard University Press.

Barnett, H.G. 1953. *Innovation: The Basis of Cultural Change.* New York: McGraw-Hill.

Bellush, Jewel, and Murray Hausknecht. 1967. *Urban Renewal: People, Politics, and Planning.* New York: Doubleday Anchor Books.

Clark, Terry N. 1968a. "Community structure and decision-making." Pp. 91–126 in Terry N. Clark (ed.), *Community Structure and Decision-Making: Comparative Analyses.* San Francisco: Chandler.

———. 1968b. "Community structure, decision-making, budget expenditures, and urban renewal in 51 American communities." *American Sociological Review* 33 (August): 576–593.

Coleman, James S. 1957. *Community Conflict.* New York: Free Press.

Crain, Robert L., and Donald B. Rosenthal. 1967. "Community status as a dimension of local decision-making." *American Sociological Review* 32 (December): 970–984.

Crain, Robert L., Elihu Katz, and Donald B. Rosenthal. 1969. *The Politics of Community Conflict: The Fluoridation Decision.* Indianapolis: Bobbs-Merrill.

Dahl, Robert A. 1961. *Who Governs? Power and Democracy in an American City.* New Haven: Yale University Press.

Duggar, George. 1961. "The relationship of local government structures to urban renewal." *Law and Contemporary Problems* 26 (Winter): 49–69.

Dye, Thomas R. 1968. "Urban school segregation: A comparative analysis." *Urban Affairs Quarterly* 4 (December): 141–165.

Elazar, Daniel J. 1967. " 'Fragmentation' and local organizational response to federal-city programs." *Urban Affairs Quarterly* 4 (June): 30–46.

Evan, William. 1966. "The organization-set: Toward a theory of interorganizational relations." Pp. 173–191 in James D. Thompson (ed.), *Approaches to Organizational Design.* Pittsburgh: University of Pittsburgh Press.

Froman, Lewis A., Jr. 1968. "An analysis of public policies in cities." *Journal of Politics* 29 (February): 94–108.

Gold, David. 1969. "Statistical tests and substantive significance." *American Sociologist* 4 (February): 42–46.

Greenstone, J. David, and Paul E. Peterson. 1968. "Reformers, machines, and the war on poverty." Pp. 267–292 in James Q. Wilson (ed.), *City Politics and Public Policy.* New York: Wiley.

Hawley, Amos H. 1963. "Community power structure and urban renewal success." *American Journal of Sociology* 68 (January): 422–431.

Hunter, Floyd. 1953. *Community Power Structure.* Chapel Hill: University of North Carolina Press. Anchor edition, 1963.

Jacob, Herbert, and Michael Lipsky. 1968. "Outputs, structure, and power: An assessment of the changes in the study of state and local politics." *Journal of Politics* 30 (May): 510–538.

Lineberry, Robert L., and Edmund P. Fowler. 1967. "Reformism and public policies in American cities." *American Political Science Review* 61 (September): 701–716.

Lowi, Theodore J. 1964a. *At the Pleasure of the Mayor.* New York: Free Press.

———. 1964b. "American business, public policy, case studies, and political theory." *World Politics* 16 (July): 677–715.

Mansfield, Edwin. 1963. "The speed of response of firms to new techniques." *Quarterly Journal of Economics* 22 (May): 290–311.

Mohr, Lawrence B. 1969. "Determinants of innovation in organization." *American Political Science Review* 63 (March): 111–126.

Morrison, Denton E., and Ramon E. Henkel. 1969. "Significance tests reconsidered." *American Sociologist* 4 (May): 131–139.

Mott, Paul E. 1970. "Configurations of power." In Michael Aiken and Paul E. Mott (eds.), *The Structure of Community Power: An Anthology.* New York: Random House.

Pinard, Maurice. 1963. "Structural attachments and political support in urban politics: A case of a fluoridation referendum." *American Journal of Sociology* 68 (March): 513–526.

Rogers, Everett M. 1962. *Diffusion of Innovations.* New York: Free Press.

Salisbury, Robert H. 1968. "The analysis of public policy: A search for theories and roles." Pp. 151–175 in Austin Ranney (ed.), *Political Science and Public Policy.* Chicago: Markham.

Sharkansky, Ira. 1969. *Spending in the American States.* Chicago: Rand McNally.

Sogg, Wilton S., and Warren Wertheimer. 1967. "Legal and governmental issues in urban renewal." Pp. 126–188 in James Q. Wilson (ed.), *Urban Renewal: The Record and the Controversy.* Cambridge: The M.I.T. Press.

Stinchcombe, Arthur. 1968. *Constructing Social Theories.* New York: Harcourt, Brace and World.

Straits, Bruce C. 1965. "Community adoption and implementation of urban renewal." *American Journal of Sociology* 71 (July): 77–82.

Terreberry, Shirley. 1968. "The evolution of organizational environments." *Administrative Science Quarterly* 12 (March): 590–613.

Thompson, Victor A. 1965. "Bureaucracy and innovation." *Administrative Science Quarterly* 10 (June): 1–20.

27

WILLIAM KORNHAUSER, Power and Participation in the Local Community

Let me begin with a paradox: those elements in a community that do *not* have power often win controversies. For example, when a fluoridation controversy breaks out, the powerful and prestigeful people generally are arrayed on the side of fluoridation—yet fluoridation often loses.

In order to understand this kind of situation, it is necessary to distinguish between the fate of community problems under routine conditions and during crisis situations. Most of the literature on power and participation is concerned with what happens on a day-to-day basis in the life of a community. However, you cannot understand what happens in a community in times of crisis by understanding what happens under routine conditions.

As we explore the character of participation in community controversies, it will be helpful to keep in mind two considerations. First, the problem is not to abolish controversy or conflict in the community; controversy and conflict are the lifeblood of a democratic community, and their suppression would be the antithesis of democracy and freedom. Secondly, a democratic community is not *necessarily* one in which there is continuous participation in community affairs on the part of large numbers of people. The most active populations in the world are populations in totalitarian societies, and this fact should throw doubt on the old idea that high levels of participation entail democratic practices.

What we know about fluoridation controversies fits in very well with what we know about other kinds of controversies, and therefore will serve as an illustration of the general problem.

In 1955, of 104 communities in which there had been referenda on fluoridation, the issue lost in fifty-seven cases, or more than 50 percent of the time. There are, of course, many more communities which have adopted fluoridation without any referenda—in 1955, something over 1,000. Most of the latter cases were handled in a routine manner, but many of the referenda were held under conditions of widespread tension. Let us examine the result of two studies of fluoridation referenda which involved a severe community crisis.

The fluoridation controversy in Northampton, Massachusetts, developed in the following manner (as reported by the Mosners in *Scientific American*, February 9, 1955):

William Kornhauser, "Power and Participation in the Local Community," *Health Education Monograph No. 6*, pp. 28–37. Copyright 1959 by the Society of Public Health Educators, Inc., Oakland, California. Reprinted by permission.

A local committee of a dental society recommended fluoridation after an investigation of its merits made at the mayor's request. The city council held hearings, voted approval and appropriated money to carry it out. A leading opponent of fluoridation, a professional chemist, was elected mayor three months later. At that time he tried to halt appropriations for fluoridation, and secured an injunction for this purpose. The injunction was subsequently withdrawn, but in the meantime the opponents of fluoridation had obtained the signatures of 10 percent of the town voters on a petition demanding a referendum, and the referendum was placed on the ballot the following November. At that election, fluoridation lost two to one.

The following observations can help us to understand the defeat of fluoridation. First, the leaders of the pro-fluoridation side—mainly professional people and more specifically dentists, but also, later, public officials—did not go all-out in fighting for fluoridation. They did not do so—I am reading between the lines of Mosner's report—because they did not want to alienate large numbers of people. You cannot fight very hard if you are a dentist, for example, because you lose those patients who are against fluoridation. You cannot fight very hard if you are a public official because you lose votes. The opponents of fluoridation, on the other hand, are generally those *without* commitments or responsibilities in the community, and are therefore capable of putting on a much stronger fight. They are not exposed to the usual restraints on responsible people who have economic and political interests in the community. So the anti-fluoridation forces in Northampton really put on a vigorous campaign, and the pro-fluoridation forces did not. The anti-fluoridation forces kept up an active telephone and letter-writing campaign, published ads in the newspapers, circulated rumors, and so on.

The second observation I wish to call to your attention is that the anti-fluoridation group—and again this is very typical—treated fluoridation as a *conspiracy*. Among other things, they accused the American Dental Association and the United States Public Health Service of having in effect been caught up in a conspiracy by the Aluminum Company of America, which presumably was going to benefit by being able to sell a waste product for the purpose of fluoridation. Another indication of the conspiratorial view of the anti-fluoridation forces was given in an ad they ran in the local newspaper the night before the election. Let me quote from that ad: "Do you know that fluoridation is mass medication regardless of the needs or wishes of the people? that fluoride is a poisonous waste from aluminum manufacture? that fluoride is a powerful poison? that fluoride could play into the hands of our enemies? America is too big to be conquered by invasion, but with fluoridation machines at the reservoirs the population in important centers could easily be wiped out or made non-resistant." This belief in a conspiracy is crucial; you will find it again and again in community controversies. The idea presented is that the "little people" are fighting against certain mysterious forces that can create havoc and destruction among us.

The third observation is this: the people who supported the anti-fluoridation group—this is based on a survey of voters before the election—were, on the average, those of less education, lower occupational status, and lower incomes.

In summary, the pro-fluoridation forces were led by the powerful and prestigeful people in the community and local government, while the anti-fluoridation forces were led by people who did not occupy positions of responsibility in the community. As a result, the anti-fluoridation forces were much less restrained than the pro-fluoridation forces in fighting for their position. The anti-fluoridation forces made their main appeal by charging the pro-fluoridation forces with conspiracy. The strongest response to this appeal came from the less educated and poorer section of the community.

An unpublished study of a California community conducted by Arnold Rogow of the University of Iowa includes additional material on fluoridation controversies.

Rogow found that the pro-fluoridation forces were community leaders, and the anti-fluoridation forces were the alienated and weakly attached elements of the community. The main community leadership was made up of business executives and managers of new industries. These leaders exercised their influence primarily through civic clubs and the Chamber of Commerce. The city council was also very closely related to the Chamber of Commerce, with many of the same people involved. On the other side, certain individuals were opposed to both the personnel and the policies of the current administration. To quote Rogow, "The opposition was for the most part based on grievances and grudges which have not yet been effectively merged into either organization or program, but certain broad groupings of opposition opinion had begun to form."

These groupings are largely confined to elements that make up what are termed the "discontinued classes." The "discontinued classes" include the older residents who have found it difficult to adjust to the fast pace of development. These are people who, by and large, have been left out as the community modernized; for the most part, they are members of the "old middle class," especially small farmers and small businessmen. These classes Rogow calls the "discontinued classes" because of the revolution that has been taking place in our society over the past several generations—the growth of large-scale organization and the increasing tendency for people to be employees rather than entrepreneurs. Most people in our society today work for others, and this includes, of course, even the top executives in big business. One hundred years ago, our society was based primarily on people who owned productive property, either farm or business. Today, as Peter Drucker has said, we are an "employee society." This transformation has been very hard on those who still seek to make their way on the basis of family capitalism. As a consequence, these people very often harbor strong resentment against the modernization of the community.

Fluoridation is closely identified with modernization. It represents a scientifically validated program for the community. Therefore, it very readily brings out the resentment of people who have suffered by virtue of modernization. So, to return to the California community, Rogow found that the orchard growers and the farmers, the small retailers, etc., expressed strong resentment against community leadership, which was increasingly composed of the new businessmen and industrial managers. The retailers were made insecure by the larger brand stores and by shopping centers; the small farmers were made insecure by industries buying up the orchards; both retailers and farmers experienced loss of power and status in the community.

These people challenged the community leadership on two issues, and both, I think, are very nice illustrations of their anti-modernization orientation. The first issue concerned the integration and establishment of civil service in the police and fire departments. Prior to integration, both the police and fire departments were immersed in politics, patronage and favoritism. The volunteer fire department, in fact, functioned as a kind of social club for the old residents, from which the newcomers to the community were excluded. When the new leaders won integration and civil service, this change immediately undercut and antagonized the older residents, who were by and large the small property owners I have mentioned. So, to quote Rogow again, "The integration of the fire department provoked sharp protests from the individuals affected and their supporters, and was eventually responsible for the wholesale resignation of the volunteer fire department. The older residents in particular were opposed to integration, and the action was used by others to illustrate the remoteness of the city government from the 'true spirit' of the community."

The second issue revolved around fluoridation. The issue began after the city council unanimously proposed buying two water fluoridating machines for the community. The Chamber of Commerce, the local newspaper, the dentists and others in the community were behind fluoridation. Within a week or two after the council's decision, a citywide committee sprang up among the older residents who opposed fluoridation. The city council had not expected opposition, and was initially unprepared to deal with it. The opposition was strong enough to force an immediate referendum.

When we look at the arguments used against fluoridation, we again find elements of the conspiratorial view of society. In this case, a strong racist element was introduced, namely that fluoridation was a Jewish plot to weaken Christian Americans; as well as being destructive of bone tissue, a cause of cancer, etc. The most effective action of the antifluoridation committee was a telephone campaign directed at 2,000 registered voters. The vote was 1,565 for fluoridation and 2,057 against. The local turnout was the heaviest in the history of the town's elections. Forty percent of the voters participated as compared with an average of 15 percent in previous elections.

Ordinarily in local elections the turnout is low, consisting primarily of the most active citizens, those most attached to community affairs. James Coleman writes (*Community Conflict*): "We would expect that when an issue becomes heated, creating a large turnout, the vote results would include a larger component of persons uninvolved and unattached to community affairs. These 'added' voters, free to vent their aggressions against the administration, would be perhaps less in favor of administration-sponsored fluoridation plans. Thus . . . the higher the turnout the less likely that a fluoridation measure will pass." A tabulation of the results of fluoridation referenda held between 1951 and 1955 shows that where the turnout was less than 10 percent, fluoridation won 58 percent of the time; but where the turnout was at least three times greater—over 30 percent—fluoridation won only 37 percent of the time and lost 63 percent of the time. In other words, in a majority of cases fluoridation won when the turnout was low and lost when the turnout was high.

To return to the California community, several of the anti-fluoridation leaders were close friends or relations of men who were in the former police and fire departments. They were, again, the older residents of the community, the ones who by and large were feeling persecuted by and resentful of the new leadership. Their supporters also were drawn disproportionately from the "discontinued classes." A comparison of the six precincts that were most in favor of fluoridation with the six precincts that were most against it shows that the pro-fluoridation people were likely to be the newer residents with the better homes and the more active record of participation in community organization. The older, anti-fluoridation voters did not belong to community organizations, and the average value of their houses was about $4,000 less than that of the pro-fluoridation voters.

In summary, fluoridation forces tend to be represented by the leading elements in the community, while anti-fluoridation forces tend to be represented by the more alienated elements, especially those alienated by the modernization of the community. The anti-fluoridation forces often win, in spite of their general lack of power and prestige, because in many cases they are able to mobilize people who, like themselves, are only poorly attached to the community.

The effects of social isolation

I now wish to consider the more general pattern of cause and effect which underlies such cases as the fluoridation controversy. The central factor is the strength or weakness of community attachment.

There are two main consequences of the lack of community attachment for participation in community affairs. Usually the lack of attachment to community groups leads to apathy, but under critical conditions it may lead to extremist responses.

Under routine conditions, people who do not participate in any kind of social group in the community—civic clubs, trade unions, church-affiliated groups, or even social and athletic clubs—tend to be indifferent toward everything beyond their immediate private concerns. The way people get interested in what is happening outside their private world is by being exposed to others who have such interests. Whole segments of communities, however, having no such contacts, develop little interest in the larger world. People who belong even to a social club are more likely to develop interest in community affairs than are people who do not have group attachments of any kind.

Furthermore, people who do not participate in any way in the community are much less likely to understand what is going on, and this lack has particularly serious consequences. For when a crisis does appear and these people become involved in community controversy, their actions and opinions are not tempered by an understanding of the true nature of the situation. Thus you get highly irrational and extremist interpretations of events, such as the belief in a conspiracy.

Coleman, in *Community Conflict,* concludes from his analysis of community conflicts all over the country—whether they involved fluoridation, a school issue, a riot as in Peekskill, or a desegregation—that:

> People who feel apart and unidentified are quickest to overstep the bounds of legitimate methods and carry the dispute into disruptive channels. When there are few or none who are identified, then there are essentially no norms to restrain the opposing sides [in the controversy]. Conversely, if most people and organizations in the community are identified with the community as a whole, then the potentially disruptive effects of the dispute are felt by all; there are conscious attempts at reconciliation.

Another measure of the difference between attached and unattached people with respect to community affairs is provided in a study made by Samuel A. Stouffer of Harvard on the question, broadly speaking, of who in the community is willing to support the exercise of free speech by nonconformists. Stouffer asked such questions as, "Are you willing to permit a socialist to speak in a public hall?" or "Are you willing to permit an atheist to teach at a university?" or "Should a communist be allowed to talk over the radio?" His most interesting finding was that community leaders of all kinds were much more tolerant of nonconformists than the general run of the community. Mayors of the communities studied in 60 percent of the cases expressed relatively strong support for the constitutional liberties of nonconformists. Among presidents of school boards, 62 percent were relatively tolerant; 79 percent of the presidents of library boards; 70 percent of chairmen of Republican county central committees; 64 percent of chairmen of Democratic county central committees; 65 percent of presidents of the local chamber of commerce; 62 percent of the local labor leaders; 85 percent of the local newspaper publishers; 82 percent of the chairmen of community chests; 77 percent of the presidents of the bar associations; 68 percent of the presidents of the PTA; 49 percent of presidents of women's clubs; 48 percent of the regents of the DAR; and 46 percent of the commanders of the American Legion. The average score for all community leaders was 66 percent. But, taking a cross-section of the populations of these same communities, only 32 percent expressed a relatively strong willingness to support the rights of nonconformists.

If you look at the results of public opinion polls of the general population, you will find that the differences in support of civil liberties are directly related to the levels of education and income of the people involved. That is, people with lower income and education and a manual occupation are by and large less supportive of civil liberties than are those with more education, higher income, and a business, professional, or white-collar occupation. For example, on the question of opposing the right of newspapers to criticize the government, 41 percent of those with less than a high school education would oppose this right of newspapers, whereas 27 percent of those with some high school and 14 percent of those with some college education would do likewise. Among those opposing job equality for Negroes we find 13 percent with college education and over twice as many among those with less than high school education. And this, by the way, is true not only of this country; public opinion data from Germany, Japan and Australia, among others, show the same patterns.

People in the lower economic and educational brackets also have fewer attachments to the community. If you study the membership of almost any kind of community group, you will find that almost all the leaders and active members are middle class. People in the working class have very few memberships or attachments to the community. The tendency for people in the lower classes is not even to have frequent association with their co-workers, compared with people in the middle class. Thus, the higher the status, the more people interact with their fellows. There is only one kind of interaction that seems to be at least as frequent, if not more so, in the lower classes—and that is socializing with relatives.

People who have fewer attachments to the community are less likely to support the rules according to which community affairs are generally conducted. Such people are less likely to support the right of those with whom they do not agree to express their opinions. And such people are by and large disproportionately represented in the lower educational and occupational strata. The people who occupy lower status in the community are especially susceptible to the belief that all personal misfortunes are due to conspiracies against them, and that the world is divided into people who "run things" and people "like us." They are readily attracted to ideologies that paint moral issues in rigid and absolutistic colors.

I do not mean to suggest that the people I call "social isolates" are completely without social ties of any kind. What I am suggesting is that people can be considered to be social isolates insofar as the community is concerned when they have no ties to community affairs but only to family and friends. Most of the lower-class social isolates do have family ties. There is a very important difference between complete personal isolation and isolation from the community. Mental health deteriorates under complete personal isolation; but the health of the community deteriorates only when many people are isolated from the community itself, even though they have family ties.

The effects of centralization

It is within the experience of all of us that development of our society is in the direction of increasing concentration of decision-making on the national level, which means the loss of considerable local autonomy and self-government on the community level. This change has been due primarily to the sheer force of industrialization and urbanization. The consequences of this shift in power from the local to the national scene are many. It is much more difficult, even for people who are attached to community groups, let alone for people without such attachments, to acquire information and understanding concerning the larger society. Not only in the political realm but also in all other realms we find the tendency for national leadership to take over functions formerly fulfilled by local groups. For example, the national union takes over functions of the local union, so that even those who are members of self-governing groups are more and more removed from effective participation and control in their own organization. It is increasingly difficult for people to order affairs in their own communities and associations in the face of increasing centralization of all kinds of organized group life. The problem has been well-stated by Robert Nisbet in his book *Quest for Community:*

> The labor unions, legal or medical associations, or the church will become as centralized and as remote as the national state itself unless these great organizations are rooted in a smaller relationship which gives meaning to the ends of the large association. To conceive of a great labor union, industrial enterprise or church as an association of individual members is but to intensify the processes of atomization which such associations can and should counteract. No large association will remain an object of personal allegiance, no matter how crucial its goals may be, unless it is consequently sensitive to the existence of the informal but potent relationships of which it is really composed. It has surely become evident by this time that the most successful and allegiance-evoking business and cultural associations in modern life are those that regard themselves as associations of groups, not of raw individuals. To recognize the existence of informal social relationships, to keep central purposes constantly alive in these small groups, and to work toward the increased spontaneity and

autonomy of these groups is the cardinal responsibility of the great private associations. Only thus will the large formal associations remain important agencies of order and freedom in democracy, only thus will they succeed in arresting and banishing the augmenting processes of insecurity and moral isolation which now paralize individual wills and strike at the roots of stable culture.

This comment raises the question as to how new modes of social participation and association develop in the modern community. I shall conclude by briefly indicating three areas of development in our society which may presage new modes of community participation. One is the tremendous growth of suburbanism since the war. New forms of community may grow out of the proliferation of suburbs, because the suburbs are small relative to the cities from which their residents came, and also because they are new and socially homogenous communities. An increasing number of studies on the quality of suburban living are being undertaken to find out whether the new suburbs favor the development of genuine community life or rather only a compulsive "social ethic."

A second area concerns the increase in leisure time. The fact is very clear that leisure is upon us with a vengeance for increasing portions of our population, and may, like atomic energy, provide either a new source of creative energy or a disintegrating influence on the community. In the history of human society, work has been a major link between men and their community, and has taken up most of their waking hours. Yet within the next fifty years, if we live in peace, it is possible for the great bulk of our industrial labor force to be working something like a twenty-hour week. The threat and the promise of that much leisure time is tremendous. If it ends in extreme apathy, it may become a powerful force undermining the social order. On the other hand, it may result in more creative use of one's time than has been possible in industrial work— which, no matter what you do to improve it, remains a damnably boring daily experience for a great many people. So the new leisure class is going to be the industrial workers, while the new "working class" will be composed of professional people.

This thought leads me to a third area of development in our society, the growth of the professions. In all kinds of organizations, as well as in the older professions, there is developing a class of people who are conscious of their special training and competence, and by virtue of that fact are developing close ties with one another as fellow professionals. Even in business there is a tendency toward mutual identification among executives, as opposed to identification with the company—although this is still only an incipient trend. Of course this kind of thing has long been evident among such professions as medicine and law. I am sure it is happening among public health people, as well as among social workers, scientists, and so forth. This tendency to professionalize is both a threat and a

promise. It is a promise insofar as it favors higher standards and greater responsibility on the part of those who deal in services for the community.

28

JON VAN TIL & SALLY BOULD VAN TIL, Citizen Participation in Social Policy: The End of the Cycle?

The participation of citizens is a basic aspect of liberal democracy. The process
of democratic governance is often valued more highly than its end product, as
Mill (1875:39) argued: "The most important point of excellence which any
form of government can possess is to promote the virtue and intelligence of the
people themselves." To Mill, and the Anglo-American tradition that followed
him, political participation was to be a great force for citizen education as well
as system legitimation.

The concept of "citizen participation" is a uniquely American variant
of the general concept of participation. It has become a key element in the
postwar development of programs to contend with the crisis in the American
city and society—particularly in the programs of urban renewal, community
action, and model cities. However, the poverty program, with its bold attempt
to foster citizen participation, has inspired as thorough a denunciation of the
concept of citizen participation as was brought forth by the urban renewal
program. Social scientists and government officials seem to have arrived at
similar conclusions from these two experiences: citizen participation in social
policy defeats the instrumental goals of policy reform and implementation.

A typology of meanings of citizen participation

This paper distinguishes between six forms of citizen participation in recent
social policy and notes certain patterns by which two modes appear to predominate. In urban renewal programs, for example, the concept was originally
interpreted to mean the involvement of civic leaders in an advisory capacity to
the local planning agency. Over time, however, the concept began to include the
activities of ordinary citizens in quite different roles. We contend that the
variety of meanings of citizen participation in urban renewal may be compre-

Jon Van Til and Sally Bould Van Til, "Citizen Participation in Social Policy: The End of the
Cycle?" *Social Problems,* vol. 17 (Winter 1970), pp. 313–323. Reprinted by permission of
the authors and the Society for the Study of Social Problems.
    This is a revised version of a paper read at the meetings of the American Sociological
Association, September 4, 1969.

Table 1.   A typology of meanings of citizen participation in urban renewal

	Participation focuses on	
Participation is by	*Administrative concerns only*	*Political and administrative concerns*
Elites only	Elite coalition	Politics of renewal
Elites and non-elites	Citizen advice	Pluralist participation

hended by a typology that distinguishes between two aspects of participation: the range of citizenry involved, and the focus of their participation.[1]

Citizen participation in renewal involved either civic leaders only, or civic leaders as well as citizens affected by the renewal. Thus, the range of participation involved elites only, or non-elites as well as elites. Similarly, the focus of issues to which the participants directed their attention varied between questions of both ends and means, and questions of means only. In the first case, the focus of participation was on both the politics and administration of renewal; in the latter, the focus was only on administration. Table 1 presents four types of meanings of citizen participation that emerge from the combination of the two dimensions.

Citizen participation in urban renewal

The "elite coalition," the involvement of elite only in questions of policy implementation, was the original form of citizen participation in urban renewal. It met the requirements of the "workable program," which demanded only the existence of a community-wide committee, which, it is suggested, should contain at least one representative of each civic group interested in the program (U.S. Housing and Home Finance Agency, 1961:4).   This type of participation stresses the values of cooperation, education, and consensus; it rather clearly implies that what is crucial is the harmonious realization of the renewal plans as drawn up by the experts.[2]

Evidence from early renewal experiences in Newark, Boston, New York, and San Francisco, indicates the presence of this form (cf. McQuade, 1966; Kaplan, 1963). In Newark, for example, Kaplan notes (1963:12) that the renewal officials often say that "their clearance decisions are made on the basis of 'technical' rather than 'political' criteria, and that the projects are planned in a 'nonpolitical' environment." The elites who rubber-stamp the plans generally do not challenge that assumption, which typically reflects the coincidence of their preferences with the plans that are drawn.

The effect of the "elite coalition" is clearly reflected in the goal-displacement that has been evident in the urban renewal program. The legislation embodied two potentially conflicting goals for renewal: the redevelopment of the center city and the provision of low-cost housing. In that the former purpose has been given higher priority than the latter, the elite coalition has had its way. Urban renewal has to date destroyed far more low-income housing than it has built (cf. Greer, 1965:3; Anderson, 1964:67).

The elite coalition often yielded to the "politics of renewal;" where competition for the scarce values of land use is concerned, the conflicting interests of political elites are often manifested. Citizen participation in the politics of renewal means little more than the struggle for control of renewal planners among competing political elites. The politics of renewal shows more than the inescapability of political conflict in renewal; it also reveals how far from the interests of those citizens whose lives are touched by renewal plans are concepts of citizen participation that make room for elites only. The best studies of renewal politics (Rossi and Dentler, 1961:287; Meyerson and Banfield, 1964; Kaplan, 1963) demonstrate that the big decisions in renewal are made at supraneighborhood levels and that non-elite participation in renewal conflict is often passive in nature.

Gradually, renewal programs elicited the participation of citizens directly affected by the plans. Such "pluralist participation" saw non-elites organizing to gain access to decisions formerly made by elites (cf. Kornhauser, 1959); it also took the form in most cases, of opposing the renewal of their neighborhoods. As citizens learned of renewal experiences in other areas of their city, they became more likely to organize to meet programs proposed for their community. The first encounter between citizens and the elite coalition tended to produce an easy win for the latter—as in Lake Meadows in Chicago, the West End in Boston, and Kips Bay and Stuyvesant Town in New York (cf. Wilson, 1966:409-410; Bellush and Hausknecht, 1967:191). As the opposition became more organized, however, delays were won in implementation, and sometimes a veto was achieved.

One observer of the mobilization of residents, William Brussat (n.d.:8), noted that "People in the mass do not produce positive, systematic programs. They are constitutionally incapable . . . of making complex decisions. But the negative decision is a simple decision, and the negative power of the grass roots is incontestable. The grass roots has the power of the veto." Kaplan (1963:164) and Wilson (1966:409) have noted the rise of such veto groups, and have pessimistically evaluated their impact on the planning process.[3]

The negative consequences of the involvement of non-elites as veto groups in the renewal process, coupled with the attractiveness of the idea of the participation of non-elites, have led to the development of the fourth type of citizen participation, where non-elites serve as "citizen advisors." Such involvement may range from the merest leg-work of collecting an audience for a meeting, to a rather full participation in the planning of the project itself. Experiences in Dyersburg, Tennessee, and Washington, D.C., have been described in demonstration reports as providing extensive administrative experiences for ordinary citizens (cf. Nixon and Boyd, 1957; District of Columbia, 1964).

The demonstration report on a conservation project in the Adams-Morgan section of Washington concluded (District of Columbia, 1964:vii): "Encouraging citizen involvement in planning and improvement programs through the organization of a citizens' planning committee turned out to be the strongest single stimulus to citizen participation in Adams-Morgan." The involvement of citizens in planning is a risky business, for their competence in this area is generally suspect. Nonetheless, the Washington report recommends (1964:8) that the advice of the citizens' committee be carried out, informed by "careful technical guidance" from professional planners. While the participation of non-elites as citizen advisors provides for optimism with regard to the extension of participation in democratic society, its application was limited to those neighborhoods in which old housing was to be rehabilitated and not cleared. Its incidence was so atypical in the renewal experience that it did not affect the scholarly consensus about participation of non-elites in renewal. Thus Kaplan (1963:164) argued that renewal was inescapably involved in the process of elite politics, but urged that it be kept as far out of the realm of mass politics as possible. And Rossi and Dentler (1961:285) denied the non-elite citizen the right to amend the plans lest "the overall features of renewal are . . . undermined by small concessions that, when aggregated, amount to serious departures from the grander conception."

It is difficult to reconcile this outpouring of pessimistic conclusions toward citizen participation of non-elites in the renewal programs with the new optimism that surrounded the involvement of poor people in the war on poverty. Did not the planners know the potential explosiveness inherent in asking for the participation of the lower class in a middle-class world?

It appears clear that they did not. The poverty program framers were affiliated with a different tradition, as well as a different political climate. Drawing on the experience of the Ford Foundation grey area studies, and the work of the President's Committee on Juvenile Delinquency, as well as the growing emphasis on "participatory democracy," an active role for the poor was conceived (cf. Marris and Rein, 1967).

Citizen participation in the War on Poverty

Most broadly, the poverty program began on the sole optimistic note of the urban renewal program, seeking to develop a role for non-elites, in this case the poor, as citizen advisors. A program designed to rehabilitate people, rather than buildings, necessarily required the active involvement of the poor. Maximum feasible participation, it followed, was necessary to enable the poor to escape from the "culture of poverty" in the bootstrapping manner of previous Americans. Nevertheless, the precise role of the poor in relation to this clause was never clarified either by the framers of the legislation, or by the Congress as the bill sped through (cf. Rubin, 1967:5-6)."[4]

The primary intention of the community action programs was generally interpreted as involving the poor in a largely administrative role (Donovan, 1967:43)[5]; but the period of noncontroversial implementation was short-lived, if it in fact existed at all in the large cities. Citizen participation in the war on poverty became embroiled in ideological issues much more quickly than it did in the urban renewal case. The vagueness of the legislative intent lent fuel to that debate (cf. Raab, 1966:47), and two new conceptions of non-elite participation emerged. One position contended that the poor should have an influential, if not controlling voice, in administering their program; another claimed that the poor should be allowed to deal with political as well as administrative questions. This was almost revolutionary; never before had the poor been given credit for much expertise regarding the area of their own experience.

To accommodate this new conception of citizen participation, we must add a third level to our model, one that deals with the participation of non-elites only. Its administrative focus we shall call "client participation," and its political focus "grassroots participation."

The overall intent of the poverty program being largely administrative implies that the innovative potential of such participation was originally seen in the form of "client participation," the structure of which was defined by Frank Riessman (1965a, 1966; Riessman and Rein, 1965). Here, the emphasis was placed upon organizing and directing the demands of the poor toward the institutions which serve them so as to make those institutions more responsive to their poor clients. The clients become a "third force;" the model maintains the need for the direct involvement of the poor in helping themselves, while also seeking to meet the O.E.O. directive of a "quiet revolution."

O.E.O. was clearly sympathetic to this interpretation of citizen participation in its definition of the problem of the poor, being "that they are not in a position to influence the policies, procedures, and objectives of the organizations responsible for their welfare" (O.E.O. Workbook quoted in Donovan, 1967:43).

Nevertheless, such participation was not agreeable to the middle-class professionals who ran the service agencies, nor to city hall, nor to the radical

Table 2.   A typology of meanings of citizen participation in social policy

Participation is by	Participation focuses on	
	Administrative concerns only	Political and administrative concerns
Elites only	Elite coalition	Politics of reform
Elites and non-elites	Citizen advice	Pluralist participation
Non-elites only	Client participation	Grassroots participation

organizers with even more ambitious plans for the poor. Even as the program was being formulated, the conflict in the Mobilization for Youth program over the involvement of the poor in running their schools indicated the political potential of client participation (cf. Riessman, 1965b).

It is not surprising, then, that the poverty program became embroiled in political questions, at both elite and non-elite levels. With few exceptions, such as Mayor Daley of Chicago and Mayor Shelley of San Francisco, traditional political elites did not initiate poverty programs. Nevertheless, they quickly became involved when their authority was challenged by grassroots participation or, as was more likely, by aspiring leaders of ethnic groups heretofore excluded from power in the pluralist polity. The nature of the concerns of local elites was clarified at the Mayors' Conference in 1965. While their proposed resolution blamed the participation of the poor for "fostering class struggle" (cf. Newsweek, 1965:24), the real threat came not from the poor themselves, but from leaders who utilized the "participation of the poor" in their bid for power through ethnic politics (cf. Raab, 1966:54–56). As Mayor Shelley of San Francisco astutely noted, the poverty program "has the potential for setting up a great political organization. Not mine" (quoted in Kramer, 1969:60).

Thus, the leadership of the black community, which had emerged in the civil rights struggle, was quick to demand a central role for the poor whose interests they were prepared to represent. Often it was the leaders of CORE, or other civil rights militants, who pressed for this "representation" (Kramer, 1969:168; Raab, 1966:54). Other ethnic groups, a large proportion of whom were also found in the ranks of the poor, were also quick to demand greater representation. Often the need to "organize the poor" was recognized only after these new leaders came into power (Kramer, 1969:107).

Grassroots participation, the participation of non-elites alone in political and administrative questions, was thus more frequently discussed than found in reality. Such participation required a period of organizing the poor. Often this organization, as indicated above, was directed toward ends of boosting the mobility of individuals aspiring to be elites rather than the creation of powerful indigenous organizations among the poor themselves. The "Alinsky model," as found in the Syracuse University Community Action Training Center (cf. Knoll and Witcover, 1966), was rare indeed. In some cases the organizing of the poor led to the development of groups that became chapters of the Welfare Rights Organization (cf. Kramer, 1969:102). But these limited attempts met with ultimate defeat. The funds for the Syracuse University project were discontinued; W.R.O. has persisted only outside the boundaries of the war on poverty. And even before the Green amendment, the Kentucky political elite had successfully moved to exclude Appalachian volunteers and Vista volunteers, the primary sources of grassroots organizing in their community action programs (*The New York Times*, Aug. 19, 1967, and Sept. 29, 1967).

In the area of practical application, then, the revolutionary new concept of non-elite participation failed to materialize. Even the less politicized of the two modes, the third force strategy of client participation, did not succeed in gaining a significant foothold. The program which Riessman describes as most closely conforming to it, the non-university Syracuse Crusade for Opportunity, has been involved in a crisis of leadership, with political attacks from both right and left (*The Wall Street Journal*, August 25, 1967:1). To remain effective yet non-political is very difficult indeed. The third force may be either "cooled out" by the service agency or co-opted for the interests of city hall (cf. Riessman and Rein, 1965:13; Shostak, 1965).

Faced with these forces, it is not surprising that poverty programs retreated to the second rung of our typology, to modes involving more traditional participation of both elites and non-elites. On that level, however, the bid for power by blacks and other groups of poor usually resulted in stalemate, as in the renewal experience. The Green amendment, placing the final power in the hands of traditional political elites, as well as the new challenges to old leadership within the ethnic groups, have both contributed to this situation; the poor, seeing little in the program to help them, lose interest. Generally, enough pressure remains in the program to provide some services. Thus, the program, now old and weary, becomes depoliticized.

By this cycle, many programs end up at the point which the majority of programs never left. The role of the poor, or their representatives, is to advise service agencies. The middle-class professional plays the key role, both in planning and implementation. The involvement of the poor, once the subject of strong O.E.D. directives, is limited to individuals who are either hired by the program or "representatives" chosen by it. The proposal emerges as a noncontroversial consensus of service agencies to improve institutional output, integrate delivery, and promote civic well-being (cf. Kramer and Denton, 1967:79-80; Jencks, 1966:21-22; Levitan, 1969: 115-116).

The inability to withstand the pressures of majority interest and minority dissensus thus forced a retreat of the poverty program from the more radical interpretations of citizen participation to which it gave birth. The Green amendment of 1967 is in one sense only a legitimation of OEO's increasing reluctance to sponsor programs which were controversial. The amendment was proposed to resolve a basic contradiction between traditional American beliefs and the proposed participation of the poor in policy-making. Those who pay, say; or as Mrs. Green (quoted in *The New York Times*, Nov. 8, 1967) put it in defending her amendment for local control: "those who are helping to pay shall have a voice through elected officials."

Thus, the tie between political and economic power is maintained, and the programs are saved from domination by the poor. Again the power to propose is guarded by elites; non-elites may merely accept or reject what is offered them. Perhaps the primary legacy of the program is found in the new political elites that have risen from the ranks of minorities formerly unrepresented in the pluralism of city politics.[6] One New York observer notes also the rise of a new class of bureaucrats, the "povertycrats" (*The New York Times*, Nov. 9, 1969).

Participation in the Model Cities program

Even before the Green amendment resolved the participation dilemma in favor of elites, Congress had already defined a new approach to citizen participation in the third postwar attack on the urban crisis. While the model cities program, too, calls for widespread citizen participation, it is clear that this time the framers, learning from past experience, had developed a clearer conception of its meaning. Participation on the part of the poor was to focus on developing their "patience" and "understanding." The tactic of "involvement" is seen as "essential to quelling frustration." While they may have available to them channels to express "desires and identify with the projects being planned . . . the actual planning and decision-making rest with the demonstration city agencies" (*The Wall Street Journal,* Oct. 31, 1966). Thus, this new program was clear in its evaluation of maximum feasible participation of non-elites: it was impractical, inefficient, and politically dangerous. Concerning the advisory and planning body, the suggestion (U.S. Dept. of Housing and Urban Development, 1967:7) is that "the ultimate manifestation of public commitment is the appointment of a Board whose members represent and speak for the power structure of the community."

The model cities program, then, attempted to formalize the retreat from the less traditional modes of client and grassroots participation which the poverty program had introduced. In part, this was achieved because the poor were weary. Nevertheless, this "professionalization of reform" (the phrase is Moynihan's, 1969: ch.2) has not occurred without some protest. In Philadelphia one secretary resigned, charging that the council's professional staff stifles true citizen participation in the program and "too many interested and hopeful participants have fallen away" (*The Philadelphia Inquirer,* March 29, 1968).

In spite of the new limited form of participation, the poor and their allies have again attempted to make their voices heard. Too often this repeats the cycle toward stalemate, for while the city proposes and the community opposes, Congress cuts the overall model cities budget, assuring the perpetuation of the status quo. The major result of this new attempt at participation by non-elites may very well be the modest goal originally proposed in the legislation of providing "maximum opportunities for employing residents of the area in all phases of the program" (Demonstration Cities and Metropolitan Development Act of 1966, Title I, Section 103, a, 2). If this process is successful in opening well-paying construction jobs to blacks, it will be no mean accomplishment for non-elite citizen participation. This meaning, however, hardly embodies the high ideals normally attributed to the concept.

Conclusion

Our examination of the changing meanings of citizen participation leads us to conclude that in both the urban renewal and community action experiences, there are strong tendencies leading toward the stalemate of citizen groups and political elites, on both matters of administrative and political concern. Rather than the emergence of a creative "pluralist participation," in which elites and non-elites seek an accommodation of their interests, we find an inability of social policy to provide solutions by the mutual adjustment of the interests involved.[7] Elites tend to resist yielding the power to propose solutions to problems to non-elites. And, as the war on poverty indicates, non-elites eventually tire of this stalemate, and citizen participation comes to mean little more than the presence of a few "citizen advisors," attached to a service agency that serves as a buffer between the poor and an affluent society. When aroused again by a new social plan, as the model cities program, we already find signs of a similar progression through the cycle of participation once more toward stalemate.

Among academic analysts of social policy, civic leaders, and new left critics, the conclusion is now abroad that citizen participation has failed. Civic leaders attribute the failure to the intractable nature of the poor; the new left attributes it to the intractable nature of the "power structure;" many academics seem to have concluded that a combination of the two explanations is sufficient.

James Q. Wilson (1966b:29), for example, concludes that "effective local planning requires *less*, not more citizen participation." Citizen participation raises "unrealistic expectations" for non-elite citizens who have, according to Bellush and Hausknecht (1967b:279ff), neither "morale-cohesion," "capacity for effective membership," "leadership," "knowledge," or "awareness," all seen as "prerequisites for participation." According to Banfield and Wilson (1964), they lack the necessary "community-regarding and public-regarding political ethos." Such conclusions incline these academic critics favorably toward the "professionalization of reform."

We suggest that these interpretations, while not inappropriate to the analysis of the social experiments we have treated in this paper, ought not be used to imply the failure of all forms of citizen participation. We contend that non-elites can behave in "public-regarding" ways if provided the proper situation by social policy. As the Cahns (1968:217) note:

> People respond to the terms of the question put . . . Until recently, there has been no attempt to create forums in which the poor have been asked to make decisions as composite human beings, as human beings who have something valid to say about the allocation of resources from the point of view of the entire community. Instead, they have been forced into the role of responding as selfish, dependent individuals. By confining the poor to speaking in that role, professionals purport to prove an incapacity to function responsibly in any other role.

Similarly, Liebow (1967:64–65) notes that the poor characteristically do not defer gratifications because they have little to gain in the long run, not because they cannot behave in orientation to the future.

The cycle of citizen participation, we believe, must be moved off its direction toward stalemate by the development of a fully democratic urban pluralism.

We do not think it necessary to conclude, as have some social scientists, that democracy does not work among the poor because it is inefficient and raises conflicts. Rather, we believe that the experience with citizen participation in recent social policy demonstrates the critical importance of the development of new institutional forms that will represent the interests of the poor and will build those interests into the larger political and social structure such that these purposes can be achieved. It is growing too late to paper over class conflicts and subcultural differences with the explanation that participation will not work. The crisis of our times is too immediate, and its potential for social chaos is great.

Social policy regarding the poor seems inevitably involved in political questions in which both the poor and the nonpoor are critically interested. The critical challenge to American social policy in the decades ahead lies in developing means whereby the interests of the poor may be accommodated without arousing the countervailing power of the nonpoor against them so that change is stalemated. The alternatives to such institutional innovation would appear to be repression or rebellion.

Notes

1. Neither of these dimensions is particularly precise, but both are venerable ones in the literature of political sociology. The elite–non-elite distinction has been used outstandingly by William Kornhauser (1959); the politics-administration distinction is considered useful by Herbert Simon (1957).

2. For instance, the *Journal of Housing* stated on its cover in July 1956: "The only possible conclusion is that, in the long run, the cause of urban renewal will be advanced by having the public aware of what is going on and how it affects them. Citizen participation can save both time and money."

3. These sentiments are still heard in high circles. One high governmental official criticized Mayor Lindsay's renewal program in New York: "Community groups have gotten two very distinct ideas. One is that there's money in this, that if you raise enough hell there's money in it. Second, the city has made very clear that until it is satisfied that a particular community group is representative and makes known what it wants, the city isn't going to do anything. I think it's wild" (*The New York Times*, November 9, 1969).

Citizen participation is currently manifested in urban renewal programs through the Neighborhood Development Programs. At this writing, it is too early to judge the success of this form of "pluralist participation."

4. The task force apparently had in mind only two rather diffuse meanings for the concept. One was a concern that not all the newly-created jobs go to the middle-class professionals and that the poor themselves were to be employed by their program. Secondly, as the legislation appeared before the passage of the 1964 Civil Rights Act, this clause was to be a protection against the exclusion of Negroes in the programs in the south (Moynihan, 1966:6).

5. Donovan quotes Attorney General Robert F. Kennedy in his testimony before a House committee: "This bill calls for maximum feasible participation of residents. This means the involvement of the poor in planning and implementing programs: giving them a real voice in their institutions."

6. Ironically, President Nixon now proposes that O.E.O. focus primarily on innovation—an area it has already seemingly exhausted.

7. Gusfield (1962:25) has noted that such stalemates often occur in pluralist systems and may lead to periodic crises within them.

References

Anderson, Martin. 1964. *The Federal Bulldozer.* Cambridge: M.I.T. Press.

Bellush, Jewell, and Murray Hausknecht. 1967a. "Urban renewal and the reformer." Pp. 189–197 in Bellush and Hausknecht (eds.), *Urban Renewal: People, Politics, and Planning.* Garden City: Anchor Books.

———. 1967b. "Planning, participation, and urban renewal." Pp. 278–286 in *ibid.*

Brussat, William K. *Citizens Organization for Neighborhood Conservation.* Chicago: National Association of Housing and Renewal Officials.

Cahn, Edgar S., and Jean Camper. 1968. "Citizen participation." Pp. 211–224 in Hans B. Speigel (ed.), *Citizen Participation in Urban Development.* Washington, D.C.: NTL Institute for Applied Behavioral Science.

District of Columbia Office of Urban Renewal. 1964. *Adams-Morgan: Democratic Action To Serve a Neighborhood.* Washington, D.C.

Donovan, John C. 1967. *The Politics of Poverty.* New York: Pegasus.

Greer, Scott. 1965. *Urban Renewal and American Cities.* Indianapolis: Bobbs-Merrill.

Gusfield, Joseph R. 1962. "Mass society and extremist politics." *American Sociological Review* 27 (February): 19–30.

Jencks, Christopher. 1966. "Accommodating Whites: A new look at Mississippi." *The New Republic* 139 (April 16): 19–22.

Kaplan, Harold. 1963. *Urban Renewal Politics: Slum Clearance in Newark.* New York: Columbia University Press.

Knoll, Erwin, and Jules Witcover. 1966. "Organizing the poor." Pp. 247–253 in Herman P. Miller (ed.), *Poverty American Style.* Belmont, California: Wadsworth Publishing Co.

Kornhauser, William. 1959. *The Politics of Mass Society.* New York: The Free Press.

Kramer, Ralph M. 1969. *The Participation of the Poor.* Englewood Cliffs: Prentice-Hall.

Kramer, Ralph, and C. Denton. 1967. "Organization of a community action program: A Comparative case study." *Social Work* 12 (October): 68–80.

Levitan, Sar A. 1969. *The Great Society's Poor Law: A New Approach to Poverty.* Baltimore: Johns Hopkins Press.

Marris, Peter, and Martin Rein. 1967. *Dilemmas of Social Reform.* New York: Atherton.

McQuade, Walter. 1966. "Urban renewal in Boston." Pp. 259–277 in James Q. Wilson (ed.), *Urban Renewal: The Record and the Controversy.* Cambridge: M.I.T. Press.

Meyerson, Martin, and Edward C. Banfield. 1964. *Politics, Planning and the Public Interest.* New York: The Free Press.

Mill, John Stuart. 1875. *Considerations on Representative Government.* New York: Henry Holt and Company.

Moynihan, Daniel P. 1966. "What is community action?" *The Public Interest* 2 (Fall): 3–8.

———. 1969. *Maximum Feasible Participation: Community Action in the War on Poverty.* New York: The Free Press.

Newsweek. 1965. "Shriver and the war on poverty." *Newsweek* 66 (September 13): 22–29.

Nixon, William Bishop, and Joseph M. Boyd, Jr. 1957. *Citizen Participation in Urban Renewal.* Nashville: Tennessee State Planning Commission.

Raab, Earl. 1966. "What war and which poverty?" *The Public Interest* 1 (Spring): 45–56.

Riessman, Frank. 1965a. "Anti-poverty programs and the role of the poor." Pp. 403–412 in Margaret Gordon (ed.), *Poverty in America.* San Francisco: Chandler.

———. 1965b. "Mobilizing the poor." *Commonweal* 82 (May 21):285–289.

———. 1966. "The new anti-poverty ideology." *Poverty and Human Resources Abstracts I* (July–August): 5–16.

Riessman, Frank, and Martin Rein. 1965. "The third force: an anti-poverty ideology." *American Child* 47 (November): 10–14.

Rossi, Peter H., and Robert A. Dentler. 1961. *The Politics of Urban Renewal.* New York: The Free Press of Glencoe.

Rubin, Lillian. 1967. "Maximum feasible participation, the origins, implications and present status." *Poverty and Human Resources Abstracts* 2 (November–December): 5–18.

Shostak, Arthur. 1965. "Containment, co-optation or co-determination." *American Child* 47 (November):15–19.

Simon, Herbert A. 1957. *Administrative Behavior* (2nd ed.). New York: Macmillan.

U.S. Department of Housing and Urban Development. 1967. *Strengthening Community Services in Low Income Areas: A Field Guide.* Washington, D.C.:7.

U.S. Housing and Home Finance Agency. 1961. *Urban Renewal.* Washington, D.C.

Wilson, James Q. 1966a. "Citizen participation in urban renewal." Pp. 407–421 in Wilson (ed.), *Urban Renewal: The Record and the Controversy.*Cambridge: M.I.T. Press.

———. 1966b. "The war on cities." *The Public Interest* 3 (Spring):27–44.

Wilson, James Q., and Edward Banfield. 1964. "Public-regardingness as a value premise in voting behavior." *American Political Science Review* 58 (December): 876–887.

29

ROBERT BLAUNER, Internal Colonialism and Ghetto Revolt [1]

It is becoming almost fashionable to analyze American racial conflict today in terms of the colonial analogy. I shall argue in this paper that the utility of this perspective depends upon a distinction between colonization as a process and colonialism as a social, economic, and political system. It is the experience of colonization that Afro-Americans share with many of the nonwhite people of the world. But this subjugation has taken place in a societal context that differs in important respects from the situation of "classical colonialism." In the body of this essay I shall look at some major developments in black protest—the urban riots, cultural nationalism, and the movement for ghetto control—as collective responses to colonized status. Viewing our domestic situation as a special form of colonization outside a context of a colonial system will help explain some of the dilemmas and the ambiguities within these movements.

The present crisis in American life has brought about changes in social perspectives and the questioning of long accepted frameworks. Intellectuals and social scientists have been forced by the pressure of events to look at old definitions of the character of our society, the role of racism, and the workings of basic institutions. The depth and volatility of contemporary racial conflict challenge sociologists in particular to question the adequacy of theoretical models by which we have explained American race relations in the past.

For a long time the distinctiveness of the Negro situation among the ethnic minorities was placed in terms of color, and the systematic discrimination that follows from our deep-seated racial prejudices. This was sometimes called the caste theory, and while provocative, it missed essential and dynamic features of American race relations. In the past ten years there has been a tendency to view Afro-Americans as another ethnic group not basically different in experi-

Robert Blauner, "Internal Colonialism and Ghetto Revolt," *Social Problems,* vol. 16, no. 4 (Spring 1969), pp. 393–408. Reprinted by permission of the author and the Society for the Study of Social Problems.

ence from previous ethnics and whose "immigration" condition in the North would in time follow their upward course. The inadequacy of this model is now clear—even the Kerner Report devotes a chapter to criticizing this analogy. A more recent (though hardly new) approach views the essence of racial subordination in economic class terms: Black people as an underclass are to a degree specially exploited and to a degree economically dispensable in an automating society. Important as are economic factors, the power of race and racism in America cannot be sufficiently explained through class analysis. Into this theory vacuum steps the model of internal colonialism. Problematic and imprecise as it is, it gives hope of becoming a framework that can integrate the insights of caste and racism, ethnicity, culture, and economic exploitation into an overall conceptual scheme. At the same time, the danger of the colonial model is the imposition of an artificial analogy which might keep us from facing up to the fact (to quote Harold Cruse) that "the American black and white social phenomenon is a uniquely new world thing."[2]

During the late 1950s, identification with African nations and other colonial or formerly colonized peoples grew in importance among black militants.[3] As a result the U.S. was increasingly seen as a colonial power and the concept of domestic colonialism was introduced into the political analysis and rhetoric of militant nationalists. During the same period black social theorists began developing this frame of reference for explaining American realities. As early as 1962, Cruse characterized race relations in this country as "domestic colonialism."[4] Three years later in *Dark Ghetto,* Kenneth Clark demonstrated how the political, economic, and social structure of Harlem was essentially that of a colony.[5] Finally in 1967, a full-blown elaboration of "internal colonialism" provided the theoretical framework for Carmichael and Hamilton's widely read *Black Power.*[6] The following year the colonial analogy gained currency and new "respectability" when Senator McCarthy habitually referred to black Americans as a colonized people during his campaign. While the rhetoric of internal colonialism was catching on, other social scientists began to raise questions about its appropriateness as a scheme of analysis.

The colonial analysis has been rejected as obscurantist and misleading by scholars who point to the significant differences in history and social-political conditions between our domestic patterns and what took place in Africa and India. Colonialism traditionally refers to the establishment of domination over a geographically external political unit, most often inhabited by people of a different race and culture, where this domination is political and economic, and the colony exists subordinated to and dependent upon the mother country. Typically the colonizers exploit the land, the raw materials, the labor, and other resources of the colonized nation; in addition a formal recognition is given to the difference in power, autonomy, and political status, and various agencies are set up to maintain this subordination. Seemingly the analogy must be stretched beyond usefulness if the American version is to be forced into this model. For here we are talking about group relations within a society; the mother country—

colony separation in geography is absent. Though whites certainly colonized the territory of the original Americans, internal colonization of Afro-Americans did not involve the settlement of whites in any land that was unequivocally black. And unlike the colonial situation, there has been no formal recognition of differing power since slavery was abolished outside the South. Classic colonialism involved the control and exploitation of the majority of a nation by a minority of outsiders. Whereas in America the people who are oppressed were themselves originally outsiders and are a numerical minority.

This conventional critique of "internal colonialism" is useful in pointing to the differences between our domestic patterns and the overseas situation. But in its bold attack it tends to lose sight of common experiences that have been historically shared by the most subjugated racial minorities in America and nonwhite peoples in some other parts of the world. For understanding the most dramatic recent developments on the race scene, this common core element—which I shall call colonization—may be more important than the undeniable divergences between the two contexts.

The common features ultimately relate to the fact that the classical colonialism of the imperialist era and American racism developed out of the same historical situation and reflected a common world economic and power stratification. The slave trade for the most part preceded the imperialist partition and economic exploitation of Africa, and in fact may have been a necessary prerequisite for colonial conquest—since it helped deplete and pacify Africa, undermining the resistance to direct occupation. Slavery contributed one of the basic raw materials for the textile industry which provided much of the capital for the West's industrial development and need for economic expansionism. The essential condition for both American slavery and European colonialism was the power domination and the technological superiority of the Western world in its relation to peoples of non-Western and nonwhite origins. This objective supremacy in technology and military power buttressed the West's sense of cultural superiority, laying the basis for racist ideologies that were elaborated to justify control and exploitation of nonwhite people. Thus because classical colonialism and America's internal version developed out of a similar balance of technological, cultural, and power relations, a common *process* of social oppression characterized the racial patterns in the two contexts—despite the variation in political and social structure.

There appear to be four basic components of the colonization complex. The first refers to how the racial group enters into the dominant society (whether colonial power or not). Colonization begins with a forced, involuntary entry. Second, there is an impact on the culture and social organization of the colonized people which is more than just a result of such "natural" processes as contact and acculturation. The colonizing power carries out a policy which constrains, transforms, or destroys indigenous values, orientations, and ways of life. Third, colonization involves a relationship by which members of the colonized group tend to be administered by representatives of the dominant power. There is an experience of being managed and manipulated by outsiders in terms of ethnic status.

A final fundament of colonization is racism. Racism is a principle of social domination by which a group seen as inferior or different in terms of alleged biological characteristics is exploited, controlled, and oppressed socially and psychically by a superordinate group. Except for the marginal case of Japanese imperialism, the major examples of colonialism have involved the subjugation of nonwhite Asian, African, and Latin American peoples by white European powers. Thus racism has generally accompanied colonialism. Race prejudice can exist without colonization—the experience of Asian-American minorities is a case in point—but racism as a system of domination is part of the complex of colonization.

The concept of colonization stresses the enormous fatefulness of the historical factor, namely the manner in which a minority group becomes a part of the dominant society.[7] The crucial difference between the colonized Americans and the ethnic immigrant minorities is that the latter have always been able to operate fairly competitively within that relatively open section of the social and economic order because these groups came voluntarily in search of a better life, because their movements in society were not administratively controlled, and because they transformed their culture at their own pace—giving up ethnic values and institutions when it was seen as a desirable exchange for improvements in social position.

In present-day America, a major device of black colonization is the powerless ghetto. As Kenneth Clark describes the situation:

> Ghettoes are the consequence of the imposition of external power and the institutionalization of powerlessness. In this respect, they are in fact social, political, educational, and above all—economic colonies. Those confined within the ghetto walls are subject peoples. They are victims of the greed, cruelty, insensitivity, guilt and fear of their masters . . .
> The community can best be described in terms of the analogy of a powerless colony. Its political leadership is divided, and all but one or two of its political leaders are shortsighted and dependent upon the larger political power structure. Its social agencies are financially precarious and dependent upon sources of support outside the community. Its churches are isolated or dependent. Its economy is dominated by small businesses which are largely owned by absentee owners, and its tenements and other real property are also owned by absentee landlords.
> Under a system of centralization, Harlem's schools are controlled by forces outside of the community. Programs and policies are supervised and determined by individuals who do not live in the community . . .[8]

Of course many ethnic groups in America have lived in ghettoes. What make the black ghettoes an expression of colonized status are three special features. First, the ethnic ghettoes arose more from voluntary choice, both in the sense of the choice to immigrate to America and the decision to live among one's fellow ethnics. Second, the immigrant ghettoes tended to be a one and two generation phenomenon; they were actually way-stations in the process of acculturation and assimilation. When they continue to persist as in the case of San Francisco's Chinatown, it is because they are big business for the ethnics themselves and there is a new stream of immigrants. The black ghetto on the other hand has been a more permanent phenomenon, although some individuals do escape it. But most relevant is the third point. European ethnic groups like the Poles, Italians, and Jews generally only experienced a brief period, often less than a generation, during which their residential buildings, commercial stores, and other enterprises were owned by outsiders. The Chinese and Japanese faced handicaps of color prejudice that were almost as strong as the blacks faced, but very soon gained control of their internal communities, because their traditional ethnic culture and social organization had not been destroyed by slavery and internal colonization. But Afro-Americans are distinct in the extent to which their segregated communities have remained controlled economically, politically, and administratively from the outside One indicator of this difference is the estimate that the "income of Chinese-Americans from Chinese-owned businesses is in proportion to their numbers 45 times as great as the income of Negroes from Negro owned businesses."[9] But what is true of business is also true for the other social institutions that operate within the ghetto. The educators, policemen, social workers, politicians, and others who administer the affairs of ghetto residents are typically whites who live outside the black community. Thus the ghetto plays a strategic role as the focus for the administration by outsiders which is also essential to the structure of overseas colonialism.[10]

The colonial status of the Negro community goes beyond the issue of ownership and decision-making within black neighborhoods. The Afro-American population in most cities has very little influence on the power structure and institutions of the larger metropolis, despite the fact that in numerical terms, blacks tend to be the most sizeable of the various interest groups. A recent analysis of policy-making in Chicago estimates that "Negroes really hold less than 1 percent of the effective power in the Chicago metropolitan area. [Negroes are 20 percent of Cook County's population.] Realistically the power structure of Chicago is hardly less white than that of Mississippi."[11]

Colonization outside of a traditional colonial structure has its own special conditions. The group culture and social structure of the colonized in America is less developed; it is also less autonomous. In addition, the colonized are a numerical minority, and furthermore they are ghettoized more totally and are more dispersed than people under classic colonialism. Though these realities affect the magnitude and direction of response, it is my basic thesis that the most important expressions of protest in the black community during the recent years reflect the colonized status of Afro-America. Riots, programs of separation, politics of community control, the black revolutionary movements, and cultural nationalism each represent a different strategy of attack on domestic colonialism in America. Let us now examine some of these movements.

Riot or revolt?

The so-called riots are being increasingly recognized as a preliminary if primitive form of mass rebellion against a colonial status. There is still a tendency to absorb their meaning within the conventional scope of assimilation-integration politics: some commentators stress the material motives involved in looting as a sign that the rioters want to join America's middle-class affluence just like everyone else. That motives are mixed and often unconscious, that black people want good furniture and television sets like whites is beside the point. The guiding impulse in most major outbreaks has not been integration with American society, but an attempt to stake out a sphere of control by moving against that society and destroying the symbols of its oppression.

In my critique of the McCone report I observed that the rioters were asserting a claim to territoriality, an unorganized and rather inchoate attempt to gain control over their community or "turf."[12] In succeeding disorders also the thrust of the action has been the attempt to clear out an alien presence, white men and officials, rather than a drive to kill whites as in a conventional race riot. The main attacks have been directed at the property of white business men and at the police who operate in the black community "like an army of occupation" protecting the interests of outside exploiters and maintaining the domination over the ghetto by the central metropolitan power structure.[13] The Kerner report misleads when it attempts to explain riots in terms of integration: "What the rioters appear to be seeking was fuller participation in the social order and the material benefits enjoyed by the majority of American citizens. Rather than rejecting the American system, they were anxious to obtain a place for themselves in it."[14] More accurately, the revolts pointed to alienation from this system on the part of many poor and also not-so-poor blacks. The sacredness of private property, that unconsciously accepted bulwark of our social arrangements, was rejected; people who looted apparently without guilt generally remarked that they were taking things that "really belonged" to them anyway.[15] Obviously the society's bases of legitimacy and authority have been attacked. Law and order has long been viewed as the white man's law and order by Afro-Americans; but now this perspective characteristic of a colonized people is out in the open. And the Kerner Report's own data question how well ghetto rebels are buying the system: In Newark only 33 percent of self-reported rioters said they thought this country was worth fighting for in the event of a major war; in the Detroit sample the figure was 55 percent.[16]

One of the most significant consequences of the process of colonization is a weakening of the colonized's individual and collective will to resist his oppression. It has been easier to contain and control black ghettoes because communal bonds and group solidarity have been weakened through divisions among leadership, failures of organization, and a general disspiritment that accompanies social oppression. The riots are a signal that the will to resist has broken the mold of accommodation. In some cities as in Watts they also represented nascent movements toward community identity. In several riot-torn ghettoes the outbursts have stimulated new organizations and movements. If it is true that the riot phenomenon of 1964–68 has passed its peak, its historical import may be more for the "internal" organizing momentum generated than for any profound "external" response of the larger society facing up to underlying causes.

Despite the appeal of Frantz Fanon to young black revolutionaries, America is not Algeria. It is difficult to foresee how riots in our cities can play a role equivalent to rioting in the colonial situation as an integral phase in a movement for national liberation. In 1968 some militant groups (for example, the Black Panther Party in Oakland) had concluded that ghetto riots were self-defeating of the lives and interests of black people in the present balance of organization and gunpower, though they had served a role to stimulate both black consciousness and white awareness of the depths of racial crisis. Such militants have been influential in "cooling" their communities during periods of high riot potential. Theoretically oriented black radicals see riots as spontaneous mass behavior which must be replaced by a revolutionary organization and consciousness. But despite the differences in objective conditions, the violence of the 1960s seems to serve the same psychic function, assertions of dignity and manhood for young blacks in urban ghettoes, as it did for the colonized of North Africa described by Fanon and Memmi.[17]

Cultural nationalism

Cultural conflict is generic to the colonial relation because colonization involves the domination of Western technological values over the more communal cultures of non-Western peoples. Colonialism played havoc with the national integrity of the peoples it brought under its sway. Of course, all traditional cultures are threatened by industrialism, the city, and modernization in communication, transportation, health, and education. What is special are the political and administrative decisions of colonizers in managing and controlling colonized peoples. The boundaries of African colonies, for example, were drawn to suit the political conveniences of the European nations without regard to the social organization and cultures of African tribes and kingdoms. Thus Nigeria as blocked out by the British included the Yorubas and the Ibos, whose civil war today is a residuum of the colonialist's disrespect for the integrity of indigenous cultures.

The most total destruction of culture in the colonization process took place not in traditional colonialism but in America. As Frazier stressed, the integral cultures of the diverse African peoples who furnished the slave trade were destroyed because slaves from different tribes, kingdoms, and linguistic groups were purposely separated to maximize domination and control. Thus language, religion, and national loyalties were lost in North America much more completely than in the Caribbean and Brazil where slavery developed somewhat differently. Thus on this key point America's internal colonization has been more total and extreme than situations of classic colonialism. For the British in India and the European powers in Africa were not able—as outnumbered minorities—to destroy the national and tribal cultures of the colonized. Recall that American slavery lasted 250 years and its racist aftermath another 100. Colonial dependency in the case of British Kenya and French Algeria lasted only 77 and 125 years respectively. In the wake of this more drastic uprooting and destruction of culture and social organization, much more powerful agencies of social, political, and psychological domination developed in the American case.

> Colonial control of many peoples inhabiting the colonies was more a goal than a fact, and at Independence there were undoubtedly fairly large numbers of Africans who had never seen a colonial administrator. The gradual process of extension of control from the administrative center on the African coast contrasts sharply with the total uprooting involved in the slave trade and the totalitarian aspects of slavery in the United States. Whether or not Elkins is correct in treating slavery as a total institution, it undoubtedly had a far more radical and pervasive impact on American slaves than did colonialism on the vast majority of Africans.[18]

Yet a similar cultural process unfolds in both contexts of colonialism. To the extent that they are involved in the larger society and economy, the colonized are caught up in a conflict between two cultures. Fanon has described how the assimilation-oriented schools of Martinique taught him to reject his own culture and blackness in favor of Westernized, French, and white values.[19] Both the colonized elites under traditional colonialism and perhaps the majority of Afro-Americans today experience a parallel split in identity, cultural loyalty, and political orientation.[20]

The colonizers use their culture to socialize the colonized elites (intellectuals, politicians, and middle class) into an identification with the colonial system. Because Western culture has the prestige, the power, and the key to open the limited opportunity that a minority of the colonized may achieve, the first reaction seems to be an acceptance of the dominant values. Call it brainwashing as the Black Muslims put it; call it identifying with the aggressor if you prefer Freudian terminology; call it a natural response to the hope and belief that integration and democratization can really take place if you favor a more commonsense explanation, this initial acceptance in time crumbles on the realities of racism and colonialism. The colonized, seeing that his success within colonialism is at the expense of his group and his own inner identity, moves radically toward a rejection of the Western culture and develops a nationalist outlook that celebrates his people and their traditions. As Memmi describes it:

> Assimilation being abandoned, the colonized's liberation must be carried out through a recovery of self and of autonomous dignity. Attempts at imitating the colonizer required self-denial; the colonizer's rejection is the

indispensible prelude to self-discovery. That accusing and annihilating image must be shaken off; oppression must be attacked boldly since it is impossible to go around it. After having been rejected for so long by the colonizer, the day has come when it is the colonized who must refuse the colonizer.[21]

Memmi's book, *The Colonizer and the Colonized,* is based on his experience as a Tunisian Jew in a marginal position between the French and the colonized Arab majority. The uncanny parallels between the North African situation he describes and the course of black-white relations in our society is the best impressionist argument I know for the thesis that we have a colonized group and a colonizing system in America. His discussion of why even the most radical French anticolonialist cannot participate in the struggle of the colonized is directly applicable to the situation of the white liberal and radical vis-à-vis the black movement. His portrait of the colonized is as good an analysis of the psychology behind Black Power and black nationalism as anything that has been written in the U.S. Consider for example:

Considered *en bloc* as *them, they,* or *those,* different from every point of view, homogeneous in a radical heterogeneity, the colonized reacts by rejecting all the colonizers *en bloc.* The distinction between deed and intent has no great significance in the colonial situation. In the eyes of the colonized, all Europeans in the colonies are de facto colonizers, and whether they want to be or not, they are colonizers in some ways. By their privileged economic position, by belonging to the political system of oppression, or by participating in an effectively negative complex toward the colonized, they are colonizers . . . They are supporters or at least unconscious accomplices of that great collective aggression of Europe.[22]

The same passion which made him admire and absorb Europe shall make him assert his differences; since those differences, after all, are within him and correctly constitute his true self.[23]

The important thing now is to rebuild his people, whatever be their authentic nature; to reforge their unity, communicate with it, and to feel that they belong.[24]

Cultural revitalization movements play a key role in anti-colonial movements. They follow an inner necessity and logic of their own that comes from the consequences of colonialism on groups and personal identities; they are also essential to provide the solidarity which the political or military phase of the anticolonial revolution requires. In the U.S. an Afro-American culture has been developing since slavery out of the ingredients of African worldviews, the experience of bondage, Southern values and customs, migration and the Northern lower-class ghettoes, and most importantly, the political history of the black population in its struggle against racism.[25] That Afro-Americans are moving toward cultural nationalism in a period when ethnic loyalties tend to be weak (and perhaps on the decline) in this country is another confirmation of the unique colonized position of the black group. (A similar nationalism seems to be growing among American Indians and Mexican-Americans.)

The movement for ghetto control

The call for Black Power unites a number of varied movements and tendencies.[26] Though no clear-cut program has yet emerged, the most important emphasis seems to be the movement for control of the ghetto. Black leaders and organizations are increasingly concerned with owning and controlling those institutions that exist within or impinge upon their community. The colonial model provides a key to the understanding of this movement, and indeed ghetto control advocates have increasingly invoked the language of colonialism in pressing for local home rule. The framework of anticolonialism explains why the struggle for poor people's or community control of poverty programs has been more central in many cities than the content of these programs and why it has been crucial to exclude whites from leadership positions in black organizations.

The key institutions that anticolonialists want to take over or control are business, social services, schools, and the police. Though many spokesmen have advocated the exclusion of white landlords and small businessmen from the ghetto, this program has evidently not struck fire with the black population and little concrete movement toward economic expropriation has yet developed. Welfare recipients have organized in many cities to protect their rights and gain a greater voice in the decisions that affect them, but whole communities have not yet been able to mount direct action against welfare colonialism. Thus schools and the police seem now to be the burning issues of ghetto control politics.

During the past few years there has been a dramatic shift from educational integration as the primary goal to that of community control of the schools. Afro-Americans are demanding their own school boards, with the power to hire and fire principals and teachers and to construct a curriculum which would be relevant to the special needs and culture style of ghetto youth. Especially active in high schools and colleges have been black students, whose protests have centered on the incorporation of Black Power and black culture into the educational system. Consider how similar is the spirit behind these developments to the attitude of the colonized North African toward European education:

> He will prefer a long period of educational mistakes to the continuance of the colonizer's school organization. He will choose institutional disorder in order to destroy the institutions built by the colonizer as soon as possible. There we will see, indeed a reactive drive of profound protest. He will no longer owe anything to the colonizer and will have definitely broken with him.[27]

Protest and institutional disorder over the issue of school control came to a head in 1968 in New York City. The procrastination in the Albany State legislature, the several crippling strikes called by the teachers union, and the almost frenzied response of Jewish organizations makes it clear that decolonization of education faces the resistance of powerful vested interests.[28] The situation is too dynamic at present to assess probable future results. However, it can be safely predicted that some form of school decentralization will be institutionalized in New York, and the movement for community control of education will spread to more cities.

This movement reflects some of the problems and ambiguities that stem from the situation of colonization outside an immediate colonial context. The Afro-American community is not parallel in structure to the communities of colonized nations under traditional colonialism. The significant difference here is the lack of fully developed indigenous institutions besides the church. Outside of some areas of the South there is really no black economy, and most Afro-Americans are inevitably caught up in the larger society's structure of occupations, education, and mass communication. Thus the ethnic nationalist orientation which reflects the reality of colonization exists alongside an integrationist orientation which corresponds to the reality that the institutions of the larger society are much more developed than those of the incipient nation.[29] As would be expected the movement for school control reflects both tendencies. The militant leaders who spearhead such local movements may be primarily motivated by the desire to gain control over the community's institutions—they are anticolonialists first and foremost. Many parents who support them may share this goal also, but the majority are probably more concerned about creating a new education that will enable their children to "make it" in the society and the economy as a whole—they know that the present school system fails ghetto children and does not prepare them for participation in American life.

There is a growing recognition that the police are the most crucial institution maintaining the colonized status of black Americans. And of all establishment institutions, police departments probably include the highest proportion of individual racists. This is no accident since central to the workings of racism (an essential component of colonization) are attacks on the humanity and dignity of the subject group. Through their normal routines, the police constrict Afro-Americans to black neighborhoods by harassing and questioning them when found outside the ghetto; they break up groups of youth congregating on corners or in cars without any provocation; and they continue to use offensive and racist language no matter how many intergroup understanding seminars have been built into the police academy. They also shoot to kill ghetto residents for alleged crimes such as car thefts and running from police officers.[30]

Police are key agents in the power equation as well as the drama of dehumanization. In the final analysis they do the dirty work for the larger system by restricting the striking back of black rebels to skirmishes inside the ghetto, thus deflecting energies and attacks from the communities and institutions of the larger power structure. In a historical review, Gary Marx notes that since the French revolution, police and other authorities have killed large numbers of demonstrators and rioters; the rebellious "rabble" rarely destroys human life. The same pattern has been repeated in America's recent revolts.[31] Journalistic accounts appearing in the press recently suggest that police see themselves as defending the interests of white people against a tide of black insurgence; furthermore the majority of whites appear to view "blue power" in this light. There is probably no other opinion on which the races are as far apart today as they are on the question of attitudes toward the police.

In many cases set off by a confrontation between a policeman and a black citizen, the ghetto uprisings have dramatized the role of law enforcement and the issue of police brutality. In their aftermath, movements have arisen to contain police activity. One of the first was the Community Alert Patrol in Los Angeles, a method of policing the police in order to keep them honest and constrain their violations of personal dignity. This was the first tactic of the Black Panther Party which originated in Oakland, perhaps the most significant group to challenge the police role in maintaining the ghetto as a colony. The Panthers' later policy of openly carrying guns (a legally protected right) and their intention of defending themselves against police aggression has brought on a series of confrontations with the Oakland police department. All indications are that the authorities intend to destroy the Panthers by shooting, framing up, or legally harassing their leadership—diverting the group's energies away from its primary purpose of self-defense and organization of the black community to that of legal defense and gaining support in the white community.

There are three major approaches to "police colonialism" that correspond to reformist and revolutionary readings of the situation. The most elementary and also superficial sees colonialism in the fact that ghettoes are overwhelmingly patrolled by white rather than by black officers. The proposal—supported today by many police departments—to increase the number of blacks on local forces to something like their distribution in the city would then make it possible to reduce the use of white cops in the ghetto. This reform should be supported, for a variety of obvious reasons, but it does not get to the heart of the police role as agents of colonization.

The Kerner Report documents the fact that in some cases black policemen can be as brutal as their white counterparts. The Report does not tell us who polices the ghetto, but they have compiled the proportion of Negroes on the forces of the major cities. In some cities the disparity is so striking that white police inevitably dominate ghetto patrols. (In Oakland 31 percent of the population and only 4 percent of the police are black; in Detroit the figures are 39 percent and 5 percent; and in New Orleans 41 and 4.) In other cities, however, the proportion of black cops is approaching the distribution in the city: Philadelphia 29 percent and 20 percent; Chicago 27 percent and 17 percent.[32] These figures also suggest that both the extent and the pattern of colonization may vary from one city to another. It would be useful to study how black communities differ in degree of control over internal institutions as well as in economic and political power in the metropolitan area.

A second demand which gets more to the issue is that police should live in the communities they patrol. The idea here is that black cops who lived in the ghetto would have to be accountable to the community; if they came on like white cops then "the brothers would take care of business" and make their lives miserable. The third or maximalist position is based on the premise that the police play no positive role in the ghettoes. It calls for the withdrawal of metropolitan officers from black communities and the substitution of an autonomous indigenous force that would maintain order without oppressing the population. The precise relationship between such an independent police, the city and county law enforcement agencies, a ghetto governing body that would supervise and finance it, and especially the law itself is yet unclear. It is unlikely that we will soon face these problems directly as they have arisen in the case of New York's schools. Of all the programs of decolonization, police autonomy will be most resisted. It gets to the heart of how the state functions to control and contain the black community through delegating the legitimate use of violence to police authority.

The various Black Power programs that are aimed at gaining control of individual ghettoes—buying up property and businesses, running the schools through community boards, taking over antipoverty programs and other social agencies, diminishing the arbitrary power of the police—can serve to revitalize the institutions of the ghetto and build up an economic, professional, and political power base. These programs seem limited; we do not know at present if they are enough in themselves to end colonized status.[33] But they are certainly a necessary first step.

The role of whites

What makes the Kerner Report a less-than-radical document is its superficial treatment of racism and its reluctance to confront the colonized relationship between black people and the larger society. The Report emphasizes the attitudes and feelings that make up white racism, rather than the system of privilege and control which is the heart of the matter.[34] With all its discussion of the ghetto and its problems, it never faces the question of the stake that white Americans have in racism and ghettoization.

This is not a simple question, but this paper should not end with the impression that police are the major villains. All white Americans gain some privileges and advantage from the colonization of black communities.[35] The majority of whites also lose something from this oppression and division in society. Serious research should be directed to the ways in which white individuals and institutions are tied into the ghetto. In closing let me suggest some possible parameters.

1. It is my guess that only a small minority of whites make a direct economic profit from ghetto colonization. This is hopeful in that the ouster of white businessmen may become politically feasible. Much more significant, however, are the private and corporate interests in the land and residential property of the black community; their holdings and influence on urban decision-making must be exposed and combated.

2. A much larger minority have occupational and professional interests in the present arrangements. The Kerner Commission reports that 1.3 million nonwhite men would have to be upgraded occupationally in order to make the black job distribution roughly similar to the white. They advocate this without mentioning that 1.3 million specially privileged white workers would lose in the bargain.[36] In addition there are those professionals who carry out what Lee Rainwater has called the "dirty work" of administering the lives of the ghetto poor: the social workers, the school teachers, the urban development people, and of course the police.[37] The social problems of the black community will ultimately be solved only by people and organizations from that community; thus the emphasis within these professions must shift toward training such a cadre of minority personnel. Social scientists who teach and study problems of race and poverty likewise have an obligation to replace themselves by bringing into the graduate schools and college faculties men of color who will become the future experts in these areas. For cultural and intellectual imperialism is as real as welfare colonialism, though it is currently screened behind such unassailable shibboleths as universalism and the objectivity of scientific inquiry.

3. Without downgrading the vested interests of profit and profession, the real nitty-gritty elements of the white stake are political power and bureaucratic security. Whereas few whites have much understanding of the realities of race relations and ghetto life, I think most give tacit or at least subconscious support for the containment and control of the black population. Whereas most whites have extremely distorted images of black power, many—if not most—would still be frightened by actual black political power. Racial groups and identities are real in American life; white Americans sense they are on top, and they fear possible reprisals or disruptions were power to be more equalized. There seems to be a paranoid fear in the white psyche of black dominance; the belief that black autonomy would mean unbridled license is so ingrained that such reasonable outcomes as black political majorities and independent black police forces will be bitterly resisted.

On this level the major mass bulwark of colonization is the administrative need for bureaucratic security so that the middle classes can go about their life and business in peace and quiet. The black militant movement is a threat to the orderly procedures by which bureaucracies and suburbs manage their existence, and I think today there are more people who feel a stake in conventional procedures than there are those who gain directly from racism. For in their fight for institutional control, the colonized will not play by the white rules of the game. These administrative rules have kept them down and out of the system; therefore they have no necessary intention of running institutions in the image of the white middle class.

The liberal, humanist value that violence is the worst sin cannot be defended today if one is committed squarely against racism and for self-determination. For some violence is almost inevitable in the decolonization process; unfortunately racism in America has been so effective that the greatest power Afro-Americans (and perhaps also Mexican-Americans) wield today is the power to disrupt. If we are going to swing with these revolutionary times and at least respond positively to the anticolonial movement, we will have to learn to live with conflict, confrontation, constant change, and what may be real or apparent chaos and disorder.

A positive response from the white majority needs to be in two major directions at the same time. First, community liberation movements should be supported in every way by pulling out white instruments of direct control and exploitation and substituting technical assistance to the community when this is asked for. But it is not enough to relate affirmatively to the nationalist movement for ghetto control without at the same time radically opening doors for full participation in the institutions of the mainstream. Otherwise the liberal and radical position is little different than the traditional segregationist. Freedom in the special conditions of American colonization means that the colonized must have the choice between participation in the larger society and in their own independent structures.

Notes

1. This is a revised version of a paper delivered at the University of California Centennial Program, "Studies in Violence," Los Angeles, June 1, 1968. For criticisms and ideas that have improved an earlier draft, I am indebted to Robert Wood, Lincoln Bergman, and Gary Marx. As a good colonialist I have probably restated (read: stolen) more ideas from the writings of Kenneth Clark, Stokely Carmichael, Frantz Fanon, and especially such contributors to the Black Panther Party (Oakland) newspaper as Huey Newton, Bobby Seale, Eldridge Cleaver, and Kathleen Cleaver than I have appropriately credited or generated myself. In self-defense I should state that I began working somewhat independently on a colonial analysis of American race relations in the fall of 1965; see my "Whitewash Over Watts: The Failure of the McCone Report," *Trans-action*, 3 (March—April 1966), pp. 3—9, 54.

2. Harold Cruse, *Rebellion or Revolution*, New York: 1968, p. 214.

3. Nationalism, including an orientation toward Africa, is no new development. It has been a constant tendency within Afro-American politics. See Cruse, *ibid.*, esp. chaps. 5—7.

4. This was six years before the publication of *The Crisis of the Negro Intellectual*, New York: Morrow, 1968, which brought Cruse into prominence. Thus the 1962 article was not widely read until its reprinting in Cruse's essays, *Rebellion or Revolution, op. cit.*

5. Kenneth Clark, *Dark Ghetto*, New York: Harper and Row, 1965. Clark's analysis first appeared a year earlier in *Youth in the Ghetto*, New York: Haryou Associates, 1964.

6. Stokely Carmichael and Charles Hamilton, *Black Power*, New York: Random, 1967.

7. As Eldridge Cleaver reminds us, "Black people are a stolen people held in a colonial status on stolen land, and any analysis which does not acknowledge the colonial status of black people cannot hope to deal with the real problem." "The Land Question," *Ramparts*, 6 (May 1968), p. 51.

8. *Youth in the Ghetto, op. cit.,* pp. 10–11; 79–80.

9. N. Glazer and D.P. Moynihan, *Beyond the Melting Pot,* Cambridge, Mass.: M.I.T., 1963, p. 37.

10. "When we speak of Negro social disabilities under capitalism, . . . we refer to the fact that he does not own anything—*even what is ownable in his own community.* Thus to fight for black liberation *is to fight for his right to own.* The Negro is politically compromised today because he owns nothing. He has little voice in the affairs of state because he owns nothing. The fundamental reason why the Negro bourgeois-democratic revolution has been aborted is because American capitalism has prevented the development of a black class of capitalist owners of institutions and economic tools. To take one crucial example, Negro radicals today are severely hampered in their tasks of educating the black masses on political issues because Negroes do not own any of the necessary means of propaganda and communication. The Negro owns no printing presses, he has no stake in the networks of the means of communication. Inside his own communities he does not own the house he lives in, the property he lives on, nor the wholesale and retail sources from which he buys his commodities. He does not own the edifices in which he enjoys culture and entertainment or in which he socializes. In capitalist society, an individual or group that does not own anything is powerless." H. Cruse, "Behind the Black Power Slogan," in Cruse, *Rebellion or Revolution, op. cit.,* pp. 238–39.

11. Harold M. Baron, "Black Powerlessness in Chicago," *Trans-action,* 6 (Nov., 1968), pp. 27–33.

12. R. Blauner, "Whitewash Over Watts," *op. cit.*

13. "The police function to support and enforce the interests of the dominant political, social, and economic interests of the town" is a statement made by a former police scholar and official, according to A. Neiderhoffer, *Behind the Shield,* New York: Doubleday, 1967 as cited by Gary T. Marx, "Civil Disorder and the Agents of Control," *Journal of Social Issues,* forthcoming.

14. Report of the National Advisory Commission on Civil Disorders, N.Y.: Bantam, March 1968, p. 7.

15. This kind of attitude has a long history among American Negroes. During slavery, Blacks used the same rationalization to justify stealing from their masters. Appropriating things from the master was viewed as *"taking* part of his property for the benefit of another part; whereas *stealing* referred to appropriating something from another slave, an offense that was not condoned." Kenneth Stampp, *The Peculiar Institution,* Vintage, 1956, p. 127.

16. Report of the National Advisory Commission on Civil Disorders, *op. cit.,* p. 178.

17. Frantz Fanon, *Wretched of the Earth,* New York: Grove, 1963; Albert Memmi, *The Colonizer and the Colonized,* Boston: Beacon, 1967.

18. Robert Wood, "Colonialism in Africa and America: Some Conceptual Considerations," December 1967, unpublished paper.

19. F. Fanon, *Black Skins, White Masks,* New York: Grove, 1967.

20. Harold Cruse has described how these two themes of integration with the larger society and identification with ethnic nationality have struggled within the political and cultural movements of Negro Americans. *The Crisis of the Negro Intellectual, op. cit.*

21. Memmi, *op. cit.,* p. 128.

22. *Ibid.,* p. 130.

23. *Ibid.,* p. 132.

24. *Ibid.,* p. 134.

25. In another essay, I argue against the standard sociological position that denies the existence of an ethnic Afro-American culture and I expand on the above themes. The concept of "Soul" is astonishingly parallel in content to the mystique of "Negritude" in Africa; the Pan-African culture movement has its parallel in the burgeoning Black culture mood in Afro-American communities. See "Black Culture: Myth or Reality" in Peter Rose, editor, *Americans From Africa,* Atherton, 1969.

26. Scholars and social commentators, black and white alike, disagree in interpreting the contemporary Black Power movement. The issues concern whether this is a new development in black protest or an old tendency revised; whether the movement is radical, revolutionary, reformist, or conservative; and whether this orientation is unique to Afro-

Americans or essentially a black parallel to other ethnic group strategies for collective mobility. For an interesting discussion of Black Power as a modernized version of Booker T. Washington's separatism and economism, see Harold Cruse, *Rebellion or Revolution, op. cit.,* pp. 193−258.

27. Memmi, *op. cit.,* pp. 137−138.

28. For the New York school conflict see Jason Epstein, "The Politics of School Decentralization," *New York Review of Books,* June 6, 1968, pp. 26−32; and "The New York City School Revolt," *ibid.,* 11, no. 6, pp. 37−41.

29. This dual split in the politics and psyche of the Black American was poetically described by Du Bois in his *Souls of Black Folk,* and more recently has been insightfully analyzed by Harold Cruse in *The Crisis of the Negro Intellectual, op. cit.* Cruse has also characterized the problem of the black community as that of underdevelopment.

30. A recent survey of police finds "that in the predominantly Negro areas of several large cities, many of the police perceive the residents as basically hostile, especially the youth and adolescents. A lack of public support—from citizens, from courts, and from laws—is the policeman's major complaint. But some of the public criticism can be traced to the activities in which he engages day by day, and perhaps to the tone in which he enforces the "law" in the Negro neighborhoods. Most frequently he is 'called upon' to intervene in domestic quarrels and break up loitering groups. He stops and frisks two or three times as many people as are carrying dangerous weapons or are actual criminals, and almost half of these don't wish to cooperate with the policeman's efforts." Peter Rossi *et al.,* "Between Black and White—The Faces of American Institutions and the Ghetto," in Supplemental Studies for The National Advisory Commission on Civil Disorders, July 1968, p. 114.

31. "In the Gordon Riots of 1780 demonstrators destroyed property and freed prisoners, but did not seem to kill anyone, while authorities killed several hundred rioters and hung an additional 25. In the Rebellion Riots of the French Revolution, though several hundred rioters were killed, they killed no one. Up to the end of the summer of 1967, this pattern had clearly been repeated, as police, not rioters, were responsible for most of the more than 100 deaths that have occurred. Similarly, in a related context, the more than 100 civil rights murders of recent years have been matched by almost no murders of racist whites." G. Marx, "Civil Disorders and the Agents of Social Control," *op. cit.*

32. Report of the National Advisory Commission on Civil Disorders, *op. cit.,* p. 321. That black officers nevertheless would make a difference is suggested by data from one of the supplemental studies to the Kerner Report. They found Negro policemen working in the ghettoes considerably more sympathetic to the community and its social problems than their white counterparts. Peter Rossi *et al.,* "Between Black and White—The Faces of American Institutions in the Ghetto," *op. cit.,* chap. 6.

33. Eldridge Cleaver has called this first stage of the anticolonial movement *community* liberation in contrast to a more long-range goal of *national* liberation. E. Cleaver, "Community Imperialism," Black Panther Party newspaper, 2 (May 18, 1968).

34. For a discussion of this failure to deal with racism, see Gary T. Marx, "Report of the National Commission: The Analysis of Disorder or Disorderly Analysis," 1968, unpublished paper.

35. Such a statement is easier to assert than to document but I am attempting the latter in a forthcoming book tentatively titled *White Racism, Black Culture,* to be published by Little Brown, 1970.

36. Report of the National Advisory Commission on Civil Disorders, *op. cit.,* pp. 253−256.

37. Lee Rainwater, "The Revolt of the Dirty-Workers," *Trans-action,* 5 (1967), pp. 2, 64.

30

HARVEY MOLOTCH, Oil in Santa Barbara and Power in America

More than oil leaked from Union Oil's Platform A in the Santa Barbara Channel—a bit of truth about power in America spilled out along with it. It is the thesis of this paper that this technological "accident," like all accidents, provides clues to the realities of social structure (in this instance, power arrangements) not otherwise available to the outside observer. Further, it is argued, the response of the aggrieved population (the citizenry of Santa Barbara) provides insight into the more general process which shapes disillusionment and frustration among those who come to closely examine and be injured by existing power arrangements.

A few historical details concerning the case under examination are in order. For over fifteen years, Santa Barbara's political leaders had attempted to prevent despoilation of their coastline by oil drilling on adjacent federal waters. Although they were unsuccessful in blocking eventual oil leasing (in February 1968) of *federal* waters beyond the three-mile limit, they were able to establish a sanctuary within *state* waters (thus foregoing the extraordinary revenues which leases in such areas bring to adjacent localities—e.g., the riches of Long Beach). It was therefore a great irony that the one city which voluntarily exchanged revenue for a pure environment should find itself faced, on January 28, 1969, with a massive eruption of crude oil—an eruption which was, in the end, to cover the entire city coastline (as well as much of Ventura and Santa Barbara County coastline as well) with a thick coat of crude oil. The air was soured for many hundreds of feet inland and the traditional economic base of the region (tourism) was under threat. After ten days of unsuccessful attempts, the runaway well was brought under control, only to be followed by a second eruption on February 12. This fissure was closed on March 3, but was followed by a sustained "seepage" of oil—a leakage which continues, at this writing, to pollute the sea, the air, and the famed local beaches. The oil companies had paid $603,000,000 for their lease rights and neither they nor the federal government bear any significant legal responsibility toward the localities which these lease rights might endanger.

Harvey Molotch, "Oil in Santa Barbara and Power in America," *Sociological Inquiry*, vol. 40 (Winter 1970), pp. 131–144. Reprinted by permission.

This paper was written as Working Paper No. 8, Community and Organization Research Institute, University of California, Santa Barbara. It was delivered at the 1969 Annual Meeting of the American Sociological Association, San Francisco. A shorter version has been published in *Ramparts*, November 1969. The author wishes to thank his wife, Linda Molotch, for her active collaboration, and Robert Sollen, reporter for the *Santa Barbara News-Press*, for his cooperation and critical comments on an early draft.

If the big spill had occurred almost anywhere else (e.g., Lima, Ohio; Lompoc, California), it is likely that the current research opportunity would not have developed. But Santa Barbara is different. Of its 70,000 residents, a disproportionate number are upper class and upper middle class. They are persons who, having a wide choice of where in the world they might live, have chosen Santa Barbara for its ideal climate, gentle beauty, and sophisticated "culture." Thus a large number of worldly, rich, well-educated persons—individuals with resources, spare time, and contacts with national and international elites—found themselves with a commonly shared disagreeable situation: the pollution of their otherwise near-perfect environment. Santa Barbarans thus possessed none of the "problems" which otherwise are said to inhibit effective community response to external threat: they are not urban villagers (cf. Gans, 1962); they are not internally divided and parochial like the Springdalers (cf. Vidich & Bensman, 1960); nor emaciated with self-doubt and organizational naïveté as is supposed of the ghetto dwellers. With moral indignation and high self-confidence, they set out to right the wrong so obviously done them.

Their response was immediate. The stodgy *Santa Barbara News-Press* inaugurated a series of editorials, unique in uncompromising stridency. Under the leadership of a former state senator and a local corporate executive, a community organization was established called "GOO" (Get Oil Out!) which took a militant stand against any and all oil activity in the Channel.

In a petition to President Nixon (eventually to gain 110,000 signatures), GOO's position was clearly stated:

> . . . With the seabed filled with fissures in this area, similar disastrous oil operation accidents may be expected. And with one of the largest faults centered in the channel waters, one sizeable earthquake could mean possible disaster for the entire channel area . . .

> Therefore, we the undersigned do call upon the state of California and the Federal Government to promote conservation by:
> 1. Taking immediate action to have present off-shore oil operations cease and desist at once.
> 2. Issuing no further leases in the Santa Barbara Channel.
> 3. Having all oil platforms and rigs removed from this area at the earliest possible date.

The same theme emerged in the hundreds of letters published by the *News-Press* in the weeks to follow and in the positions taken by virtually every local civic and government body. Both in terms of its volume (372 letters published in February alone) and the intensity of the revealed opinions, the flow of letters was hailed by the *News-Press* as "unprecedented." Rallies were held at the beach; GOO petitions were circulated at local shopping centers and sent to friends around the country; a fund-raising dramatic spoof of the oil industry was produced at a local high school. Local artists, playwrights, advertising men, retired executives and academic specialists from the local campus of the University of California (UCSB) executed special projects appropriate to their areas of expertise.

A GOO strategy emerged for a two-front attack. Local indignation, producing the petition to the President and thousands of letters to key members of Congress and the executive would lead to appropriate legislation. Legal action in the courts against the oil companies and the federal government would have the double effect of recouping some of the financial losses certain to be endured by the local tourist and fishing industries while at the same time serving notice that drilling would be a much less profitable operation than it was supposed to be. Legislation to ban drilling was introduced by Cranston in the U.S. Senate and Teague in the House of Representatives. Joint suits by the city and County of Santa Barbara (later joined by the state) for $1 billion in damages was filed against the oil companies and the federal government.

All of these activities—petitions, rallies, court action, and legislative lobbying—were significant for their similarity in revealing faith in "the system." The tendency was to blame the oil companies. There was a muckraking tone to the Santa Barbara response: oil and the profit-crazy executives of Union Oil were ruining Santa Barbara—but once our national and state leaders became aware of what was going on, and were provided with the "facts" of the case, justice would be done.

Indeed, there was good reason for hope. The quick and enthusiastic responses of Teague and Cranston represented a consensus of men otherwise polar opposites in their political behavior: Democrat Cranston was a charter member of the liberal California Democratic Council; Republican Teague was a staunch fiscal and moral conservative (e.g., a strong Vietnam hawk and un-relenting harrasser of the local Center for the Study of Democratic Institutions). Their bills, for which there was great optimism, would have had the consequence of effecting a "permanent" ban on drilling in the Channel.

But from other quarters there was silence. Santa Barbara's representatives in the state legislature either said nothing or (in later stages) offered minimal support. It took several months for Senator Murphy to introduce Congressional legislation (for which he admitted to having little hope) which would have had the consequence of exchanging the oil companies' leases in the Channel for comparable leases in the under-exploited Elk Hills oil reserve in California's Kern County. Most disappointing of all to Santa Barbarans, Governor Reagan withheld support for proposals which would end the drilling.

As subsequent events unfolded, this seemingly inexplicable silence of the democratically elected representatives began to fall into place as part of a more general problem. American democracy came to be seen as a much more complicated affair than a system in which governmental officials actuate the desires of the "people who elected them" once those desires come to be known. Instead, increasing recognition came to be given to the "all-powerful oil lobby," to legislators "in the pockets of Oil," to academicians "bought" by Oil, and to regulatory agencies which lobby for those they are supposed to regulate. In other words, Santa Barbarans became increasingly *ideological,* increasingly *sociological,* and in the words of some observers, increasingly *"radical."*[1] Writing from his lodgings in the area's most exclusive hotel (the Santa Barbara Biltmore), an irate citizen penned these words in his published letter to the *News-Press:*

> We the people can protest and protest and it means nothing because the industrial and military junta are the country. They tell us, the People, what is good for the oil companies is good for the People. To that I say, Like Hell!

> Profit is their language and the proof of all this is their history (*SBNP,*[2] Feb. 26, 1969, p. A-6).

As time wore on, the editorials and letters continued in their bitterness.

The Executive Branch and the regulatory agencies: Disillusionment

From the start, Secretary Hickel's actions were regarded with suspicion. His publicized associations with Alaskan Oil interests did his reputation no good in Santa Barbara. When, after a halt to drilling (for "review" of procedures) immediately after the initial eruption, Hickel one day later ordered a resumption of drilling and production (even as the oil continued to gush into the channel), the government's response was seen as unbelievingly consistent with conservationists' worst fears. That he backed down within 48 hours and ordered a halt to drilling and production was taken as a response to the massive nationwide media play then being given to the Santa Barbara plight and to the citizens' mass outcry just then beginning to reach Washington.

Disenchantment with Hickel and the executive branch also came through less spectacular, less specific, but nevertheless genuine activity. First of all, Hickel's failure to support any of the legislation introduced to halt drilling was seen as an *action* favoring Oil. His remarks on the subject, while often expressing sympathy with Santa Barbarans[3] (and for a while placating local sentiment) were revealed as hypocritical in light of the action not taken. Of further note was the constant attempt by the Interior Department to minimize the extent of damage in Santa Barbara or to hint at possible "compromises" which were seen locally as near-total capitulation to the oil companies.

Volume of Oil Spillage. Many specific examples might be cited. An early (and continuing) issue in the oil spill was the *volume* of oil spilling into the Channel. The U.S. Geological Survey (administered by Interior), when queried by reporters, broke its silence on the subject with estimates which struck as incredible in Santa Barbara. One of the extraordinary attributes of the Santa Barbara locale is the presence of a technology establishment among the most sophisticated in the country. Several officials of the General Research Corporation (a local R & D firm with experience in marine technology) initiated studies of the oil outflow and announced findings of pollution volume at a "minimum" of ten-fold the Interior estimate. Further, General Research provided (and the *News-Press* published) a detailed account of the methods used in making the estimate (cf. Allan, 1969). Despite repeated challenges from the press, Interior both refused to alter its estimate or to reveal its method for making estimates. Throughout the crisis, the divergence of the estimates remained at about tenfold.

The "seepage" was estimated by the Geological Survey to have been reduced from 1,260 gallons per day to about 630 gallons. General Research, however, estimated the leakage at the rate of 8,400 gallons per day at the same point in time as Interior's 630 gallon estimate. The lowest estimate of all was provided by an official of the Western Oil and Gas Association, in a letter to the *Wall Street Journal.* His estimate: "Probably less than 100 gallons a day" (*SBNP*, August 5, 1969: A-1).

Damage to Beaches. Still another point of contention was the state of the beaches at varying points in time. The oil companies, through various public relations officials, constantly minimized the actual amount of damage and maximized the effect of Union Oil's cleanup activity. What surprised (and most irritated) the locals was the fact that Interior statements implied the same goal. Thus Hickel referred at a press conference to the "recent" oil spill, providing the impression that the oil spill was over, at a time when freshly erupting oil was continuing to stain local beaches. President Nixon appeared locally to "inspect" the damage to beaches, and Interior arranged for him to land his helicopter on a city beach which had been cleaned thoroughly in the days just before, but spared him a close-up of much of the rest of the county shoreline which continued to be covered with a thick coat of crude oil. (The beach visited by Nixon has been oil stained on many occasions subsequent to the President's departure.) Secret servicemen kept the placards and shouts of several hundred demonstrators safely out of Presidential viewing or hearing distance.

Continuously, the Oil and Interior combine implied the beaches to be restored when Santa Barbarans knew that even a beach which looked clean was by no means restored. The *News-Press*, through a comprehensive series of interviews with local and national experts on wildlife and geology, made the following points clear:

1. As long as oil remained on the water and oil continued to leak from beneath the sands, all Santa Barbara beaches were subject to continuous doses of oil—subject only to the vagaries of wind change. Indeed, all through the spill and up to the present point in time, a beach walk is likely to result in tar on the feet. On "bad days" the beaches are unapproachable.

2. The damage to the "ecological chain" (a concept which has become a household phrase in Santa Barbara) is of unknown proportions. Much study will be necessary to learn the extent of damage.

3. The continuous alternating natural erosion and building up of beach sands means that "clean" beaches contain layers of oil at various sublevels under the mounting sands, layers which will once again be exposed when the cycle reverses itself and erosion begins anew. Thus, it will take many years for the beaches of Santa Barbara to be completely restored, even if the present seepage is halted and no additional pollution occurs.

Damage to Wildlife. Oil on feathers is ingested by birds; continuous preening thus leads to death. In what local and national authorities called a hopeless task, two bird-cleaning centers were established to cleanse feathers and otherwise administer to damaged wildfowl. (Oil money helped to establish and supply these centers.) Both spokesmen from Oil and the federal government then adopted these centers as sources of "data" on the extent of damage to wildfowl. Thus, the number of dead birds due to pollution was computed on the basis of number of fatalities at the wildfowl centers.[4] This of course is preposterous, given the fact that dying birds are provided with very inefficient means of propelling themselves to such designated places. The obviousness of this dramatic understatement of fatalities was never acknowledged by either Oil or Interior—although noted in Santa Barbara.

At least those birds in the hands of local ornithologists could be confirmed as dead—and this fact could not be disputed by either Oil or Interior. Not so, however, with species whose corpses are more difficult to produce on command. Several observers at the Channel Islands (a national wildlife preserve containing one of the country's largest colonies of sea animals) reported sighting unusually large numbers of dead sea-lion pups—on the oil-stained shores of one of the islands. Statement and counter-statement followed, with Oil's defenders arguing that the animals were not dead at all—but only appeared inert because they were sleeping. Despite the testimony of staff experts of the local Museum of Natural History and the Museum Scientist of UCSB's Biological Sciences Department that the number of "inert" sea-lion pups was far larger than normal and that field trips had confirmed the deaths, the position of Oil, as also expressed by the Department of the Navy (which administers the stricken island), remained adamant that the sea animals were only sleeping (cf. *Life,* June 13, 1969; July 4, 1969). The dramatic beaching of an unusually large number of dead whales on the beaches of Northern California—whales which had just completed their migration through the Santa Barbara Channel—was acknowledged, but held not to be caused by oil pollution. No direct linkage (or non-linkage) with oil could be demonstrated by investigating scientists (cf. *San Francisco Chronicle,* March 12, 1969: 1-3).

In the end, it was not simply Interior, its U.S. Geological Survey and the President which either supported or tacitly accepted Oil's public relations tactics.

The regulatory agencies at both national and state level, by action, inaction, and implication had the consequence of defending Oil at virtually every turn. Thus, at the outset of the first big blow, as the ocean churned with bubbling oil and gas, the U.S. Coast Guard (which patrols Channel waters regularly) failed to notify local officials of the pollution threat because, in the words of the local commander, "the seriousness of the situation was not apparent until late in the day Tuesday and it was difficult to reach officials after business hours" (*SBNP*, January 30, 1969: A-1, 4). Officials ended up hearing of the spill from the *News-Press*.

The Army Corps of Engineers must approve all structures placed on the ocean floor and thus had the discretion to hold public hearings on each application for a permit to build a drilling platform. With the exception of a single *pro forma* ceremony held on a platform erected in 1967, requests for such hearings were never granted. In its most recent handling of these matters (at a point long after the initial eruption and as oil still leaks into the ocean) the Corps changed its criteria for public hearings by restricting written objections to new drilling to "the effects of the proposed exploratory drilling on *navigation or national defense*" (*SBNP*, August 17, 1969: A-1, 4). Prior to the spill, effects on *fish and wildlife* were specified by the Army as possible grounds for objection, but at that time such objections, when raised, were more easily dismissed as unfounded.

The Federal Water Pollution Control Administration consistently attempted to understate the amount of damage done to waterfowl by quoting the "hospital dead" as though a reasonable assessment of the net damage. State agencies followed the same pattern. The charge of "Industry domination" of state conservation boards was levelled by the State Deputy Attorney General, Charles O'Brien (*SBNP*, February 9, 1969: A-6). Thomas Gaines, a Union Oil executive, actually sits as a member on the State Agency Board most directly connected with the control of pollution in Channel waters. In correspondence with complaining citizens, N.B. Livermore, Jr., of the Resources Agency of California, refers to the continuing oil spill as "minor seepage" with "no major long-term effect on the marine ecology." The letter adopts the perspective of Interior and Oil, even though the state was in no way being held culpable for the spill (letter, undated to Joseph Keefe, citizen, University of California, Santa Barbara Library, on file).

With these details under their belts, Santa Barbarans were in a position to understand the sweeping condemnation of the regulatory system as contained in a *News-Press* front page, banner-headlined interview with Rep. Richard D. Ottinger (D–NY), quoted as follows: "And so on down the line. Each agency has a tendency to become the captive of the industry that it is to regulate" (*SBNP*, March 1, 1969: A-1).

The Congress: disillusionment

Irritations with Interior were paralleled by frustrations encountered in dealing with the Congressional establishment which had the responsibility of holding hearings on ameliorative legislation. A delegation of Santa Barbarans was scheduled to testify in Washington on the Cranston bill. From the questions which Congressmen asked of them, and the manner in which they were "handled," the delegation could only conclude that the Committee was "in the pockets of Oil." As one of the returning delegates put it, the presentation bespoke of "total futility."

At this writing, six months after their introduction, both the Cranston and Teague bills lie buried in committee with little prospect of surfacing. Cranston has softened his bill significantly—requiring only that new drilling be suspended until Congress is convinced that sufficient technological safeguards exist. But to no avail.

Science and technology: disillusionment

From the start, part of the shock of the oil spill was that such a thing could happen in a country with such sophisticated technology. The much overworked phrase, "If we can send a man to the moon . . ." was even more overworked in Santa Barbara. When, in years previous, Santa Barbara's elected officials had attempted to halt the original sale of leases, "assurances" were given from Interior that such an "accident" could not occur, given the highly developed state of the art. Not only did it occur, but the original gusher of oil spewed forth completely out of control for ten days, and the continuing "seepage" which followed it remains uncontrolled to the present moment, seven months later. That the government would embark upon so massive a drilling program with such unsophisticated technologies, was striking indeed.

Further, not only were the technologies inadequate and the plans for stopping a leak, should it occur, nonexistent, but the area in which the drilling took place was known to be ultra-hazardous from the outset. That is, drilling was occurring on an ocean bottom known for its extraordinary geological circumstances—porous sands lacking a bedrock "ceiling" capable of containing runaway oil and gas. Thus the continuing leakage through the sands at various points above the oil reservoir is unstoppable, and could have been anticipated with the data *known to all parties involved.*

Another peculiarity of the Channel is the fact that it is located in the heart of earthquake activity in that region of the country which, among all regions, is among the very most earthquake prone.[5] Santa Barbarans are now asking what might occur in an earthquake: if pipes on the ocean floor and casings through the ocean bottom should be sheared, the damage done by the Channel's *thousands* of potential producing wells would be devastating to the entire coast of Southern California.[6]

Recurrent attempts have been made to ameliorate the continuing seep by placing floating booms around an area of leakage and then having workboats skim off the leakage from within the demarcated area.[7] Chemical dispersants, of various varieties, have also been tried. But the oil bounces over the sea booms in the choppy waters; the work boats suck up only a drop in the bucket and the dispersants are effective only when used in quantities which constitute a graver pollution threat than the oil they are designed to eliminate. Cement is poured into suspected fissures in an attempt to seal them up. Oil on beaches is periodically cleaned by dumping straw over the sands and then raking up the straw along with the oil it absorbs.

This striking contrast between the sophistication of the means used to locate and extract oil compared to the primitiveness of the means to control and clean it up was widely noted in Santa Barbara. It is the result of a system which promotes research and development which leads to strategic profitability rather than to social utility. The common sight of men throwing straw on miles of beaches within sight of complex drilling rigs capable of exploiting resources thousands of feet below the ocean's surface, made the point clear.

The futility of the cleanup and control efforts was widely noted in Santa Barbara. Secretary Hickel's announcement that the Interior Department was generating new "tough" regulations to control off-shore drilling was thus met with great skepticism. The Santa Barbara County Board of Supervisors was invited to "review" these new regulations—and refused to do so in the belief that such participation would be used to provide the fraudulent impression of democratic responsiveness—when, in fact, the relevant decisions had been already made. In previous years when they were fighting against the leasing of the Channel, the Supervisors had been assured of technological safeguards; now, as the emergency continued, they could witness for themselves the dearth of any means for ending the leakage in the Channel. They had also heard the testimony of a high-ranking Interior engineer who, when asked if such safeguards could positively prevent future spills, explained that "no prudent engineer would ever make such a claim" (*SBNP*, February 19, 1969: A-1). They also had the testimony of Donald Solanas, a regional supervisor of Interior's U.S. Geological Survey, who had said about the Union Platform eruption:

I could have had an engineer on that platform 24 hours a day, 7 days a week and he couldn't have prevented the accident.

His "explanation" of the cause of the "accident": "Mother earth broke down on us" (*SBNP*, February 28, 1969: C-12).

Given these facts, as contained in the remarks of Interior's own spokesmen, combined with testimony and information received from non-Interior personnel, Interior's new regulations, and the invitation to the County to participate in making them, could only be a ruse to preface a resumption of drilling. In initiating the County's policy of not responding to Interior's "invitation," a County Supervisor explained: "I think we may be falling into a trap" (*SBNP*, April 1, 1969).

The very next day, the Supervisors' suspicions were confirmed. Interior announced a selective resumption of drilling "to relieve pressures." (*News-Press* letter writers asked if the "pressure" was geological or political.) The new tough regulations were themselves seriously flawed by the fact that most of their provisions specified those measures, such as buoyant booms around platforms, availability of chemical dispersants, etc., which had proven almost totally useless in the current emergency. They fell far short of minimum safety requirements as enumerated by UC Santa Barbara geologist Robert Curry who criticized a previous version of the same regulations as "relatively trivial" and "toothless"[8] (*SBNP*, March 5, 1969: C-9).

On the other hand, the new regulations did specify that oil companies would henceforth be financially responsible for damages resulting from pollution mishaps. (This had been the *de facto* reality in the Union case; the company had assumed responsibility for the cleanup, and advised stockholders that such costs were covered by "more than adequate" insurance.[9]) The liability requirement has been vociferously condemned by the oil companies—particularly by those firms which have failed to make significant strikes on their Channel leases (*SBNP*, March 14, 1969). Several of these companies have now entered suit (supported by the ACLU) against the federal government charging that the arbitrary changing of lease conditions renders Channel exploitation "economically and practically impossible," thus depriving them of rights of due process (*SBNP*, April 10, 1969: A-1).

The weaknesses of the new regulations came not as a surprise to people who had already adapted to thinking of Oil and the Interior Department as the same source. There was much less preparation for the results of the Presidential Committee of "distinguished" scientists and engineers (the DuBridge Panel) which was to recommend means of eliminating the seepage under Platform A. Given the half-hearted, inexpensive and primitive attempts by Union Oil to deal with the seepage, feeling ran high that at last the technological sophistication of the nation would be harnessed to solve this particular vexing problem. Instead, the panel—after a two-day session and after hearing testimony from no one not connected with either Oil or Interior—recommended the "solution" of drilling an additional fifty wells under Platform A in order to pump the area dry as quickly as possible. The process would require ten to twenty years, one member of the panel estimated.[10]

The recommendation was severely terse, requiring no more than one and a half pages of type. Despite an immediate local clamor, Interior refused to make public the data or the reasoning behind the recommendations. The information on Channel geological conditions was provided by the oil companies; the Geological Survey routinely depends upon the oil industry for the data upon which it makes its "regulatory" decisions. The data, being proprietary, could thus not be released. Totally inexplicable, in light of this "explanation," is Interior's continuing refusal to immediately provide the information given a recent clearance by Union Oil for public release of all the data. Santa Barbara's local experts have thus been thwarted by the counter-arguments of Oil-Interior that "if you had the information we have, you would agree with us."

Science was also having its non-neutral consequences on the other battlefront being waged by Santa Barbarans. The chief Deputy Attorney General of

California, in his April 7 speech to the blue-ribbon Channel City Club of Santa Barbara, complained that the oil industry

> is preventing oil drilling experts from aiding the Attorney General's office in its lawsuits over the Santa Barbara oil spill (*SBNP*, Aug. 8, 1969).

Complaining that his office has been unable to get assistance from petroleum experts at California universities, the Deputy Attorney General further stated:

> The university experts all seem to be working on grants from the oil industry. There is an atmosphere of fear. The experts are afraid that if they assist us in our case on behalf of the people of California, they will lose their oil industry grants.

At the Santa Barbara Campus of the University, there is little Oil money in evidence and few, if any, faculty members have entered into proprietary research arrangements with Oil. Petroleum geology and engineering is simply not a local specialty. Yet it is a fact that Oil interests did contact several Santa Barbara faculty members with offers of funds for studies of the ecological effects of the oil spill, with publication rights stipulated by Oil.[11] It is also the case that the Federal Water Pollution Control Administration explicitly requested a UC Santa Barbara botanist to withhold the findings of his study, funded by that Agency, on the ecological consequences of the spill (*SBNP*, July 29, 1969: A-3).

Except for the Deputy Attorney General's complaint, none of these revelations received any publicity outside of Santa Barbara. But the Attorney's allegation became something of a statewide issue. A professor at the Berkeley campus, in his attempt to refute the allegation, actually confirmed it. Wilbur H. Somerton, Professor of petroleum engineering, indicated he could not testify against Oil

> because my work depends on good relations with the petroleum industry. My interest is serving the petroleum industry. I view my obligation to the community as supplying it with well-trained petroleum engineers. We train the industry's engineers and they help us. (*SBNP*, April 12, 1969, as quoted from a *San Francisco Chronicle* interview.)

Santa Barbara's leaders were incredulous about the whole affair. The question—one which is more often asked by the downtrodden sectors of the society—was asked: "Whose University is this, anyway?" A local executive and GOO leader asked, "If the truth isn't in the universities, where is it?" A conservative member of the State Legislature, in a move reminiscent of SDS demands, went so far as to ask an end to all faculty "moonlighting" for industry. In Santa Barbara, the only place where all of this publicity was occurring, there was thus an opportunity for insight into the linkages between knowledge, the University, government, and Oil and the resultant non-neutrality of science. The backgrounds of many members of the DuBridge Panel were linked publicly to the oil industry. In a line of reasoning usually the handiwork of groups like SDS, a *News-Press* letter writer labeled Dr. DuBridge as a servant of Oil interests because, as a past President of Cal Tech, he would have had to defer to Oil in generating the massive funding which that institution requires. In fact, the relationship was quite direct. Not only has Union Oil been a contributor to Cal Tech, but Fred Hartley (Union's President) is a Cal Tech trustee. The impropriety of such a man as DuBridge serving as the key "scientist" in determining the Santa Barbara outcome seemed more and more obvious.

Taxation and patriotism: disillusionment

From Engler's detailed study of the politics of Oil, we learn that the oil companies combat local resistance with arguments that hurt: taxation and patriotism (cf. Engler, 1961). They threaten to take their operations elsewhere, thus depriving the locality of taxes and jobs. The more grandiose argument is made that oil is necessary for the national defense; hence, any weakening of "incentives" to discover and produce oil plays into the hands of the enemy.

Santa Barbara, needing money less than most locales and valuing environment more, learned enough to know better. Santa Barbara wanted oil to leave, but oil would not. Because the oil is produced in federal waters, only a tiny proportion of Santa Barbara County's budget indirectly comes from oil, and virtually none of the city of Santa Barbara's budget comes from oil. *News-Press* letters and articles disposed of the defense argument with these points: (1) oil companies deliberately limit oil production under geographical quota restrictions designed to maintain the high price of oil by regulating supply; (2) the federal oil import quota (also sponsored by the oil industry) which restricts imports from abroad, weakens the country's defense posture by forcing the nation to exhaust its own finite supply while the Soviets rely on the Middle East; (3) most oil imported into the U.S. comes from relatively dependable sources in South America which foreign wars would not endanger; (4) the next major war will be a nuclear holocaust with possible oil shortages a very low level problem.

Just as an attempt to answer the national defense argument led to conclusions the very opposite of Oil's position, so did a closer examination of the tax argument. For not only did Oil not pay very much in local taxes, Oil also paid very little in *federal* taxes. In another of its front-page editorials the *News-Press* made the facts clear. The combination of the output restrictions, extraordinary tax write-off privileges for drilling expenses, the import quota, and the 27.5 percent depletion allowance, all created an artificially high price of U.S. oil—a price almost double the world market price for the comparable product delivered to comparable U.S. destinations.[12] The combination of incentives available creates a situation where some oil companies pay no taxes whatever during extraordinarily profitable years. In the years 1962–1966, Standard of New Jersey paid less than 4 percent of profits in taxes, Standard of California, less than 3 percent, and twenty-two of the largest oil companies paid slightly more than 6 percent (*SBNP*, February 16, 1969: A-1). It was pointed out, again and again to Santa Barbarans, that it was this system of subsidy which made the relatively high cost deep-sea exploration and drilling in the Channel profitable in the first place. Thus, the citizens of Santa Barbara, as federal taxpayers and fleeced consumers were subsidizing their own demise. The consequence of such a revelation can only be *infuriating.*

The mobilization of bias

The actions of Oil and Interior and the contexts in which such actions took place can be reexamined in terms of their function in diffusing local opposition, disorienting dissenters, and otherwise limiting the scope of issues which are potentially part of public controversies. E.E. Schattschneider (1960:71) has noted:

> All forms of political organization have a bias in favor of the exploitation of some kinds of conflict and the suppression of others because *organization is the mobilization of bias.* Some issues are organized into politics while others are organized out.

Expanding the notion slightly, certain techniques shaping the "mobilization of bias" can be said to have been revealed by the present case study.

1. *The pseudo-event.* Boorstin (1962) has described the use of the pseudo-event in a large variety of task accomplishment situations. A pseudo-event occurs when men arrange conditions to simulate a certain kind of event, such that certain prearranged consequences follow as though the actual event had taken place. Several pseudo-events may be cited. *Local participation in decision making.* From the outset, it was obvious that national actions vis-à-vis Oil in Santa Barbara had as their strategy the freezing out of any local participation in decisions affecting the Channel. Thus, when in 1968 the federal government first called for bids on a Channel lease, local officials were not even informed. When subsequently queried about the matter, federal officials indicated that the lease which was advertised for bid was just a corrective measure to prevent drainage of a "little old oil pool" on federal property adjacent to a state lease producing for Standard and Humble. This "little old pool" was to draw a high bonus bid of $21,189,000 from a syndicate headed by Phillips (*SBNP*, February 9, 1969: A-17). Further, local officials were not notified by any government agency in the case of the original oil spill, nor (except after the spill was already widely known) in the case of any of the previous or subsequent more "minor" spills. Perhaps the thrust of the federal government's colonialist attitude toward the local community was contained in an Interior Department engineer's memo written to J. Cordell Moore, Assistant Secretary of Interior, explaining the policy of refusing public hearings prefatory to drilling: "We preferred not to stir up the natives any more than possible."[13]

(The memo was released by Senator Cranston and excerpted on page 1 of the *News-Press*.)

Given this known history, the Santa Barbara County Board of Supervisors refused the call for "participation" in drawing up new "tougher" drilling regulations, precisely because they knew the government had no intention of creating "safe" drilling regulations. They refused to take part in the pseudo-event and thus refused to let the consequences (in this case the appearance of democratic decision-making and local assent) of a pseudo-event occur.

Other attempts at the staging of pseudo-events may be cited. Nixon's "inspection" of the Santa Barbara beachfront was an obvious one. Another series of pseudo-events were the Congressional hearings staged by legislators who were, in the words of a local well-to-do lady leader of GOO, "kept men." The locals blew off steam—but the hearing of arguments and the proposing of appropriate legislation based on those arguments (the presumed essence of the Congressional hearing as a formal event) certainly did not come off. Many Santa Barbarans had a similar impression of the court hearings regarding the various legal maneuvers against oil drilling; legal proceedings came to be similarly seen as ceremonious arrangements for the accomplishing of tasks not revealed by their formally-stated properties.

2. *The creeping event.* A creeping event is, in a sense, the opposite of a pseudo-event. It occurs when something *is* actually taking place, but when the manifest signs of the event are arranged to occur at an inconspicuously gradual and piecemeal pace, thus eliminating some of the consequences which would otherwise follow from the event if it were to be perceived all-at-once to be occurring. Two major creeping events were arranged for the Santa Barbara Channel. Although the great bulk of the bidding for leases in the Channel occurred simultaneously, the first lease was, as was made clear earlier, advertised for bid prior to the others and prior to any public announcement of the leasing of the Channel. The federal waters' virginity was thus ended with only a whimper. A more salient example of the creeping event is the resumption of production and drilling after Hickel's second moratorium. Authorization to resume *production* on different specific groups of wells occurred on these dates in 1969: February 17; February 21; February 22; and March 3. Authorization to resume *drilling* of various groups of new wells was announced by Interior on these dates in 1969: April 1, June 12, July 2, August 2, and August 16. (This is being written on August 20.) Each time, the resumption was announced as a safety precaution to relieve pressures, until finally on the most recent resumption date, the word "deplete" was used for the first time as the reason for granting permission to drill. There is thus no *particular* point in time in which production and drilling was re-authorized for the Channel—and full resumption has still not been officially authorized.

A creeping event has the consequences of diffusing resistance to the event by holding back what journalists call a "time peg" on which to hang "the story." Even if the aggrieved party should get wind that "something is going on," strenuous reaction is inhibited. Non-routine activity has as its prerequisite the crossing of a certain threshold point of input; the dribbling out of an event has the consequence of making each of the revealed inputs fall below the threshold level necessary for non-routine activity. By the time it becomes quite clear that "something *is* going on" both the aggrieved and the sponsors of the creeping event can ask why there should be a response *"now"* when there was none previously to the very same kind of stimulus. In such manner, the aggrieved has resort only to frustration and a gnawing feeling that "events" are sweeping him by.

3. *The "neutrality" of science and the "knowledge" producers.* I have already dealt at some length with the disillusionment of Santa Barbarans with the "experts" and the University. After learning for themselves of the collusion between government and Oil and the use of secret science as a prop to that collusion, Santa Barbarans found themselves in the unenviable position of having to demonstrate that science and knowledge were, in fact, not neutral arbiters. They had to demonstrate, by themselves, that continued drilling was not safe, that the "experts" who said it was safe were the hirelings directly or indirectly of Oil interests and that the report of the DuBridge Panel recommending massive drilling was a fraudulent document. They had to document that the University *petroleum* geologists were themselves in league with their adversaries and that knowledge unfavorable to the Oil interests was systematically withheld by virtue of the very structure of the knowledge industry. As the SDS has learned in other contexts, this is no small task. It is a long story to tell, a complicated story to tell, and one which pits lay persons (and a few academic renegades) against a profession and patrons of a profession. An illustration of the difficulties involved may be drawn from very recent history. Seventeen Santa Barbara plaintiffs, represented by the ACLU, sought a temporary injunction against additional Channel drilling at least until the information utilized by the DuBridge Panel was made public and a hearing could be held. The injunction was not granted and, in the end, the presiding federal judge ruled in favor of what he termed the "expert" opinions available to the Secretary of the Interior. It was a function of limited time for rebuttal, the disorienting confusions of courtroom procedures, and also perhaps the desire to not offend the Court, that the ACLU lawyer could not make his subtle, complex, and highly controversial case that the "experts" were partisans and that their scientific "findings" follow from that partisanship.

4. *Constraints of communication media.* Just as the courtroom setting was not amenable to a full reproduction of the details surrounding the basis for the ACLU case, so the media in general—through restrictions of time and style—prevent a full airing of the details of the case. A more cynical analysis of the media's inability to make known the Santa Barbara "problem" in its full fidelity might hinge on an allegation that the media are constrained by fear of "pressures" from Oil and its allies; Metromedia, for example, sent a team to Santa Barbara which spent several days documenting, interviewing and filming for an hour-long program—only to suddenly drop the whole matter due to what

is reported by locals in touch with the network to have been "pressures" from Oil. Such blatant interventions aside, however, the problem of full reproduction of the Santa Barbara "news" would remain problematic nonetheless.

News media are notorious for the anecdotal nature of their reporting; even so-called "think pieces" rarely go beyond a stringing together of proximate "events." There are no analyses of the "mobilization of bias" or linkages of men's actions and their pecuniary interests. Science and learning are assumed to be neutral; regulatory agencies are assumed to function as "watch-dogs" for the public. Information to the contrary of these assumptions is treated as exotic exception; in the manner of Drew Pearson columns, exception piles upon exception without intellectual combination, analysis or ideological synthesis. The complexity of the situation to be reported, the wealth of details needed to support such analyses require more time and effort than journalists have at their command. Their recitation would produce long stories not consistent with space requirements and make-up preferences of newspapers and analogous constraints of the other media. A full telling of the whole story would tax the reader/viewer and would risk boring him.

For these reasons, the rather extensive media coverage of the oil spill centered on a few dramatic moments in its history (e.g., the initial gusher of oil) and a few simple-to-tell "human interest" aspects such as the pathetic deaths of the sea birds struggling along the oil-covered sands. With increasing temporal and geographical distance from the initial spill, national coverage became increasingly rare and increasingly sloppy. Interior statements on the state of the "crisis" were reported without local rejoinders as the newsmen who would have gathered them began leaving the scene. It is to be kept in mind that, relative to other local events, the Santa Barbara spill received extraordinarily extensive national coverage.[14] The point is that this coverage is nevertheless inadequate in both its quality and quantity to adequately inform the American public.

5. *The routinization of evil.* An oft quoted American cliché is that the news media cover only the "bad" things; the everyday world of people going about their business in conformity with American ideals loses out to the coverage of student and ghetto "riots," wars and crime, corruption and sin. The grain of truth in this cliché should not obfuscate the fact that there are *certain kinds of evil* which, partially for reasons cited in the preceding paragraphs, also lose their place in the public media and the public mind. Pollution of the Santa Barbara Channel is now routine; the issue is not whether or not the Channel is polluted, but *how much* it is polluted. A recent oil slick discovered off a Phillips Platform in the Channel was dismissed by an oil company official as a "routine" drilling byproduct which was not viewed as "obnoxious." That "about half" of the current oil seeping into the Channel is allegedly being recovered is taken as an improvement sufficient to preclude the "outrage" that a big national story would require.

Similarly, the pollution of the "moral environment" becomes routine; politicians are, of course, on the take, in the pockets of Oil, etc. The depletion allowance issue becomes not whether or not such special benefits should exist at all, but rather whether it should be at the level of 20 or 27.5 percent. "Compromises" emerge such as the 24 percent depletion allowance and the new "tough" drilling regulations, which are already being hailed as "victories" for the reformers (cf. *Los Angeles Times,* July 14, 1969:17). Like the oil spill itself, the depletion allowance debate becomes buried in its own disorienting detail, its ceremonious pseudo-events and in the triviality of the "solutions" which ultimately come to be considered as the "real" options. Evil is both banal and complicated; both of these attributes contribute to its durability.[15]

The struggle for the means to power

It should (although it does not) go without saying that the parties competing to shape decision making on oil in Santa Barbara do not have equal access to the means of "mobilizing bias" which this paper has discussed. The same social structural characteristics which Michels has asserted make for an "iron law of oligarchy" make for, in this case, a series of extraordinary advantages for the Oil-government combine. The ability to create pseudo-events such as Nixon's Santa Barbara inspection or controls necessary to bring off well-timed creeping events are not evenly distributed throughout the social structure. Lacking such ready access to media, lacking the ability to stage events at will, lacking a well-integrated system of arrangements for goal attainment (at least in comparison to their adversaries) Santa Barbara's leaders have met with repeated frustrations.

Their response to their relative powerlessness has been analogous to other groups and individuals who, from a similar vantage point, come to see the system up close. They become willing to expand their repertoire of means of influence as their cynicism and bitterness increase concomitantly. Letter writing gives way to demonstrations, demonstrations to civil disobedience. People refuse to participate in "democratic procedures" which are a part of the opposition's event-management strategy. Confrontation politics arise as a means of countering with "events" of one's own, thus providing the media with "stories" which can be simply and energetically told. The lesson is learned that "the power to make a reportable event is . . . the power to make experience" (Boorstin, 1962:10).

Rallies were held at local beaches; Congressmen and state and national officials were greeted by demonstrations. (Fred Hartley, of Union Oil, inadvertently landed his plane in the midst of one such demonstration, causing a rather ugly name-calling scene to ensue.) A "sail-in" was held one Sunday with a flotilla of local pleasure boats forming a circle around Platform A, each craft bearing large anti-oil banners. (Months earlier boats coming near the platforms were sprayed by oil personnel with fire hoses.) City-hall meetings were packed with citizens reciting "demands" for immediate and forceful local action.

A City Council election in the midst of the crisis resulted in the landslide election of the Council's bitterest critic and the defeat of a veteran Councilman suspected of having "oil interests." In a rare action, the *News-Press* condemned the local Chamber of Commerce for accepting oil money for a fraudulent tourist advertising campaign which touted Santa Barbara (including its beaches) as restored to its former beauty. (In the end, references to the beaches were removed from subsequent advertisements, but the oil-financed campaign continued briefly.)

In the meantime, as a *Wall Street Journal* reporter was to observe, "a current of gloom and despair" ran through the ranks of Santa Barbara's militants. The president of Şloan Instruments Corporation, an international R & D firm with headquarters in Santa Barbara, came to comment:

> We are so God-damned frustrated. The whole democratic process seems to be falling apart. Nobody responds to us, and we end up doing things progressively less reasonable. This town is going to blow up if there isn't some reasonable attitude expressed by the Federal Government—nothing seems to happen except that we lose.

Similarly, a well-to-do widow, during a legal proceeding in Federal District Court in which Santa Barbara was once again "losing," whispered in the author's ear:

> Now I understand why those young people at the University go around throwing things . . . The individual has no rights at all.

One possible grand strategy for Santa Barbara was outlined by a local public relations man and GOO worker:

> We've got to run the oil men out. The city owns the wharf and the harbor that the company has to use. The city has got to deny its facilities to oil traffic, service boats, cranes and the like. If the city contravenes some federal navigation laws (which such actions would unquestionably involve), to hell with it.

> The only hope to save Santa Barbara is to awaken the nation to the ravishment. That will take public officials who are willing to block oil traffic with their bodies and with police hoses, if necessary. Then federal marshals or federal troops would have to come in. This would pull in the national news media (*SBNP,* July 6, 1969, p. 7).

This scenario has thus far not occurred in Santa Barbara, although the use of the wharf by the oil industries has led to certain militant actions. A picket was maintained at the wharf for two weeks, protesting the conversion of the pier from a recreation and tourist facility to a heavy industrial plant for the use of the oil companies.[16] A boycott of other wharf businesses (e.g., two restaurants) was urged. The picket line was led by white, middle-class adults—one of whom had almost won the mayorality of Santa Barbara in a previous election. Hardly a "radical" or a "militant," this same man was several months later representing his neighborhood protective association in its opposition to the presence of a "Free School" described by this man (somewhat ambivalently) as a "hippie hotel."

Prior to the picketing, a dramatic Easter Sunday confrontation (involving approximately 500 persons) took place between demonstrators and city police. Unexpectedly, as a wharf rally was breaking up, an oil service truck began driving up the pier to make delivery of casing supplies for oil drilling. There was a spontaneous sit-down in front of the truck. For the first time since the Ku Klux Klan folded in the 1930s, a group of Santa Barbarans (some young, some "hippie," but many hard-working middle-class adults), was publicly taking the law into its own hands. After much lengthy discussion between police, the truck driver and the demonstrators, the truck was ordered away and the demonstrators remained to rejoice their victory. The following day's *News-Press* editorial, while not supportive of such tactics, found much to excuse—noteworthy given the paper's long standing *bitter* opposition to similar tactics when exercised by dissident Northern blacks or student radicals.

A companion demonstration on the water failed to materialize; a group of Santa Barbarans was to sail to the Union platform and "take it"; choppy seas, however, precluded a landing, causing the would-be conquerors to return to port in failure.

It would be difficult to speculate at this writing what forms Santa Barbara's resistance might take in the future. The veteran *News-Press* reporter who has covered the important oil stories has publicly stated that if the government fails to eliminate both the pollution and its causes, "there will, at best be civil disobedience in Santa Barbara and at worst, violence." In fact, talk of "blowing up" the ugly platforms has been recurrent—and is heard in all social circles.

But just as this kind of talk is not completely serious, it is difficult to know the degree to which the other kinds of militant statements are serious. Despite frequent observations of the "radicalization"[17] of Santa Barbara, it is difficult to determine the extent to which the authentic grievances against Oil have generalized to a radical analysis of American society. Certainly an SDS membership campaign among Santa Barbara adults would be a dismal failure. But that is too severe a test. People, especially basically contented people, change their worldview only very slowly, if at all. Most Santa Barbarans go about their comfortable lives in the ways they always did; they may even help Ronald Reagan to another term in the statehouse. But I do conclude that large numbers of persons have been moved, and that they have been moved in the directions of the radical left. They have gained insights into the structure of power in America not possessed by similarly situated persons in other parts of the country. The claim is thus that some Santa Barbarans, especially those with most interest and most information about the oil spill and its surrounding circumstances, have come to view power in America more intellectually, more analytically, more sociologically—more *radically*—than they did before.

I hold this to be a general sociological response to a series of concomitant circumstances, which can be simply enumerated (*again!*) as follows:

1. *Injustice.* The powerful are operating in a manner inconsistent with the normatively sanctioned expectations of an aggrieved population. The aggrieved population is deprived of certain felt needs as a result.
2. *Information.* Those who are unjustly treated are provided with rather complete information regarding this disparity between expectations and actual performances of the powerful. In the present case, that information has been provided to Santa Barbarans (and only to Santa Barbarans) by virtue of their own observations of local physical conditions and by virtue of the unrelenting coverage of the city's newspaper. Hardly a day has gone by since the initial spill that the front page has not carried an oil story; everything the paper can get its hands on is printed. It carries analyses; it makes the connections. As an appropriate result, Oil officials have condemned the paper as a "lousy" and "distorted" publication of "lies."[18]
3. *Literacy and Leisure.* In order for the information relevant to the injustice to be assimilated in all its infuriating complexity, the aggrieved parties must be, in the larger sense of the terms, literate and leisured. They must have the ability and the time to read, to ponder and to get upset.

My perspective thus differs from those who would regard the radical response as appropriate to some form or another of social or psychological freak. Radicalism is not a subtle form of mental illness (cf. recent statements of such as Bettelheim) caused by "rapid technological change," or increasing "impersonality" in the modern world; radicals are neither "immature," "underdisciplined," nor "anti-intellectual." Quite the reverse. They are persons who most clearly live under the conditions specified above and who make the most rational (and moral) response, given those circumstances. Thus radical movements draw their membership disproportionately from the most leisured, intelligent, and informed of the white youth (cf. Flacks, 1967), and from the young blacks whose situations are most analogous to these white counterparts.

The accident as a research methodology

If the present research effort has had as its strategy anything pretentious enough to be termed a "methodology," it is the methodology of what could be called "accident research." I define an "accident" as an occasion in which miscalculation leads to the breakdown of customary order. It has as its central characteristic the fact that an event occurs which is, to some large degree, unanticipated by those whose actions caused it to occur. As an event, an accident is thus crucially dissimilar both from the pseudo-event and the creeping event. It differs from the pseudo-event in that it bespeaks of an authentic and an unplanned happening; it differs from the creeping event in its suddenness, its sensation, in the fact that it brings to light a series of preconditions, actions and consequences all at once. It is "news"—often sensational news. Thresholds are reached; attentions are held.

The accident thus tends to have consequences which are the very opposite of events which are pseudo or creeping. Instead of being a deliberately planned contribution to a purposely developed "social structure" (or, in the jargon of the relevant sociological literature, "decisional outcome"), it has as its consequence the revelation of features of a social system, or of individuals' actions and personalities, which are otherwise deliberately obfuscated by those with the resources to create pseudo- and creeping events. A resultant convenience is that the media, at the point of accident, may come to function as able and persistent research assistants.

At the level of everyday individual behavior, the accident is an important lay methodological resource of gossipers—especially for learning about those possessing the personality and physical resources to shield their private lives from public view. It is thus that the recent Ted Kennedy accident functioned so well for the purpose (perhaps useless) of gaining access to that individual's private routines and private dispositions. An accident such as the recent unprovoked police shooting of a deaf mute on the streets of Los Angeles provides analogous insights into routine police behavior which official records could never reveal. The massive and unprecedented Santa Barbara oil spill has similarly led to important revelations about the structure of power. An accident is thus an important instrument for learning about the lives of the powerful and the features of the social system which they deliberately and quasi-deliberately create. It is available as a research focus for those seeking a comprehensive understanding of the structure of power in America.

Finale

Bachrach and Baratz (1962) have pointed to the plight of the pluralist students of community power who lack any criteria for the inevitable *selecting* of the "key political decisions" which serve as the basis for their research conclusions. I offer accident as a criterion. An accident is not a decision, but it does provide a basis for insight into whole series of decisions and non-decisions, events and pseudo-events which, taken together, might provide an explanation of the structure of power. Even though the local community is notorious for the increasing triviality of the decisions which occur within it (cf. Schulze, 1961; Vidich and Bensman, 1958; Mills, 1956), accident research at the local level might serve as "micro"-analyses capable of revealing the "second face of power" (Bachrach and Baratz), ordinarily left faceless by traditional community studies which fail to concern themselves with the processes by which bias is mobilized and thus how "issues" rise and fall.

The present effort has been the relatively more difficult one of learning not about community power, but about national power—and the relationship between national and local power. The "findings" highlight the extraordinary intransigence of national institutions in the face of local dissent, but more importantly, point to the processes and tactics which undermine that dissent and frustrate and radicalize the dissenters.

The relationship described between Oil, government, and the knowledge industry does not constitute a unique pattern of power in America. All major sectors of the industrial economy lend themselves to the same kind of analysis as Oil in Santa Barbara. Where such analyses have been carried out, the results are analogous in their content and analogous in the outrage which they cause. The nation's defeat in Vietnam, in a sense an accident, has led to analogous revelations about the arms industry and the manner in which American foreign policy is waged.[19] Comparable scrutinies of the agriculture industry, the banking industry, etc., would, in my opinion, lead to the same infuriating findings as the Vietnam defeat and the oil spill.

The national media dwell upon only a few accidents at a time. But across the country, in various localities, accidents routinely occur—accidents which can tell much not only about local power, but about national power as well. Community power studies typically have resulted in revelations of the "pluralistic" squabbles among local sub-elites which are stimulated by exogenous interventions (cf. Walton, 1968). Accident research at the local level might bring to light the larger societal arrangements which structure the parameters of such local debate. Research at the local level could thus serve as an avenue to knowledge about *national* power. Sociologists should be ready when an accident hits in their neighborhood, and then go to work.

Notes

1. See the report of Morton Mintz in the June 29, 1969, *Washington Post.* The conjunction of these three attributes is not, in my opinion, coincidental.

2. *SBNP* will be used to denote *Santa Barbara News-Press* throughout this paper.

3. Hickel publicly stated and wrote (personal communication) that the original leasing was a mistake and that he was doing all within discretionary power to solve this problem.

4. In a February 7 letter to Union Oil shareholders, Fred Hartley informed them that the bird refuge centers had been "very successful in their efforts." In fact, by April 30, 1969, only 150 birds (of thousands treated) had been returned to the natural habitat as "fully recovered," and the survival rate of birds treated was estimated as a miraculously high (in light of previous experience) 20 percent (cf. *SBNP*, April 30, 1969: F-3).

5. Cf. "Damaging Earthquakes of the United States through 1966," Fig. 2, National Earthquake Information Center, Environmental Science Services Administration, Coast and Geodetic Survey.

6. See Interview with Donald Weaver, Professor of Geology, UCSB, *SBNP*, Feb. 21, 1969, p. A-1, 6. (Also, remarks by Professor Donald Runnells, UCSB geologist, *SBNP*, Feb. 23, 1969, p. B-2.) Both stress the dangers of faults in the Channel, and potential earthquakes.

7. More recently plastic tents have been placed on the ocean floor to trap seeping oil; it is being claimed that half the runaway oil is now being trapped in these tents.

8. Curry's criticism is as follows:

"These new regulations make no mention at all about in-pipe safety valves to prevent blowouts, or to shut off the flow of oil deep in the well should the oil and gas escape from the drill hole region into a natural fissure at some depth below the wellhead blowout preventers. There is also no requirement for a backup valve in case the required preventer fails to work. Remember, the runaway well on Union Platform A was equipped with a wellhead blowout preventer. The blowout occurred some 200 feet below that device.

"Only one of the new guidelines seems to recognize the possible calamitous results of earthquakes which are inevitable on the western offshore leases. None of the regulations require the minimization of pollution hazards during drilling that may result from a moderate-magnitude, nearby shallow-focus earthquake, seismic sea wave (tsunami) or submarine landslide which could shear off wells below the surface.

"None of the regulations state anything at all about onshore oil and gas storage facilities liable to release their contents into the oceans upon rupture due to an earthquake or seismic seawave.

"None of the new regulations stipulate that wells must be cased to below a level of geologic hazard, or below a depth of possible open fissures or porous sands, and, as such, none of these changes would have helped the present situation in the Santa Barbara Channel or the almost continuous blowout that has been going on since last year in the Bass Straits off Tasmania, where one also finds porous sands extending all the way up to the sea floor in a tectonically active region—exactly the situation we have here."

9. Letter from Fred Hartley, President of Union Oil, to "all shareholders," dated February 7, 1969.

10. Robert Curry of the geography department of the University of California, Santa Barbara, warned that such a tactic might in fact accelerate leakage. If, as he thought, the oil reservoirs under the Channel are linked, accelerated development of one such reservoir would, through erosion of subterranean linkage channels, accelerate the flow of oil into the reservoir under Platform A, thus adding to the uncontrolled flow of oil through the sands and into the ocean. Curry was not asked to testify by the DuBridge Panel.

11. Verbal communication from one of the faculty members involved. The kind of "studies" which oil enjoys is typified by a research conclusion by Professor Wheeler J. North of Cal Tech, who after performing a one-week study of the Channel ecology under Western Oil and Gas Association sponsorship, determined that it was the California winter floods which caused most of the evident disturbance and that (as quoted from the Association Journal) "Santa Barbara beaches and marine life should be back to normal by summer with no adverse impact on tourism." Summer came with oil on the beaches, birds unreturned, and beach motels with unprecedented vacancies.

12. Cf. Walter J. Mead, "The Economics of Depletion Allowance," testimony presented to Assembly Revenue and Taxation Committee, California Legislature, June 10, 1969, mimeo; "The System of Government Subsidies to the Oil Industry," testimony presented to the U.S. Senate Subcommittee on Antitrust and Monopoly, March 11, 1969. The ostensible purpose of the depletion allowance is to encourage oil companies to explore for new oil reserves. A report to the Treasury Department by Consad Research Corp. concluded that *elimination* of the depletion allowance would decrease oil reserves by only 3 percent. The report advised that more efficient means could be found than a system which causes the government to pay $10 for every $1 in oil added to reserves. (Cf. Leo Rennert, "Oil Industry's Favors," *SBNP*, April 27, 1969, pp. A-14, 15, as reprinted from the *Sacramento Bee*.)

13. Cranston publicly confronted the staff engineer, Eugene Standley, who stated that he could neither confirm or deny writing the memo. (Cf. *SBNP*, March 11, 1969, p. A-1).

14. Major magazine coverage occurred in these (and other) national publications: *Time* (Feb. 14, 1969); *Newsweek* (March 3, 1969); *Life* (June 13, 1969); *Saturday Review* (May 10, 1969); *Sierra Club Bulletin; Sports Illustrated* (April 10, 1969). The last three articles cited were written by Santa Barbarans.

15. The notion of the banality of evil is adapted from the usage of Arendt, 1963.

16. As a result of local opposition, Union Oil was to subsequently move its operations from the Santa Barbara wharf to a more distant port in Ventura County.

17. Cf. Morton Mintz, "Oil Spill 'Radicalizes' a Conservative West Coast City," *Washington Post*, June 29, 1969, pp. C-1, 5.

18. Union Oil's public relations director stated: "In all my long career, I have never seen such distorted coverage of a news event as the *Santa Barbara News-Press* has foisted on its readers. It's a lousy newspaper." (*SBNP*, May 28, 1969, p. A-1).

19. I have in mind the exhaustively documented series of articles by I.F. Stone in the *New York Review of Books* over the course of 1968 and 1969, a series made possible, in part, by the outrage of Senator Fulbright and others at the *mistake* of Vietnam.

References

Allen, Allan A. 1969. "Santa Barbara Oil Spill." Statement presented to the U.S. Senate Interior Committee, Subcommittee on Minerals, Materials and Fuels, May 20, 1969.

Arendt, Hannah. 1963. *Eichmann in Jerusalem: A Report on the Banality of Evil.* New York: The Viking Press.

Bachrach, Peter, and Morton Baratz. 1962. "The Two Faces of Power." *American Political Science Review,* 57 (December), 947–952.

Boorstin, Daniel J. 1961. *The Image.* New York: Atheneum Press.

Engler, Robert. 1961. *The Politics of Oil.* New York: Macmillan.

Flacks, Richard. 1967. "The Liberated Generation." *Journal of Social Issues,* 22 (December), 521–543.

Gans, Herbert. 1962. *The Urban Villagers.* New York: The Free Press of Glencoe.

Mills, C. Wright. 1956. *The Power Elite.* New York: Oxford University Press.

Schattschneider, E.E. 1960. *The Semisovereign People.* New York: Holt, Rinehart & Winston.

Schulze, Robert O. 1961. "The Bifurcation of Power in a Satellite City." Pp. 19–81 in Morris Janowitz (ed.), *Community Political Systems.* New York: The Free Press of Glencoe.

Vidich, Arthur, and Joseph Bensman. 1958. *Small Town in Mass Society.* Princeton: Princeton University Press.

Walton, John. 1968. "The Vertical Axis of Community Organization and the Structure of Power." Pp. 353–367 in Willis D. Hawley and Frederick M. Wirt (eds.), *The Search for Community Power.* Englewood Cliffs, N. J.: Prentice-Hall.

CHAPTER 7

Contents

THE CHANGING CHARACTER OF URBAN POLITICS

This section deals with social change and what we may be able to expect for the future of urban political systems. As recent discussions in the media and the councils of government indicate, the problems are immense. Schools, health care, pollution, ghettoes, housing, welfare, declining tax bases, and overcrowding only begin to suggest the range of problems which some analysts estimate would require a cool trillion-dollar commitment of public and private resources for even short-term solutions. The selections that follow suggest some of the more and less optimistic views of alternative futures for the city and its political institutions. Henry Cohen's article on the constraints on the governing process very neatly lists dimensions of the problem. Irving Horowitz intelligently discusses some virtues and pitfalls in proposed systems which would decentralize urban governments.

In his article on Gary, Indiana, Edward Greer treats a specific instance of a clearly emerging phenomenon, the changing basis of ethnic control and the black mayor. While Gary—like Newark, Cleveland, and Fayette—is a unique case, it does illustrate many problems that confront mayors and reformist political organizations. To update Greer's discussion, it is interesting to note that Gary's Mayor Hatcher was reelected in the spring of 1971. John Walton's article builds on the community power and decision-making literature discussed in Chapter 6. Of particular importance here is the suggestion that a phenomenon increasingly characteristic of American cities—namely, their growing interdependence with the institutions of national society—is causally related to the advent of more competitive political systems. If such proves to be the case, we may be able to expect, in the future, more representative policy decisions. In any event, it is clear that city politics must be viewed in the context of their connection to state and national corporate institutions.

The article by Daniel Bell and Virginia Held is a choice illustration of some latent or unintended consequences of recent federal programs designed to fight poverty. While these programs may have had minimal effectiveness, the authors argue that they left a legacy of political awareness and organization that will figure prominently in future policy issues. Another illustrative change in the involvement of institutions in the urban scene is Andrew Gordon's discussion of the university and action programs. The article is based on the author's experience with Northwestern University's Center for Urban Affairs and indicates both the potential role and the limitations of the university as a change agent.

The final three selections treat various new styles of citizen participation in policy-related issues. From a large-scale study of fifteen major American cities, Richard Berk and his associates argue that the form of participation—the elitist or populist model—appears to vary as a consequence of the particular issue under consideration. The analysis is suggestive of a resolution of many problems raised in the previous section, as well as broader generalization. Walter Gove and Herbert Costner provide an interesting evaluation of a specific action program in Seattle and suggest some conditions under which similar efforts might meet with more success in the future. Finally, in another essay written for this volume, Allan Schnaiberg traces the development of the environmentalist movement. Of special interest is his analysis of the social-class dimensions of the movement. From his discussion, one might be able to infer the kinds of political movements to be expected in the future and their likely effects.

Generally speaking, all of these selections attempt to provide a sense of where we are moving as an urban political society. The picture is a complex one, though the essays attempt to provide some general prospectus.

31

HENRY COHEN, Governing Megacentropolis: The Constraints

The difficulties of governing our large metropolitan cities are manifested in the increasingly severe survival problems of large-city mayors, the struggle to maintain service standards in a number of traditional municipal activities such as sanitation, the extension of blight despite sizable renewal and housing programs in many communities, and the inability to respond effectively to demands for changes in programs and services. The disgovernance syndrome (as distinct from non-, mal-, and un-) has developed during a decade when municipal governments as a group have broadened their responsibilities, have attempted to do more and better, and have in fact been more responsive to problems of human welfare than ever before. We may expect during the '70s and '80s that municipal

Henry Cohen, "The Constraints," from "Governing the Megacentropolis: A Symposium," *Public Administration Review,* vol. 30 (September/October 1970), pp. 488–497. Reprinted by permission.

governments as a group will further broaden their responsibility, and that they will try to do more rather than less with respect to the social and economic well-being of their citizens. In order to consider what changes are needed to enable them to broaden their efforts and be more effective, it is essential to examine the ingredients of the disgovernance syndrome.

Some of these factors are those of scale and expanse. Some are primarily political, and some administrative and managerial. Others are more clearly sociological or cultural in character. All are, however, many-sided and so inter-related with one another that they become difficult to group into a typology. Individually, the factors might be dealt with; it is their simultaneous occurrence which creates the disgovernance syndrome.

Twelve factors, by no means a complete list, contribute significantly to current difficulties in mega-urban management.

1. The size of the metropolitan cities
2. The increasing bureaucratization and professionalism of municipal services
3. The growing distance between central decision and points of impact
4. The explosion in public demand and expectation
5. The complexities of federal-state-local arrangements
6. The increasing breakdown of formal political machinery at the local level
7. The scale and character of the postwar migration
8. The interdependency in urban living
9. The metropolitanization of many urban problems
10. The inadequacy of the arrangements for sheltering the municipal chief executive
11. The inability to renew the older sections of the large cities
12. The pervasiveness of a mood of alienation and powerlessness

1. The size of the metropolitan cities. The largeness of the metropolis has many beneficial qualities. Administratively, it provides a basis for stimulating special-ization and achieving efficiencies and economies which are difficult to obtain in small units. Economically, it offers a diversified labor force, concentrated markets, and opportunities for creativity that lead to growth, high levels of pro-ductivity, better paid workers, and possibilities for higher standards of living for more people. Socially, it provides diversity, stimulation, greater opportunities for the exchange of ideas. In many ways, because of this, it contributes to the liberation of man. On the one hand it provides greater opportunities for privacy and thereby freedom from the more crushing and repressive features of parochial communities, and on the other hand it provides an environment in which rigid thought and value systems (parochial rigidities) are difficult to sustain because of their constant exposure to fresh ideas and perspectives.

However, the very largeness of the city contributes to the development of many problems which cannot be easily dispelled by concentration alone on the "benefit" side of the equation. In order that the large city function, many aspects of operation must become systematized and reduced to regularity. The regularities themselves frequently become automatic and rigid, and therefore not easy to change. These new "systems" rigidities become difficult to deal with, and if they persist long enough in the face of complaint, opposition, and "reason," they are felt to be as oppressive as the "parochial" rigidities. As we shall see, the consequences of the systems rigidities are clearly observable in the increasing bureaucratization of municipal services, and the growing distance between central decision and local impact.

Students of municipal government who concentrate on efficiency and management principles are sanguine over the size issue. They tend to overlook or minimize the deeper political and sociological consequences of many of the traditional political or administrative reforms.

2.   The increasing bureaucratization and professionalization of municipal services. The bureaucratization and professionalization of municipal services have many positive aspects, more than can here be recited. For example, without ignoring many valid current concerns over a variety of environmental conditions, it is nothing short of remarkable that so much is right about big-city public health. Water supplies are generally safe to drink, milk is uncontaminated, and most communicable disease is under control. The anxieties of plague and pestilence have largely been dispelled for urban dwellers in the United States. Despite some breakdowns in recent years due to increases in utilization and overload, most urban dwellers take rapid transit services, the provision of gas, electricity, and telephone services for granted. These positive achievements are in great measure the function of technological advancement on the one hand and the invention and management of large service delivery systems.

While cities were growing and expanding, and new technologies were arising, the systems rigidities had little time to crystallize or were less noticeable and offensive than today. Progressively, however, the bureaucratic and professional systems have become more and more impervious to review and change. What started at first as efforts to define criteria to assure technical and professional competence have become closed systems to protect a class. What started as a means of assuring a community objective—high quality of service—has become a small group objective-protection of role and status. The functionaries who manage and operate the city system develop a stake in the "system," and over time consider changes in the system from their point of view rather than from the point of view and interest of the consumer. As the functionaries organize and become the primary factors in defining the elements, practices, and character of the particular system, political leadership and the receivers and consumers of the public services becomes less capable of influencing the systems of public service. The public sector, more than the private sector, becomes increasingly unresponsive to consumer demand. Not only do the functionaries vote, but because they are highly organized, they are able to have a disproportionate influence on elections by virtue of their ability to funnel campaign contributions and provide cadres of workers. In addition, since they are sophisticated in managing the system, they appreciate the significance of voting in primary elections where turnouts are typically low.

This displacement of objectives has contributed to crisis conditions in many large cities. Increasing expenditures are matched only by increasing public dissatisfaction. Its most serious overt form is evidenced in the barriers to program changes and involvement that the prevailing rules and practices present to the newcomer groups—the Negroes, Puerto Ricans, and Mexican-Americans. However, the rigidities are serious, apart from the racial factor. For example, the high costs of providing medical care under Medicare and Medicaid are not primarily a function of the presence in the cities of the ethnic poor, they are more significantly a function of the practices and arrangements for providing medical care.

3. The growing distance between central decision and points of impact. The largeness of the city and the growth of large service systems through which to carry out the public business have contributed substantially to the sense of alienation of the receiver of services from the systems which serve him. The receivers of service feel they are not getting what they want, when they want it, and how they want it. The receivers of services who have begun to look upon themselves as citizens with rights do not want to be treated as clients on the dole. They seek a new citizen-customer relationship to the system which is difficult to develop without the realities of currency transactions, competition, and the incentives of profit. Central decision makers laying out rules, patterns of service, and personnel policies are frustrated over their inability to translate intent into practice. The systems over which they preside do not deliver the services as they would like those services to be delivered.

The enormous variations from neighborhood to neighborhood in the need for different types of services, and in the character of the services provided, cannot easily be coped with in the face of the "system" rigidities. Decentralization, so appealing a solution, cannot easily overcome the differences in resource availability, area by area, nor the function of the center in resources allocation.

The need to systematize activities, procedures, and methods in the large metropolis tends to leave less discretion to the individual public servant, and tends to make public services less responsive to individual or localized needs and conditions.

The levers of change from the point of view of the receiver of service are remote. In the public sector, in contrast to the private sector, there are few incentives for the renderer of service in the field to satisfy the customer. The electoral process offers the voter little relief from the impersonal and impervious administrative structures of the large city. The resulting alienation is not confined to the blacks, Puerto Ricans, and Mexican-Americans; it is endemic among many groups in the large city.

4. The explosion in public demand and expectations. The rapidity of change since World War II—the change in character of the civil rights quest, the increased unionization of public employees, and the radicalization of large portions of the youth population—have severely weakened the ability of local political and administrative leadership to cope with problems by resorting to incremental strategies. Incrementalism has become a devalued currency. It is still in use, in fact there may be no alternative to it, but it enjoys no public confidence. During the '50s, the northern and western cities attempted to deal with the increased migration from the South and from Puerto Rico with incremental strategies. The problem of absorption would be solved, it was thought, if a few more remedial reading teachers were added, foster care services expanded, casework services more effectively coordinated, and additional public housing units constructed. The large cities were being hit by a tidal wave, but their informed leadership—in and out of government—was tilting with windmills. By the early 1960s, more than half of black America, for the first time, lived outside the states of the old confederacy, and growing numbers of black youth born and raised in the freer environment of the northern and western cities were coming of age. Their demand was not for incremental improvement, but for parity—freedom now. Incremental strategies were based on assumed relationships and program targets which were no longer acceptable. Though parity could not be achieved overnight, the "reasonable" objectives of the old incremental strategies became passé. The '60s was a decade in which new targets and objectives were defined and negotiated. Their achievement was clearly beyond the means and capability of municipal leadership. This explosion in expectation was not limited to the blacks. Comparable revolutions in the patterns of demand erupted among public employees, the young, and other interest groups.

Public leadership, caught in the crossfire of demands, is overwhelmed. Raising tax revenues is not easier and bureaucratic resistance to change is if anything greater than heretofore. At a deeper level, the knowledge base needed for problem solving is not keeping up with the multiplication and intensification of the problems. The demand for radical change and improvement has become universal. While municipal governments try to do more, the limits to improvement and resistance to change become formidable. There seems to be no way to break away from incrementalism which we may not want to live with but without which we cannot survive.

5.   *The complexity of federal-state-local arrangements.* The intergovernmental system of the United States is unsymmetrical. Different federal programs involve the locality through a variety of arrangements. Similarly, the states do not have uniform responsibilities, and the patterns of state-city relationships are varied. The character, scope, and structure of municipal and county governments is also extremely variegated. This infinitely varied system is a product of regional and historical differences in the country. This lack of symmetry in the intergovernmental system has had many advantages in preserving flexibility in the arrangements by which the system operates over the American continent. Nevertheless, the difficulties for localities in managing the federal system are

immense. For one thing, responsibility and power are diffused. One need but examine any number of programs which are intergovernmental in character, such as welfare, manpower, and model cities, to appreciate how difficult it is to assess accountability, and how even more difficult it is for local leadership (which is the target of popular wrath) to affect the programs substantially. The administrative and political hazards of managing many of the New Frontier programs in the face of erratic congressional funding have driven many mayors to distraction.

The lack of accountability which flows from these complex intergovernmental arrangements contributes to the difficulties local government faces in broadening its responsibilities to its citizens in the absence of sufficient locally generated tax revenues.

6. The increasing breakdown of formal political machinery at the local level. Local political machines have come into increasing disrepute over the past hundred years. Civic reform, going back to the muckraking period late in the last century, has steadily eroded the strength of local political structures. The reforms took many forms: nonpartisan government, the city manager system, the civil service system, and competitive bidding, among others. Reform came on the heels of scandals, widespread corruption, and incompetence. Whatever its weaknesses, and it had many, the system of local politics had many benefits for which we have not yet provided effective substitutes.

At the ward or district level, the leader or captain, in contact with his constituents, was able to mediate within the governmental system for them. He could overcome rules and bypass the chain of command. He preserved some flexibility in a system which size, technology, and bureaucracy was beginning to make increasingly rigid.

At the citywide level, the political system functioned to get things done. It might exact a price, but subways would get built, roads paved, and aqueducts constructed. Dissidents would be quieted, bought off, or removed. Legislators from districts with competing claims would be permitted to represent their districts, but others would be kept in line, not free to express their moral qualms. With the political machine, the balance in decision making was more towards doing things and doing things faster. The public system had some of the aspects of the private system—particularly money incentive. Since the machine in one manner or another took a cut, the premium was on high-volume turnover. The more that was done, the greater the profit.

The emphasis in civic reform was in substituting technocracy and professionalism for politics. The mediating role that the political machine played was lost or largely reduced. Local citizens in need of service had to cope with the bureaucracy directly, with its rigidities untempered by the softening influence of politics. With no controlling group in the system having a stake in getting things done, projects and decisions were left to the mercy of elongated administrative and consultative processes where the veto dominates and the decisive act is a rarity. With no relatively coherent political machine, every legislator feels freer to play for the most parochial advantage. The executive is left to manage as best he can, without the disciplining, mediating, and humanizing properties of the political machine.

7. *The scale and character of the postwar migration.* Since World War II, Negro migration to the North and West has changed the character of white-black relations in the nation as a whole, and has created some of the most difficult problems confronting the medium and large cities. In New York City alone, almost two and a quarter million blacks and Puerto Ricans have migrated or been born in the last twenty-five years. This largest of the nation's cities had to accommodate and absorb a preindustrial population equal to over one-quarter of the population which resided in the city over this period. In most of the other large cities the proportion to be absorbed has been even greater. The demands on resources, talent, knowledge, and political skill have taxed municipal government and municipal leadership.

The recent migration has focused on certain deficiencies in the pattern of municipal services which until recently were all but ignored. The bulk of municipal services are provided on what can be described as a self-service basis. The potential user of the service must recognize his need for the service and seek it out. This applies to most welfare and social services, health services, and library services. It applies also to education, even though here state laws establish schooling as compulsory. In the other than the human resource area, the self-service system applies to certain aspects of zoning, and to a variety of licensing and other regulatory matters. Thus, the local service system contains an assortment of services or requirements with respect to which the individual citizen must make his own decisions as to need or applicability. He must then exercise the initiative to secure the service, license, or approval. Historically, the bulk of the service system has never successfully coped with the problems of providing services for people or groups who are incapable of brokering the system themselves. Only for situations where there is a clear and present danger (public safety, public health, or other potential catastrophe) have the municipal services been organized for intervention. The new migration pointed up the inadequacy of the assumptions underlying the municipal service patterns, and created the political imperatives which made it essential to deal with these inadequacies. The new migrants were unfamiliar with the service systems, and, in many instances, they had difficulty with the language. They were unable to broker the system for themselves or their children. In comparison to the migrants in earlier years, the new migrants were U.S. citizens, and the levels of expectations of the public service systems were higher. Thus, the municipal services suddenly came under attack because of the inadequacy of their outreach capability, and municipal workers who had been working conscientiously under one set of assumptions were suddenly under attack because the rules were changed. Stemming from the migration, the demand to modify services, enrich services, extend services, and create new services has added to the pressures of limited financial resources. One need not detail here the riots and other dramatic forms of conflict, to underscore how the new migration has attributed to the added burdens of managing the cities.

8. The interdependency in urban living. The highly technical system essential for maintaining life and activity in the city creates a high degree of interdependency. The technical system, broken at any point, creates friction and enormous inconvenience. Relatively small numbers of individuals can thus tie up the system. Strikes among public employees can bring to a halt major subsystems of activity—transportation, sanitation services, hospitals, and others. Demonstrators and sit-ins can consume executive energy, so that general planning, program development, and management are neglected. Priorities are distorted in favor of those who are employed in activities, the curtailment of which makes the community at large most vulnerable, or of those whose tactics, regardless of purpose, are most dramatic or appealing. Traditional systems of voicing concern—in meetings, conferences, and public hearings—lose their value. The escalation of demands, the extremeness of expression, and the disruption of daily life have become the norm.

9. The metropolitanization of many urban problems. The increasing interdependency in urban living extends beyond the central city boundaries to the assorted jurisdictions surrounding the city. Many of the residents of these outer zones are former central city dwellers who have moved outward in search of less dense residential areas. Partly the outward movement reflects a desire to escape some of the social and financial burdens of central-city living, including the problems of crime and delinquency. It is natural, therefore, to expect suburbanites to resist those metropolitan approaches which will transfer some of the central-city burdens to them. Beyond the crucial physical and economic development concerns, such as transportation, water supply, and water pollution, are a series of regional problems which defy easy solution. For example, fiscal inequities arise from the variations in the regional distribution of business properties, commuter population, and low-income population. Some communities, including most of the central cities, carry disproportionate costs in meeting the requirements of business and industry from which the whole region benefits and in meeting the needs of low-income people who concentrate in the cities. The demographic equation in most central cities, because it creates such a concentrated burden on the center, requires a regional strategy for the redistribution of low-income population throughout the region. The economic well-being of all in the region depends on preventing the central cities from being crushed by the overload of problems. Yet, most suburbanites will not willingly share the burden. Unless the state governments intervene strongly, which is unlikely, the cities will thus continue to live with intolerable problems for at least the next generation or two.

10. The inadequacy of arrangements for sheltering the municipal chief executive. In strong mayor cities, where the political machine has been weakened, mayors are left with relatively little shelter from the all-consuming crossfires of municipal life. They are also deprived of the out-reach capability and intelligence network which a political machine in touch with ordinary citizens can provide. In the city manager cities, the city council, to which the manager reports, does provide to some extent both shelter for the manager and a corrective balance that keeps government in touch with the people. In the larger cities, the mayors have little strength for dealing with the bureaucracies when they attempt to make them more responsive to constituency demands and winds of change. These mayoralty difficulties are exacerbated by the growth of intergovernmental programs which are usually administered by vertical bureaucracies in which the professionals and administrators within each program track at every level of government mutually reinforce one another against intrusion from political executives or generalist administrators. Few federal programs are designed to strengthen the mayor's capability to cope with complex local issues and relations. Unlike the council-manager system or the collegial system which exists in many European cities, the mayor alone in American big-city government bears performance responsibility. With performance becoming more and more difficult, the mayor's job has become exposed and dangerous.

11. The inability to renew the older sections of the large cities. Building on vacant land, though it has its problems, is not comparable to the difficulties confronting built-up cities with substantial sections of decay. The difficulties in tenant relocation and the increased militancy of neighborhood groups have made urban renewal all but impossible. In addition to the problems arising from the large substandard housing stock, others arise from the lack of an adequate system of public facilities. Despite the enormous need for modern schools, hospitals and other health facilities, community centers and libraries, and for space for a growing array of community activities, formidable obstacles lay in the way of constructing public facilities in the ghetto. The community consultation process, essential as it may be, nevertheless causes lengthy delays in the processing of projects from conception to completion. Not only do these delays lead to significant increases in costs of construction, but they impede progress in dealing with deep problems because of the inadequacy of existing facilities.   Municipal government is constantly caught between the Scylla of insufficient attention to community interest, and the Charybdis of slow action and delay. We can expect this problem to become worse, not easier.

12. The pervasiveness of a mood of alienation and powerlessness. Feelings of alienation and powerlessness are not confined to the blacks, the Puerto Ricans, and the Mexican-Americans. These feelings are present among many young people, and among many others of all ages caught in the web of complex public and private organizational systems, and of dense urban neighborhoods.

The changing social structure of urban family life has drastically modified the living style of the aged, who nationally represent 10 percent of central city population. Social Security and Medicare may improve some of the conditions of living, but they do not deal with the psycho-social rupture between the aged and others in the urban setting.

The failure to cope adequately with the large migrations from the South and Puerto Rico, and the failure to date to integrate the blacks and the browns into our social and economic life, have contributed to rises in crime and delinquency which create fear and anxiety among all groups in the population, and add to the tensions among the races.

The city, among other things, is a competitive arena, where men and women compete for improved opportunity, status, and recognition. In the bigger cities the competition is heightened, for the stakes and the rewards are potentially greater. Even for those who achieve relative states of affluence, life in the city is like a slippery slope.

While there are, obviously, differences in the degree and character of alienation and powerlessness or helplessness among different groups, it is important to recognize how pervasive these phenomena are.

The interdependency of modern living, while it assures freedom in some ways, limits it in others. Mounting dissatisfaction and frustration erupts in attacks on existing organizational arrangements and procedures. Some of the protest is directed at overcoming inequity and injustice, while other protest is directed at the apparent senselessness of so much bureaucratic behavior and anachronistic practice. The distance between the individual and the amorphous forces which affect him contributes on the one hand to a state of helplessness, and on the other to attacks on the faceless establishment in which all power appears to reside. The difficulty is further seen in the anomaly of our progress. We know by the indicators that most measurable conditions are getting better, but most immeasurable things are also getting worse. For the minorities, even to the extent that conditions have become somewhat better, the gap seldom narrows and the pain deepens. As the decibel count of protest rises, it becomes more and more difficult to do anything in public life, yet the demands for accomplishment go up, not down. Not only are the people alienated and powerless, but so are the organization men, and the political leadership. So, alienation and powerlessness are pervasive and cannot be relieved simply by improving this or that service, or satisfying this or that constituency.

Can cities assume ultimate responsibility for human welfare?

Considering the difficulties in organizing communal existence to deal with already defined responsibilities, it is rather mystical to hold out hope that cities can organize themselves to assume ultimate responsibility for human welfare, even if ultimate responsibility could be defined.

An examination of the intergovernmental system shows how elusive a pastime it would be for city governments to attempt to assume ultimate responsibility.

Though increased financial resources would help the cities cope with some of their problems, it should be clear from the above discussion that money alone will not be sufficient. Similarly, managerial improvements to deliver services more effectively would help, but will not be sufficient. What is needed are changes in a variety of political arrangements. The following notions are intended to suggest only a few directions we may have to pursue.

1. Intergovernmental arrangements must be simplified so that it becomes easier for local political and executive leadership to organize programs and to define the relationships among programs. The existing system of categorical grants places too much of the balance of power into the vertical bureaucracies, vis-à-vis the city political leadership. It also places too much power into the hands of state government, where the political equation is different from that of city governments. The intervention of state bureaucracies merely adds delays and complications. Building on the bloc grant principle embodied in model cities legislation, big-city mayors would be strengthened in their efforts to cope with city problems and with the wide array of conflicting interest groups.

2. Because of the growing power of the bureaucrats and professionals, steps need to be taken to strengthen the role and participation of consumers and receivers of services in the decision-making process. Most of the experimentation with community action programs in the last seven years has been somewhat to the side of the regular governmental and political structure. It is perhaps time to begin efforts to regularize these activities in a number of ways, such as holding elections to community and neighborhood boards on days when municipal voting normally takes place.

In addition, changes in the structure of local legislative bodies should be considered. In large cities we should perhaps reverse the trend towards smaller councils and begin to enlarge the councils in a number of ways. The doubling of wards or districts would provide representation responsive to smaller constituencies. The addition of more at-large seats would provide representation for interest groups which are not geographically concentrated. The introduction of proportional representation in at-large elections would assure participation of an assortment of citywide interests. Such measures should be accompanied by a strengthening of council committee structure which should be provided with funds for adequate staffing. Larger councils, while more unwieldy than smaller bodies, would at least concentrate more of the furious conflict within the legislative bodies where in the end, decisions must be made, budgets approved, and taxing policy set. By channeling more of the demands and frustrations into the legislative arena, the bargaining should hopefully become more realistic and the expectations more realizable. There is great educational value in investing groups with performance responsibility. While in the short run, such new legislative bodies might make the life of the mayor and executive agencies more miserable, in the long run it should help them. It would regularize some of the random conflict and organize it around real choices. Much of the conflict would be within the legislative bodies among different interest groups, and not directed as much at the executive. Furthermore, as the executive agencies became more sensitive to consumer demand, the areas of conflict should lessen.

3. There has been much discussion in recent years about the delegation of certain local government functions to community groups. Actually, there is a long history of contracting out certain functions to private health, welfare, and recreation agencies. There are also substantial precedents in which local governments purchase services from other governments. Recently, some of the discussion has centered around the development of two-tier governmental arrangements within big cities, following the London pattern. Some of the reviews of the London borough system indicate that this system does not produce more efficient, effective, or responsive service. Apparently, citizen involvement is not increased, and the bureaucratic rigidities that plague the large-city systems exist in the borough governments. Nevertheless, the distrust in American cities of the large government agencies cannot be ignored. There are benefits that could accrue from a pluralistic system of service delivery in the large cities. It can stimulate new leadership and new ideas, and by introducing competition into the system, it could keep everyone on his toes. We should be searching for ways to delegate certain functions, recognizing that each such effort will have hazards and drawbacks. Certain recreation functions can be delegated to local groups; why do central agencies have to run programs in local schools or parks? Certain housing functions can be delegated; why can local groups not be given responsibilities for some housing inspection functions? Why not delegate some of the local sanitation services? Why not delegate some of the responsibilities for standing traffic violations? This list could be lengthened. The New York experience with school decentralization should be observed carefully; it may provide some insight into ways of moving towards a two-tier system of local government in the U.S.

4. Local governments need to expand their coordinative capabilities at the neighborhood level, and improve the information and referral services for individual citizens. A large variety of efforts have been undertaken along these lines: the Citizens Advice Bureau in England, the neighborhood multiservice centers in a number of American cities, and the model cities programs among others. None is yet so successful a model that we can extend it rapidly. Recent attempts in New York and Boston to extend the mayoralty outreach into neighborhoods, in distinction to a functional department outreach, bear watching. The expansion of services, while important, is no substitute for improvement of methods of linking people to services and making services more responsive to individual needs.

Conclusion

The disgovernance syndrome in the big cities embodies political and sociological factors more than it does managerial and administrative factors. It represents matters of mood and feeling which are not easily quantifiable. It represents a sense of malaise with things as they are, despite the social and economic improvements in life for so many. It also represents some of the consequences of America's unresolved racial problems. For cities to deal with these problems will require more funds, a strengthening of the central executive vis-à-vis the governmental bureaucracies, a strengthening of consumer groups vis-à-vis the providers of the public services, the invention of new political mechanisms which bring the competing interests more effectively into the decision-making system, and the creation of administrative mechanisms which assist citizens in getting more nearly what they need and what is their right. If we can resolve more effectively these political and administrative issues, then cities will be able to serve their citizens better. If we cannot, then people will have to look elsewhere.

32

IRVING LOUIS HOROWITZ, "Separate But Equal": Revolution and Counterrevolution in the American City

City finances: from affluence to austerity

The political system of alderman, councilman, borough presidents, and mayors, was laid out at a time when the city was a viable and growing community. Today, when the city must be considered anything but viable or expanding, these same political structures with their built-in constraints and mutual responsibilities have made of the mayor's post an office that is more readily described in psychological than political terms. As former Mayor Joseph Barr of Pittsburgh recently declared: "You are beat like a bag of sand all day. You leave the office and you really feel like you've been clubbed all day."

It is an old adage that wealth breeds corruption. However, the corollary is rarely drawn: poverty breeds austerity. And in the history of the American city, corruption has been a vital input in getting essential tasks done—from building bridges and highways to making the necessary payoffs to racial and ethnic leaders that help prevent ghetto explosions. But now the padding has gone out of city budgets. Apart from the fact that most of the financial obligations are ongoing in character, i.e., salaries to police, fireman, and other service personnel, little in the way of new money is entering the city treasury.

Increasing city taxes helps little, since those best able to pay such taxes

Irving Louis Horowitz, " 'Separate But Equal': Revolution and Counterrevolution in the American City." Copyright © from *Social Problems*, vol. 17, no. 3 (Winter 1970), pp. 294–312. Reprinted by permission of the author and the Society for the Study of Social Problems.

have moved to the suburbs. Local debt per capita has quadrupled since 1946 while the per capita federal debt has declined substantially (Piven and Cloward, 1967). New York City provides a classic model. One out of five people now lives in poverty. The concentration of poverty among minority groups indicates that such trends will persist. These minority groups are pouring into the city, while the middle classes are leaving in equal numbers. An interesting statistic is that from the 1960 Census to 1966, Bronx median family income declined from $5,830 to $5,525, this in the face of an annual inflationary rate of 3 to 4 percent. Further, the number of families in the Bronx earning less than $3,000 per annum increased from 16 percent to 21 percent. To the economic data one must add the geographic problems. The total population in New York's chief ghettoes, such as Central and East Harlem, has decreased by as much as 25 percent; however, at the same time the numbers of Negroes and Puerto Ricans in these ghettoes have increased—so that in Bedford-Stuyvesant, there are now 93 to 95 percent blacks, in contrast to 85 percent only six years earlier (cf. Lurie, 1963; Manso, 1969; Olson, 1969).

This brief capsule of economic and ecological information is well known. What is not well appreciated, however, is how this condition deprives the cities of the necessary financial "fat" to do business as usual. The possibility of building low-rent housing, taking care of block mayors, "fixing" the right people at the right time, are all thoroughly reduced in this era or urban economic austerity. To this must be added the drive toward "clean government" that is perhaps more enforced by the desperate needs of a city for federal and state funds than by any alteration in the moral climate of the city. That the cities have become "cleaned up" may thus work more to the disadvantage of the poor than to their advantage. The cities, in effect, are more cleaned out than they are cleaned up (Hartman, 1967).

Meanwhile, the ideology of how to run a city has not changed even among "newcomers" to political power. Certainly, nothing in the pre-election statements of Hatcher in Gary or Stokes in Cleveland indicated an awareness that this structure was no longer the way to maintain political authority. But clearly at the same time the costs of education, welfare, and health increase, the local tax base has dissolved (Tax Foundation, 1969). The same payoffs no longer obtain for the mayor; and in turn the mayor cannot guarantee the same network of rewards to party stalwarts or to personal cronies.

In the light of the erosion of the fiscal condition of most large American cities, the interesting question is: Will the simple act of electing Negro mayors serve to "keep the lid" on the black population? It has been suggested by black militants that the Negro mayor is the glorified "block captain" of yesteryear. The new mayor and the old block captain manage the crumbs by means of which the seething ghetto mass simmers down. But just as the Negro block captain had fewer jobs to dole out and less money to spread on friends and party stalwarts than their white counterparts, the new Negro mayors find themselves with little but promises and hope to offer their constituents. It seems dubious that the tactic of employing Negro mayors of powderkeg cities can contain the sort of militancy prevalent in the black ghettoes—a militancy which perhaps has become as harsh in its condemnation of "Negroes" as it is of "Honkies."

The flight of talent

As any novice will testify, the first law of the political jungle is survival. Even electoral losses serve to test the mettle of those who enter politics with a soft skin versus those who enter with the will to win. The Jamesian dictum of the "tough minded" versus the "tender hearted" has traditionally applied in the American political arena. Yet despite such an obvious dictum of survival, the summer of 1969 witnessed the resignations and announcements of retirement of mayors of several major cities. Among the casualties were Joseph Barr of Pittsburgh, Jerome P. Cavanagh of Detroit, Arthur Naftalin of Minneapolis, and Richard C. Lee of New Haven. The men were more than local figures. They were architects of national policies toward urban areas. Their activities ranged from holding office in the prestigious United States Conference of Mayors to framing the federal Model Cities program.

Many factors may have contributed to their decisions: the ethnic and religious bases of support that put the special appeal politician into office have largely turned suburban; the potential of the mayor's office as a stepping stone for national frame and power has given way to gubernatorial and senatorial figures—wielders of far greater power; being mayor is no longer a sinecure, but very hard, often unrewarded work; and with the loss of the city tax base there has been a corresponding loss of the patronage pile that in former eras kept disbelievers and dissidents in line. Finally, the loss of funds has exacerbated conditions to the point where the generally "civilized" forms of mayoral control—bribery and graft—have given way to increasingly "uncivilized" confrontations between police power and poor man's power.

Allied to the flight of funds has been the flight of talent available to the mayor's office. In an earlier age, political appointments had a certain strategic and status value; but now, these same positions are far less enticing. The options open to technically trained personnel in private enterprise are extensive, and the risks run are far fewer. Thus, even if and when a man of talent can be found for the mayor's post, the back-up posts are increasingly filled by semicompetent or even downright unqualified people. In the face of such a situation, the ability to generate public-spirited behavior at a citywide level is at least as difficult as doing so at a statewide or federal level—only without even the rewards of these state and national offices.

Like major administrative posts in universities, the office of city mayor is no longer a high-status, low-work position. It is usually a terminal post and rarely leads to higher office. It is increasingly a post which demands the juridical skills of an eighteenth-century lawyer, rather than the verbal skills of a turn of the century ward heeler. The "fun" has gone out of the position almost with the same degree of rapidity as the trough has been emptied of surplus.

Getting exact information on the character of city experts is, to say the least, very difficult. A big city mayor does have the supplemental support of federal and state agencies assigned to city affairs (often unwanted support, viewed as interference). And the mayor's office can count on foundations and private organizations who provide free resources in small amounts, but resources that are relatively unencumbered with bureaucratic sloth. The programming of the Ford Foundation in the New York and Cleveland areas during 1968 and 1969 is a good illustration of instances where experts made the difference between "hot" and "cool" summers. However, the foundation personnel remain only marginally linked to city administrations. And so the problem of getting high-level personnel into local city government remains.

In a perceptive essay on "The Mayors vs. the Cities" in the Focus on New York issue of *The Public Interest,* James Q. Wilson (1969:31) points out both the difficulties in getting needed expert help, and the liberal liability they can become once acquired.

> For all the talk about cities being "where it's at," very few able administrators seek out employment in the low-prestige, low-paying jobs that city hall has to offer. There are such people, but they are small in number and young in age. To get the best of them, or even any at all, every big-city mayor is in competition with every other one. The mayor that runs (however well advised) a business-as-usual administration is at a profound disadvantage in this competition. Indeed, the would-be mayor must often start seeking them out when he decides to run for office so that they can give him the speeches, the position papers, and the "task force reports" that increasingly are the hallmark of a campaign that wins the sympathy of the media. The process of tuning the mayor to be responsive to the audience begins, therefore, even before he becomes mayor. And if he should ever entertain any thoughts about taking a "tough line" or going after the "backlash vote" (however rational such a strategy might be), he would immediately face a rebellion among his younger campaign and staff assistants.

Of course, in some sense, the problem of keeping middle-echelon appointees intact is a reflection of the larger problem of keeping the office of the mayor nationally important. Very few mayors seem able to achieve higher offices, such as governorships and senatorial nominations. Since doing a good job as mayor becomes an impossible achievement, the use of the office to create a sound political image becomes similarly impossible. And as the office of the mayor becomes a political dead end, the opportunities to build a sound cadre around the office diminish.

The city divided

Another prime explanation of the problem of the urban governability malaise is to be found in an ecological pattern that concentrates black population in the cities, white populations in the county, but white political systems in both areas, with relatively interlocking structures. Ethnic politics, particularly in the large Eastern and Midwestern cities, continue as usual: the mayoralty continues to be the plum of Irish Catholics (Cavanagh in Detroit, Daley in Chicago, Yorty in Los Angeles, Collins in Boston, Tate in Philadelphia) and increasingly of Italian and Spanish Catholics (Alioto in San Francisco, Cervantes in St. Louis, Addonizio in Newark). By the time the blacks assume the mayoralty, the tax base of the inner cities is so eroded that the finances of these cities are drastically inadequate to permit the exercise of normal local corruption: patronage jobs from the local armory to newspaper delivery stands, smalltime graft guaranteeing rapid construction work and electrical and plumbing installations, the manipulation of the size of police and fire departments to guarantee jobs for overzealous and undertrained youth, and the satisfactory management of a welfare system to prevent starvation from within and looting from without. All of these sub rosa "services" collectively added up in the past to keep the political machine working effectively. The voting base, padded by these marginal personnel, thus reinforced the incumbent and his party apparatus.

Of the total population growth of cities in the last 20 years, nearly 80 percent of the nonwhite increase has been in the central cities, while approximately the same percentage of the white increase has been outside the inner city regions. But of course these distributions of population signify much more than simple ecological transformation. The gap between death rates for white and nonwhite infants has become wider, increasing from 66 percent in 1950 to 90 percent in 1964. Living areas inhabited by blacks and Mexican-Americans contain 3.5 times the proportion of substandard housing that is to be found in white areas. Nonwhite unemployment rates consistently run two to four times that of white rates, with rates among young males as high as 40 percent in some cities. As recently as 1964, a nonwhite American with four years of college education could expect to earn less in his lifetime ($185,000) than a white who had only completed his eighth grade ($191,000). Black Median income as a percentage of white median income has actually dropped to 53 percent from a previous figure of 57 percent (U.S. Dept. of Labor, 1966; U.S. Dept. of Commerce, 1966, 1967). These figures only underscore the economic and social sources of political instability. They do not really explain this instability, for if some indicators are worse, others are better or at least getting better (Olsen, *et al.* 1969).

The exacerbation of racial tensions is further reinforced by the fact that efforts at racial balance, slum clearance, and urban improvements *per se* have a strong racist bias. The rise of racial voting in cities like Milwaukee and Los Angeles only underscore the intense racial separatism that has come to define the city. The city is now two cities—divided not so much by educational and income levels as by racial types. And attempts to break down this separation have only taken forms such as the Hemisfair in San Antonio which displaced blacks and browns, but not middle-class whites, or magnificent baseball and football stadiums in the middle of still unrenewed black ghettoes in cities such as Atlanta and St. Louis, or more subtly, racially "balanced" communities in areas formerly deep in the ghetto regions, which provide buffer zones under the guise of integrated living quarters. Whether such decisions are made consciously or otherwise, they have the same consequence of dividing black and white citizens, and hence making "two cities" within a city, ungovernable by a single mayor (cf. Schrag, 1969).

The process of polarization is a pleasant phrase which disguises a very unpleasant situation. A great deal has been said of the militancy of the Black Panthers in Oakland, the Revolutionary Action Movement in New York, the Liberators of St. Louis, the Blackstone Rangers of Chicago, etc. But the fact is that the white working class has been mobilizing its own efforts in paramilitary defense. *The New York Magazine* of April 14, 1969, reports the following:

> The revolt involves the use of guns. In East Flatbush, and Corona, and all those other places where the white working class lives, people are forming gun clubs and self-defense leagues and talking about what they will do if real race rioting breaks out. It is a tragic situation, because the poor blacks and the working-class whites should be natural allies. Instead, the black man has become the symbol of the working-class white man's resentments. "I never had a gun in my life before," a 34-year old Queens bartender named James Giuliano told me a couple of weeks ago. "But I got me a shotgun, license and all. I hate to have the thing in the house because of the kids. But the way things are goin', I might have to use it on someone. I really might. It's comin' to that. Believe me, it's comin' to that."

The task of making allies, "natural" or otherwise, out of enemies is exacerbated by a white working class that cannot get beyond the bills of the week, reading about welfare mothers organizing for the purpose of getting credit cards. Even if community control does not guarantee economic equality, it would at least permit the emergence of countervailing pressure groups that would lessen the present age of urban anxiety.

The response from mayors has not exactly been illuminating. A marked note of architectural monumentalism has crept into the thinking of leaders of such cities as Philadelphia, Pittsburgh, and St. Louis. Each seems bent on making their cities major tourist attractions and in developing multimillion dollar projects that lead to the creation of pavillions, malls, plazas, cultural centers, etc. that bring visitors for a week or suburbanites for an evening, but do next to nothing for the inner-city dweller, who continues to live in the interstices of the city. This architectural monumentalism has the support of real estate and banking interests and easily generates matching federal funds, but call it "Fun City," "The Iron Triangle," "Gateway to the West," this monumentalism is itself a large part of the problem and hardly a solution to it. It too only reinforces the fact that one mayor is being asked to preside over two cities, or more to the point, two virtually sealed-off sets of racial and social classes.

Federal programs vs. local power

The agony of the mayoralty results also because at the very moment the city tax base is eroding, there is also a militant resistance on the part of state and federal agencies to shoulder any more financial responsibility. The Pennsylvania legislature has repeatedly rejected requests for city payroll taxes that would obligate those who live in the suburbs but work in the cities to pay for the privilege; and the same fate has befallen efforts at indirect levies in New Jersey and elsewhere that call for a new tax on banks and lending institutions, a tax earmarked for use to ease the plight of the urban poor. When this has been coupled with the cutback in federal programs sponsored by the Office of Economic Opportunity, and in its various training and welfare centers, the magnitude of resentment by the cities has been equalled by the magnitude of resistance by the suburban regions to pay any increased freight. The war on poverty has come to look more like a war on the poor, as both federal and state bureaucracies remain unwilling to act.

Under the circumstances, the routes open to the cities are considerably fewer than they were even ten years ago. The riots and looting that have intimidated urban dwellers serve to reinforce the death wish of suburbanites to bottle up the cities, to put a cork on them economically and educationally, and let them become sources of warfare between blue-collar workers and black-faced welfarers (Gans, 1969).

The old protest that urban renewal means nigger removal has been borne out by the vivid and livid description of federally sponsored housing projects in big centers like Harlem or Watts. James Baldwin has called such projects prison houses for the poor blacks, and his descriptions only underscore the widespread feeling that such planning is a racial monstrosity: the constant failure to attract residents to these projects in such low-income areas as the Pruitt-Igoe district in St. Louis indicates the failure of bureaucracy, if not the failure of planning for, rather than by, people. That sociologists like Herbert Gans (1962) and Lee Rainwater (1967) have documented these charges many times over does nothing to erase a quarter century of planning activities that took into account the political needs of the mayor's office, the economic needs of the federal authority and the engineering needs of the housing authority—but not the human needs of the inhabitants.

The obvious is also true. The physical and social structures of virtually every large city in the nation have become increasingly unable to meet the needs of rapidly growing populations for jobs, housing, education, and other services. They are decreasingly in a position to cope with massive violence, population concentration, and postindustrial pollution (Boulding, 1963). But the trigger mechanism of these constants is the racial variable. The absolute rate of urban decline is important, but much less so than the relative living conditions of white and black, rich and poor, suburb and inner city residents.

The solutions put forward under both Democratic and Republican welfare administrations accentuate federal support programs at the expense of local authorities. This has the dramatic effect of weakening still further the mayor's authority by creating a link between city welfare leaders and national directors that bypass city government. The differences between the welfare programs of Nixon vis-à-vis Johnson relate to the relative controls of welfare funds by local versus national figures, but they do not serve to restore the lost fiscal power of the urban mayor. The poverty gap is now roughly $10.8 billion. By expending this amount, in addition to the $8 billion already allotted to the welfare programs, all thirty million Americans now in the underclass can be brought above the poverty threshhold. Such income maintenance programs have built-in levers for work incentives. Thus, even Nixon cannot get away from increasing the urban poverty indebtedness, nor can he possibly restore the authority of the mayor—since the funding process continues to cycle in from the government to the neighborhood.

The difficulty here is that the enormous cost of the bureaucracy to maintain and establish this program would eat up most of these funds; it would reinforce precisely the sort of federal involvement that has worked so ineffectively in the past, and it would further weaken any sense of local autonomy or even mayoral control of the urban areas governed. What is so tragic is that the very men who advocate even greater expenditure of federal funds in income maintenance programs and guaranteed annual wages, do appreciate more keenly than most that it is precisely these programs that in the past have accentuated rather than alleviated the "income gap" between the rich and the poor. One such figure, Philip M. Klutznick, board Chairman of the Urban Investment and Development Company of Chicago, and the American Bank and Trust Company of New York, put the matter quite directly (even though he went on blithely to support bigger and better bureaucratic programming).

> State and now federal aid to education is meant to better educational opportunity for all. Actually, it has widened the gap between expenditures for education in the suburbs as against the inner city. Yet, the pressing and demanding need was the reverse. Likewise, in housing, the FHA and public housing programs were supposed to help everybody. Yet, the first worked to accelerate the white man's escape to the suburbs and the second increased the number of Negro ghettoes in the inner city (1969).

Under such circumstances to argue the case for an enlarged bureaucracy seems ingenuous if not worse.

The difficulties in the life of the city, or the life of the mayor for that matter, ought not to be confused with the character of the continuing impulse toward urbanization. By 1964 the percent of the population living in metropolitan regions had reached 65 percent; and 70 percent by 1970 is projected. But in 1900 over 60 percent of this metropolitan population lived within central cities; by 1965 the number had declined to under 50 percent. In a nutshell, the growth of suburbia has been staggering, ranging from New Orleans with a suburban increase of 109.0 percent in one decade (1950–1960) to Dallas, where the suburbs increased by 30.7 percent. In the meantime, the inner cities of New York, Chicago, Philadelphia, Detroit, Baltimore, Cleveland, Washington, St. Louis, and Boston, were undergoing varying degrees of economic decline and political polarization. An analysis of economic pattern yields some basic explanations. Residents of the inner city in 1950 earned roughly 88.5 percent of the income of their compatriots in the suburbs. This figure of median family income shows a widening gap; by 1960 the ratio was 86.2 percent—or for the average sub-urban family an income of $7,772. The inner city income median was $6,697. Thus economically as well as demographically, the gulf between the inner city and the suburban regions is widening in the same way as the gap between under-developed and properly developing regions (cf. Seligman, 1965; Laumann, 1966; Downes, 1968; Lockard, 1968). Only this problem takes place at the opposite end of the historical spectrum: it is the problem of overdevelopment, not under-development, that defines the inner city. We sometimes forget that the gulf between the properly developing society and the underdeveloped society is paral-leled by a gulf between it and the overdeveloped society. By overdeveloped society I mean: facilities available (like parks and malls) that are not used; factories that underemploy; subway stations and highways that break down as a result of an overproduction and overuse of cars. The problems of too much, rather than too little, characterize the American city. And as such, the problem is not the search for avenues to "modernization" but for ways to curb the effects of modernization.

Mayors today often confront the same dilemma that rulers of under-developed nations face: they are responsible for the formulation of realistic plan-ning objectives in difficult and treacherous circumstances. Rarely are there well-developed information resources about conditions; and hence, to distinguish between would be and should be becomes impossible. Furthermore, the distilla-tion of common social goals at a high level of abstraction is easy enough—every-one wants to reduce crime, expand education, eliminate racial discrimination. But when it comes to the nitty-gritty of these things, questions change from "principles" to "priorities:" from what a society should provide in the way of services, to which services deserve attention.

The crisis in our cities is perhaps best understood as part of the crisis in the federalist system of representative democracy. When one person represents one hundred people, the town hall concept of direct responsibility can be maintained; when one man represents one hundred thousand, the representational concept of general-will responsibility can be maintained. But when one man represents one million people, any notion of democracy becomes strained and tenuous, and ultimately it must break down. The political space between ruler and ruled becomes so great that the very notion of participation itself disintegrates. And this is precisely what seems to have happened in the large cities (Davidson, 1969; Slayton, 1969).

The big metropolis is the setting for bitter struggles among competing interest groups—ethnic, racial, class, etc.—thus planning mechanisms must solicit a consensus on what the problems are, what the causes are, and what kind of city is desired, all of which assumes an agreement between the very groups involved in a political fallout to begin with (cf. Smith and McGrail, 1969). The worth of community control is that it reduces the magnitude of the planning process and at the same time makes possible more effective small-scale planning by bypassing the interaction of antagonistic interest groups—since these interest groups would themselves form the nucleus of the new community. Clearly this is an idea/ vision—but at least it permits the creation of an urban policy of scale—something clearly lacking in the present competition of interest groups in a zero sum game.

Again, it is not so much a question of the mayoralty changing, as of the quantitative ratios changing so drastically that the very concept of urban rule collapses. Neither in access nor in control do people of a city like New York feel that they have any real part in the political apparatus. The political party system, itself an elitist inheritance, only serves to further isolate the political processes from the intimate social processes. This was the kernel of truth in the Norman Mailer campaign. He appreciated the degree to which alienation has become a fact of urban political life, affecting leaders no less than citizens (Manso, 1969). What he failed to realize is the next step—the need for New York to be broken down, and not built up into a fifty-first state.

Recently, it has become fashionable to raise questions about "the price of community control" (Beck, 1969: 14–20). It is said that most serious programs for welfare or education require such a high expenditure of risk capital that only citywide units can possibly manage such amounts rationally and economically. Another argument against community control is that "liberalism" itself would be sacrificed if the city was sacrificed. The size of the unit is equated with its politics, i.e., ghetto ideologies function at community levels and integrationist ideologies function at the macro-levels. Therefore, the city is said to be a bulwark against fanaticisms of right and left, black and white. While both arguments have *prima facie* merits, they overlook (or suppress) important parts of the community control argument. Let us take each one separately.

While the costs of welfare and education programs are extremely high and growing higher (the cost of educating one child varies from $1,000 to $1,500 per annum), the ability and willingness to absorb such increased costs could more readily come from communities running a gamut of class elements, than from racially sealed ghettoes such as now exist. Behind the community control approach is not a threat to present levels of federal support but only to the arrogant control of these funds by outside agencies. In the long run, however, community control may indeed lessen federal support, as local communities discover they can better manage their own affairs and determine the long run benefits and costs of federal and state aid programs.

This proposal for a polity of scale would parallel an economy of scale. I am not suggesting simple localism, that is, "neighborhood control" or "block participation." These schemes, similar in content if not in form to the community participation programs in isolated areas of Latin America, fail to take into account the ineffectual and unmanageable nature of simple anarchism, not to mention the "colonizing" role of the metropolitan center. What I am suggesting is that areas such as Bedford-Stuyvesant with its 300,000 people and Harlem with its 500,000 represent quite large-scale cities—in fact they are comparable to many middle-sized cities in the United States—yet lack any comparable autonomy or political clout. The mechanical theory that people first associate themselves with blocks, then with neighborhoods, and only then with communities—and that social reorganization of urban affairs should move in parallel fashion—simply ignores the fact that social and political life has a reality of its own quite apart from the natural history of individual political socialization. In short, the needs of large groups do not necessarily have to move in the same cognitive groove as the growing-up process of individuals.

The ragged argument that liberalism operates with unique worth at the city level forgets that the foundation of liberalism (with a small "l") is not the size of federal work and welfare programs, but having each man count as one—not less than one and not more than one. Even if the cities could deal more adequately with the problems of jobs and income and thereby take the heat off current education and welfare debates, it would not alter the fact that liberalism for many has come to be defined in terms of adequate living standards guaranteed by a government agency. All sectors of the political spectrum are intent on guaranteeing everyone minimal standards of living conditions. The character of liberalism, however, is uniquely linked to the quality of life—specifically of political life, because even the enfranchisement of the 40 percent or so of non-mobilized and nonparticipating citizens depends on a sense of community and a sense of mission. These sensibilities are much more easily nurtured by direct control at a community level than by indirect control at an impersonal bureaucratic level. The ploy which distinguishes community control from "administrative decentralization" is just that—since the latter is a consequence of the former and not an option to community control. Thus, the argument that guarantees of adequate living standards—the "ends of liberalism"—would be frustrated by community control seems spurious and part of a general campaign to perpetuate a political party process that, whatever its worth at the gubernatorial or national levels, has proven woefully inadequate at the city level.

Economic and political elites

The relationship between size and governability of a city is only slightly less critical than the crisis of representative government as such. The movement toward community control is as powerful among the "left" as it is on the "right," as motivating a factor in the behavior of the black underclass as it is in the white working class. In New York City, the movement for "community control" of the educational system at Ocean Hill district is but a forerunner of a citywide struggle of racial and ethnic minorities to decentralize the Board of Education—if not entirely dismantle it. Given the bureaucratic, unresponsive, and notoriously undemocratic history of the Board, the only wonder is that demands for local control did not come sooner. The trouble is that the taxes from which the apportionment of funds for these school districts are drawn are collected on a citywide, statewide, and ultimately nationwide basis. Thus the search for political and educational control comes up against the hard facts of economic and financial "responsibility" being lodged in remote quarters. Here the mayor is caught in a crossfire, not simply of racial versus ethnic interests (largely spurious divisions, it might be added), but the much more real bifurcation of powerful community political life and equally powerful economic interests—neither of which are particularly responsive or responsible to the mayor's office. Nor is this a New York phenomenon. The same sort of bind affects the mayor of St. Louis in relation to welfare and health services. Such services are either provided by local business elites or federal political elites, again neither of which is responsive or responsible to the mayor's office. Thus, the political bases of power have become smaller and smaller—down to the community and block levels, while the economic bases of power have become larger and larger—up to the state and federal levels. At either end of the spectrum, the city mayor has become obsolete.

The Ocean Hill-Brownsville experiment in local control of education is simply the first straw indicating that beyond local discontent is community control. That it will be a long, arduous task, that many good people will be hurt in the process, that exaggerations will arise along with innovations, all of this should caution us in blueprinting the forms of community political life; but it certainly does not lead to the abandonment of the originating premise, namely, the collapse of the city as a viable institution of social control or political participation.

In line with this, social planning has become extremely difficult. First, planning must be coordinated with federal bureaucrats, who themselves are often hamstrung and impotent to make financial decisions. Second, social planning requires the kind of rezoning legislation that realty interests and banking interests jointly sabotage; and finally, the type of social planning done in the past has made the beneficiaries of such programs increasingly suspicious.

Dis-annexation

Urbanologists have a convenient fiction that people living in suburbs "need" the city—as a place to work and as a place to get away and play. This is sheer nonsense. The rise of industrial parks and the decentralization of industrial plants as such have led to an industrial exodus from the city at least as rapid as the population exodus. A city like New York, for instance, has lost a large share of its garment and clothing manufacturing—and did so long before the Jews, Italians, and Irish left the inner city. Further, as for the city providing for recreation and enjoyment, these facilities too have been relocated. Theaters playing first-run films and performing live plays in earlier years could only be seen in the inner city; now they exist in nearly every suburban region. Further, most new stadiums are built in suburban rather than urban regions—San Francisco's Candlestick Park and New York's Shea Stadium are more easily reached from the mid-peninsula and Long Island, respectively, than by roads linked to the inner city—ask any driver, he will tell you.

A mortifying dilemma arises at two ends: first, new mini-cities are in fact able to provide a total network of services for counties that make participation in the life of the inner city superfluous; and second, when urban renewal in the inner city is tried, it is usually in areas inhabited exclusively by black and minority groups, thus serving only to intensify an already raw racial separation. To speak of solutions, therefore, without questioning the very content of the city government and urban economics, is simply ludicrous. The problem of the mayoralty situation is in the final analysis the problem of urban viability itself.

A deep tragedy in this so-called new philosophy for cities is the fallacious assumption that the central city and the suburbs form a single unitary entity. According to Charles Abrams (1964, 1965), the able urbanologist, city and suburb depend upon each other for job opportunities, services, recreation, escape, variety, and progress. The plain fact is that this is decreasingly the case. The relative total autonomy of suburban regions is now a full fact if not a particularly full philosophy. In a recent television documentary, "Sixteen in Webster Groves," few of the youngsters interviewed had ever been to the inner St. Louis city—even though it is but a ten-mile car ride away! Indeed, only curiosity coupled with the impulse to social good led to their going to St. Louis even at age sixteen. Indeed, with the present superhighway system, it is possible to get from the county to a destination within the center city without going through the urban interstices. Whatever else this says, it is clear that the suburban regions do provide a total life package quite apart from the urban city which perhaps explains why movements for amalgamation and fusion of city and county districts have failed so decisively (cf. Bollens and Schmandt, 1965: 491–524).

Nor is this a simply ethnographic observation or unique event to one mid-western city. In each and every major industrial region there are now industrial parks of a size and scope that obviate any further contact with the inner city. The industrial park is, to date, the most powerful development recruiting the blue collar to the suburbs, following their white-collar brethren by one decade. Coupled with the movement of industry is the growth of huge shopping plazas providing everything from banking services to bowling tournaments. It is a tragic mistake to think that the excitement of the city, the lure of the inner loop, is irresistible. To the white collar, the inner city represents an established evil as ferocious in mythic proportions as the nineteenth century Protestant rural fears of the urban life. To the blue collar, these suburbs represent escape from ethnicity and proximity to the black population. To the offspring of both these major class sectors, the suburb is an uncontested way of life—and if anything, their impulses are for nostalgia and more retreatism—and not for involvement in urban affairs. Even though urban communities of the young sometimes display political concerns in demonstrations, marches, and vigils, they show negligible interest in traditional party or electoral politics.

The thunder on the racial left is well known. But no less ominous than black demands for community control, are the increasing demands for community control and for "dis-annexation" coming from the white working-class and ethnic blue-collar workers. The more the whites feel that they occupy "enclaves" in cities that they once dominated, the more they begin to react in terms of autonomous, self-government proposals. The situation in Mayor Richard Hatcher's Gary, Indiana, is probably typical of sentiments elsewhere. Indeed, the probability is that were Shaker Heights an incorporated part of Cleveland, Ohio, a similar opposition to Mayor Stokes would be exhibited.

Eugene Kirtland, head of the "secessionist" movement in Gary's quasi-fashionable Glen Park division, recently put the matter this way in a *Harper's* interview (Frady, 1969:41–42).

The small, middle-class property owners out here look on dis-annexation as a defense for their investments. Oh, there are many reasons—people feel we would have better economic development under our own government, for one thing. Gary's like every other middle-class community, I suppose: the good people don't say anything until it's almost too late—but then watch out!

Beneath the rhetoric of threatened mass violence is the antifederalist theme that has become the common denominator for animus on the Right and Left. "I think people just generally feel institutions are getting too big, too remote, and impersonal and unresponsive to individuals—that goes for business and government too. And now you've got all these taxes to finance social change, and it's the average Joe in the middle of the block who's having to pay them, but for what? He doesn't really know how they're spent, why they're spent, or how much is spent—he just knows it's a lot, and he's paying it." One might argue that this is just the black-white struggle being presented in covert fashion. But I suspect that whether or not this is the case, the fact that both black and white are responding in the identical "anti-civic" fashions indicates that the end of the city as a politically viable unit may fast be approaching.

The community level of politics is hardly limited to representational forms of struggle. It is beginning to characterize confrontational politics as well. Some of the smaller Eastern cities, e.g., Plainfield and New Brunswick in New Jersey, have witnessed situations in which public officials, fearful of the cost in lives of trying to reassert control over the area, cordon it off but do not allow police to enter. Then for a period which may last from a day to a week, state authority over the embattled community is held in abeyance as militant armed youth exercise a *de facto* control. Finally, the standoff is broken by negotiations between public officials and representatives of the rioters. H. Rap Brown has encouraged the development of what sociologist Martin Oppenheimer (1969) has called the urban guerrilla. "Look what the brothers did in Plainfield. The brothers got their stuff. They got 46 automatic weapons. Then they went back to their community . . . and they told that peckerwood cop: 'Don't come in my community.' He didn't come. And the only reason he didn't come was 'cause he didn't want to get killed. And the brothers had the material to do it. They had 46 carbines down there. That's what he respects—power. He respects that kind of power.''

Under such circumstances, it is pointless to ask whether the community represents a viable option of politicization to the city. The more pointed question is the future of the city precisely to the extent that its officials must be able to deal with community "leaders" on a basis of parity. Thus, confrontation politics may be the forward wedge in the legal redefinition of urban affairs.

The solution is *not* making states out of our big cities. Indeed, this would only compound the dilemmas by further bureaucratizing urban regions and separating them even more firmly from the rest of the country.

The solution is *not* incorporating vast stretches of country into the big cities, first and foremost because such steps have been vigorously resisted by county dwellers, who fear the loss of their autonomy; and second, because like the plan for statehood, the incorporation of counties into cities only deepens the bureaucratic malaise by encouraging precisely the kind of gigantism that is at the root of the problem to begin with.

The solution is *not* an increase in taxes people pay—either on income or property. These are already at maximum figures and serve to further drive the much maligned middle sectors to the suburban regions. Furthermore, these taxes most often affect the city residents and leave relatively unaffected those who use urban facilities but do not live within the urban centers.

The solution is *not* to ban automobiles or other vehicular forms of transportation. For to deprive the inner city of such transportation, that is to "countryfy" the city, is precisely to deprive the city of the throb and vitality that made it great to begin with. The creation of "downtown malls" is furthermore not to touch the problem of the urban poor—it is only to make the life of middle-class shoppers more comfortable. A more rational and more equitable form of transportation may be indicated, particularly public transportation programs such as Bay Area Transit Authority, but this is no solution.

In the first stage, New York might be divided into five cities—with each borough becoming an incorporated, legal entity distinguishable in its administration from every other borough. After that, the boroughs themselves should be split into organic neighborhoods—something which is remarkably simple to accomplish in some cities and more difficult, but still not impossible, in other cities. Bensonhurst, Borough Park, Coney Island, Hamilton Parkway, Sea Beach, and Brighton Beach area, each of these already shows profound sociological commonalities, boundaries which are fixed by ethnic, racial, religious conventions that superseded the customary legal boundaries of the borough system.

I am suggesting that the question of politics is always one of control, and that in turn, the quest for community is always a thirst for politics (Greer and

Minar, 1968). For it is control which defines the extent and the limits of power. The present "controls" have clearly broken down. What is needed is not restorationism, not law and order, not bigger and better budgets, but the exercise of power, the establishing of intimacy between rulers and ruled. If this strikes some as restorationism of another variety, of the town hall variety, then so be it. The fact that a model from an earlier age in American history exists is neither an argument for or a refutation of this proposal. Indeed, the urban dweller does perceive himself as living in a neighborhood (not even a district) and often on a block (where even the neighborhood may be the enemy).

This raises the additional consideration that community control and disannexation or decentralization in general are not mutually exclusive. Alan K. Campbell has recently made this point decisively.

> Although students of American federalism have for generations tried to divide the functions of government among the levels in a clear-cut and precise fashion, such a division is impossible. It is not functions which are assigned to parts of the governmental system, but rather power. It is quite possible to design a system where local communities are given substantial influence in the administration of functions, even though those functions must, for technological and economic reasons, be performed on an area-wide basis . . . The desire for community involvement, the need for citizens to have a participating role in the system, goes far beyond disadvantaged blacks and discontented young people. Underlying, in part, the movement to suburbia by the white middle-class was a search for community (Campbell, 1970:208).

The struggle around "decentralization" is perhaps the key opening wedge in the larger struggle for what Saarinen (1943) long ago called "organic integration." Every major city has "real" neighborhoods that can form the backbone of any relocation of authority into the community. People do their living in these smaller units—all the way from the block to the borough. In this form, the people have themselves already answered the question of the feasibility of community control of urban America (cf. Heilbrun and Wellisz, 1968).

Natural divisions exist in San Francisco, with districts like Fillmore, Haight-Ashbury, Russian Hills. Similar divisions exist in New York between Greenwich Village, Sheepshead Bay, Bay Parkway, etc. What is lacking, therefore, is not the existence of the community, but the juridical sanctions for the community. The present level of political struggle is thus centered on securing legal status. And in this way the citizenry moves beyond professional sanctity toward community needs (cf. Gittell, 1868:70–71).

The community city offers distinct advantages for all sectors of the urban population. It presents the first clear indication of the reduction, if not the end, of the welfare system; an end to the psychic state of anomie and impotence caused by living in "ungovernable" surroundings; an end to arbitrary and profoundly resented schemes for creating racial balance that never really touch the actual imbalances of income and housing; and it represents a real break with conventional party politics that would permit new coalitional formations and new groupings along the interest lines that exist now in the third part of the twentieth century rather than those left over from the last part of the nineteenth century. But above all, it creates a condition of proximate parity between the inner city and the suburban minicenters—by giving them similar structural forms and by granting its citizenry similar rights and obligations. The inner city will only become desirable when it incorporates the major positive features of suburban living: spacious housing, good highway systems, a public education network good enough to absorb all sectors of the population, etc. For the city to remain an "amusement capital" or a "leisure playland," or even the "center of banking and commerce," is to guarantee the perpetuation of an artificial division between inner city and outer suburb—a division whose very existence makes a solution to our domestic ailments impossible.

The most effective deterrent to the breakup of the central city into various middle-sized cities is the inability of the city's inhabitants to know how to execute such proposals, and a larger and mostly unstated fear that there would be a loss of federal funds for support of the poor. The principle of the urban poor is territoriality. The principle of the working class is expropriation. Thus, the poor, despite their many deficits and disadvantages in the organization of political appeal, have a larger advantage: they are defending the neighborhood, a very real fact of geographic and ecological integrity. It needs no utopian programming or blueprinting; and it is largely capable of uniting diffuse class interests (i.e., the black poor and the white working class), and hence represents a healing revolution rather than an abrasive revolution.

The differences between centralized and community systems of governing obviously affect specific policies on everything from fluoridation to floating school bonds; the contradiction for most liberal-minded people is that they prefer the goals of big government but would like to see that they are brought about through community control. This is not to be. One has to accept certain bridling of enlightened policies if one wants community control; whereas one has to accept the bureaucratic apparatus if we want certain welfare programs. As the operations of the Community Action Program during its first four years indicate, a choice must be made in terms of a theory of government and also in terms of a set of specific policies (cf. Levitan, 1969).

What can be said is that the centralized approach has received a far greater trial run that decentralized approaches—this because it squares better with the federalist ideology that has dominated American life since its Constitutional fathers formulated it. But if the problem of police brutality is going to be resolved, community control is necessary. And this will mean, too, an increase in segregated communities (on both black and white sides). Community control is not a panacea, and not without high risks. For instance, it may temporarily stimulate rather than settle inequalities in the distribution of material perquisites (cf. Greenstone and Peterson, 1968). But such risks seem eminently worth taking at a point when the struggle for improved services depends increasingly on the consciousness of citizens—and people will pay for what they can see is beneficial, not for what big government agencies say is beneficial. And big cities are big governments—and are so perceived by the people they rule. Because cities have not and cannot act against national interests, community control seems a necessary as well as feasible response to urbanized anomie.

The high irony of the present situation, viewed ideologically, is that the doctrine of pluralism in the hands of its prime advocates, such as Robert Dahl (1961) and Nelson Polsby (1963), represents a celebration of American democracy and the countervailing elite formations that add up to a *laissez-faire* polity. But it resolves itself in a quite different way in the current situation. For men like Nathan Hare (1969) and Charles Hamilton (1967), the same doctrine of pluralism is a justification of the breakdown of American democracy, a statement that pluralism is separatism and conflict politics and not the hidden hand of consensus politics. Aside from proving that any doctrine can be used in just about any way, it shows how the oligarchical potentials of separate principates do not quite die out in a democracy, but rather come back in the form of the local party boss or "block captain." The cry of pluralism in the hands of the decentralizers is a demand for making democracy viable at the expense of the national orchestration of politics that was envisioned by classical political pluralism with its veto effects and interest group formations. But this too means that even the rhetoric of conventional liberal wisdom has been undermined by the new urban condition.

We turn a full circle: if the city is ungovernable in its death throes, then the community is governable in its resurgence. This in turn is but a particularistic manifestation of the decline of federalism at the political level and "mass society" at the economic level. Masses are turning into publics. The push toward bigness translates itself into a search for privacy and intimacy. The pluralism which saw its pinnacle in the play of interest groups within the city, has increasingly become realized in the play of interest groups between communities. It is all too easy to dismiss Nathan Hare's assertion of his faith in the pluralistic ideal as simple demagoguery. Quite the contrary, his is indeed a touching faith precisely in the substance of liberalism: the system of political checks and balances that truthfully, accurately represents and reflects real interests in contrast to contrived interests. If the cities seem to have a bleak future on the face of it, there is nevertheless no need to fret. The community, that clustering of human souls and ecological boundaries under direct supervision of the inhabitants of an area, has been revitalized—and with it, let us hope that the Greek ideal of democracy exercising its magic within the community can protect us from the worst excesses of anomic gigantism and bureaucratic anti-humanism.

References

Abrams, Charles. 1964. *Man's Struggle for Shelter in an Urbanizing World.* Cambridge, Mass.: M.I.T. Press.
——. 1965. *The City Is the Frontier.* New York: Harper & Row.

Beck, Bertram, M. 1969. "Community control: A distraction, not an answer." *Social Work,* 14 (October 1969): 14–20.

Bollens, John C., and Henry J. Schmandt. 1965. *The Metropolis: Its People, Politics, and Economic Life.* New York: Harper & Row.

Boulding, Kenneth. 1963. "The death of the city: A frightened look at post civilization." Pp. 133–145 in Oscar Handlin and John Burchard (eds.), *The Historian and the City.* Cambridge, Mass.: M.I.T. Press.

Campbell, Alan K. 1970. *The States and the Urban Crisis.* Englewood Cliffs, N.J.: Prentice-Hall, Inc.

Community Relations Service. 1969. Mimeographed Reports on Urban Population. Washington, D.C.: United States Department of Justice.

Dahl, Robert. 1961. *Who Governs? Democracy and Power in an American City.* New Haven: Yale University Press.

Davidson, Robert H. 1969. "The war on poverty: Experiment in federalism," *The Annals* of the American Academy of Political and Social Science. 385 (September 1969): 1–13.

Downes, Bryan T. 1968. "Social and political characteristics of riot cities: A comparative study." *Social Science Quarterly.* 49 (December 1968): 504–520.

Frady, Marshall. 1969. "Gary, Indiana." *Harper's Magazine.* 239 (August 1969): 35–45.

Gans, Herbert J. 1962. *The Urban Villagers: Group and Class in the Life of Italian Americans.* New York: The Free Press.

———. 1969. "The future of the suburbs." Pp. 282–295. In Alan Shank (ed.), *Political Power and the Urban Crisis.* Boston: Holbrook Press, Inc.

Gittell, Marilyn. 1968. "Community control of education." *Proceedings* of The Academy of Political Science. 29:1 (July): 60–71.

Greenstone, J. David, and Paul E. Peterson. 1968. "Reformer, machines, and the war on poverty." Pp. 267–292 in James Q. Wilson (ed.), *City Politics and Public Policy.* New York: John Wiley & Sons, Inc.

Greer, Scott, and Davie W. Minar. 1968. "The political side of urban development and redevelopment." Pp. 301–314 in Scott Greer, Dennis L. McElrath, David W. Minar, and Peter Orleans (eds.), *The New Urbanization.* New York: St. Martin's Press.

Hamilton, Charles, and Stokely Carmichael. 1967. *Black Power.* New York: Random House, Inc.

Hare, Nathan. 1969. "The case for separatism: Black perspective." Pp. 233–234 in James McEvoy and Abraham Miller (eds.), *Black Power and Student Rebellion: Conflict on the American Campus.* Belmont, Calif.: Wadsworth Publishing Co.

Hartman, Charles W. 1967. "The politics of housing." *Dissent* 14 (November–December): 701–714.

Heilbrun, James, and Stanislaw Wellisz. 1968. "An economic program for the ghetto." *Proceedings* of the Academy of Political Science 29 (July): 72–85.

Laumann, Edward O. 1966. *Prestige and Association in an Urban Community: An Analysis of an Urban Stratification System.* Indianapolis–New York: The Bobbs-Merrill Co., Inc.

Levitan, Sar A. 1969. "The community action program: A strategy to fight poverty." *The Annals* of the American Academy of Political and Social Science 285 (September 1969): 63–75.

Lockard, Duane. 1968. *Toward Equal Opportunity: A Study of State and Local Antidiscrimination Laws.* New York: The Macmillan Company.

Lurie, Ellen. 1963. "Community action in East Harlem." Pp. 246–258 in Leonard J. Duhl (ed.), *The Urban Condition: People and Policy in the Metropolis.* New York: Basic Books, Inc.

Manso, Peter (ed.). 1969. *Running Against the Machine: The Mailer-Breslin Campaign.* Garden City, New York: Doubleday and Company, Inc.

National Resources Committee. 1937. *Our Cities.* Washington, D.C.: U.S. Government Printing Office.

Olson, Mancur, *et al.* 1969. *Toward A Social Report* (U.S. Department of Health, Education, and Welfare). Washington, D.C.: U.S. Government Printing Office.

Oppenheimer, Martin. 1969. *The Urban Guerrilla.* Chicago: Quadrangle Books.

Piven, Frances Fox, and Richard A. Cloward. 1967. "Black control of cities." *The New Republic* 157 (September 30 and October 7, 1967): 19–21 and 15–19.

Polsby, Nelson. 1963. *Community Power and Political Theory.* New Haven: Yale University Press.

Rainwater, Lee. 1967. "Open letter on white justice and the riots." *Trans-action,* 4, (September 1967): 22–32.

Saarinen, Eliel. 1943; *The City: Its Growth, Its Decay, Its Future.* New York. Reinholdt Publishing Company.

Schrag, Peter. 1969. "The forgotten American." *Harper's Magazine.* 239, (August 1969): 27–34.

Seligman, Ben B. (ed.) 1965. *Poverty as a Public Issue.* New York: The Free Press, Macmillan Co.

Slayton, William L. 1969. "A national urbanization policy." Pp. 71–80 in Jean Brand and Lowell H. Watts (eds.), *Federalism Today.* Washington, D.C.: Graduate School Press, U.S. Department of Agriculture.

Smith, David Horton, and Richard F. McGrail. 1969. "Community control of schools: A review of issues and options." *Urban and Social Change Review,* 3 (Fall 1969). Pp. 2–9.

United States Department of Commerce. 1966. *Americans at Mid-Decade.* Series P-23, No. 16 (March) Washington, D.C.: U.S. Government Printing Office.

——. 1967. *Provisional Estimates of the Population of the Largest Metropolitan Areas. July 1, 1966.* Series P-25, No. 378 (November) Washington, D.C.: U.S. Government Printing Office.

United States Department of Labor. 1966. *The Negroes in the United States: Their Economic and Social Situation.* Bulletin 511 (June) Washington, D.C.: U.S. Government Printing Office.

Wilson, James Q. 1969. "The mayors vs. the cities." *The Public Interest,* 16 (Summer): 25–40.

33

EDWARD GREER, The "Liberation" of Gary, Indiana

In silhouette, the skyline of Gary, Indiana, could serve as the perfect emblem of America's industrial might—or its industrial pollution. In the half-century since they were built, the great mills of the United States Steel Corporation—once the largest steel complex on earth—have produced more than a quarter-trillion tons of steel. They have also produced one of the highest air pollution rates on earth. Day and night the tall stacks belch out a ruddy smoke that newcomers to the city find almost intolerable.

Apart from its appalling physical presence, the most striking thing about Gary is the very narrow compass in which the people of the city lead their lives. Three-quarters of the total work force is directly employed by the United States Steel Corporation. About 75 percent of all male employment is in durable goods manufacture and in the wholesale-retail trades, and a majority of this labor force is blue-collar. This means that the cultural tone of the city is solidly working-class.

But not poor. Most Gary workers own their own homes, and the city's median income is 10 percent above the national average. The lives of these people, however, are parochial, circumscribed, on a tight focus. With the exception of the ethnic clubs, the union and the Catholic church, the outstanding social edifices in Gary are its bars, gambling joints and whorehouses.

Company town

The city of Gary was the largest of all company towns in America. The United States Steel Corporation began construction in 1905, after assembling the necessary parcel of land on the Lake Michigan shore front. Within two years, over $40 million had been invested in the project; by now the figure must be well into the billions.

Gary was built practically from scratch. Swamps had to be dredged and dunes leveled; a belt-line railroad to Chicago had to be constructed, as well as a port for ore ships and of course a vast complex of manufacturing facilities including coke ovens, blast furnaces and an independent electrical power plant. The city was laid out by corporation architects and engineers and largely developed by the corporation-owned Gary Land Company, which did not sell off most of its holdings until the thirties. Even though the original city plan included locations for a variety of civic, cultural and commercial uses (though woefully little for park land), an eminent critic, John W. Reps, points out that it "failed sadly in its attempt to produce a community pattern noticeably different or better than elsewhere."

The corporation planned more than the physical nature of the city. It also had agents advertise in Europe and the South to bring in workers from as many different backgrounds as possible to build the mills and work in them. Today over fifty ethnic groups are represented in the population.

This imported labor was cheap, and it was hoped that cultural differences and language barriers would curtail the growth of a socialist labor movement. The tough pioneer character of the city and the fact that many of the immigrant workers' families had not yet joined them in this country combined to create a lawless and vice-ridden atmosphere which the corporation did little to curtail. In much more than its genesis and name, then, Gary is indelibly stamped in the mold of its corporate creators.

Labor and the Left

During the course of the First World War, government and vigilante repression broke the back of the Socialist party in small-town America, though it was not very strong to begin with. Simultaneously, however, the Left grew rapidly as a political force among the foreign-born in large urban centers. As the war continued, labor peace was kept by a combination of prosperity (full employment and overtime), pressures for production in the "national interest," and Wilsonian and corporate promises of an extension of democracy in the workplace after the war was over. The promises of a change in priorities proved empty, and in 1919 the long-suppressed grievances of the steelworkers broke forth. Especially among the unskilled immigrant workers, demands for an industrial union, a reduction of the workday from twelve to eight hours and better pay and working conditions sparked a spontaneous movement for an industry-wide strike.

For a time it appeared that the workers would win the Great Steel Strike of 1919, but despite the capable leadership of William Z. Foster the strike was broken. The native white skilled-labor aristocracy refused to support it, and the corporation imported blacks from the South to scab in the mills. This defeat helped set back the prospect of militant industrial trade unionism for almost a generation. And meanwhile, racism, a consumer-oriented culture (especially the automobile and relaxed sexual mores) and reforms from above (by the mid-twenties the eight-hour day had been voluntarily granted in the mills) combined to prevent the Left from recovering as a significant social force.

It was in this period between World War I and the Depression that a substantial black population came to Gary. Before the war only a handful of black families lived there, and few of them worked in the mills. During World War I, when immigration from abroad was choked off, blacks were encouraged to move to Gary to make up for the labor shortage caused by expanding production. After the war this policy was continued, most spectacularly during the strike, but rather consistently throughout the twenties. In 1920 blacks made up 9.6 percent of the population; in 1930 they were 17.8 percent—and they were proportionately represented in the steel industry work force.

When the CIO was organized during the depression, an interracial alliance was absolutely essential to the task. In Gary a disproportionate number of the union organizers were black; the Communist party's slogan of "black and white unite and fight" proved useful as an organizing tactic. Nevertheless, it was only during World War II (and not as the result of the radicals' efforts) that black workers made a substantial structural advance in the economy. Demography, wartime full employment and labor shortages proved more important to the lot of black workers than their own efforts and those of their allies.

As after the First World War, so after the second, there came a repression to counter the growth of the Left. The Communist component of the trade union movement was wiped out, and in the general atmosphere of the early cold war black people, too, found themselves on the defensive. At the local level in Gary, the remaining trade union leaders made their peace with the corporation (as well as the local racketeers and Democratic party politicians), while various campaigns in the forties to racially integrate the schools and parks failed utterly.

Finally, in the early fifties, the inherently limited nature of the trade union when organized as a purely defensive institution of the working class—and one moreover that fully accepts capitalist property and legal norms—stood fully revealed. The Steelworkers Union gave up its right to strike over local grievances, which the Left had made a key part of its organizing policy, in return for binding arbitration, which better suited the needs and tempers of the emerging labor bureaucrats.

Corporate racism

The corporation thus regained effective full control over the work process. As a result, the corporation could increase the amount of profit realized per worker. It could also intensify the special oppression of the black workers; foremen could now assign them discriminatorily to the worst tasks without real union opposition. This corporate racism had the additional benefit of weakening the workers' solidarity. For its part, the union abolished shop stewards, replacing them with one full-time elected "griever." This of course further attenuated rank-and-file control over the union bureaucracy, aided in depoliticizing the workers and gave further rein to the union's inclination to mediate worker/employer differences at the point of production, rather than sharpen the lines of struggle in the political economy as a whole.

The corporate and union elites justified this process by substantial wage increases, together with other benefits such as improved pension and welfare plans. For these gains a price was paid. Higher product prices, inflation and a rising tax burden on the workers all ensued from the union's passive acceptance of corporate priorities.

There were extremely important racial consequences as well. For as the union leadership was drawn further and further into complicity with corporate goals, a large segment of the industrial working class found itself in the apparently contradictory position of opposing the needs of the poorest workers for increased social welfare services. A large part of the material basis for white working-class racism originates here. Gary steelworkers, struggling to meet their home mortgage payments, are loath to permit increased assessments for additional municipal services which they view as mostly benefitting black people.

United States Steel

Needless to say, the corporation helped to develop, promote and protect the Gary working class's new ways of viewing itself and its world.

In the mill, the corporation systematically gave the black workers the dirtiest jobs (in the coke plants, for example) and bypassed them for promotion—especially for the key skilled jobs and as foremen. Nor has that policy changed. Although about a third of the employees in the Gary Works are black, and many of them have high seniority, and although virtually all the foremen are promoted directly from the ranks without needing any special qualifications, there are almost no black (or Spanish-speaking) foremen. According to figures submitted by the United States Steel Corporation to the Gary Human Relations Commission, as of 31 March 1968, out of a total of 1,011 first-line supervisors (foremen) only 22 were black.

The corporation not only practices racism directly, it also encourages it indirectly by supporting other discriminatory institutions in Gary. Except for some free professionals and small business, the entire business community is a de facto fief of the corporation. The Gary Chamber of Commerce has never to my knowledge differed from the corporation on any matter of substance, though it was often in its economic self-interest to do so. This has been true even with regard to raising the corporation's property assessment, which would directly benefit local business financially. And in its hiring and sales practices, as well as in its social roles, this group is a leading force for both institutional racism and racist attitudes in the community. For instance, it is well known that the local banks are very reluctant to advance mortgage money in black areas of town, thus assuring their physical decline. White workers then draw the reasonable conclusion that the movement of blacks into their neighborhoods will be at the expense of the value of their homes and react accordingly. The local media, completely dependent financially on the local business community, can fairly be described as overtly racist. The story of the voting fraud conspiracy to prevent the election of the present mayor, Richard Hatcher, a black man, didn't get into the local paper until days after it made the front page of the *New York Times.*

The newspaper publisher is very close to the national Catholic hierarchy and the local bishop, who in turn is closely linked to the local banks. The church is rhetorically moderately liberal at the diocesan level, but among the ethnic parishes the clergy are often overtly racist.

Political considerations

While the United States Steel Corporation has an annual budget of $5 billion, the city of Gary operates on some $10 million annually. (This figure applies only to municipal government functions; it excludes expenditures by the schools, welfare authorities, the Sanitary Board and the Redevelopment Commission.)

And the power of the city government, as is usually the case in this country, is highly fragmented. Its legal and financial authority is inadequate to carry out the public functions for which it bears responsibility. The power of the mayor is particularly limited. State civil service laws insulate school, welfare, fire, and police personnel from the control of City Hall. Administrative agencies control key functions such as urban renewal, the low-income housing authority, sanitation, the park system and the board of health. Appointive boards, with long and staggered terms of tenure, hire the administrators of these agencies; and although in the long run a skillful mayor can obtain substantial control over their operations, in the short run (especially if there are sharp policy differences) his power may well be marginal.

Two other structural factors set the context in which local government in Gary—and in America generally—is forced to operate. First, key municipal functions increasingly depend upon federal aid; such is the case with the poverty program, urban renewal, low-income housing and, to a substantial degree, welfare, education, and even police and sanitation. Thus, the priorities of the federal government increasingly shape the alternatives and options open to local officials, and their real independence is attenuated.

Second, the tax resources of local governments—resting for the most part on comparatively static real estate levies—are less and less able to meet the sharply rising costs of municipal services and operations. These costs reflect the increased social costs of production and welfare, costs that corporations are able to pass on to the general public.

This problem is particularly acute in Gary because of the ability of the corporation to remain grossly underassessed. As a result, there are implacable pressures to resist expansion of municipal services, even if the need for them is critical. In particular, since funds go to maintain existing services, it is virtually impossible for a local government to initiate any substantive innovations unless prior funding is assured. In this context, a sustained response to the urban crisis is prevented not only by a fragmentation of power but also by a lack of economic resources on a scale necessary to obtain significant results.

For the city of Gary, until the election of Mayor Hatcher, it was academic to talk about such considerations as the limits of local government as an instrument of social change and improvement of the general welfare. Before him, municipal government had been more or less content simply to mediate between the rackets on the one hand and the ethnic groups and business community on the other.

The Democratic Party, structured through the Lake County machine, was the mechanism for accomplishing a division of spoils and for maintaining at least a formal legitimacy for a government that provided a minimum return to its citizenry. Left alone by the corporation, which subscribed to an inspired policy of live and let live where municipal politics were concerned, this political coalition governed Gary as it saw fit.

In return for the benevolent neutrality of the corporation toward its junior partner, the governing coalition refrained from attempting to raise the corporation's tax assessments or to otherwise insinuate itself into the absolute sovereignty of the corporation over the Gary Works. Air pollution activities were subjected only to token inspection and control, and in the entire history of the city the Building Department never sent an inspector into the mill. (These and other assertions about illegal or shady activities are based on reports from reliable informants and were usually verified by a second source. I served under Mayor Hatcher as director of the Office of Program Coordination until February 1969.)

In this setting—particularly in the absence of a large middle class interested in "good government" reform—politics was little more than a racket, with the city government as the chief spoils. An informal custom grew up that representatives of different ethnic minorities would each hold the mayor's office for one term. The mayor then, in association with the county officials, would supervise the organized crime (mostly gambling, liquor, and prostitution) within the community. In effect, the police force and the prosecutor's office were used to erect and centralize a protection racket with the mayor as its director and organized crime as its client. Very large sums of money were involved, as indicated by the fact that one recent mayor was described by Internal Revenue officials as having an estimated annual income while in office of $1.5 million.

Besides the racket of protecting criminal activity, other sources of funds contributed to the large illicit incomes of city officials. There were almost 1,000 patronage jobs to distribute to supporters or sell to friends. There were proceeds from a myriad of business transactions and contracts carried out under municipal authority. Every aspect of municipal activity was drawn into the cash nexus.

For instance, by local ordinance one had to pass an examination and pay a $150 fee for a contractor's license to do repair or construction work within city limits. The licensing statute was enacted to maintain reasonable standards of performance and thus protect the public. In reality, as late as 1967, passing the exam required few skills, except the ability to come up with $1,200 for the relevant officials, or $1,500 if the applicant was unfortunate enough to have black skin.

Gary municipal affairs also had a racist quality. The black population continued to rise until in the early sixties it composed an absolute majority. Yet the benefits of the system just outlined were restricted to the less scrupulous of the leaders of other ethnic groups, which constituted altogether only 40 percent of the population. The spoils came from all: they were distributed only among whites.

And this was true not only for illegal spoils and patronage but also for legitimate municipal services. As one example, after Hatcher became mayor, one of the major complaints of the white citizenry concerned the sharp decline in the frequency of garbage collection. This resulted, not from a drop in efficiency of the General Services division, as was often charged, but from the fact that the garbage routes were finally equalized between white and black areas.

In short, the city government was itself just another aspect of the institutionalized structure of racism in Gary. To assure the acquiescence of Gary's blacks to the system, traditional mechanisms of repression were used: bought black politicians and ward leaders, token jobs, the threat of violence against rebels and the spreading of a sense of impotence and despair. For instance, it was a Gary tradition for the Democratic machine to contribute $1,500 each week to a black ministers' alliance for them to distribute to needy parishioners—with the tacit understanding that when elections came around they would help deliver the vote.

Hatcher's campaign

The successful insurgency of Richard Gordon Hatcher destroyed the core of this entire relationship.

Hatcher developed what can best be described as a black united front, inasmuch as it embraced all sectors of the black community by social class, occupation, ideology, and temperament. The basis of this united front was a commonly held view that black people as a racial group were discriminated against by the politically dominant forces. Creating it required that Hatcher bridge existing divisions in the black community, which he did by refusing to be drawn into a disavowel of any sector of the black movement either to his left or right—except for those local black politicians who were lackeys of the Democratic machine. Despite immense public pressure, for example, Hatcher refused to condemn Stokley Carmichael, even though scurrilous right-wing literature was widely circulated calling him a tool of Carmichael and Fidel Castro. Actually, the rumor that hurt Hatcher the most was the false assertion that he was secretly engaged to a white campaign worker—and it was so damaging in the black community that special pains had to be taken to overcome it.

Muhammad Ali was brought to the city to campaign for Hatcher, but Hubert Humphrey was not invited because of the bitter opposition of white antiwar elements within his campaign committee. It is worth noting that a substantial portion of Hatcher's financial and technical assistance came from a very small group of white liberals and radicals, who, while they played a role disproportionate to their numbers, suffered significant hostility from their white neighbors for involving themselves openly with Hatcher. Their support, however, made it possible for the campaign to appeal, at least rhetorically, to all the citizens on an interracial basis.

Of course, this support in the white community did not translate into votes. When the count was complete in the general election, only 13 percent of Gary's overwhelmingly Democratic white voters failed to bolt to the Republicans; and if one omits the Jewish professional and business section of town, that percentage falls to 6 percent (in blue-collar Glen Park)—a figure more explicable by polling booth error than goodwill.

Even in the Democratic primary against the incumbent mayor, Hatcher barely won, although he had the support of a large majority of the Spanish-speaking vote and overwhelming support (over 90 percent) of the black vote. His victory was possible, moreover, only because the white vote was split almost down the middle due to the entry of an insurgent and popular "backlash" candidate.

Hatcher's primary victory was particularly impressive given the obstacles he had to face. First, his entire primary campaign was run on less than $50,000, while the machine spent an estimated $500,000 in cash on buying black votes alone. Second, the media was openly hostile to Hatcher. And third, efforts were made to physically intimidate the candidate and his supporters. Death threats were common, and many beatings occurred. Without a doubt, the unprecedented action of the Hatcher organization in forming its own self-defense squads was essential in preventing mass intimidation. It was even necessary on primary day for armed groups to force open polls in black areas that would otherwise have remained inoperative.

These extraordinary methods demonstrated both how tenuous are the democratic rights of black people and what amazing organization and determination are necessary to enforce them when real shifts of power appear to be at stake. When the primary results came in, thousands of black citizens in Gary literally danced in the streets with joy; and everyone believed that the old Gary was gone forever.

Hatcher's temptations

Immediately after the primary victory, the local alignment of forces was to some degree overshadowed by the rapid interposition of national ones. Until Hatcher won the primary, he was left to sink or swim by himself; after he established his own independent base of power, a new and more complex political process began: his reintegration into the national political system.

The county Democratic machine offered Hatcher a bargain: its support and $100,000 for the general election campaign in return for naming the chief of police, corporation counsel, and controller. Naturally, Hatcher refused to accept a deal that would have made him a puppet of the corrupt elements he was determined to oust from power. Thereupon the county machine (and the subdistrict director of the Steelworkers Union) declared itself for, and campaigned for, the Republican.

But the question was not left there. To allow the Democratic Party to desert a candidate solely because he was black would make a shambles of its appeal to black America. And dominant liberal forces within the Democratic Party clearly had other positive interests in seeing Hatcher elected. Most dramatically, the Kennedy wing of the Democratic party moved rapidly to adopt Hatcher, offering him sorely needed political support, financial backing, and technical assistance, without any strings attached. By doing this, it both solidified its already strong support from the black community and made it more reasonable for blacks to continue to place their faith in the Democratic Party and in the political system as a whole.

As a necessary response to this development (although it might have happened anyway), the Johnson-Humphrey wing of the Democratic Party also offered support. And this meant that the governor of Indiana and the Indiana state Democratic Party endorsed Hatcher as well—despite the opposition of the powerful Lake County machine. Thus Hatcher achieved legitimacy within the political system—a legitimacy that he would need when it came to blocking a serious voting fraud plot to prevent his winning the election.

Despite clear evidence of what was happening, the Justice Department nevertheless refused to intervene against this plot until Hatcher's campaign committee sent telegrams to key federal officials warning them that failure to do so would result in a massive race riot for which the federal officials would be held publicly responsible. Only by this unorthodox maneuver, whose credibility rested on Hatcher's known independent appeal and constituency, was the federal executive branch persuaded to enforce the law. Its intervention, striking 5,000 phony names from the voter rolls, guaranteed a Hatcher victory instead of a Hatcher defeat.

The refusal of the Justice Department to move except under what amounted to blackmail indicated that the Johnson-Humphrey wing of the party was not enthusiastic about Hatcher, whose iconoclastic and often radical behavior did not assure that he would behave appropriately after he was in power. But its decision finally to act, together with the readiness of the Kennedy forces to fully back Hatcher, suggests that there was a national strategy into which the Hatcher insurgency could perhaps be fitted.

My own view of that national strategy is that the federal government and the Democratic party were attempting to accommodate themselves to rising black insurgency, and especially electoral insurgency, so as to contain it within the two-party system. This strategy necessitated sacrificing, at least to a degree, vested parochial interests such as entrenched and corrupt machines.

Furthermore, black insurgency from below is potentially a force to rationalize obsolete local governments. The long-term crisis of the cities, itself reflecting a contradiction between public gain and private interest, has called forth the best reform efforts of the corporate liberal elite. Centered in the federal government, with its penumbra of foundations, law firms, and universities, the political forces associated with this rationalizing process were most clearly predominant in the Kennedy wing of the Democratic party.

The economic forces whose interests are served by this process are first the banks, insurance companies, and other sections of large capital heavily invested in urban property and, more generally, the interests of corporate capital as a whole—whose continued long-range profit and security rest on a stable, integrated, and loyal population.

Thus the support given to Hatcher was rational to the system as a whole and not at all peculiar, even though it potentially implied economic and political loss for the corporation, United States Steel, whose operations on the spot might become more difficult. The interests of the governing class as a whole and of particular parts of it often diverge; this gap made it possible for Hatcher to achieve some power within the system. How these national factors would shape the amount and forms of power Hatcher actually obtained became quite evident within his first year of office.

Mosaic of black power

When I arrived in the city five months after the inauguration, my first task was to aid in the process of bringing a semblance of order out of what can fairly be described as administrative chaos.

When the new administration took over City Hall in January 1968, it found itself without the keys to offices, with many vital records missing (for example, the file on the United States Steel Corporation in the controller's office) and with a large part of the city government's movable equipment stolen. The police force, for example, had so scavenged the patrol cars for tires and batteries that about 90 percent of them were inoperable. This sort of thing is hardly what one thinks of as a normal process of American government. It seems more appropriate to a bitter ex-colonial power. It is, in fact, exactly what happened as the French left Sekou Toure's Guinea.

There were no funds available. This was because the city council had sharply cut the municipal budget the previous summer in anticipation of a Hatcher victory. It intended, if he lost, to legislate a supplemental appropriation. But when he won without bringing in a council majority with him, its action assured that he would be especially badly crippled in his efforts to run the city government with a modicum of efficiency. Moreover, whenever something went wrong, the media could and did blame the mayor for his lack of concern or ability.

Not only did Richard Hatcher find his position sabotaged by the previous administration even before he arrived, but holdovers, until they were removed from their positions, continued to circumvent his authority by design or accident. And this comparatively unfavorable situation extended to every possible sphere of municipal activities.

Another problem was that the new administrators had to take over the management of a large, unwieldly and obsolete municipal system without the slightest prior executive experience. That there were no black people in Gary with such experience in spite of the high degree of education and intelligence in the black community is explicable only in terms of institutionalized racism—blacks in Gary were never permitted such experiences and occupational roles. Hatcher staffed his key positions with black men who had been schoolteachers, the professional role most closely analogous to running a government bureaucracy. Although several of these men were, in my view, of outstanding ability, they still had to learn everything by trial and error, an arduous and painful way to maintain a complex institution.

Furthermore, this learning process was not made any easier by the unusually heavy demands placed on the time of the mayor and his top aides by the national news media, maneuvering factions of the Democratic Party, a multiplicity of civil rights organizations, universities and voluntary associations, and others who viewed the mayor as a celebrity to be importuned, exploited, or displayed. This outpouring of national interest in a small, parochial city came on top of and was almost equal to, the already heavy workload of the mayor.

Nor were there even clerical personnel to answer the mail and phone calls, let alone rationally respond to the deluge. The municipal budget provided the mayor with a single secretary; it took most of the first summer to make the necessary arrangements to pay for another two secretaries for the mayor's own needs. One result was that as late as June 1968 there was still a two-month backlog of personal mail, which was finally answered by much overtime work.

In addition to these problems, there were others, not as common to American politics, such as the threat of violence, which had to be faced as an aspect of daily life. The problem of security was debilitating, especially after the King and Kennedy assassinations. In view of the mayor's aggressive drive against local organized crime, the race hatred whipped up during and after the campaign by the right wing, and the history of violence in the steel town, this concern with security was not excessive, and maintaining it was a problem. Since the police were closely linked with the local Right, it was necessary to provide the mayor with private bodyguards. The presence of this armed and foreboding staff impaired efficiency without improving safety, especially since the mayor shrugged off the danger and refused to cooperate with these security efforts.

In addition, the tremendous amounts of aid we were offered by foundations, universities, and federal officials proved to be a mixed blessing. The time needed to oversee existing processes was preempted by the complex negotiations surrounding the development and implementation of a panoply of new federal programs. There had never been a Concentrated Employment Program in Gary, nor a Model Cities Program, nor had the poverty program been locally controlled. Some of these programs weren't only new to Gary, they hadn't been implemented anywhere else either. The municipal bureaucracy, which under previous administrations had deliberately spared itself the embarrassment of federal audits, didn't have the slightest idea as to how to utilize or run these complex federal programs. Moreover, none of the experts who brought this largesse to Gary had a clear understanding of how it was to be integrated into the existing municipal system and social structure. These new federal programs sprang up overnight—new bureaucracies, ossified at birth—and their actual purposes and effects bore little relation to the legislative purposes of the congressional statutes that authorized them.

Needless to say, ordinary municipal employees experienced this outside assistance as a source of confusion and additional demoralization, and their efficiency declined further. Even the new leadership was often overwhelmed by, and defensive before, the sophisticated eastern federal bureaucrats and private consultants who clearly wanted only to help out America's first black mayor. The gifts, in other words, carried a fearful price.

Bureaucratic enemies

Except for the uniformed officials and the schools, which were largely outside the mayor's control, the standing city bureaucracy was a key dilemma for Mayor Hatcher.

The mayor had run on a reform program. His official campaign platform placed "good government" first, ahead of even tax reform and civil rights. Hatcher was deeply committed to eliminating graft and corruption, improving the efficiency of municipal government—especially the delivery of services to those sectors of the citizenry that had been most deprived—and he did not view his regime as merely the substitution of black faces for white ones in positions of power.

But he also had a particular historic injustice to rectify: the gross underrepresentation of blacks in the city government, and their complete exclusion from policy-making positions. Moreover, implicit in his campaign was a promise to reward his followers, who were mostly black. (At least most participants in the campaign assumed such a promise; Hatcher himself never spoke about the matter.)

Consequently, there was tremendous pressure from below to kick out everyone not covered by civil service protection and substitute all black personnel in their places. But to do so would have deepened the hostility of the white population and probably weakened Hatcher's potential leverage in the national Democratic Party. He resisted this pressure, asserting that he believed in an interracial administration. However, in addition to this belief (which, as far as I could determine, was genuine), there were other circumstances that dictated his course of action in this matter.

To begin with, it was always a premise of the administration that vital municipal services (police and fire protection, garbage collection, education, public health measures) had to be continued—both because the people of Gary absolutely needed them and because the failure to maintain them would represent a setback for black struggles throughout the country.

It also appeared that with a wholesale and abrupt transition to a totally new work force it would be impossible to continue these services, particularly because of a lack of the necessary skills and experiences among the black population—especially at the level of administration and skilled technical personnel. In this respect Hatcher faced the classic problem faced by all social revolutions and nationalist movements of recent times: after the seizure of power, how is it possible to run a complex society when those who traditionally ran it are now enemies?

The strategy Hatcher employed to meet this problem was the following. The bulk of the old personnel was retained. At the top level of the administration (personal staff, corporation counsel, chief of police, controller) new, trustworthy individuals were brought in. Then, gradually, new department heads were chosen, and new rank-and-file people included. If they had the skill already, they came at the beginning; if they didn't, they were brought in at a rate slow enough to provide for on-the-job training from the holdovers, without disrupting the ongoing functions of the particular department.

The main weakness of this gradualist strategy was that it permitted the old bureaucracy to survive—its institutional base was not destroyed.

The result was that the new political priorities of the administration could not be implemented with any degree of effectiveness in a new municipal political practice. City government remained remarkably like what it had been in the past, at least from the perspective of the average citizen in the community.

While the political leadership was tied up with the kinds of problems I noted earlier, the bureaucracy proceeded on its own course, which was basically one of passive resistance. There were two aspects to this: bureaucratic inertia, a sullen rejection of any changes in established routine that might cause conflicts and difficulties for the employees; and active opposition based on politics and racism, to new methods and goals advocated by the mayor.

To cite just one example, the mayor decided to give a very high priority to enforcement of the housing codes, which had never been seriously implemented by preceding administrations. After much hard work, the Building Department was revamped to engage in aggressive inspection work. Cases stopped being "lost," and the number of inspections was increased by 4,000 percent while their quality was improved and standardized. Then it was discovered that cases prepared for legal enforcement were being tabled by the Legal Department on grounds of technical defects.

I personally ascertained that the alleged legal defects were simply untrue. I then assumed that the reason for the legal staff's behavior was that they were overburdened with work. Conferences were held to explain to them the mayor's priorities so they could rearrange their work schedule. Instead, a series of bitter personal fights resulted, culminating in my removal from that area of work since the staff attorneys threatened to resign if there were continued interference with their professional responsibility. In the course of these disputes, both black and white attorneys expressed the opinion that they did not consider themselves a legal aid bureau for Gary's poor, and furthermore the root of the city's housing problem was the indolent and malicious behavior of the tenants. In their view, it was therefore unjust to vigorously enforce the existing statutes against the landlords. Thus, despite the administration's pledge, black ghetto residents did not find their lives ameliorated in this respect.

Gradually, then, the promise of vast change after the new mayor took office came to be seen as illusory. Indeed, what actually occured was much like an African neocolonial entity: new faces, new rhetoric and people whose lives were scarcely affected except in their feelings towards their government.

This outcome was not due to a failure of good faith on the part of the Hatcher administration. Nor does it prove the fallacious maximalist proposition that no amelioration of the people's conditions of life is possible prior to a revolution. Instead, it was due to the decline of the local mass base of the Hatcher administration and the array of national political forces confronting it.

Most black people in Gary were neither prepared nor able to take upon themselves the functions performed for them by specialized bureaucracies. They relied upon the government for education, welfare, public health, police and fire protection, enforcement of the building codes and other standards, maintenance of the public roads, and the like. Unable to develop alternative popularly based community institutions to carry on these functions by democratic self-government, the new administration was forced to rely upon the city bureaucracy— forced to pursue the option that could only result in minor changes.

Aborted liberation

The most significant consequence of the Hatcher administration's failure to transcend the structural terrain on which it functioned was political, the erosion of popular support after the successful mobilization of energies involved in the campaign. The decline of mass participation in the political process contributed in turn to the tendency of the new regime to solve its dilemmas by bureaucratic means or by relying on outside support from the federal government.

The decline in mass support ought not to be confused with a loss of votes in an election. Indeed, Hatcher is now probably as secure politically as the average big city mayor. The point is that the mass of the black population is not actively involved in helping to run the city. Thus, their political experiences are not enlarged, their understanding of the larger society and how it functions has not improved, and they are not being trained to better organize for their own interests. In short, the liberating process of the struggle for office was aborted after the initial goal was achieved—and before it could even begin to confront the profound problems faced by the mass of urban black Americans.

For example, after the inauguration, old supporters found themselves on the outside looking in. For the most part, since there was no organized effort to continue to involve them (and indeed to do so could not but conflict with the dominant strategy of the administration), they had to be content to remain passive onlookers. Moreover, the average citizen put a lot of faith in the mayor and wanted to give him an opportunity to do his job without intruding on the process.

Even among the most politicized rank-and-file elements there was a fear of interfering. Painfully conscious of their lack of training and experience, they were afraid of "blowing it." Instead they maintained a benevolent watchfulness, an attitude reinforced by the sense that Hatcher was unique, that his performance was some kind of test of black people as a race. (Whites were not the only people encouraged by the media to think in these terms.) There were of course some old supporters who were frankly disillusioned: they did not receive the patronage or other assistance they had expected: they were treated rudely by a bureaucratic holdover or were merely unable to reach the ear of a leader who was once accessible as a friend.

The ebbing away of popular participation could be seen most markedly in the Spanish-speaking community, which could not reassure itself with the symbolic satisfaction of having a member of its group in the national spotlight. With even less education and prior opportunity than the blacks, they found that the qualifications barrier to municipal government left them with even less patronage than they felt to be their due reward. This feeling of betrayal was actively supported by the former machine politicians and criminal elements, who consciously evoked ethnic prejudices to isolate the mayor and weaken his popular support.

What happened in the first year of the new administration, then, was a contradiction between efficiency and ethnic solidarity. At each point the mayor felt he had to rely upon the expert bureaucracy, even at the cost of increasing his distance from his mass base. And this conflict manifested itself in a series of inexorable political events (the appointment of outside advisors, for example), each of which further contributed to eroding the popular base of the still new leadership.

As Antonio Gramsci pointed out, beneath this contradiction lies a deeper one: a historic class deprivation—inflicted on the oppressed by the very structure of the existing society—which barred the underclass from access to the skills necessary for it to run the society directly in its own interests and according to its own standard of civilization. Unless an oppressed social group is able to constitute itself as what Gramsci characterizes as a counterhegemonic social bloc, its conquest of state power cannot be much more than a change in leaders. Given the overall relation of forces in the country at large, such an undertaking was beyond the power of the black community in Gary in 1968. Therefore, dominant national political forces were able quickly to reconstitute their overall control.

National power

What happened to Richard Hatcher in Gary in his first year as mayor raises important questions—questions that might be of only theoretical interest if he were indeed in a unique position. He is not. Carl Stokes, a black, is mayor of Cleveland. Charles Evers, a black, is mayor of Fayette, Mississippi. Thomas Bradley, a black, very nearly became mayor of Los Angeles. Kenneth Gibson, a black, is now mayor of Newark. The list will grow, and with it the question of how we are to understand the mass participation of blacks in electoral politics in this country and the future of their movement.

I believe that until new concepts are worked out, the best way of understanding this process is by analogy with certain national liberation movements in colonial or neocolonial countries. Of course, the participants—in Gary as in Newark—are Americans, and they aren't calling for a UN plebiscite. But they were clearly conscious of themselves as using elections as a tool, as a step toward a much larger (though admittedly ill-defined) ultimate goal—a goal whose key elements of economic change, political power, dignity, defense of a "new" culture and so forth are very close to those of colonial peoples. It is because Hatcher embraced these larger objectives (without, of course, using precisely the rhetoric) that his campaign can be thought of as part of a nationalist process that has a trajectory quite similar to that of anticolonial liberation movements.

In its weakened local posture, the Hatcher administration was unable to resist successfully a large degree of cooptation by the national political authorities. Despite a brave vote at the Democratic National Convention for Reverend Channing Philips, Hatcher was essentially forced to cooperate with the national government and Democratic Party—even to the extent of calling on the sheriff of

Cook County to send deputies to reinforce the local police when a "mini-riot" occurred in the black ghetto.

Without either a nationally coordinated movement or an autonomous base of local insurgency—one capable of carrying out on a mass scale government functions outside the official structure—Hatcher's insurgency was contained within the existing national political system. Or, to express it somewhat differently, the attempt by black forces to use the electoral process to further their national liberation was aborted by a countervailing process of neocolonialism carried out by the federal government. Bluntly speaking, the piecemeal achievement of power through parliamentary means is a fraud—at least as far as black Americans are concerned.

The process by which the national power maintained itself, and even forced the new administration to aid it in doing so, was relatively simple. As the gap between the popular constituency and the new government widened, like many another administration, Hatcher's found itself increasingly forced to rely upon its "accomplishments" to maintain its popularity and to fulfill its deeply held obligation to aid the community.

Lacking adequate autonomous financial resources—the mill remained in private hands, and it still proved impossible to assess it for tax purposes as its true value—accomplishments were necessarily dependent upon obtaining outside funds. In this case, the funds had to come from the federal government, preferably in the form of quick performance projects to maintain popular support and to enable everyone to appear to be doing something to improve matters.

These new programs injected a flow of cash into the community, and they created many new jobs. In his first year in office, the mayor obtained in cash or pledges more federal funds than his entire local budget. Hopes began to be engendered that these programs were the key to solving local problems, while the time spent on preparing them completed the isolation of the leadership from the people.

Then, too, the stress of this forced and artificial growth created endless opportunities for nepotism and even thievery. Men who had never earned a decent living before found themselves as high-paid executives under no requirement to produce any tangible results. Indeed, federal authorities seemed glad to dispense the funds without exercising adequate controls over their expenditures. A situation arose in which those who boasted of how they were hustling the system became prisoners of its largesse.

Even the most honest and courageous leader, such as Mayor Hatcher, could not help but be trapped by the aid offered him by the federal authorities. After all, how can any elected local executive turn down millions of dollars to dispense with as he sees fit to help precisely those people he was elected to aid? The acceptance of the help guaranteed the continuation of bonds of dependence. For without any real autonomous power base, and with new vested interests and expectations created by the flow of funds into the community, and with no available alternate path of development, the relation of power between the local leader and the national state was necessarily and decisively weighted toward the latter.

In Gary, Indiana, within one year after the most prodigious feat in the history of its black population—the conquest of local political power—their insurgency has been almost totally contained. It is indeed difficult to see how the existing administration can extricate itself from its comparative impasse in the absence of fresh national developments, or of a new, more politically coherent popular upsurge from below.

There is, however, no doubt that the struggle waged by the black people of Gary, Indiana, is a landmark on their road to freedom; for the experiences of life and struggle have become another part of their heritage—and thus a promise for us all.

34

JOHN WALTON, Differential Patterns of Community Power Structure: An Explanation Based on Interdependence

In the relatively brief period since its inception, the study of community power has attracted a wide range of enthusiasts. Researchers of diverse backgrounds have found their particular interests coalesce around the assumption that local leadership processes are of central importance to the explanation of community action. The research implications of this approach have been explored in a variety of areas including urban renewal, social welfare, health and hospital services, community conflict, and ethnic relations.[1] Though often divided on issues of how the leadership process is organized and the extent to which power is effectively exercised, investigators are in agreement concerning the viability of research problems suggested by the approach.

In addition to these fertile substantive applications, much has been done to develop the research methods of power structure studies.[2] The conflict which prevailed a few years ago between proponents of rival methods seems to have subsided with the recognition that different methods tap different dimensions of the total power scene. Investigators now appear to agree on the need for methodologically balanced, comparative, and longitudinal studies. This trend is manifest in several notable works that have appeared recently.[3]

"Differential Patterns of Community Power Structure: An Explanation Based on Interdependence," by John Walton from *Community Structure and Decision Making: Comparative Analyses* (edited by Terry N. Clark) from pages 441–459. Reprinted by permission of Intext Educational Publishers.

In spite of these convergences, however, there has been almost no progress in one vital respect; the development of theoretical explanations of the reported findings. Elaborate documentation of the atheoretical character of the field hardly seems necessary. One has only to peruse a portion of the literature to discover that the principal issues are almost entirely concerned with method and conflicting interpretations of how broadly power is distributed. Only rarely are some of the initial steps in theorizing represented by conceptual considerations and the development of propositional inventories.[4]

The purpose of this paper is to develop a theoretical explanation of how power is distributed in local communities, and to consider briefly how various power arrangements may account for different forms of community action. The analysis incorporates earlier theoretical discussions of the community and a systematic review of the power structure literature. Anticipating the conclusions for a moment, it will be argued that as communities become increasingly interdependent with extracommunity institutions, changes in the local normative order ensue producing more competitive power arrangements.

Starting with a review of previous research, the argument moves on to consider the adequacy of certain theoretical approaches and, finally, to develop the propositions concerning power structure and community action.

Findings of previous research

In an earlier paper the findings of thirty-three power structure studies dealing with fifty-five communities were analyzed in order to determine the relationship between a number of substantive and methodological variables and the dependent variable type of power structure.[5] Subsequently that analysis was replicated using a somewhat larger number of studies.[6] The selection of studies was intended to be exhaustive of the published literature in social science devoted specifically to the study of community power structure. By dealing with the published literature some unpublished studies were excluded, especially dissertations. Confining the analysis to the social science literature excluded journalistic reports. Finally, the criterion that the research be specifically concerned with community power excluded a number of community studies dealing with stratification, local government, and related aspects of social and political life. These criteria were employed in a screening of the literature, and the resulting list of studies was checked against several lengthy bibliographies to ensure its inclusiveness. Thus the studies are regarded as a universe, defined by the above criteria, rather than a sample.

Each study was reviewed and, when sufficient information was available, coded in terms of a number of self-explanatory independent variables (for example, region, population size, industrialization, economic diversity, and the like). Similarly, the type of power structure identified in each report was coded in terms of four categories: (1) pyramidal—a monolithic, monopolistic, or single cohesive leadership group; (2) factional—at least two durable factions that compete for advantage; (3) coalitional—leadership varies with issues and is made up of fluid coalitions of interested persons and groups; (4) amorphous—the absence of any persistent pattern of leadership or power exercised on the local level.

Table 1 indicates those few associations which were found to be significant or meaningful.[7]

In contrast to these positive findings, a large number of variables, including region, population size, population composition, industrialization, economic diversity, and type of local government, were *not* found to be related to type of power structure.

Taking these results as a summary of the present status of research, it appears that no firm generalizations are suggested. The findings fail to conform to any neat pattern such as an association between competitive power structures and greater complexity of local social and economic organization. The inadequacies of such an explanation are underscored by the negative findings. The evidence may, however, be suggestive of some less obvious explanation. In order to explore that possibility some implicitly theoretical positions in the area of community power and a major theoretical work on American communities will be examined, considering, in both cases, how they square with the above findings and how they might inform the present analysis.

Theoretical approaches

In one of the first attempts to bring some order out of the confusion of results, Rogers developed a series of propositions concerning community political systems.[8] His dependent variable, type of political system, was made up of the categories monolithic and pluralistic. In stating the relationship between these and a number of characteristics of community social structure, Rogers hypothesized that the following would be associated with a pluralistic system: a high degree of industrialization, a large population, a socially heterogeneous population, a polity differentiated from the kinship and economic systems, a local government of extensive scope, two or more political parties and the unionization, or other political and economic organization, of working-class groups. The underlying theme in this series of propositions, what has been referred to as the implicit theory, centers on the effects of industrialization, and attendant processes of urbanization and bureaucratization, the outcome of these being structural differentiation which contributes to a pluralistic power situation. The approach is, of course, central to contemporary social science whether stated in terms of *gemeinschaft* and *gesellschaft* or any other of a variety of polar types.

Hawley has presented a somewhat more specific approach.[9] Here power is defined as a system property whose distribution can be measured by the ability to mobilize resources and personnel. In any total system, such as a community, this ability lies in the various component subsystems and is exercised through their managerial functions. Hence, operationally, the greater the number of managerial personnel, the greater the concentration of power. If it is granted

Table 1.[a] Community characteristics and community power structure[b,c]

	Pyramidal	Factional, coalitional and amorphous	Total
Absentee ownership			
Present	2	18	20
Absent	12	9	21
Total	14	27	41
	$Q = -.85$ $.01 > p > .001$		
Economic resources[d]			
Adequate	9	17	26
Inadequate	6	5	11
Total	15	22	37
	$Q = -.39$ $.30 > p > .20$		
Type of city[e]			
Independent	14	22	36
Satellite	2	10	12
Total	16	32	48
	$Q = -.52$ $.20 > p > .10$		
Party competition			
Competitive	0	10	10
Noncompetitive	10	12	22
Total	10	22	32
	$Q = -1.0$ $.02 > p > .01$		
Change in power structure			
Dispersion	2	17	19
Concentration	0	0	0
No change	3	4	7
Oscillation	2	1	3
Decline locally	1	2	3
Total	8	24	32

[a]The cell entries in the table represent communities, rather than studies, since a single study often dealt with two or more towns.

[b]The variable power structure was originally coded in terms of four categories. The categories are collapsed here to avoid small Ns and to provide a contrast between more and less concentrated power arrangements.

[c]The Ns in each of the subtables vary because the studies coded do not uniformly provide data on each variable.

[d]Operational definitions of the following three variables are indicated by the type of information coded under each category. Adequate economic resources—includes towns with a reportedly prosperous business community, low rates of poverty, and unemployment; inadequate economically—underdeveloped with high rates of poverty and unemployment. Independent city—includes central cities of metropolitan areas and independent manufacturing, commercial or agricultural centers; satellite city—suburb or town dominated by a nearby city. Party competition—the existence of two or more local parties (or affiliates in formally nonpartisan cities) which regularly contend for public office; noncompetitive—a one-party town.

[e]When the zero-order level findings on economic resources and type of city are examined controlling for research method, a factor associated with type of power structure identified, the differences here do not persist. The findings are reported here because they are suggestive and because the low quality of the data may be obscuring significant associations. That is, the lower the quality of the data, the more difficult it is to demonstrate statistically significant relationships and the more likely it is that such relationships may be obscured. That is, in the present context I have gone beyond a strict interpretation of the earlier findings in an attempt to draw some meaningful generalizations.

that success in a collective action requires the mobilization of resources and personnel, and that this ability is greatest where power is most highly concentrated, then it follows that the greater the concentration of power in a community the greater the *probability* of success in any collective action. In a recent paper, inspired in part by the Hawley piece, Butler and Pope have suggested another measure of power concentration—the number of profile or key industries and the concentration of managerial functions within these.[10]

It should be noted that the Hawley and Butler and Pope papers are concerned chiefly with community action; for each the premise is that more concentrated power situations are conducive to concerted action. Unlike Rogers, they are not trying to explain patterns of power distribution but, rather, employ these to explain community action. Nevertheless, they are pertinent here because they imply a theoretical position involving the saliency of managerial functions in the determination of community power structures.

How do these explanatory schemes square with the findings culled from the existing literature? Considering first the hypotheses formulated by Rogers, the evidence runs counter to his notions of the effects of industrialization, population size, and population heterogeneity. On the positive side, his proposition about political parties, though not entirely equivalent to party competition, is supported. Unfortunately, no data are available on the remaining three propositions. What evidence exists, however, indicates that Rogers's propositions do not fare very well within the present context, though they may have greater predictive power in a cross cultural or historical perspective. For our purposes the implication is that the theoretical approach implicit in these propositions is in need of revision. Perhaps it will be necessary to abandon the simplified notion of a unilinear relationship between the growing complexity of industrial society and more pluralistic local power arrangements, in favor of a more limited, yet more discriminating explanation.[11]

The evidence presented previously is not directly relevant to the Hawley and Butler and Pope approaches since these attempt to explain community action. If, however, it is assumed with these authors that concentrated power structures are associated with community action, and then the antecedent link in their chain of reasoning is examined, it is found that those community characteristics allegedly conducive to power concentration (ones engendering a large number of managerial functions)—industrialization, economic diversity, proportion of absentee ownership, and economic resources—are either unrelated or associated with the less concentrated power structures in the data. This fact can hardly be taken as a refutation of the positions presented. What it does indicate is that the number of managerial functions appears to be a poor indicator of type of power structure (though it may indicate the number of potentially powerful people in community action).

In short, the analysis thus far demonstrates the need for theoretical statements which are both more explicit and account better for the available data.

Warren's analysis of *The Community in America*[12] provides a pertinent general framework for dealing theoretically with the specific questions of power structure. Warren's central thesis is that American communities are undergoing a drastic transformation of their entire structure and function; "(this) 'great change' in community living includes the increasing orientation of local community units toward extracommunity systems of which they are a part, with a decline in community cohesion and autonomy."[13] Although Warren analyzes these changes along seven fundamental dimensions of community life, a summary statement indicates their relevance for present purposes:

> In the first place, they signalize the increasing and strengthening of the external ties which bind the local community to the larger society. In the process, various parts of the community—its educational system, its recreation, its economic units, its governmental functions, its religious units, its health and welfare agencies, and its voluntary associations—have become increasingly oriented toward district, state, regional, or national offices and less and less oriented toward each other.
>
> In the second place, as local community units have become more closely tied in with state and national systems, much of the decision-making prerogative concerning the structure and function of these units has been transferred to the headquarters or district offices of the systems themselves, thus leaving a narrower and narrower scope of functions over which local units, responsible to the local community, exercise autonomous power.[14]

On the basis of these observations concerning the "great change" and with the simultaneous recognition that communities (that is, 'combinations of social units and systems which perform the major functions having locality reference') do persist as meaningful units, Warren finds useful a distinction between the *horizontal* and *vertical axes* of community organization. The vertical axis refers to connections between community organizations and extracommunity centers, and the horizontal axis refers to connections between community organizations. The "great change" involves an increase in the former type of connections often at the cost of the latter.

In what follows several propositions will be developed which relate Warren's approach specifically to the question of how power is distributed on the local level. His concept of a vertical axis of community organization has particular importance for this analysis.

An explanation of differential patterns of community power structure

Power is defined here as *the capacity to mobilize resources for the accomplishment of intended effects with recourse to some type of sanction(s) to encourage compliance.*[15] This definition includes the elements of both potential and actualized power in that capacity for mobilizing resources refers to potential while the application of sanctions refers to actualized power. *Capacity* also implies a distinction from *right* such that *authority* is not confused with the definition. Following Lasswell and Kaplan, the threat of sanctions, positive or negative, distinguishes *influence* from power—influence refers only to the capacity to mobilize resources.

Power structure is defined as *the characteristic pattern within a social organization whereby resources are mobilized and sanctions employed in ways that affect the organization as a whole.*

For the sake of simplicity competitive and monopolistic power structures will be dealt with here.[16] Monopolistic power structures characterize social organizations in which the capacity for mobilizing resources and recourse to sanctions are the exclusive property of a group with similar interests. In competitive situations the capacity for mobilizing resources and recourse to sanctions are possessed by two or more groups with different interests.

The basic assumption of the theoretical statement to be developed here is that a monopoly of power produces a situation in which consensus is the most important factor underlying the use of power. This consensus may, but need not, imply agreement on values and objectives. What it does imply is agreement concerning the capabilities of those holding power to realize their own intentions over a wide range of community relevant issues. In such a monopolistic situation, expectations concerning the norms prescribed by the existing power arrangement tend to be widely recognized. That is, the limits of allowable (nonsanctionable) deviance and opposition are narrow and clear. As a result of these congruent expectations, potential rather than manifest power is more commonly the mechanism by which compliance is encouraged; overt conflict and coercion are relatively infrequent occurrences because compliance can be realized without them. Merriam captured the sense of this assumption when he wrote, "Power is not strongest when it uses violence, but weakest."[17]

By contrast, in competitive situations the exercise of power moves from a reliance on consensus to more overt applications of sanctions. This becomes necessary to the extent that competing groups become capable of restricting the scope of each other's sanctions. Claims to power must be supported by effective action. Greater normative diversity, with attendant diversity in expectations, characterizes this situation. Such circumstances result in a greater incidence of conflict stemming from the fact that those who would exercise power are required to make evident their claim through the use of sanctions.

It should be added that each of these circumstances contains elements of the other. Monopolistic power arrangements do, at times, generate divergent norms and expectations just as they occasionally have recourse to overt applications of coercion. More important, the role of consensual expectations and potential power are critical to all forms of social organization and can be observed in many of the transactions carried on in competitive power settings. In this connection conflict is probably most characteristic of those transitional periods in which power is becoming more or less diffused since it is at this point that the normative order is most uncertain and expectations least clear.[18] In the

event that this transition is one from monopolistic to competitive it may culmin-
ate in a new set of rules defining community power arrangements which, while
more conducive than the monopolistic situation, produces less conflict than the
transitional phase.

Because at first glance this assumption may appear to be a truism, its
nontrivial character will be demonstrated. Presthus' study of two New York communities which differed on a pluralist-elitist continuum is valuable here. Discussing the more elitist of the two, Presthus reasons:

> In Riverview sharper class and economic differences and resulting dispari-
> ties in expectations, values and consensus seem to have placed a premium
> on more centralized, imperative leadership. As organizational theory and
> studies of group behavior suggest, social support, shared values, and com-
> mon expectations make possible the minimization of overt power and
> authority. When community consensus is limited, leaders tend to function
> in a more unilateral manner.[19]

Here the minimization of overt power and authority is equated with a more
pluralistic (competitive) power situation. The present argument agrees with the
prior notion that common expectations result in a minimization of overt power
(and conflict), but this is taken to be characteristic of a monopolistic situation.
Thus, when community consensus is limited the leadership process tends to be
more competitive.[20]

Obviously the relationship identified in my assumption may operate in
either direction; changes in the competitiveness of the power situation can
produce changes in norms and expectations and, similarly, changes in norms and
expectations can lead to changes in power arrangements. This approach is concerned with developing an explanation of the change in power structures, that is,
in the latter direction of the causal complex.

This section has reasoned that normative expectations bear a particular
relationship to power structure and that conflict can be taken as an indicator of
that relationship.[21] In what follows an attempt will be made to elaborate the connection between normative expectations and types of power structure in terms
of the data drawn from existing community studies.

Returning to the data in Table 1, the question of how the ideas presented
would account for the findings can now be raised. It will be recalled that the data
indicate a relationship between competitive power structures and the presence of
absentee-owned corporations, competitive party politics, adequate economic
resources, and satellite status. Further, in those communities where change was
studied, the trend was in the direction of a greater dispersion of power. Do these
findings suggest some underlying explanation?

Upon closer examination the evidence does point to an explanation. Each
of the variables associated with competitive power structures reflects the interdependence of the community and extracommunity centers of power or increased emphasis on the vertical axis. For example, a high proportion of absentee-

owned industry suggests that many community relevant decisions are controlled by the personnel and interests of national corporate bodies whose influence may stem from either a deliberate intervention in local affairs or from the more characteristic aloofness to local responsibility.[22] Similarly, competitive political parties may often reflect the involvement of county, state, and national party organizations in a struggle for control of local constituencies.[23] While it could be reasonably argued that inadequate economic resources result in substantial intervention and control by state and federal agencies which extend aid to local bodies, the position taken here is that communities with more adequate economic resources maintain a greater number of interdependent ties to extracommunity institutions such as suppliers, markets, investors, and other economic units. Finally, in the case of type of city, the connection is apparent. Suburban municipalities and smaller towns which form satellites of larger urban centers are interdependent in a variety of economic and political activities including municipal services, jobs, consumer behavior, and the like. If, at points, the relationship between each of these variables and community interdependence is not unambiguous, the position taken here is enhanced by the pattern they suggest when taken together.

Drawing together all that has been said up to this point, the proposition which seems to account best for the findings can be stated as follows: *to the extent that the local community becomes increasingly interdependent with respect to extracommunity institutions (or develops along its vertical axis), the structure of local leadership becomes more competitive.*[24]

Theoretically this proposition derives from the more general statement concerning norms and power arrangements. That is, the mechanism by which interdependence, or increasing relevance of the vertical axis of community organization, affects the distribution of community power is the disruption of the local normative order associated with the existing power structure. Development along the vertical axis involves the introduction of new interests and new institutional relationships implying new definitions of the community, and these have the effect of disrupting consensual normative expectations.

In addition to a differentiation of allegiances, these changes include the introduction of new *resources* and *sanctions* into the community. Local organizations with verticle ties to extracommunity institutions frequently share in the capital and human resources of the larger entity making it possible for them to sustain a broader scope of activities than would otherwise be the case. For example, absentee-owned corporations may receive funds and skilled personnel for a desired expansion of local operations making them more important as local tax contributors, employers and suppliers. Such resources carry with them potential sanctions. In the above example some of these would include the threat to locate elsewhere,[25] threat of cutbacks or other actions having an adverse effect on the local economy, support or nonsupport in local elections. What has been said here of absentee-owned corporations could also be said, though perhaps in less dramatic ways, of other vertical community organizations. The point to be emphasized is that these organizations introduce new sources of power into the local picture and, being interdependent, they also have stakes in the local decision-making process which occasionally must be defended. The greater the number of community organizations with vertical ties, the more frequent and the more inclusive are contests surrounding the decision-making process.

In summary, the theoretical statement advanced here states that the introduction of organizations with vertical ties produces a greater interdependence between community and extracommunity centers of power. This interdependence brings changes in the local normative order, as well as new resources and sanctions, creating circumstances conducive to the emergence of competing power centers. Accordingly, variables which reflect the interdependence of the community and the "carrying society"—absentee ownership, party competition, adequate economic resources, and satellite status—are associated with competitive power structures; whereas those variables which reflect only intra-community change—economic diversity, population increase, etc.—are not so associated.[26]

Parenthetically, it is instructive to note certain parallels between this argument and Banfield's theoretical treatment of the exercise of power. Defining power as "the ability to establish control over another" (that is, "the ability to cause another to give or withhold action"),[27] Banfield states that any actor has a limited stock of power which he spends or invests in ways that he believes will maintain and enhance his ability to control. When "investment opportunities" change so does the structure of influence. For example, he offers the following proposition; "As the number of autonomous actors increases, control tends to become less structured. Structures of control, that is, relationships which are stable from proposal to proposal, are expensive to maintain. The value of a structure—and thus the amount that will be invested in it—tends to decline as the outcome of the process becomes less and less subject to control."[28] In the present context the number of "autonomous actors" increases as a result of changes in normative expectations and the effectiveness of sanctions. Similarly, the result here is a less concentrated structure of power.

Returning to my own explanatory scheme, one loose end can be tied up. The findings on change in Table 1 indicated that community power structures are tending to become more competitive. This trend is a predictable consequence of the spread of "metropolitan dominance"[29] and its implications for greater community interdependence. That is, if Bogue and others are correct, and there seems to be ample evidence that they are, the spread of metropolitan dominance would lead one to predict a corresponding trend toward competitive power arrangements according to our explanation. That is, in fact, what the findings indicate.

Discussing the effects of increasing interdependence, Greer summarizes the consequences for the "locality group" in terms of a loss of autonomy, exposure to conflicting norms, and the fragmentation of local normative order. In connection with the latter he identifies many of the events and explanations embodied in the theoretical statement developed here.

Fragmentation of the local normative order is a predictable consequence; some of the members of the local group must conform to patterns from afar, since they are dependent upon the large, extended organization for their livelihood. Others take advantage of the local group's loss of coercive power to exploit added degrees of freedom; they experiment with new means to old ends, they exercise freedom of choice. Others, still, are dependent upon the local order for social position and rewards; their life is controlled by its norms, but with the attrition of dependence (and therefore the basis for order), they find it impossible to communicate or to enforce compliance. (The cutting edge of the sanctions depended, after all, upon the interdependence of the local group.) When individuals become committed to groups centering outside the locality, the new dependence brings a measure of independence from their neighbors.[30]

This fragmentation of the local normative order, accomplished through changes in expectations concerning power leads, according to this theoretical statement, to changes in the structure of community power, and specifically to more competitive power arrangements.

Metropolitan politics and community action

Recalling that the purpose of this paper was to develop an explanation of how power is distributed in local communities, *and* how power arrangements may account for community action, some comments on the latter question are called for. Explanation may be particularly useful for two reasons: first, the foregoing analysis bears directly on the subject of community action and, second, the discussion serves to integrate another perspective on power and decision-making into this explanation.

In his well known essay describing the local community as an "ecology of games,"[31] Long argues that the concept of "power structure" suffers from misplaced concreteness, that when we look more closely at cities we find no such structured decision-making institution.

What is characteristic of metropolitan areas is the lack of overall decision-making institutions. This does not mean that there are not institutions with power in metropolitan areas. It does mean that there are no institutions with sufficient power and overall responsibility to make decisions settling metropolitan issues and solving metropolitan problems . . .[32]

Rather, Long conceives of metropolitan issues as having careers in which interested and powerful parties—governments, groups and institutions—interact and "develop a system of largely unintended cooperation through which things get done . . ."[33] In this process actors deal with metropolitan problems from a limited point of view, that is, one confined to their particular interest and institutional base.

There are at least two reasons why Long's empirically persuasive approach has stymied students of community power. One would appear to be the fact that much of this research has been conducted in places other than metropolitan areas where decisions settling local issues are possible. Second, the well known controversy over pluralism and elitism in the literature—because it is a debate over who makes local decisions, a small, cohesive group or a large, diverse one—may have obscured the possibility that no one makes such decisions.

In the present explanation metropolitan areas are prototypes of interdependent, vertically organized communities. Here a highly fragmented and competitive power arrangement in which the scope of any group or institution would be limited to prime interest areas could be expected. That is, the competitive process would militate against generalized influence and require that actors work to maintain their position within the system. Long and Banfield concur with this prediction in the stress they put on metropolitan politics as going systems in which institutions and groups seek to maintain and enhance their power in particular areas, public policy representing the results of their cooperation.[34]

Under these circumstances one would expect to find a fragmented and competitive pattern of community action. Community action in American cities seems increasingly to fit this pattern. The most apparent illustrations are found in the activities of civil rights, antipoverty, and peace groups which often possess resources conferred by extracommunity institutions and are beginning to seriously involve themselves in the local political process. Here, of course, they encounter opposition from other local and vertically organized groups. As a result, coordinated community action becomes more problematic, and public policy represents less a reflection of consensus than a byproduct of the competitive process in which power is differentially exercised. Discussing the resurgence of radical politics in Chicago, Cleveland, Pittsburgh, Gary, and several other cities, one author concludes "In the midwest, this tendency is general, and holds promise of becoming the outstanding fact of urban political life in America by the end of the decade."[35] In another vein, several studies which have touched on the consequences of increasing involvement of the federal government in local affairs find, contrary to political folklore, an enhancement of competitive, democratic processes.[36]

Notable among deviant cases is the Vidich and Bensman study[37] where involvement of state and county governments resulted in an abdication of responsibility on the part of local leaders. While it is significant that these changes diluted the power of Springdale's elite, it is also recognized that the consequences of extracommunity involvement were not those we would predict. In this regard the theory presented here may be in need of modification. Recalling that Springdale is a town of 2,500 people and that its extracommunity ties center chiefly around state subsidies, it is reasonable to infer that both the nature of the community and of the vertical ties are contingent elements in the theory presented here. Perhaps it is the case, for example, that changes along the vertical axis lead to greater competitiveness only in those communities which possess a certain minimum of institutional viability and that without this the same changes spell the demise of local leadership.

Conclusion

The explanation offered here is an attempt to push the study of community power beyond a disproportionate emphasis on technique and toward a concern for testing propositions derived from explicit theoretical statements. There seems little doubt that this alternative is best suited for resolving the controversies over how power is distributed in local communities, and for generalizing research in this area to the larger problems of social organization and change.

The theory developed in this paper states that the introduction into the local community of the institutions and influences of national-urban culture produces a "fragmentation of local normative order" or a disruption of consensual expectations concerning the norms prescribed by existing power arrangements. As expectations are altered and interests are differentiated, new resources are exploited for the creation of competing power groups.

The theory focuses on one direction of influence in what is undoubtedly a complex process. In so doing, however, it has the virtue of generating a number of testable propositions. Future comparative studies could evaluate, on the basis of first-hand data, the fundamental proposition regarding community interdependence and the advent of competitive power arrangements. A sampling of related propositions includes:

1. Changes, other than interdependence, which challenge the local normative order lead to more competitive power arrangements.
2. Intracommunity change which does not challenge the normative order does not lead to greater competitiveness.
3. Vertical ties which do not alter the normative order do not lead to the exploitation of new resources and more competitive power arrangements.
4. Normative diversity within a community leads to a greater frequency of application of overt sanctions (Presthus).
5. The greater the number of vertical ties in a community, the smaller the scope of local power groups.
6. The greater the number of vertical ties (and competitiveness) the more difficult (less frequent) is coordinated community action.

In addition to suggesting propositions, the theory implies a new direction for research in that it locates the source of local change in the relationship between the community and extracommunity institutions. It is expected that researchers will find this theory informative as they become increasingly aware of what it implies for the choice of an appropriate unit of analysis in future community power studies. If the theory is correct, the appropriate unit of analysis is not the community per se but, rather, the relationship between the community and the institutions of national-urban culture.

Notes

1. See, for example, Amos Hawley, "Community Power and Urban Renewal Success," also included in this present volume, pp. 393–405; Warner Bloomberg and Morris Sunshine, *Suburban Power Structures and Public Education: A Study of Values, Influence and Tax Effort* (Syracuse: Syracuse University Press, 1963); Ralph B. Kimbrough, *Political Power and Educational Decision Making* (Chicago: Rand McNally & Co., 1964); Irving A. Fowler, "Local Industrial Structure, Economic Power and Community Welfare," *Social Problems*, 6 (Summer 1958), 41–51; Ivan Belknap and John Steinle, *The Community and Its Hospitals* (Syracuse: Syracuse University Press, 1963); Floyd Hunter, Ruth Connor Schaffer, and Cecil G. Sheps, *Community Organization: Action and Inaction* (Chapel Hill: University of North Carolina Press, 1956); James S. Coleman, *Community Conflict* (New York: The Free Press, 1957); William A. Gamson, "Rancorous Conflict in Community Politics," *American Sociological Review*, 31 (February 1966), 71–81; James McKee, "Community Power and Strategies in Race Relations," *Social Problems*, 6 (Winter 1958–59), 41–51.

2. L. Vaughn Blankenship, "Community Power and Decision Making: A Comparative Evaluation of Measurement Techniques," *Social Forces*, 43 (December 1964), 207–216; William V. D'Antonio and Eugene Erickson, "The Reputational Technique as a Measure of Community Power: An Evaluation Based on Comparative and Longitudinal Studies," *American Sociological Review*, 27 (June 1962), 362–376; Linton C. Freeman, *et al.*, "Locating Leaders in Local Communities: A Comparison of Some Alternative Approaches," *American Sociological Review*, 28 (October 1963), 791–798.

3. Robert Presthus, *Men at the Top: A Study in Community Power* (New York: Oxford University Press, 1964); Robert E. Agger, Daniel Goldrich, and Bert E. Swanson, *The Rulers and the Ruled: Political Power and Impotence in American Communities* (New York: John Wiley & Sons, 1964); William V. D'Antonio and William H. Form, *Influentials in Two Border Cities: A Study in Community Decision-Making* (Notre Dame: University of Notre Dame Press, 1965).

4. For some efforts in this direction see Agger, *et al., ibid.;* Presthus, *ibid.;* M. Herbert Danzger, "Community Power Structure: Problems and Continuities," *American Sociological Review*, 24 (October 1964), 707–717; Terry N. Clark, "Community or Communities?"

5. John Walton, "Substance and Artifact: The Current Status of Research on Community Power Structure," *American Journal of Sociology*, 71 (January 1966), 430–438.

6. John Walton, "A Systematic Survey of Community Power Research" in Michael T. Aiken and Paul E. Mott, *The Structure of Community Power: Readings* (in press).

7. A complete summary of the findings, positive and negative, is to be found in Walton, *ibid.*

8. David Rogers, "Community Political Systems: A Framework and Hypotheses for Comparative Studies," in Bert E. Swanson, ed., *Current Trends in Comparative Community Studies* (Kansas City: Community Studies Inc., 1962). A similar but more comprehensive formulation is Terry N. Clark, "Power and Community Structure: Who Governs, Where, and When?" *The Sociological Quarterly*, Summer 1967.

9. Hawley, *op. cit.*

10. Edgar W. Butler and Hallowell Pope, "Community Power Structures, Industrialization and Public Welfare Programs," paper read at the 61st annual meeting of the American Sociological Association, Miami Beach, Florida, August 1966.

11. This conclusion applies to similar propositional inventories based on the "evolutionary" or "continuum" notion. See, for example, Delbert C. Miller and William H. Form, *Industry, Labor, and Community* (New York: Harper, 1960).

12. Roland L. Warren, *The Community in America* (Chicago: Rand McNally & Co., 1963) and "Toward a Reformulation of Community Theory," *Human Organization*, 15 (Summer 1962), 8–11.

13. Warren, *The Community in America, op. cit.*, p. 53.

14. *Ibid.*, p. 5.

15. This definition derives from a number of discussions of the concept of power. Some of the most relevant writings include Bertrand Russell, *Power: A New Social Analysis* (New York: Barnes and Noble, 1962); Max Weber, *The Theory of Social and Economic*

Organization, trans., A. M. Henderson and Talcott Parsons (New York: Oxford University Press, 1947); Talcott Parsons, "On the Concept of Political Power," *Proceedings of the American Philosophical Society*, 107 (June 1963), 232–262; Harold Lasswell and Abraham Kaplan, *Power and Society: A Framework for Political Inquiry* (New Haven: Yale University Press, 1950).

16.   This is not meant to imply that such a dichotomy is the most useful framework, though it tends to preoccupy the literature, for example, Presthus *op. cit.*, D'Antonio and Form, *op. cit.* Etzioni has offered four types of control structure based on the means of control available to various positions within an organization; see *A Comparative Analysis of Complex Organizations* (New York: The Free Press, 1961). Agger, *et al.*, characterize power structures with two variables, "distribution of power" and "convergence of leadership ideology," and a resulting four-fold table. Construing the second variable as an indicator of leadership cohesiveness, the formulation provides an important distinction between truly competitive systems and cases where power is shared among a number of groups but similarity of interests unites them in a monopolistic power arrangement. Many controversies in the field stem from a failure to make this distinction.

17.   In a more elaborate statement Merriam writes, "In most communities the use of force is relatively uncommon in proportion to the number of regulations, and the success of the organization is not measured by the amount of violence in specific cases but by the extent to which violence is avoided and other substitutes discovered." Charles E. Merriam, *Political Power*, Collier Books edition (New York: The Macmillan Company, 1964), p. 36.

18.   Although the present concern is with community conflict, this argument closely parallels Durkheim's thesis on suicide and changes in the normative order.

19.   Presthus, *op. cit.*, p. 427.

20.   A more precise treatment of this relationship would specify types of conflict and how these are associated with various power arrangements. For example, monopolistic power structures may suppress dissent and conflict, they may manage it within innocuous limits or they may engender revolutionary conflict. Competitive power structures, on the other hand, may encourage conflict which results in a stalemate or in effective argument and nonrevolutionary change.

21.   James S. Coleman, *Community Conflict* (New York: The Free Press, 1957), accords with this point by arguing that whenever the pattern of control is so complete that certain elements can see no way of moving into a position of power, there may be sporadic conflict but no organized opposition (nor, presumably, regular conflict).

22.   For studies documenting this see Robert O. Schulze, "The Bifurcation of Power in a Satellite City," in Morris Janowitz, (ed.), *Community Political Systems* (Glencoe: The Free Press, 1961), 19–80; Roland J. Pellegrin and Charles H. Coates, "Absentee-owned Corporations and Community Power Structure," *American Journal of Sociology*, 61 (March 1956), 413–419.

23.   On this point there is little evidence pro or con and I present it only as a plausible hypothesis.

24.   It should be noted that the inferences about change are drawn primarily from cross-sectional data and thus run the risk of incorrectly inferring trends. Given the nature of available data, there is no alternative other than recommending future longitudinal studies following the lead of Agger, *et al.*, and D'Antonio and Form, *op. cit.* Other studies which attempt to replicate earlier work include Delbert C. Miller, "Decision-Making Cliques in Community Power Structures: A Comparative Study of an American and an English City," *American Journal of Sociology*, 64 (November 1958), 299–310; David A. Booth and Charles R. Adrian, "Power Structure and Community Change: A Replication Study of Community A," *Midwest Journal of Political Science*, 6 (August 1962), 277–296; Donald A. Clelland and William H. Form, "Economic Dominants and Community Power: A Comparative Analysis," *American Journal of Sociology*, 69 (March 1964), 511–521; M. Kent Jennings, *Community Influentials: The Elites of Atlanta* (New York: The Free Press, 1964).

25.   For a discussion of this ploy and other sanctions available to economic institutions see Arnold Rose, *The Power Structure: Political Processes in American Society*, (New York: Oxford University Press, 1967), chapter 3.

26.   The point to be emphasized here is that greater complexity and specialization **are not** necessarily conducive to the changes under consideration, but only insofar as these

developments produce greater interdependence. At some point, of course, complexity and specialization do necessitate greater interdependence but it would seem that this is not always the case at every level of community development. We would expect that some of these variables are confounded such that increasing size, for example, will be related to competitive power structures at that point in a community's development when size and interdependence vary together. According to this argument such an association would be spurious. This may be the case though the available data are too crude and provide too few observations to allow an unequivocal solution.

27. Edward C. Banfield, *Political Influence: A New Theory of Urban Politics* (New York: The Free Press Paperback Edition, 1965), p. 348.

28. *Ibid.*, p. 318.

29. Don J. Bogue, *The Structure of the Metropolitan Community* (Ann Arbor: Horace H. Rackham School of Graduate Studies, University of Michigan, 1949).

30. Scott Greer, *The Emerging City: Myth and Reality* (New York: The Free Press, 1962), pp. 50–51.

31. Norton E. Long, "The Local Community as an Ecology of Games," *American Journal of Sociology* 44 (November 1958), 251–266.

32. Norton E. Long, *The Polity* (Chicago: Rand McNally & Co., 1962), p. 157.

33. *Ibid.*

34. Also relevant to this characterization is Wallace S. Sayre and Herbert Kaufman, *Governing New York City: Politics in the Metropolis* (New York: Russell Sage Foundation, 1960).

35. Stephen A. Booth, "The New Politics Goes Local," *The Nation* 204, no. 22 (May 29, 1967).

36. Presthus, *op. cit.;* William V. D'Antonio, "Community Leadership in an Economic Crisis: Testing Ground for Ideological Cleavage," *American Journal of Sociology* 71 (May 1966), 688–700.

37. *Small Town in Mass Society,* (Princeton: Princeton University Press, 1958).

35

DANIEL BELL & VIRGINIA HELD, The Community Revolution

> *. . . Two neighbors may agree to drain a meadow, which they possess in common: because it is easy for them to know each other's mind; and each must perceive, that the immediate consequence of his failing in his part, is the abandoning the whole project. But it is very difficult, and indeed impossible, that a thousand persons should agree in any such action; it being difficult for them to concert so complicated a design, and still more difficult for them to execute it; while each seeks a pretext to free himself of the trouble and expense, and would lay the whole burden on others. Political society easily remedies both these inconveniences. . . . Thus, bridges are built, harbours opened, ramparts raised, canals formed, fleets equipped, and armies disciplined, everywhere, by the care of government,*

Daniel Bell and Virginia Held, "The Community Revolution." *The Public Interest*, no. 16 (Summer 1969), pp. 142–177. Copyright © National Affairs, Inc., 1969. Reprinted by permission.

which, though composed of men subject to all human infirmities, becomes,
by one of the finest and most subtle inventions imaginable, a composition
which is in some measure exempted from all these infirmities.
—David Hume, *A Treatise of Human Nature*

One cliché of contemporary political discourse is that "the people have no real voice—or, less and less of a voice—in their political affairs," a view reinforced by a ponderous academic sociology that asserts "a decline or eclipse of the local community" and a change wherein "all groupings based on traditional criteria such as shared ethnic descent and inheritance of status are undermined . . . "

We believe both assertions to be quite wrong. In fact, the opposite may be true—that there is more participation than ever before in American society, particularly in the large urban centers such as New York, and more opportunity for the active and interested person to express his political and social concerns. That very state of affairs leads to a paradox because it is the increase in participation which creates a sense of powerlessness and consequent frustration.

A person who is socially conscious wants results, particularly *his* results, and he wants them immediately. But the very fact that there is an increase in the number of claimants leads, inevitably, to lengthier consultation and mediation, and more importantly, to a situation wherein thousands of different organizations, each wanting diverse and contradictory things, simply check each other in their demands. As a Mrs. Gladys Gonzales, vice-president of the Parents Teachers Association of Junior High School 71, is reported as saying at the public hearings of the Board of Education on the school decentralization plan, "You graciously allow us to say what is on our mind and then turn around and do what you want to do anyway." But this is precisely what *every* speaker, whatever his point of view, feels and says at such a meeting; and the result is rancor and a sense of frustration.

Forty years ago, a Tammany political boss could give an order to a mayor. Today, no such simple action is possible. On each political issue—decentralization or community control, the mix of low income and middle income housing, the proportion of blacks in the city colleges, the location of a cross-Manhattan or cross-Brooklyn expressway, etc.—there are dozens of active, vocal, and conflicting organized opinions. The difficulty in governing New York—and many other cities as well—is not the "lack of voice" of individuals in city affairs, or the "eclipse of local community," but the babel of voices and the multiplication of claimants in the widened political arena. In this new participatory democracy the need is for the creation of new political mechanisms that will allow for the establishment of priorities in the city, and for some effective bargaining and tradeoffs between groups; without that the city may end in a shambles.

The multifarious associations

Writing on his trip to the United States in 1904, Max Weber could comment, after Tocqueville, "In the past and up to the present, it has been a characteristic precisely of the specifically American democracy that it did *not* constitute a formless sandheap of individuals, but rather a buzzing complex of strictly exclusive, yet voluntary associations."

No count has ever been made of the number of voluntary associations in the United States or in any major American city. In New York, the *Directory of Social and Health Agencies of New York City* lists 1200 welfare organizations, voluntary and public, excluding civic, educational, and religious organizations. Ten years ago, Sayre and Kaufman in *Governing New York City* remarked, "No careful census of these nongovernmental groups in the city has ever been made, but the number seems to run at least to *tens of thousands.* This estimate comprises only those groups sufficiently well organized to have letterheads, telephones and/or to appear in some published directory" (our italics).

Whatever the total ten years ago, the number of groups, particularly local block associations, tenants organizations, welfare councils—name the issue and a dozen groups spring into being—have since multiplied spectacularly. The chief reason has been the revolution in the political structure of urban life that was initiated by the Kennedy-Johnson administrations, a development obscured and to some extent distorted by the Vietnam war. Just as the Wagner Act of 1935 facilitated—indeed, shaped—the organization of the economic workplace by trade unions, so the community action provisions of the Poverty Act of 1964 established the basis for neighborhood organization by community groups. In so doing, it has created a potential for political bargaining on urban community issues just as there is economic bargaining on issues in the workplace.

There are substantial differences of course. The Wagner Act created a rule-making institution in the National Labor Relations Board with well-defined contestants, specific issues, and real payoffs. The structure of political bargaining in the community is still inchoate. Whether it will function is moot. The system has been quickly repudiated, in part, by the Johnson and Nixon administrations; the militants, who initially sought to take advantage of the system to gain a place in society, have turned to more radical and direct action tactics; and the established political machines have fought the community action programs and in many places have taken them over. Yet the potential remains, particularly in New York City, for disadvantaged groups—or more specifically their indigenous leaders—to get "a share of the action" or at a minimum to act as veto groups in the system. The full thrust of community organization may have been blunted in these last couple of years, but it would be foolish to ignore what may yet be one of the great structural changes in the political system of American urban society.

The patterns of communal life

Going back sixty years or more—there has been an extensive network of participation by different kinds of groups in the communal life of New York City, and these have tied into the political system in different ways. For purposes of analysis, one can identify three different kinds of communal systems in the city life.

The first might be called the *civic associations*. These are the old, established, predominantly upper middle class, business, and "good government" organizations. They include such groups as the Citizens Union (established in 1897 growing out of the City Reform Club whose members included Theodore Roosevelt and elected reform mayor William L. Strong), the Citizens Budget Commission (business-supported), the Citizens' Committee for Children (primarily wealthy, liberal Jewish women), the Men's and Women's City Clubs, the Civil Service Reform Association, the Public Education Association, the Citizens Housing and Planning Council, the Commerce and Industry Association, the League of Women Voters, etc. These are all politically-minded, politically active, "clean government," reform movements.

The second is the more numerous and more diffuse *fraternal and service organizations* built, traditionally, around the religious and ethnic groups. These consist of the Protestant Council, the Catholic Charities, the Federation of Jewish Philanthropies, the hospitals, family service centers, old age homes, child care centers, parochial schools, and the like. They are represented in the large, coordinating, research and information agencies, such as the Community Council of Greater New York, and in major service groups, such as the Community Service Society of New York. These agencies, plus the many "old country" associations, particularly among the Jews and the Irish, have provided the means whereby the poor immigrants of an earlier era were helped to settle in New York. These organizations have been the backbone of the communal, self-help structures of New York.

And third, there has been the large network of *neighborhood organizations:* settlement houses, parent-teachers associations, block associations, tenants associations, local churches and synagogues. The center of these activities was often the local political club. City aldermen, state assemblymen, and state senators kept in touch with these organizations which meant grievances or needs were funneled through the elected representatives.

In the past, almost all of these three "communal systems" were private and voluntary. They were sustained by the monies and time of individuals who gained status, political visibility, or simple personal satisfaction through these activities. They were maintained by professional staffs who provided the day-to-day services, as well as structural continuity through time, and who often "recruited" new leaders for these organizations in order to sustain the monies and activities.

In addition, the political system itself was the main "brokerage" agency for patronage, reward, wealth, status, and power. New immigrants could get jobs through "pull" at city hall or through the large number of business concerns whose existence depended in part on political favor; for example, Consolidated Edison, pier stevedore concerns, construction companies, and truckers. The quid pro quo was jobs for votes.[1] The political clubs serviced the new and unorganized poor (on the lower east side before World War I, it was not uncommon for a person who had an appendicitis attack, to go to his precinct captain, because he often didn't know where the hospital was, and he certainly did not have a telephone). They told city hall what was needed in the neighborhoods. In the current jargon, the political clubs were the chief modes of communication and control.

Over the past decades, the political machines that were the structure of government in New York have broken down. Under the New Deal, the locus of power and attention shifted to Washington, and the major jobs and finances of the society came under federal control. The rise of middle-class liberal reformers within the Democratic Party—reform, previously, had always operated outside the party, usually in some "fusion" slate—cracked the singular power of the old bosses because the reform clubs were oriented more to issues than to jobs. The extension of the merit system in the 1960s, "upward, outward and downward," reduced the role of patronage. More and more frequently, administrators of the top agencies came from career ranks and party background almost became a mark of disqualification. As Theodore Lowi observed, "The triumph of Reform really ends in paradox: *Cities like New York became well-run but ungoverned.*"[2]

In the past thirty years, the influx of Negro and Puerto Rican migrants brought a double problem. They lacked the resources and often the will to build voluntary community structures. They arrived on the scene at a time when the older political mechanisms were in disarray. The blacks did achieve some political power, with the votes of Harlem as a base. When Hulan Jack became borough president in Manhattan in 1953, it became clear that for the foreseeable future this post would be a black prerogative. (And so it has been with his successors, Constance Motley and Percy Sutton. But the other rewards—political contracts, the protection of rackets, the patronage to the lawyers and professionals—that had gone in the past to the ethnic minorities did not follow this political power: in part, because such rewards were no longer available and, in part, because there were few blacks able to claim them. The chief point here is that the blacks lacked the communal network that could interact with the political base, and thus provide the basis for the kind of advancement that had been made by earlier ethnic groups.[3]

It has always been the case in modern society that the three fundamental hierarchies are power, wealth, and status. In the past, wealth commanded power or power commandeered wealth. But for the ethnic groups in the United States, these two were reinforced through the *communal* structures, which provided status and prestige for the wealthy and powerful, and which also provided a cohesion for the group coming into the society.[4] The communal structures set up a network of full-time professionals who would advance the interests of the ethnic groups and their activities furthered and reinforced the contacts and social ties which aided the lawyer, the businessman, the financier in their business and professional careers.

The problem for the blacks, thus, was that at the time they were coming into urban life the political base was restricted and their communal structures were weak. In time, the two weaknesses would doubtless have been corrected. It is only in the last decade, after all, that the blacks have become primarily urban and concentrated in the north. But time is no longer available. What took the Irish three generations, the Italian two, and the Jews one to achieve—the security of middle class status—is something the blacks want immediately. They have been here the longest, and have been held down the most. They no longer want to wait. What they are asking for is power and resources; these have to come through the community.

The redemption of the cities

To this political and sociological crisis is added another crucial fact: the multiplication of social problems arising from the demographic transformation of the country. The population of the country is being concentrated in metropolitan areas, the older sections of the cities are dilapidated, the transportation systems are choked and swollen, and services are lagging. It is easy, and deceptive, to blame this simply on "capitalism," or, more ambiguously on "the system." But this crisis derives in the first instance from one of the most fundamental facts about modern society: *the increase in number and movement of persons, and the increased demand for a level of services and amenities for all which has been hitherto unknown in the society.* Sixty-five years ago, a million persons a year could pour into the country in a steady stream for a decade, and jam together in crowded ghettoes, with little direct impact on the settled middle-class lives of the older inhabitants, but that is no longer possible today. Each person wants full access to education and to services; and today each middle class person, sitting in his car, among 80 million others, wants a free and unobstructed highway.

These demands for services underscore what has been evident for a long time: that the administrative structure of the cities, organized as they are in a crazy-quilt pattern of counties, townships, and districts, are out of whack with the times. The United States may have the most modern economy and technology in the world, but its administrative structure, as Samuel Huntington has observed, is a Tudor polity. This is particularly evident in New York. The population of New York *City* (not of the metropolitan region) is *twice* the population of Norway, and is greater than the population of Austria or Sweden. But the city's political structure is wholly incongruent with the social realities. The mayor almost has to keep in touch with every birth, briss, confirmation, wedding, national day, death, and memorial service of the multifarious nationality groups in the city in his ceremonial duties; but in his administrative role, the mayor is unable to be in control of the day-to-day functions of the city or to determine its long-range planning requirements.

In 1947, the Citizens Union proposed the division of New York City into districts "for more orderly planning and decentralization of municipal services and community development." The report recommended the grouping of city services in one location in each district, and proposed that each district would develop its own plan in cooperation with the City Planning Commission. In 1950, the City Planning Commission took up the idea and proposed sixty-six districts as "logical units for the planning of schools, housing, hospitals, libraries, playgrounds, local street systems and other public facilities as well as for consideration of land use and zoning patterns." As Borough President of Manhattan in 1951, Robert Wagner set up a Community Planning Council, consisting of fifteen to twenty members, for each of the twelve Manhattan districts suggested by the City Planning Commission. In part, Wagner did this because the local political clubs that had been the source of information and mediation between the districts and the city had largely ceased to function, and the administrative agencies increasingly were being overwhelmed by the local groups who took their claims and grievances directly to the city heads. Through these Local Planning Boards, Wagner sought to set up a mediating mechanism against the anarchic onslaught of the multiple organizations in the city.

Thus, the idea of decentralization and local community organizations as the basis of new administrative and political functions was underway, slowly, haltingly, and confusedly, in the 1950s.

To this the Kennedy administration added a new ideology, the ideology of "participation." The upsurge of the blacks, the discovery of the poor, the argument that these groups could not help themselves because they were powerless, all led to the conception that in programs fostered by government one should encourage the creation of new communities. In this way, new structures could be built that could provide help and training for the poor through institutions under their control or influence. In these communities, new, indigenous leaderships would emerge who would lead their constituents "into" the society. Thus the groundwork was laid for a change in the structure of American urban life, a transformation fostered by and financed by the federal government. It is a story unique in American history.

The ideology of participation

The heart of the participation ideology was the Poverty Program, and the section entitled the Community Action Programs (CAP) which provides for participation by the poor in the programs that will affect their lives. The key phrase in the section was "maximum feasible participation," a phrase which for some was rhetoric, for some ideology, and for some an instrumental means whereby the poor would gain a sense of political identity. As Daniel P. Moynihan observes, "Community action with citizen participation was a coherent and powerful idea working its way into national policy, albeit little noticed or understood at the time."

One of the earliest pamphlets produced by CAP, entitled "A Hometown Fight," sets forth this idea in its instructions to communities on how to apply for community-action grants:

> Local community action programs are central to the war on poverty.
> . . . The individual community decides how best to attack poverty in its
> midst. Initiative and direction must come from the community itself.
> . . . In a community with limited resources, local leaders can begin a com-

munity action program in stages. For example, with the "building block" approach a community might start a child development program including health services. . . . The major goal of community action programs is to help individuals help themselves.

The assumptions behind these propositions were quite clear. As John G. Wofford indicates, "There was to be no federal blueprint, no magic formula worked out in Washington that would be imposed on local problems. . . . Problems of decaying mining towns in Kentucky, of Indian reservations, of rural Mississippi, and of urban slums were seen as too different to permit meaningful detailed federal direction." There was also a more important reason, as Mr. Wofford details it:

> Planning itself was seen as a form of action. The very process of getting communities to think about their problems was viewed as an essential means of mobilizing local resources most of which had been either unused or diffused in the past. In communities throughout the country, at the time of the enactment of the antipoverty legislation, most programs dealing with local poverty were "single-tracked." School boards, city halls, departments of welfare, juvenile courts, settlement houses, were going their separate ways without significant contact with each other. The person who suffered programmatic insularity was, of course, the poor person himself; his problems were segmented into traditional molds, and he was rarely, if ever, viewed as one human being with connected crises, needs and styles of life. Thus "linkage" of programs at the local level became an important goal, and the local planning needed to develop these linkages was conceived as the first and one of the most important forms of community action.[5]

While the rationale and intentions of the "participation" idea are clear, the political history of its emergence and realization is still somewhat of a mystery. The Wagner Act had behind it a large social movement, a long history of agitation, and a political ideology. The Community Action Program had none of these. It was initiated almost completely from the "top," by professionals, rather than by the poor, and on the basis of a mystique of participation.[6]

Much of the original push in this direction came from the Ford Foundation through the proddings of its public affairs director, Paul Ylvisaker, a former philosophy professor at Swarthmore. In the 1950s, American communities had little awareness of the huge problems ahead. Urban renewal, which had been initiated by the Housing Act of 1949, had brought physical change to the center of the cities, but the social changes, particularly the displacement of the poor, were largely ignored. Through Ylvisaker, the Ford Foundation "Gray Areas" programs gave substantial grants to cities to set up community agencies in such fields as youth employment, education, and community services. Ylvisaker had no specific program for social reform—the very idea went against his grain—but he believed in the method of self-help through which communities could bring forth programs suitable to their needs.

A very different source of the participation ideology was a group that had gathered around Robert Kennedy when he was Attorney-General. Kennedy had become concerned with the growing extent of youth crime and he had set up a President's Committee on Juvenile Delinquency and Youth Crime, actually an interagency team from the departments of Labor, Justice, and Health, Education and Welfare, directed by David Hackett, a close friend. This committee accepted a theory of delinquency that had been advanced by two sociologists from the Columbia University School of Social Work, Richard Cloward and Lloyd Ohlin, a theory derived from Robert Merton's hypothesis of the relation between "social structure and *anomie.*" Delinquency, they argued, is not an individual pathology, to be "cured" by psychiatric or social work therapies. Lower-class youths, they said, do have conventional goals (e.g., success), but face a disparity between what "they are led to want and what is actually available to them." Delinquency then, is an illegitimate means of achieving what the society prescribes. In the formal language of the two sociologists, "delinquency is not . . . a property of individuals . . . it is a property of social systems in which these individuals and groups are enmeshed." The major task, therefore, for those who wish to eliminate delinquency must be to reorganize the slums and to create new "functional substitutes for traditional structures." In short, one must provide the slum youngsters with realistic opportunities for social mobility, and to do this one has to create, not just jobs, but a whole new way of life, a new community.

This theory was translated into practice in Mobilization for Youth, a project on the lower east side of New York. By 1963, to cite Sundquist, "the work of the President's Committee on Juvenile Delinquency and Youth Crime had become 'a $30 million test of Ohlin's opportunity theory.' " The MFY demonstration included employment programs, work preparation, evaluation and guidance, skills training, antidiscrimination activities, remedial education, home visits, and neighborhood service centers. More importantly, the Cloward and Ohlin theories about community action, and Ylvisaker's faith in the efficacy of experiment as the means whereby community goals would emerge out of experience and self-organization (a quixotic fusion of John Dewey and Quaker philosophy), became the ideology of the Kennedy-Johnson antipoverty program and the basis of a putative "participation revolution" in American politics.

The intention to change

There is no legislative history as to the meaning and intent of Congress in providing for maximum feasible involvement of the poor in the Economic Opportunity Act's definition of "community action." Adam Yarmolinsky, one of the legislative drafters of the act, recalls that "the requirement of 'maximum feasible participation' was incorporated into the language of the bill from its very first draft; but it was thought of simply as the process of encouraging the residents of poverty areas to take part in the work of community action programs and to perform a number of jobs that might otherwise be performed by professional social workers. . . . The possibility of major conflict between the organized poor and the politicians in city hall was simply not one that anybody worried about during this period, although Shriver and his associates did see the possibility of conflicts between city hall and the poverty community on the one side and the organized social work hierarchy on the other side." [7]

But this vague intention did contain an implicit commitment. As Wofford puts it, the "key—and often unstated—objective of the Community Action Program [was] institutional change." And, as Leonard Chazen, in a study of the act (in the *Yale Law Journal*, March 1966) writes: "section 202 (a) (3) . . . has been commonly interpreted as a mandate for federal assistance in the effort to create political organizations for the poor."

None of this was "planned" by social scientists. It was implicit in the intention of the Great Society to include the poor and the blacks into the society, just as the New Deal had included labor and the farmers. As James L. Sundquist writes, in summing up the American Academy of Arts and Sciences Project: "The decision to set the new and revolutionary institution in the midst of every American community, all at once, was made not by social theorists but by politicians—or, more precisely, their speech writers. The key word that ordained all that followed was neither 'maximum,' 'feasible,' nor 'participation,' but 'unconditional' from President Johnson's declaration of 'unconditional war on poverty.' That set the tone from which there could be no retreat. That this would mean the organization of the poor for a frontal assault on the power structure in city after city—merging inevitably into racial conflict—was not planned by those who wrote the language of the Economic Opportunity Act any more than it was foreseen by those who accepted and enacted it."

What some of the social scientists only dimly sensed quickly became a reality: that for the indigenous leaders of the poor, particularly the militant blacks, the movement for "participation" became a drive for "power." This challenge was aimed at the local political machines, and was correctly understood as such by the local politicos. In San Francisco, black leaders succeeded early in 1965 in taking over control of the Poverty Program, and they sought to use the program to build a political base for black control. Plans were laid to have a part-time community organizer for almost every block and a full-time organizer for every eight blocks. Little of the monies went into services for the residents. In the political struggle within the black community, and between it and city hall, the original black leaders lost out. In Philadelphia, a program dominated by independent blacks was pulled back to city hall influence, though not with total city hall control. In New York City, the situation was reversed. The Poverty Program was used by the Lindsay administration to build a new political base by putting the black militants on the community action payrolls, tying them in with the Urban Action Task Forces, and using them as a battering ram against the older political machines.

Whatever the political outcome, the fact remains that a new institutional structure began to be built into the American political system. The question whether local community groups will *control* particular programs—schools, health, housing—is still being fought out. But the *participation* of the community is no longer in doubt. The Johnson administration felt that the Poverty Program had gone too far; but in setting up the Model Cities program it realized that little could be done without community participation, and that act stipulates that local community groups have to be consulted in the drawing up of new neighborhood plans. (Mindful of the experience of the Poverty Program, it provides that the control and final decisions over the plans are to be lodged in the mayor's office and in city hall.) The Nixon administration has chosen to expand the Model Cities program, rather than the Poverty Program, as its instrument for the basis of a coherent urban polity, and the participation of the local community will be further institutionalized under that scheme. How far and how effective the "community revolution" will be in American political life, remains to be seen. In the remainder of this essay we shall explore the extent of that change, as it has become manifest in New York City, and raise some questions about the meanings and extent of "community participation" for the political structure of the society.

The community revolution in New York

The "community revolution" has been more extensive—and, one might say, explosive—in New York than in any other city in the United States. The reasons for this lie largely in the inchoate nature of the political system of the city.

First, as we have noted earlier, there was a receptivity to the idea of decentralization, and this had led to the establishment of local planning boards in Manhattan and the demarcation of planning districts in other boroughs.

Second, there was strong ideological support for the creation of local community structures, both from the reform elements and from the liberal establishment in the city, particularly the foundations. Depending on the ideological position one holds, one can describe these efforts as either helping the blacks to full citizenship, or as "cooling" a tense and heated situation (particularly after the rioting in Watts and Newark), as (as the SDS puts it) a "counter-insurgency" tactic by McGeorge Bundy to blunt a revolutionary upsurge by the exploited. However one depicts the motive, the fact is that a number of the "activist" foundations (Ford, Taconic, New World) financed a significant number of community demonstration projects in different parts of the city. The two most contentious were the Ocean Hill-Brownsville school districts and the I.S. 201 complex in Harlem. These two educational efforts were given a high degree of autonomy by the Board of Education and, until the teachers strikes, had come under considerable "community control."

A third, and somewhat different, impetus were the decisions by Kennedy and Lindsay to cultivate the blacks and the poor in order to create a new political base as against the older dilapidated machines. Kennedy, aided by wealthy Wall Street friends, such as André Meyer of Lazard Frères, set up a corporation in Brooklyn's Bedford-Stuyvesant district to help rehabilitate the neighborhood and he brought in a former Justice Department assistant, John Doar, to head up this effort. Through the Poverty Program and the Urban Action Task Forces, Lindsay built an extensive network of contacts in the ghettos, and put a large number of street leaders on the Human Resources Administration payroll.

Encouraged by these attentions, but in greater measure arising out of the new upsurge of black militancy, a large number of new, indigenous leaders emerged in the neighborhoods to play a role as community activists. What they quickly discovered is that their ability to "holler" and to threaten violence would give them, if not control, then at least a veto over government projects in their neighborhoods. Thus, the rise of CORE in Harlem, or the Afro-American Teachers Association, or the dozens of other new organizations, became a fourth dimension in the community revolution.

But behind all this there is the simple fact that in every major area which touches on the lives of people, especially in social services, the prevailing federal legislation now calls for community participation, and in New York, because of the political climate and official encouragement, the community movement has spilled over into more areas than in any other city in the country.

Nine community systems

Despite the importance and proliferation of the community efforts, the extra-ordinary fact is that nowhere in the city administration is there a single office which keeps track of all the community and neighborhood programs, coordinates the information about (let alone the overlapping jurisdictions of) these programs, or maintains a register of community leaders in each neighborhood and in each program, in order to assess the representativeness of the participation.

From what we have been able to piece together, there are nine different "community systems" in the city—nine areas, each comprising a number of different programs in which "the community" is supposed to have a voice. The nine are:

▪ *Planning;* On March 1, 1968, the City Planning Commission adopted a map delineating sixty-two community planning districts. (It would be difficult to say that these districts follow historic boundaries or encompass the politically or sociologically identifiable neighborhoods—a point we shall consider later.) Twelve of these districts are in Manhattan, fourteen in the Bronx, eighteen in Brooklyn, fourteen in Queens, and four in Staten Island. The Planning Boards, which are mandated in the City Charter, counsel each Borough President on needs and facilities in each district. These boards are largely advisory and have few powers. Yet in any further movement to decentralize administrative functions of the city, it is possible that these districts would become, as in the case of the London County Councils, the basis of new political functions. For this reason, many persons have been concerned about the boundaries of the districts.

■ *Community Development.* This is the euphemism for the Poverty Program. Under the jurisdiction of the Human Resources Administration—one of the ten new "super" agencies in the city—there is a citywide Council Against Poverty made up of fifty-one persons, half of whom are representatives of local poverty areas, and there are twenty-five Community Corporations, one-third of whose members are elected by the poor in each district. The Community Corporations, the heart of the program, are supposed to organize a comprehensive set of services, adapted to local needs (e.g., community action bureaus to work for better housing and more jobs, child care centers, youth programs), and to administer these programs.

■ *Health.* Health Districts have long been a feature of the city, and the demographic data from Health Districts as well as from census tracts form the basis for nearly all the social statistics in the city. In 1940, the New York City Health Department adopted a master plan to attain units of manageable size for health services. The city was divided into thirty Health Districts, each one having roughly equal units of 250,000 population. Each district was then subdivided into smaller units, known as Health Areas, each with about 25,000 population. In recent years, because of the revolution in medical practice—e.g., the extraordinary decline in virus diseases—there has been a new emphasis on "community medicine." Large hospitals have established extensive community service agencies. A major impetus, however, has come from the Kennedy bill requirement of community participation in the new mental health programs. Thus, in addition to local groups that work with the city's Municipal Health Centers, Community Mental Health Advisory Boards are presently being established. The creation of these community boards has led to a new kind of conflict between "the community" and the "professionals."

■ *Housing and Urban Renewal.* Since 1962 the Housing and Development Administration consults with a community urban renewal council when it designates an area for urban renewal. Last year this policy was made national and mandatory by a Department of Housing and Urban Development administrative directive. Each renewal countil is the judge of its own membership. The Morningside Urban Renewal Council, for example, has sixty membership organizations ranging from local churches, institutions, tenants associations, all the way over to the SDS. Renewal councils are funded by the city and provide legal and other services for persons affected by urban renewal. Because an urban renewal plan is often the main instrument for the reorganization of a neighborhood, the question of who is "the community" comes into its sharpest focus in these council debates. There are local groups participating in renewal activities in twenty areas.

■ *Model Cities.* To a considerable extent, the Model Cities program supersedes urban renewal, and is designed to provide a comprehensive overhaul of a limited number of selected areas, concentrating new housing, rehabilitation, and various services for maximum impact. Under the law, any Model Cities program has to be worked out in conjunction with community groups, and in the three areas designated by New York as Model City areas, the processes of consultation that are being worked out are very much in flux.

■ *Police.* For many minority persons, the police is the "enemy." Only about 7 percent of the police in New York City are black, a figure that has changed little in the past decade. Yet, even the police are involved in community relations programs. The Police Athletic League is an effort, now over fifty years old, to create neighborhood athletic teams. Since 1966, Police Precinct Councils made up of local residents have been meeting with police representatives to discuss community problems in the seventy-six Police Precincts.

■ *Youth Services.* A wide variety of programs are aimed today at youth in the city, though there is no central coordinating agency. These touch on such matters as career development, vocational training, recreational facilities, and narcotics addiction. In each of these instances, programs are set up in neighborhoods and involve some community advisory boards.

■ *Urban Action Task Force.* The Task Forces are primarily communication and "cooling" devices. The idea evolved after the East New York (Brooklyn) disorders in the summer of 1966, when the neighborhood Task Force was set up to identify local leaders, to establish contact, to hear grievances, and to funnel complaints to appropriate city agencies. When disorders have threatened, the Task Force has been able to enlist local leaders to "cool" a situation. There are now twenty-two neighborhood Task Forces, both in low-income and middle-class neighborhoods. Each is headed by a city official and has two staff members from the community, paid for by the city.[8] Along with the Task Forces, the Lindsay administration has set up five "Neighborhood City Halls," usually in a storefront, to receive complaints. Last year, 71,000 complaints were handled by these offices. The offices use city personnel but are financed by foundations and private individuals, because the Democratic-controlled city council has nullified all budget requests on the ground that the mayor was trying to use city funds to establish his own type of political clubhouse.

■ *Schools.* Local School Boards have been in existence in New York since early in the century, but typically such boards were without power and consisted of local luminaries nominated by the political clubs. When the issue of integration and busing became salient, local feeling began to run high, and local groups began to pay attention to the schools. Since 1962, members of the Local School Boards have been screened by panels of local parent and community organizations and appointed by the Board of Education. More recently the issue of the "community control" of schools has become the most fractious political issue in New York. Under the decentralization plan passed by the New York State legislature in 1969, the city will be divided into thirty to thirty-three School Districts each having a Local School Board elected by proportional representation. Although the central board retains the power to employ and assign teachers, the local boards will have some influence in the choice of principals, and boards in disadvantaged communities will have some power to select special teachers who they think may be effective.[9]

In all these areas, as we said, "the community" is supposed to be involved. But what does this mean? We can try to gauge what participation means, in practice, by considering two programs. Poverty and the Model Cities.

The Poverty Program

Although the idea of community participation may have been launched in the Poverty Program somewhat inadvertently, its career is by now quite deliberately molded. A significant number of persons have acquired a stake in its future and do their best to swell its tide. A significant number of others fear the consequences of the escalation of demands upon the political system, to which community participation contributes, and would like to curb its rise. By now, the latter intent is probably futile and possibly dangerous. As Jeremy Bentham noted long ago, it is psychologically harder to lose than simply not to gain, and as the urban poor have almost acquired the status of having something to lose, they are not about to give it away quietly.

The question is no longer *whether* but *how* to involve "the community" in the processes of decision; and officials, planners, reformers, and politicians now vie with one another in claiming that their programs and methods achieve the most and the best of that elusive attribute, participation. There is widespread recognition that once the original phases of dramatic chaos and exciting turmoil have been outgrown, the militant young hotheads often do not participate in the developed processes of participation—the meetings between community groups and government officials, the public hearings, the elections for local boards, the consultations and deliberations. But there is also a growing recognition that, in providing the possibilities for meaningful participation, the supports on which the militants erect their rhetoric are weakened. "The difference between us and them," said a well-dressed, hard-working black poverty program official in his thirties, "is ten years. We used to think, too, that the only thing to do was to tear it down, but now we're trying to change the system from the inside, and sometimes we think there's a chance."

The Poverty Program's claim to have developed a significant degree of participation by the inhabitants of the ghetto in the planning and operation of services designed to help them is a fair one. In some ways New York City has gone further than most other cities; twenty-five of the fifty-one-member citywide Council Against Poverty (set up in September 1966) are representatives of the poor who are selected by the twenty-five communities designated by the city as poverty areas. On the Council Against Poverty are also seventeen public officials, including the mayor, borough presidents, the superintendent of schools and the administrator of the Housing and Development Administration. Nine seats represent labor, business, religious, racial, and civic groups designated by the mayor as eligible to send a representative. Council Against Poverty sets priorities among antipoverty efforts, gives final approval to program grants using both city and federal funds, and supervises the setting up of what are called—one does not yet know whether the term is unfortunate or instructive—local "Community Corporations." In New York City, one-third of the members of Community Corporation boards must be directly elected by the poor; two-thirds of the members must be residents of the area; and, in most plans, one-third of the members must be, in the literal sense, poor—that is, have incomes below the poverty line. The Community Corporations screen and recommend program requests and operate programs or subcontract for them with "delegate agencies" at an even more local level. Twenty-five Community Corporations have now been formed.

The numbers of poor people who have taken part in the elections for these boards are not large, and are sometimes cited as percentages of the total inhabitants of an area to discredit the reality of participation: 5,276 voters out of a total Bedford-Stuyvesant population of 250,000, and 3,991 out of 190,000 residents of East Harlem, are not high percentages, although the numbers of eligible voters who take part in these elections sometimes run as high as 10 percent.[10] The more significant issue is how these levels of participation compare with whatever participation existed before, and here the picture is more impressive. Participation in the Poverty Program has involved much more than mere reshuffling—the reorganization of people already caught up in the block associations and parent organizations into new groups. It has drawn in many new members, and propelled them through its processes to a point where a sanitation worker from Bedford-Stuyvesant chairs a Council Against Poverty committee on which some of the highest officials of the city government sit.

What has not always been anticipated is that the more the community is drawn into the process of consultation, participation, and advocacy of its own interests, the closer it may come to demanding that it be the final authority as well as a source *for* its own programs, able to summon outside funds and expert advice, but maintaining the most prized and constantly sought power—the final say. When one set of persons moves closer to power, however, another set is displaced; and the Poverty Program's early efforts to achieve the specified "maximum feasible participation" by organizing the poor to pressure the politicians has led to an inevitable reluctance on the part of those in the established structures to be shouted at or bypassed. The result has been a compromise. In 1967 Congress amended the original Economic Opportunity Act to require that one-third of the membership of bodies allocating Poverty Program funds consist of public officials.

In New York City, efforts to combat poverty are coordinated through the Human Resources Administration, which includes a large number of operating agencies. Through its Department of Social Services, it disburses welfare payments to more than a million persons. The Manpower and Career Development Agency operates twenty Neighborhood Manpower Service Centers which provide job recruitment and counseling services. The Community Development Agency handles the antipoverty efforts, but is subject to policies that are determined by the Council Against Poverty.

This year, apart from the $1.3 billion spent on the payment and administration of welfare and medical assistance to welfare recipients, $155 million is being spent on programs for one million poor people: $70 million through the Community Development Agency, $54 million through the Manpower and Career Development Agency, the rest through smaller agencies that deal with such problems as drug addiction.

In all, city and federal antipoverty funds finance 1,000 delegate agencies operating more than 250 all-year and 1,000 summer programs. Some of the 1,000 delegate agencies are long-established organizations, such as the YMHA, the Urban League, United Neighborhood Houses, the Roman Catholic Archdiocese of New York, etc.; but most of them are newer, strictly local organizations developed and run by residents for the poor from their neighborhoods.[11]

More than 14,300 persons are employed by the antipoverty program in New York City. Of these, 400 are on the central staff of the Community Development Agency, but 80 percent of the 13,900 others who work in the poor communities are local residents. The human resources administrator, Mitchell Ginsberg, proudly claims that 80 percent of New York City's local initiative programs "are run by grassroots, nontraditional social agencies; in Los Angeles, it's 54 percent, Chicago 10 percent and Detroit 2 percent."

This has also led to considerable confusion, and, in a number of instances, as federal audits have shown, to a considerable number of financial defalcations and embezzlements by free-wheeling local entrepreneurs. "Honest graft," as George Washington Plunkitt once called it, was the price of Tammany Hall for its services. As Mitchell Ginsberg phrases it in the locutions of social work, "inasmuch as one of the primary goals of the community action program is to give community people the opportunity to learn the ways of organized effort and to thus enter the mainstream of society, they must be allowed to learn by doing."

Brownsville

What is a poverty "community" and how does it "participate"? Of New York City's twenty-five poverty communities, some have as many inhabitants as Pasadena or Salt Lake City. The lines that have been drawn encompass as few as 18,000 and as many as 300,000 persons, but each area is high in what are taken to be the most significant indices of poverty: total persons receiving welfare per 1,000 population, percent of live births in hospital wards, and juvenile delinquency offenses per 1,000 youths between the ages of 7 and 20. Compared to a citywide average of 61.0 persons per 1,000 receiving welfare in 1965, east Harlem, for instance, had 182.0 and Morrisania, in the Bronx, 196.4. Compared to a citywide average of 48.4 percent of births in hospital wards, central Harlem had 93.2 percent and Bushwick, in Brooklyn, 73.2 percent. Central Harlem had 112.2 juvenile delinquency offenses per 1,000 youths between the ages of 7 and 20, and Bedford-Stuyvesant 123.6, compared to an average of 52.2 for the whole of New York City.

As Raleigh Davenport, the staff director of the Council Against Poverty explains, poverty area lines "determine which organizations and individuals are eligible to receive, respectively, money and services. . . . It should not be surprising, then, that a great deal of interaction [sic!] . . . preceded the maps" which defined New York City's poor communities.

Brownsville, in central Brooklyn, is one New York City poverty community. Once a well-known Jewish area, its population of 150,000 in 1960 was 32.5 percent black, 21 percent Puerto Rican. Now its somewhat higher population is approximately 65 percent black and 30 percent Puerto Rican. About half of the people in Brownsville are on welfare. It was the first poverty area to set up a Community Corporation, the plans for which were drawn up by ninety-four preexisting groups, such as block associations, church groups, and parent associations. Its Community Corporation now coordinates twenty-six programs, and allocates nearly $3 million of antipoverty funds. Among the programs are a Consumer Education Program that teaches low income and welfare consumers how to shop efficiently, and promotes a credit union to encourage savings and the development of a consumer cooperative; a Family Planning Unit; a Mental Health Project that involves whole families; and the Brownsville Young Troupers that draws young people between the ages of 6 and 21 into the performing arts, social activities, and sports. Trouper membership grew from 172 in 1964 to 589 in 1968.

Brownsville now has 9,000 persons registered to vote in the special elections for Community Corporation representatives. Three open hearings a month, between September 1968 and January 1969, on a master plan for Brownsville gave the members of the community a chance to air their complaints. According to Paul Cooper, the director of the Brownsville Community Corporation, between 50 and 150 people attended these meetings, nearly all of them new participants at each meeting. The Corporation's open meetings are efficiently conducted, and parliamentary procedures generally prevail over emotional outpourings. At a recent meeting, candidates were presented for the unpaid offices on the Local Governing Boards in five areas of Brownsville to which the BCC will delegate various responsibilities. Beneath the surface were the tensions without which politics would not be what it is; but at the suggestion that the residents of Brownsville are tired of having the people in Washington making plans for this community, there was loud and universal applause.

Model Cities

The road to participation is, of course, not as straight as some advocates of the war on poverty have presented it. Because community participation threatened to develop into a drive for community control, a different mode was devised within the Model Cities program. There it is emphasized that participation does *not* mean control, and when a New York City Model Cities neighborhood director is pressed to discuss how the line is drawn for the Model Cities program, he repeats his most carefully chosen words, "It is the *mayor's* program."

The federal Demonstration Cities and Metropolitan Development Act was passed in 1966. In New York City an executive order by the mayor in 1967 set up a Model Cities Committee composed of the director of city planning as chairman, the director of the budget, and four other persons including the HRA administrator and the acting chairman of the Council Against Poverty. Mrs. Eugenia Flatow, a former co-leader of the reform Riverside Democrat Club, became executive secretary.

Three areas in the city, populated by some 900,000 residents, have been designated as Model Cities Neighborhoods and have received planning grants from the federal government's Housing and Urban Development agency. These are Central Brooklyn (including Bedford-Stuyvesant, Brownsville, and East New York), Harlem-East Harlem, and South Bronx (including parts of Mott Haven, Morrisania, and Hunts Point). Sixty-five million dollars were set aside for these three areas, $28.8 million of it for Central Brooklyn. Plans for the expenditure of the total $65 million were approved by HUD in June 1969, and HEW has made another $5 million available.

Although the Nixon administration has decided to spread the effort more evenly and more thinly, the Model Cities approach in New York has been to concentrate its efforts on a multiplicity of ills in a few selected areas. Planning proceeds under the rubrics of physical development, education, economic development, sanitation and safety, and multiservices. As Mrs. Flatow explains the guidelines under which the Model Cities program operates, existing city agencies are given "first crack" at getting accomplished what needs to be done—whether it be rehabilitating houses or improving police-community relations. But where an existing agency "cannot or will not" operate a needed program, Model Cities can and will develop and carry out alternative means.

Spelling this out in greater detail, staff members explain that if local residents want, more than anything else, to get the garbage service improved, the Model Cities staff will seek to circumvent the contract provisions whereby the city's sanitation workers refuse to go beyond the building line in front of which all garbage is to be placed—which leaves yards and alleys and vacant lots untouched. And if the local residents want the paying jobs involved, instead of hiring outsiders, Model Cities planners will try to devise a way to hire trucks and give the local people jobs as sanitation "assistants"—so that the sanitation "workers" will not call a citywide strike to protest this threat to their job waiting lists and their prestige. Again, if the poor in Brooklyn express their opposition to outside builders from Queens constructing their projects, arrangements will be made to put aside the usual bidding requirements, demanded by the Comptroller's Office, in order to favor possibly less efficient local contractors, who will give jobs to local blacks and Puerto Ricans, many of whom will have tried, unsuccessfully, to join building and construction trade unions.

The furthest developed program so far is the one for Central Brooklyn. It calls for the expenditure of $188 million—by far the largest segment—on physical development alone to be funded from Model Cities funds, Title I funds, City Capital Budget, and "mortgage money." Its programs—seventy in all—are described in terms of "long-range objectives, one-year objectives, and five-year objectives." Under the heading of physical development, the one year objective is to "start construction of 4,150 new dwelling units . . . assemble and initiate site acquisition to support 4,157 new housing units; let construction contracts for about 20 percent of these units." A one-year job objective is to "employ at least 50 percent minority workers in all building and maintenance projects in the area." The five-year objective is to complete 70,000 new units. And since the area's residents prefer buildings no higher than five stories, this is the height stipulated. The five-year objective for elementary and intermediate education is to "bring at least 70 percent of school population up to grade level."

Inevitably, the relation between the city and the local community has involved tension. Efforts to bring Central Brooklyn community residents into Model Cities planning began in September 1967. Elected officials, representatives of community boards, of planning committees, of civil rights organizations, of school groups and businesses were invited to a meeting. The more than fifty persons present selected a committee to screen candidates for the position of Neighborhood Director, and recommended Horace Morancie, a black, for the post. Lindsay appointed him. The committee also proposed the creation of three twenty-five member committees, one each for the three communities within the area. In February 1968, information about the Model Cities program and election procedures for these area committees was mailed to over 800 organizations in the Central Brooklyn area; and in the following months, at meetings attended by from 250 to 700 persons, members of these committees were elected at meetings within each of the three communities.

Well aware of the vast mistrust felt by the poor towards city hall, Morancie has tried to temper the community's demands and at the same time to meet its accusations that he has "sold out." Speaking in the summer of 1968 to representatives of the community about his difficult role, he suggested that his head was on the block, and would be "chopped off downtown or here," unless the community got down to business. Half a year later, the plan for Central Brooklyn was complete. Although there had been many consultations with representatives of the community, the plan was essentially written downtown, by the "suspect powers" themselves.

But in the Harlem-East Harlem area, where open hearings were still in progress to allow residents to air their frustrations—and to make their dramatic appeals for understanding that "the poor are *people*"—there was, until a few weeks before the deadline for submission of a plan to HUD, no plan. Model Cities' staff members have persuaded some of those working on proposals that statements about middle-class teachers profiting from the "educational genocide" of black children might be less effective in drawing funds to the area than softer phraseology, and local spokesmen for the "let's-get-on-with-the-job" middle were beginning to emerge, but resistance to the hand of "governmental bureaucracy" was still formidable.

In order not to forfeit the federal money at stake, the Lindsay administration rescinded some aspects of the participation process for Harlem-East Harlem and for the South Bronx areas, and proceeded with plans that could not be said to represent "what these communities wanted," especially not the extent of local control some members of them wanted.

The differences in approach have engendered some rivalry between the HRA and the Model Cities program. Some Model Cities staff members are not altogether displeased with the allegations of money mismanagement by the antipoverty agencies, while some HRA defenders doubt the sincerity of Model Cities' participation efforts.

The rivalry has been distinctly visible in Brownsville, where the local Community Corporation has charged it is being bypassed in the Model Cities planning and that its programs will be duplicated. The Model Cities neighborhood director has replied that much of the antagonism in the community toward anything emanating from government must be blamed on the antipoverty programs, which raised the expectations of so many that a breakthrough would occur, and which is seen now by many among the poor as mere appeasement.

On balance, what are the gains and what are the losses of participation? There is some dispute as to whether or not it actually lengthens the time required for action to be accomplished. Major Owens, head of the Community Development Agency, and an ardent advocate of participation, estimates that the benefits are worth the effort even though it "at least doubles the amount of time required to accomplish any task in the areas of planning, budgeting, and evaluation." Donald Elliott, chairman of the City Planning Commission, claims that, in the long run, working with community groups shortens the time needed for planning urban renewal projects before construction can begin. To go ahead without participation, and then to meet strong opposition, causes the most serious delays. "Obviously," he says, "if the city is going to give community groups the responsibility to determine their own destiny, it has to allow them to resolve their own internal struggles. We have found that the community, when given the actual responsibility of having to resolve problems by themselves, solves them better without interference from the city administration."

One seasoned black participant admits with some sadness his conclusion that "leaders don't grow on trees," but he remains convinced that if efforts are to be more than temporary handouts, they must contribute to the organizing of the poor to assert themselves.

Some of the political problems that have arisen have been serious. There have been ugly battles over who truly represents whom, racial differences among the poor have been exacerbated, racial hatreds towards those with jobs and power have been inflamed, and the whole question of the effectiveness and wisdom of inciting the poor to pressure the politicians has been questioned by knowledgeable students of American society and by friends of the poor.

At a theoretical level, one might wish to assert that, if there were no costs involved in arriving at decisions, everyone should participate in every decision, even to the extent of yielding nothing involuntarily. James Buchanan and Gordon Tullock, in their book *The Calculus of Consent,* have written that "if the costs of organizing decisions voluntarily should be zero, *all* externalities [i.e., disadvantages to persons] would be eliminated by voluntary private behavior of individuals. . . . There would, in this case, be no rational basis for state or collective action. . . . The choice between voluntary action, individual or cooperative, and political action, which must be collective, rests on the relative costs of organizing decisions, on the relative costs of social interdependence."

But in the real world the costs in time, energy, delay, and wasted funds, of decisions in which individuals talk out their differences and voluntarily arrive at agreement, can be very high. And the more numerous the individuals participating in the deliberations, the higher such costs become. The less justifiable these costs for a given kind of issue appear to be, the more attractive becomes the alternative of imposing a decision from above, by a federal or city bureaucracy. But there the costs are hidden by administrative procedures and by the seeming "efficiency" of issuing decrees or plans by fiat. Such procedures do not gain consent, and the virtues of a participatory scheme—despite the rancors and irrationalities it may engender—are that the final product is the work of those whose lives are affected by the decisions that are made.

The commitment to participation, it seems to us, is inescapable in the kind of multigroup society in which we live. The real sociological problem—and this is the set of issues to which we finally turn—is the definition of the participating unit itself—the neighborhood or community—and its relations with the other political and sociological entities in the society.

The boundaries of community

To sum up: two problems have emerged for city government in recent years, that of the decentralization of functions because of the unwieldy administrative structures, and the claims of community decision (particularly in the black areas) over these functions. The two are not necessarily the same. Decentralization, in most instances, as in government or corporate enterprise, means giving a high degree of autonomy to subordinate administrative *officials* within a centralized policy structure. Community decisions represent a political shift in the locus of control. In recent years, the two modes have become fused. Decentralization has come to mean community decisions and, as in the campaign program of Norman Mailer, the cry has even become "*all* power to the local neighborhoods." The difficulty with this slogan, so redolent of an earlier revolutionary time, is in the complication of defining a neighborhood both in communal and administrative terms.

A neighborhood becomes a community when there is a shared life and purpose built around local institutions. In New York, one can identify, historically, six overlapping types of neighborhoods. Traditionally, there are the neighborhoods built around kin and church, family life and synagogues. Religious buildings are the oldest symbol of community, and within a strange area they are the first marks of identification. Thus, there are the Catholic, Protestant, and Jewish neighborhoods.

There are, second, the ethnic clusters, such as Polish, Irish and Italian, who, even though all Catholic, still congregate among their own; as do, of course, German, Ukranian, Jewish, Chinese, etc. The distinctive food stores and specialty shops make these sections visible.

There are, third, subethnic clusters of a highly defined kind—the Hassidic Jews in Williamsburg, the Sephardic Jews in Bensonhurst, the West Indian Negroes in Harlem—who cling to each other even more tenaciously than do the larger ethnic groups of which they are a part, intermarry more frequently, engage in specialized crafts and occupations (diamonds for the Hassidim, embroidery for the Bensonhurst Sephardi) and maintain a high clannishness among themselves in distinct geographic districts.

There is, fourth, the segregation by income and class, as in the upper east side along Central Park, or in Brooklyn Heights or Riverdale.

Fifth, there is the neighborhood defined by function, such as the university enclave around Morningside Heights.

And, finally, there are the *quartiers* marked off by a distinct style of life, such as Greenwich Village or East Village, or, more numerous, yet less well known, the neighborhoods of rooted middle-class home ownership such as in Bay Ridge, east Flatbush, north Bronx or Staten Island, which, too, have a distinctive style of life.

Most of the "natural" neighborhoods of the city are in Brooklyn, north Bronx and the older sections of Queens and Staten Island. These are "natural" clusters, self-defined by individuals in relation to each other. The continual shifting about which takes place because of upward social mobility, or changes in the life cycle (i.e., having small children, or children leaving home), tends to redefine neighborhoods, such as the departure of the Italians out of east Harlem into home ownership in the north Bronx, or the movement of the Germans out of Yorkville, the Irish from the west side, etc. But in the last twenty years this process has been distorted by a number of rigidities. Rent control has frozen movements which would have taken place under normal circumstances, such as keeping elderly persons and small families in large apartments along West End Avenue and Riverside Drive. More importantly, deliberate social policy, by the federal government and the city, has sought to mix income classes and neighborhoods by placing low-income projects in high land-cost areas, or by mixing low-income and middle-income housing projects. The very act of beginning slum clearance during a tight housing shortage shortly after World War II, and locating these new projects in dense and high land-cost acquisition areas, wreaked further havoc. At that time, Nathan Straus, then housing administrator, proposed that any new low-cost housing be located in Staten Island, Queens, the north Bronx, and the outlying sections of the city. There, low-rise garden type developments could be built cheaply. But he was shouted down by political leaders in Harlem who feared the dispersion of their voting base, and attacked by liberal reformers for proposing that low-income persons be forced to travel a considerable distance to work. The result was that, as the city began to remake the faces of east Harlem and the East River drive with project housing, the displaced inhabitants were

dumped onto the west side, where landlords began cutting up the large apartments into small rabbit warrens, and the pattern of neighborhoods became a
shambles.

The large influx of Negroes and Puerto Ricans in the postwar years, amidst
the upheaval in social mobility, created a further problem of definition of community. Once jammed largely into Harlem, the blacks (and Puerto Ricans) have
spilled over into south Bronx (Hunts Point and Morrisania), east Harlem, the
lower east side, Brownsville and Bedford-Stuyvesant in Brooklyn, and pockets of
the west side in Manhattan—taking over, largely, the areas vacated by Italians, the
Irish, and the Jews. Here are concentrated the dilapidated and slum housing,
the oldest school buildings, and antiquated hospitals and clinics.

But even Harlem, as a once settled area, has suffered the fate of the other
ethnic sections of New York. From the 1920s to the 1940s, Harlem had its own
"Society"—the Negro doctors, lawyers, ministers and entertainers who lived in
Hamilton Grange, Sugar Hill, Edgecombe Avenue—the sections in north Harlem
and the rocky heights fronting the Harlem River facing the Bronx. These persons
gave a coherence to the area. Today, while many may still work there, the Negro
middle and upper class lives in Hastings, New Rochelle, Amityville, and other
suburbs in Westchester or Long Island. Dances once held in the Savoy Ballroom
are now held in the Americana Hotel. What is left is the street gangs and the
jungle.

There is no single Harlem "community," a veteran observer of black life
has remarked. There are different groups of activists, each of whom has staked
out a claim on an issue. If you want to open a business in Harlem—a branch say,
of a brokerage house or a bank—you go to the Harlem Chamber of Commerce,
or to Roy Innis of CORE, and clear it with them. If you want to appoint a principal of a school, you go to another group. The Harlem Architects Committee
(ARCH), which led the fight against Columbia's intention to build a gymnasium
in Morningside Park, has no constituency, but it has the ability, as do many of
the multifarious groups in Harlem, to put any "outsider" on the spot. What
unites all of Harlem is essentially an anger at "The Man," and groups compete in
utilizing and exacerbating this anger. The new activists, thus, have no authority,
but they do have power: the power to interfere, to raise hell, to shut things down.

This process has been accelerated to a considerable extent by the Lindsay
administration which, in seeking to make contacts in the ghettoes, has provided
recognition, some status, and some patronage for the militants. As one of the
heads of the Urban Action Task Force explained: "When you have to go in and
cool the ghetto, the older, established church groups or political clubs don't
count; you have to find the local 'influential.' " As anthropological lore, or for
political firefighting, all of this is very true and highly relevant. But what the
Lindsay administration has also sought to do is to use this indigenous leadership
as the base for its own political machine and to bypass the established groups
who, traditionally, have been allied to the Democratic Clubs. In short, what the
Poverty Program and the Lindsay administration have tended to do is to "place ⁄

their bets" on the militants and activists as the source of new community leadership. What may be effective for local political base building is not, however, functional for institution-building and strengthening of community ties.

The decentralized crazy-quilt

If it is difficult, sociologically, to define neighborhood communities in New York, then, administratively, there is a worse mess. There are, as we have pointed out, at least nine community systems now operative in the city, plus other services which have local offices: 62 Planning Districts, 25 Community Corporations, 35 Urban Renewal areas, 3 Model Cities projects, 30 Health Districts, 76 Police Precincts, 30 School Districts, 22 Urban Action Task Forces, 5 Neighborhood City Halls, 58 Sanitation districts, 15 Fire Department divisions, 42 welfare centers, 14 offices of the Bureau of Emergency Repair Services, etc.

The Citizens Union, when it proposed dividing New York City into districts "for more orderly planning and decentralization of services," recommended, it may be recalled, that all city services in each district be grouped in one location so that each district could develop its own plan in cooperation with the City Planning Commission. But the startling fact is that almost *none* of the present community boundaries, as it turns out, correlate with divisions of police, school, planning, etc. Neither is there much relation between the community planning districts and the political boundaries of districts, especially the councilmanic. If the city councilman is supposed to be the local representative in city hall, as the state assemblyman or state senator is in Albany, then the major political lines should have some determinate relation to the service and administrative boundaries; but they do not.

The City Planning Commission, which most recently had to wrestle with the problem of defining communities, had no real guide. The 1961 City Charter, which mandated community planning boards, stated: "Such districts shall coincide, so far as is feasible, with the historic communities from which the city has developed and shall be suitable as districts to be used for the planning of community life within the city." But there is not in the charter, perhaps prudently, any definition of what is meant by "historic communities" and no elaboration about the orbit of concerns which are to be encompassed in "the planning of community life" within the city. The commission, in setting down the boundary lines, sought to use "old names," but its chief criteria for districts was the identification of certain "cores" (e.g., Morningside Heights, Greenwich Village, Bay Ridge, Ridgewood) and to look for "communication barriers" such as waste land or major highways as the boundary lines. As the commission noted, in its own defense; "Stable and continuous areas containing persons with the same culture, have not been characteristic of New York. From its earliest beginnings, as an outpost of the Dutch West India Company, the city has consisted of a thrashing diversity of peoples, tongues, customs, national backgrounds and beliefs existing in proximity of each other."

Community and institutions

Assuming for the purposes of analysis that one can define "the community," and then locate "its leaders," a host of other questions still arise. One, for example, is the balance of rights between "the community" (defined as residents) and "institutions," in this instance, schools, churches, hospitals, etc. When these institutions seek to expand, physically, as have the institutions on Morningside Heights, who is to make the decisions on such plans, and how? The frustrations of these institutions is, itself, a case study in the problematics of community action.

In 1947, the institutions on Morningside Heights[12] banded together to fight the deterioration of the area. Under their leadership, the decrepit area which bounded it on the north, La Salle Street, was renovated. The institutions financed the construction of Morningside Gardens, a middle-income residential area of 1,000 apartments, and the city built, adjacent to it, the Grant Houses with 2,000 apartments. These 3,000 units replaced 3,200 slum apartments. The area, which was previously 51 percent white, became 30 percent black and Puerto Rican in Morningside Gardens, and 95 percent black and Puerto Rican in the Grant houses.

These developments were completed in 1956–1957. In 1959, Morningside Heights Inc., the planning agency of the institutions, proposed a large scale reorganization of the area which would have created a new "city" of 100,000 persons on 600 acres (the size of Wilmington, Delaware), maintaining the existing population by high-rise developments, but doubling the land area allotted to the institutions.

At that time, the institutions were popular with the politicians because it was felt that, backed as they were by David Rockefeller and the Rockefeller interests, they were all powerful. Hulan Jack, the borough president of Manhattan, therefore demanded that west Harlem, below the Heights, be included in the renewal plan as the price of his support. And Puerto Rican elements, living south of Morningside, in Manhattan Valley (the area from 110th Street to 103rd Street), demanded inclusion as well. The city, under the Housing Development Board, drew up a General Neighborhood Renewal Plan, dividing the area into five districts, with the Cathedral Parkway area (around 110th Street) slated first for urban renewal. A Morningside Renewal Council, consisting of organizations in "the neighborhood," was set up, with government money to advise the city of "neighborhood" wishes. But in the process, the "core" Morningside Heights area, which is a neighborhood primarily made up of Columbia faculty and employees of other institutions found itself outvoted, and outshouted, by the other two groups. What then was *the* neighborhood for urban renewal?

In ten years, literally nothing has been accomplished. Tenants' organizations on the Heights have resisted bitterly any effort to displace existing buildings. Student organizations have decried any efforts to "change the character" of the neighborhood, though in the decade the character of the neighborhood was indeed changed, largely by greedy landlords who cut up well-built houses and jammed them full of welfare cases, gaining exorbitant rents from the city. The reform Riverside Democrats began attacking the expansion plans of the institutions, claiming that tenants' needs and housing should have priority over institutional claims. (Curiously enough, no public outcry came when City College demolished a number of blocks during this period for its expansion.)

The institutions, losing confidence in the ability of the city to act, in self-defense began buying property in the neighborhood, in part to clean it up, in part to assure space for their own needs. The "Bryn Mawr" was a case in point. An apartment house on 121st Street and Amsterdam Avenue, it had been converted to Single Room Occupancy, containing 190 rooms. The building itself was sublet to an operator who operated it as a transient business. The turnover was rapid, and it was populated largely by junkies, whores, alcoholics, and welfare families who were placed there temporarily by the city. In 1964, Barnard College bought the building and began to convert it into use for a student dormitory. At first, the college was applauded for "cleaning up" the neighborhood. But within a year, it came under attack for "heartlessness" in the treatment of the poor, the blacks, and the Puerto Ricans, and its effort to "change the character" of the neighborhood.[13] The institutions, as landlords, are feared by tenants who claim, quite accurately, that the institutions want the apartments for their own members, or the land for expansion. But whose needs are to take precedence?

The institutions on Morningside Heights—apart from their educational and medical services—represent one of the major economic resources of the city. They employ 20,000 persons (half of them professional and administrative) and have a payroll of $140 million a year. Of the 35,000 persons living in the "core area" of Morningside Heights (from 110th Street to 125th, and from Riverside Drive to Morningside Drive), one-third are "institutionally-related." A host of small businesses in the area are dependent on the institutions, and in particular on the 5,600 students living within the core area.

How is one to assess the balance of rights between tenants and institutions? When Columbia proposed to build a gymnasium in Morningside Park to avoid the displacement of tenants, it was accused, suddenly, of taking away parkland from "the people."[14] When it seeks to deconvert SROs, it is accused of becoming antipoor. But how is the character of the neighborhood to be determined?

To a great extent, the influx of the blacks and Puerto Ricans, particularly through the SROs and the cutting up of old large apartments, was determined by the market, through the action of private landlords. When the institutions seek to use the same market mechanisms, their actions come under attack. Yet in any rational planning, the needs of a great intellectual and economic resource, providing jobs for many thousands of persons (particularly now of blacks) has to be taken into account in the balance of things. Such a task, inevitably, can't be performed by the neighborhood itself, for tenants have a vested interest in the rent controlled apartments they occupy.[15] It is a responsibility of the city to understand the needs of the institutions—for offices, laboratories, classrooms, dormitories—while seeking to expand the stock of housing to accommodate those who are displaced. But in the face of the multiplicity of pressures, the city has virtually abdicated all responsibility.

The accommodation of conflict

A number of extraordinary changes are taking place in American life and, in conclusion, we can deal only schematically with these changes and the problems they pose.

There is, first, the increasing "politicalization" of society, particularly in urban affairs. Activities which were once allocated through the market are now subject to political decisions or political controls. Previously the question of who was to be housed where, would be settled through a "rationing by purse." Today, the decisions as to where housing is to be sited, what tax abatements are to be given, what proportion is to be reserved for low income or for municipal housing, etc. are made politically. And this carries over into many other areas as well. The sociological question is whether a society, this society, can carry such an increasing burden. The classical effects of politicalization are clear: the decision points are visible, rather than dispersed. The consequences are plain, for people know "whose ox will be gored." There is an overconcentration on law and legislation, and an increasing burden on administration. All of this, inevitably, increases the potential for group conflict. One of the chief reasons why in the last twenty years New York has been deemed to be "ungovernable" is the increasing politicalization of decision-making.

Second, a group of "new men" have come into the political system, specifically among the blacks. They are angry and they feel deprived. Their goal, in many instances, is not integration or the sharing of power but the control of their "own" institutions and enclaves. Yet two things are remarkable about this movement. The projects in which a large number of the new leaders are employed are federally-funded. And second, other than schools and a few local services such as health and the like, there is little possibility that the blacks will achieve control of major economic or political resources, for the locus of these resources are not in the neighborhood or community. To this extent, a whole series of unrealistic expectations are being generated in the black communities which may boomerang badly. What the black leadership may be able to achieve is a significant bargaining power, or even a veto in many instances, of city policies, but the talk of the ultramilitants about gaining control of the "major" institutions of society is unreal. The outcome will either be some accommodation or an increase in senseless rage. Despite the ultramilitant talk, the likelihood, still, is of accommodation.

Finally, we have seen the emergence, in a formal way, of the idea of "group rights" as the means whereby disadvantaged groups, particularly the blacks, can establish their claims in the system. The focal point here is education and it lies in the demands of the blacks for control of the schools in black districts, and for a quota or some preferential system in the colleges. This demand has brought the militant blacks squarely into conflict with the teachers union, which has felt its position threatened by the demand. It has raised the ugly spectre of anti-Semitism because a number of the blacks, particularly those in the leadership of the Afro-American Teachers Association, have deliberately made anti-Semitic statements in order to frighten away Jewish teachers and particularly Jewish principals from schools in the ghetto.

Three issues are involved in the argument for group rights. One is that of merit: the question whether a person should or should not achieve a position on the basis of his demonstrated ability, or whether a proportion of posts should be allotted on the basis of group membership. The second, allied to it, is that of common culture. The argument, made by Rhody McCoy at Ocean Hill, for example, was that any principal from the civil service list would be white, but that a white principal could not understand or guide a black child. Such an argument strikes at the traditional understanding of a common education and raises the question whether, in the future, all education in the major American cities may not be parochial or segmented by class or race. Third is the question of representation. Should there be majority rule or proportional representation; and if the latter, by geography or by group? When the New York State legislature proposed the election of a city Board of Education by boroughs, the Rev. Milton A. Galamison cried that the bill "deprives the blacks and Puerto Rican people of representation . . . Whenever we get into this nose-counting business, it's to the disadvantage of blacks and Puerto Ricans." And the administrator of Harlem's IS 201 district, Charles Wilson, agreed, saying: "The notion that the elected board will democratize the system is not so." What are the appropriate answers?

These divisive questions of political rights and political philosophy conjoin with a different set of problems that arise out of the nature of the size of the polis in a modern society. In a brilliant essay in the *American Political Science Review,* for December 1967, "The City in the Future of Democracy," Robert A. Dahl raised the question, "which is no longer a subject of discussion among political scientists," of what "is the optimum size for a city." And, he remarks, "the evidence seems to me . . . that the all-round optimum size for a contemporary American city is probably somewhere between 50,000 and 200,000, which, even taking the larger figure, may be within the threshold for wide civic participation."[16]

Not only has there been little discussion on the optimum size of a city or a "quarter" of a large city, but there has been little thought as to what is the appropriate size and scope of the appropriate social unit to handle what problems: i.e., what services and functions can be left to a neighborhood or community, what has to be handled on a borough or city level, what has to be conducted in a region, and what has to be federalized? All that we have are shibboleths. We have the traditional decentralizers such as Paul Goodman, or the regionalists, or the federalizers. But nowhere is there a detailed examination of what functions of government are best handled at what levels of government.

A few suggestions may be hazarded, but they must be tentative. They involve ways of separating kinds of decisions in such a way that some are best decided at the periphery by participatory discussion and voluntary agreement, and some are best decided at more central levels, not only in order to arrive at such decisions with dispatch, but also to be able to bring local interests into line with wider, more regional considerations. An example of such a division of decision-making power is the way the Human Resources Administration divides antipoverty funds between the various poverty areas according to impartial, mathematical calculations of the areas' poverty index. But then, once the amounts have thus been centrally fixed on the basis of such formulas, decisions on how to spend these funds are allowed to reflect the ebbs and flows of local sentiment and preference. Another example is the way the central Council Against Poverty decided this year, also on the basis of general and quantifiable criteria, to establish priorities to which all Community Corporations would be expected to allocate 70 percent of their funds. These priorities are "education action, manpower action, economic development and consumer education, and housing." Within the bounds of these general requirements, the localities can then pursue these objectives in ways that satisfy the particular moods, tastes, and non-quantifiable enthusiasms of their members. In the field of housing, central and long-range decisions on appropriate relative proportions of low and middle-income housing units can be recommended, within which communities can develop the housing projects that seem to them most humane and habitable. And central decisions on the allocation of funds for education according to fairly abstract principles of justice can still make possible neighborhood determination of the particular ways to spend such funds.

Behind the notion of optimum level is not just the question of administrative efficiency. There is the larger question, which is the theme of this essay, of participation. One virtue of participation is a simple one. It not only creates a basis of community, by allowing people to share in decisions that affect their lives, it is also a deeply conservatizing institution for, like property, it gives people a stake in the decision which becomes binding on all.

Participation, however, is not the end of politics, as it seems to be in some of the rhetoric of the new left. It is the beginning, for politics arises in the first instance when one realizes that there is no such thing as *the* people—that no single decision can please all people. There are only *peoples,* with contradictory and conflicting ideas and interests. Suggest a jetport near some builtup area and a committee will arise to save 'our' community; locate an airport on a swamp, and there will be a committee to protect the wildlife; suggest a floating airport and a group will form to keep our lakes and waters clear of pollution.

A rational politics, to the extent there can be one, is bounded by economics, that is the recognition of the principle of relative scarcity and the necessity, therefore, of bargaining as a means of allocation and adjudication within some principle of justice. If in a multigroup society, within which there is to be effective participation, social conflict is to be regulated within bounds, then, just as mechanisms for economic bargaining were worked out in the 1940s and 1950s which brought the trade unions in the society, so mechanisms for political bargaining have to be established which allow for a tradeoff of objectives between groups. This means a more formal recognition of political groups, just as there was recognition of trade unions, and the establishment of rules of the game, within boundaries of defined communities within which the bargaining can take place.

But if economics deals with relative scarcity, politics includes the effort to gain relative advantage; and this is a never-ending process in human affairs. The political problem is to make sure that the process takes place within bounds and does not tear the society apart. And this possibility can only be realized if one strengthens that most fragile of social relations—the trust that each person has in the other that the rules of the game will be observed and that each will have his chance to participate.

Notes

1. How far back all this goes can be seen from the entries in the diaries of George Templeton Strong, stalwart of the New York Bar, trustee of Columbia College, and a founder of the Columbia Law School in 1856, whose diaries over a forty-year period remain one of the great sources of social history of New York. On November 6, 1838, Strong notes in his diary: "It was enough to turn a man's stomach—to make a man adjure republicanism forever—to see the way they were naturalizing this morning at the Hall. Wretched, filthy bestial-looking Italians and Irish, and creations that looked as if they had risen from the lazarettos of Naples for this especial object; in short, the very scum and dregs of human nature filled the clerk of Common Pleas office so completely that I was almost afraid of being poisoned by going in."

2. Theodore Lowi, "Machine Politics—Old and New," *The Public Interest*, no. 9 (Fall 1967).

3. In Chicago, the political structure is still sufficiently strong to serve as an integrative mechanism. Negroes coming into Bronzeville (the long central strip on the south side in which blacks are congregated) are met by the local precinct captain who provides services, information, and job leads, in exchange for votes. For in Chicago, the political machines are still operative. (To reverse the Lowi paradox, Chicago is governed, but not well-run.) The rackets, and the revenues derived from them, are still intertwined with the machines, and unlike Harlem, the major black political organization in Chicago has a monopoly on the rackets in the black areas.

4. In most societies, the status system was transmitted through "family," and "old families" were at the top of status hierarchies. The family system was joined to the economic enterprise and provided continuity through inheritance. In the more fluid society of the U.S., particularly for immigrant groups, the family system could not as easily fulfill this function, and status was achieved largely through holding office in the communal organizations; among the Jews, for example, through positions in the temple, the community center, welfare fund, hospital, "defense" organizations such as the American Jewish Committee or the B'nai Brith, etc.

5. "The Politics of Local Responsibility," in James Sundquist, ed., *On Fighting Poverty* (New York: Basic Books, 1969). This volume, and its companion *On Understanding Poverty*, edited by Daniel P. Moynihan, derive from a seminar on the Origins of the Poverty Program sponsored by the American Academy of Arts and Sciences.

6. Daniel P. Moynihan, "The Professionalization of Reform," *The Public Interest*, no. 1 (Fall 1965).

7. "The Beginnings of O.E.O.," in the Sundquist volume, *op. cit.*

8. If one looks at the typical services of a neighborhood Task Force, it is clear that it is performing the functions of an old-style political club or the kind of services which an aggressive councilman could provide. The Flushing-Bayside task force, for example, is headed by a Deputy Commissioner of Public Events; it has arranged programs for elderly citizens, provided for five traffic lights in the area, helped support a summer day camp for children, worked to extend the size of some nursery schools, helped set up a playground in Pomonok Houses, and cleaned up Alley Pond Park.

9. Almost all the public attention has been centered on the elementary and secondary schools in the city, but a state law also sets up "community education districts" to deal with vocational training and "upgrading" of learning of school dropouts and adults. Control of these programs has been a political issue as well.

10. Typically, in many towns, the "slide-off" in voting, from national presidential elections to local contests, is from 50-60 percent in the former to 15-20 percent in the latter.

11. For example, the Poverty Program pays for some 200 storefront centers operated by welfare groups in New York. A typical one, as reported in the *New York Times,* is the United Welfare League in a storefront at 105th Street and Columbus Avenue. Its rent and personnel are paid for by funds from the Office of Economic Opportunity. Its field director is Mrs. Sydelle Moore who went from being on welfare to her present job. One of her jobs is to bring people to welfare. "We go through the buildings on the west side, knocking on doors, talking to people in their rooms, finding out if they need help. We've located a lot of people who needed welfare but who wouldn't have been found dead in a welfare center," she said. "We tell them about the Social Welfare Law. We let them know what their legitimate rights are, and we help them get through the intake process. . . ." She has more than 3,500 cases in her file.

12. The institutions are Columbia University, Barnard College, Teachers College, the Riverside Church, Union Theological Seminary, the Interchurch Center, St. Luke's Hospital, St. Hilda and St. Hugh's School, Jewish Theological Seminary, International House, Corpus Christi Church and School, Home for Old Men and Aged Couples, Cathedral of St. John the Divine.

13. In 1961, thirty-three buildings in the Morningside Heights core area were tenanted as single room occupancies, commonly referred to as SROs, with 5,426 rooms. By the end of 1967, twenty buildings had been removed from SRO use, eighteen of these being converted to institutional use, the other two to apartment use by private owners. The thirteen remaining SRO buildings contained 2,085 rooms, a reduction of 61 percent from the original total. Institutional expansion, as proposed by Morningside Heights, Inc., would remove nine of the remaining SROs over the next ten years.

14. Roger Starr, "The Case of the Columbia Gym," *The Public Interest,* no. 13 (Fall 1967).

15. One factor which has enormously complicated the situation is the money some tenants can now make by resisting evictions to the end. City College pays $750 to a tenant who is displaced for a city building. But private institutions may be forced to pay whatever a tenant can successfully demand. Recently, the Jewish Theological Seminary, which sought to use two adjacent buildings for expansion, offered $2,000 each to seventeen remaining tenants in the building to help them relocate. The faculty proposed doubling this amount to $4,000, but the tenants refused. Columbia students threatened to occupy the apartments to force the Seminary to give up its expansion plans. Meanwhile, the lawyers for the tenants have asked $25,000 a family! With building costs going up 5 to 10 percent a year, the institutions increasingly are forced to pay large sums to obtain complete possession of a building. St. Luke's Hospital, two years ago, paid $4,000 each to twenty-two tenants. Bank Street College, which has planned to move up to the Heights, paid $7,500 to each of fifteen tenants, for it risked losing $3,500,000 of federal funds if it could not submit construction plans by a specified date.

16. Dahl says further: "There is, for example, no worthwhile evidence that there are any significant economies of scale in city governments for cities over about 50,000. The few items on which increasing size does lead to decreasing unit costs, such as water and sewerage, are too small a proportion of total city outlays to lead to significant economies; and even these reductions are probably offset by rising costs for other services such as police protection.

"Per capita city expenditures increase with the size of city, at least in the United States. In 1960 the mean expenditure for U.S. cities over 150,000 was $123 per capita compared with $70 per capita for cities in the 35–50,000 range. Yet there is no evidence that these higher costs per capita provide residents of large cities with a better life, taking it in the round, than the life enjoyed by residents of smaller cities. If it costs more in a city of a million than in a city of 25,000 to build, maintain and police a park within walking distance of every citizen, then higher per capita expenditures for parks in big cities hardly signify that their residents have better public services than residents of smaller cities . . . "

"The oft-cited cultural advantages of metropolis are also largely illusory. On the basis of his research on American cities, [Otis Dudley] Duncan estimates that the requisite population base for a library of desirable minimum professional standards is '50,000–75,000, for an art museum, 100,000, with a somewhat higher figure for science and historical museums'. . ."

36

ANDREW C. GORDON, University-Community Relations: Problems and Prospects

INTRODUCTION

Studies of contemporary problems, of public and private bureaucracies, of social services, or of the poor have been traditional for academicians; their approach to this research, however, has not been impartial. For example, scholarly research on corporations has often been at the request of the organization, perhaps for a consultant's fee. Studies of urban problems are frequently undertaken for government agencies. The poor, or social service recipients, or delinquents, have been scrutinized for purely theoretical reasons, or for the benefit of a social agency which mediates academic contact with program recipients. Findings which imply action or political consequences usually have been relegated to scholarly journals, where they are read by a limited, elitist audience.

The "ivory tower" nature of academic pursuits is largely overemphasized. University personnel have a well-documented history of involvement in applied research, but the application has usually served the interests of the powerful. The distinction is not in the nature of the research: academicians have cooperated fully in advancing the machinery of war, as well as the efficiency of factory work. These efforts have been justified on the grounds of their potential theoretical impact, or perhaps undertaken with minimal academic justification. Academic research is contracted, paid for, and delivered to identifiable clientele.

The Center for Urban Affairs at Northwestern University is struggling to modify the predominating imbalance which normally exists in extra-university research relationships. Rather than implementing research which is designed to inform our own methods and theories—and which gives little priority to the

This article is original to this book.

immediate relevance of the outcome to respondents, due consideration is given to the inclusion of information which is expected to benefit the traditional subjects of social science.

We have, in effect, attempted to implement a stance of *mutuality,* within which, for example, government service recipients are treated as co-investivators. The research undertaken contains a mix, both theoretical and pragmatic in appeal. These attempts have involved new priorities and strategies, and have thrown us into relationships with professional and nonprofessional personnel outside the university, relationships for which we were unprepared.

We believe that reflective thought and experience can lead to the development of skills which will facilitate research which is socially useful as well as intellectually enlightening. The intent of this paper is to explore some areas of difficulty that we have encountered in our serious attempt to implement this revised academic stance, and to suggest some new directions for the future.

An outline of representative studies conducted through the Center will provide a framework for the observations which follow. These studies illustrate the range of experiences in which the Center has been involved, and will be referred to throughout the rest of the paper.

Contract buying

In the late 1960s the Contract Buyer's League (CBL) was established in Chicago to identify, inform, and serve black persons who had purchased homes on contract. Contract buying, common throughout the Midwest, is more costly and more hazardous than mortgage buying. A contract buyer normally needs only a small down payment, but builds no equity in his home until it is fully paid for—often thirty years or longer—or until the contract is converted to a mortgage.

On behalf of thousands of blacks for whom it was argued that the racially discriminatory character of the housing market forced "unconscionable" contract arrangements, a class suit was initiated in federal court, with contract sellers, savings and loan associations, and federal housing agencies as defendants. The plaintiffs include, but are not limited to, the members of the Contract Buyers League. Legal services on behalf of the plaintiffs, who otherwise could not afford adequate representation, have been donated by a prestigious Chicago firm. The lawyer-client relationship has provided a unique experience for the lawyers: many of the plaintiffs have withheld contract payments or resisted eviction against the advice of counsel. The definition of the plaintiff class ensures the inclusion of contract buyers who may never have heard of the case. The extent and nature of the data exceed the normal experience of law firms.

Academicians have been involved in the collection and analysis of the data, the design and rationale of a sample of the universe of buyers contracts, and the design and administration of a questionnaire for securing legally valid data from the plaintiff sample. In addition, personnel at the Center have explored solutions to the methodological and theoretical difficulties imposed by real-world constraints (e.g., selectively missing data, unreachable contract buyers) on the initial sample.

Our job is unfinished. We have been involved for nearly two years, and the federal case is still in preparation. During that time we have worked with the community organization, its leadership, and the voluntary legal staff. The ultimate outcome of the case is yet to be decided. Out-of-court settlements by the defendant-sellers already have resulted in a $2 million saving to contract buyers.

Community self-determination

The Kenwood-Oakland Community Organization (KOCO), located in a particularly blighted and ignored area of Chicago, received a five-year grant for business and social development. The Community Renewal Society (CRS), a church-related Chicago organization, was to encourage business, foundations, and religious institutions to invest unrestricted funds in an effort to demonstrate that strict community self-determination could be efficacious. The corporate donors were being asked to give their funds under at least two unusual conditions. First, they were to invest in a high-risk venture whose payoff would not be easily measurable. Second, it was said that they were to have limited control over the use of the funds.

The relations between the CRS and KOCO were formalized in a covenant of agreement. Through its component agencies KOCO was to employ the guaranteed funds to develop housing, business and social services in a neighborhood with powerful youth nations, and with few established businesses and lacking critical public services.

The covenant between KOCO and the CRS obligated the parties to an independent evaluation which would identify the strengths and weaknesses of the organization's efforts. The evaluation was to be used for possible modification of the organization and for the benefit of future organization efforts elsewhere. A small staff at the Center attempted to implement that evaluation. Our best attempts were met with difficulties for which we were unprepared. Some of these problems are explored in this paper.

Access to public information

Throughout the nation there are statutes which outline the public right to information held by public agencies. The laws often liberally interpret the citizen's right to know. We are presently attempting to explore in some detail the critical determinants of one's access to public information. In the process of implementing our research, we have encountered striking and often unexpected resistance from public information sources, and other investigators have reported similar problems. By means of an appropriate field-experimental design and subsequent observation we are trying to ascertain some of the variables which affect the actual availability of public information, including the nature and reputation of the inquirer, the nature of the source-agency from whom it is requested, the labor necessary to extract the data, and the inquirer's anticipated use of the information.

Social service delivery

One of the initial projects of the Illinois Institute for Social Policy was the Woodlawn Service Program (WSP). The governor's office guaranteed WSP administrative control over state social services in Woodlawn, a predominately black neighborhood near the University of Chicago. The task of the program was to design and administer a comprehensive, integrated program for the delivery of state social services, a delivery responsive to the needs of the community and sufficiently evaluated so that successful strategies could be implemented statewide.

We at the Center served in an advisory capacity to the administrators, suggesting how, with minimal embarrassment to program recipients, one might gauge community needs and thereby begin to provide a service package which was acceptable to the community and capable of being evaluated. Our task was not to advise on the content of the program, but merely on the forms of data collection which would yield comprehensive and useful information.

There has been a staffing turnover at the IISP, and our advisory capacity has been terminated, due largely to difficulties of the kind which are explored in this paper. We have attempted to broaden our experience in this area, and have continued to develop models for the systematic inclusion of data from recipients of agency services (Gordon and Campbell, 1971).

Minority business

The Opportunity Funding Corporation (OFC) is a private agency largely funded by the Office of Economic Opportunity (OEO). The task of the OFC is to leverage investment in, and support for, minority businessmen. They are attempting to implement a range of programs, including deposit guarantees and interest subsidies to minority banks, and credit support for minority contractors.

Before programs will be approved for funding, it must be demonstrated that they can be evaluated to OEO's satisfaction. The OFC is primarily concerned with success as a demonstration program, but also wishes to guarantee the infusion of funds into poverty-area businesses. Answerable formally or informally to many groups, OFC is immeshed in an intricate web of interested parties. A team from Northwestern has been engaged in designing persuasive and competent evaluations of these programs for OFC.

The Center staff is regularly contacted by established or nascent community organizations who, because it has been required of them or because they wish to know, are seeking advice and support for surveys of the needs and interests of persons in the Chicago area.

Public school discrimination

The Center undertook an investigation of the distribution of staffing expenditures by race and class in the Chicago Public Schools, with the expectation that the funding allocations might discriminate against predominately black schools. Most of the data was readily available in public documents, and the Chicago Board of Education cooperated when asked. The data were consistent with expectations. From one point of view, the bulk of the discrepancy could be explained by the voluntary placement of senior faculty in predominately white schools, and with respect to that analysis, the onus falls on the teachers' union rather than on the Board of Education. Careful revision in expenditures was proposed by the Board of Education soon after the publication of these data. This revision balances the allocations as measured by our indices while, in the opinion of many, preserving the fundamental inequities in the schools. Center staff are continuing to monitor adjustments in the allocation of monies (Berk, Mack, and McKnight, 1971).

The Law-Enforcement Study Group

The Law Enforcement Study Group (LESG) is a broadly sponsored organization which is attempting to determine whether public officials are administering the criminal law on a nondiscriminatory basis. Most of their research is conducted through the Center of Urban Affairs. These studies have involved us in a broad range of experiences, some of which are briefly described below.

Court reform

There had developed in Evanston, Illinois, a persistent but undocumented belief that the local court bonding practices and availability of counsel were unfair. A mayor's committee was established in response to the death in jail of a young Evanston citizen. For that committee, a team of lawyers and social scientists associated with the Center undertook a systematic analysis, largely based on readily available court and legal records, of counsel and bonding practices in the Evanston courts in 1970. The report and committee recommendations, (Mercer, Gordon, and Fahey, 1971), largely critical of present practices, were submitted to the mayor, who expressed great enthusiasm for the findings and recommendations. Some proposals, such as ticketing for misdemeanors, have been implemented. Others, including far-reaching court reforms, are under consideration by City Council committees.

Other LESG reports which also have sparked controversy include an investigation of the Chicago coroner's office which suggests that the office merely ratifies police judgments about the nature and cause of deaths; and a report on the juvenile court which illustrates local anachronisms in the treatment of juveniles as adult offenders. All these studies have been undertaken largely with publically available data, and each has been widely discussed.

The research briefly outlined above is a sampling of the studies undertaken through the Center for Urban Affairs. They are a varied lot, and form the experiential basis for the discussion which follows. This is a preliminary statement, and reflects my belief that a thorough airing of these issues may benefit others who are attempting to implement a revised university-community relationship. The details of these studies and others are available in papers issued through the Center.

The following discussion is organized around four major themes, though the dividing lines between them are nebulous. First, I shall briefly discuss some reasons why the academic community might advantageously accept these new strategies. Next, I shall focus on issues regarding access to the community organizations with whom we attempt to work. Then I shall discuss issues which arise with attempts to implement this research. Finally, I shall explore ways in which findings are distributed, internally and externally. In a brief summary, I attempt to suggest possible revisions through which these relationships might be more easily facilitated.

A. WITHIN THE UNIVERSITY

There are many sound reasons why academicians, particularly academic social scientists, should welcome a new stance with regard to what constitutes appropriate research. These reasons include: *theoretical and methodological concerns.* Theory building should integrate many diverse viewpoints, while traditional procedures have represented community opinions only through biased intermediaries. Particularistic methodologies should give way to others which recognize inherent biases and attempt to overcome them through a variety of approaches, (e.g., the triangulation of deliberately diverse measures [Campbell and Fiske, 1959]). Our support for new directions for academic research should also be motivated by *pragmatic concerns.* Organized community interests actively shun research which does not involve some benefit to them. Students rebel at an uninvolved or self-serving social science in an era of pressing social concerns. Finally, there is the concern for *democratic principles.* The systematic exclusion or misrepresentation of legitimate interests in a society which supports academic pursuits is inconsistent with genuine democracy. As institutions of a free society, universities, too, should strive to balance these interests.

Methodological issues

A major objection to academic research on social problems has been the lack of methodological sophistication (Evans, 1969). There is some validity to this point of view, though much criticism of the imprecision of field-implemented research may come from an inflated notion of the precision of "laboratory" or "pure" academic research. *Whenever* a concept or theory is translated into a measurable index of that concept, imprecision results. Measurement error, unreliability, confounding with other concepts which are being unintentionally included in the index, respondent confusion about the meaning of a question, deliberate fabrication, equipment error, the complexity of the information borne by physiological channels, the trivializing of a complex concept with a simple index—all of these and more plague the laboratory or armchair theorist; the same is true in the field.

Recent literature reflects attempts to refine measurement and conceptualization, and emphasizes that no single measure will ever suffice and that global measures are often uninterpretable. This recognition has prompted the deliberate inclusion of multiple measures, each imperfect and misleading. The best measures are chosen to minimize correlated error, in order to triangulate asymptotically on the concept of interest.

Just as laboratory work suffers from inexactness, so do field studies; they add some errors and eliminate others. For example, field settings are realistic where the laboratory is not. The solutions to the methodological and theoretical problems which originate in laboratories are of certain principal types, but the exact solutions are idiosyncratic. The same is true in nonlaboratory research, or in the analysis of data generated for purposes other than research.

The field implementation of rigorous research is difficult and often frustrating. Since studies of the nature discussed here are likely to have important policy implications, it is critical that they be conducted with particular care. Grievous errors can be committed in even the most expensive field research. Despite the heavy investment in the well-documented Ohio-Westinghouse evaluation of Headstart (Williams and Evans, 1969), for example, it has been persuasively demonstrated that the "controls" for Headstart recipients were predestined to achieve better than the Headstart pupils and therefore to underestimate the success of the program (Campbell and Erlebacher, 1970). No single control would have sufficed, and precision could only be approached with a more complex design. The design chosen, however, guaranteed seriously misleading results which had the effect of reflecting eeroneously and disadvantageously on Headstart.

Another widely publicized study of an entirely different kind is Heussenstamm's demonstration of police harrassment of students whose cars bore Black Panther bumper stickers (Heussenstamm, 1970). Fifteen students who had not had any traffic violations during the preceding twelve months attached Black Panther bumper stickers to their cars. Within seventeen days they had received a total of thirty-three traffic violations and at least $500 in fines. The shock value of the results is not disputed, but there are some unfortunate methodological difficulties which render the data difficult to interpret, and certainly weaken its efficacy for legal action. For example, the students knew when their cars bore the stickers, and had they wished, they could have deliberately provoked the police. Heussenstamm acknowledges that the study was only intended as a pilot, but has had trouble getting funds for replication.

It appears to us that social science studies of controversial issues must be as rigorous as possible. Our response to a request to advise on a tighter demonstration of this differential treatment had difficulties of its own (Gordon and Myers, 1970). The original study was cheap; the more precise replication is expensive, for example. And we faced the unresolved legal issue of whether there was entrapment of the police. We abandoned our design when we were convinced that experimental participants were potentially in mortal danger, so deep is the animosity between the police and the Black Panthers. We are continuing to investigate alternative designs, however, because of legal assurance that the documentation of alleged harrassment would be a valuable contribution.

Many of the field studies in this form of social research have encountered important methodological problems. It would be foolish to expect rigorous field work without the experience of failure. We need careful documentation of those experiences and serious attempts to reflect on and learn from the failures. This is where much of the exciting methodological work is taking place and where the academic community can profitably be involved.

Achieving clear results

The clairty achievable in the laboratory manipulation of variables, imprecise as it is, is intellectually satisfying, and this clarity is the model for which to strive in nonlaboratory, field experimental or quasi-experimental situations. It is also often true that clarity is achieved at great expense. The artificial simplicity of controlled manipulation may skirt the complex interactions which bear the true explanation of an effect. Further, the unreality imposed in the laboratory may more severely affect behavior than the intrusion of a social scientist in a field setting, where the research is *relatively* unimportant (Becker, 1970).

In their search for precision, researchers have too long shunned situations where precision is more difficult and have thereby foreclosed efforts to bring precision to the more realistic field setting. Because they are slow to consider an hypothesis validated, academicians often refuse to commit themselves to the validity of field findings. Lawyers, politicians, and community leaders who are not so protective of scientific pretension demand a right to know, now, and the scientist often cannot respond. Time is frequently a critical factor for the community organization that may be trying to fulfill a pressing need, or for the government agency responding to a legislative deadline. The academic demand for time to tool up before researchers feel fully prepared to engage in research; the academic rhythm which makes university researchers available in some seasons but not in others; and the demand for time to consider all aspects of research findings may considerably erode the potential usefulness of academicians.

Academicians need a revised procedure which either allows a quicker, if attenuated faith, in research findings, or a public conviction to proceed along a course of action which may be subject to a revised evaluation when firmer results become available. The community organization leader or the politician, on the other hand, must respond to the immediate needs or demands of the community, or of the funding agency, or of corporate donors. Organization leaders or the political sponsor of a program want evaluations to praise chosen procedures and to avoid any focus on failures—a situation that poses many dilemmas for the committed social scientist.

Political naïveté

The credential prerequisite to a university appointment, and the "other worldliness" which is normally necessary to gain that credential, assures that relatively little political savvy will creep into academe. The rarefied nature of academic theory and empirical research have been justified by the need to guarantee precision of measurement and analysis. But these prerequisites, too, have buffered academicians from political realities, and have had the consequence of squelching serious efforts to develop inclusive theoretical and methodological schemes. Recently, for example, methodologies have been available for credible evaluative research, but we lack the skills and understanding to implement them. To a large extent our design attempts flounder because they still make demands exceeding real-world realities. Clients, community or governmental, openly refuse to cooperate, or they conceal data. Critical methodological suggestions, acknowledged as such, are never operationalized. Staff members with direct responsibility for research are swamped by "more pressing" tasks. And so it goes.

Naïveté is best modified by experience, and the appropriate experiences frequently cannot be brought to the campus. Some have suggested systematic placement of academicians in government agencies for real-world exposure (Cowhig, 1971). Others are developing a voucher system through which community organizations can purchase university services of their own choosing, a strategy designed to ensure consideration of the mutual needs of both parties (Epperson, 1970).

Adjustments in research and dissemination of results may prove also to be effective remedies for some of the student dissent and disenchantment with academia. Students are justifiably concerned about their lack of a voice in university affairs; if they shared with faculty the opportunity to submit minority reports, and if there were a fuller disclosure of research decisions, much of this criticism would be answered. Students issue demands for relevance, and scholars mistake their unease for laziness of thought or action, assuming that students are inventing excuses for inactivity. Some of this is surely the case; some students are so fully disenchanted that total escapism can overtake them. Professors who modify their teaching should be warned by those students who are soon disillusioned with classes which emphasize relevance at the expense of scientific merit—a panacea sought by some teachers. But honest intellectual pursuit which at the same time explores pressing social issues, with the same academic intensity which is associated with "purer" stuff, kindles interest and energy which many of us have been encouraged to witness returning to the campuses.

B. ACCESS

Trust

Outsiders are viewed with alarm in many of the governmental and community organizations which interest us. Academicians are hardly immune from this lack of trust. Resources are often limited, and any new commitment, especially one with a distant payoff, is viewed as a potential drain on those resources. Universities, often located in or near ghettos, have frequently advanced their own interests at the expense of the community. The universities in Woodlawn (Chicago) and in Morningside Heights (New York), for example, have been considered by some to be among the most powerful and amoral community adversaries.

Specific experience with university researchers has not always mollified this portrait, even when there has been academic interaction with community organizations, social services recipients, and the poor. Academicians have frequently entered the community, asked embarrassing questions, and promised some vague and future benefit from the research. Frequently these research efforts provide no immediate payoff for the host organization, and often these projects are undertaken at the expense of short-range community goals. Epperson and Detzel (1971) systematically surveyed the experience of university personnel with urban clients. Among those professionals who acknowledged any involvment with the community, interviews revealed that the vast majority of their contacts had been at the behest of and to the advantage of an intermediary, government or private agency, and not with regard to priorities determined by the community. Of the very few academicians who even attempted direct communication with the community, all considered their ventures to be failures, and the difficulties often included the denial of client trust and cooperation.

In the climate of apprehension, which frequently accompanies academic-community cooperative efforts, unwelcome turns of events may bear useful side effects.

In the case of contract buying, the lawyers decided that questions which could not be strongly argued as essential to the court case would have to be dropped. Items about the buyer's attitudes, which represented a major theoretical benefit from our cooperation, were eliminated. A major component of the data from an academic perspective was therefore eviscerated, though important methodological issues remained. Our relationship to the organization was probably strengthened, however, for our continuing cooperation balanced the nagging suspicion that our efforts were only self-serving.

Because of the historical university stance, the academician is seriously mistrusted by the street researcher. When the academician attempts to cooperate in ameliorative efforts, he frequently becomes the least protected representative of establishment interest. A large measure of his task may be to modify that opinion, and to learn its subtle truth.

Overpromise or interpreted overpromise

The heady enthusiasm which carries the day when real-world research is undertaken sometimes gives way to gloom and disillusion when the results are in. There are several reasons why these occur. One of the most frequently encountered reasons is the lack of understanding about how much careful work is involved in creditable field research. Often the research team is not prepared for the difficulties which arise in persuading the organization to remain accountable to the researchers. For numerous reasons, a researcher who has involved himself in cooperative research may feel certain that appropriate methodological advice will produce data which will serve the organizations' purposes. However, once the data collection is under way it may become clear that problems encountered in the process of data collection are formidable, perhaps insurmountable in the immediate instance, and that as a result the data are no longer as clear or supportive as he envisioned they would be. There even may be deliberate deceit on one side or the other where, for example, the researcher has promised supportive results in order to gain access, or where the community organizer has promised access in order to gain the cover, legitimacy, and publicity which the cooperation with a university normally provides.

Center personnel have sometimes found that once a research team has demonstrated faith in the organization's work by accepting a cooperative role, the organization will expect the researchers to operate as committed advocates, rather than as researchers. The organization may expect the research team, for example, to participate in the irregular manipulation or misleading presentation of data. Refusal to do so may be regarded as betrayal.

Often, in large part because of their lack of experience, researchers expect that scrupulous research will be far more advantageous to the organization than it actually is. Many organizations contend with such huge difficulties, and the problems they intend to ameliorate are so vast, that their relatively trivial tactics and political pressures stand no chance of making major inroads. The involvement of academicians with community organizations in the theory or methodology of an intervention has often led to disappointment on all sides, either because the potential political thrust has been misinterpreted or because their enthusiasm led researchers to promise more than they could deliver.

Given the present state of the art of evaluation, for example, it is usually guaranteed that when researchers seem to receive full evaluative cooperation, one of two things is happening: (1) crucial and potentially damaging data are being subverted; or (2) the cooperative agency knows very well in advance what the proper analysis of their data will reveal, and want to ensure credibility by having the analysis done by an independent source. In the latter case, the data may be intended for partisan political purposes, with which the researcher may or may not have sympathy. When the data for a critical examination of the Evanston courts were made readily available by the courtroom officers, it was because they recognized the dissolution of the court system and felt that only the publicity which would accompany an analysis would produce the changes they desired (Mercer, Gordon, and Fahey, 1971). When the Chicago Board of Education was fully cooperative with a study which demonstrated a racial disparity in school expenditures (Berk, Mack, and McKnight, 1971), they knew that the differential was accounted for by the requested placement of senior teachers in white neighborhoods. The Board, too, suffered from the union-supported seniority privileges, and were seeking the publicity which would accompany the disclosure of these data.

There is another, radical criticism which those who advocate an academic-community liaison must recognize, the recognition of which may support efforts to impede access. However these strategies are implemented, their aim is to serve the public good through the fullest and most interpretable disclosure of information. The premise is that genuine improvement will accompany proper research and the accumulation of rigorous data. From one point of view, all these tactics are ameliorative and rooted in a mistaken analysis. From this perspective, genuine structural change is impossible, for the preservation of the poor and disenfranchised is too functional for the un-poor, both the slightly better off and the truly rich (Gans, 1971). It is, by this analysis, misleading to offer even high-powered services to organizations so poorly placed that their efforts are futile. A true democracy is an illusion. Highly placed political figures are too entangled ever to respond to pressure for full disclosure, and so, once again, the imbalance will only cement their control. No matter how scrupulous the attempts to include the impoverished in the decision-making process, they can never receive more than lip-service and cooption. By this analysis, the major purpose surveys of need, better information systems and evaluations serve is to forestall effective action. Because the personnel with whom we speak of cooperating are so trivially financed compared to the systems whose nature they try to alter, rigorous methods can only fully document their failure, destroy illusions, and aggravate their frustrations.

C. IMPLEMENTATION

Overcommitment

Because the skills which are critical to the success of competent research are diverse, and because there are relatively few people engaged in this kind of work, field- and community-oriented academicians find themselves spread thin. They are expected to represent a wide variety of interests and skills, rather than to reflect the far narrower abilities and training that they possess. The pressure to comment and advise on everything academic absorbs time and energy which, if fully dedicated to the skills they actually can bring to a problem area, might result in more meaningful programs. Researchers are often asked, essentially, to pretend or to develop renaissance skills. Succumbing to these pressures can instead lead to efforts which are shallow, corrupt, and useless.

We can predict dilettantism from those who try to master several skills, however critical those skills may be. Since we collectively lack some essential skills, particularly political ones, perhaps we should develop structural encouragements for specialists, whose expertise links established disciplines. An enlightened university hiring and recognition policy which incorporates the resources of non-academicians who can provide necessary linkages with extra-university constituencies is an important step in this direction. This suggestion is developed later in this paper.

Process vs. outcome

There is a distinction frequently encountered in the literature on research—between studies of *process* (i.e., the various techniques and components of community or governmental action) and studies of *outcome* (i.e., the eventual results of such action). The distinction is often misleading, conceptually and empirically. Researchers are frequently called in after programs are fully developed, under the assumption that outcomes can be studied quite apart from process, and after data collection. Usually, however, it is no longer possible to recover the preprogram information against which change can be measured. The intuitive indices which sometimes exist are often too global to be useful, and there is insufficient knowledge about extra-organizational pressures or seasonal or secular trends to provide a context for interpreting whatever change may have occurred as a result of the program. The solutions to these difficulties are of the same genre whether the research focuses on the effects of specific program components, or attempts to illustrate and evaluate the efficacy of the overall program. The emphasis here has been on futile attempts to recoup errors resulting from belated attention to research requirements. But even where the data needs of researchers have been entertained from the onset, the research is often so low in program priority that it is eviscerated through resource allocation. The priorities of community organizations rarely emphasize theoretical payoff to academicians. To guarantee that their interests mesh with those of the community, university personnel may willingly accept reduced resources for research. In the short run this may be reasonable, even necessary, to ensure a continuing relationship. In the long run, it may be costly.

Organizational persistence

The pace and priorities of traditional scholarly work are disruptive of the routine activities of most extra-university organizations. Community organizations focus on local issues and, with few resources to spare, cooperate in the research effort, mostly out of a conviction that such cooperation will in the end, serve their own purposes. The viability of a community organization is tied to the achievement of local victories, apparent or real, which support energy and enthusiasm. Human and financial resources must be directed toward the solution of immediate problems. As one community leader told us when we seemed to be imposing on his time, "We are not in the business of producing Ph.D.'s." Similarly, political agencies, hoping to influence governmental appropriation by demonstrated success, insist that researchers produce clear findings which will be persuasive in Congress, and sometimes force premature closure, or definitive analysis before the definitive data exist. If researchers can cooperate in these publicity efforts without prostituting themselves, for instance by presenting existing data in the most graphic, least obscure manner, the efforts should be made. If instead, the demand is for the falsification or selective elimination of data, then, at least, in the long-range interests of these efforts, such support must be denied.

Staff ineptitude

Trained and sensitive talent in community organizations is often so scarce that the talented quickly move to the top; those who have the time and responsibility for liaison with researchers are often underskilled for the task. In governmental agencies, researchers often deal with bureaucrats whose dedication or training is not sufficient to ensure effective cooperation. Evaluation research, for instance, has only recently become academically respectable. Persons hired for their background in this area may impose a research framework which is harmful rather than valuable to the organization. Academicians, on the other hand, may possess the technical skills to design an appropriate evaluation, but have neither the time nor the ties to the organization which are necessary to implement their plans. Their too-direct intervention may appear to be a lack of confidence in the skills of the organizational researchers, which may result in the loss of future cooperation.

Lack of client cooperation

Some of the strongest arguments which have been mounted against university involvement in political and extra-university affairs have involved the impracticality of securing the data this research demands. No matter how skillfully nonreactive techniques are utilized, much of the fundamental data must come from persons who have come to view the university as exploitative. As an example of how those prejudices can compromise research, consider the outspoken leader of the Kenwood-Oakland community organization who was arrested for murder and held for several months without trial and unavailable for comment. Just as surely as the organization knew he was innocent, they knew that on the basis of some unrevealed information he had been arrested and held, and they knew we were present, asking questions whose immediate purpose was unclear. It was no surprise to us that cooperation flagged, and that data which we considered critical to an even-handed process study were no longer available. After the leader had spent six months in jail, the judge threw out the state's case as completely without foundation, a bitter organization victory, but irretrievably late to recover our original research purposes.

Normally, an irreducible necessity for proper research is some basis for comparison. If, for example, an attempt at social amelioration is introduced, it is impossible appropriately to evaluate the effect of the program in most instances without comparative information from similarly situated others who are *not* recipients of the program. There are infrequent situations in which these comparisons are unnecessary, e.g., programs in which a massive program departs so drastically from previous policy that the effects are obvious. These occurences are extremely rare.

Far more common is the initiation of a local and relatively meager program, in one or a limited number of locations. Limited resources for reform guarantee that across-the-board reforms are unlikely. Necessarily limited programs should therefore be implemented in the most evaluable way, and this includes systematic allocation so that nonrecipients approximate true controls (Campbell, 1969). Any control or comparison group is necessarily inexact. In the best designs there must be several control-groups, each comprised of people who either receive no amelioration or one that is vastly different (weaker, less diversified, etc.) from the one about which the program planners were undoubtedly enthusiastic.

The logic of comparative information included from the onset of a program is straightforward, but experience with planned comparison groups in social reform is meager. In structuring an experimental state social service program in Peoria, the staff of the Illinois Institute for Social Policy (IISP) has given serious thought to interpretable comparisons. Though the financial community is notoriously resistant to evaluation, our suggestions for an information system for the Opportunity Funding Corporation which would maximize interpretability met little resistance, once it was designed to be as undisruptive as possible.

There have been administration matters, where the decisions were theirs to make. In the case of social services, the valuable information must often be obtained from the recipients themselves. Administrative staffs have assumed—and it is an assumption which has defeated several otherwise creditable evaluations—that even if the staff understood the logic of comparative information, program recipients would clearly balk at the blatant exploitation: data collection without remuneration and without a noticeable change in their lives.

Our suspicions have paralleled those of the administrators. At best, we have expected differential dropout rates between program recipients and the imperfect controls, which create difficulties of interpretation. When the community has been asked directly, however, rather than through administrative intermediaries, for their reactions to these design niceties, the experience has been than they are far more understanding than professionals expect. Such innocent misrepresentation of client feelings by service worker intermediaries is not unusual and is, in fact, one of the strongest reasons we argue for systematic and direct feedback from all constituencies, most especially, program recipients. In the New Jersey Negative Income Tax Experiment, the design was tighter than most because of enormous planning, and the availability of "control" individuals who received no subsidy, beyond $10 per month for filling out questionnaires. Many fewer of the controls than expected balked at this procedure, and those who did were easily persuaded that chance decisions about program inclusion were quite lottery-like and reasonable—the lack of the draw. Some differential dropout rates occurred, but not enough to ruin the data. In short, we fear a misplaced liberalism among program administrators as well as among academicians, which distorts the opinions of program recipients. It is frequently the administrator and not the clients who say the client won't understand and won't cooperate.

The following case provides a concrete example of the possible misrepresentation of community attitudes by program administrators. In our advisory capacity to the Woodlawn program for the improved delivery of social services that the inherited arrangement meant that the administrators had to receive program approval from a community board. We were told that if we had proposals for gauging community opinions of and experiences with social services, those forms would have to be revised and approved by that board. We were advised that the board would have to be carefully handled, for they would find academic procedures obscure and inappropriate. We viewed our appearance before the board as an opportunity rather than a threat. We wished to explain the strategies we had developed, to gain their advice on the most comprehensible wording of the items, to incorporate those they wished to include, and to be advised on the best local strategy for implementing the pretest. The community board was in fact cautious; they were fed up with academic surveys, and had already rejected one which was typically embarrassing and cumbersome. We thought our presentation was successful and that the board was highly receptive. To our surprise, strong dissention came the next day from the program administrator who felt we had provided the board with too much potential leverage, so much so that the administration would not be able to function without community scrutiny.

Resources

As mentioned above in another context, community agencies and government bureaus are often strapped for funds. With some forethought a reasonable evaluation often costs no more than a sloppy one, but the funds may be committed for neither. Instead, an organization may construct a public relations piece out of whole cloth, or ignore evaluation altogether. Prerequisite "evaluation" agreements often accompany government or corporate grants, but they do not guarantee an adequate evaluation, and sometimes they only produce corruption. Some projects cannot be evaluated in the present climate, or with the present skills and tools, and such a prerequisite may only ensure fabrication. So long as it is known that the refunding of an agency or the position of an administrator rests on the narrowly defined "success" of his program, administrators cannot afford to cooperate in even-handed evaluation research (Campbell, 1969).

When collection of intellectually or methodologically satisfying data is beyond the financial means of fringe or extra-establishment organizations, or when research would so drain the limited resources that funds would be better spent in other ways, university-based research advisors whose interests are aligned with the organizations may donate their time for the methodological and practical experience. But the residual research costs may still be insurmountable. It would be a new and terrible immorality if, for the sake of expensive methodologies, academicians interfered with the intent of community activists. When precision is within the means of such groups, it should be demanded. Careful evaluation is unusual, but it is consistent with recent government policy statements. When serious evaluation would therefore in itself be an effective means for advancing a group's interests or for soliciting financial support, that should be made clear at the policy level. If the evaluation cannot be done on a shoestring, and only a shoestring is available, the long-range benefit to precise evaluation will only be gained by the social scientist's refusing to cooperate in the effort.

Starr (1970) has described an alternative research strategy. The method was developed with an ad hoc community organization which was attempting to affect bail reform in Chicago. The Chicago courts had not been influenced by the Vera Foundation (Ares, *et al.,* 1963) demonstration that persons with ties in the community, released on their own recognizance, are as likely to appear in court as those on bond. The early attempts to contact officers of the court were frustrated. Rather than being receptive to the study of procedures which had ameliorated bonding situations elsewhere, an important judge responded: "Who gave you the authority to do this? All you want to do is let murderers and rapists on the streets." With this and the temperance advised by other organizations who were trying (unsuccessfully) to reform the bail system, the ad hoc committee found it difficult to sustain enthusiasm. Further, it was clear that the colorless documentation of specific procedures in Chicago would have no satisfactory local impact. Starr described the evaluation of a research strategy with enormous publicity value. Up to fifty concerned citizens at once inundate the court room, all are bent on objectively recording the information which would document the bond-related procedures in Chicago and provide the data for alternatives. The problems here are enormous, methodologically and otherwise, but in this instance the courts responded to the publicity as they never have to other pressures, and have modified their bail procedures. Participation in this study revivified the community organization as well. These alternatives tactics deserve exploration for the lessons they bear, and for the problems alleviated as well as those introduced.

Inadequately prepared research strategies have undesirable repercussions for further research. Normal politeness, a respect for the lives of the researched which exceeds the traditional lot of the laboratory subject, is to be exercised. During one academic period the Uptown community of Chicago was deluged by large numbers of enthusiastic and unprepared undergraduates in a hastily planned research project. The hostile community reaction resulted in the threat of public interest class action enjoining academicians from any further disruptive activity in that area. Surely this unfortunate experience renders any future thoughtful and concerned research activity more difficult.

The strategy described by Starr, which involved concerned citizens as co-data-gatherers, is a better model. The publicity value of their court attendance *en masse* forced the legal remedy demanded. However, publicity value is likely to decrease with repeated instances, and it is also likely to be less valuable in those instances where the desires of the target are not aligned with the research cause.

D. DISSEMINATION

Lack of communication channels

It would be foolish to expect scholars to refine the skills which would produce truly effective commentary on policy, without experience accumulated from many such attempts. But the standards and prerequisites which govern the selection of articles for respected academic journals virtually guarantee that the experience gained cannot be passed through normal channels. Research is judged by its precision, often according to irrelevant criteria; priority is granted to studies whose findings appear clearcut and relatively unambiguous. At the present stage of development even the best field-oriented work is not likely to produce such findings. Admissions of difficulties are normally excised from a manuscript or consigned to footnotes. Yet only through the detailed communication of these difficulties and attempted solutions, with difficulties *emphasized* rather than elided or obscured, can researchers in varied settings can begin to discern patterns and possible avenues toward their amelioration.

Scientific advancement has been secured through the fullest revelation of data, and the alternative analyses and interpretations of others within the community of scholars who reject a certain point of view. The same general rules may apply in a rigorously applied social science. Those who disagree with analyses and demand the opportunity to reanalyze our data should have it.

Communication to organization

Since it is unlikely that some community organizations will ever be able to fully trust academic personnel, perhaps one of the most effective ways to provide academic support for such efforts would be to prepare a handbook which demythologizes the research process, and circulates the basic information organizations need to perform their *own* research, either for internal purposes, or for presentation to others. We can count on this strategy to produce another sieve through which only seemingly successful research strategies or supportive results reach the public. But, this may only place community organizations on a par with public agencies, who selectively declare "confidential" any findings that are embarrassing or shoddy. But at least we'll all know where we stand. No one can be expected, particularly in the pursuit of a defined goal, to recognize and equally weigh everyone's interests. An approximation of that mix of interests would be a broad availability of the capacity to do persuasive research, and an acceptance of, if not an enthusiasm for, the advocate reanalysis of controversial findings.

Becoming public relations

No matter how openly an organization may have entertained the notion of honest evaluation, the final report is likely to be buried and uninfluential if it is not an enthusiastic endorsement rather than an equivocal evaluation. This possibility is bound to provoke despair among honest researchers and may seem sufficient reason for retreating to the purity of the laboratory or inapplicable theoretical stances. Our "solution" in one instance where rumors and realities of governmental infiltration and harrassment of a community organization had rendered certain data simply unobtainable, and a realistic evaluation therefore impossible, was to attempt to construct an "interim report" which said nothing untrue, but which so painfully hedged with careful sentences that it could be described at best, as it was by an insider, as "a masterful piece of tightrope walking." Though some organization members were clearly pleased with an honest, equivocal evaluation, we also understood that no better cooperation was forthcoming, and that we would continue to dishonestly fulfill the role of "objective" evaluators required by the donors. We terminated our relationship as comfortably as possible.

Later, our equivocal interim report was publicized as entirely "favorable." Writing it brought to mind problems of a critic of a wishy-washy movie who cautiously words his review so no choice phrases can be lifted out of context and used for publicity. But our best writing efforts were unsuccessful; excerpts from our piece became a cornerstone for future fundraising. For the sake of our future research in this content area, and for the sake of our own integrity as social scientists, we felt we had to terminate our relationship.

In this instance, the likely and erroneous interpretation is that we left in disgust, because of a lack of cooperation. Instead, we felt that the project, however laudable, simply could not be evaluated in the present political climate. This decision was not an easy one, for our faith in the possible benefits of an even-handed evaluation remained. Some of the organization's best efforts were stymied, we felt, by entrenched and powerful political interests greater than the organization and beyond its control, and we believe that a critical evaluation of that position would be a useful service. But it was clear that because of internal and external strife the organization could not entrust researchers with the data which might have supported this case, and we also felt that we would not be privy to the data which would allow an effective intra-organizational study (Gordon and Mack, 1971).

Polemic vs. reality in reporting

As a practical matter, it often occurs that the community or political interests with whom researchers work assert with some justification that the usefulness of the research is eroded by super caution, or by minutely correct but generally incomprehensible wording. A workable compromise seems to be one in which the research methodology is laid out in detail, and the cautions which a careful researcher demands in the interpretation of the data be included, but relegated to footnotes or methodological appendices. The research is coupled with the full report, but the amplifications, theorizing, or polemicism which exceed the data are clearly noted as such. The complex and justifiable hedgings which the researcher demands are usually ignored no matter where they are placed, and there is little gained by interrupting the flow of the argumentation with precision. The solutions to these matters include sidestepping these research involvements altogether in order to preserve academic purity (a conclusion we will not accept) or guaranteeing the inclusion of the methodological or theoretical cautions, and making the data fully available for analysis by advocates for alternative views.

Data confidentiality

Because of whatever trust that has been established, we have in several organizations, within and without the government, been privy to critical data which, if interpreted out of context, could be fundamentally damaging, or could provoke litigation against the organization or individuals within. In legal actions, since we have collected much of our data from the files of defendants, we have been required to sign agreements which enjoin us to obey established laws of discovery. That agreement restricts what can be revealed or published without the permission of the court.

One moral dilemma is clear. Academic pursuit at its best involves the free and open pursuit of knowledge, unfettered by the political necessities which necessarily are of paramount concern to activists. Our bias insists that no data should be confidential, beyond the protection of the personal lives of the "subjects" interviewed. Rarely has the issue come up, for rarely has social science data been of any interest to outsiders. Those concerned with re-analysis had no interest in the identity of individual respondents.

In more directly relevant research, the data unearthed through the research process, or indirectly discovered because of the access which the research relationship made possible, may be of crucial legal and/or political relevance to outsiders. We have frequently encountered this set of circumstances. Doctor-patient and lawyer-client relationships are legally confidential, but the social researcher enjoys no such privileges. It appears that the present state of the legal situation is such that academic research records are fully subpoenable.

The press has had its right to protect its sources reaffirmed by the courts, but we cannot assume that this vital protection applies to sources in action-oriented research. We feel certain that many honest and exacting researchers are naïvely holding on to data which they do not realize could be demanded through legal action. Researchers should acknowledge this clearly and in advance to those from whom they collect information. The researcher could, for example, either state that he cannot guarantee the protection of whatever confidential information the source might provide, or give personal, extralegal assurances. Proposals have been advanced about various technical precautions, for example, scrambling data so they are uninterpretable to the uninitiated, or aggregating data so that individuals cannot be identified (Borouch, 1971); nevertheless, existing law is such that a researcher could be asked to provide his tactics for data-scrambling.

Even if data could be fully protected, what is the academician's responsibility about data revelation? Poor analyses have been the norm, and faults are often uncovered only through independent re-analysis. If we are to enter into such research, particularly at this crucial time when the appropriate skills are only now being developed, for the sake of free inquiry and technical advancement, re-analysis must be received enthusiastically for the sake of free inquiry and technical advancement.

Once one has agreed to cooperate with an organization in a research venture the results of which are crucially important, where lies the moral choice between breaking the promise made to protect discovered information, and being true to what seem to be larger interests? The dilemma is not new, and the choices are never easy. Daniel Ellsberg was privy, through his capacity with the Rand Corporation, to documents the revelations of which he believed would end the war in Vietnam. He argued that the authors of those documents and of government policy were the victims of a policy created by predecessors from which they could not extract themselves. After futile attempts to reveal the information through channels, he broke laws and trusts by making his extraordinary revelations (Ellsberg, 1971).

Reporters became aware that because of established practices which forbid them to cite verbatim or for attribution information available through government "backgrounders," they had become tools for the manipulation of news rather than representatives of a free press. Similar instances on a more mundane scale may easily occur when the access made available through promises of confidentiality to an organization leads to the discovery of information which is more generally vital than it at first appeared.

CONCLUSION

We at the Center have had a broad array of illuminating experiences in our attempts to implement a revised university-community relationship. Our experiences have taught us much, and, of course, there is more to learn. We are attempting to incorporate our new understandings into theoretical and methodological models which will move us further along. I will conclude with a brief outline of some of the proposed models which are scattered throughout this paper. They have in common the attempt to develop mechanisms (1) for short-circuiting some of the academic problems which have occurred, and (2) for creating situations for the continuing growth both of the scholar and the extra-university personnel, without sacrificing scholarship.

Many of the difficulties we have encountered in our new relationships with nonuniversity persons might be alleviated with a simple and honest document, e.g., a handbook, which communicates our capacities and our skills. The handbook could explore the frequent misconceptions both of the scholar and of the community personnel with whom he has worked, and should comment on the limits of such involvements. The document should detail the extent to which confidentiality can be guaranteed. It should be specific about the cooperation which we have learned is necessary in order for the research to be of any mutual advantage and it should comment on the kinds of cooperation any research arrangement will necessitate.

Enhanced experience

We should work toward institutional structures which maximize the exposure of our students to areas of social and political concern, in a manner which allows them to reflect on what they are learning in the classroom. Academic standards should not be sacrificed; the aim is a program which emphasizes action *and* reflection. We should give academicians who have an interest in applying their skills to these areas of concern an opportunity to expose themselves systematically to extra-academic influences which confront this research, e.g., through placement in a government agency. It is the *combination* of exposure and opportunity for reflection which is vital here.

Likewise, we should encourage and offer opportunities for the training of personnel. In disadvantaged organizations these skills are most clearly lacking. The training would have the effect, not of creating an imbalance, but of distributing necessary skills more democratically.

Client feedback

Because it would correct another crucial imbalance, we should support attempts to encourage the systematic feedback from the recipients of social service programs. Such feedback must include their opinions of the nature of their experience with the governmental or private agency. Frequently recipients have been asked how badly off they are, though in no way has an evaluation scheme followed which allowed them to comment on whether governmental programs run on their behalf were making a difference. These feedback systems should be designed to maximize the likelihood that the information will be responded to, so that the recipients can evaluate the nature of the response (Gordon and Campbell, 1971).

Vouchers

Through the Center, Epperson (1971) has initiated a proposal for an experimental voucher system which would allow less-advantaged community organizations to purchase services of their choice at participating universities. The plan would involve certificates for the purchase of definitional, strategic, or tactical services, in such a way that maximum information about the universities' interests and capacities to respond are gauged, as are the organizations' ability to utilize the services. The proposal appears to be an effective means to encourage the redefinition of university-community relations and the balanced capacity to respond which we seek.

There are no panaceas presented here. The instigation of any of these proposals would include new challenges. We recognize that specifying the ground rules for the relationship, such as with the handbook, or creating vouchers for services would be difficult. But our proposals are based on the urgency of the need, and we are better able to anticipate and overcome many of these difficulties now, with the benefit of the experience we have had. What we are proposing are more opportunities for experience, experience which will further the responsible involvement of the university in community affairs.

Note

Many thanks to Howard S. Becker, Donald Campbell, Denis Detzel, Margo Gordon, John McKnight, Raymond W. Mack, and John Walton for their comments on an earlier draft of this paper.

References

Ares, C., A. Rankin, and H. Sturz. 1963. "The Manhattan Bail Project: An interim report on the use of pretrial parole." *New York University Law Review* 38: 67–95.

Becker, Howard S. 1970. "Field Work Evidence." Pp. 39–62 in Becker, *Sociological Work.* Chicago: Aldine Publishing Company.

Berk, R., R. Mack, and J. McKnight. 1971. *Race and Class Differences in Per Pupil Expenditures in Chicago, 1969–1970.* Evanston: Northwestern University, Center for Urban Affairs.

Boruch, R. 1971. "Assuring Confidentiality of Response: A note on strategies." *The American Sociologist* (November).

Campbell, D. 1969. "Reforms as Experiments." *American Psychologist* 24 (4).

Campbell, D. T., and A. Erlebacher. 1970. "How regression artifacts in quasi-experimental evaluations can mistakenly make compensatory education look harmful." Pp. 185–210 in J. Hellmuth (ed.), *Compensatory Education: A National Debate.* New York: Brunner/Mazel, Inc.

Campbell, D. T., and D. Fiske. 1959. "Convergent and discriminant validation by the multitrait-multimethod matrix." *Psych. Bulletin* 56: 81–105.

Cowhig, James. 1971. "Federal grant-supported social research and 'relevance': Some reservations." *American Sociologist* (June): 65–68.

Ellsberg, Daniel. 1971. Comments on the ABC Television Network.

Evans, John. 1969. "Evaluating social action programs." *Social Science Quarterly* 50 (3): 4–22.

Epperson, David. 1971. *The Scholar's Response to Urban Discontent.* Evanston: Northwestern University, Center for Urban Affairs.

Epperson, David, and D. Detzel. 1971. *The Scholar in Urban Problem Solving: Rhetoric, Reality, Remedies and Recommendations.* Evanston: Northwestern University, Center for Urban Affairs.

Gans, Herbert. 1971. "The uses of poverty: The poor pay all." *Social Policy* (July/ August): 20–24.

Gordon, A., and D. T. Campbell. 1971. "Recommended accounting procedures for the evaluation of improvements in the delivery of state social services." Report to the Illinois Institute for Social Policy. Evanston: Northwestern University, Center for Urban Affairs. 51 pp.

Gordon, A., and R. Mack. 1971. *The Kenwood-Oakland Community Organization and Toward Responsible Freedom.* Evanston: Northwestern University, Center for Urban Affairs.

Gordon, A., and J. Meyers. 1970 *Methodological Recommendations for Extensions of the Heussenstamm Bumper Sticker Study.* Evanston: Northwestern University, Center for Urban Affairs (September).

Mercer, S., A. Gordon, and R. Fahey. 1971. *Release on Bond and Legal Representatives of Criminal Defendants Arrested in Evanston, Illinois, in 1970.* Evanston: Northwestern University, Center for Urban Affairs.

Reissman, Frank. 1969. "Community control and human services." New York University (mimeo).

Rossi, Peter. 1969. "Practice, method and theory in evaluating social action programs." In D. Moynihan (ed.), *On Understanding Poverty: Perspectives from the Social Sciences.* New York: Basic Books, Inc.

Starr, Joyce. 1971. *Taking Research Out of Academia and Into the Street.* Evanston: Northwestern University, Department of Sociology.

Weiss, R., and M. Rein. 1969. "The evaluation of broad-aim programs: A cautionary case and a moral." *The Annals* of the American Academy of Political and Social Science, September: 133–142.

37

RICHARD A. BERK, PETER H. ROSSI, DAVID BOESEL, BETTYE EIDSON & W. EUGENE GROVES, Characteristics of Public Issues as Determinants of Political Behavior

Discussions about the existence of a power structure functioning at the local level usually focus on the city or town as the unit of analysis. Employing either the intensive case study (Hunter, 1953; Dahl, 1961; Banfield, 1961: etc.) a broader multicity technique (Clark, 1968; Crain, 1969; Walton, 1971; Aiken and Alford, 1970), or controlled case comparisons, (Agger, *et al.*, 1964) researchers describe the distribution of influence for an entire city—an approach that has seemed appropriate since one normally thinks of city boundaries as enclosing a meaningful and relatively self-contained arena in which power is exercised.

Though investigators usually agree on the utility of using the city as the unit of analysis, a perusal of the literature on community power structure quickly reveals that attempts to characterize entire cities and/or groups of cities have lead to heated debates in which researchers have been divided by ideology as well as by methodology and social science discipline (Polsby, 1963). Traditionally, sociologists have tended to fall into a camp arguing for a "power elite" description of "who governs," while political scientists have generally favored a pluralist interpretation (Walton, 1966). Adding further intensity to the debate are the practical day-to-day interests of city leaders who correctly note that describing a city as ruled by a power elite has important implications in a society that prides itself on its democratic principles.

In spite of strong temptation to join the battle, this paper will not take sides in the debate, at least as it has generally been defined. Rather, we will attempt to show that positions on both sides might be more accurately argued if researchers employing analyses of decisional processes in order to examine power relations within cities were to place more emphasis on studying a *variety* of issue areas within a large sample of cities. There are at least three reasons why this broader approach would be productive.

First, many researchers recognize that the life cycles of potentially salient public issues reveal much about the power structure in a city, and some have even argued that an analysis of decisions on public issues is the only way to examine the exercise of power* (Dahl, 1958). However, studies that have tried to inves-

This article is original to this volume.
*The authors here are less convinced, believing that there are severe problems with the "decisional" approach and that positional and reputational methodologies are frequently useful techniques. (For a good discussion of the issues see Rose, 1967, chapter 8.)

tigate a variety of issues have usually been limited to one or a small number of cities, making generalization extremely difficult.

Second, those who have tried to look across many cities have too frequently limited themselves to one or two issues (Crain, 1969) and introduced the implicit assumptions that there is one power structure for each city and that it can be meaningfully analyzed through the history of a few issues. Ruled out is the possibility that different issues can be associated with different arrangements of power, because even those investigators who study several separate issues typically aggregate their findings into a single power structure interpretation.

Third, there has been little concentration on characteristics of potential issues themselves, suggesting that the inherent nature of issues is unimportant. Actually, the character of potential issues per se may frequently have crucial implications for the distribution and use of power. For example, in Dahl's analysis of the political structure of New Haven, interest in urban renewal appeared to be generated primarily by the business community, while passage of a school bond showed extensive and diverse citizen participation. Not only were the interested parties different in the two issues, but the distribution of power appeared to vary. Data from a recent study more directly to the point (part of the study will be summarized in this paper) indicate that mobilizing people around the issue of police brutality is often easier than mobilizing them around exploitation by retail merchants. Consequently, the concentration of political power is different in the two instances (Rossi and Berk, 1970). In short, analyses of urban power structures which ignore potential constraints that issues place on political processes may misrepresent the functioning of power by crediting political actors with too much influence independent of the issue context.

This paper will focus on potentially salient issues themselves and attempt to demonstrate that studies of community power structure which employ issue life cycles (a kind of decisional methodology) should consider characteristics of issues which are independent of political actors. Were this impact on the powerful better understood, one might be able to do more meaningful analyses of community power structure.

METHODS

In order to make the strongest case that issues have characteristics with important effects on political actors, one should have details on the entire life history of each potential and actual issue in a wide variety of cities. We do not have material of that caliber, but we do have sufficiently detailed information from fifteen of the thirty largest American cities (with the exception of Gary, Indiana, which is not in the top thirty) on five important kinds of controversies to permit an examination of how the issues were generated. In other words, we have reasonably good data on how political controversy emerges.*

---

*The sample includes eleven of the fifteen largest cities in the United States and nine of the ten largest located in Northeast and North Central regions.

The material is not as limited as it might appear. First, fifteen of the largest American cities is a substantively meaningful universe. It would be an important contribution to improve the understanding of power relations in just these fifteen. Second, using fourteen out of the thirty largest cities makes generalizations about the remaining sixteen and others of similar size a reasonable endeavor. Third, the issues are important. Frequently the headlines of metropolitan newspapers include police brutality, discrimination in employment, the quality of public education, consumer protection, and the operation of the public welfare system. Fourth, how a potential issue becomes salient has crucial political implications. One of the most important powers that city influentials have is the ability to both generate and "cool-out" issues. For example, if no one has enough information to evaluate the quality of education (such information might be held by boards of education), the issue is less likely to emerge, and actors who would be hurt by such disclosures can avoid having to defend themselves. Restated, the ability to set the agenda of issues in a city is a vital kind of power, and understanding the processes by which issues are raised provides important insights into the impact of potential issues on political actors.

The data for this paper was gathered in early April 1968 before the wave of civil disorders triggered by the death of Dr. Martin Luther King, Jr. The cities sampled can be seen in Table 1.

Notice none of the cities are southern, though three are located in border states. Consequently, it may be unwise to have too much confidence in generalizations to large southern American cities. Further, the sampling process was not random, but based on the design of a study undertaken to examine local causes of civil disorders.* Cities were selected to maximize the variation in riot experience. Five were chosen because they had experienced severe civil disorders in 1967 (Newark, Detroit, Milwaukee, Boston, and Cincinnati). Five were chosen because they had experienced no civil disorder as of the summer of 1967 (Washington, Baltimore, Gary, Pittsburgh, and St. Louis). And five were chosen

Table 1. Cities included in the sample

Newark	Pittsburgh
Detroit	St. Louis
Milwaukee	Brooklyn (New York City)
Boston	Cleveland
Cincinnati	Chicago
Washington, D.C.	Philadelphia
Baltimore	San Francisco
Gary	

*The study was conducted under the auspices of the President's Commission on Civil Disorders (Kerner Commission) and funded by the Ford Foundation and the National Institute of Mental Health.

because they had experiences civil disorders sometime during the four years prior to 1967 (Brooklyn, Cleveland, Chicago, Philadelphia, and San Francisco). However, when three of the five "non-riot" cities had civil disorders in the spring of 1967, it became abundantly clear that presence or absence of a ghetto riot was not an especially sensitive measure of variability in urban discontent, and our interest then shifted to more subtle indicators of city political processes, such as how public controversy was generated.

In order to collect information about the emergence of salient issues in a city, one must first complete the difficult task of specifying relevant actors and groups. This is problematic because the generation of public controversy typically involves several political actors and/or groups who represent different interests in the city and who interact in complicated ways. Spheres of interest can conflict or overlap (Long, 1958). For example, local schoolteachers might be allied with neighborhood residents on one issue but allied with the city government on another. Similarly, the city government and local groups may or may not be opponents. Sometimes groups of teachers are themselves divided, as frequently occurs during attempts at unionization. Given the complexity of city coalitions, any conceptualization of relevant constituencies is clearly a dangerous simplification. Nevertheless, one must use categories in all attempts at analysis. Our scheme has the city divided into three levels: a level of city leaders, a level of "delivery system personnel," and a level of the general population.

Gathering data from these three different levels required three somewhat different techniques. For the city leaders, we employed reputational criteria and a snowball sample to select an average of forty civic leaders from each of the cities. In-depth interviews (the interviewers had an outline to follow but no questionnaire) were obtained with such people as the mayor, police chief, head of the NAACP, school board members, members of the chamber of commerce, newspaper editors, and the leaders of various community groups. The people selected were used both as respondents and informants.

In a middle level, we gave questionnaires to five occupational groups evaluated to be of great importance in the functioning of any city. Included were policemen, schoolteachers, caseworkers, retail merchants, and heads of personnel for major city employers. The first four groups only included people who had direct interactions with ghetto residents. The policemen worked in black precincts, the teachers in inner-city schools, the caseworkers had primarily black clients, and the retail merchants had stores in the city's ghetto. The personnel chiefs had little direct contact with inner-city blacks but had great influence in hiring policy and hiring implementation for their firms. Notice also that the first three occupational groups operated in the public sector and the last two in the private.*

At the third level was a sample of inner-city blacks averaging approximately 200 in number for each of the fifteen cities. These population samples were

---

*The field work was done by Audits & Surveys, Inc., New York, New York.

Table 2. Groups sampled and sample size

Level	Categories	Average number per city
City leaders	Snowball sample	40
Mediating personnel (delivery systems)		
	Police (from ghetto precincts)	40
	Schoolteachers (from inner-city schools)	20
	Caseworkers (based in the city)	30
	Retail merchants (owners and/or managers of ghetto stores)	30
	Heads of personnel (of major employers)	30
Inner-city residents		200

gathered by the Survey Research Center of the University of Michigan employing questionnaires authored by Howard Schuman and Angus Campbell.

The groups interviewed and their sample sizes can be seen in Table 2. It is important to recall that the categories of people (three levels within each city and five occupational groups within the delivery system level) were chosen because they frequently function as active political units. Police lobby against civilian review boards, city leaders push for a new expressway, ghetto blacks vote as a block for a black mayor, and so on. This is not to say that the levels and groups represent completely homogeneous aggregates. However, for many important issues there will often be more variability of political stance between the levels and groups than within. Further, if one's goal is to build a theoretical model of the power relations in cities, the categories represent several different kinds of roles (leaders, followers, mediators, implementors, etc.) that one would expect to be vital.

Models of the generation of political issues

In this paper we are primarily interested in the processes by which abrasive objective conditions in a city become translated into salient issues, a salient issue being operationally defined as high visibility of that particular issue (e.g., police brutality) in the interviews with city leaders. In other words, an issue is salient when it frequently appears in the text of elite interviews.*

For heuristic purposes one can think of two kinds of processes through which issues might be generated. At one pole is a populist model in which objective conditions in a city arouse its population who in turn communicate their

---

*Recall that city leaders were used both as informants and respondents so that high salience could appear because a city leader consciously labeled an issue as controversial or because the information he disclosed probably meant that an issue was controversial. Usually, if issues were important in a city, the interviewee consciously noted it, and indirect information from the interview supported the labeling by the leader.

feelings about these conditions to city leaders. The people react to the conditions before elites are aware of potential controversy and force leaders at least to acknowledge the presence of an issue. The other pole is an elite model in which abrasive objective conditions are sensed directly by city leaders who then may choose to communicate their feelings to the people by publicly labeling the conditions as an issue. (The labeling may involve public statements or indicative actions.) The conditions become a salient issue without the help of the public. Only later, through actions of city leaders, does the population become involved.

In actual practice, few controversial issues neatly fit under a populist or elite model because there is usually some exchange of information between leaders and the populace as the issue becomes defined. Further, additional variables such as the demography of the city have important impacts that complicate the picture. Nevertheless, some kinds of issues do appear to be generated by processes enough like either of the two models to make use of the models productive.

Whether the emergence of an issue follows a populist or elitist model has important implications for one's analysis of the power structure of the city. If one were to look at a single city at a specific time, the processes by which the issue evolves will suggest the extent of centralized control of the city's agenda of issues. In other words, if any issue become salient through populist-type processes, one can argue that, for that city and that issue, the appearance of the issue on the city's agenda is primarily the result of masses communicating their needs to leaders. More generally, if more issues emerge from below, a city's leaders would appear to have limited agenda control. In contrast, an elite process argues for control of the agenda from above. However, looking at a single city, it is extremely difficult to separate the effect of the people on the issue from the effect of the issue on the people. For example, if police brutality becomes a salient issue in a city through a populist model it is hard to say if leadership control of the city's agenda is weak or if police brutality per se favors a populist kind of generation mechanism.

In order to examine the *independent* effects of issues on political actors, we will analyze data from all of the fifteen cities and see if certain kinds of issues consistently emerge through either a populist or elite model. If such consistency exists, then one can make a plausible argument that the issues have impacts of their own, independent of particular political actors. That is, if given issues consistently appear to follow either a populist or elite model, one can infer that there are characteristics of the issues per se that determine the process of generation.[*]

OVERVIEW OF THE FINDINGS

Findings illustrating elite and populist models will be presented in diagrammatic form. Arrows indicate the relations between variables from the three city levels

[*]One could also infer that consistency reflects, not independent characteristics of issues, but similar power structures in all fifteen cities. This is certainly logically possible but, we feel, unlikely, given the variety of cities in the sample.

we have sampled.* For simplicity, numerical values used to estimate the arrows and their effects will be excluded, but pluses and minuses will show the direction of change in the dependent variable resulting from changes in the independent variable.**

It should be clear that the diagrams include only variables that we have been able to measure, while other variables that could have important effects which we could not measure are not included. Further, the presentation will ignore variables that we did measure but which seemed to have small or negligible impact. Finally, the models reflect an attempt to fit the empirical patterns of relationships between variables to our two models and such statistical manipulation does not produce results having the credibility of experimental designs or data gathered at several points in time. Thus, the diagrams should be considered tentative summaries of complex processes (Blalock, 1961; Heise, 1969).

The welfare system as an issue

No one seems especially satisfied with the welfare system. The existence of the National Welfare Rights Organization indicates dissatisfaction from the recipients of welfare, and the variety of proposed reforms discussed in Congressional debate attest to dissatisfaction from above. Middle America, torn between knowledge that some people in the United States live in poverty and a reluctance to give a "hand-out," look ambivalently at both the current system and proposed changes.

Analysis of the material in our interviews of city leaders indicated that, as in much of America, the quality of welfare was frequently a salient issue in our fifteen cities. Welfare was never the most controversial issue in a city, but it appeared with some consistency in the leader interviews in all of the cities sampled.

The proposed model can be seen in Figure 1; arrows indicate populist processes.† Performance of caseworkers is specified as a cause of dissatisfaction in welfare clients who in turn affect city leaders. One can infer that objective conditions affect welfare recipients and they communicate their feelings to the elites. Additionally, the diagram shows some interesting directions in causal effects and the absence of some variables one might have expected to appear. Especially noticeable for its absence is any measure of the monthly payment for

---

*Variables gathered from sources other than our interviews (primarily the 1960 Census) will also be employed.

**A full presentation of the data can be found in a forthcoming book written by the authors of this article. In the diagrams presented here, zero-order correlations associated with arrows ranged from approximately .35 to .75 in absolute value, with most clustered around .50. A correlation of .50 was necessary to attain statistical significance at less than the .05 level.

†Recall that the causal relations are based on statistical manipulations (i.e., path analysis), and in the absence of a more technical presentation the reader's only criteria for the validity of a causal diagram are its logic, parsimony, and theoretical reasonableness.

Figure 1. Quality of welfare system an issue

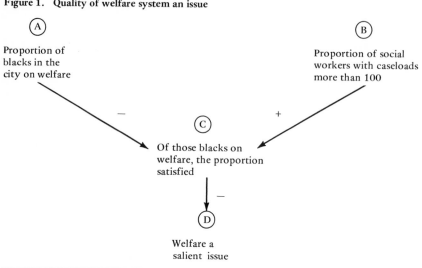

Operationalization of the variables

(A) Estimate of the percentage of the city's black population that is on welfare. The estimate was based on the percentage of black respondents from the general population survey who said they were on welfare.

(B) Percentage of caseworkers in the caseworker sample of a city who say they have caseloads of more than 100.

(C) Of those blacks from the population samples who are on welfare in each city, the percentage who say they are satisfied with the welfare system.

(D) After reading the approximately forty in-depth interviews from leaders in each of the fifteen cities, four raters independently scored each city (0–9) on quality of welfare as a salient issue in that city. A mean was calculated for each city with a high mean indicating high salience. The intercorrelations between the scores of each rater were very high.

each recipient. Estimates of both the average payment in each city per month and the average payment in each city per month weighted by the cost of living in each city failed to correlate highly with other variables of interest.*

Of the variables present, the higher the proportion of the city's black population that is on welfare, the less likely blacks are to be satisfied; and the higher the percentage of caseworkers with caseloads over 100, the *more* likely are black welfare recipients to be satisfied. The caseload variable is associated with two measures of caseworker performance: number of visits to clients per month and the length of time for each visit (the data are not presented here). Caseworkers with larger caseloads visit their clients less frequently and for shorter periods, whether one analyzes the data for individual caseworkers or for aggregate rates of each city. In other words, in cities where caseworkers have heavier

*The absence of an effect does not necessarily mean that the size of payment is not important. It only implies that *variability* in payment has no impact.

caseloads, they generally see less of their clients. However, clients in cities where caseworkers have large caseloads are more satisfied than in cities where loads are light. It seems that clients are happier when they see less of their caseworker! (For the information of the skeptical, the zero order correlation is .62.)

The effect of the proportion of blacks in the city who are on welfare can probably best be understood by focusing on the group processes functioning in the general population during the generation of public awareness. The higher the proportion of blacks in the city who are on welfare, the more likely that one person who is on welfare will know others who are on welfare. And given the reality of residential segregation in urban areas, the percentage would not have to be very large for there to be considerable interaction between welfare recipients. Such interpersonal contact is necessary if large numbers of people are to understand their plight and mobilize around their grievances. Thus, one can think of proportion of blacks on welfare as a structural variable affecting the conditions under which public expression can emerge. However, only those who want change initially have reason to organize, so the structural variable will have its largest impact on those who are dissatisfied. This accounts for the negative sign in the causal relationship.

The final link in the causal model (between public sentiment and leader perception of the issue) is the key to the populist interpretation of the data. Clearly, actions in the general population are affecting leaders, and a reasonable inference is that welfare recipients communicate their grievance to elites either as individuals or, more likely, through groups such as the National Welfare Rights Organization. This populist model undermines theories which attempt to explain activism in the black community (and in this case welfare recipients) primarily on the basis of "outside agitators" and "troublemakers." More generally, the validity of any populist model demonstrates that public issues can be raised by people reacting to their actual plight (e.g., abrasive caseworkers). Certainly political organizers can help mobilize their constituencies, but the people can be aroused because they commonly perceive a set of objectionable circumstances.

Exploitation by ghetto retail merchants as an issue

During the wave of civil disorders that struck urban areas of the United States in the late 1960s, one frequent target of black hostility was the ghetto retail merchant. Clearly, retail merchants operating in ghetto areas have been the center of much controversy and, even when not targets of violence, are frequently criticized for allegedly taking advantage of ghetto customers.

The causal diagram for exploitation by ghetto merchants can be seen in Figure 2. The directions of the arrows indicate that generation of the issue of exploitation by retailers follows largely an elite model, though one of the independent variables feeds directly into black dissatisfaction with merchant practices.

Starting at the top of Figure 2, variable B—merchant "sharp practices"—directly affects the salience of merchant exploitation as an issue. The more

Figure 2.   Exploitation by ghetto merchants an issue

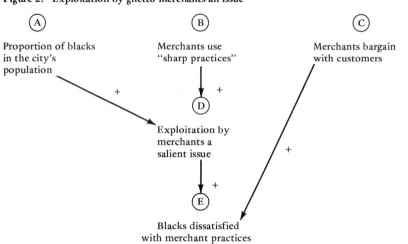

Operationalization of the variables

(A)   Proportion black: Proportion of blacks in city population (1960 Census).

(B)   Merchant "sharp practices" index: Composed of two items from merchant questionnaires: Merchants were asked to express agreement or disagreement to ". . .merchants feel that in business the main thing in a neighborhood like this is to learn how to price their merchandise to cover the extra costs of poor credit risks, petty thievery, and the like," and ". . .merchants say the main thing to do is buy bargain merchandise so that they can keep their retail prices low enough for people to afford."

(C)   Merchant bargaining: Composed of an item asking the extent of merchant agreement with the statement ". . .[merchants] feel that the best way to stay in business in a neighborhood like this is to bargain with each customer and take whatever breaks you can get."

(D)   Merchant exploitation as an issue: Protocols of qualitative interviews with public and civic leaders were pooled for each community and read by four raters, who made judgments on a ten-point scale as to how salient merchant exploitation was as an issue in the black community of that city. Ratings were done independently and achieved a high degree of consensus.

(E)   Black dissatisfaction with retail merchants: Composed of responses to three items in SRC questionnaire covering whether respondents felt they were overcharged in local stores, sold inferior goods, or treated disrespectfully by merchants.

merchants in a city who engage in "sharp practices," the more salient the issue. "Sharp merchant practices" is an index made up of two items: one asking if merchants felt it good business policy to increase the price of their goods to cover the "unusual overhead" of doing business in their neighborhood (a ghetto), and another asking if merchants thought it good policy to buy bargain wholesale merchandise. For both questions we argue that if the merchants in a city tend to agree, they will probably be passing on to their customers a poorer dollar value. In the first case, though the merchants may be justified for business reasons in raising their prices to cover the extra costs of poor credit risks, petty thievery, and the like, the result would be a poorer dollar value for the typical customer.

In the second case, for small retailers, which most ghetto businesses are, buying bargain merchandise may frequently mean buying goods of lesser quality because of the inability to purchase on the large scale needed for real bargain prices.

The second link in the causal chain runs from the salience of the issue to black dissatisfaction with merchant practices. The more salient the issue, the more blacks are dissatisfied. Clearly, this is an elite model because leaders are reacting directly to an objective condition and only later inform the public. Plausibility for the elite model is increased when one considers the kinds of knowledge a ghetto customer would need in order to discover that he was getting a poor dollar value in ghetto stores. Comparative price information would be required for the wide variety of consumer goods. In other words, he would need extensive comparative shopping data, and such data is rarely available without cooperation from leaders and concerned groups. Thus, information that stores are not giving ghetto consumers a good dollar value would be more readily available to leaders than the common citizen, and emergence of exploitation by merchants as an issue would be more likely to follow an elite pattern.

Looking again at the top of Figure 2, the proportion of blacks in a city also appears to operate through an elite model. The higher the proportion of blacks in a city, the more salient the issue of merchant exploitation. The impact may be best understood using two related approaches. First, as in the case of the percentage of people in a city who are on welfare, the proportion of blacks in the city's population may produce the demographic structure necessary for the issue to emerge. The higher the proportion of blacks in the city, the higher the percentage of people who are potential victims of exploitive practices by ghetto merchants. Second, the higher the proportion of blacks, the more that leaders will be likely to raise issues like exploitation of blacks by retail merchants in order to enhance their own popularity. The proportion of blacks is one gauge of potential political mileage to be gained through the issue.

The impact of variable C—merchants bargaining with customers—appears to have its effect directly on black dissatisfaction. The more the merchants bargain with customers, the more blacks are dissatisfied. This measure of retail practices is based on a question asking merchants if they thought it good business practice to bargain with customers and take whatever breaks one could get. Though such practices are usually legal and in some enterprises even expected (e.g., car sales, pawning items, etc.), they can frequently be abrasive and unfair to customers. More specifically, the bargaining process can make naive customers vulnerable to unethical practices such as "one for 11 cents, two for 30," and the increase of prices on the days that welfare checks arrive.

It is important to notice that "sharp practices" follows an elite pattern while "merchants bargaining with customers" affects the common people directly. Such differences in process are probably a consequence of characteristics of the two kinds of practices. "Sharp practices" requires subtle and widespread information for translation of individual experience into a grievance. "Bargaining" can be immediately recognized by the customer as abrasive and potentially exploitative.

Thus, the former practice will probably require an overview presented to the people by leaders, while the latter practice will probably be perceived as a grievance without instigation from elites.

Police brutality as an issue

In Figures 1 and 2 we saw examples of populist and elite models, and in both cases, objective conditions existed around which people could mobilize. Further, some objective conditions were more likely to need labeling from above ("sharp practices"), while others could be perceived as common grievances without help from leaders (abrasive caseworkers). Generalizing from this analysis, one would expect that objective conditions easily labeled as unacceptable by the man in the street would be likely to emerge as issues through a populist model.

Among all of the objective conditions in a city that could be defined as unacceptable, abrasive practices by police would probably be among the easiest for the general population to perceive without the aid of leadership. It is relatively easy to decide that being called insulting names, for example, is objectionable. Figure 3 illustrates processes by which police brutality emerges as an issue. Indeed people directly affect city leaders, and a populist model is the result.

Starting at the top of the figure, we notice that the higher the percentage of blacks in a city, the more the police chief is rated as responsive to the needs of the black population.* Apparently the police chief is reacting to real political pressure. Also, the higher the percentage of blacks in the city, the more likely police are to know personally black residents who live in their precinct. The best explanation may be that patrolmen also respond to demands from the black community for better police protection and better police-community relations. The responses of the police chief and the patrolmen to political power of the black population are both direct results of demographic conditions, and *not* a result of the police chief responding to political pressure and then requiring patrolmen to be more public relations-oriented. In short, any statistical association between a responsive police chief and community knowledgeable policemen is not a consequence of actions of the police chief.* *

In contrast to the noncausal relationship between a responsive police chief and community knowledgeable patrolmen, the link between a responsive police chief and the tendency of police in a city to employ potentially abrasive street practices is causal. The more responsive the police chief, the less likely are police to engage in potentially abrasive street practices. Apparently, the chain of

---

*The evaluation of the police chief is based on information in the leader interviews. Again, interviewees were used as respondents and informants.
**In statistical terms, the relationship between a responsive police chief and a public relations-oriented police force is spurious. The spuriousness is inferred solely from the patterns of correlations in the data but because of the simplified style of presentation, the reader will have to look at the data in our forthcoming book and/or our 1970 article (Berk and Rossi) for the details of how the inferences were made.

Figure 3.   Police brutality as an issue

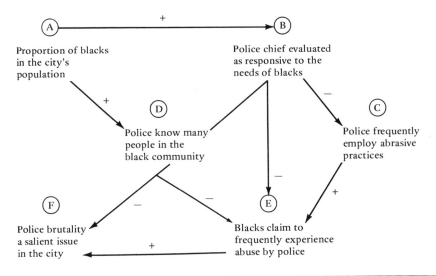

Operationalization of variables
(A)   Proportion of blacks in city population (1960 Census).
(B)   Police Chief Responsiveness Index based on composite ratings (0–9) from the in-depth interviews of city leaders of police chief as accessible to black leaders, sympathetic to black grievances, and responsive to such grievances. As with other material from these interviews, the rating was done independently by four researchers on the project and achieved a high degree of consensus.
(C)   Police Abusive Practices Index based on items in police interviews asking about frequency with which police stop and frisk suspicious people, search on suspicion without a warrant, break up loitering groups, and interrogate suspected drug users.
(D)   Police Community Knowledge Index based on how many people policemen knew from the following categories: important adult leaders, residents in general, youth leaders, and "continual" troublemakers.
(E)   An index composed of three items:
"Some people say that the police don't show respect for people or they use insulting language. Has it ever happened to you?"
"Some people say the police frisk or search people without good reasons. Has it ever happened to you?"
"Some people say the police rough up people unnecessarily when they are arresting them or afterwards. Has it ever happened to you?"
(F)   After reading the approximately forty in-depth interviews from leaders from each city, four raters independently scored each city (0–9) on salience of police brutality as an issue. A mean was calculated for each city (there was high consensus between raters) with a high mean indicating high salience.

command functions with regard to police practices that are more explicitly of a law enforcement nature.

How then do people come to say that they have experienced abusive police practices? Three objective conditions appear to be operating. First, the more that policemen in a city personally know people in the black community, the less likely are people to claim they have experienced police abuse. Second, the more the police chief is rated as responsive, the less likely are people in that city to claim they have experienced police abuse. Third, the more police in a city employ potentially abrasive street practices, the more likely people are to claim they have experienced police abuse. Note that police knowledge of community residents has no impact on the kinds of street tactics police employ; it is not the case that in cities where police know more people on their beat, the knowledge is directly translated into less abrasive practices. Rather, in cities where police know more people in the community, potentially abrasive patrolling practices are less likely to be *perceived* by residents as abuse from police! In other words, any association between police knowledge of the community and police practices is noncausal.

The impact of a responsive police chief on the frequency of complaints about abuse is a bit more complicated. A responsive police chief not only functions to reduce the amount of potentially abrasive street practices employed by police in his city, but, if he is favorably evaluated by the black population, blacks will be less likely to interpret their experiences with police as objectionable. Public relations seems to have an important impact, at least within the range of police patrolling practices whose frequency we were able to estimate.

Finally, consistent with a populist model, the issue of police brutality becomes salient after members of the black community claim to have experienced police abuse. However, once again public relations has an independent effect. If the police chief is viewed as responsive to the issue, police brutality will generally be less salient. Apparently, city leaders will be less likely to believe black complaints about police if the police chief has a sympathetic and responsive reputation. An overview of Figure 3, then, sees police brutality becoming an issue through populist processes, but the salience of the issue being muted by a police chief who is evaluated as responsive to black demands.

Discrimination in employment as an issue

The three models presented so far were rather easily labeled either elite or populist. For the issue salience of discrimination in employment the interpretation is considerably more ambiguous (see Figure 4).

The higher the proportion of blacks in a city, the more likely are blacks to be employed (at unskilled levels).* The higher percentage of employed blacks in the unskilled work force may result from black political pressure and/or a relatively larger black labor pool in cities having higher proportions of blacks.

---

*We chose unskilled levels because we thought in 1967 controversy around discrimination in employment would be best understood by looking at objective conditions affecting the largest numbers of potential black employees. However, we have done the same analysis for skilled levels and the results are substantially the same.

Figure 4. Employment discrimination of blacks an issue

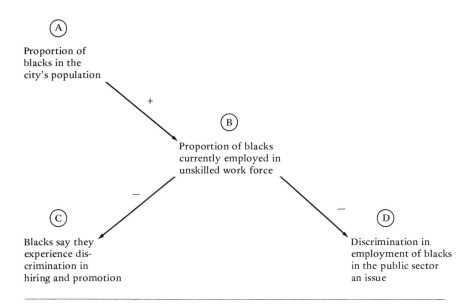

Ⓐ
Proportion of
blacks in the
city's population

+

Ⓑ
Proportion of blacks
currently employed in
unskilled work force

−

Ⓒ
Blacks say they
experience dis-
crimination in
hiring and promotion

−

Ⓓ
Discrimination in
employment of blacks
in the public sector
an issue

Operationalization of the variables
Ⓐ   Proportion of blacks in city population (1960 Census).
Ⓑ   Directors of personnel in the approximately thirty companies sampled in each city were asked the percentage of blacks in their unskilled work force. The mean percentage was then calculated for each city.
Ⓒ   A scale made up of two items asking the blacks sampled in each city how frequently they had experienced discrimination in hiring and promotion.
Ⓓ   As with the other measures of issue salience, a mean rating for each city based on the scores of four raters.

The next links in the chain produce difficulties in attempting to construct either a populist or elite model. The higher the proportion of blacks employed at unskilled levels, the less likely are blacks to claim they have experienced discrimination in hiring and promotion. Also, the higher the proportion blacks employed, the less likely employment discrimination will be a salient issue. However, any association between black grievances and issue salience is for this sector (employment) noncausal. Both are independently caused by the objective condition of proportion of blacks employed*

The absence of a causal link between black grievances about employment and issue salience means that neither a populist nor an elite model are appropriate. In cities where there is a low proportion of blacks employed at unskilled levels,

*As with several links in the police brutality model, the data base from which the relationship was judged spurious can be found in other works by the authors.

people in the inner city are more likely to say they have experienced discrimination in hiring and promotion, and the more likely discrimination in employment will be an issue. But both reactions to the objective conditions occur simultaneously; and *neither is produced by the other.* Apparently, the general population and city leaders can independently react to the employment situation, independently evaluate the facts, and arrive at similar conclusions. This does not mean there will be no cooperation or conflict between levels eventually; it means that in the *generation* of consciousness about the objective condition there is no causal link between city leaders and the black population.

Quality of education as an issue

In Figure 4 we saw how an issue can emerge when both the general population and city leaders react similarly to the objective employment situation of blacks. The data supported neither an elite nor populist but a "simultaneous" model. For the salience of issues surrounding quality of public education the generation process has some characteristics of a simultaneous model (see Figure 5), but closer inspection reveals additional complexity.

Figure 5. Quality of public schools as an issue

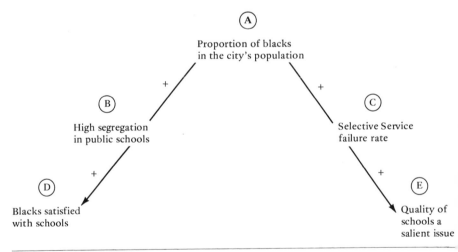

Operationalization of the variables
(A)   Proportion of blacks in city population (1960 Census).
(B)   Estimate of school segregation—percentage of schools in city over 90 percent black.
(C)   Proportion of draftees failing Selective Service preinduction mental test (from Jones and Flax, 1970).
(D)   Proportion of blacks who say they are satisfied with the quality of public schools.
(E)   Similar to other measures of issue salience, a mean rating for each city based on the scores of four raters.

Starting at the top of the diagram, the higher the proportion of blacks a city, the greater the school segregation. Similarly, the higher the proportion of blacks, the higher the Selective Service mental examination failure rate. The former causal link is probably a direct result of demographic pressure; the higher the proportion of blacks in a city, the higher the proportion of blacks in public schools. The latter link does not have such a straightforward explanation. First, it is not clear what underlying traits the Selective Service mental test measures; basic school skills, intelligence, or a middle-class world view. Second, for each of the many things it could be measuring there are several potential intervening variables to explain a positive association between the failure rate and proportion of blacks in the city. An attempt to unravel such issues is beyond the scope of this paper, and fortunately, such an endeavor is probably not necessary. The Selective Service mental examination can be simply thought of as a measure of what the larger society feels are prerequisite skills for the soldier and civilian. Consequently, the data indicates that the higher the proportion of blacks in a city, the higher the rate of failure in this test of "skills."*

Returning to Figure 5, the greater the degree of school segregation in a city, the *more* likely that blacks will be satisfied with the school system. This is a controversial finding to interpret. The correlation is .55, large enough to have to deal with. Possibly, the black community is more satisfied when schools are more segregated because segregated black schools are easily controlled by black neighborhoods. In other words, school segregation is a measure of community control. It may also be that in 1968 (when the data was collected), the black community was in general less critical of the quality of education than the white community and/or less sophisticated in assessing educational processes (or they may be employing different criteria). Consequently, the more segregated the school, the less potential for dissatisfaction. Yet another explanation may lie in the larger number of black teachers and administrators who are probably employed in cities that have greater numbers of segregated schools. School segregation may lead to greater job opportunities for black educators and greater visibility of black professionals in the school system.

For all three interpretations above, no causal link is included between segregation and the Selective Service failure rate, or between black satisfaction and the failure rate. Any statistical associations that exist are noncausal. Thus, segregation has no effect on whatever the failure rate is measuring, and blacks do not react to either the test results or what it represents.

Although the Selective Service failure rate and/or what it represents has little impact on the black community, it does have an effect on city leaders. The

*One must be careful not to automatically assume that characteristics of black per se are raising the failure rate. This may be true, but our data reflect associations at the city level, so inferences about individuals are not likely to be valid. Further, even if it is true that the black population directly increases the failure rate, one must think carefully about the kinds of skills such tests measure and be very cautious about one's interpretations.

higher the failure rate, the more likely the quality of schools will be an issue. Apparently city leaders respond to objective conditions which are reflected by the test. (It is unlikely that city leaders use the test itself to evaluate the quality of public education.)

It should now be clear why the data for this issue is problematic. In the first issue areas (welfare, ghetto measures, and police) either the population aroused the elites or the elites aroused the population. In the fourth issue area (employment discrimination) neither group agitated the other; rather, both agreed on the objective conditions and responded similarly (a simultaneous model). But for quality of education, the black community and city leaders seem to be reacting to different aspects of the school scene and arriving at conflicting evaluations. In short, evaluating the quality of schools seems a difficult matter leading to ambiguous results.

Such an interpretation of the data is not as *post hoc* as it sounds. Recall that for earlier issue areas we tried to examine characteristics of objective conditions that helped determine the emergence of public controversy (as analyzed through a causal model). Since the objective condition of abuse by police, for example, was seen as easily interpretable by the man in the street, we argued that populist processes were feasible. In contrast, "sharp practices" of ghetto merchants required an overview of leaders and the operation of elite processes. But the kinds of evaluations necessary to rate the quality of education in a city are probably so unclear that no one, neither leaders nor the general population, can react with much consistency. With educators, community leaders, political agitators, social scientists, and concerned parents unsure how to measure the quality of education (for example, see the Coleman report), it is very difficult to state what objective conditions should be studied and how an evaluation could be accomplished. Given such ambiguous objective conditions, the issue loses the specific characteristics that help determine its evolution through populist or elite processes.

SUMMARY AND CONCLUSIONS

The findings we have discussed are an initial attempt to unravel a complex problem. The sample and statistical analysis add further vulnerabilities to the analysis. Therefore, it is useful to organize the many implications of the paper into an overview in order to aid the reader in his evaluation of the material.

1. By employing data from three levels within our fifteen cities and additional material from public sources such as the census, we have been able to build an analysis of political processes from several *independent* data bases. Consequently, the patterns of relationships carry more credence than if the data were from only one source.

2. For every sector, popular dissatisfaction or issue salience was highly related to objective conditions, indicating that discontent was in part based

on real events and not exclusively on the skills of political agitators.
3. Salient issues emerged through several different models, in the clearest cases either populist or elite.
4. The kind of processes by which the issue became salient seemed determined in part by characteristics of the objective conditions. The more readily the objective conditions were interpretable by the man-in-the-street, the more likely a populist model. The greater the necessity of an overview for interpretation of the objective conditions, the more likely an elite model. When the general population and the leaders could independently evaluate objective conditions, we found a simultaneous model. Finally, if all parties found it difficult to evaluate the objective conditions, there was little consensus and no clear-cut issue appeared. In this case, there was controversy, but of a relatively undefined nature.
5. Finally, the consistency found in each of the sectors across the fifteen cities argues that characteristics of the objective conditions have important impacts on the shape of the public controversy. Political actors face constraints in their attempts to set city agendas; and consequently, analyses of city power structure must consider the nature of issues when employing decisional type methodology.

References

Agger, Robert E., *et al. The Rulers and the Ruled: Political Power and Impotence in American Communities,* New York: John Wiley & Sons, Inc., 1964.

Aiken, Michael, and Robert A. Alford. "Community Structure and Innovation: The Case of Urban Renewal." *American Sociological Review* 35 (August 1970), pp. 650–665.

Alford, Robert A. *Bureaucracy and Participation: Political Cultures in Four Wisconsin Cities.* Chicago: Rand McNally, 1969.

Banfield, Edward. *Political Influence,* New York: The Free Press, 1961.

Blalock, Hubert M., Jr. *Causal Inferences in Nonexperimental Research.* Chapel Hill: University of North Carolina Press, 1961.

Clark, Terry N. "Community Structure, Decision-Making, Budget Expenditures, and Urban Renewal in 51 American Communities." *American Sociological Review* 33 (August 1968), pp. 576–593.

Crain, Robert L. *The Politics of School Desegregation.* New York: Doubleday Anchor Books, 1969.

Dahl, Robert A. "A Critique of the Ruling Elite Model." *American Political Science Review* 52 (June 1958), pp. 463–469.

———. *Who Governs?* New Haven: Yale University Press, 1961.

Heise, David R. "Problems in Path Analysis and Causal Inference." In Edgar F. Borgatta (ed.) *Sociological Methodology 1969.* San Francisco: Jossey-Bass, Inc., 1969.

Hunter, Floyd. *Community Power Structure.* Chapel Hill: University of North Carolina Press, 1953.

Jones, Martin V., and Michael J. Flax. "The Quality of Life in Metropolitan Washington (D.C.): Some Statistical Benchmarks." Paper from The Urban Institute, Washington, D.C., March 1970.

Long, Norton E. "The Local Community as an Ecology of Games." *American Journal of Sociology* 64 (November 1958), pp. 251–261.

Polsby, Nelson W. *Community Power and Political Theory.* New Haven: Yale University Press, 1963.

Rose, Arnold M. *The Power Structure: Political Processes in American Society.* New York: Oxford University Press, 1967.

Rossi, Peter H., and Richard A. Berk. "Local Political Leadership and Popular Discontent in the Ghetto." *The Annals* of the American Academy of Political and Social Science 391 (September 1970), pp. 111–127.

Walton, John. "Development Decision-Making: A Comparative Study in Latin America." *American Journal of Sociology* 75 (March 1970), pp. 828–851.

———. "Discipline, Method and Community Power: A Note on the Sociology of Knowledge." *American Sociological Review* 32 (October 1966), pp. 684–689.

———. "A Methodology for the Comparative Study of Power: Some Conceptual and Procedural Applications." *Social Science Quarterly* 53 (June 1971), pp. 39–60.

38

WALTER GOVE & HERBERT COSTNER, Organizing the Poor: An Evaluation of a Strategy

Most social scientists, as Haggstrom has noted, have agreed that the poor (1) live on a moment-to-moment basis and rarely plan their activities; (2) perceive the world from a concrete personal perspective, being largely limited to self, family and neighborhood; and (3) typically feel envious and hostile towards the more affluent.[2] The poor are also typically perceived as fatalistic in their outlook on life and as lacking in social and instrumental skills.[3] It is now recognized that the lifestyle and perspective of the poor are attributable not only to their financial impoverishment, but also to a poverty culture[4] which is produced, at least in part, by a feeling of powerlessness.[5]

A traditional way of resolving problems in the United States has been through the development of local self-improvement associations.[6] In spite of the fact that the above characteristics of the poor suggest that they would not participate effectively in voluntary associations, many intervention programs reflect the belief that self-help associations constitute an important, if not an indispensable, ingredient for breaking the poverty culture.[7] There appear to be two main goals sought through local self-help organizations of the poor. First, it is believed that participation in self-help associations will help alleviate feelings of powerlessness which will lead to other changes in perspective and behavior and ultimately to a break with the poverty culture. This assumption remains largely untested, although Levens[8] has provided evidence that participants in self-help organizations do have a stronger feeling of destiny control than nonparticipants. Second, it is assumed that such organizations will be helpful in bringing about institutional changes that will benefit the poor. This may be a more important goal, for the proportion of poor involved in self-help organizations will typically be small, and if the sole accomplishment of a self-help organization is the improved self-

Walter Gove and Herbert Costner, "Organizing the Poor: An Evaluation of a Strategy." *Social Science Quarterly*, vol. 50 (December 1969), pp. 643–656. Reprinted by permission.

concept of those involved, the majority of the poor may remain unaffected by such organizations. To change the orientation of nonparticipants, it is probably necessary to implement concrete changes in the world they encounter.

Organizing the poor on their own behalf can be attempted either in conjunction with the prevailing social order, as in the community action programs sponsored by the Office of Economic Opportunity, or in opposition to the prevailing order, as in programs associated with Saul Alinsky or the new student left.[9] Organizing the poor in opposition to the prevailing social order does not elicit support from established social institutions,[10] but may provide the drama and the emotional appeal that will motivate participation by a substantial segment of the poor population. On the other hand, organizing within the framework of the existing social order may produce strong institutional support, but it limits the targets and tactics of organizational strategy. Local neighborhood self-improvement associations seem to provide a "safe" type of organization whose goals—neighborhood improvement, improved public services for the area, playgrounds for children, and so forth—would elicit broad support from established institutions. A concern with relatively small, concrete goals would presumably enhance the likelihood of successful accomplishments and hence maximize the potential for alleviating feelings of powerlessness. Furthermore, the focus on the immediate neighborhood would seem to be in accord with the concrete personal perspective that characterizes the poor. On the other hand, the main problems perceived by the impoverished seem to extend beyond the confines of the immediate neighborhood, and the diffuse unrest of such a population may be difficult to focus on neighborhood problems.

The remainder of this paper describes one attempt to develop neighborhood self-help associations among the poor and the fate of this attempt. An evaluation of this attempt leads to a summary of general problems encountered in organizing the poor.

The neighborhood organizations

Late in 1965, the Central Area Motivational Program (CAMP), a part of OEO in Seattle, began a program of organizing neighborhood clubs in its service area. Nineteen such neighborhood clubs were eventually listed, along with their membership, in the records of CAMP. The clubs were given names indicative of their intended focus and purpose—"Neighborhood Concern," "Trinity Motivation Council," "Coleman Community Club," "Willing Workers," "27th Avenue Improvement Club," and so on. Each listing represented the effort of a community organizer, a paid member of the CAMP staff, whose responsibilities included organizing a neighborhood group for a specific geographic area and providing assistance to the group in identifying and resolving neighborhood problems. The geographic base of each club was comprised of a few blocks rather than a broad geographic area of the city.

CAMP anticipated that, as the clubs became established, the members would assume the major responsibility for the operation of the club activities and that the community organizer would serve primarily as an adviser and as liaison with the parent organization, CAMP. As CAMP envisioned the program, the clubs would discuss neighborhood problems, devise projects to alleviate these problems (e.g., build playgrounds on vacant lots, press for improved public services in their area, and so forth), stage small fund-raising events to support their projects, assist in resolving the problems of individual families in the neighborhood and cooperate with other clubs and agencies in the area in matters of common interest.

The community organizers were "indigenous workers," that is, residents of the general impoverished area (though not necessarily of the immediate neighborhood served by the club they advised) who were recruited from those not gainfully employed. Most were housewives before becoming community organizers. Formal training or experience in similar roles was not required, although one consideration in selection was the potential for working effectively with such neighborhood groups, and an attempt was made to provide on-the-job training. All of the community organizers and almost all of the club members were Negro women.

Study design

The study was aimed at making an evaluation of the effectiveness of this particular strategy of organizing the poor. In particular, it was concerned with: (1) the extent of participation in the clubs, especially by those who constitute the "hard core" poor, (2) the goals and actual accomplishments of the clubs, and (3) the characteristics that distinguished effective clubs from ineffective clubs.

The data for this study were collected in interviews with a sample of 112 adult residents of the CAMP service area and with *all* interviewable persons on the available membership lists of *all* the neighborhood clubs sponsored by CAMP. Five community organizers were also interviewed. Club members were asked the same series of questions asked of nonmembers, and, in addition, a series of questions pertaining to their own neighborhood club. Interviews were conducted by a team of nine paid student interviewers, eight of whom were black.

The sample of nonmembers was actually a sample of households, one from each of 112 randomly selected blocks. In six of these households no respondent was found at home, and in four, the respondent refused to be interviewed. Each of these ten missing respondents was then replaced by another draw. Hence, a total of 122 interviews were attempted with 112 completions for a completion rate of 92 percent.

All listed members of the neighborhood clubs were target respondents. The membership lists obtained from CAMP contained the names of 132 persons. CAMP was unable to supply the addresses for seven of these persons and attempts to locate them by another means proved fruitless, leaving 125 to be interviewed.

Table 1. Results of attempts to contact persons listed as club members

	N	Percent	N	Percent
Not interviewed			52	39
Moved, no new address	31	23		
Never an address available	7	5		
Not at home on any of five contact attempts	7	5		
Refused to be interviewed	4	3		
Ineligible[a]	3	2		
Interviewed			80	61
Stated that they were at present a member of one of the clubs (3 did not know the name of club)	20	15		
Stated that they were at present a member of one of the clubs but named a club whose name did not approximate any on CAMP list	12	9		
Stated that they had been but no longer were a member of one of the clubs (8 did not know the name of club)	14	11		
Stated that they had been but no longer were a member of one of the clubs but named a club whose name did not approximate any on the CAMP list	3	2		
Stated that they had never been a member of one of the CAMP neighborhood clubs	31	23		
Total			132	100

[a]Persons who could not have been club members, e.g., a seven-year-old boy, a senile, 85-year-old woman cared for by her daughter.

Club membership

The study was initiated with the assumption that all of the neighborhood clubs listed in the CAMP records were operating, and that they had been operating since their initiation several months previously. That assumption was erroneous; some of the clubs were operating, many were not. Table 1 shows the results of attempts to interview persons on the membership lists and the responses pertaining to club identification and participation among those who were interviewed. Table 2 shows other aspects of these same data tabulated for each club separately. Several features of the tables require comment.

First, approximately one out of every four persons listed as club members had moved since the listing approximately eighteen months previously. The data

Table 2.   Selected characteristics of 19 neighborhood clubs

Club	Number of members on original list	Number interviewed	Number interviewed who claimed member- ship at time of interview[a]	Inferred status of club at time of interviews
A	10	8	7	active
B	3	1	0	not active
C	4	3	1[b]	not active
D	7	5	3	active
E	6	2	0	not active
F	5	5	1[b]	not active
G	7	3	2	active
H	8	8	4	active
I	8	6	1[c]	not active
J	5	4	1	(?) active
K	4	3	1	(?) active
L	4	1	0	not active
M	5	2	1[c]	not active
N	6	3	1[d]	not active
O	10	8	4	active
P	7	5	0	not active
Q	9	7	2	active
R	15	6	3	active
S[e]	9	0	0	not active
Total	112	80	32	

[a]Includes those who claim membership but who do not know the name of the club or who give a club name not correspondent to name in CAMP record.

[b]Respondent listed as "acting chairman" or "president" did not know the club name.

[c]Respondent listed as "president" denied ever having been a member.

[d]Although one person claimed current membership the community organizer reported it to be inactive.

[e]A community organizer informed us that club "S" was not a neighborhood club (although it was listed as such) but was an alliance of state employees and students, which had never functioned. None of the listed members could be located.

from the community sample indicates that the overall mobility rate for persons living in the area serviced by CAMP is even higher than this: of those interviewed in the sample, 47 percent indicated that they had changed their residence at least once during the past two years. Such a high rate of mobility implies that almost any association which is based on the local neighborhood, as these clubs were, will experience a heavy and rapid attrition of members. Since many of these movers undoubtedly move to other parts of the general area served by CAMP, the attrition rate due to moving would probably be less for a special-interest group than for a geographically based association.

Second, at least one out of every four persons listed as a club member, had, in fact, never been a club member, and the proportion may well be higher. Many persons listed as members denied having ever been affiliated with the clubs, while a few others were obviously ineligible for membership. The only reasonable interpretation for the inclusion of the "ineligibles" is that the membership lists were "padded"; the most generous interpretation of the inclusion of persons who denied ever having been affiliated with any such club is that in some contact with the community organizer they made remarks that indicated that they might be interested in participating. The conclusion seems unmistakable that the efforts of the community organizers to bring together neighborhood residents to form a club were frequently casual. Apparently, for some of the community organizers, the assignment was beyond their experience and they did not know how to go about it.

Third, at the time of the interviews only half of the clubs gave any evidence of continuing to operate and only four of the clubs (A, H, O, and R) were clearly active at the time of the interviews. Of the forty-nine persons who apparently started as members of the clubs (i.e., all those interviewed except those who denied ever having been affiliated with any of the clubs), approximately one out of three remain in the neighborhood but do not remain active members for as long as eighteen months. Among the thirty-two persons who identified themselves as current members at the time of the interview, one-third reported that they had not participated in any club activities for over one month. It would appear that the clubs were generally unable to sustain the initial interest of their members.

Taken together, these results indicate that the general program of neighborhood clubs was never fully activated. A more intensive organizing effort than that undertaken in this program would be required, and it seems highly doubtful that housewives recruited primarily because they need employment are well suited to the task.

Characteristics of the club members

The contribution of self-help associations toward breaking the poverty culture presumably can be realized only if participants include the carriers of that culture. With some exceptions, areas of a city that are designated "poverty areas" are not populated by residents who are uniformly poor, and such areas frequently include a minority rather than a majority of "hard core" poverty cases who are the primary carriers of the poverty culture. Consequently, neighborhood associations in poverty areas may fail to include the very persons to whom participation would presumably be of the greatest benefit. Carriers of the poverty culture typically are concentrated among those who have a low income and who frequently are unemployed and supported by welfare. We would expect them to have a high proportion of broken homes and to participate in voluntary associations only infrequently. Furthermore, it might be anticipated that the hard core poor would have a distinctive perception of the problems of their area that would set them apart from the more advantaged. We turn now to a description of those characteristics of the club participants that serve as indicators of their status as carriers or noncarriers of the poverty culture. As indicated by Table 3, there is little basis for assuming that the club participants were typically hard core poverty cases embedded in the poverty

Table 3. Comparison of neighborhood club members and nonmembers on selected characteristics (in percent)

	Neighborhood club members (N = 49)	Nonmembers (N = 112)
Race		
Negro	94	57
Caucasian	6	39
Oriental	0	4
Marital status		
Married	71	56
Separated or divorced	8	20
Widowed	10	7
Never married	10	13
Children		
No children in household	10	32
Age		
Under 30	22	26
30–50	59	38
Over 50	19	36
Education		
Completed high school	49	54
Amount of income		
$4,000 or more/yr.[a]	81	73
Main source of income		
Wage or salaries	76	71
Welfare	10	10
Other	14	19
Occupation class		
White collar	20	17
Blue collar	63	53
Unemployed	2	9
Housewife	8	6
Student or retired	6	10
Not ascertained	0	5
Church[b]		
Member, attends regularly	61	39
Member, attends occasionally or never	25	28
Not a member	14	33
Voluntary organizations other than church or CAMP[b]		
Regular attendance in one or more organizations	49	39
Occasional attendance in one or more organizations	37	29
Never attends (including nonmembers)	14	31

[a]Twelve of the club members and 28 persons in the community sample did not reply to this question.

[b]For four persons in the community sample, this information was not ascertained.

culture. Most were employed, married with spouse present, and had incomes greater than $4,000 a year. The most striking difference between club members and nonmembers is that fact that almost all (94 percent) of the club members were black, while the area population was just slightly more than half black (57 percent). The heavy predominance of Negroes in the clubs seems to be a result of the fact that the community organizers were themselves black and the parent organization, CAMP, was largely oriented to the blacks in the area. Other differences between members and nonmembers are less striking. They do, however, indicate that the club members, far from being the least affluent in the area, were somewhat advantaged in comparison to the area as a whole. Club members were more likely to be between 30 and 50 years old, to be married, and to have children in the household. The general picture of the neighborhood serviced by CAMP is that of a relatively poor working-class area, but one in which the majority of persons are not hard core poverty cases. Furthermore, the club members have been drawn primarily from those who are slightly more favorably situated than their neighbors and they are in the middle years of a relatively stable family life cycle.

Members of the neighborhood clubs were much more frequently involved in voluntary associations than nonmembers (see Table 3). The most common voluntary association was church membership, with club members belonging much more frequently than nonmembers. Church-affiliated groups (e.g., a missionary society), civil rights and labor organizations predominated among the other associational memberships. For purposes of summarizing participation in voluntary associations other than churches and CAMP, each respondent was classified as to (1) regular attendance in one or more organizations, (2) occasional attendance in one or more organizations, and (3) never attends. The data in Table 3 indicate that, even omitting church membership and attendance, the members of neighborhood clubs were more likely to be "joiners" than were the nonmembers of the area.

The respondents were asked to indicate if they were satisfied or dissatisfied with fourteen different conditions in their own neighborhood—play space for children, housing, police protection, public transportation, and so forth. Club members indicated more dissatisfaction than the nonmembers on every condition, suggesting a greater sensitivity to or awareness of neighborhood problems. Only "play space for children" elicited a response indicating dissatisfaction by as many as half of the nonmembers. In contrast, six of the fourteen conditions—housing, play space, appearance of the area, traffic safety, police protection, condition of streets—elicited a response of dissatisfaction by half or more of the club members.

In addition, respondents were asked what they felt was the "most important community problem" facing the residents of their general area; responses to this open-ended question suggest there is no general consensus since no single problem was named by more than 17 percent of the respondents. Among the club members, however, 47 percent named housing. In contrast, the very poor nonmembers (incomes less than $4,000) most frequently named crime and employment.

Club members, then, appear to view the problems of the area from a somewhat different perspective than do the hard core poverty cases. A further illustration of this tendency comes from an interview with a community organizer who reported that one of her clubs was composed entirely of home owners. The focus of a series of club meetings was how to force three or four of their renting neighbors to clean up the property they were renting, as their behavior was forcing down the financial values of other property in the neighborhood.

The general characteristics of the club members indicate that club membership was not concentrated among the very poor and that club members were not likely to be carriers of the poverty culture. Furthermore, our data indicate that the clubs were not comprised primarily of persons who would otherwise have been lacking in voluntary association participation; indeed it appears that members of the neighborhood clubs were already rather heavily involved in voluntary associations. Finally, there is some evidence that club members have a different view of the "most important problem of the area" than the very poor.

Accomplishments of the clubs
and factors related to club success

Even though the neighborhood clubs varied in their degrees of success over a very limited range, the existence of this variation permits a preliminary exploration of some of the factors that contribute to success or failure. Success may be judged either in terms of the benefits presumably accruing from the concrete accomplishments of the clubs or in terms of the self-perceived achievement of club goals.

Each club member interviewed (who did not deny club affiliation) was asked to name the goals sought by his own club, to describe the activities undertaken in an attempt to achieve these goals, and to indicate if he felt the goal had been accomplished. The lack of consensus in many clubs suggested that they had not developed clear goals. Furthermore, for many of the club members, successful accomplishment of a goal meant that the club had discussed a problem on a particular occasion, or that a telephone call had been made, or a letter written. These interviews, as well as those with the community organizers, indicated that most of the club members had no conception of the type of activities necessary to put pressure upon governmental or commercial agencies, to say nothing of knowing how to organize and implement such activities.

The ratio of goals perceived as accomplished to goals named was low—even with the very liberal meaning of "accomplish" used by the respondents. Members named 107 goals for their respective clubs; in 37 cases (34 percent) the respondent naming the goal indicated that it had been accomplished. The low rate of perceived success may have been one of the reasons for the high dropout rate.

The concrete accomplishments of the clubs were, if anything, even less spectacular, and they can be listed in their entirety very briefly. One club succeeded in establishing a "tot lot" playground on land donated by a club member. Another club painted one building, while a different club, with the aid of their community organizer, obtained a donation of paint which they attempted to give to others in the neighborhood who needed it. (They reported plaintively, however, that no one would accept it.) Two clubs, in an attempt to provide assistance to the needy, staged small fund-raising events (a rummage sale and a raffle). The most spectacular accomplishment of any neighborhood club was the role one club played in the establishment of a crosstown bus route. The idea for the route initially came from the club; however, implementation required CAMP officials and other important community leaders to organize and carry out the campaign eventually leading to the bus route establishment.

Two members of the research team independently made a "dichoto-mized" judgment of the relative success of each club based on the information available. These judges agreed on the placement of all but two of the clubs, and these disagreements were resolved by discussing the characteristics of these clubs and arriving at a common decision.[11] Six clubs (A, H, K, N, O, and R in Table 2) were categorized "more successful" while the remainder were categorized "less successful."

The members of the more successful and less successful clubs were com-pared with only trivial differences between the two sets of club members in terms of age, socioeconomic status, other organizational memberships, or in atti-tudes toward the community or toward CAMP. Although the differences are not great enough to rule out random variation as a source of difference, the members of the more successful clubs had fewer children, fewer persons in the household, and were less likely to be employed outside the home. These differences, although slight, suggest that members of more successful clubs may have had more time available to devote to club activities. Members of the more successful clubs also tended to be slightly more personally "optimistic" (i.e., more anticipated that five years from now they would occupy a more favorable position).

Probably the most significant difference between successful and unsuccess-ful clubs was club size. The average size of the initial membership listed for the more successful clubs was 8.8 persons as contrasted to an initial membership of 5.8 persons for the unsuccessful clubs. The less successful clubs were only slightly more likely to have listed members who moved away or who denied ever belonging to the club.[12] However, the loss of any particular club member was more of a serious threat to a small club than to a large one.

Very small clubs appear to be disadvantageous for a number of reasons.[13] First, when mobility is high and dropouts are likely, as in this case, a larger mem-bership can sustain some losses from these sources without diminishing the membership to one or two lone survivors. Second, it is difficult to undertake projects of any consequence, and thereby sustain motivation and interest through activity and accomplishment, if the membership is too small. It is difficult, for example, for a club of three or four members to muster the courage to go to city hall or the energy to start a clean-up campaign because the social support from within the group for such an undertaking is so limited. Third, it is probably difficult for a club of three or four members to develop a sense of being a club at all; in a club with only three or four members the absence or inactivity of one or two members turn the "club meeting" into a tête-a-tête, and any feeling of accomplishment is difficult to muster under such circumstances.

More than one-third of the neighborhood clubs organized by CAMP community organizers had an initial membership list of five or fewer members, and with one exception these very small clubs had ceased to be active by the time of the interviews. Allowing for the possibility of people moving and dropping out, almost all of the neighborhood clubs started with a precariously small membership which may have been a major source of their difficulty. It is conceivable that the "local neighborhood" is simply too small an area to provide a population base for workable self-improvement associations among the poor.

Discussion and conclusions

The strategy of organizing the poor described in this paper—an attempt to develop local neighborhood self-improvement associations through the efforts of an indigenous community organizer—was a failure. The types of problems encountered appear to be common, and other attempts based on a similar strategy will probably be similarly unsuccessful. The major problems are these:

1. Indigenous community organizers working without close expert guidance and supervision are likely to find the task of organizing difficult and frustrating. As a consequence, their efforts may be perfunctory and records may exaggerate the degree of organization accomplished.

2. Community residents most easily recruited and most likely to continue as participants seem to be the relatively advantaged residents of the area who are already participating in other associations, rather than the "hard core" poor. Whatever the presumed benefits of participation, the unaffiliated and unintegrated are not likely to be reached, nor are their viewpoints necessarily well represented by their slightly more advantaged neighbors.

3. Although residents of poverty areas, and especially club members, respond to questions about area problems in ways that suggest moderately high dissatisfaction with prevailing neighborhood conditions, they apparently lack knowledge of how to deal effectively with the sources of dissatisfaction. Even very small and limited goals are rarely accomplished.

4. Residents of poverty areas typically have pressing personal concerns and are particularly geared to immediate concrete rewards.[14] The slow processes of accomplishing ends through organization seem to provide little satisfaction and dropouts are frequent. Club participation seems to be lacking in any zeal and, if it has any effect on psychological outlook, probably adds to a sense of frustration rather than imparting any feeling of accomplishment and power.

5. Associations with a neighborhood base are likely to be too small to make for organizational continuity in the face of mobility and dropouts, too small to generate and sustain a feeling of being a real organization, and too small to undertake some of the tasks that would presumably be necessary to alleviate sources of dissatisfaction. The larger neighborhood clubs had a better chance of achieving

some success than the smaller ones, but the local neighborhood seems to be an inappropriate unit for dealing with many of the problems of the impoverished.

Strategies for organizing the poor that can overcome these difficulties should enjoy a more favorable prognosis for success than would a repetition of the strategy described here. An organizational focus around a common problem rather than a shared locality might provide a more realistic base for organizing the poor, and might also assist in recruiting a higher proportion of the hard core poor and a larger membership base. Involvement of professionals in relevant specialties and citizens other than the poor and near poor might assist in overcoming some of the other organizational problems (listed above) by providing information and guidance as well as encouragement in the face of delayed achievement.

A strategy embodying such points has recently been described by Zurcher and Key.[15] In such a program the poor act as experts on what goals need to be accomplished, while persons already skilled in the intricacies of community activity play a major role in achieving these goals. This "Overlap Model," as Zurcher and Key have named it, when viewed from the standpoint of the now conventional objectives of organizing the poor, appears to present a dilemma of its own: How can an organizational "model" that is built in part around the dependency of the poor help reduce the feeling of powerlessness of the poor? The feeling of powerlessness among the poor, however, is reality, not illusion, and its significance for the poor may lie not so much in the psychological adaptions that emerge from the *feeling* of powerlessness as in the limited life chances that emerge from the *reality* of powerlessness. In the long run, organization among the poor may be most effective if participation by the poor is viewed in terms of its instrumental contributions to goal achievement rather than in terms of its social-emotional contributions to psychological change. The program discussed in this paper suggests that the contributions of the poor to goal attainment can be best achieved if they work closely with others who have the skills which the poor lack. The fate of this program also suggests that neighborhood-based associations are ill-suited for changing the reality of powerlessness.

Notes

1. The research reported in this paper was performed pursuant to Contract #1375 with the Office of Economic Opportunity, Washington, D.C. 20506.

2. Warren C. Haggstrom, "The Power of the Poor," in Frank Riessman, Jerome Cohen, and Arthur Pearl (eds.), *Mental Health of the Poor* (New York: The Free Press, 1964).

3. See, for example, Oscar Lewis, *The Children of Sanchez: Autobiography of a Mexican Family* (Vintage, N.Y.: Alfred A. Knopf, 1963); Walter Miller, "Focal Concerns of Lower Class Cultures," and Murray Hausknecht, "The Blue Collar Joiner," in Arthur Shostak and William Gomberg (eds.), *Blue Collar World: Studies of the American Worker* (Englewood Cliffs, N.J.: Prentice-Hall, Inc., 1964).

4; Michael Harrington, *The Other America: Poverty in the United States* (Baltimore: Penguin Books, 1962).

5. See, for example, Marshall B. Clinard, *Slums and Community Development: Experiments in Self-Help* (New York: The Free Press, 1966); Haggstrom, "Power of the

Poor," *op. cit.*, and Patricia C. Sexton, *Spanish Harlem: Anatomy of Poverty* (New York: Harper and Row, 1965).

6. For example, Alexis de Tocqueville, in his classic commentary on life in the United States in the early nineteenth century, noted the prominence of the "principle of association" in the resolution of collective problems in America as compared to alternative forms of resolving problems in Europe. Bradford Smith in *A Dangerous Freedom* (New York: J. B. Lippincott, Co., 1952), has chronicled the successes of dozens of special-purpose associations in the United States from the nineteenth to the middle of the twentieth century, many representing attempts of local citizens to solve local problems.

7. For example, Warner Bloomberg, "Notes on Poverty and Dependency," unpublished paper, sees the organization of the poor as an effective strategy in combatting feelings of dependency, while Nathan Cohen in "A National Program for the Improvement of Welfare Services and the Reduction of Welfare Dependency," in Margaret S. Gordon (ed.), *Poverty in America* (San Francisco: Chandler Publishing Co., 1965) maintains that the way to alleviate a feeling of powerlessness is by socially and politically organizing the poor to deal with the problems that directly confront them. Haggstrom, "Power of the Poor," *op. cit.*, suggests that participation in powerful neighborhood conflict organizations will enhance the poor's conception of their own worth and will overcome their feeling of powerlessness.

8. Helene Levens, "Organizational Affiliations and Powerlessness: A Case Study of the Welfare Poor," *Social Problems*, 16 (Summer 1968), pp. 18–32. Her finding of greater degree of destiny control among participants, however, may be a consequence of the selection process involved in becoming a member of such an organization. Although Levens attempts to control for this possibility, she is unable to rule out the selectivity hypothesis as she only has cross-sectional data.

9. Frank Riessman, "A Comparison of Two Social Action Approaches: Saul Alinsky and the New Student Left," unpublished paper.

10. Warren Haggstrom, "On Eliminating Poverty: What We Have Learned," in Warren Bloomberg, Jr., and Henry Schmandt, (eds.), *Power, Poverty and Urban Policy* (Beverly Hills: Sage Publications, 1968).

11. These judgments were then compared against four objective indicators of success: (a) number of tasks attempted, (b) ratio of tasks accomplished to tasks attempted, (c) proportion of members on the membership list who could be identified as active members, and (d) the ratio of all attendances at club meetings during the month preceding the interview to the number of members. The judgments had a higher association with each of the other indicators than these other indicators had with each other.

12. Twenty-one percent of those appearing on the membership lists of the "more successful" clubs had moved by the time of the interviews, as compared to 25 percent of those on the lists for the "less successful" clubs. The percentage denying ever belonging to the club was 23 percent in the "more successful" and 27 percent in the "less successful" clubs. Eight percent of the membership list of the "more successful" clubs were dropouts, as compared to 19 percent in the "less successful" clubs.

13. Since the community organizers assumed the responsibility for assembling the club members initially and also for continuing to work with the clubs, the possibility arises that the more energetic community organizers had both larger and more successful clubs, membership size itself making no contribution to club success. We do not have a detailed record of the activities of the community organizers, but the meager evidence available on this point suggests that this interpretation of the relation between club size and success is untenable. Approximately one-third of the members of the "less successful" clubs, as compared to only one-sixth of the members of the "more successful" clubs reported that the community organizers had focused the problem for the club. This suggests that, if there were any differences in community organizer activity between the more and the less successful clubs, the community organizer was more dominant in those clubs that were less successful.

14. See, for example, Elizabeth Herzog, "Some Assumptions About the Poor," *Social Service Review*, 37 (December 1963), pp. 391–400; Lawrence L. LeShan, "Time Orientation and Social Class," *Journal of Abnormal and Social Psychology*, 47 (June 1952), pp. 589–592; S. M. Miller, Frank Riessman, and Arthur A. Seagull, "Poverty and Self-Indulgence: A Critique of Non-Deferred Gratification Pattern," in Louis Ferman, Joyce

Kornbluh, and Alan Haber (eds.), *Poverty in America* (Ann Arbor: University of Michigan Press, 1965), pp. 285-302.

15. Louis Zurcher and William Key, "The Overlap Model: A Comparison of Strategies for Social Change," *Sociological Quarterly*, 10 (Winter 1968), pp. 85-96.

39

ALLAN SCHNAIBERG, Politics, Participation, and Pollution: The "Environmental Movement"

The city dweller of the early 1960s who thought that American urban problems had reached their zenith with the pressures generated by the civil rights movement was an optimist, as things have subsequently turned out. Not only did the 1960-1970 period produce an urban-based "war on poverty" and an anti-Vietnam war movement, but in the last years there emerged still another problem-oriented social movement—the "environmental movement."

But, like the other major social and political problems that had been imposed on the consciousness (and conscience) of urban Americans, environmental issues became ever more complex and solutions appeared farther and farther on the horizon. Short-term solutions were often unworkable and even more frequently inadequate to *halt* the continuing degradation of the environment. They were still more inadequate to *reverse* the cumulative degradation of decades and even centuries that existed in the urban (and rural) American environment.

However, what was accomplished by the end of the decade was the creation of a large-scale social movement of "environmentalists." If success is defined in the American context in terms of size and rate of growth, it is clear that the environmental movement is far more successful than its predecessors, such as the civil rights movement. Organizations like the Sierra Club and Environmental Action have compiled lists of the many thousands of organizations that have been involved in some form of environmental action, and a recent list for Illinois alone produced some 250 names.[1] Likewise, it is an indisputable fact that mass media awareness of the dimensions of the environmental problem has *grown* in the United States,[2] whether one measures this in terms of column-inches, numbers of stories (a six-fold increase from 1955 to 1963)[3] or editorials. And finally, the distribution of concern about pollution and environmental degradation is distributed throughout the United States,[4] not being confined initially to one segment of the country, as the early civil rights movement was concentrated on the South.

Yet, in spite of this phenomenal "success" in educating the public and

This article is original to this book. The assistance of the Center for Urban Affairs, Northwestern University, is gratefully acknowledged.

creating a viable organization, the degree to which the environmental movement has accomplished its stated goal, that of improving environmental quality, is at best extremely limited. Although some short-term actions, such as limited glass and paper recycling, have had some beneficial environmental impacts, it is not at all clear that any major workable long-term solutions have been given a firm foothold. In order to comprehend why this has happened, the environmental movement must be placed in its proper historical and sociopolitical setting. The central question to be posed is: Given the universal approval to improving our (universal) environment, why is it that the environmental movement has had limited success, and has, in the process, generated substantial community conflict which threatens the future viability of the movement? How is it that in a period of perhaps three to five years we have moved from a focus on environment as the means for achieving national unity to a position, by the Chairman of the Board of Directors of General Motors, attacking some environmentalists as seeking to destroy the American way of life?

> . . . the short term political advantage offered by spectacular but unsound consumer legislation can do lasting *damage* to the very consumers it purports to help. The consumer is the loser when *irresponsible* criticism and *ill-conceived* legislation break down faith in our economic system, when *harassment* distracts us from our modern challenge, when the very idea of free enterprise is diminished in the eyes of the young people who must one day manage our businesses. Corporate responsibility is a catchword of the *adversary* culture that is so evident today. If something is wrong with American society, *blame* business . . . The dull cloud of *pessimism* and *distrust* which some have cast over free enterprise is impairing the ability of business to meet its basic economic responsibilities—not to mention its capacity to take on newer ones[5] [emphasis mine] .

Historical basis

In an attempt to either discredit or justify the environmental "bandwagon" effect, a number of authors have cited the long history of environmental degradation that existed in England and other societies early in the Industrial Revolution.[6] Furthermore, they have cited the "alarmists" or "Jeremiahs" of these periods, warning of the imminent decline of cities, and indeed of civilizations, if environmental problems were not solved. At the very least, this indicated merely that history, like Scripture, can be quoted by the devil for his own purposes.

Let us grant the long history of the degradation of the environment; the question arises as to why a *movement* emerged in the late 1960s, aimed at confrontation with the forces leading to such degradation. The most common explanation is that a consciousness or awareness of the quality of the environment did not emerge until then. But this merely begs the question: if the degradation has been occurring for at least a century why did this awareness emerge only in the late 1960s?[7] One possible answer is that the scientific basis for evaluating the degradation was nonexistent until this point: a glance at the volumes of any major scientific publication, any major engineering or planning journal or the like will surely dispel such a naïve assumption. Technical information, whether on water quality, the effects of pesticides on animal food chains, air pollution, or water resources, mineral resources, etc., have all been available in some form for several decades, at the very least.

Clearly, then, it was neither a sudden crisis nor a totally new type of information that created the preconditions for the environmental movement. Two components, I will argue, were necessary and sufficient to provide the impetus. The first is the precedent set by the two major movements of young Americans, the more important of which was the civil rights movement, which spanned the late 1950s and the early 1960s. It might not be misleading to cite the uniqueness of this movement, involving massive numbers of individuals struggling in a cause that went beyond their immediate economic concerns (unlike many other earlier social movements in the United States), and a confrontation with various levels of the power structure. It was the first social movement to capture the energies of substantial numbers of the college population, shifting their concerns from private to public goals. And it was the first to extend and develop new techniques of *participation* in resistance to existing social forces, using sit-ins, mass demonstrations, marches, picketing, leafletting and media contact for *public* interests (unlike labor unions, which had used some of these, but largely for the private ends of the membership).[8] The second movement, the anti-Vietnam-war organization, served to further develop some of these techniques and to build a base for an ecology movement to a limited extent (along with providing a competitive movement in the later 1960s).[9] The Vietnam movement indicated that the civil rights techniques could be applied to other public issues, thereby generalizing the process of *participatory mobilization*[10] around social issues.

Both these major social movements shared one additional quality, which was transmitted to the environmental movement, as we shall see. Whether in civil rights or antiwar causes, the evaluation of *success* proved to be extremely difficult, even though "equality" or "peace" had some intuitive and simple appeal at the start of the movements. The questions that nagged leaders of both movements were centered around the adequacy of public awareness or arousal about the issues, legislation, litigation, limited enforcement, and the like. In other words, though there was initial acceptance of common *ultimate* goals, there emerged a proliferation of intermediate organizational goals (which were themselves means to the achievement of the ultimate goal). Faced with these dilemmas of self-evaluation, many groups responded in the classical sociological mold: the growth of their organization became the measure of their success. This particular type of "goal displacement"[11] appears to have disseminated to the environmental movement as well, as we shall presently observe.

I have said that there was a second major precondition for the ecology movement: this was the emergence of a popularized perspective on environmental problems. It would appear likely that this honor falls to Rachel Carson, whose *The Silent Spring,* published in 1962,[12] became the touchstone of the ecology movement. Why, it may be asked, was this popularized work necessary for the creation of a movement, when the evidence of pollution existed much earlier in the form of smog and the like in metropolises like Los Angeles and New York, and water pollution in virtually every major body of water? One possible interpretation is that Carson's book provided a much more sinister worldview, one in which the forces undermining the ecosystem operated much less dramatically but with greater impact than any lay observor could appreciate. Furthermore, Carson's work exposed some of the social and economic *and* scientific infrastructure that had *knowingly* permitted ecological degradation to occur. Put in other terms, Rachel Carson provided convincing evidence for a lack of a constituency that supported environmental systems, and an eloquent plea for the creation of such a constituency. The validation of the thesis that no substantial constituency existed is contained in the fact that it was approximately eight years before a "National Environmental Teach-In" was organized. In those eight years, a large proportion of the educated and general population made do with the convenient rationalizations that "someone else was the expert in charge," as David Miller[13] has put it. To a great extent, as we shall see, many of these rationalizations continue today, within the environmental movement, as well as in the general population.

Several caveats should be noted at this point, concerning the above observations. In the first instance, there have been organizations devoted to preserving some portions of our environment for some considerable period in America, ranging from conservation (and conservative)[14] groups to organic farming proponents and organic food advocates.[15] But few of these, in spite of public rhetoric to the contrary, were actively concerned about the total environmental system, and fewer still were acting to prevent what they believed was an imminent apocalypse of environmental collapse. Correspondingly, none of these movements ever captured the attention of large numbers of people, nor did they mount the political campaigns to convince the political and economic elites of the seriousness of the situation. That is, the present movement is unique in its scope and intensity.

A second caveat is that of multiple causation. I have discussed two central factors in the emergence of the movement, one dealing with techniques and the other dealing with goals and mobilizing ideologies. Yet there were many other influences that led to the emergence as well. Among these might be the growing interest in wilderness recreation and camping,[16] in part a reflection of continued metropolitan decay and the expansion of urbanized areas (with suburbs effectively removing a green or "natural" belt around the central cities, thus further removing urbanites from contact with nature). The growth of camping and natural-area recreation had a variety of impacts; for one thing, they placed tremendous pressures on existing facilities, leading to a national concern about the present inadequacy and future paucity of recreational areas; in addition, they exposed the degradation of many of these areas through the "multiple-use" by logging and ranching and mining interests, approved in the name of the people of the United States by the Department of the Interior and its subsidiaries.[17] In addition to this pressure, numerous other pressures mounted in the period before and during the movement's emergence to reinforce and expand the urgency associated with environmental preservation, many of these associated with particular population groups and/or particular regions of the country.[18] A full discussion of these factors is beyond the scope of this work.

The final caveat which should be noted here is that the prime movers in the creation of the movement differed for groups of participants. While some substantial segment of the action groups emerged from direct experience with the civil rights movement, the "war on poverty," or the antiwar movement, this is by no means true of all the groups (a simple observation of the age of many young environmentalists would suffice to show that they were too young to have acted in the civil rights movement, for example). Thus the movement consisted of the "veterans" of prior social action, as well as the new environmental "recruits," many of whom had totally different social backgrounds and ideologies, and an interest only in the preservation of the "environment." This diversity of backgrounds, as we shall presently observe, is an important aspect of the movement.

Definitions of the problem and concomitant actions

The scope of the environment, and consequently the scope of environmental problems, is both the strength and weakness of the ecology movement. The strength lies in the fact that every citizen is in some way touched by environmental quality, and thus everyone is a potential activist in the "cause." Furthermore, as was stated repeatedly in the early days of the movement, no one could deny the *ultimate* goal of environmental preservation, i.e., it was a universal objective. In this sense it differed considerably from its predecessors, the civil rights, antipoverty and antiwar movements. Yet the differences, as I will demonstrate, were only in degree. The very breadth of the environmental problems that exist permitted, indeed required, some degree of specialization among the participants, since no group could mount sufficient social and political pressures on all environmental fronts, given a general lack of resources. Furthermore, the fact that environmental problems touched every citizen was in part a corollary of the fact that every citizen's activities in turn *affected* the environment.

At the outset, there was some attempt (Machiavellian or otherwise) to stress the *universal* contribution to environmental problems, as a rallying cry for massive participation in environmental improvement.[19] But this universality was clearly a double-edged sword: if everyone's actions contributed to environmental decay, then environmental improvement programs were bound to have an impact upon everyone's *actions* ultimately. A trivial statement perhaps, yet the possible profundity of this observation has escaped the consciousness of many of the current and past participants, although it has likely influenced the *non*participation of many citizens! That is, it may be precisely the expectation of such consequences that has deterred some segments of the population from participation in environmental groups. Put most simply, the message here is a variant of the Black Panther perspective: If you're part of the problem, then you are affected by the solution.

What precisely do we mean when we link "actions" to environmental problems? One simple view is the classification of actions into *consumption* and *production;* insofar as we consume and/or produce, our action has some environmental consequences. In every such action, material is transformed in some fashion, and always involving some energy loss (the Second Law of Thermodynamics), which we might term depletion of energy resources.[20] In addition to the energy loss, there are frequently byproducts of the consumption/production processes, such that new materials are formed, which are discharged into the environment; these might properly be called pollution, which in turn is a special case of the general problem of depletion of *usable* resources. Material, unlike energy, is conserved, so that we transform by combustion a usuable resource such as coal into a nonusable (at some level) byproduct or "pollutant" like sulfur dioxide or dust particles. Thus pollution and resource usability depletion are part of the same process, and are intimately linked to *every* act of consumption or production in a society. Again, once stated, this principle appears to border on the trivial, yet only a handful of the ecology movement participants, I would claim, fully appreciate this set of linkages between the economic sphere and the ecological. Everyone involved sees a part, has a "piece of the action," yet few recognize the wholistic and *universal* applicability of these principles. The evidence for this statement lies in the public outcries of many ecological activists for a "technological" solution to environmental degradation;[21] any good physicist could tell them that this is equivalent to asking for a perpetual motion machine which would negate the Second Law of Thermodynamics, a privilege which is not accorded even to the most powerful nation in the world. Technological proposals such as the catalytic auto muffler, cooling towers for nuclear power plants, larger urban sewage treatment plants, and so on, all have *resource* costs associated with their production and use, and thus all have some negative environmental impact along with their obvious positive functions.

If few environmentalists see the whole picture, what "pieces" do they perceive, and what types of corrective actions are proposed by or engaged in by the several groups? On a simple level, we can outline four major types of "movement" participants, recognizing that this is merely a first approximation to describing the various approaches currently being attempted. These types are (a) cosmetologists, (b) meliorists, (c) reformists, and (d) radicals.[22] Each of these types, which will presently be described, has operationalized its "piece of the action" on either or both of two planes: the individual level of action and the collective level. What follows is a brief description of the definition of *the* environmental problem modally used by the group, and the concomitant solutions or actions proposed by the group.

(*a*) *Cosmetologists*   For this group, the prime mover is the most immediate sense perception of the group. In the urban areas, one of the most conspicuous consequences of consumption is waste of various types, discarded in both public and private locales. The generic concept for such waste is "litter," so that the cosmetologists are primarily engaged in an "anti-litter" campaign of one or another types. This might be termed a "postconsumption" level of action, since it deals only with the byproducts of consumption, basically consumer goods packaging. It should be stressed that this type is neither concerned directly about consumption nor about production functions. Their primary concern is with the *disposal* process; a typical successful environmental action would be collection of paper and other wastes from public places (or vacant lots, etc.) and transporting it to city incinerators or sanitary land fills. What happens to the solid wastes after this point is of no direct concern to these groups, by their criterion of success.

It would not be unfair to state that these groups are the most naïve environmentalists, for a variety of reasons. In the first place, they ignore the fundamental social and economic behaviors which cause "litter," thus engaging in a never-ending (recurrent expenditure, in economic terms) struggle. They neither criticize the consumption habits of the population, which engages in waste production of various types, including litter, nor do they criticize the production behavior, which engages in an ever-increasing proliferation of disposable packaging, thus perpetuating the problem. And finally, they fail to recognize the ecological facts of life, in that the materials they aggregate may merely increase concentrated air and water and land pollution or degradation, through municipal waste-disposal procedures.

The fact that their definition of the problem is an immediate sense perception (visual litter) is correlative of the backgrounds of these environmentalists. Typical civic groups of this type are Boy Scout groups, ladies' Garden Clubs, PTA groups, and the like. Most of the participants were unaffiliated with any prior sociopolitical movement, like the civil rights campaign, and indeed may be precisely from the lower-middle or upper-middle classes which strongly opposed such movements. In other words, these are groups which have been drawn into the environmental movement *de novo*, and view the environmental problem as isolated from most other major social issues. They are thus the groups most likely to be supported by industrialists engaged in the creation of the problem, e.g., soft drink bottlers, glass producers, paper companies, and to be totally insensitive to the environmental impact of these latter groups.

In terms of individual pro-environment actions, participants in this group engage in careful disposal of solid wastes (though not necessarily of liquid wastes, since this is not as visible a form of pollution). On a collective or group action basis, they may form clean-up committees, particularly in poor neighborhoods, or public urban places such as parks and playgrounds; they may also sponsor anti-litter advertising, circulate litterbags, provide additional litter containers in public places, and so on.

In many ways, the cosmetologists represent one pole of environmental awareness, and perhaps are most representative of the American population in terms of consciousness of processes leading to environmental decay, as well as of the nature and extent of this decay. They have also become one of the "straw men" for critiques by more sensitive environmentalists, especially the radical groups.

(b) Meliorists. Like the cosmetologists, this group focuses primarily on consumption-related activities. In many other ways, they are similar to the cosmetologists, in terms of perspective on the socioeconomic origins of environmental problems. But there is a greater knowledge of the extent of environmental problems, and the physical processes that directly affect the urban environment. For example, a prime example of their activity would be glass, paper, or aluminum can recycling. Unlike the cosmetologists, these participants understand that incineration or compacting or sludge dispersal is not the "final" solution for waste disposal. Indeed, many of them recognize that concentration of such waste often exacerbates the problem, since this may mean an overload on the local water system, air flows, or open land quality and availability. They recognize the potential in the application of the Law of Conservation of Matter (and Energy) through the social organization of recycling programs. Thus the aim is to transform "waste" into "usable material," rather than merely disposing of waste into an environmental "sink," and accepting the *social* definition of waste.[23]

Unfortunately, they share with the cosmetologists a great deal of naïveté and limited worldviews. They do not attempt to locate the source of the waste in the areas of production, or at a later stage, in the realm of consumer preferences (and lack of consumer sovereignty). Programs are organized on a local basis, with no carryover to regional or national groups, in many cases. Moreover, they often fail to appreciate the economics of recycling, thereby permitting (indeed, encouraging) producers to gain excessive profits from recycling procedures, e.g., using volunteer community labor to man recycling stations, and perhaps even to transport the recycled material directly (or through municipal agencies) to the packaging factory. Though some municipal agencies have utilized producer payments for support of costs of transportation and allocation of space for recycling material storage, there has been little or no attempt to evaluate objectively the profit margins of producers in resale of the recycled material. Furthermore, many of these meliorist action groups are in part supported by these same producers, a point which critics frequently stress.[24]

On an individual level, participants engage in directing their own waste products (glass bottles and jars, aluminum drink containers, old newspapers) to recycling areas. At the collective level, they may help to set up such recycling stations, contacting producers or other purchasers of recyclable material, engaging in negotiations for sites, manning these sites, and providing community publicity for such activities. Most communities now have such "Citizens for a Better Environment" types of organization, usually created for such specific recycling types of activity.

The cosmetologists and the meliorists may both be placed in the laissez-faire, grassroots, or populist sociopolitical orientation. They share a faith in aggregated *voluntary* action, both on their own part and on the part of the local citizenry. At the upper limit, they may attempt to negotiate with local elites (political and economic) to gain support for their advertising or recycling programs, but with only the vaguest self-definition of an "interest group." By and large their self-view is one of interlocuter, attempting to *coordinate* or *organize* the *preexisting* proto-environmental orientations of the population. There is some differentiation made by many of these groups on a social class basis, but this is mainly of the superficial type. For example, cosmetologists may observe that the poor "litter" more, in that they observe greater waste in poor areas (never questioning the differentials in sanitary department service in poor and affluent areas of the city). Likewise, the meliorists may reason that a greater effort is required to recycle disposable materials from poorer areas, because of communication barriers, lack of auto transportation, etc. (again, never probing beyond this level of observation for alternative explanations of poverty, other than lack of skills, etc.). It is likely that prior movement experiences have been quite limited for much of this group, although the objectives of civil rights and other movements may have been supported.

(c) Reformists. This is the first group which begins to consider both the consumption and production aspects of environmental decay. In addition, they are generally more knowledgeable about the physical-biological aspects of environmental processes, as contrasted with the cosmetologists and many of the meliorists. For example, in considering a glass recycling program, such groups may question the environmental economics (as well as the standard economics), on an environmental-social cost-benefit basis. That is, they might weigh the energy costs of melting silica for glass, distributing the glass, then crushing the glass and remelting it for a second use, as against the multiple-use of returnable bottles (which may make twenty to twenty-five trips) from a single melting operation. Obviously, the information required to make such assessments is detailed and requires considerable expertise and organizational skill to use and obtain. Yet this is clearly the direction in which societies will ultimately have to go, to maximize the protection of the environment.[25]

In addition to gathering and analyzing such detailed environmental and production data, however, such reformist groups engage quite self-consciously in a variety of lobbying activities, as special-interest groups.[26] They tend to be the groups that attend public hearings at local, state, and even national levels. They mount the campaigns against particular producers, or classes of producers, that provide products which are degrading of the environment in their production stage and/or their final-use stage. And finally, they also engage in consumer education campaigns. Perhaps the most notable success such groups have had is in the phosphate-detergent campaign. Taking as a starting point the evidence that high phosphate levels of water promote the rapid growth of algae, which subsequently die and absorb a lake's oxygen supply (eutrophication process), they have engaged in a multi-tiered environmental action. This has included the chemical analysis of major detergents (often with findings quite different from manufacturers' analyses), the publication of findings and circulation to the public newspapers, supermarket shopping areas, etc. And simultaneously, they have brought pressure to bear on local political administrations to ban high-phosphate detergents, with success in at least two states. They have argued with city officials on a hard economic basis, rather than simply playing the "moral environmentalist" role, and have varied their level of arguments according to the various audiences they have approached. Similar kinds of activities have taken shape in the areas of auto pollution, highway construction, land fill operations, construction of nuclear power facilities, and so on. Many of these are activities that are properly termed "participatory technology,"[27] emphasizing the use of technology in the production phase of economic activity.

Unlike the cosmetologists and the meliorists, the reformists have not restricted themselves to a grassroots movement, arousing consumer ire and changing their buying behavior. Rather, they have recognized that in many areas, there is in fact little "consumer sovereignty" in terms of environmentally benign alternative products. Hence their public and political pressures on the major producers (e.g., Campaign GM),[28] along with the somewhat less effective consumer boycotts. Along with the greater appreciation for the "web of nature" (which they share with the meliorists), they have developed the beginnings of a similar appreciation for the "web of society," which intersects with the former. In part this stems from the high level of professional and technical skills possessed by this group, and very likely from the prior movement experiences of many of the participants. This joint grassroots-elitist strategy is highly reminiscent of the civil rights campaigns as well as the later antiwar and antipoverty campaigns, reflecting such movement experiences and conventional local political experience for some participants. In the Chicago area, the most prominent experienced group is the "Businessmen for the Public Interest," but other inexperienced groups such as "Northwestern Students for a Better Environment" have been equally active and effective.

On an individual level, many participants attempt to reduce some elements of consumption (e.g., substituting bicycles for auto transport, buying unleaded gasoline, low-phosphate detergents, etc.), in addition to proselytizing for particular campaigns and a wider environmental worldview of colleagues, friends, voluntary associations, etc. At the collective level, strategies vary widely, from simple media advertising to major journalistic efforts, creation of new action organizations, provision of technical expertise, Congressional and local lobbying activities, etc. Clearly the most conspicuous representative of this movement is Ralph Nader, whose background is *consumer* protection, rather than *environmental* protection activity. Others in this area include Barry Commoner and Paul Ehrlich, though none of these individuals can be adequately classified in the present scheme.

(d) Radicals. The differences between radicals and reformers may be termed differences of degree, or of kind, depending on the observer. Whereas reformists stress the need for control and revision, radical environmentalists aim at total restructuring of the social and especially the economic system. This varies from a direct attack on capitalist economic systems per se, to a rather more wide-reaching critique of industrial society in general (although with a heavy emphasis on the United States). This is the only group which ever engages in an *international* scale of analysis, in large part because the backgrounds of many of these participants is in the antiwar movement, with its internationalist "Third World" orientation, and thus links resource utilization in the United States to an economic imperialism which systematically depletes resources of most underdeveloped countries.

One major difference between reformists and radicals is the former's emphasis on *means* of achieving environmental quality, or procedures for implementing goals, whereas radical environmentalists concentrate on the social-philosophical goals of a society in adaptation to the natural environment, and the necessary major value shifts required in America to move in this direction. A harsher evaluation might be that radical actions are utopian, unlike the more pragmatic reformist directives. But the radical perspective also indicates the fundamental incompatability of an expansive industrial society with the preservation of environmental quality. The role of government (including regulatory agencies) is viewed differently by the two groups as well: whereas reformists see government as the major lever of environmental change, imperfect as governmental organization may be, radicals see little opportunity for mediation by the government. What is interesting about this contrast is that it reflects a very different orientation, on the part of the two groups, to the degree of "representativeness" of government (urban, state, and national): reformists see governments as insufficiently representative of the "public interest," whereas radicals see governments as all too representative of the "false consciousness" of the producers and consumers in America. Hence the stronger emphasis on grassroots participation on the reformists' part, as contrasted with the cynicism of the radical environmentalists, who view themselves as a handful of "true believers."[29]

Because of the emphasis on goals rather than means, the radical environmental movement is highly fractionated. On an individual level, the range is from "alternative life styles," involving low levels of material consumption, concentrating on a Zen- or Maoist-like discipline and concentration on environmental impact, to a much more active political strategy (a range not unlike that among blacks, from "cultural nationalism" to civil rights activism).[30] At a collective level, there is a similar range, from urban and rural communes to direct and disruptive strategies at the political and economic level.[31] Groups such as the Council on Economic Priorities attempt to gather heretofore secret company data on pollution, along with data on other major social problems. For the radicals, there is little meaning in separating environmental problems from the "corporate" or "industrial state," and the inequalities therein. Although there may be periodic cooperation with reformist groups, by and large radical environmentalists presume that such groups share the "false consciousness" of the bulk of American society, and that their efforts are bound to have little impact.[32] Where such cooperation has occurred, the results have often been important: the reformists maintain their demands, while remaining "negotiable," and the pressures created by radical tactics often drive industrialists or politicians into serious negotiation with reformist groups. In part, the suspicion of "Establishment politics" derives from the considerable experience many of the radicals have had in the anti-Vietnam movement (and some civil rights experience).

Some consequences of environmental actions

One of the major criticisms leveled at "environmentalists" by radical political groups is the political and social naïveté of the former. Since the movement developed at precisely the peak of the anti-Vietnam movement, there has been deep suspicion that this "unifying" movement was a distraction (although this conveniently ignores the rise of environmental movements in most European societies not directly involved in the war), created with the connivance of politicians and major industrialists. Unfortunately, the activities of several of the groups listed appear supportive of such a claim; in particular, cosmetologists and meliorists generally engage in activities at least cosponsored by major industries (or local political administrations). And politicians at all levels have used such actions and concerns to distract attention from issues like the Vietnam war, in fact. Although the direct effects of such activity may be positive and highly visible, this very visibility has much greater side-effects, runs the radical argument. It provides some direct evidence that "things are getting better," thereby increasing the public's receptivity to the "eco-pornography" of the major producers.[33] In particular, the cosmetologists and meliorists themselves are most susceptible to this perception, both by predisposition and by the fact that the "success" of their activity has resulted from the cooperative nature of the major producers (and politicians). From this, it follows that there is a reinforcement of a perception that "we're all part of the problem, and will all work together for a solution."

It would thus not be unfair to state that cosmetologists and meliorists find their expectations *confirmed* by their environmental action. That is, they continue to believe that environmental problems are solvable, that they are capable of solution at minor costs and minor inconvenience, and that there is no opposition in this country to environmental improvement. Whether this is viewed as a Machiavellian manipulation of such groups by economic elites, or merely a self-fulfilling prophecy depends on one's perspective.

Turning to reformist groups, a rather different picture appears to emerge. For those who have emerged from considerable experience in the civil rights, antiwar, or antipoverty programs and movements, the environmental problem arena is seen as a resultant of the same processes as have been observed previously, at least among the major elite groups. Venality, shortsightedness, corruption, self-interest—all of these operate in the environmental impact area as well as for other major social issues. However, for those with little or no background in direct political action, the environmental area is fraught with new social learning. For social inequalities enter into environmental effects, in spite of the early reductionist perspective of our "one environment, shared by all." Indeed, the question for many sensitive reformists has become "who owns the environment?" Who is the "public" for whom the "public interest" is being served by current political and economic policies?

At the very least, the discoveries of many reformists include the following: (a) a new awareness of the complexity of society, and the corresponding complexity of the ecosystem—on the one hand, a new insight into the meaning of the "division of labor in society" (without the necessary integration, at many points), and its consequences for the "web of nature"; (b) discovery of the power, and powerlessness, of grassroots organizations—a painful awareness of the efforts required to mobilize citizenry, and the limits on responsiveness of elites even to a mobilized group; (c) a recognition of the close interrelationships (power elite) among key economic and political elites in most metropolitan areas, so that the analytic distinction between economic and political power becomes highly blurred; (d) a growth in awareness of social inequalities in the socioeconomic structure, and therefore of some of the causes of the resulting differentials in the evaluation of environmental problems; (e) institutional control—the degree to which the current economic and political policies have been reinforced by a variety of institutions, from educational to religious, raises the question as to where the control of the major social institutions in America *in fact* rests.[34] Some of these issues will be discussed below in greater detail.

Finally, for the radical groups, their activity has tended to reinforce their worldview, concerning the basic materialism and undemocratic nature of American society.[35] Since their concentration has been on ends, not means, this is both understandable and comforting for such groups. The response may in many cases simply be a form of retreatism, into a communal (often rural rather than urban) life style, and a separation from the degraded environment—or at least, a perception of such isolation.

On the basis of the above formulation, it appears to be the reformists that have been transformed most markedly in the environmental action field. These are the "liberals" of the environmental action movement, and like the many liberal political groups in other social arenas, they have been most affected, and most bifurcated, by their experiences. For many, it has led to intense politicization and a Marxist socioeconomic worldview, while for others the response has been a form of retreatism, similar to the radical response, with one difference: the liberal retreatism is more often a return to the status quo, not to an alternative life style.[36]

Some causes of nonparticipation
in the environmental movement

Thus far, the analysis of the environmental movement has been phrased in terms of the major participants in the movement. Clearly, such a frame of reference is highly limited, since it ignores the vast numbers of Americans who have not directly participated in any movement actions. Since the majority of participants in the movement appear to be middle class,[37] it would appear that the most significant social groups here are the poor (or at least the less affluent), and the most affluent classes. Although participation in any voluntary association has repeatedly been demonstrated to be strongly associated with the social class of the individual,[38] the environmental movement appears to be somewhat of an exception to this sociological rule of thumb. For there appears to be an underrepresentation of the rich in the movement, along with the "normal" low levels of participation of the poor (and most conspicuously, the black poor).[39] What are the likely explanations for this distribution?

In order to approach an explanation, the social and economic realities of environmental degradation need to be clarified. Some approach to this has been made in the discussion of reformist and radical environmental groups, but the issues need to be clarified further. We need to start by first differentiating between the total impact of a social group on the environment, and the "per capita" or individual contribution. The latter appears most appropriate here, since we are concerned with the reasons why *individuals* of a given social class are more likely not to participate in the environmental movement, rather than explaining the distribution of total environmental impact of a social *class.*

If we discuss environmental impacts from and on individuals of a given social class, one useful framework is a general "cost-benefit" approach, a standard tool of economists and increasingly used for a variety of evaluation schemes. At the outset of the environmental movement, a serious attempt was made by a variety of politicians and industrialists to infuse the movement with the following assumption: Regardless of what the net costs of environmental degradation are, this same net cost is borne equally by all citizens. And strange as it may seem, this element of social and political propaganda held sway for some considerable period in the movement—and still does, for the cosmetologists and the meliorists at the very least. Why intelligent and cynical observers of social reality ever seriously adhered to such a preposterous position is a question which cannot be readily answered here. Among other postulated explanations, the most important one appears to be the extreme division of American society at the start of the movement, and the widespread quest for the elusive "national unity" via a new "national purpose" (especially one that was "constructive," unlike the Vietnam war).

Given that no social scientist, on the basis of decades of evidence of social inequalities in the United States, could accept the equality of citizens of various social classes with regard to any issue, what were (and are) the underlying realities? If we turn to costs of environmental degradation, the following appears to be an accurate statement: regardless of the particular cost dimension examined, environmental costs to the individual are consistently higher for the poor than for the more affluent. Whether in terms of air pollution (higher in central city areas, where high concentrations of poor reside), water pollution (more severe in high-density areas, again where the poor reside), or land pollution (impact of DDT spraying is most severe for migrant farm laborers, for example), the poor are in a position of entrapment.[40] That is, they generally have little freedom to move away from areas of highest pollution which have, in part at least, *become* undesirable because of pollution. This is true for the familiar reasons of economic and racial discrimination, leading to a poor (and in many cases black) central city, with middle- and upper-class white suburban rings surrounding it. Though it is by no means universally true that all types of environmental decay are most severe in the central city, it is certainly true that the poor suffer from whatever metropolitan-areawide degradation exists to a greater extent than do the more affluent suburbanites. Even if we were to discount the differential possibility of relocating within the metropolitan area as irrelevant, the more affluent still possess considerably more resources to seek recreation, a second home, health resorts, and other amenities to alleviate the persistent effects of environmental decay. And, if we project current environmental decay to the apocalypse that many forecast, one would have to be incredibly naïve to believe that such a catastrophe would strike uniformly across social lines. If air deteriorates, oxygen is available to the more affluent; if water deteriorates, water purifiers or bottled water will go to the highest bidders; and the choicest land already belongs to the corporate elite![41] Short of massive civil insurrection and the revolt of the military against the "military-industrial" complex, in other words, the environmental decay will continue to strike hardest against the least affluent.[42]

Turning to the *benefits* that have accrued over the years from systematic free use of the environmental resources of air and water, again we find significant differentiation. It is true that producers produce for the consumers in a society, but it is equally true that in a society with unequal income distribution the levels of consumption differ markedly. Thus the most affluent, the economic elite of America, have benefitted in a twofold manner from such systematic environmental exploitation: in terms of their roles as producers (and major stockholders),[43] they have reaped enormous profit levels from industrial and related enterprises. And second, as the largest consumers, they have benefitted from the lower costs of consumer goods to a substantially greater extent than those with lower levels of consumption.[44]

If we view our society in a simple-minded tripartite division of lower, middle and upper classes, the following cost-benefit picture emerges. The lower classes have maximum costs and minimum benefits from environmental decay. The upper classes have minimum cost and maximum benefits. It may be assumed that the middle classes are intermediate on both issues: they incur moderate levels of cost (although some might argue that their costs are closer to those of the lower classes than to the upper), and moderate levels of benefit (although again, their level may be somewhat closer to the lower than the upper classes). The middle-class position may be closer to that of the poor than the rich because of the similar dependence of each on labor market situations, and the much smaller differentials in income and tax burdens in the former comparison. In terms of *net* cost-benefit, then, the lower classes have maximal *net* costs, and the upper classes have minimal *net* costs (or maximal net benefits, put more directly), with the middle classes intermediate.

Accepting the above as a rough indication of the ordering of the major social classes, the reason for the nonparticipation of the upper classes is clear: they are merely acting so as to maximize their net benefits, by continuing to use environmental systems for profit maximization. Yet on the basis of the above, we have failed to account for the low participation of the poor or lower classes in the movement, in addition to the middle class component of the movement. One element is needed to complete this explanation: the control over social and economic organization of the United States by the urban-industrial elites.

Whether we examine environmental improvement suggestions, from one or another movement (especially reformist) and nonmovement groups, the one commonality is the element of cost incurred. This is true whether the path to pollution abatement[45] is through legislation—via tax credits, fines, direct subsidies; or through litigation—fines, delays in construction, shut-downs, etc. In the case of "carrot" (positive) incentives, some group of taxpayers and/or consumers ultimately foots the bill, in the form of taxes paid, or increased prices. For "stick" (disincentive) actions, increased prices and decreased employment are frequently the concomitants. Given the power of the industrial elite to influence the legislative processes at every level, from gathering of information[46] to directing campaign contributions for "sensitive" candidates, it is clear that legislation will have the most pro-elite orientation that money can purchase—and even more so, in the case of enforcement.[47] The legal powers of the corporation are wide enough to discourage and delay enforcement of environmental legislation interminably, as reformists have been painfully learning over the past five years.[48] Yet the costs of fines, legal costs, abatement equipment, etc., must ultimately be borne by some group. And it is here that the lower classes are apprehensive, and rightfully so, to a considerable extent. Whether as consumer, taxpayer (including every level of tax, from municipal to federal), aid recipient, or employee, they already bear an economically regressive burden; there is little reason for them not to expect the anticipated environmental improvement costs to fall disproportionately on their shoulders.[49]

Indeed, it should be stressed, the realities have been demonstrated even at this early date. For example, the increased electricity rates granted one Illinois power company recently, which were contingent on the company's installing substantially improved air pollution abatement equipment, have had this impact. Any price increase in a necessary consumer good like electricity provides a disproportionately large impact on the poor—a standard inflationary situation. As environmental groups successfully take on other industrial titans, similar inflationary effects will be felt, and their impact on the poor has been well documented by economists.

Hence the resistance of the poor to the environmental movement,[50] along with resistance of the rich. Is this the answer to our earlier hypothetical question "who owns the environment?" Furthermore, what does this suggest for the future of the environmental movement? One gloomy, though by no means unlikely, prospect is for the emergence of a coalition between the poor and the rich, to sabotage the environmental activists. Indeed, the reactions of the Chairman of the Board of General Motors bears a striking similarity to those of many of the leaders of the poor. . . . Can it be that a new "war on poverty" rhetoric will emerge, with the casuality of the war being the environment? (And with poverty left undiminished, to serve as a rallying cry in future threats to the elite?) Can it really be that the tangible and intangible environment of the United States is so differently perceived by these several social classes that such a result is possible? One need merely to contrast the recent coverage of environmental problems by the editors of *Fortune,* on the one (and upper-class) hand, and those of *Ramparts,*[51] on the other. A search of the *Fortune* reports reveals very little assessment of differential benefits from environmental degradation, and equally little concern with differential allocation of costs of environmental improvement. The *Ramparts* approach focuses almost exclusively on precisely these differentials, and the related issues of social justice and environmental control. It continuously confronts and attacks the simplistic (and self-serving) view of *Fortune* that environmental control be conceived of as a "national mission," arguing that the differential control and concern *within* the "nation" is the crucial lever for environmental change.

Looking forward

We have seen that there are very different answers to the question "where do we go from here?" Recent environmental events have, in fact, largely ignored the crucial social dimensions of this question. What legislation has been enacted has been relatively weak either in its legislative form or in the actual enforcement of such legislation. Yet there have been *some* important environmental controls initiated nonetheless, which have short and long term effects, e.g., in sulfur dioxide emissions from coal, some detergent phosphate reductions.

But, what is virtually universally true of current legislation is that it ignores the questions of social justice that have been raised. There is no provision in such legislation for apportioning costs of environmental improvement on any basis other than the "market," in spite of a growing awareness among some environmentalists of the social-class differentials in the cost-benefit parameters. If we project into the future the legislative trends of the past four to five years, two things become apparent: (1) there will be no provision whatsoever for allocating pollution costs on the basis of *cumulative* benefits derived by the upper classes from environmental decay; and (2) it is almost as unlikely that such costs will be allocated without the upper classes deriving *present* and *future* benefits from environmental improvement.

This second point requires some clarification. If an automobile manufacturer installs pollution emission equipment on an auto, then the manufacturing cost of such equipment is certain to be passed on to the consumer. However, it is also likely that the "normal" margin of profit the company (especially the major stockholders) obtains will be applied to this equipment, as well as the rest of the auto. Thus the company in fact makes an additional profit on the pollution equipment. Here industrialists might be expected to show less reluctance to change (although with a careful eye on demand curves), since they will profit from pollution abatement as they profited from pollution! But consumers, especially lower income groups, will be more likely to be adverse to such courses of environmental improvement, for the major beneficiaries of such action are the upper classes, and those bearing the costs are the middle and lower classes.

An even more subtle example is that of "regulated utilities," e.g., electric and gas companies. Here companies apply for a higher rate, in order to install new plant pollution abatement equipment. But this new equipment is now part of the company's *capital,* which is thereby increased, and at the next rate hearing, another rate increase is likely to be approved so that the "fair rate of return" (i.e., profit divided by *capital*) allowed the utility by law will be maintained. Thus consumers, and especially the poor, will have borne a double burden by this "normal" process of rate regulation, all in the name of environmental quality, but largely benefiting the major shareholders of utilities.

These examples and projections afford a gloomy outlook, as well as an explanation for the current lack of substantial environmental improvement. The major controllers of industry are already maximizing their net benefits from the environment, and have little to gain; the middle and especially the lower classes can expect to bear the main costs of environmental improvement. Hence, aside from the most active environmentalists, there is little constituency for environmental improvement. What changes have occurred and will occur are going to increase the burdens on the middle and lower classes, while permitting a continuation of profit maximization by the upper classes. Thus the likely outcome, at best, is a substitution of social exploitation for environmental exploitation . . . Only a well-organized, politically skilled environmental movement that will devote its resources to informing the larger public of these threats can intercede in this "normal market process" occurring.

An alternative scenario

Lest we end on a Jeremaic note,[52] some alternative paths to environmental quality should be noted. If we accept as a premise that the reformist group holds the greatest pragmatic promise for improving the environment of the over-two-hundred-million in the United States, then what changes need to occur to prevent the success of the possible anti-environmental coalition of rich and poor cited above or the substitution of social for environmental exploitation? At the outset, the harsh socioeconomic realities underlying the nonparticipation of these two groups must be recognized and dealt with, seriously and consistently. On the one side, the likely and powerful opposition of the elite to any "meaningful" program of action should be anticipated, and planned for. By "meaningful," I mean a program for environmental improvement which will not be paid for disproportionately (or even proportionately, for that matter) by the poor. Industrialists may overcome their natural inertia and accept programs which lay the burdens on the door of the middle class and poor—but that cannot be construed as a "meaningful" environmental program, since the resulting *social environmental* degradation may far outweigh any gain in the *physical* environment, and the "quality of life" may suffer irreparable damages.

Therefore, any proposal for environmental action must clearly incorporate the elements of social justice, and there must be a commitment of the middle-class proponents to *explicitly* build in such considerations. This is a political necessity, as well as a moral prerequisite, since the coalition of rich and poor is sufficient to doom any proposal. But the coalition of the poor and the middle class *may* sufficiently offset the existing political imbalance to provide passage of significant proposals.[53]

One example, in closing, neatly illustrates the potential involved in a meaningful environmental movement. In the Chicago area, a program for paper recycling was recently established.[54] This involved the collection of newspapers from middle- and upper-class white suburban areas, and the transportation of the newsprint to a black community development organization in Chicago, which packages and sells the newsprint to paper companies for recycling. Here is a situation in which the environmental movement had provided the impetus for newspaper transport, on the part of middle- and upper-class individuals, to a point where lower-class groups benefitted from the operation. On one level, one can dismiss this cynically as a trivial operation—yet it contains all the elements of a meaningful environmental movement. For this action represents a form of income transfer from more to less affluent groups,[55] while contributing to the preservation of trees and lowering water pollution (in newspaper production).

How many such scenarios can we write? We will only discover this through trying; the stakes certainly merit the effort.

Notes

1. Among other sources, environmental action groups are listed in the *Guide to Organized Environmental Efforts* (Washington, D.C.: Environmental Resources, Inc., 1971). A brief list and references also appear in *Earth Day—the Beginning* (New York: Arno Press/New York Times, 1970), edited by the National Staff of Environmental Action. The Illinois List was compiled for the Illinois Science Related Information Center (ISRIC), an affiliate of the national Scientists' Institute for Public Information (SIPI).

2. A summary of public opinion polls from the 1960—70 period supports this contention: see Cecile Trop and Leslie L. Roos, Jr., "Public Opinion and the Environment," pp. 52—63 in Leslie L. Roos, Jr. (ed.), *The Politics of Ecosuicide* (New York: Holt, Rinehart & Winston, Inc., 1971).

3. *Ibid.;* and John C. Maloney and Lynn Slovonsky, "The Pollution Issue: A Survey of Editional Judgments" (p. 64), in Roos (ed.), *op. cit.*

4. Trop and Roos, *op. cit.*

5. This address by James M. Roche to the Executive Club of Chicago is excerpted in "Defending Big Business," *The New York Times,* April 21, 1971 (p. 47).

6. For England, an interesting history of pollution and its opponents is contained in Jack Bregman and Sergei Lenormand, *The Pollution Paradox* (New York: Spartan Books, 1966), chapter 1; and William Wise, *Killer Smog* (New York: Audubon/Ballantine, 1968), pp. 8–63. A cynical interpretation is provided by Alexander King, "The Environmental Bandwagon, And Some Other Matters Concerning the Future of the Human Race," pp. 189–201 in Clifton Fadiman and Jean White, *Ecocide . . . And Thoughts Toward Survival* (Palo Alto, California: James E. Freel and Associates, 1971).

7. Some discussion of the peaks and troughs of environmental concern is found (for England) in Wise, *op. cit.*, and more recently (for the U.S.) in Trop and Roos, *op. cit.*

8. Although many activists, in their truncated sense of history, conveniently forget this, there was considerable precedence in the 1950s for nonviolent protest. Not only labor unions, but a variety of interest groups, including the unemployed, had used most of the *techniques* of the civil rights movement earlier (and examples abound in other societies, such as India, France, Italy), with the possible exception of the sit-in (and there had earlier been similar union activity in plants). What was unique about the movement was the *goal*—a societal, humanitarian objective, not the self-interested activity of earlier periods.

9. For example, note the decline in *New York Times* coverage of the environment, Trop and Roos, *op. cit.*, p. 57. A succinct statement on this is I. F. Stone, "Con Games," in Environmental Action Staff (ed.), *Earth Day—The Beginning, op. cit.*

10. The classic statement on "social mobilization" is Karl Deutsch, "Social Mobilization and Political Development," *American Political Science Review* 55 (September 1961), 493–511. "Participatory mobilization" here refers to the self-conscious pattern of action involved in social movements, a special form of mobilization process.

11. This concept emerged in David Sills, "The Succession of Goals," pp. 146–59 in Amitai Etzioni (ed.), *Complex Organizations: A Sociological Reader* (New York: Holt, Rinehart & Winston, Inc., 1960). [The larger study, from which this was drawn, is *The Volunteers* (Glencoe, Illinois: The Free Press, 1957)]. In situations like this, the survival of the organization becomes transformed from an instrumental objective to a consummatory one—and the organizational leadership frequently devises a new set of "goals" to rationalize the continuation of the organization.

12. Rachel Carson, *The Silent Spring* (Boston: Houghton Mifflin Company, 1962).

13. David C. Miller, "Ecology—The Last Fad," pp. 303–310 in Fred Carvell and Max Tadlock (eds.), *It's Not Too Late . . .* (Beverly Hills: Glencoe Press, 1971). Miller lists six rationalizations (p. 304) for "choosing not to be an active agent" in the formation of the future.

14. Groups like the Sierra Club, whose broader interests in environmental (as opposed to simply *wilderness*) preservation has expanded its membership phenomenally in recent years, from 15,000 in 1960 to over 85,000 in 1970 [*Congressional Quarterly Almanac* (Washington, D.C.: Congressional Quarterly Service, January 30, 1970), p. 282]. Part of the recent success of such groups has been their coalition with other active environmental interest groups, as suggested by Daniel R. Grant, "Carrots, Sticks, and Consensus," in Lynton K. Caldwell (ed.), *Environmental Studies—Papers on the Politics of Public Administration of Man-Environment Relationships* (Bloomington: Institute of Public Administration, Indiana University, 1967). A brief history of the government's role in conservation is David C. Coyle, *Conservation: An American Story of Conflict and Accomplishment* (New Brunswick: Rutgers University Press, 1957).

15. The most notable example being the late J. I. Rodale, author of the standard American works on organic gardening and farming, and publisher in recent years of such environmental journals as the *Environmental Action Bulletin* and its predecessor, the *Eco-Bulletin.*

16. See, for example, the growth in membership of organizations like the Sierra Club (note 14).

17. One of the many examples is the U. S. Forest Service: see Luther J. Carter, "Timber Management: Improvement Implies New Land-Use Policies," *Science* 170 (December 25, 1970), 1387–1390.

18. Numerous examples have been treated: see, for example, Jeremy Main, "Conservationists at the Barricades," pp. 167–180; and Judson Gooding, "Victory on San Francisco Bay," pp. 181–188, both in *The Environment: A National Mission for the Seventies* (New York: Perennial Library/Harper and Row, 1969), by the editors of *Fortune.*

19. Characteristic of this position is the recent statement of President Nixon, pp. 11–13 in *The Environment: . . . (Fortune* editors), *op. cit.*

20. A simple and readable explanation of these principles is provided in Kenneth E. Boulding, "The Economics of the Coming Spaceship Earth," in Henry Jarrett (ed.), *Environmental Quality in a Growing Economy.* (Baltimore: The Johns Hopkins Press, 1966).

21. One pessimistic critique of such demands is Beryl L. Crowe, "The Tragedy of the Commons Revisited," *Science* 166 (November 28, 1969), pp. 1103–1107.

22. This typology draws in part on a much earlier classification by Robert K. Merton, "Social Structure and Anomie," chapter IV in his *Social Theory and Social Structure* (New York: The Free Press, 1957), revised edition.

23. For an interesting contrast of the U. S. and China on the uses of waste, see Leo A. Orleans and R. P. Suttmeier, "The Mao Ethic and Environmental Quality," *Science* 170 (December 11, 1970), pp. 1173–1176.

24. A brief example from the *Washington Post* of April 23, 1970, is reprinted (p. 133) in Environmental Action's *Earth Day—The Beginning, op. cit.*

25. Some general overviews on this are contained in Boulding, *op. cit.;* Eugene P. Odum, "The Strategy of Ecosystem Development," *Science* 164 (April 18, 1969), 262–270; and J. Alan Wagar, "Growth vs. the Quality of Life," *Science* 168 (June 5, 1970), 1179–1184, among others.

26. David Brower, who left the leadership of the Sierra Club to found Friends of the Earth, was one of the long-time conservationists who recognized the need for such direct political action—and thus formed the Friends as a non-tax-exempt organization in order to carry out such lobbying activity in a direct (and hopefully) effective manner.

27. This term was used by James D. Carroll ["Participatory Technology," *Science* 171 (February 19, 1971), 647–653] to describe recent activist efforts, as well as to advocate future movements. The strained (and tangential) relationships of ecologists to technology are discussed in William Murdoch and Joseph Connell, "The Ecologist's Role and the Non-solution of Technology," pp. 47–62 in Fadiman and White, *op. cit.*

28. A brief summary of "Campaign GM" and its pressures on universities (and other institutions) appears in Luther J. Carter, "Campaign GM: Corporation Critics Seek Support of Universities," *Science* 168 (April 24, 1970), 452–455.

29. A representative statement by the Berkeley Ecology Center, entitled "Four Changes," is reprinted in Garrett de Bell (ed.), *The Environmental Handbook* (New York: Ballantine Books, 1970), pp. 323–333. See also Katherine Barkley and Steve Weissman, "The Eco-Establishment," pp. 15–24 in *Eco-Catastrophe* (San Francisco: Canfield Press, 1970), edited by *Ramparts* staff.

30. *Ibid.*

31. A variety of "underground" ecology periodicals (such as *Clear Creek*) provide a sense of this range of action, as does the editorial by the *Ramparts* editors, pp. vi–xii in *Eco-Catastrophe, op. cit.,* and the report by Sol Stern, "Rural Renewal: Trouble in Paradise," pp. 146–158 in *ibid.,* citing the conflict between radical environmentalists and the "consumer society."

32. Barkley and Weissman, *op. cit.,* among others. For a counterview, see Kenneth E. F. Watt, "Whole Earth," p. 5–25 in Environmental Action, *Earth Day—The Beginning, op. cit.*

33. Jerry Mander (*sic*), "The Media and Environmental Awareness," (pp. 253–262), and Thomas Turner, "Eco-Pornography, or How To Spot an Ecological Phony," (pp. 263–267), both in *The Environmental Handbook, op. cit.,* deal with this.

34. Some of the reasons for the lack of awareness of many of these social structural inequalities are discussed in Norbert Wiley, "America's Unique Class Politics: The Interplay of the Labor, Credit and Commodity Markets," *American Sociological Review* 32 (August 1967): 525–541. An example of the new awareness is in Harvey Molotch, "Santa Barbara: Oil in the Velvet Playground," pp. 84–105 in *Eco-Catastrophe, op. cit.*

35. One reductionist approach has been the attribution of the problem to "cultural" values, specifically the Judeo-Christian ethic [Lynn White, Jr., "The Historical Roots of Our Ecologic Crisis," *Science* 155 (March 10, 1967), 1203–1207]. An attack on this position and some of the simplistic radical critiques is found in Lewis W. Moncrief, "The Cultural Basis for Our Environmental Crisis," *Science* 170 (October 30, 1970), 508–512.

36. Many of these differences in responses have been predicted—Marx discusses the outcomes and strategies of scientists, but his observations are applicable to the entire environmental movement. Leo Marx, "American Institutions and Ecological Ideals," *Science* 170 (November 27, 1970): 945–952.

37. Though no systematic inventory of the activists exists, the results of many public opinion polls point to the middle class as having the greatest concern for environmental degradation. For a national report, see Trop and Roos, "Public Opinion . . .", *loc. cit.;* a recent survey of the Chicago area supports this—see Calvin P. Bradford, *et al.,* "Public Attitudes and Social Trends in Chicago: An Annual Inventory," Center for Urban Affairs, Northwestern University, (April 1971), especially pp. 11–15.

38. A summary of such findings appears in Arnold M. Rose, *Sociology: The Study of Human Relations,* second edition (New York: Alfred A. Knopf, 1965), chapter 10.

39. See, among many others, Harold Sprout, "The Environmental Crisis in the Context of American Politics," Center for International Studies, Princeton University (March 1970).

40. A point stressed by many participants in "Earth Day." See the brief (but pointed) observations by Freddie Mae Brown *et al.,* Adam Walinsky, Charles A. Hayes, and others, in *Earth Day—The Beginning, op. cit.*

41. Peter Barnes, "Land Reform in America," *The New Republic* (June 5, 12, and 19, 1971).

42. Yet it is the more affluent, or better educated, respondents (though not necessarily the economic elite) who indicate a greater impact of environmental decay on their lives. See Trop and Roos, *op cit.,* pp. 53, 58–59; and *The United States Public Considers Its Environment* (Princeton: American Institute of Public Opinion, February 1969).

43. This is one of the repeated findings in consumer finance surveys: see James N. Morgan, "Contributions of Survey Research to Economics," in Charles Y. Glock (ed.), *Survey Research in the Social Sciences* (New York: Russell Sage Foundation, 1967), especially p. 224.

44. Although it should be noted that consumption of material goods is not perfectly correlated with income, i.e., lower income elasticity of demand at higher income levels.

45. The economics of environmental control have been discussed in many places: for example, Neil H. Jacoby, "Corporations, Government and the Environment: Policy Approaches to a Better Urban America," pp. 169–188 in Fadiman and White, *op. cit.;* Harold Sprout, *op. cit.;* Sanford Rose, "The Economics of Environmental Quality," pp. 65–87 in *The Environment* (Fortune), *op. cit.* A radical critique of the underlying social equity issues is in Martin Gellen, "The Making of a Pollution-Industrial Complex," pp. 73–83 in *Eco-Catastrophe, op. cit.*

46. The extent of industrialists' control over environmental data-collection has recently been indicated: see Vic Reinemer, "Budget Bureau: Do Advisory Panels Have an Industry Bias?" *Science* 169 (July 3, 1970), 36–39.

47. The failure of federal regulatory agencies is a long and sordid history. One recent example is in: Luther J. Carter, "Timber Management: Improvement Implies New Land-Use Policies," *Science* 170 (December 25, 1970): 1387–1390.

48. As reported in Michael Kitzmiller, "Environment and the Law," pp. 149–168 in Fadiman and White, *op. cit.;* and Victor J. Yannacone, "Sue the Bastards," pp. 179–195 in *Earth Day—The Beginning, op. cit.*

49. The most simple and eloquent statement of this position was by the head of the National Welfare Rights Organization: George Wiley, "Ecology and the Poor," pp. 213–216 in *Earth Day—The Beginning, op. cit.* Evidence of public attitudes on taxation and transfer of environmental funds from other areas is found in Trop and Roos, *op. cit.;* and the attitudes (and behavior) of major industrialists are reported in Robert S. Diamond, "What Business Thinks About Its Environment," pp. 55–64 in *The Environment* (Fortune), *op. cit.*

50. Clearly, this is not the only factor for their underrepresentation. Rather, it is a serious compounding effect, over and above the "normal" problems of creating action organizations among the poor. Furthermore, the "failure" of the poor to perceive their pressing environmental problems also contribute to this low participation. Whether this is a perceptual problem (due to lack of contact with particular media sources, etc.) or merely

represents the greater press of problems of health, unemployment, security, etc., on their consciousness is not clear. Bradford *et al., op. cit.,* indicate in their recent survey of the Chicago metropolitan area that for all the *non*environmental problem issues, it is the poor (and/or the black) who perceive the problem is most severe.

51. *The Environment* (Fortune), *op. cit.; Eco-Catastrophe, op. cit.* Industrial-oriented authors frequently cite the need for *growth* to solve environmental *and* social equity problems (Rose, *op. cit.;* Jacoby, *op. cit.*), whereas few radical (or committed reformist) authors take this position. One of the few sociologists taking a stance similar to the *Fortune* perspective is Samuel Z. Klausner, *On Man in His Environment* (San Francisco: Jossey-Bass, Inc., 1971).

52. Akin to that of Anthony d'Amato, "The Politics of Ecosuicide," pp. 10–28 in Roos, *op. cit.,* or Crowe, *op. cit.*

53. A point stressed by Sprout, *op. cit.*

54. This is the STEP (*Save Trees, Eliminate Pollution*) program.

55. A more pessimistic scenario is contained in Arthur Simon, "Battle of Beaufort," *The New Republic* (May 23, 1970), all of the major themes above are represented, and the outcome led to the poor (and black) residents paying for conservation and water quality. The dilemma of community development vs. environmental quality is further illustrated by taking proposals for *de*centralization of urban power (e.g., Irving Louis Horowitz, " 'Separate But Equal': Revolution and Counter-Revolution in the American City," *Social Problems* 17, no. 3 (Winter 1970): 294–312; and projecting the urban environmental outcomes of such proposals. [See pp. 466–485 of this book.]

CHAPTER 8

CONTENTS

CITIES ANd THE fUTURE

Let us begin by agreeing upon the obvious: no one *knows* what the future will bring in any area of life. All we can hope to do, in relation to cities of the future, is study trends which appear in past and present cities and do our best to extend them into the future. Variation occurs, of course, in which trends one selects for attention and what kind of model is used to extend the present—linear, dialectic, curvilinear, or other.

The first decision, the one concerning substantive matters (and also to a certain extent, the change model itself), is usually a value judgment, which in turn is closely related to the sort of training a person has received or, if an activist or utopian, the vision of the future most congenial to his ideology. Thus, for example, many science fiction writers create utopian or dystopian cities in their fiction, depending upon whether the positive or negative mode is dominant in their writing style; but both creations reflect what is usually a common underlying theme: a desire for simplification, for a return to an unalienated state of mankind in which work and living are more closely tied to total units and experiences: the small group, the individually hand-crafted product, nature, and so forth. An example of a negative utopia (dystopia) may be found in Kurt Vonnegut's *Player Piano,* a terrifying view of a totally automated society, specifically an automated city, the mythical "Ilium," New York. Positive utopias abound in the works of men like Robert Heinlein: the noble quest, individual success against the forces of society, the role of good citizen in societies of the future, and so forth.

Insofar as possible, we have tried to gather readings for this final chapter which reflect *realistic* thinking about the future of cities. We do not mean to disparage other kinds of projections as necessarily unrealistic; in fact the world of *Player Piano* could, under certain circumstances, be the future city which Melvin M. Webber discusses in the last article of this chapter. But we sense that predictions or proposals about the future city will be more useful to the student if they are intimately grounded in known or suspected trends in cities of today— the 1970s—especially those in the developed West.

The first selection in this chapter, Jane Jacobs's "Some Patterns of Future Development," is an excellent illustration of this kind of approach—a direct and imaginative extrapolation of trends coupled with her views of the potential health of cities which do or do not correspond to the patterns she predicts. Briefly stated, she argues that manufacturing is inevitably diversifying, that is moving away from a strictly mass-market concept. To the extent a city is fixed in a decaying form of production (e.g., mass production of tractors), it is at the same time part of the establishment (that is, it possesses power currently) and is becoming increasingly irrelevant and possibly unproductive in terms of total growth and change in the economy of the society. At the same time, cities in the forefront because they have newer industries catering to newer, more diversified and specialized markets, especially in the service rather than strictly production orientation toward consumers, will show more positive signs of future economic health; at the same time, these are less powerful than the older, mass-production cities. The real power struggles of the future, according to Jacobs, will be between entrenched and emerging concepts of the economy. At the same time, Jacobs's view is a critique of the mass-society technocrats who have been predicting for so long the eventual elimination of most jobs, including white-collar ones, through automation. Jacobs actually predicts a proliferation of types of work in newer societies which become founded on diversified services and limited production concepts, a trend fully in line with the postindustrial society idea and the apparent development of an incredible array of life styles and specialized needs among the young and, increasingly, their elders.

It is significant that the Nixon administration secured governmental subsidies to shore up the ailing Lockheed Corporation; monies were allocated in 1970 for the Penn Central Railroad. By definition, both industries are powerful, for their economic utility is founded on a technology that has been around for a relatively long time. These companies and industries have intimate ties with the polity and, perhaps more importantly, with American cultural values as they modally exist today. Such activities will be retained long past their economic usefulness because of the companies' power; while newer, more risk-prone industries will try and fail, and perhaps eventually succeed. But in that way the entire economic system will change imperceptibly as more and more risk-takers venture forth.

Thus Jacobs provides for us an analysis of the basic underpinnings of all modern Western cities—the economic process—and by showing how changes are occurring in that base, she enables us to imagine which cities will survive in what ways and, perhaps more importantly, what kind of jobs and social roles we can expect in cities of the future.

"Toward a National Urban Policy," by Daniel P. Moynihan, is a ten-point policy statement about American cities which, if adopted, would at least provide both a focus for and a unifying codification of present federal, state, and local efforts to change and improve urban areas. Note that Moynihan's first and most pressing point concerns the poverty and social isolation of American urban minorities, especially blacks. One suspects that if this alone became the overriding urban policy statement for the United States, and *if* in ten years it could be dealt with substantially, then most other urban problems would become more manageable. Not that other things do not need to be done—environmental pollution and mass transport are only two—but Moynihan's article is less a program statement than a plea for policy and statement of values. Thus, he notes that existing programs and quasi-policies, which inhibit rather than encourage solutions to urban problems, should be changed immediately, for they are incongruent with long-term planning for change. Among these are programs that encourage an imbalance of power in cities, not only among elements of the private sector, but also among the divisions of local government and its services. Thus, many proposed plans for metropolitan government which have been soundly defeated at the polls by suburban residents might stand a better chance if federal and state policies provided strong economic encouragements. After reading Moynihan, one undoubtedly will wonder how cities manage to exist today at all; the answer is that they all exist, but few function well. But we have here the start toward future solutions, written by a man formerly close to the top of the pyramid of power in this society.

The next selection, "Alternative Futures for the American Ghetto," by Anthony Downs, was included for two reasons. First, it concerns the overarching problem mentioned in reference to Moynihan's article: separation and inequality in cities. Second, Downs attacks the problem not at the level of policy or program but by examining several alternative *strategies* for urban ghetto change, alternatives which encompass the broad range of real possibilities and rise above patchwork tactics of the past several years. Downs's discussion is far too involved and broadly based to summarize here. The reader should simply keep in mind that the contributions by Downs and Moynihan are complements to each other, and together provide a fairly coherent overview of what *could* be done in American cities under given circumstances and, by implication, what *will* happen if nothing is done.

The scope of the last selection is quite broad, for Melvin Webber deals with changing technologies, the decreasing emphasis on work, the uses of leisure in public affairs, and finally, planning in an environment of rapid and universal change. His point of view is at times at odds with the Jacobs article, especially on the issue of the withering away of work, for Webber tends to regard automation as more immediately upon us than Jacobs does (or to be more precise, to have a more wide-reaching effect). But Webber's outlook seems, in essence, at least hopeful, although he warns that predicting the future and then planning for it is a risky business. The reader will appreciate how risky after reading his article.

As we started out saying, no one knows or can know the future until he experiences it. But the four articles in Chapter 8 represent some of the best attempts to understand future trends, both from the point of view of prediction and from the perspective of influencing what will happen. For it is our ability to knowledgeably understand urban dynamics that will give rise to our capability to control, and thus to improve, the quality of urban life in the future.

40

JANE JACOBS, Some Patterns of Future Development

We now have in hand all the major processes at work in a growing city economy. First, the city finds in an older city or cities an expanding market for its initial export work, and it builds up a collection of numerous local businesses to supply producers' goods and services to the initial export work. Second, some of the local suppliers of producers' goods and services export their own work. The city builds up an additional collection of local businesses to supply producers' goods and services to the new export work. Some of these new local suppliers take to exporting their own work. The city builds up more local businesses to supply producers' goods and services to them, and so on. The city earns a growing volume and growing diversity of imports.

Third, many of the imports the city has been earning are replaced by goods and services produced locally, a process that causes explosive city growth. The city, at the same time, shifts the composition of its imports. Its local economy grows large (and diverse) in proportion to the volume of the city's exports and imports. Owing to the powerful multiplier effect of the replacement process, the local economy contains room for entirely new kinds of goods and services, that is, goods and services formerly neither imported nor locally produced. Among these can be unprecedented goods and services. The replacement of imports causes total economic activity to expand rapidly. Fourth, the city's greatly enlarged and greatly diversified local economy becomes a potential source of numerous and diversified exports, including many consumer goods and services as well as producers' goods and services, and still other exports built upon local goods and services. The city's exporting organizations arise by (a) adding the export work to other people's local work; (b) adding the export work to different local work of their own; and (c) exporting their own local work. By generating new exports, the city earns more imports. But many of the new exports merely compensate for older exports the city loses through obsolescence of older exports, transplants of some exporting organizations into the rural world, and replacement of its exports by local production in former customer cities.

Jane Jacobs, "Some Patterns of Future Development." From *The Economy of Cities*, by Jane Jacobs. Reprinted by permission of Random House, Inc.

Fifth, from this time on, the city continues to generate new exports and earn imports; replace imports with local production; generate new exports and earn imports; replace imports with local production, and so on.

All of these processes, taken together, compose two interlocking, reciprocating systems; the first triggers off the second. (A diagram correlating the two reciprocating systems appears in Section IV of the Appendix.) If any one process fails, the entire system fails and the city stagnates economically.

Among the producers' goods and services that form in the course of these events are those that supply capital to new goods and services that are forming and growing, as well as to older goods and services. The root process is the adding of new work to older divisions of labor, thus multiplying the divisions of labor, to some of which still newer activities can be added. This underlying process, which I have symbolized as $D + A \rightarrow nD$, makes possible all the others.

The emergence of differentiated production

These processes and the systems they compose are old and predictable, though the goods and services they cast up change and are not necessarily predictable. As the new goods and services emerge, certain dominant patterns of economic organization also change. These are large, gradual and cumulative movements. For example, the dominant form of manufacturing used to be craftwork. This has been succeeded in currently advanced economies by mass production, a sequence, incidentally, which occurs in ancient as well as modern times. Mohenjo-daro and Harappā had their mass-production industries, and cities of the Roman Empire developed mass-produced lamps, pottery, and other utensils. Machines developed in the industrial revolution of the nineteenth century have been strikingly successful means of carrying out mass production, but the concept and practice are older. Is mass production the ultimate type of manufacturing? Or is there a more advanced type?

Before touching on that question, let us notice another large pattern that has changed over time: organizational work. Merchants used to organize manufacturing; in the main, the type of manufacturing they organized was craftwork. Trade was not only the work of arranging exchanges of goods, it was also the activity that organized other economic activities. Manufacturers used to aspire to become merchants because merchants were the organizers. But now we do not find automobile manufacturers, say, aspiring to become dealers. Manufacturing now tends to be the economic activity around which other activities center, including many forms of trade and services. Manufacturing has become not only the work of making things, but also an activity that organizes other economic activities. This change has corresponded, in time, with the rise of mass-production manufacturing. For those who would like to see these movements shown schematically, a little diagram appears in Section V of the Appendix.

When Adam Smith looked at England, the most advanced economy of the eighteenth century, he found clues to future patterns of economic development.

Mass production was not then the dominant form of manufacturing, but neverthe-less Smith saw it as a coming thing. I think, from the symptoms to be observed, that the economy of the United States is in process of stagnating.* Nevertheless, it is still the most advanced economy to be found. Therefore, no matter what its own future may be, it is a suitable economy in which to look for clues to patterns that may be found in more highly developed economies of the future—wherever those economies may prove to be.

Garment making, I think, affords an interesting clue to future manufac-turing because it exemplifies manufacturing of three distinctly different kinds. The oldest is craftwork, the method of hand tailors and seamstresses. It persists to this day in fine custom tailoring and in the work of couturiers. The second is mass production. This is the method used for making overalls, army uniforms, men's popularly priced shirts, most socks, nylon stockings, and many standard items of underclothing. Mass-production manufacturing of garments in the United States began in the 1860s. At that time, it would have appeared that garment manufacturing was to be done in a few very large organizations turning out highly standardized products. One of the first successes, described by Ishbel Ross in *Crusades and Crinolines,* was a small hoop skirt turned out in the factory of Ellen Demorest, a remarkable innovator of many developments in garment manufacturing, pattern manufacturing, and fashion journalism. The skirt she mass-produced was "one of the wonders of the crinoline age and achieved immense popularity and distribution." A writer of the time, quoted by Miss Ross, said, "Madame Demorest deserves grateful remembrance for being the first to introduce a really excellent, cheap hoop skirt; and so popular did they immedi-ately become, that other manufacturers were compelled to reduce their prices, although none have ever pretended to vie with these in cost, quality of material used, and amount of labor expended upon them." It was these skirts to which *Fortune* was referring in a survey of the New York garment industry almost a century later, when it noted that one-third of all those employed in the industry in New York in the 1860s worked in one establishment that made hoop skirts, "certainly the closest approach that there has ever been to a General Motors in the [women's] clothing trade." While no one organization did come to dominate the mass-production clothing industry, the greatest successes in mass-produced garments were made by firms that concentrated upon finding large common denominators in the clothing market.

The third method of garment manufacturing has arisen chiefly during this century, has grown much more rapidly than the other two, and has become the dominant form. For lack of any present generic name, let us call it differentiated

---

*I would not venture to prophesy how decisive this stagnation is. If it proves to be pro-found and unremitting, it could be comparable to that of the later Roman Empire or to that of many another economy in which revitalization, if it has occurred at all, has followed only upon revolution. If stagnation is still reversible in the United States, then by definition vigorous city-development processes not only can, but will, start into motion again.

production. This method produces relatively modest amounts of each item as compared with mass production, yet it is not craft manufacturing either. In some ways it resembles mass-production work more than it resembles craftwork. Thanks to this third kind of garment making, one can look at a crowd of thousands of persons in a large city park on a fine day or gathered to watch a parade, and be hard put to find two women or two children dressed in identical outfits. One also sees in the same crowd more variety in men's clothing than one would have found a generation ago. This is the kind of garment manufacturing that used to amaze visiting Europeans; they took back the extraordinary news that even shopgirls and factory girls in the United States were fashionably clothed in a dazzling variety of dresses. Europeans now use this kind of manufacturing themselves. In America it is this manufacturing that renders the poor deceptively invisible, as Michael Harrington has pointed out. They do not wear a uniform of the poor, nor do they dress in rags. Because of their clothing, they look more prosperous than they are, an amazing economic achievement on the part of the garment industry.

The salient distinction between mass production and differentiated production is in the way the manufacturers look at the market—or, if one prefers, at the need for garments. A mass-production manufacturer seeks common denominators in the market; he exploits similar needs. A differentiated-production manufacturer depends on differences to be found in the market. He deliberately exploits the fact that people have differing tastes in styles, fabrics, and colors, differing clothing budgets and, as individuals, reasons for needing diverse clothing (e.g., garments for going to parties, lounging, sports, work, city activities, country activities). The two different approaches to the market give rise to other distinctions between mass production and differentiated production. Mass production churns out far greater numbers of identical items than does differentiated production. Much more design and development work goes into differentiated production than into mass production, in proportion to the volume of output.

Mass-production manufacturing introduces variations into total output only if great expansion in volume justifies variations which can also be produced in large volumes. A producer of black socks may devote part of his expanding volume to production of brown socks, much as automobile makers have introduced new models when their markets expanded. But the variations thus introduced in mass production are almost invariably superficial and they too are calculated to satisfy major common denominators in the potential market. The variations created through differentiated production are precisely what permit this production at all; *variations are not a result of expanded volume in differentiated production,* they are primary.

Consider, in this light, what has been happening to newspapers in the United States. The mass-production city dailies, aimed at common denominators in the market for newspapers, seem to have passed their heyday. They have declined steeply in number; many of those remaining have declined in circulation. In the meantime, city and suburban weekly newspapers have been growing rapidly both in number and circulation. The new weeklies aim at differences within the city newspaper markets. They carry news and features which are of vital importance or of interest to people in this or that district, but may be of little importance or interest elsewhere. Some cut across geography to aim at special communities of interest. These weeklies are not a return to the old-fashioned country and small-town weeklies run off on hand presses by their editors. In their production methods, the new papers are more like the mass-production newspapers. Nor are they, as a rule, culturally backward. Some make the mass-production newspapers seem old-fashioned in their writing, layouts, photography and subject matter. The weeklies are doing a job that was left undone, and that must inherently be left undone, in mass production. The reason the mass-production dailies are declining is not, however, that there are no significant similarities in a city's total market for news, but that the job once done by mass-production newspapers has been largely duplicated by television and radio news and feature programs, and by the mass-production weekly news magazines.

Also, there is a market for standard agricultural tractors and their accessories which are aimed at widespread similarities of needs among farmers, though this is no longer the kind of farm-equipment business that is growing appreciably. As far back as 1961, *Fortune* reported that the giant, mass-production farm-equipment manufacturers were in economic trouble. Their business was static or declining, and they were saddled with huge factories working below capacity and numerous retail outlets that no longer paid their way. The rapidly growing farm-equipment business was going disproportionately to more than a thousand small manufacturers who were aiming precisely at differences within the market. The big companies had stayed too long with "the mass concept," *Fortune* commented. "Less of [the farmers'] equipment money goes for the standard items . . . Today a small company can manufacture a highly specialized item of equipment just as easily as a large firm, and often at a better profit." Again, the relatively small-scale differentiated equipment production is not a return to craft methods.

In *The Silent Spring*, Rachel Carson attacked the practice of applying chemical pesticides wholesale—the mass-production approach to pest infestations. Instead, she advocated differentiated production based upon sophisticated biological controls of varying kinds, according to circumstances. This is a far cry from depending on the barnyard cat and the fly swatter, and resigning oneself to watching the locusts consume the year's work. It is a far more advanced approach than indiscriminate, wholesale use of chemicals. Miss Carson also advocated differentiation of crops within geographical localities, pointing out that mass production in farming itself—great factory farms devoted to one kind of cash crop—leads inherently to drastic imbalances of natural life and tends to increase the potential ravages of plant diseases and pests. (It also, I might add, can be economically disastrous to a rural region and often has been. A rural economy with all its eggs in one basket is bound to lose out from changes in markets.) As we might expect, Miss Carson's point has been heeded first in cities. Not many years ago, for instance, New York City was using the mass-production approach to street-tree planting. All the trees planted were London planes which were raised in great mass-production tree nurseries. As Robert Nichols, a landscape architect, had been pointing out, some twenty different varieties of trees do quite as well as London planes on the city streets; but the city had been committed, under a powerful administrator, Robert Moses, to mass production in this as in all things affecting parks or supervised by the parks department. Now, realizing the wholesale disaster that a London plane tree blight would bring, the city has begun differentiated planting of street trees.

I have brought trees and agricultural equipment into this discussion not only because they illustrate that there is more reason to produce for differences than variations of whims or tastes, but also to show that differentiated production is not a luxury and another term for "custom made." Differentiated production, in spite of its disproportionate requirements for design and development work, is not an extravagance. In real life, real and important differences abound, whether in nature or in a market, whether in the resistance of trees to diseases or in the information about current events needed by people in differing districts. And with economic development all kinds of differentiations increase; they do not diminish.

For some economic needs, mass production is superb. The common denominators are valid and enduring. Mass production is well suited, for example, to brick manufacturing, making screwdrivers, bed sheets, paper, electric light bulbs, and telephones. I am not proposing that mass production will disappear from economic life. Farmers still need their standard tractors; people still need standard denim pants or their equivalents. The point is that for some goods, mass production is a makeshift. It represents only an early stage of development and is valid only as an inadequate expedient until more advanced differentiated production has been developed. Consider transportation. The automobile is overdepended upon as an expedient for replacing the still less adequate horse; it is largely a makeshift in lieu of still undeveloped types of vehicles and methods of surface transportation for short and long distance. Still, it is unlikely that the automobile will be supplanted by some other mass-produced vehicle. Rather, it will be supplanted by many different kinds of vehicles and many new kinds of transportation services based not upon crude common denominators of moving people and goods, but on differentiations. Nor will the automobile be wholly supplanted. It will be valid for some of these needs, although no doubt it will be radically changed and also more differentiated. Other vehicles will be completely different from automobiles. New forms of swift and smooth water travel will almost surely be developed, possibly making use of hydrofoils of many designs and sizes. These will first be used on waterways for express transportation within cities and between cities. Their manufacture will most likely begin in cities where they are used first.

In still other kinds of manufacturing, mass production is so unsuitable that it cannot be used even as an expedient. In such cases, if the industry is to develop at all, it must be based on differentiated production from the beginning. The electronics industries are an illustration of this kind of manufacturing. Many business analysts have pointed out that electronics manufacturing has developed differently from automobile manufacturing in which hundreds of enterprises were reduced to very few as the industry grew. The hundreds of early electronics enterprises did not reduce to a few huge mass-production companies. Instead, the hundreds increased to thousands and most have remained relatively small. The radical difference is not accidental. Electronics manufacturing is based only slightly on similarities of needs for electronic devices; it must satisfy immense numbers of diverse needs within the total market.

The construction industries have emerged only rather recently from the craft-manufacturing stage, of which many vestiges linger. As mass production became predominant in many other types of manufacturing, construction was a case of arrested development. Now construction seems to be arrested in the mass-production stage, although mass-production building is clearly a makeshift. For example, back in 1961 New York City proposed rebuilding the neighborhood in which I lived. The idea was to wipe out virtually every structure that occupied the land and mass-produce a new "neighborhood," formed for the most part of large, identical buildings. Even if the plan had been to construct identical small buildings it would have been the same approach in essence. The idea was to build for similarities of need, similarities of use and, by means of clearance, to impose similarities of sites that could accommodate mass-production construction. The project was to have cost an estimated $35,000,000. Because of the wholesale destruction of more than seven hundred already existing dwellings, the expenditure would have resulted in a net gain of about 300 dwelling units and a net loss of 156 businesses that employed about 2,500 persons. Some of these businesses might have relocated elsewhere, at additional economic costs not included in the $35,000,000, but most would have represented a total loss. They would have disappeared from the economy.

This scheme was defeated. Residents and property owners in the neighborhood, through their civic organization, the West Village Committee, then hired a firm of architects and planners and instructed them to work out a wholly different scheme. New buildings, gardens and public sidewalk plazas were to be added in already vacant sites, abandoned plots, and makeshift parking lots, without destroying a single existing dwelling or requiring the removal of any business, other than the random and usually illegal parking. The architects met these requirements by working out designs for three different sizes of relatively small buildings (most, of ten apartments each) that could be fitted into existing vacant and abandoned sites individually and in combinations. The buildings themselves were capable of many differentiations, not only into apartments of differing sizes, but also of differing uses such as retail stores and workshops. This scheme, costing an estimated $8,700,000 instead of $35,000,000 (both at 1964 prices), provided a net increase of 475 dwelling units, instead of 300, and destroyed no businesses. This second plan was a far cry from the old craft manufacturing of dwellings; indeed, it was designed to use a number of building techniques and materials more advanced than those being currently employed by mass-production builders. But it is a long way from mass-producing a neighborhood.*

With growth of differentiated production in developing economies of the future, we may expect to find other changes in economic life. The average size of manufacturing enterprises will be smaller than at present. But the numbers of manufacturing enterprises will greatly increase and so will the total volume of manufactured goods. Most mass-production enterprises that have not been made obsolete by differentiated production—and many will remain—will have been transplanted to the countryside and into inert towns. There, with their low requirements of labor, their large requirements of space, and their relative self-sufficiency, these industries can operate more efficiently than in cities. Mass-production manufacturing will no longer be regarded as city work. Cities will manufacture even more goods than they do today, but these will be almost wholly differentiated production goods, made in relatively small, or very small, organizations.

Manufacturing work will, I think, no longer be the chief activity around which other economic activities are organized, as it is today and as the work of merchants once was. Instead, services will become the predominant organizational work, the instigators of other economic activities, including manufacturing. For an obvious example, consider what has been happening in the case of office machines. The older sorts—typewriters, dictating machines, adding machines and so on—are bought simply as machines. If a service is also bought along with them, it is a minor appendage: maintenance checking and repair, brief instructions to users of the machines, a trade-in service when a new machine is bought to replace an old one. But some of the new kinds of office machines are not bought in this way. Rather, what is bought is first and foremost a service: the service of analyzing and programming the work of an office, such as billing, payroll preparation, and sales and inventory analyzing. The machines are bought as an appendage to accommodate the system prescribed by the analytical service. Sometimes the machines are not even bought. Instead, an office may buy services from a computer or data-processing center, and it will be the service organization that buys or leases the necessary machines. In either case, service work is the organizing activity for the other work, including the manufacturing of the machines.

It is not likely that manufacturers of vehicles will organize the transportation of the future, as they do now, to a considerable extent. The organizing

*Apparently it was too advanced. Although the differentiated-production plan was prepared in 1962, and building could have begun that year, the city bureaucracies—whose philosophy and also rules and regulations were all shaped by the mass-production approach to construction and planning—opposed it adamantly until 1967, when they at last permitted it to begin inching its way through red tape, a process still under way as this is written. In the meantime, mass-production construction has continued, and vast amounts of money have of course been spent for an amazingly small yield of improved housing accommodations; the shortage of habitable housing has thus been increasing, not diminishing, as deterioration has outrun net construction.

forces, rather, will be transportation services, including even the services of renting differentiated automobiles for different purposes to individual users. The manufacturing will be done specifically to meet needs of these various services. When I was conjecturing, in Chapter Three [of Jacobs's *The Economy of Cities*] how waste recycling systems might be organized in developing economies of the future, I suggested that services would be the key work in such industries, and that the service organizations would be customers for many kinds of waste-collecting equipment. This conjecture was based upon the logic of the work, but it corresponds to what I suspect is the coming trend in economic organization generally. Service organizations in developing economies of the future are likely to draw upon products made by many different manufacturers, and are likely to be larger than manufacturing organizations. Even so, they will begin as small businesses and expand as they add innovations.

No doubt, to English-speaking people of the future, especially if they happen to live in developing and highly advanced economies, it will seem quaint that "service" carries a connotation of servants' work, and even quainter that these economically important and awesomely large organizations should, in many cases, have sprung from such menial work as cleaning, minor maintenance, or chauffeuring. The case will seem, no doubt, as quaint as it seems to us that manufacturing arose upon servants' work, or that merchants originated from vagabonds and beggars who were even lowlier than the manorial servants of their time.

Economic conflict

There is no point in pretending that economic development is in everyone's interest. Development of petroleum for lamp fuel was not good for the American whaling industry nor for those whose economic and social power were bound up with that industry. Development of new forms of public transit would not be good for today's petroleum industry or highway builders or automobile manufacturers, nor for anyone whose economic or social power is bound up with those industries. Development of economically important new goods and services by blacks would not be to the interests, as they see them, of white racists, including unconscious racists and paternalists.

In developing economies, even the well-established activities that are not directly affected adversely by new goods and services are indirectly affected, and so are the people whose economic and social power are tied up with those established activities. It is a question of sharing power. As an economy grows, its older, well-established economic interests grow less important and less powerful as a part of the whole. Furthermore, the most meteoric rises (starting at almost nothing) occur in new activities. The older activities do not necessarily decline in absolute size and wealth—indeed, they or their changing derivatives often expand in response to the general expansion—but they suffer at least a relative decline. And so do the people who derive their social and economic power from them.

In Çatal Hüyük it is unlikely that the huntsmen ruled the roost as they must have at an earlier, remote time when there was no trading in the ancestral society and no way of getting food and craft materials other than hunting. The malapportioned state legislatures of the United States, elected by votes disproportionately weighted in favor of rural areas, small towns, and little stagnant cities, were an anachronism. But they were an accurate picture of political, social and economic power at the time apportionments were first made. And then they were clung to by precisely the groups in American life—the farmers, the people in inert towns—whose importance in the whole had declined as the rest of the economy developed more swiftly. In short, economic development, no matter when or where it occurs, is profoundly subversive of the status quo.

Marx thought that the principal conflict to be found in economic life, at any rate in industrialized countries, was the deep disparity of interests between owners and employees, but this is a secondary kind of conflict. If one accepts Marx's conception, then revolutions should occur (as indeed he expected) in the most industrialized societies, rather than in economically backward and stagnant countries. Also, if one accepts his conception, much of the behavior of labor unions becomes impossible to understand. In real life, unions, once they have become institutionalized, can successfully deal with employers; and the interests of the two, to a large extent, then coincide. It is to the interests of construction workers that a great deal of construction be undertaken, and if this hurts other workers by wiping out the businesses to which their jobs are attached, so much the worse for them. It is also in the interests of labor unions that their industries should not change technologically; this, of course, often puts unions in conflict with employers—but even more so, in conflict with the interests of industries (and workers in those industries) that produce new technological devices. The inherent solidarity of the working class is an economic fiction.

Nor do the interests of already well-organized workers inherently correspond with the interests of those who have no well-established work to pursue, who are "redundant" in a stagnant economy, and thus short-changed on the goods and services they receive. Should the creativity of such people be allowed to flourish, it must change things as they are, upset the status quo, make some well-established activities obsolete and reduce the relative importance of others. Of course, the creativity of "redundant" people would make the economy develop, prosper and expand; but it is also a threat to all those workers and employers attached to activities potentially threatened by development. It is no accident that demands by blacks for control of ghetto education are desperately opposed not only by school boards (employers) but also by associations of school principals and by teachers' unions (employees); if anything, more implacably by the latter than the former. That the change may be to the benefit of children, and might result in significant development of education, is beside the point to those threatened. To be sure, when almost no workers in an economy believe they are becoming better off, and almost all are coming to hate the status quo, they may join in an attack upon it. But an economy must already have become profoundly flawed before this occurs, especially if the assault is to succeed.

The primary economic conflict, I think, is between people whose interests are with already well-established economic activities, and those whose interests are with the emergence of new economic activities. This is a conflict that can never be put to rest except by economic stagnation. For the new economic activities of today are the well-established activities of tomorrow which will be threatened in turn by further economic development. In this conflict, other things being equal, the well-established activities and those whose interests are attached to them, must win. They are, by definition, the stronger. The only possible way to keep open the economic opportunities for new activities is for a "third force" to protect their weak and still incipient interests. Only governments can play this economic role. And sometimes, for pitifully brief intervals, they do. But because development subverts the status quo, the status quo soon subverts governments. When development has proceeded for a bit, and has cast up strong new activities, governments come to derive their power from those already well-established interests, and not from still incipient organizations, activities and interests.

In human history, most people in most places most of the time have existed miserably in stagnant economies. Developing economies have been the exceptions, and their histories, as developing economies, have been brief. Now here, now there, a group of cities grows vigorously by the processes I have been describing in this book and then lapses into stagnation for the benefit of people who have already become powerful. I am not one who believes that flying saucers carry creatures from other solar systems who poke curiously into our earthly affairs. But if such beings were to arrive, with their marvelously advanced contrivances, we may be sure we would be agog to learn how their technology worked. The important question however, would be something quite different: What kinds of governments had they invented which had succeeded in keeping open the opportunities for economic and technological development instead of closing them off? Without helpful advice from outer space, this remains one of the most pressing and least regarded problems.

Provided that some groups on earth continue either muddling or revolutionizing themselves into periods of economic development, we can be absolutely sure of a few things about future cities. The cities will not be smaller, simpler or more specialized than cities of today. Rather, they will be more intricate, comprehensive, diversified, and larger than today's, and will have even more complicated jumbles of old and new things than ours do. The bureaucratized, simplified cities, so dear to present-day city planners and urban designers, and familiar also to readers of science fiction and utopian proposals, run counter to the processes of city growth and economic development. Conformity and monotony, even when they are embellished with a froth of novelty, are not attributes of developing and economically vigorous cities. They are attributes of stagnant settlements. To some people, the vision of a future in which life is simpler than it is now, and work has become so routine as to be scarcely noticeable, is an exhilarating vision. To other people, it is depressing. But no matter. The vision is irrelevant for developing and influential economies of the future. In highly developed future economies, there will be more kinds of work to do than today, not fewer. And many people in great, growing cities of the future will be engaged in the unroutine business of economic trial and error. They will be faced with acute practical problems which we cannot now imagine. They will add new work to older work.

* * *

APPENDIX

IV. *The two reciprocating systems of city growth*

The various processes that have been diagramed operate as two major reciprocating systems. The first system is the process of simple export generating in a young city. Producers' goods and services become exports. The export multiplier increases the numbers and varieties of producers' goods and services. More producers' goods and services become exports, and so on, the process sustaining itself as indicated by the curved arrows. Simultaneously, the city's earned imports grow in volume and variety:

The second system is set in motion. Imports, having grown, are replaced. The versatile export generating of a large city becomes possible. So do subsequent episodes of import replacing:

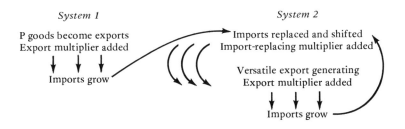

V.   Changing patterns of economic activities

As suggested . . . , the predominant methods of manufacturing change as an economy develops. So do the kinds of activities around which—and also by which—other economic activities are organized. Let us correlate these changes, and also relate them to the situation in currently highly developed economies:

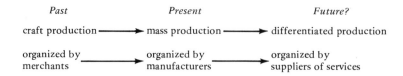

Past	*Present*	*Future?*
craft production ⟶	mass production ⟶	differentiated production
organized by merchants ⟶	organized by manufacturers ⟶	organized by suppliers of services

41

DANIEL P. MOYNIHAN, Toward a National Urban Policy

In the spring of 1969, President Nixon met in the Cabinet room with ten mayors of American cities. They were nothing if not a variegated lot, mixing party, religion, race, region in the fine confusion of American politics. They had been chosen to be representative in this respect, and were unrepresentative only in qualities of energy and intelligence that would have set them apart in any company. What was more notable about them, however, was that in the interval between the invitation from the White House and the meeting with the President, four had announced they would not run again. The mayor of Detroit who, at the last minute, could not attend, announced *his* noncandidacy in June.

Their decisions were not a complete surprise. More and more, for the men charged with governance of our cities, politics has become the art of the impossible. It is not to be wondered that they flee. But we, in a sense, are left behind. And are in trouble.

At a time of great anxiety—a time that one of the nation's leading news magazines now routinely describes as "the most serious domestic crisis since the Civil War," a time when Richard Rovere, writing of the 1972 elections, can add parenthetically, "assuming that democracy in America survives that long"—these personal decisions may seem of small consequence; yet one suspects they are not.

All agree that the tumult of the time arises, in essence, from a crisis of authority. The institutions that shaped conduct and behavior in the past are being

Daniel P. Moynihan, "Toward a National Urban Policy," *The Public Interest*, no. 17 (Fall 1969), pp. 3–20. Copyright © National Affairs, Inc., 1969. This article is Chapter 1 in Moynihan's book, *Toward a National Urban Policy* (New York: Basic Books, Inc., Publishers, © 1970). Reprinted by permission of National Affairs, Inc., and Daniel P. Moynihan.

challenged or, worse, ignored. It is in the nature of authority, as Robert A. Nisbet continues to remind us, that it is consensual, that it is not coercive. When authority systems collapse, they are replaced by power systems that *are* coercive.[1] Our vocabulary rather fails us here: the term "authority" is an unloved one, with its connotations of "authoritarianism," but there appears to be no substitute. Happily, public opinion is not so dependent on political vocabulary, certainly not on the vocabulary of political science, as some assume. For all the ambiguity of the public rhetoric of the moment, the desire of the great mass of our people is clear. They sense the advent of a power-based society and they fear it. They seek peace. They look to the restoration of legitimacy, if not in existing institutions, then in new or modified ones. They look for a lessening of violent confrontations at home, and, in great numbers, for an end to war abroad. Concern for personal safety on the part of city dwellers has become a live *political* fact, while the re-appearance—what, praise God, did we do to bring this upon ourselves?—of a Stalinoid rhetoric of apocalyptic abuse on the left, and its echoes on the right, have created a public atmosphere of anxiety and portent that would seem to have touched us all. It is with every good reason that the nation gropes for some means to weather the storm of unreason that has broken upon us.

It would also seem that Americans at this moment are much preoccupied with the issue of freedom—or, rather, with new, meaningful ways in which free-dom is seen to be expanded or constrained. We are, for example, beginning to evolve some sense of the meaning of group freedom. This comes after a century of preoccupation with individual rights of a kind which were seen as somehow opposed to, and even threatened by, group identities and anything so dubious in conception as *group* rights.

The Civil Rights Act of 1964 was the culmination of the political energies generated by that earlier period. The provisions which forbade employers, universities, governments, or whatever to have any knowledge of the race, religion, or national origin of individuals with which they dealt marked in some ways the high-water mark of Social Darwinism in America; its assumption that "equality" meant *only* equal opportunity did not long stand unopposed. Indeed, by 1965 the federal government had already, as best one can tell, begun to require ethnic and racial census of its own employees, and also of federal contractors and research grant recipients. To do so violated the spirit if not the letter of the Civil Rights Act, with its implicit model of the lone individual locked in equal—and remorseless—competition in the marketplace, but very much in harmony with the emerging sense of the 1960s that groups have identities and entitlements as well as do individuals. This view is diffusing rapidly. In Massachusetts, for example, legislation of the Civil Rights Act period, which declared any public school with more than 50 percent black pupils to be racially "imbalanced" and in consequence illegal, is already being challenged—by precisely those who supported it in the first instance. Insofar as these demands have been most in evidence among black Americans, there is not the least reason to doubt that they will now diffuse to

[1] "The Twilight of Authority," *The Public Interest*, no. 15, Spring 1969.

other groups, defined in various ways, and that new institutions will arise to respond to this new understanding of the nature of community.

In sum, two tendencies would appear to dominate the period. The *sense of general community is eroding,* and with it the authority of existing relationships; simultaneously, a powerful *quest for specific community is emerging* in the form of ever more intensive assertions of racial and ethnic identities. Although this is reported in the media largely in terms of black nationalism, it is just as reasonable to identify emergent attitudes in the "white working class," as part of the same phenomenon. The singular quality of these two tendencies is that they are at once complementary and opposed. While the ideas are harmonious, the practices that would seem to support one interest are typically seen as opposing the other. Thus, one need not be a moral philosopher or a social psychologist to see that much of the "crisis of the cities" arises from the interaction of these intense new demands, and the relative inability of the urban social system to respond to them.

Programs do not a policy make

Rightly or otherwise—and one is no longer sure of this—it is our tradition in such circumstances to look to government. Social responses to changed social requirements take the form, in industrial democracies, of changed government policies. This had led, in the present situation, to a reasonably inventive spate of program proposals of the kind the New Deal more or less began and which flourished most notably in the period between the presidential elections of 1960 and 1968, when the number of domestic programs of the federal government increased from 45 to 435. Understandably, however, there has been a diminution of the confidence with which such proposals were formerly regarded. To say the least, there has been a certain nonlinearity in the relationship between the number of categorical aid programs issuing forth from Washington and the degree of social satisfaction that has ensued.

Hence the issue arises as to whether the demands of the time are not to be met in terms of *policy,* as well as program. It has been said of urban planners that they have been traumatized by the realization that everything relates to everything. But this is so, and need paralyze no one; the perception of this truth can provide a powerful analytic tool.

Our problems in the area of social peace and individual or group freedom occur in urban settings. Can it be that our difficulties in coping with these problems originate, in some measure, from the inadequacies of the setting in which they arise? Crime on the streets and campus violence may mark the onset of a native nihilism: but in the first instance they represent nothing more complex than the failure of law enforcement. Black rage and white resistance. "Third World" separatism, and restricted neighborhoods all may define a collapse in the integuments of the social contract: but, again, in the first instance they represent for the most part simply the failure of urban arrangements to meet the expectations of the urban population in the areas of jobs, schools, housing, transportation, public health, administrative responsiveness, and political flexibility. If all these are related, one to the other, and if in combination they do not seem to be working well, the question arises whether the society ought not to attempt a more coherent response. In a word: ought not a national urban crisis to be met with something like a national urban policy? Ought not the vast efforts to control the situation of the present be at least informed by some sense of goals for the future?

The United States does not now have an urban policy. The idea that there might be such is new. So also is the Urban Affairs Council, established by President Nixon on January 23, 1969, as the first official act of his administration, to "advise and assist" with respect to urban affairs, specifically "in the development of a national urban policy, having regard both to immediate and to long-range concerns, and to priorities among them."

What happened

The central circumstance, as stated, is that America is an urban nation, and has been for half a century.

This is not to say Americans live in *big* cities. They do not. In 1960 only 9.8 percent of the population lived in cities of one million or more. Ninety-eight percent of the units of local government have fewer than 50,000 persons. In terms of the 1960 census, only somewhat more than a quarter of congressmen represented districts in which a majority of residents lived in central city areas. The 1970 census will show that the majority of Americans in metropolitan areas in fact live in suburbs, while a great many more live in urban settlements of quite modest size. But they are not the less urban for that reason, providing conditions of living and problems of government profoundly different from that of the agricultural, small town past.

The essentials of the present "urban crisis" are simple enough to relate. Until about World War II, the growth of the city, as Otto Eckstein argues, was "a logical, economic development." At least it was such in the northeastern quadrant of the United States, where most urban troubles are supposed to exist. The political jurisdiction of the city more or less defined the area of intensive economic development, that in turn more or less defined the area of intensive settlement. Thereafter, however, economic incentives and social desires combined to produce a fractionating process that made it ever more difficult to collect enough power in any one place to provide the rudiments of effective government. As a result of or as a part of this process, the central area ceased to grow and began to decline. The core began to rot.

Two special circumstances compounded this problem. First, the extraordinary migration of the rural southern Negro to the northern city. Second, a postwar population explosion (90 million babies were born between 1946 and 1968) that placed immense pressures on municipal services, and drove many whites to the suburbs seeking relief. (Both these influences are now somewhat attenuating, but their effects will be present for at least several decades, and indeed a new baby boom may be in the offing.) As a result, the problems of economic stagnation of the central city became desperately exacerbated by those of racial tension. In the course of the 1960s tension turned into open racial strife.

City governments began to respond to the onset of economic obsolescence and social rigidity a generation or more ago, but quickly found their fiscal resources strained near to the limit. State governments became involved, and much the same process ensued. Starting in the postwar period, the federal government itself became increasingly caught up with urban problems. In recent years resources on a fairly considerable scale have flowed from Washington to the cities of the land, and will clearly continue to do so. However, in the evolution of a national urban policy, more is involved than merely the question of programs and their funding. Too many programs have produced too few results simply to accept a more or less straightforward extrapolation of past and present practices into an oversized but familiar future. *The question of method has become as salient as that of goals themselves.*

As yet, the federal government, no more than state or local government, has not found an effective *incentive* system—comparable to profit in private enterprise, prestige in intellectual activity, rank in military organization—whereby to shape the forces at work in urban areas in such a way that urban goals, whatever they may be, are in fact attained. This search for incentives, and the realization that present procedures such as categorical grant-in-aid programs do not seem to provide sufficiently powerful ones, must accompany and suffuse the effort to establish goals as such. We must seek, not just policy, but policy allied to a vigorous strategy for obtaining results from it.

Finally, the federal establishment must develop a much heightened sensitivity to its "hidden" urban policies. There is hardly a department or agency of the national government whose programs do not in some way have important consequences for the life of cities, and those who live in them. Frequently—one is tempted to say normally!—the political appointees and career executives concerned do *not* see themselves as involved with, much less responsible for the urban consequences of their programs and policies. They are, to their minds, simply building highways, guaranteeing mortgages, advancing agriculture, or whatever. No one has made clear to them that they are simultaneously redistributing employment opportunities, segregating or desegregating neighborhoods, depopulating the countryside and filling up the slums, etc.: all these things as second and third order consequences of nominally unrelated programs. Already this institutional naïveté has become cause for suspicion; in the future it simply must not be tolerated. Indeed, in the future, a primary mark of competence in a federal official should be the ability to see the interconnections between programs immediately at hand and the urban problems that pervade the larger society.

The fundaments of urban policy

It having been long established that, with respect to general codes of behavior, eleven precepts are too many and nine too few, ten points of urban policy may be set forth, scaled roughly to correspond to a combined measure of urgency and importance.

1. The poverty and social isolation of minority groups in central cities is the single most serious problem of the American city today. It must be attacked with urgency, with a greater commitment of resources than has heretofore been the case, and with programs designed especially for this purpose.

The 1960s have seen enormous economic advances among minority groups, especially Negroes. Outside the south, 37 percent of Negro families earn $8,000 per year or more, that being approximately the national median income. In cities in the largest metropolitan areas, 20 percent of Negro families in 1967 reported family incomes of $10,000 or over. The earnings of *young* married black couples are approaching parity with whites.

Nonetheless, certain forms of social disorganization and dependency appear to be increasing among the urban poor. Recently, Conrad Taeuber, associate director of the Bureau of the Census, reported that in the largest metropolitan areas—those with one million or more inhabitants—"the number of black families with a woman as head increased by 83 percent since 1960; the number of black families with a man as head increased by only 15 percent during the same period." Disorganization, isolation, and discrimination seemingly have led to violence, and this violence has in turn been increasingly politicized by those seeking a "confrontation" with "white" society.

Urban policy must have as its first goal the transformation of the urban lower class into a stable community based on dependable and adequate income flows, social equality, and social mobility. Efforts to improve the conditions of life in the present caste-created slums must never take precedence over efforts to enable the slum population to disperse throughout the metropolitan areas involved. Urban policy accepts the reality of ethnic neighborhoods based on free choice, but asserts that the active intervention of government is called for to enable free choice to include integrated living as a normal option.

It is impossible to comprehend the situation of the black urban poor without first seeing that they have experienced not merely a major migration in the past generation, but also that they now live in a state almost of demographic siege as a result of population growth. What demographers call the "dependency ratio"—the number of children per thousand adult males—for blacks is nearly twice that for whites, and the gap widened sharply in the 1960s.

It is this factor, surely, that accounts for much of the present distress of the black urban slums. At the same time, it is fairly clear that the sharp escalation in the number of births that characterized the past twenty-five years has more or less come to an end. The number of Negro females under age five is now exactly the number aged five to nine. Thus the 1980s will see a slackening of the present

Table 1. Children per 1000 adult males		
	1960	*1966*
White	1,365	1,406
Negro	1,922	2,216

severe demands on the earning power of adult Negroes, and also on the public institutions that provide services for children. But for the decade immediately ahead, those demands will continue to rise—especially for central city blacks, whose median age is a bit more than ten years below that for whites—and will clearly have a priority claim on public resources.

2. Economic and social forces in urban areas are not self-balancing. Imbalances in industry, transportation, housing, social services, and similar elements of urban life frequently tend to become more rather than less pronounced, and this tendency is often abetted by public policies. A concept of urban balance may be tentatively set forth: a social condition in which forces tending to produce imbalance induce counterforces that simultaneously admit change while maintaining equilibrium. It must be the constant object to federal officials whose programs affect urban areas—and there are few whose do not—to seek such equilibrium.

The evidence is considerable that many federal programs have induced sharp imbalances in the "ecology" of urban areas—the highway program, for example, is frequently charged with this, and there is wide agreement that other, specifically city-oriented programs such as urban renewal have frequently accomplished just the opposite of their nominal objectives. The reasons are increasingly evident. Cities are complex social systems. Interventions that, intentionally or not, affect one component of the system almost invariably affect second, third, and fourth components as well, and these in turn affect the first component, often in ways quite opposite to the direction of the initial intervention. Most federal urban programs have assumed fairly simple cause and effect relationships that do not exist in the complex real world. Moreover, they have typically been based on "common sense" rather than research in an area where common sense can be notoriously misleading. In the words of Jay W. Forrester, "With a high degree of confidence we can say that the intuitive solution to the problems of complex social systems will be wrong most of the time."

This doubtless is true, but it need not be a traumatizing truth. As Lee Rainwater argues, the logic of multivariate analysis, and experience with it, suggest that some components of a complex system are always vastly more important than others, so that when (if) these are accurately identified a process of analysis that begins with the assertion of chaos can in fact end by producing quite concise and purposeful social strategies.

3. At least part of the relative ineffectiveness of the efforts of urban government to respond to urban problems derives from the fragmented and obsolescent structure of urban government itself. The federal government should constantly encourage and provide incentives for the reorganization of local government in response to the reality of metropolitan conditions. The objective of the federal government should be that local government be stronger and more effective, more visible, accessible, and meaningful to local inhabitants. To this end the federal government should discourage the creation of paragovernments designed to deal with special problems by evading or avoiding the jurisdiction of established local authorities, and should encourage effective decentralization.

Although the "quality" of local government, especially in large cities, has been seen to improve of late, there appears to have been a decline in the vitality of local political systems, and an almost total disappearance of serious effort to reorganize metropolitan areas into new and more rational governmental jurisdictions. Federal efforts to recreate the ethnic-neighborhood-based community organization, as in the poverty program, or to induce metropolitan area planning as in various urban development programs, have had a measure of success, but nothing like that hoped for. Meanwhile the middle-class norm of "participation" has diffused downward and outward, so that federal urban programs now routinely require citizen participation in the planning process and beyond; yet somehow this does not seem to have led to more competent communities. In some instances it appears rather to have escalated the level of stalemate.

It may be we have not been entirely candid with ourselves in this area. Citizen participation, as Elliott A. Krause has pointed out, is in practice a "bureaucratic ideology," a device whereby public officials induce nonpublic individuals to act in a way the officials desire. Although the putative object may be, indeed almost always is, to improve the lot of the citizen, it is not settled that the actual consequences are anything like that. The ways of the officials, of course, are often not those of the elected representatives of the people, and the "citizens" may become a rope in the tug-of-war between bureaucrat and representative. Especially in a federal system, "citizen participation" easily becomes a device whereby the far-off federal bureaucracy acquires a weapon with which to battle the elected officials of local government. Whatever the nominal intent, the normal outcome is federal support for those who would diminish the legitimacy of local government. But it is not clear that the federal purposes are typically advanced through this process. To the contrary, an all-round diminishment rather than enhancement of energies seems to occur.

This would appear especially true when "citizen participation" has in effect meant putting indignant citizens on the payroll. However much these citizens may continue to "protest," the action acquires a certain hollow ring. Something like this has already happened to groups that have been openly or covertly supported by the federal government, seeking to influence public opinion on matters of public policy. This stratagem is a new practice in American democracy. It began in the field of foreign affairs, and has now spread to the domestic area. To a quite astonishing degree it will be found that those groups that nominally are pressing for social change and development in the poverty field, for example, are in fact subsidized by federal funds. This occurs in protean ways—

research grants, training contracts, or whatever—and is done with the best of intentions. But, again, with what results is far from clear. Can this development, for example, account for the curious fact that there seems to be so much protest in the streets of the nation, but so little, as it were, in its legislatures? Is it the case, in other words, that the process of public subsidy is subtly debilitating?

Whatever the truth of this judgment, it is nevertheless clear that a national urban policy must look first to the vitality of the elected governments of the urban areas, and must seek to increase their capacity for independent, effective, and creative action. This suggests an effort to find some way out of the present fragmentation, and a certain restraint on the creation of federally financed "competitive governments."

Nathan Glazer has made the useful observation that in London and Tokyo comprehensive metropolitan government is combined with a complex system of "subgovernments"—the London Boroughs—representing units of 200,000–250,000 persons. These are "real" governments, with important powers in areas such as education, welfare, and housing. In England, at all events, they are governed through an electoral system involving the national political parties in essentially their national postures. (Indeed, the boroughs make up the basic units of the parties' urban structure.) It may well be there is need for social inventions of this kind in the great American cities, especially with respect to power over matters such as welfare, education, and housing that are now subject to intense debates concerning "local control." The demand for "local control" is altogether to be welcomed. In some degree it can be seen to arise from the bureaucratic barbarities of the highway programs of the 1950s, for example. But in the largest degree it reflects the processes of democracy catching up with the content of contemporary government. As government more and more involves itself in matters that very much touch on the lives of individual citizens, those individuals seek a greater voice in the programs concerned. In the hands of ideologues or dimwits, this demand can lead to an utter paralysis of government. It has already done so in dozens of urban development situations. But approached with a measure of sensitivity—and patience—it can lead to a considerable revitalization of urban government.

4. A primary object of federal urban policy must be to restore the fiscal vitality of urban government, with the particular object of ensuring that local governments normally have enough resources on hand or available to make local initiative in public affairs a reality.

For all the rise in actual amounts, federal aid to state and local government has increased only from 12 percent of state-local revenue in 1958 to 17 percent in 1967. Increasingly, state and local governments that try to meet their responsibilities lurch from one fiscal crisis to another. In such circumstances, the capacity for creative local government becomes least in precisely those jurisdictions where it might most be expected. As much as any other single factor, this condition may be judged to account for the malaise of city government, and especially for the reluctance of the more self-sufficient suburbs to associate themselves with the nearly bankrupt central cities. Surviving from one fiscal deadline to another, the central cities commonly adopt policies which only compound their ultimate difficulties. Yet their options are so few. As James Q. Wilson writes, "The great bulk of any city's budget is, in effect, a fixed charge the mayor is powerless to alter more than trivially." The basic equation, as it were, of American political economy is that for each one percent increase in the Gross National Product, the income of the federal government increases one and one-half percent, while the normal income of city governments rises half to three-quarters of a point at most. Hence both a clear opportunity and a no less manifest necessity exist for the federal government to adopt as a deliberate policy an increase in its aid to urban governments. This should be done in part through revenue sharing, in part through an increase in categorical assistance, hopefully in much more consolidated forms than now exist, and through credit assistance.

It may not be expected that this process will occur rapidly. The prospects for an enormous "peace and growth dividend" to follow the cessation of hostilities in Vietnam are far less bright than they were painted. But the fact is that as a nation we grow steadily richer, not poorer, and we can afford the government we need. This means, among our very first priorities, an increase in the resources available to city governments.

A clear opportunity exists for the federal government to adopt as a deliberate policy an increase in its aid to state and local governments in the aftermath of the Vietnam war. Much analysis is in order, but in approximate terms it may be argued that the present proportion of aid should be about doubled, with the immediate objective that the federal government contribution constitute one-third of state and local revenue.

5. Federal urban policy should seek to equalize the provision of public services as among different jurisdictions in metropolitan areas.

Although the standard depiction of the (black) residents of central cities as grossly deprived with respect to schools and other social services, when compared with their suburban (white) neighbors, requires endless qualification, the essential truth is that life for the well-to-do is better than life for the poor, and that these populations tend to be separated by artificial government boundaries within metropolitan areas. (The people in between may live on either side of the boundaries, and are typically overlooked altogether.) At a minimum, federal policy should seek a dollar-for-dollar equivalence in the provision of social services having most to do with economic and social opportunity. This includes, at the top of the list, public education and public safety. (Obviously there will always be some relatively small jurisdictions—"the Scarsdale school system"— that spend a great deal more than others, being richer; but there can be national or regional norms and no central city should be allowed to operate below them.)

Beyond the provision of equal resources lies the troubled and elusive question of equal results. Should equality of educational opportunity extend to equality of educational achievement (as between one group of children and another)? Should equality of police protection extend to equality of risks of criminal victimization? That is to say, should there be not only as many police, but also as few crimes in one area of the city as in another? These are hardly simple questions, but as they are increasingly posed it is increasingly evident that we shall have to try to find answers.

The area of housing is one of special and immediate urgency. In America, housing is not regarded as a public utility (and a scarce one!) as it is in many of the industrial democracies of Europe, but there can hardly be any remaining doubt that the strong and regular production of housing is nearly a public necessity. We shall not solve the problem of racial isolation without it. Housing must not only be open, *it must be available.* The process of filtration out from dense center city slums can only take place if the housing perimeter, as it were, is sufficiently porous. For too long now, the production of housing has been a function, not of the need for housing as such but rather of the need to increase or decrease the money supply, or whatever. Somehow a greater regularity of effective demand must be provided the housing industry, and its level of production must be increased.

6. The federal government must assert a specific interest in the movement of people, displaced by technology or driven by poverty, from rural to urban areas, and also in the movement from densely populated central cities to suburban areas.

Much of the present urban crisis derives from the almost total absence of any provision for an orderly movement of persons off the countryside and into the city. The federal government made extraordinary, and extraordinarily successful, efforts to provide for the resettlement of Hungarian refugees in the 1950s and Cuban refugees in the 1960s. But almost nothing has been done for Americans driven from their homes by forces no less imperious.

Rural to urban migration has not stopped, and will not for some time. Increasingly, it is possible to predict where it will occur, and in what time sequence. (In 1968, for example, testing of mechanical tobacco harvesting began on the east coast and the first mechanical grape pickers were used on the west coast.) Hence, it is possible to prepare for it, both by training those who leave, and providing for them where they arrive. Doubtless the United States will remain a nation of exceptionally mobile persons, but the completely unassisted processes of the past need not continue with respect to the migration of impoverished rural populations.

There are increasing indications that the dramatic movement of Negro Americans to central city areas may be slackening, and that a counter movement to surrounding suburban areas may have begun. This process is to be encouraged in every way, especially by the maintenance of a flexible and open housing market. But it remains the case that in the next thirty years we shall add 100 million persons to our population. Knowing that, it is impossible to have no policy with respect to where they will be located. *For to let nature take its course is a policy.* To consider what might be best for all concerned and to seek to provide it is surely a more acceptable goal.

7. *State government has an indispensable role in the management of urban affairs, and must be supported and encouraged by the federal government in the performance of this role.*

This fact, being all but self-evident, tends to be overlooked. Indeed, the trend of recent legislative measures almost invariably prompted by executive initiatives, has been to establish a direct federal-city relationship. States have been bypassed, and doubtless some have used this as an excuse to avoid their responsibilities of providing the legal and governmental conditions under which urban problems can be effectively confronted.

It has, of course, been a tradition of social reform in America that city government is bad and that, if anything, state government is worse. This is neither true as a generalization nor useful as a principle. But it is true that, by and large, state governments (with an occasional exception such as New York) have *not* involved themselves with urban problems, and are readily enough seen by mayors as the real enemy. But this helps neither. States *must* become involved. City governments, without exception, are creatures of state governments. City boundaries, jurisdictions, and powers are given and taken away by state governments. It is surely time the federal establishment sought to lend a sense of coherence and a measure of progressivism to this fundamental process.

The role of state government in urban affairs cannot easily be overlooked (though it may be deliberately ignored on political or ideological grounds). By contrast, it is relatively easy to overlook county government, and possibly an even more serious mistake to do so. In a steadily increasing number of metropolitan areas, it is the county rather than the original core city that has become the only unit of government which makes any geographical sense. That is to say, the only unit whose boundaries contain most or all of the actual urban settlement. The powers of county government have typically lagged well behind its potential, but it may also be noted that in the few—the very few—instances of urban reorganization to take place since World War II, county government has assumed a principal, even primary role in the new arrangement.

8. *The federal government must develop and put into practice far more effective incentive systems than now exist whereby state and local governments, and private interests too, can be led to achieve the goals of federal programs.*

The typical federal grant-in-aid program provides its recipients with an immediate reward for promising to work toward some specified goal—raising the education achievement of minority children, providing medical care for the poor, cleaning up the air, reviving the downtown business district. But there is almost no reward for actually achieving such goals—and rarely any punishment for failing to do so.

There is a growing consensus that the federal government should provide market competition for public programs, or devise ways to imitate market conditions. In particular, it is increasingly agreed that federal aid should be given directly to the consumers of the programs concerned—individuals included—thus enabling them to choose among competing suppliers of the goods or services that the program is designed to provide. Probably no single development would more enliven and energize the role of government in urban affairs than a move from the *monopoly service* strategy of the grant-in-aid programs to a *market* strategy of providing the most reward to those suppliers that survive competition.

In this precise sense, it is evident that federal programs designed to assist those city-dwelling groups that are least well off, least mobile, and least able to fend for themselves must in many areas move beyond a *services* strategy to an approach that provides inducements to move from a dependent and deficient status to one of independence and sufficiency. Essentially, this is an *income* strategy, based fundamentally on the provision of incentives to increase the earnings and to expand the property base of the poorest groups.

Urban policy should in general be directed to raising the level of political activity and concentrating it in the electoral process. It is nonetheless possible and useful to be alert for areas of intense but unproductive political conflict and to devise ways to avoid such conflict through market strategies. Thus conflicts over "control" of public education systems have frequently of late taken on the aspect of disputes over control of a monopoly service, a sole source of a needed good. Clearly some of the ferocity that ensues can be avoided through free choice arrangements that, in effect, eliminate monopoly control. If we move in this direction, difficult "minimum standard" regulation problems will almost certainly arise, and must be anticipated. No arrangement meets every need, and a good deal of change is primarily to be justified on grounds that certain systems need change for their own sake. (Small school districts, controlled by locally elected boards may be just the thing for New York City. However, in Phoenix, Arizona, where they have just that, consolidation and centralization would appear to be the desire of educational reformers.) But either way, a measure of market competition can surely improve the provision of public services, much as it has proved an efficient way to obtain various public paraphernalia, from bolt-action rifles to lunar landing vehicles.

Here as elsewhere, it is essential to pursue and to identify the *hidden* urban policies of government. These are nowhere more central to the issue than in the matter of incentives. Thus, for better than half a century now, city governments with the encouragement of state and federal authorities have been seeking to direct urban investment and development in accordance with principles embodied in zoning codes, and not infrequently in accord with precise city plans. However, during this same time the tax laws have provided the utmost incentive to pursue just the opposite objectives of those incorporated in the codes and the plans. It has, for example, been estimated that returns from land speculation based on zoning code changes on average incur half the tax load of returns from investment in physical improvements. Inevitably, energy and capital have diverted *away* from pursuing the plan and *toward* subverting it. It little avails for government to deplore the evasion of its purposes in such areas. Government has in fact established two sets of purposes, and provided vastly greater inducements to pursue the implicit rather than the avowed ones. Until public authorities, and the public itself, learn to be much more alert to these situations, and far more open in discussing and managing them, we must expect the present pattern of self-defeating contradictions to continue.

9. The federal government must provide more and better information concerning urban affairs, and should sponsor extensive and sustained research into urban problems.

Much of the social progress of recent years derives from the increasing quality and quantity of government-generated statistics and government-supported research. However, there is general agreement that the time is at hand when a general consolidation is in order, bringing a measure of symmetry to the now widely dispersed (and somewhat uneven) data-collecting and research-supporting activities. Such consolidation should not be limited to urban problems, but it must surely include attention to urban questions.

The federal government should, in particular, recognize that most of the issues that appear most critical just now do so in large measure because they are so little understood. This is perhaps especially so with respect to issues of minority group education, but generally applies to all the truly difficult and elusive issues of the moment. More and better inquiry is called for. In particular, the federal government must begin to sponsor longitudinal research, i.e., research designed to follow individual and communal development over long periods of time. It should also consider providing demographic and economic projections for political subdivisions as a routine service, much as the weather and the economy are forecast. Thus, Karl Taeuber has shown how seemingly unrelated policies of local governments can increase the degree of racial and economic differentiation between political jurisdictions, especially between cities and suburbs.

Similarly, the extraordinary inquiry into the educational system begun by the U. S. Office of Education under the direction of James S. Coleman should somehow be established on an on-going basis. It is now perfectly clear that little is known about the processes whereby publicly-provided resources affect educational outcomes. The great mass of those involved in education, and of that portion of the public that interests itself in educational matters, continue undisturbed in its old beliefs. But the bases of their beliefs are already thoroughly undermined and the whole structure is likely to collapse in a panic of disillusion and despair unless something like new knowledge is developed to replace the old.

Here again, longitudinal inquiries are essential. And here also, it should be insisted that however little the new understandings may have diffused beyond the academic research centers in which they originated, the American public is accustomed to the idea that understandings do change and, especially in the field of education, is quite open to experimentation and innovation.

Much of the methodology of contemporary social science originated in clinical psychology, and perhaps for that reason tends to be "deficiency-oriented." Social scientists raise social *problems,* the study of which can become a social problem in its own right if it is never balanced by the identification and analysis of social *successes.* We are not an unsuccessful country. To the contrary, few societies work as hard at their problems, solve as many, and in the process stumble on more unexpected and fulsome opportunities. The cry of the decent householder who asks why the social science profession (and the news media which increasingly follow the profession) must be ever preoccupied with juvenile delinquency and never with juvenile decency deserves to be heard. Social science like medical science has been preoccupied with pathology, with pain. A measure of inquiry into the sources of health and pleasure is overdue, and is properly a subject of federal support.

10. The federal government, by its own example, and by incentives, should seek the development of a far heightened sense of the finite resources of the natural environment, and the fundamental importance of aesthetics in successful urban growth.

The process of "uglification" may first have developed in Europe; but, as with much else, the technological breakthroughs have taken place in the United States. American cities have grown to be as ugly as they are, not as a consequence of the failure of design, but rather because of the success of a certain interaction of economic, technological, and cultural forces. It is economically efficient to exploit the natural resources of land, and air, and water by technological means that the culture does not reject, albeit that the result is an increasingly despoiled, debilitated, and now even dangerous urban environment.

It is not clear how this is to change, and so the matter which the twenty-second century, say, will almost certainly see as having been the primary urban issue of the twentieth century is ranked last in the public priorities of the moment. But there *are* signs that the culture is changing, that the frontier sense of a natural environment of unlimited resources, all but impervious to human harm, is being replaced by an acute awareness that serious, possibly irreparable harm is being done to the environment, and that somehow the process must be reversed. This *could* lead to a new, nonexploitive technology, and thence to a new structure of economic incentives.

The federal establishment is showing signs that this cultural change is affecting its actions, and so do state and city governments. But the process needs to be raised to the level of a conscious pursuit of policy. The quality of the urban environment, a measure deriving from a humane and understanding use of the natural resources together with the creative use of design in architecture and in the distribution of activities and people, must become a proclaimed concern of government. And here the federal government can lead. It must seek out its hidden policies. (The design of public housing projects, for example, surely has had the consequence of manipulating the lives of those who inhabit them. By and large the federal government set the conditions that have determined the disastrous designs of the past two decades. It is thus responsible for the results, and should force itself to realize that.) And it must be acutely aware of the force of its own example. If scientists (as we are told) in the Manhattan Project were prepared to dismiss the problem of longlived radioactive wastes as one that could be solved merely by ocean dumping, there are few grounds for amazement that business executives in Detroit for so long manufactured automobiles that emitted poison gases into the atmosphere. Both patterns of decision evolved from the primacy of economic concerns in the context of the exploitation of the natural environment in ways the culture did not forbid. There are, however, increasing signs that we are beginning to change in this respect. We may before long evolve into a society in which the understanding of and concern about environmental pollution, and the general uglification of American life, will be both culturally vibrant and politically potent.

Social peace is a primary objective of social policy. To the extent that this derives from a shared sense of the aesthetic value and historical significance of the public places of the city, the federal government has a direct interest in encouraging such qualities.

Daniel J. Elazar has observed that while Americans have been willing to become urbanized, they have adamantly resisted becoming "citified." Yet a measure of "citification" is needed. There are perhaps half a dozen cities in America whose disappearance would, apart from the inconvenience, cause any real regret. To lose one of those six would plunge much of the nation and almost all the immediate inhabitants into genuine grief. Something of value in our lives would have been lost, and we would know it. The difference between these cities that would be missed and the rest that would not, resides fundamentally in the combination of architectural beauty, social amenity, and cultural vigor that sets them apart. It has ever been such. To create such a city and to preserve it was the great ideal of the Greek civilization, and it may yet become ours as we step back ever so cautiously from the worship of the nation-state with its barbarous modernity and impotent might. We might well consider the claims for a different life asserted in the oath of the Athenian city-state:

> *We will ever strive for the ideals and sacred things of the city,*
> *both alone and with many;*
> *We will unceasingly seek to quicken the sense of public duty;*
> *We will revere and obey the city's laws;*
> *We will transmit this city not only not less, but greater, better and*
> *more beautiful than it was transmitted to us.*

42

ANTHONY DOWNS, Alternative Futures for the American Ghetto

In the past few years, the so-called "ghetto" areas of large American cities have emerged as one of the major focal points of national and local concern. Yet there have been very few attempts to develop a comprehensive, long-run strategy for dealing with the complex forces that have created our explosive ghetto problems.

Historically, the word "ghetto" meant an area in which a certain identifiable group was compelled to live. The word retains this meaning of geographic constraint, but now refers to two different kinds of constraining forces. In its *racial* sense, a ghetto is an area to which members of an ethnic minority, particularly Negroes, are residentially restricted by social, economic, and physical pressures from the rest of society. In this meaning, a ghetto can contain wealthy and middle-income residents as well as poor ones. In its *economic* sense, a ghetto is an area in which poor people are compelled to live because they cannot afford better accommodations. In this meaning, a ghetto contains mainly poor people, regardless of race or color.

Considerable confusion arises from failure to distinguish clearly between these different meanings of the word "ghetto." In the remainder of this analysis, I will use the word in its racial sense unless otherwise noted.[1]

The population of ghettos

In March 1966, there were 12.5 million nonwhites living in all U. S. central cities, of whom 12.1 million were Negroes. Since the Negroes were highly segregated residentially, this number serves as a good estimate of the 1966 ghetto population in the racial sense. Approximately 39 percent of these racial ghetto residents had incomes below the "poverty level" (the equivalent of $3,300 per year for a four-person household), based upon data for 1964 (the latest available).[2]

On the other hand, in 1964 the total number of persons with incomes below the "poverty level" in all U. S. central cities was about 10.1 million. Approximately 56 percent of these persons were white and 44 percent were

Anthony Downs, "Alternative Futures for the American Ghetto," *Daedalus,* vol. 97, no. 4 (Fall 1968), pp. 1331–1378. Reprinted by permission.

nonwhite.[3] Since there were about 11.3 million nonwhites altogether in central cities in 1964, the ghetto in its purely economic sense contained about 11 percent fewer people than in its racial sense. Moreover, about 4.4 million persons were doubly ghetto residents in 1964—they were central-city citizens who were both poor and nonwhite.[4]

No matter which ghetto definition is used, it is clear that the population of ghettos is a small fraction of total U. S. population—less than 7 percent. Moreover, future growth in the ghetto population will be dwarfed by future growth in the suburbs of metropolitan areas, which are predominantly white. From 1960 through 1980, those suburbs will gain about 40.9 million persons.[5] Thus the *growth* of suburban population in this period will be almost twice as large as the *total size* of all U. S. ghettos by 1980.

Any policies designed to cope with the ghetto must recognize that the concentrations of Negro population in our central cities are growing rapidly. In 1950, there were 6.5 million Negroes in central cities. In 1960, there were 9.7 million. This represents an increase of 49.2 percent, or an average of 320,000 persons per year. In the same decade, the white population of central cities went from 45.5 million to 47.7 million, an increase of 2.2 million, or 4.8 percent. However, in the largest central cities, the white population actually declined while the Negro population rose sharply.[6]

Since 1960, the growth of nonwhite population in central cities has continued unabated. White population growth in all those cities taken together has, however, ceased entirely. In 1966 the total Negro population of all central cities was about 12.1 million. This is a gain of 2.4 million since 1960, or about 400,000 persons per year. Thus the *absolute* rate of growth of ghettos per year has gone up to its highest level in history. In contrast, the white population of central cities in 1965 was 46.4 million, or 1.3 million *less* than in 1960. So for all 224 central cities considered as a whole, all population growth now consists of gains in Negro population.[7]

Moreover, nearly all Negro population growth is now occurring in ghettos, rather than in suburbs or rural areas. From 1960 to 1966, 89 percent of all nonwhite population growth was in central cities, and 11 percent was in suburbs. Nonmetropolitan areas (including the rural South) actually *lost* nonwhite population. This indicates that heavy out-migration from rural areas to cities is still going on.[8]

Future ghetto growth
if present policies continue

All evidence points to the conclusion that future nonwhite population growth will continue to be concentrated in central cities unless major changes in public policies are made. Not one single significant program of any federal, state, or local government is aimed at altering this tendency or is likely to have the unintended effect of doing so.[9] Moreover, although nonwhite fertility rates have declined since 1957 along with white fertility rates, ghetto growth is likely to remain rapid because of continued in-migration, as well as natural increase.

Recent estimates made by the National Advisory Commission on Civil Disorders indicate that the central-city Negro population for the whole U. S. will be about 13.6 million in 1970 and could rise to as high as 20.3 million by 1985. These estimates assume continued nonwhite in-migration at about the same rate as prevailed from 1960 to 1966. But even if net in-migration is reduced to zero, the 1985 central-city Negro population would be about 17.3 million.[10]

Within individual cities, rapid expansion of segregated ghetto areas will undoubtedly continue. Our 1967 field surveys in Chicago show that about 2.9 city blocks *per week* are shifting from predominantly white to nonwhite occupancy, mainly on the edge of already nonwhite areas. This is somewhat lower than the 3.5 blocks-per-week average from 1960 to 1966, but above the average of 2.6 from 1950 to 1960.[11] If such "peripheral spread" of central-city ghettos continues at nearly the same rate—and there is no present reason to believe it will not—then a number of major central cities will become over 50 percent Negro in total population by 1985. These cities include Chicago, Philadelphia, St. Louis, Detroit, Cleveland, Oakland, Baltimore, New Orleans, Richmond, and Jacksonville. Washington, D. C., Newark, and Gary are already over 50 percent Negro. The proportion of nonwhites in the public school systems in most of these cities now exceeds 50 percent. It will probably be approaching 90 percent by 1983—unless major changes in school programs and districting are adopted before then.[12]

This future growth has critical implications for a great many policy objectives connected with ghettos. For example, it has been suggested that school district boundaries within central cities should be manipulated so as to counteract *de facto* segregation by creating districts in which many Negroes and many whites will jointly reside. This solution is practical over the long run only when there is reasonable stability in the total size of these two groups. But when one group is rapidly expanding in a city where there is no vacant land to build additional housing, then the other group must contract. The only alternative is sharp rises in density which are not occurring. Therefore, as the Negro population expands in such cities, the white population inevitably falls. So possibilities for ending *de facto* segregation in this manner inexorably shrink as time passes. For this and other reasons, no policy toward ghettos can afford to ignore this rapid expansion of the Negro population.

The complexity of the ghetto population and ghetto problems

To be accurate, every analysis of ghettos and their problems must avoid two tempting oversimplifications. The first is conceiving of the ghetto population as a single homogeneous group, all of whose members have similar characteristics, attitudes, and desires. Thus, because many ghetto residents are unemployed or "underemployed" in low-paying, transient jobs, it is easy—but false—to think of all ghetto households as plagued by unemployment. Similarly, because some ghetto residents have carried out riots and looting, whites frequently talk as though *all* ghetto dwellers hate whites, are prone to violence, or are likely to behave irresponsibly. Yet all careful studies of recent riots show that only a small minority of ghetto residents participated in any way, a majority disapprove of such activity, and most would like to have more contact with whites and more integration.[13]

In reality, each racial ghetto contains a tremendous variety of persons who exhibit widely differing attitudes toward almost every question. Many are very poor, but just as many are not. Many have radical views—especially young people; many others are quite conservative—especially the older people. Many are "on welfare," but many more are steadily employed.

This diversity means that public policy concerning any given ghetto problem cannot be successful if it is aimed at or based upon the attitudes and desires of only one group of persons affected by that problem. For example, take unemployment. Programs providing job training for young people could, if expanded enough, affect a large proportion of ghetto dwellers. But the inability of many adult ghetto men to obtain and keep steady, well-paying jobs is also a critical ghetto problem.[14] Also, many women with children cannot work because no adequate day-care facilities are available. Thus, public policy concerning every ghetto problem must have many complex facets in order to work well.

A second widely prevalent oversimplification of ghetto problems is concentration of remedial action upon a single substandard condition. For instance, improving the deplorable housing conditions in many slums would not in itself eliminate most of the dehumanizing forces which operate there. In fact, no single category of programs can possibly be adequate to cope with the tangled problems that exist in ghettos. Any effective ghetto-improvement strategy must concern itself with at least jobs and employment, education, housing, health, personal safety, crime prevention, and income maintenance for dependent persons. A number of other programs could be added, but I believe these are the most critical.[15]

The location of new jobs

Most new employment opportunities are being created in the suburban portions of our metropolitan areas, not anywhere near central-city ghettos.[16] Furthermore, this trend is likely to continue indefinitely into the future. It is true that downtown office-space concentrations in a few large cities have created additional jobs near ghettos. But the outflow of manufacturing and retailing jobs has normally offset this addition significantly—and in many cases has caused a net loss of jobs in central cities.

If we are going to provide jobs for the rapidly expanding ghetto population, particularly jobs that do not call for high levels of skills, we must somehow bring these potential workers closer to the locations of new employment opportunities. This can be done in three ways: by moving job locations so new jobs are created in the ghetto, by moving ghetto residents so they live nearer the new jobs, or by creating better transportation between the ghetto and the locations of new jobs. The first alternative—creating new jobs in the ghetto—will not occur in the future under normal free-market conditions, in my opinion.

That nearly all *new* job opportunities will be located in suburbs does not mean that central cities cannot provide *any* employment to their Negro residents. There are still millions of jobs located in central cities. Just the turnover in workers regarding those jobs will open up a great many potential positions for Negro central-city residents in the future—if employers and other workers cease racial discrimination in their hiring and promotion practices. Nevertheless, as the total numbers of Negro central-city job-seekers steadily rises, the need to link them with emerging sources of new employment in the suburbs will become more and more urgent as a means of reducing unemployment in Negro neighborhoods.

Recently, a number of proposals have been advanced to create public subsidies or guaranteed profits encouraging free enterprise to locate new jobs in ghettos.[17] It is possible that they might work to some extent if the promised profits are high enough to offset the risks and disadvantages involved. Any ghetto improvement strategy must, however, face the problem of linking up persons who need employment with those firms which can provide it or those public agencies assigned to create it.

The future "cost squeeze" on local governments

Traditionally, individual productivity has risen faster in the manufacturing, mining, construction, and agricultural sectors of our economy than in sectors where personal services are dominant—such as finance, insurance, and real estate; retailing; services; and government. The ability to employ larger amounts of capital per worker, coupled with technological change, has caused much larger increases in hourly output-per-worker in the former sectors than in the latter.

All sectors compete with one another for talent and personnel, and all use many of the same products as basic inputs. This means that wages and salaries in the service-dominated sectors must generally keep up with those in the capital-dominated sectors. This tends to place a "squeeze" on the cost of those activities for which individual productivity is hard to increase.

A recent analysis of the performing arts by economists William Baumol and William Bowen highlighted this type of "cost squeeze" as the major reason why it is so difficult to sustain theaters, opera, symphonies, and ballet companies on a self-supporting basis.[18] A pianist cannot perform Chopin's Minute Waltz in 30 seconds, or spend half as much time learning how to play it, to improve efficiency. Yet his salary and the salaries of all the electricians, accompanists, administrators, and others needed for the performing arts are constantly raised to keep their living standards comparable with those of people in the sectors where wage gains can be offset by productivity increases.

Baumol has argued that a similar "cost squeeze" is one of the reasons why state and local expenditures have risen so fast in the postwar period. They increased 257 percent from 1950 to 1966, as compared to 159 percent for Gross National Product and 206 percent for federal expenditures.[19] Moreover, Baumol believes that this pressure to increase service-oriented wages and salaries faster than real output-per-man-hour in the service-oriented sectors will generate an even bigger "explosion" of local and state government costs in the future. For one thing, a higher fraction of society is now and will be employed in public activities than ever before. So there is a steady increase in the proportion of persons whose compensation tends to rise faster than their real output. This reflects both rapid automation in non-service-oriented sectors and an increasing shift of consumer demand toward such services as education, entertainment, and government activities of all types.

The resulting upward pressure on local and state government costs—and tax needs—will undoubtedly be offset to some extent by two forces. The first is greater automation of services themselves through use of computers, closed-circuit TV, duplicating machines, and other devices. The second is the partial substitution of semiskilled and low-skilled assistants for highly-skilled professionals. For example, teachers' aids could relieve professional teachers of immense amounts of administration and paperwork, thereby freeing the latter for more effective use of their time.

Nevertheless, the huge future growth of suburban population will almost certainly force a continuance of the trend toward rising local and state taxes that has now gone on for twenty years. Similar upward pressure on revenue needs will be felt even more strongly by central-city governments. Center cities will contain ever higher proportions of low-income residents who need more services per capita than wealthier suburbanites.

This future "cost squeeze" is important to our analysis because of its impact upon the willingness of suburban taxpayers to help finance any large-scale programs aimed at improving ghetto conditions. Such programs would almost certainly require significant income redistribution from the relatively wealthy suburban population to the relatively poor central-city population. Yet suburbanites will be experiencing steadily rising local and state tax burdens to pay for the services they need themselves.

The "law of dominance"

The achievement of stable racial integration of both whites and nonwhites in housing or public schools is a rare phenomenon in large American cities. Contrary to the views of many, this is *not* because whites are unwilling to share schools or residential neighborhoods with nonwhites. A vast majority of whites of all income groups would be willing to send their children to integrated schools or live in integrated neighborhoods, *as long as they were sure that the white group concerned would remain in the majority* in those facilities or areas.

The residential and educational objectives of these whites are not dependent upon their maintaining any kind of "ethnic purity" in their neighborhoods or schools. Rather, those objectives depend upon their maintaining a certain degree of "cultural dominance" therein.[20] These whites—like most other middle-class citizens of any race—want to be sure that the social, cultural, and economic milieu and values of their own group dominate their own residential environment and the educational environment of their children. This desire in turn springs from the typical middle-class belief of all racial groups that everyday life should be primarily a *value-reinforcing* experience for both adults and children, rather than primarily a *value-altering* one. The best way to ensure that this will happen is to isolate somewhat oneself and one's children in an everyday environment dominated by—but not necessarily exclusively comprised of—other families and children whose social, economic, cultural, and even religious views and attitudes are approximately the same as one's own.

There is no intrinsic reason why race or color should be perceived as a factor relevant to attaining such relative homogeneity. Clearly, race and color have no necessary linkage with the kinds of social, cultural, economic, or religious characteristics and values that can have a true functional impact upon adults and children. Yet I believe a majority of middle-class white Americans still perceive race and color as relevant factors in their assessment of the kind of homogeneity they seek to attain. Moreover, this false perception is reinforced by their lack of everyday experience and contact with Negroes who are, in fact, like them in all important respects. Therefore, in deciding whether a given neighborhood or a given school exhibits the kind of environment in which "their own" traits are and will remain dominant, they consider Negroes as members of "another" group.

It is true that some people want themselves and their children to be immersed in a wide variety of viewpoints, values, and types of people, rather than a relatively homogeneous group.[21] This desire is particularly strong among the intellectuals who dominate the urban planning profession. They are also the strongest supporters of big-city life and the most vitriolic critics of suburbia. Yet I believe their viewpoint—though dominant in recent public discussions of urban problems—is actually shared by only a tiny minority of Americans of any racial group. Almost everyone favors at least some exposure to a wide variety of viewpoints. But experience in our own society and most others shows that the overwhelming majority of middle-class families choose residential locations and schools precisely in order to provide the kind of value-reinforcing experience described above. This is why most Jews live in predominantly Jewish neighborhoods, even in suburbs; why Catholic parents continue to support separate school systems; and partly why so few middle-class Negro families have been willing to risk moving to all-white suburbs even where there is almost no threat of any harassment.

However demeaning this phenomenon may be to Negroes, it must be recognized if we are to understand why residential segregation has persisted so strongly in the United States, and what conditions are necessary to create viable racial integration. The expansion of nonwhite residential areas has led to "massive transition" from white to nonwhite occupancy mainly because there has been no mechanism that could assure the whites in any given area that they would remain in the majority after nonwhites once began entering. Normal population turnover causes about 20 percent of the residents of the average U. S. neighborhood to move out every year because of income changes, job transfers, shifts in life-cycle position, or deaths. In order for a neighborhood to retain any given character, the persons who move in to occupy the resulting vacancies must be similar to those who have departed.

But once Negroes begin entering an all-white neighborhood near the ghetto, most other white families become convinced that the area will eventually become all Negro, mainly because this has happened so often before. Hence it is difficult to persuade whites not now living there to move in and occupy vacancies. They are only willing to move into neighborhoods where whites are now the dominant majority and seem likely to remain so. Hence the whites who would otherwise have moved in from elsewhere stop doing so.[22] This means that almost all vacancies are eventually occupied by nonwhites, and the neighborhood inexorably shifts toward a heavy nonwhite majority. Once this happens, the remaining whites also seek to leave, since they do not wish to remain in an area where they have lost their culturally dominant position.

As a result, whites who would be quite satisfied—even delighted—to live in an integrated neighborhood *as members of the majority* are never given the opportunity to do so. Instead, for reasons beyond the control of each individual, they are forced to choose between complete segregation or living in an area heavily dominated by members of what they consider "another group." Given their values, they choose the former.

Many—especially Negroes—may deplore the racially prejudiced desire of most white middle-class citizens to live in neighborhoods and use schools where other white middle-class households are dominant. Nevertheless, this desire seems to be firmly entrenched among most whites at present. Hence public policy cannot ignore this desire if it hopes to be effective. Moreover, this attitude does not preclude the development of racial integration, as long as whites are in the majority and believe they will remain so. The problem is convincing them that their majority status will persist in mixed areas in the face of past experience to the contrary. Even more difficult, the people who must be persuaded are not those now living in a mixed area, but those who must keep moving in from elsewhere to maintain racial balance as vacancies occur through normal population turnover.

Clearly, the dynamic processes related to this "Law of Dominance" are critical to any strategy concerning the future of American ghettos. They are especially relevant to strategies which seek to achieve stable residential or educational integration of whites and nonwhites, instead of the "massive transition" and "massive segregation" which have dominated the spatial patterns of non-white population growth in the past twenty years. Such stable integration will occur in most areas only if there is some way to guarantee the white majority that it will remain the "dominant" majority. This implies some form of "quotas" concerning the proportion of nonwhites in the facility or area concerned—even legally supported "quotas."

Unless some such "balancing devices" are *explicitly* used and reinforced by public policies and laws to establish their credibility, whites will continue to withdraw from—or, more crucially, fail to keep entering—any facility or area into which significant numbers of nonwhites are entering. This means a continuation of *de facto* segregation and a reinforcement of the white belief that any nonwhite entry inevitably leads to "massive transition." Even more importantly, it means continued failure to eliminate white perception of race as a critical factor by encouraging whites and nonwhites to live together in conditions of stability. Thus, in my opinion, the only way to destroy the racial prejudice at the root of the "Law of Cultural Dominance" is to shape current public policy in recognition of that "Law" so as to encourage widespread experience that will undermine it.[23]

The concept of social strategy

Americans typically do not attempt to solve social problems by means of be-havior patterns that could reasonably be considered "strategies." The concept of strategy implies development of a single comprehensive, long-range plan to cope with some significant social problem. But U. S. decision-making concerning domestic issues is too fragmented and diffused to permit the formulation of any such long-range plan regarding a given problem. Instead, we approach most social problems through a process which has been aptly labeled "disjointed incremental-ism."[24] Each decision-maker or actor makes whatever choices seem to him to be most appropriate at that moment, in light of his own interests and his own view of the public welfare. For two reasons, he pays little attention to most of the consequences of his action upon others—especially the long-run consequences. First, no one has the detailed knowledge and foresight necessary to comprehend all those consequences. Second, no one has the time nor the energy to negotiate in advance with all others likely to be affected by his actions. So instead he acts "blindly" and waits for those who are hurt to complain or those who are bene-fited to applaud.

A process of mutual adjustment ensues. Those who are unduly harmed by each decision supposedly recoup their losses by exercising whatever economic, moral, or political powers are available to them. Those who benefit use their powers to encourage more of the same. Presiding over this melee is a set of mainly "reactive" governments and other public agencies. They keep altering the "rules of the game" and their own programs and behavior so as to correct any grievous imbalances that appear.

There is no guarantee that the checks and balances built into this unco-ordinated process will effectively counteract every destructive condition or trend that emerges from it. It is certainly possible that each individual will be motivated by the incentives facing him to take actions that, when combined with those taken by others acting in a similar individualistic fashion, will lead to collective disaster.

So far in history, the system has been remarkably effective at avoiding such outcomes. Part of this success undoubtedly results from society's ability to generate in most of its citizens a single set of basic values and even broad policy objectives that exert a cohesive influence on their supposedly individualistic decisions. But another important ingredient in the system's success is the ability of enough significant actors in it to perceive threatening trends in time to formu-late and carry out ameliorating policies.

This means they must accurately forecast any potentially dire outcome of current trends. They must also visualize alternative outcomes that would be preferable and are within the capabilities of society. Finally, they must devise policies and programs that will shift individual incentives so one of those alterna-tives will occur. In some cases, the ongoing trends that threaten society are strongly entrenched in its institutional structure. If so, alternatives that avoid the pending threats may not be attainable without fundamental changes in institu-tions. Those changes in turn may be possible only if a preponderance of power-ful people in society share at least a broad concept of the need for change and the kinds of objectives motivating it. This concept closely resembles a social strategy. It visualizes a certain desired outcome, implies a wide range of policies by various actors necessary to attain that outcome, and serves as a "hidden coordinator" of seemingly individualistic behavior.

The above reasoning implies two conclusions crucial to this analysis. First, strategic thinking about social problems can play a vital role in stimulating social change even where decision-making is dominated by disjointed incrementalism. Second, the alternative outcomes conceived in such thinking can usefully include some which could not be achieved without major changes in existing institutions or values. For example, some of the strategies discussed herein require a high-ly coordinated set of policy decisions. Such coordination is unlikely to occur in the presently fragmentalized governmental structures of our metropolitan areas unless major changes in the incentives facing these governments are created.

I will therefore formulate several alternative strategies for coping with the problems posed by future ghetto growth, even though carrying out some of them would require a far more consciously coordinated development of social change than has been typical of America in the past.

Formulation of major alternative strategies

Because of the immense complexity of our society, an infinite number of alternative future strategies regarding ghettos could conceivably be designed. But for purposes of practical consideration, this number must be narrowed drastically to a few that highlight the major choices facing us. Selecting these few is inescapably arbitrary—there is no "scientific" way to do it. I believe, however, that the narrowing of alternative ghetto futures can best be accomplished by focusing upon the major choices relating to the following three questions:

To what extent should future nonwhite population growth be concentrated within the central cities, as it has been in the past twenty years?

To what extent should our white and nonwhite populations be residentially segregated from each other in the future?

To what extent should society redistribute income to relatively depressed urban areas or population groups in society in a process of "enrichment"?

Each of these questions can be answered with any one of a whole spectrum of responses from one extreme to the other. But for purposes of analysis, I believe we can usefully narrow these answers down to just two points on the spectrum for each question. This allows us to reduce the alternatives to the following:

Degree-of-Concentration Alternatives

1. Continue to concentrate nonwhite population growth in central cities or perhaps in a few older suburbs next to central cities. (*Concentration*)
2. Disperse nonwhite population growth widely throughout all parts of metropolitan areas. (*Dispersal*)

Degree-of-Segregation Alternatives

1. Continue to cluster whites and nonwhites in residentially segregated neighborhoods, regardless of where they are within the metropolitan area. (*Segregation*)
2. Scatter the nonwhite population, or at least a significant fraction of it, "randomly" among white residential areas to achieve at least partial residential integration. (*Integration*)

Degree-of-Enrichment Alternatives

1. Continue to provide relatively low-level welfare, educational, housing, job-training, and other support to the most deprived groups in the population—both those who are incapable of working, such as the vast majority of public-aid recipients, and those who might possibly work, but are unemployed because of lack of skills, discrimination, lack of desire, or any other reason. (*Non-enrichment*)
2. Greatly raise the level of support to welfare, educational, housing, job-training, and other programs for the most deprived groups, largely through federally aided programs. (*Enrichment*)

Even narrowing the alternatives in this fashion leaves a logical possibility of eight different combinations. A number of these can, however, be ruled out as internally inconsistent in practice. For example, I believe it is extremely unlikely that any strategy of dispersing the nonwhite population throughout metropolitan areas could be accomplished without provision of substantially greater incentives to both nonwhites (to get them to move) and whites (to increase their willingness to accept large numbers of nonwhite in-migrants without strong resistance). Thus no combination of both dispersal and non-enrichment need be considered.

Similarly, in the very long run, concentration of future nonwhite population growth within central cities is probably inconsistent with integration. Many of those cities will become so preponderantly nonwhite that integration within their borders will be impossible. Admittedly, it may take two or more decades for this to occur in some central cities, and it might never occur in others. Nevertheless, some types of integration (such as in the public schools) will become impossible long before that if a concentration policy is followed. For these reasons, I will consider only one special combination containing both concentration and integration. This consists of continued concentration, but a build-up of a gradually expanding inner-city core of fully integrated housing and public facilities created through massive urban renewal. For reasons explained below, this strategy would require a significant enrichment program too.

This whole process of elimination leaves five basic alternative strategies relevant to future development of ghettos. For convenience, each has been assigned a short name to be used throughout the remainder of this article. These strategies can be summarized as follows:

1. *Present Policies:* concentration, segregation, non-enrichment.
2. *Enrichment Only:* concentration, segregation, enrichment.
3. *Integrated Core:* concentration, integration (in the center only), enrichment.
4. *Segregated Dispersal:* dispersal, segregation, enrichment.
5. *Integrated Dispersal:* dispersal, integration, enrichment.

Before these strategies are examined in detail, two things about them should be emphasized.

First, they apply to individual metropolitan areas. Therefore, it would be at least theoretically possible to adopt different strategies toward the ghetto in different metropolitan areas. There are, in fact, some convincing reasons why this would be an excellent idea.

Second, these strategies are formed from relatively extreme points on the relevant ranges of possibilities. Hence they could actually be adopted in various mixtures, rather than in the "pure" forms set forth above. This further strengthens the case for using a variety of approaches across the country. For purposes of analysis, however, it is fruitful to examine each of these strategies initially as though it were to be the sole instrument for coping with ghetto problems in all metropolitan areas.

The present-policies strategy

In order to carry out this strategy, we need merely do nothing more than we do now. Even existing federal programs aimed at aiding cities—such as the Model Cities Program—will continue or accelerate concentration, segregation, and non-enrichment, unless those programs are colossally expanded.

I do not wish to imply that present federal and local efforts in the anti-poverty program, the public housing program, the urban renewal program, health programs, educational programs, and many others are not of significant benefit to residents of ghettos. They are. Nevertheless, as both recent investigations and recent violence have emphasized, existing programs have succeeded neither in stemming the various adverse trends operating in ghetto areas nor in substantially eliminating the deplorable conditions there. Therefore, the strategy of continuing our present policies and our present level of effort is essentially not going to alter current conditions in ghettos.

This may make it seem silly to label continuation of present policies as a specific antighetto strategy. Yet failure to adopt effective policies is still a strategy. It may not be a successful one, but it nevertheless is an expression of society's current commitment and attitude toward the ghetto.

Thus, if we maintain our current programs and policies, segregated areas of residence in our central cities will continue to expand rapidly and to suffer from all the difficult problems inherent in both racial and economic ghettos.

The enrichment-only strategy

The second fundamental ghetto future strategy I call "enrichment only." This approach is aimed at dramatically improving the quality of life within the confines of present ghetto areas and those nearby areas into which ghettos will expand in the future if concentration continues. I presume that any such policy would apply to the poverty meaning of ghetto more than the racial one—that is, any enrichment strategy would aim at upgrading the lowest-income and most disadvantaged citizens of our central cities, regardless of race. Nevertheless, a sizable proportion of such persons are nonwhites. Moreover, programs aimed at reducing racial discrimination in employment and in the quality of public services would form an important part of any strategy aimed at upgrading the most deprived groups. So the enrichment-only strategy would still concentrate upon the same areas as if it were to follow a racial policy.

The basic idea underlying the enrichment-only strategy (and part of every other strategy involving enrichment) is to develop federally financed programs that would greatly improve the education, housing, incomes, employment and job-training, and social services received by ghetto residents. This would involve vastly expanding the scale of present programs, changing the nature of many of them because they are now ineffective or would be if operated at a much larger scale, and creating incentives for a much greater participation of private capital in ghetto activities. Such incentives could include tax credits for investments made in designated ghetto areas, wage subsidies (connected with on-the-job training but lasting longer than such training so as to induce employers to hire unskilled ghetto residents), rent or ownership supplements for poor families, enabling them to rent or buy housing created by private capital, and others.[25]

It is important to realize that the enrichment-only strategy would end neither racial segregation nor the concentration of nonwhites in central cities (and some older adjoining suburbs). It would help many Negroes attain middle-class status and thus make it easier for them to leave the ghetto if they wanted to. Undoubtedly many would. But, by making life in central-city ghettos more attractive without creating any strong pressures for integration or dispersal of the nonwhite population, such a policy would increase the in-migration of nonwhites into central cities. This would speed up the expansion of racially segregated areas in central cities, thereby accelerating the process of "massive transition" of whole neighborhoods from white to nonwhite occupancy.

The integrated-core strategy

This strategy is similar to the enrichment-only strategy because both would attempt to upgrade the quality of life in central-city ghettos through massive federally assisted programs. The integrated-core strategy would also seek, however, to eliminate racial segregation in an ever expanding core of the city by creating a socially, economically, and racially integrated community there. This integrated core would be built up through large-scale urban renewal programs, with the land re-uses including scattered-site public housing, middle-income housing suitable for families with children, and high-quality public services—especially schools.

All of these re-uses would be based upon "managed integration"—that is, deliberate achievement of a racial balance containing a majority of whites but a significant minority of Negroes. Thus, the integrated-core strategy could be carried out only if deliberate racial discrimination aimed at avoiding *de facto* segregation becomes recognized by the Supreme Court as a legitimate tactic for public agencies. In fact, such recognition will probably be a necessity for any strategy involving a significant degree of integration in public schools, public housing, or even private residential areas. This conclusion was recently recognized by the Chicago Board of Education, its staff, and its consultants, who all recommended the use of quotas in schools located in racially changing neighborhoods to promote stable integration.[26]

The integrated-core strategy essentially represents a compromise between an ideal condition and two harsh realities. The ideal condition is development of a fully integrated society in which whites and Negroes live together harmoniously and the race of each individual is not recognized by anyone as a significant factor in any public or private decisions.

The first harsh reality is that the present desire of most whites to dominate their own environment means that integration can only be achieved through deliberate management and through the willingness of some Negroes to share schools and residences as a minority. The second harsh reality is the assumption that it will be impossible to disperse the massive Negro ghettos of major central cities fast enough to prevent many of those cities from eventually becoming predominantly, or even almost exclusively, Negro in population. The development of predominantly Negro central cities, with high proportions of low-income residents, ringed by predominantly white suburbs with much wealthier residents, might lead to a shattering polarization that would split society along both racial and spatial lines.

This strategy seeks to avoid any such polarization by building an integrated core of white and nonwhites in central cities, including many leaders of both races in politics, business, and civic affairs. Negro leadership will properly assume the dominant position in central-city politics in many major cities after Negroes have become a majority of the municipal electorates there. By that time, integration of leadership within those cities will, it is to be hoped, have become a sufficient reality so that leaders of both races can work together in utilizing the central city's great economic assets, rather than fighting one another for control over them.

Thus, the integrated-core strategy postulates that a significant movement toward racial integration is essential to keep American society from "exploding" as a result of a combined racial-spatial confrontation of central cities vs. suburbs in many large metropolitan areas. It also postulates that development of integration in the suburbs through massive dispersal cannot occur fast enough to avoid such a confrontation. Therefore, integration must be developed on an "inside-out" basis, starting in the core of the central city, rather than in the suburbs.

The concept of dispersal

The two dispersal strategies concerning the future of ghettos are both based upon a single key assumption: that the problems of ghettos cannot be solved so long as millions of Negroes, particularly those with low incomes and other significant disadvantages, are required or persuaded to live together in segregated ghetto areas within our central cities. These strategies contend that large numbers of Negroes should be given strong incentives to move voluntarily from central cities into suburban areas, including those in which no Negroes presently reside.

To illustrate what "large numbers" really means, let us postulate one version of dispersal which I call the "constant-size ghetto strategy." This strictly hypothetical strategy aims at stopping the growth of existing central-city ghettos by dispersing enough Negroes from central cities to the suburbs (or to peripheral central-city areas) to offset potential future increases in that growth. Taking the period from 1970 through 1975, estimates made by the National Advisory Commission on Civil Disorders show that the nonwhite population of all U. S. central cities taken as a whole would, in the absence of any dispersal strategy, expand from about 13.6 million to about 15.5 million.[27] Thus, if dispersal of nonwhites were to take place at a scale large enough to keep central-city racial ghettos at their 1970 level during the five subsequent years, there would have to be an out-movement of 1.9 million Negroes into the suburbs. This amounts to 380,000 per year.

From 1950 to 1960, the suburban Negro population of all U. S. metropolitan areas grew a total of only 60,000 per year. In that decade, the white population of suburban portions of our metropolitan areas (the so-called "urban fringe") increased by about 1,720,000 persons per year. Thus, 96.6 percent of all suburban population growth consisted of whites. From 1960 to 1966, the Negro population growth in all suburban areas declined sharply to a rate of 33,300 per year. In fact, there was actually in-migration of Negroes from suburbs to central cities. But the white population in all suburbs went up an average of 1,750,000 per year. Thus the proportion of suburban growth made up of whites climbed to 98.1 percent—an even higher fraction than in the decade from 1950 to 1960.[28] Undoubtedly, some of this white population increase was caused by an exodus of whites from central cities in response to the growth therein. If future Negro population growth in central cities were stopped by a large-scale dispersion policy, then white population growth in the suburbs would be definitely smaller than it was from 1950 through 1966. The size of the resulting decline would depend upon the fraction of white exodus from central cities that occurs in response to Negro growth, as opposed to such other factors as rising incomes, the aging central-city housing stock, and shifts in life-cycle position. If whites leave central cities in a one-to-one ratio with the expansion of Negro population therein, then a cessation of Negro ghetto growth would result in a large drop in white suburban growth. In that case, future suburban population increases would consist of about 23 percent Negroes (based on very rough calculations). This contrasts with proportions of less than 5 percent from 1950 through 1960 and less than 3 percent from 1960 through 1966.

Clearly, such dispersal would represent a radical change in existing trends. Not only would it stop the expansion of Negro ghettos in central cities, but it would also inject a significant Negro population into many presently all-white suburban areas. It is true that policies of dispersal would not necessarily have to be at this large a scale. Dispersal aimed not at stopping ghetto growth, but merely at slowing it down somewhat could be carried out at a much lower scale. Yet even such policies would represent a marked departure from past U. S. practice.

Such a sharp break with the past would be necessary for any significant dispersal of Negroes. Merely providing the *opportunity* for Negroes to move out of ghettos would, at least in the short run, not result in many moving. Even adoption of a vigorously enforced nationwide open-occupancy law applying to *all* residences would not greatly speed up the present snail's-pace rate of dispersion. Experience in those states that have open-occupancy ordinances decisively proves this conclusion.

Hence, positive incentives for dispersion would have to be created in order to speed up the rate at which Negroes voluntarily move from central cities and settle in suburban areas. (Certainly no policy involving *involuntary* movement of either whites or Negroes should ever be considered.) Such incentives could include rent supplements, ownership supplements, special school-support bonus payments linked to the education of children moving out from ghettos, and other devices which essentially attach a subsidy to a person. Then, when the person moves, he and the community into which he goes get credit for that subsidy. This creates incentives both for him to move and for the community to accept him gladly. Both of the strategies involving dispersal would thus represent radical changes in existing practices.

Segregated vs. integrated dispersal

One of the fundamental purposes of any dispersal strategy is providing Negro Americans with real freedom of choice concerning housing and school accommodations. The experience of other ethnic groups indicates that Negroes would exercise that choice in suburban areas in a combination of two ways. Some individual Negro households would become scattered "randomly" in largely white residential areas. But other Negro households—probably a larger number—would voluntarily cluster together. This would create primarily Negro neighborhoods, or even primarily Negro suburban communities. Such a combination of both *scattering* and *clustering* would occur even if Negro households had absolutely no fears of hostility or antagonism from white neighbors. It is unrealistic to suppose, however, that *all* prejudice against Negro neighbors can be eliminated from presently all-white suburbs in the immediate future. As a result, even if a dispersal strategy is carried out, there will still be some external pressure against Negro newcomers. This will encourage an even higher proportion of incoming Negro households to cluster together than would do so in the absence of all fears and antagonism. Moreover, public policies to accomplish dispersion might include deliberate creation of some moderate-sized clusters of Negro families, as in scattered-site public housing developments.

Once all-Negro clusters appear in previously all-white suburbs, there is a high probability that they will turn into "ghetto-lets" or "mini-ghettos." The same forces that produced ghettos in central cities are likely to repeat themselves in suburbs, though in a much less pathological form. Those pressures are a rapidly expanding Negro population, the "Law of Cultural Dominance" among whites, and at least some restriction of Negro choice in areas far removed from existing all-Negro neighborhoods. Therefore, once a Negro cluster becomes large enough so that Negro children dominate a local elementary school, the typical phenomenon of white withdrawal from the local residential real-estate market is likely to occur. This has already taken place regarding Jews and gentiles in many suburban areas. Thus, any dispersal strategy that does not explicitly aim at preventing segregation, too, will probably create new segregated neighborhoods in the suburbs.

This new form of *de facto* segregation will, however, have far less damaging effects upon Negroes than existing segregation concentrated in central cities. In the first place, if Negro clusters are deliberately created in almost all parts of the metropolitan area at once, whites will be unable to flee to "completely safe" suburbs without accepting impractically long commuting journeys. This will strongly reduce the white propensity to abandon an area after Negroes begin entering it. Moreover, the presence of some Negroes in all parts of suburbia will also make it far easier for individual Negro families to move into all-white neighborhoods on a scattered basis. Thus any dispersal policy that really disperses Negroes in the suburbs will immediately create an enormous improvement in the real freedom of residential choice enjoyed by individual Negro families. This will be true even if most of those families actually choose to remain in Negro clusters.

Second, any dispersal strategy would presumably be accompanied by strongly enforced open-occupancy laws applying to all housing. At present, these laws do not lead to scattering, but they would in the climate of a dispersal strategy. Then Negro willingness to move into all-white areas would rise sharply, and white antagonism toward such move-ins would drop.

Third, *de facto* residential segregation need not lead to segregated suburban schools. In relatively small communities, such as most suburbs, it is easy to bus students to achieve stable racial balance. Thus, the formation of clustered Negro housing would not have to cause the quality-of-education problems that now exist in central-city ghettos. True, if a given suburb became predominantly Negro, its schools might become quite segregated. In that case, school systems in adjoining suburbs might have to merge or at least work out student exchange procedures with the segregated community in order to counteract segregation. This may be difficult to accomplish (though in the climate of a dispersal strategy, it would be at least thinkable). Hence it is possible that some segregated school systems might appear in suburban areas. But Negro families would still have far more opportunities than they do now to move to areas with integrated schools.

A dispersal strategy that did not succeed in initially placing Negro households in almost all parts of the metropolitan area would be more likely to generate "ghetto-lets." Hence, if dispersal tactics call for initially concentrating on dispersion only to a few suburbs, it is quite possible that segregated dispersal would result. This implies that integrated dispersal could be attained in only two ways. Either the initial dispersal strategy must place Negroes in almost all suburban communities, or specific integration-furthering mechanisms—such as school and residential quotas—must be adopted.

The speculative nature of the above discussion illustrates that society needs to do much more thinking about what dispersal really means, how it might be achieved, what alternative forms it might take, and what its consequences would be.

In an article of this length, it is impossible to present an adequate analysis of each of the strategies described above. Certain factors will, however, have a crucial influence on which strategy actually prevails. These factors should be at least briefly mentioned here.

The possibility of a spatial-racial "confrontation"

Society's existing policies toward the ghetto are, by definition, those called for by the present policies strategy. Yet there are strong reasons to believe that maintenance of these policies in ghettos is not possible. The striking increase in violence in big-city ghettos is probably related to a combination of higher aspirations, reduced sanctions against the use of violence, and continued deplorable slum conditions. If so, persistence of the present-policies strategy may continue to spawn incidents, riots, and perhaps guerrilla warfare. Then existing local police forces might have to be supplemented with para-military forces on continuous alert. Thus, the present-policies strategy might lead to further polarization of whites and Negroes and even to the creation of semi-martial law in big cities.

Moreover, when Negroes become the dominant political force in many large central cities, they may understandably demand radical changes in present policies. At the same time, major private capital investment in those cities might virtually cease if white-dominated firms and industries decided the risks of involvement there were too great. In light of recent disorders, this seems very likely. Such withdrawal of private capital has already occurred in almost every single ghetto area in the U. S. Even if private investment continues, big cities containing high proportions of low-income Negroes would need substantial income transfers from the federal government to meet the demands of their electorates for improved services and living conditions.

But by that time, Congress will be more heavily influenced by representatives of the suburban electorate. The suburbs will comprise 41 percent of our total population by 1985, as opposed to 33 percent in 1960. Central cities will decline from 31 percent to 27 percent.[29] Under a present-policies strategy, this influential suburban electorate will be over 95 percent white, whereas the central-city population in all metropolitan areas together will be slightly over 60 percent white. The suburban electorate will be much wealthier than the central-city population, which will consist mainly of Negroes and older whites. Yet even the suburbs will be feeling the squeeze of higher local government costs generated by rising service salaries. Hence the federal government may refuse to approve the massive income transfers from suburbs to central cities that the mayors of the latter will desperately need in order to placate their relatively deprived electorates. After all, many big-city mayors are already beseeching the federal government for massive aid—including [former] Republicans like John Lindsay—and their electorates are not yet dominated by low-income Negroes.

Thus the present-policies strategy, if pursued for any long period of time, might lead to a simultaneous political and economic "confrontation" in many metropolitan areas. Such a "confrontation" would involve mainly Negro, mainly poor, and fiscally bankrupt larger central cities on the one hand, and mainly white, much wealthier, but highly taxed suburbs on the other hand. Some older suburbs will also have become Negro by that time, but the vast majority of suburbs will still be "lily white." A few metropolitan areas may seek to avoid the political aspects of such a confrontation by shifting to some form of metropolitan government designed to prevent Negroes from gaining political control of central cities. Yet such a move will hardly eliminate the basic segregation and relative poverty generating hostility in the urban Negro population. In fact, it might increase that population's sense of frustration and alienation.

In my opinion, there is a serious question whether American society in its present form could survive such a confrontation. If the Negro population felt itself wrongly "penned in" and discriminated against, as seems likely, many of its members might be driven to supporting the kind of irrational rebellion now being preached by a tiny minority. Considering the level of violence we have encountered already, it is hard to believe that the conditions that might emanate from a prolonged present-policies strategy would not generate much more. Yet the Negro community cannot hope to defeat the white community in a pitched battle. It is outnumbered 9 to 1 in population and vastly more than that in resources. Thus any massive resort to violence by Negroes would probably bring even more massive retaliation by whites. This could lead to a kind of urban *apartheid*, with martial law in cities, enforced residence of Negroes in segregated areas, and a drastic reduction in personal freedom for both groups, especially Negroes.

Such an outcome would obviously violate all American traditions of individual liberty and Constitutional law. It would destroy "the American dream" of freedom and equal opportunity for all. Therefore, to many observers this result is unthinkable. They believe that we would somehow "change things" before they occurred. This must mean that either the present-policies strategy would not lead to the kind of confrontation I have described, or we would abandon that strategy before the confrontation occurred.

Can the present-policies strategy avoid "confrontation"?

What outcomes from a present-policies strategy might prevent this kind of confrontation? For one thing, if incomes in the Negro community rise rapidly without any additional programs, the Negro population of central cities may enter the middle class at a fast rate. If so, the Negro electorate that comes to dominate many major central cities politically by 1985 under the present-policies strategy may consist largely of stable, well-to-do citizens capable of supporting an effective local government.

To test this possibility, we have done some projections of incomes in the nonwhite population on a rough basis through 1983, assuming a present-policies strategy. These indicate that about two-thirds of the nonwhite population at that time will have incomes *above* the existing poverty level—about the same fraction as at present. Since nonwhites will then form a much larger share of total central-city population, however, the percentage of *total* central-city population below the present poverty level might actually *rise* slightly. It is possible that nonwhite incomes might increase faster than in this forecast. Yet it is almost certain that the substitution of a relatively poor nonwhite group for a middle-income white group in central cities under a status-quo strategy will counterbalance likely increases in the incomes of nonwhites.

As a result, the electorate that will exist in major cities when Negroes become a majority will probably be just as poor as it is now (in real income terms). In contrast, the population in surrounding suburbs will be much wealthier than it is now. Thus, even if nonwhite incomes rise rapidly, there is still likely to be a significant "gap" between central-city and suburban income levels at that time—probably larger than at present.

Yet even under *present* conditions, many large central cities are critically short of revenue. Furthermore, in a generally wealthier society, it is highly probable that most central-city electorates will demand higher-than-existing levels of public service. Finally, the general cost of all government services will have risen sharply because of the productivity trends explained earlier. Hence, future central-city governments will have much higher costs, but not much greater resources than they do now. So rising incomes among nonwhites will not remove the fiscal pressure on central-city governments that is a key ingredient in the "confrontation" described above.

Moreover, the population group most responsible for violence and disturbances in central cities appears to consist of young Negro men between fifteen and twenty-four years of age. A high proportion of these people are unemployed because they lack skills (many are high school dropouts) and elementary training and motivation. This group will undoubtedly grow larger through natural increase and in-migration. Its problems are not likely to be solved under a status-quo strategy. Hence, even if the vast majority of nonwhites in central cities have increasing reason to abhor violence and riots, the *absolute size* of this more alienated group in 1975 will be 40 percent larger than in 1966, and even larger by 1985.[30] This implies that at least part of this group might start actions forcing the kind of "confrontation" I have described.

Most of the other possible developments under a non-enrichment strategy that would avoid any major "confrontation" involve abandoning concentration of Negroes in central cities. Thus, some observers argue that members of the Negro middle class will increasingly move out to suburban communities as their incomes rise with no further encouragement from public programs. In this way, Negroes would be following the precedent of other ethnic groups. Up to now, there is no evidence that this has started to occur, even though a large Negro middle class already exists. But if such a pattern did evolve, it would amount to dispersal rather than the concentration implicit in the present-policies strategy.

Can present policies be sustained?

In any event, there appears to be significant probability—which I subjectively judge to be at least 25 percent and perhaps as high as 75 percent—that the present-policies strategy will prove unsustainable. If adopted, it would probably generate major repercussions that would force it to be abandoned. Society would be compelled either to suspend traditional individual rights and adopt martial law in cities or to institute major programs to improve ghetto conditions or to move toward wider dispersal of the Negro population, or some combination of these. Admittedly, there is no certainty that the present-policies strategy will lead to these outcomes. Nevertheless, I believe the probability that it will is high enough to make this strategy essentially self-defeating. Modern life is too dynamic for the status quo to be preserved for long.

Yet the present-policies strategy is the one society has so far chosen. Almost all current public policies tend to further concentration, segregation, and non-enrichment, as mentioned earlier. The few supposedly anti-concentration devices adopted, such as open-occupancy laws, have proved almost totally ineffective. All we have to do to confirm our choice of this strategy is to continue existing policies. In fact, avoiding this strategy will be difficult, because doing so will require major changes in present attitudes as well as in existing resource allocations.

The "black power" case
for the enrichment-only strategy

The enrichment-only strategy is consistent with a current ideology that has come to be called the "Black Power" viewpoint. This viewpoint has been criticized by many, and some of its proponents have misused it to incite violence. Yet it is certainly an intellectually respectable and defensible position containing some persuasive elements.

The "Black Power" argument states that the Negro American population needs to overcome its feelings of powerlessness and lack of self-respect before it can assume its proper role in society. It can do so only by exerting power over the decisions that directly affect its own members. According to this view, a fully integrated society is not really possible until the Negro minority has developed its own internal strength. Therefore, the ideal society in which race itself is not an important factor can only come much later. It could exist only after Negroes had gained power and self-respect by remaining in concentrated areas over which they could assume political and economic control and direction. Hence this view contends that a future in which central cities become primarily Negro and suburbs almost entirely white would be an advantage rather than a disadvantage.

The "Black Power" view has several notable strong points. First, such assumption of local power would be fully consistent with the behavior of previous nationality groups, such as the Irish in New York and Boston. They, too, came up from the bottom of the social and economic ladder, where they had been insulted and discriminated against. And they did it by gaining political and economic control over the areas in which they lived.

Second, it is unquestionably true that one of the two most important factors providing Negroes with all their recent gains in legal rights and actual welfare has been their own forceful presentation of grievances and demands. (The other factor has been high-level prosperity in the economy in general.) Negro-originated marches, demonstrations, protests, and even riots have had immensely more impact in improving their actual power, income, and opportunities than all the "purely voluntary" actions of whites combined—including those of white liberals.

Third, time is on the side of the "Black Power" argument if current population growth and location trends continue. As pointed out earlier, Negroes are likely to become a majority of the electorate in many large American cities within the next fifteen years, unless radically new policies are adopted. By giving Negroes political control over these cities, this trend would provide them with a powerful bargaining position in dealing with the rest of society—a tool they now sorely lack.

Fourth, the "Black Power" viewpoint provides many key ideological supports for Negro self-development. It stresses the need for Negroes to become proud of their color and their history, more conscious of their own strengths. It also focuses their attention on the need for organizing themselves economically and politically. Hence it could provide a focal point for arousing and channeling the largely untapped self-development energies of the Negro American population. One of the greatest difficulties in improving ghettos is discovering effective ways in which the lowest-income and most deprived residents can develop their own capabilities by participating more fully in the decisions and activities that affect them. Such "learning by doing" is, in my opinion, a vital part of the process of bringing deprived people into the main stream of American society. Insofar as "Black Power" proponents could develop such mechanisms, they would immensely benefit American society.

There are, however, also significant flaws in the "Black Power" argument. First, Negroes do not in fact have much power in the U. S. Nor is it clear just how they can obtain power solely through their own efforts, particularly in the near future. "Black Power" advocates constantly talk about "taking what is rightfully theirs" because they are dissatisfied with what "whitey" is willing to turn over to them voluntarily. They also reject the condescension inherent in whites' "giving" Negroes anything, including more power. But what bargaining power can Negroes use to compel whites to yield greater control over the economic and political decisions that affect them?

There are two possible answers. First, they could organize themselves so cohesively that they would become a potent political and economic force through highly disciplined but fully legal action. Examples would be block voting and economic boycotts. So far, nearly all efforts at such internal organization have foundered on the solid rocks of apathy, lack of funds, internal dissension, and disbelief that anything could be accomplished.

Second, Negroes could launch direct action—such as demonstrations and marches—that would morally, economically, or physically threaten the white community. This approach has so far proved to be the most successful. But many Negroes believe it has not improved their situation as fast as is necessary. Hence, there is a tendency to shift the form of threat employed to more and more violent action in order to get faster and more profound results. This tendency need only influence a small minority of Negroes in order to cause a significant escalation of violence. Yet such an escalation might result in massive retaliation by the white community that would worsen the Negroes' position. What is needed is enough of a threat to cause the white community to start changing its own attitudes and allocation of resources in ways far more favorable to Negroes, but not so much of a threat as to cause withdrawal of all white cooperation and sympathy.

This conclusion points up the second flaw in the "Black Power" case: Ultimately, U. S. Negroes cannot solve their own problems in isolation, because they are fully enmeshed in a society dominated by whites. The solution to Negro problems lies as much in the white community as in the Negro community. This is especially true because whites control the economic resources needed to provide Negroes with meaningful equality of opportunity. Hence, any strategy of action by Negro leaders that totally alienates the white community is doomed to failure.

Yet "Black Power" advocates are probably correct in arguing that Negroes must develop an ideology that focuses upon self-determination and therefore has some "anti-white" tinges. They need an "enemy" against which to organize the Negro community. History proves that organization *against* a concrete opponent is far more effective than one *for* some abstract goal. They also need an abrasive ideology that threatens whites enough to open their eyes to the Negroes' plight and their own need to do something significant to improve it. The question is how they can accomplish these goals without going too far and thereby creating violent anti-white hostility among Negroes and equally violent anti-Negro sentiment among whites.

In the past few years, many Negro Americans—including prominent community leaders—have shifted their sights away from direct racial integration as a goal. Instead they have focused upon other goals more consistent with the "Black Power" viewpoint. They want better housing, better schools, better jobs, and better personal security within all-Negro areas—and a much stronger Negro voice in controlling all these things. These enrichment-only objectives have apparently eclipsed their desire for greater ability to enter directly into white-dominated portions of the society. This rather dramatic change in values appears to rule out much possibility of Negroes' accepting either dispersal strategy.

In my opinion, the main cause of this shift in objectives is the failure of white society to offer any real hope for large-scale integration. After years of seeking equality under the law, Negro leaders have discovered that even removal of legal barriers is not producing much progress toward a true sharing in the life of white-dominated society. Why should they keep knocking on the door if no one will answer? Why not turn instead to existing all-Negro communities and try to improve conditions there? Indeed, I believe continued white refusal to engage in meaningful, large-scale integration will make it impossible for any self-respecting Negroes to avoid espousing some version of the "Black Power" viewpoint. Understandably, they will not be able to accept the conclusion that most of the millions of Negroes whom whites force to live racially segregated lives must therefore be condemned to inferior educations, housing, culture, or anything else.

Rather, they will reason, there must be some way to make the quality of life in all-Negro portions of a racially segregated society just as good as it is in the all-white portions. And if equality in terms of the indices of desirability accepted by whites cannot be achieved, then some of these "Black Power" advocates will be willing to attain at least nominal equality by denouncing those indicators as specious. They will further claim—with some justification—that life in all-white portions of society cannot be better and may be morally worse because whites suffer from racial blindness.

The reason why this argument is and will be advanced so strongly is certainly understandable. Those who advance it would hardly be human if they were not at least tempted to do so. As long as present white attitudes and behavior persist, adopting any other view amounts to despairing of any chance at equality for most Negroes.

Can the enrichment-only strategy create "separate but equal" societies?[31]

The "Black Power" viewpoint essentially argues that racially separate societies in America can provide equal opportunities for all their members if Negroes are able to control their own affairs. Yet there is a great deal of evidence that this argument is false.

Certainly concerning employment, equality of opportunity for Negroes cannot possibly be attained in a segregated labor market. Negroes must be provided with full freedom and equality regarding entry into and advancement within the white-dominated enterprises that are overwhelmingly preponderant in our economy. Only in this way can they have any hope of achieving an occupational equality with whites.

In education, the evidence is far more ambiguous. The recent reports of the Office of Education and the Civil Rights Commission contend that both racial and economic integration are essential to the attainment of educational equality for Negroes.[32] Yet critics of these reports point out that many types of enrichment programs were not tested in the studies conducted by the authors. Unfortunately, most alternative approaches have not yet been tried on a scale large enough to determine whether any of them will work. Yet one conclusion does seem reasonable: Any real improvement in the quality of education in low-income, all-Negro areas will cost a great deal more money than is now being spent there, and perhaps more than is being spent per pupil anywhere.

Thus, society may face a choice between three fundamental alternatives: providing Negroes with good-quality education through massive integration in schools (which would require considerably more spending per pupil than now exists), providing Negroes with good-quality education through large-scale and extremely expensive enrichment programs, or continuing to relegate many Negroes to inferior educations that severely limit their lifetime opportunities. The third alternative is what we are now choosing. Whether or not the second choice—improving schools in all-Negro areas—will really work is not yet known. The enrichment alternative is based upon the as-yet-unproven premise that it will work.

Regarding housing, the enrichment-only strategy could undoubtedly greatly improve the quantity, variety, and environment of decent housing units available to the disadvantaged population of central cities. Nevertheless, it could not in itself provide Negroes of *any* economic level with the same freedom and range of choice as whites with equal incomes have. Clearly, in this field "separate but equal" does not mean *really* equal. Undoubtedly, all-white suburban areas provide a far greater range and variety of housing and environmental settings than can possibly be found in central cities or all-Negro suburbs alone.

Moreover, there is an acute scarcity of vacant land in many of our largest central cities. Therefore, greatly expanding the supply of decent housing for low-income families in those cities at a rapid rate requires creating many new units for them in the suburbs too.

Thus, if society adopts one of the many possible versions of the enrichment-only strategy, it may face the prospect of perpetuating two separate societies—one white and one Negro—similar to those that would develop under the present-policies strategy. If the enrichment programs carried out proved highly effective, then the gap between these two societies in income, education, housing, and other qualities of life would be nowhere near so great as under the present-policies strategy. Hence, the possibility of a potentially catastrophic "confrontation" between these two societies sometime in the next twenty years would be greatly reduced.

Nevertheless, I do not believe it will really be possible to create two separate societies that are truly equal. Therefore, even if the enrichment-only strategy proved extraordinarily successful at improving the lot of disadvantaged central-city residents of all races and colors (which is by no means a certainty), it would still leave a significant gap in opportunity and achievement between the separate white and Negro societies which would continue to emerge over the next twenty years. This gap would remain a powerful source of tension that might lead to violence, for experience proves that men seeking equality are not placated by even very great absolute progress when they perceive that a significant gap remains between themselves and others in society who are no more deserving of success than they. And that would be precisely the situation twenty years from now under the enrichment-only strategy—whether linked to "Black Power" concepts or not.

Why dispersal should be seriously considered

As pointed out earlier, either of the two dispersal strategies would require radical changes in current trends and policies concerning the location of Negro population growth. Moreover, it is likely that massive dispersal would at present be opposed by *both* suburban whites and central-city Negroes. Many of the former would object to an influx of Negroes, and many of the latter would prefer to live together in a highly urbanized environment. Why should we even consider a strategy that is not only socially disruptive, but likely to please almost nobody?

In my opinion, there are five reasons why we should give enrichment plus dispersal serious consideration. First, future job-creation is going to be primarily in suburban areas, but the unskilled population is going to be more and more concentrated in central-city ghettos unless some dispersion occurs. Such an increasing divergence between where the workers are and where the jobs are will make it ever more difficult to create anything like full employment in decent jobs for ghetto residents. In contrast, if those residents were to move into suburban areas, they would be exposed to more knowledge of job opportunities and would have to make much shorter trips to reach them. Hence they would have a far better chance of getting decent employment.

Second, the recent U. S. Office of Education and U. S. Civil Rights Commission reports on equality of achievement in education reach a *tentative* conclusion that it is necessary to end the clustering of lower-income Negro students together in segregated schools in order to improve their education significantly.[33] As I understand these reports, they imply that the most significant factor in the quality of education of any student is the atmosphere provided by his home and by his fellow students both in and out of the classroom. When this atmosphere is dominated by members of deprived families, the quality of education is inescapably reduced—at least within the ranges of class size and pupil-teacher ratios that have been tried on a large scale. Therefore, if we are to provide effective educational opportunities for the most deprived groups in our society to improve themselves significantly, we must somehow expose them to members of other social classes in their educational experience. But there are not enough members of the Negro middle class "to go around," so to speak. Hence this means some intermingling of children from the deprived groups with those from not-so-deprived white groups, at least in schools. Because of the difficulties of bussing large numbers of students from the hearts of central cities to suburban areas, it makes sense to accomplish this objective through some residential dispersal. This consideration tends to support the integrated-dispersal strategy to some extent, even though these reports have received significant criticism, as noted above.

Third, development of an adequate housing supply for low-income and middle-income families and provision of true freedom of choice in housing for Negroes of all income levels will require out-movement of large numbers of both groups from central cities to suburbs. I do not believe that such an out-movement will occur "spontaneously" merely as a result of increasing prosperity among Negroes in central cities. Even the recently passed national open-occupancy law is unlikely to generate it. Rather, a program of positive incentives and of actual construction of new housing in suburban areas will be necessary.

Fourth, continued concentration of large numbers of Negroes under relatively impoverished conditions in ghettos may lead to unacceptably high levels of crime and violence in central cities. The outbreak of riots and disorders in mostly nonwhite areas in our central cities in the past few years is unprecedented in American history. As the report of the National Advisory Commission on Civil Disorders indicates, continuing to concentrate masses of the nonwhite population in ghettos dominated by poverty and permeated with an atmosphere of deprivation and hopelessness is likely to perpetuate or intensify these disorders. This could lead to the disastrous outcome already discussed in connection with the present-policies strategy.

Fifth, a continuation of ghetto growth will, over the next three or four decades, produce a society more racially segregated than any in our history. We will have older, blighted central cities occupied by millions of Negroes, and newer, more modern suburban areas occupied almost solely by whites. Prospects for moving from that situation to a truly integrated society in which race is not a factor in key human decisions are not encouraging. In fact, by that time we will be faced with a fantastically more massive dispersal problem than the present one if we really want to achieve a society integrated in more than just words.

Thus, only the two enrichment-plus-dispersal strategies explicitly seek to create a single society rather than accepting our present perpetuation of two separate societies: one white and one Negro. Dispersal would involve specific policies and programs at least starting us toward reversal of the profoundly divisive trend now so evident in our metropolitan areas. It may seem extraordinarily difficult to begin such a reversal. But however difficult it may be now, it will be vastly more difficult in twenty years if the number of Negroes segregated in central cities is 8 million larger than it is today.

The difficulty of gaining acceptance for dispersal

I am fully aware that any strategy involving significant dispersal may now seem wholly impractical to responsible politicians and social leaders. The voluntary movement of large numbers of Negroes from ghettos to the suburbs encouraged by federal programs presupposes radical changes in existing attitudes among both suburban whites and central-city Negroes.

In spite of our social mobility, Americans are extremely sensitive to class differentiations. We have deliberately developed class-stratified suburban areas. Residents of each suburb use zoning, tax rates, lot-size requirements, and other devices to exclude persons considered farther down the ladder of social and economic prominence. As each group and each family moves upward in our mobile society, they become more concerned about creating social distance between themselves and those now below them—including those who were once equal to them.

I certainly do not deplore the historic traditions of self-improvement and protection of amenities and privileges that have been won through hard work and perseverance. These traditions should and will continue in some form, because it is proper for successful people to enjoy the fruits of their efforts.

Nevertheless, it is at least possible that the social objective of upgrading the lowest and most deprived groups in our society cannot be accomplished if we simultaneously insist upon excluding those groups from nearly all daily contact with other more fortunate people—as we do now—by maintaining extremely rigid class distinctions by geographic area. Thus, the best dispersal policy might be one that promoted day-to-day interclass and interracial experiences without changing the dominant socioeconomic character of the receiving suburban areas. This would allow persons moving out from the inner city to benefit from the existing character of those suburbs. Such a policy implies that the newcomers would comprise a minority in each area into which they went. This means that an integrated-dispersal strategy might ultimately provide the most desirable form of dispersal. It would enable the group that was already there to maintain nearly intact their conception of the proper standards for that community, while sharing the benefits of those standards with others.

Even this change in attitude, however, presupposes a shift in values of profound magnitude among white middle-class Americans. Furthermore, I doubt that most Negroes today want to live in white communities in which they would be relatively isolated from other Negroes. Hence they might prefer a segregated-dispersal strategy, if they were willing to accept dispersal at all. Yet, since most suburban areas are already incorporated into predominantly white communities, where and how could such a strategy be initiated?

Some tactical mechanisms for encouraging dispersal

Any attempt to achieve dispersal must involve specific answers to two basic questions:

1. What *mechanisms* can be designed to encourage voluntary out-movement of large numbers of Negroes into the suburbs and their peaceful acceptance and welcome by whites there?
2. What *incentives* can be developed leading particular interest groups in society to press politically for—or at least support—employment of those mechanisms?

Let us consider the mechanisms first. Americans have always used one basic approach to get people to overcome inertia and make voluntarily some socially desirable change. It consists of providing a significant economic or other reward for persons who behave in the desired manner. That reward might be free land (as for homesteaders and railroads in the nineteenth century), or tax reductions (as for homeowners or investors in equipment in the past few years), or direct payments (as for farmers), or services and income supplements tied to participation in specific programs (as for users of the G.I. Bill in education).

In the case of dispersion, I believe the system of rewards used should probably have the following characteristics:[34]

1. Advantages should accrue both to the Negro households moving out from central cities and to the suburban households into whose communities the newcomers move.

2. Whenever possible, these advantages should consist of rewards administered under metropolitan-area-wide organizations specifically set up for such a purpose. These organizations could be quasi-private bodies able to cooperate directly with existing local governments and other geographically limited organizations. Hence they would *not* be metropolitan governments.

3. Advantages to out-moving households might include the following:

a. The possibility of sending their children to top-quality schools that receive special grants because of participation in programs involving out-moving children.

b. Home-buying or renting financial aids available only to out-moving families or at least with assigned proportions of their total funding available only to such families.

c. Top-priority access to special programs concerning employment and on-the-job training in suburban industrial and other firms. In my opinion, such programs might be effectively built around the self-selection principle embodied in the G.I. Bill—that is, eligible persons would be given certificates enabling those firms who hire them to receive special benefits to compensate for their lower productivity or training costs. Such benefits might include tax credits or direct payments. The persons receiving these certificates would then make their own choice of employers among firms participating in such programs. This would preserve maximum individual choice among program participants.

4. Advantages to households already living in the receiving areas might include:

a. Special aid to schools receiving children of out-moving Negro families. Such aid should consist of funds linked to the students in such families (as Title I funding under the Elementary and Secondary Education Act is now linked to low-income families). But the per-student amount of aid given should greatly exceed the added direct cost of teaching each out-moving student. Hence the school district concerned would have a positive incentive to accept such students because of the financial "bonuses" they would bring with them. Those bonuses could be used to upgrade the entire receiving school or cut locally-borne costs therein.

b. "Bonus" community financing to participating suburban local governments. Again, the payments involved should significantly exceed the added costs of servicing in-coming families, so that each participating community would be able to improve other services too.

c. Giving higher priority in other federal programs to communities participating in out-movement programs than to those refusing to participate. These related programs could include sewer and water financing, planning aid, and selection as locations for federal installations.

5. Benefits available for out-moving families and receiving areas could be restricted by geographic area to avoid either paying people discriminately by race or wasting funds paying families who would move out anyway. A precedent for giving residents of certain neighborhoods special benefits already exists in the urban renewal and Model Cities programs. Thus, specific ghetto neighborhoods could be designated "origination" areas and largely white suburban communities designated "receiving" areas. Benefits would accrue only to persons moving from the former to the latter or to residents of the latter participating in reception programs.

6. If these programs were part of an integrated-dispersal strategy, they could be linked to quota systems concerning newcomers to each school or community involved. Thus, the special bonus aids would be available only up to a certain fraction of the total school enrollment or residential population of a given receiving community. This restriction would be aimed at retaining in the schools or communities concerned the dominance of the groups originally residing there. It is to be hoped that the result would be suburban integration, rather than a shift of massive neighborhood transition from central cities to suburbs.

The above suggestions are highly tentative and exploratory. Yet I hope they at least indicate that practical mechanisms can be created that might achieve a substantial amount of peaceful Negro out-movement—*if* they were adopted in a general atmosphere of social encouragement to dispersal.

Some aspects of the basic approach described above may seem terribly unjust. In particular, this approach rewards the advantaged (those already living in suburbs) as well as the disadvantaged (those moving out of deprived areas into suburbs) in order to get the former to accept the latter. Yet that is a key mechanism, one which free-enterprise systems have always employed when they seek to attain high-priority ends through voluntary action. Our society abounds with arrangements that provide special economic advantages to those who are already privileged, presumably in order to evoke socially desired behavior from them. Examples are oil depletion allowances, stock option plans for top executives, profitable contracts for defense firms, lower tax rates on capital gains, and subsidy payments to wealthy farmers. I am defending neither the equity nor the effectiveness of these particular examples. Yet they illustrate that we often adopt public policies that pay the rich to undertake behavior which presumably benefits society as a whole.

A second aspect of the approach to dispersal I have described which might seem harsh is that no benefits apparently accrue to disadvantaged persons who fail to move out to the suburbs. As stated earlier, however, I believe dispersal programs should only be undertaken simultaneously with large-scale ghetto enrichment programs. The latter would provide comparable, or even greater, benefits for those "left behind" in central cities—who will undoubtedly comprise the vast majority of Negroes in our metropolitan areas for many years to come.

Developing political support for dispersal

The concept of dispersal will remain nothing but an empty theory unless a significant number of Americans decide their best interests lie in politically supporting specific dispersal mechanisms. It is conceivable that such support might result from a massive "change of heart" among white suburbanites. They might view dispersal as a way to "purge themselves" of the kind of "white racism" which the National Advisory Commission on Civil Disorders described. I do not think this will occur. In fact, I believe recent urban violence has tended to make white suburbanites more hostile than ever to the idea of having Negroes live next door to them.

Yet, on the other hand, several specific groups in society are beginning to realize that dispersal might benefit them immensely. The motivation of persons in these groups varies widely, from pure moral guilt to sheer self-interest. But almost all significant social change in the United States has occurred because a wide variety of different types of people with diverse motives have formed a coalition to accomplish something. In my opinion, only through that kind of process will any of the basic strategies I have described (except the present-policies strategy) ever be achieved.

I believe the groups favorable to dispersal now include, or soon will include, the following:

1. Suburban industrialists. In many metropolitan areas, they are experiencing acute labor shortages, particularly of unskilled workers. They will soon be willing to provide open and powerful political support for the construction of low-income and moderate-income housing for Negro workers and their families in currently all-white suburbs.
2. Downtown-oriented retailers, bankers, restaurant operators, hotel operators, and other businessmen in our larger cities. In cities where disorders have penetrated into central business districts (such as Milwaukee and Washington), many former patrons have stopped visiting these areas altogether—especially at night. If disorders in these areas get worse, the impact upon both consumer patronage and future capital investment in big-city down-

towns could be catastrophic. Those whose enterprises are "locked in" such areas will soon realize they must vigorously support both stronger law enforcement and positive programs aimed at alleviating Negro discontent. At first, these programs will consist primarily of ghetto enrichment, but these groups will soon begin to support dispersal too.

3. Home builders. They would benefit from any large-scale programs of housing construction. But the delays and difficulties of carrying out such programs within central cities are much greater than they are on vacant suburban land. Hence they will eventually exert at least low-level support for dispersal if it means large-scale subsidy of privately built homes.

4. White central-city politicians in large cities. As the populations of their cities shift toward Negro majorities, they will be more and more willing to support some dispersal policies, as well as the enrichment programs they now espouse.

5. Businessmen in general with plants, offices, or other facilities "locked in" large central cities. An increasing number of such persons will realize that they will emerge losers from any major "confrontation" between black-dominated central cities and white-dominated suburbs, as described earlier.

6. Persons of all types whose consciences influence them to accept the National Advisory Commission's conclusion that dispersal of some kind is the only way to avoid perpetuating two separate societies, with the Negro one forever denied equality.

Since these groups now constitute a small minority of Americans a great many other Americans must change their existing values considerably if large-scale dispersal is ever to occur. Yet the alternatives to such a strategy—especially the one we are now pursuing—could conceivably lead us to equally grave changes in values. For example, if there is an extremely significant increase in violence in Negro ghettos which spills over into all-white areas, the white population might react with harshly repressive measures that would significantly restrict individual freedoms, as noted above. This, too, would call for a basic shift in our values. But it is a shift which I regard with much more alarm than the one required by a dispersal strategy. In fact, in this age of rapid technological change, it is naïve to suppose that there will not in the future be significant alterations in attitudes that we presently take for granted.

The scale of efforts required

The foregoing discussion emphasizes that any strategy likely to have a significant impact upon ghettos will require a very much larger effort than we are now devoting to this problem. Even a "pure" ghetto-enrichment strategy, which does not eliminate or even slow down the growth of the racial ghetto, would require a significantly greater allocation of financial and manpower resources to coping with the problems of the urban poor. A dispersal strategy that addresses itself to breaking up or at least slowing down the growth of the racial ghetto would also require even more profound changes in values and attitudes. Only the first strategy—that of continuing our present activities—requires no immediate change in effort or values. But it may eventually result in significant value changes too—and perhaps far less desirable ones than are required by the other two alternatives.

Thus, there is simply no easy way to cope with this problem. In my opinion, past federal programs and many currently suggested approaches have suffered from the desire to find a cheap solution to what is an extremely expensive problem. The problem is expensive in terms not only of money, but also of our national talents and our willingness to change our basic values. In one way or another, we must and will accommodate ourselves to this problem. We cannot evade it.

Creating the programs and incentives necessary to achieve any desired ghetto future

Each strategy contains two basic parts: a desired outcome and a set of actions designed to achieve that outcome. I have not placed equal emphasis on these two parts in discussing each of the five strategies concerning ghetto futures. For example, the present-policies strategy as I have described it is essentially a set of actions—the continuation of present policies. Hence it does not emphasize a desired outcome. In fact, I have pointed out several reasons why its outcome might be quite undesirable. Conversely, my discussion of the enrichment-only strategy has focused upon its outcome. Hence I have not made many suggestions about how that outcome might be brought about. Similar emphasis upon the outcome rather than the means of attaining it also marks the discussion of the integrated-core strategy. Even my tentative analysis of how dispersal might be carried out hardly represents a complete blueprint for action.

Any strategy is really just wishful thinking until it links the outcome it envisions with some feasible means of attaining that outcome. This is especially true regarding several of the ghetto futures I have described, since they embody such radical changes in society. They are likely to remain largely fantasies, rather than real alternatives, until specific programs for achieving them can be defined. I have made some program suggestions in connection with dispersal strategies in order to prove that dispersal is not totally unrealistic. Unfortunately, the complexity of developing similar suggestions for the other strategies involving social change prevents my attempting to do so in this article.

Nevertheless, there are five basic principles crucial to formulating such programs.

1. No proposed "solution" to ghetto problems that is not eventually supported by the majority of the white middle class can possibly succeed.[35]

2. The actions designed to bring about any desired outcome must be linked to incentives that will appeal both to the self-interest of all groups concerned and

to their consciences. In fact, the most difficult part of implementing any strategy (other than the present-policies strategy) will be providing effective incentives for the relatively well-off white majority. This group must be persuaded to expand many resources, and alter its own traditional behavior, in order to produce outcomes that appear to benefit mainly a small minority of the population. As indicated in the discussion of dispersal, each segment of the white majority (such as business, labor, suburbanites, senior citizens, farmers, and so forth) must be presented with arguments and incentives which appeal specifically to its interests. An example is the argument that business suffers great losses of potential profits and output because of the failure of poor Negroes to engage in high-level consumption and the inability of poorly educated Negro workers to help meet high demands for skilled labor.

3. Any program designed to achieve a given outcome should involve significant action by the private sector. Otherwise, society may relegate ghettos to a position of dependency upon government that is inconsistent with full equality in American life. On the other hand, it is naïve to suppose that the private sector can or will bear the huge expense of coping with ghetto problems unaided. Society as a whole must pay the extra costs of on-the-job training programs, new factories located in ghettos, union training of unskilled Negro apprentices, and other actions aimed at helping the unskilled or otherwise "left out" enter the mainstream of our economy. These actions must be carried out by nongovernmental organizations, but financed by the government through direct payments, tax credits, or other means.

4. No program involving ghettos can be effective unless it involves a high degree of meaningful participation by ghetto residents, and significant exercise of power and authority by them. We must realize that ghettos cannot be drawn into the mainstream of American life without some redistribution of authority and power, as well as income, for equality in America means exercise of significant self-determination. Admittedly, lack of skill and experience may cause that exercise to be disorderly, inefficient, and even corrupt at first—as it was among the Irish, Italians, Jews, and others in the past. Therefore, turning over more power in ghetto areas to local residents may actually cause a short-run decline in the professional quality of government there—whether in schools, the police, or local government in general. Yet it will greatly alter the attitudes of residents toward those institutions and begin to draw them into the real functioning of our society. So it should and must come.

5. The more benefits that most ghetto residents receive through programs aimed at helping them, the more dissatisfied and vocally discontent certain small parts of the ghetto community are likely to become. This makes the problem of persuading the white majority to support large-scale aid programs doubly difficult. It also means that socioeconomic programs will have to be accompanied by greatly enlarged and improved law-enforcement efforts, particularly those in which ghetto leaders themselves play significant roles. Yet emphasis on improving law enforcement alone, without massively trying to meet

the other needs of ghetto residents, will probably prove disastrous. Such one-sided emphasis on "law and order" could easily provoke steadily rising violence shifting in form toward guerrilla warfare. The need to avoid this outcome further emphasizes the importance of relying more and more on ghetto communities to develop their own internal controls of violence, with outside aid, as is consistent with the preceding principle of greater self-determination.

Merely stating these principles emphasizes how far we are from having designed practical programs to achieve most of the outcomes set forth in this article. In my opinion, one of the most important tasks facing us is the formulation and public discussion of the specific ingredients needed for such programs. But even that cannot be done until we have recognized more explicitly the various possible futures of American ghettos and weighed their relative advantages and disadvantages.

At present, most public discussion and thought about racial and ghetto problems in America suffer from a failure to define or even to consider explicit possible long-range outcomes of public policy. This is one reason why such discussion seems so confused, inchoate, and frustrating. I hope that the ideas set forth in this article can serve as a nucleus for more fruitful public discussion of this crucial topic, for the future of American ghettos will determine to a large extent the future of America itself.

References

1. The first draft of this article was written in the early summer of 1967. Subsequently, the author became a consultant to the National Advisory Commission on Civil Disorders. In that capacity, he wrote the rough drafts of several chapters in the Commission's final report. One of these (Chapter 16) contains many of the ideas set forth in this article. Nevertheless, there are sufficient differences between the contents and presentation of Chapter 16 in the Commission's Report and this article to warrant separate publication of the latter. The contents of this article express the thoughts of its author only and do not necessarily represent the views of either the National Advisory Commission on Civil Disorders or Real Estate Research Corporation.

2. Data from the Social Security Administration.

3. *Report of the National Advisory Commission on Civil Disorders* (Washington, D.C.: March 1, 1968), p. 127. This document will hereafter be referred to as the *NACCD Report.*

4. *Ibid.*, pp. 121, 127.

5. Based upon the Census Bureau's Series D projections of future population—the ones assuming the lowest of the four levels of future fertility used by the Census Bureau. See U. S. Bureau of the Census, *Statistical Abstracts of the United States, 1967* (88th Edition; Washington, D. C., 1967), pp. 8–10.

6. *NACCD Report*, p. 121.

7. *Ibid.*

8. *Ibid.*

9. Open-occupancy legislation appears to be aimed at shifting the location of some future nonwhite growth to presently all-white areas. Experience in those states which have had open-occupancy ordinances for some time indicates, however, that they have little, if any, impact in altering the distribution of nonwhite population growth.

10. *NACCD Report*, p. 227.

11. Surveys conducted annually by Real Estate Research Corporation, results unpublished.

12. *NACCD Report*, p. 216.

13. See Raymond J. Murphy and James M. Watson, *The Structure of Discontent*, Mimeographed, Los Angeles: University of California at Los Angeles, June 1, 1967.

14. *NACCD Report*, pp. 123–131.

15. Specific recommendations concerning these subjects are set forth in the *NACCD Report*, Chapter 17.

16. See John F. Kain, "The Distribution and Movement of Jobs and Industry," in *The Metropolitan Enigma*, ed. James Q. Wilson (Washington, D. C., 1967).

17. These include legislative proposals made by Senator Javits, the late Senator Robert Kennedy, and Senator Percy.

18. William Baumol and William Bowen, *The Performing Arts: The Economic Dilemma* (New York: 20th Century Fund).

19. *NACCD Report*, p. 217.

20. Insofar as I know, this principle was first formulated by my father, James C. Downs, Jr.

21. Two well-known urban specialists with such views are Jane Jacobs and Victor Gruen. See Jane Jacobs, *The Life and Death of Great American Cities* (New York, 1961), and Victor Gruen, *The Heart of Our Cities* (New York, 1964).

22. This phenomenon explains why it is so difficult to halt "massive transition" from white to nonwhite occupancy once it begins. It tends to continue even when whites originally living in the area concerned do not "panic" at all. As long as normal turnover continues to produce vacancies, and only nonwhites fill them, such transition is inescapable. The key persons whose behavior must be affected to stop transition are not the whites living in the area at the outset, but those living scattered elsewhere in the metropolitan area or even other parts of the nation. They are the persons who must move into the areas as vacancies appear in order to maintain racial balance therein. Thus, attempts to organize existing white residents so as to prevent them from fleeing almost always fail to halt transition. Organizers can rarely identify "the whites who aren't there yet," so they cannot influence the decisions of these potential future occupants, and transition continues relentlessly.

23. The U. S. Supreme Court will soon have to face up to the consequences of this "Law." In order to attack *de facto* segregation effectively, it must recognize racial discrimination in the form of school quotas as Constitutional. At present, our society cannot achieve integration or end segregation without deliberate and explicit racial discrimination by public authorities. This is true in relation to other public facilities besides schools, including hospitals and housing.

24. This term and usage were coined by Charles E. Lindblom. See Lindblom and David Braybrooke, *The Strategy of Decision* (New York, 1963).

25. See the *NACCD Report*, Chapter 17.

26. See their statements as quoted in the Chicago *Daily News*, August 25, 1967.

27. *NACCD Report*, p. 227.

28. *Ibid.*, p. 121.

29. These figures are based upon the Census Bureau's Series D population projections. If higher fertility projections are used, the suburbs would contain slightly higher proportions of total population in 1985. See the reference cited in footnote 5.

30. *NACCD Report*, pp. 216–217.

31. This section of the article was written after Chapter 16 of the *NACCD Report* had been completed and closely parallels the contents of certain parts of that chapter.

32. See James Coleman *et al.*, *Equality of Educational Opportunity* (Washington, D. C., 1966), and the U. S. Civil Rights Commission, *Racial Isolation in the Public Schools* (Washington, D. C., 1967).

33. *Ibid.*

34. Many of the programs described in this section have been recommended by the National Advisory Commission on Civil Disorders. See the *NACCD Report*, Chapter 17.

35. This fact is recognized by most Negro leaders not committed to zealously militant separatism. For example, see Kenneth Clark, *Dark Ghetto* (New York, 1965), p. 222.

43

MELVIN M. WEBBER, Planning in an Environment of Change: Beyond the Industrial Age

A new concept of the future

We are constantly amazed at the speed with which our images and attitudes absorb new ideas and new technologies. Novelty appears to have a rapid decay rate in the modern western world. Once television was made cheap enough for mass distribution, it quickly became part of people's everyday lives. Within a year after Sputnik was launched, space shots scarcely seemed remarkable any more, even though the recent satellites' experiment packages are surely far more sophisticated achievements than the vehicles that orbit them. Then, when satellite transmission of television broadcasts became work-a-day, we readily accepted simultaneous worldwide visual communication as just another clever technological novelty. By next year, heart-transplants will scarcely warrant notice by the news media. And so it has gone, step by step, each dramatic achievement—even the unanticipated big leap—has a way of becoming commonplace after the fact.

Because we have lacked adequate predictive theory of technological or social change, we have tended to confront each incremental development as it occurs, regarding it as a unitary, independent event. Few people have tried to trace the waves of repercussions that those events might in turn generate through the larger systems of which they become new component parts. Fewer still have tried to predict the chains of consequences that numerous and *cumulative* changes would then induce within the larger systems. And so we have calmly accepted each new accretion, telling ourselves that 'the more things change, the more they remain the same'.

Virtually everyone now knows that the rate of discovery and invention has been explosive during these past two decades; and yet we in the developed world seem to have accepted even that fact as a stable condition and take rapid change as a normal, no-change condition. Perhaps this is a further indication of our large adaptive capacities—in both senses of that phrase: first, that modern social systems have been able to absorb new developments without permitting them to rock the social order and, secondly, that we must *believe* that change is no-

Melvin M. Webber, "Planning in an Environment of Change. Part 1: Beyond the Industrial Age," *Town Planning Review*, vol. 39, no. 3 (October 1968), pp. 170–195. Reprinted by permission.

change, for to believe otherwise would itself upset our perceptions of social order. However, even if true in the past, this is not likely to go on. Knowledge of physical, biological, and social systems in expanding at such a fantastic rate that it is triggering off an equally fantastic expansion in the technologies through which those systems can be modified. These new intellectual resources are making it increasingly possible to anticipate future scientific discovery and technological invention and to forecast some subsequent social effects of discovery and invention. As social theory improves, we are likely to be better able to forecast social change too. In turn, better forecasts will permit us deliberately to plan our responses to those anticipated outcomes—even to select, in some fields, those of the possible outcomes that we happen to prefer. This is to say, in effect, that among the consequences of the knowledge explosion is the emergence of a new way of thinking about the future. That conception is the derivative of our new capacities for prediction, our new images of our powers for controlling future events and, hence, a new outlook suggesting that, to a considerable degree, maybe we really can invent the future.

This new concept of the future represents a remarkable change, a change that is potentially as important as any of the developments that are now building up in the developed world. Let me here simply state my thesis, which I will elaborate upon later.

Pre-industrial societies around the world all seem to be marked by a common perception that the future lies outside the field of vision and certainly outside control. The accumulating studies of peasant and primitive societies are revealing a common fatalism in virtually all of them. Some (the Sioux Indians are one example) do not even have a word for "future" in their languages. Others that do conceive of future time see its events as in the hands of the gods.

With the coming of industrialization and the commercial economy, possibilities for forward scheduling of production and the requirements for monetary credit provoked a different image of the future. Within the shortrun, managers found they could shape the institutions under their control. Observed and anticipated stability in growth rates permitted banks to make loans, with the prospect that they would be repaid. Population forecasters could extrapolate trend lines with some confidence that whatever determined birth and death rates in the immediate past would probably continue to affect them in the immediate future. Indeed, a large insurance industry was in fact built upon the actuarial estimates of probabilities that grew out of these measurements of system stability. For that matter, the whole of the industrial structure was built against the conception of the future that saw a sufficient degree of stability in the short run to justify investment. To account for those future changes that were not or could not be anticipated, the market system developed to feed information on change back into decision centers, so that managers and consumers could then adjust their predictions.

In brief, in the vernacular conception of the industrial age, the future was seen as closely resembling the present; where conditions and events would depart from the present, the response was to *accommodate* to those conditions and events.

The big change which is commented on later, is the current shift away from that image of stability and accommodative response. With the emergence of the post-industrial stage of development, the future is being seen to depart drastically from the present, and it now looks as though men will be seeking more directly to design the future. If we can characterize a single distinguishing difference between the outlooks of the industrial age and of the post-industrial age it is this: that industry and government in the recent past had to respond to change after the fact; in the post-industrial age they will be intellectually equipped to respond before. That is to say, that the coming style for confronting the future will be forecasting and planning.

We are already seeing the signs of this new post-industrial outlook in the rapid rise of new quasi-science of futurism and, in parallel, the rise of a large number of new kinds of planning institutions. These signs are seen in the projective work of such groups as Resources for the Future in Washington, Professor de Jouvenal's Futuribles group on France, The American Academy of Arts and Science's Commission on the Year 2000 and its several committees on the next ten years. In London, there are the Social Science Research Council's project on The Next Thirty Years, and the Centre for Environmental Studies' group on Developing Patterns of Urbanization. There are more. By now there is a literal flood of new institutes on the future being organized in America and elsewhere. Their counterparts are the new planning institutions with such unlikely names as CONSAD Research Corporation, the RAND Corporation, Systems Development Corporation, and the even more unlikely names Lockheed Aircraft Corporation, Aero-Jet General, Litton Industries, and so on.

The best of the new students of the future are trying to foresee latent qualitative consequences before they become manifest—in effect, to develop an early-warning-system that might signal impending disasters, as well as potentially beneficial outcomes that might be exploited were appropriate action be taken soon enough. Most important, they are attempting to trace out the alternative future histories—particularly the social and economic histories—that would be shaped by plausibly foreseen uncontrollable events and by deliberately designed ones.

Despite the excitement and fashion that is marking this activity, this is probably no fad. Had we been in the forecasting business before, the rise of futurist studies might have been foreseen as a deterministic outcome of the current knowledge explosion. More knowledge, better theory, and improved methods were bound to make conscious confrontation of emphatic and rapid social change inevitable.

Of course, neither students of the future nor practitioners of planning are new phenomena in our midst. There have been individual prophets and forecasters at work for a long time, but these men have typically been aberrants within the world of scholarship. Although scholars generally agree that the test of a theory is its capacity to predict well, theorists in the social and behavioral sciences have traditionally eschewed projective modes of thought in favor of observational modes; and they have done so just as firmly as they have declined normative interpretation in favor of positivistic accounts. The thing that is new is the emergence of a legitimate and organized activity, explicitly devoted to systematic and normative interpretation of potential future histories.

All this can be read as very good news to the city planners, who had for so long been the lonely custodians of a futurist tradition. But this new futurist enterprise can also be read as a serious challenge to the traditional thoughtways and activities of city planning. It is doubtful if city planning will ever be the same again once the impact of this new attitude toward the future, the new predictive technology, and the emerging theoretic sophistication begin to impinge upon it.

City planners have always claimed, of course, that their business is to influence, if not to shape, the future. But until recently, we have been previewing history through very inadequate binoculars. The theory we have had to rely upon has never been good enough. Data have always been too sparse and ill-suited to our wants. Our methods have been too naïve to deal with the complexities of contemporary urbanism. Further, images of the future have always been shaped by the outlook of the industrial age. On all these counts, the new futurism should supply intellectual reinforcements that we have long wished for. This is not to suggest that we shall soon find the magic that will permit us to design the ideal future city. That is neither politically possible nor ethically tolerable. The course of history cannot be controlled either for, as the old-fashioned idea holds, there are logically derivative chains of developmental steps, such that certain social or technological changes determine those that follow.

That deterministic view might seem to be in contradiction with the growing stochastic view that sees events as probabilistic outcomes, and with the older teleologic view that sees history as the resultant of purposive, goal-seeking behavior of men. These three conceptions are not in contradiction, only in competition.

As planners, we are well served by each. Insofar as our theory and their derivative models can help us to predict deterministically, we can act with greater confidence about the coming changes. Insofar as we can predict probabilistically, we can reduce the odds of error. And, insofar as we can teleologically set out goals and matching actions, we can accomplish the ends we seek. History, however, is not teleologically shaped to the degree that city planners have traditionally presumed. We *can* consciously force some events to happen. But not all. Much of the future will continue to lie outside our control, and we shall have to conform. Some can be approached only with the attitude of the gambler. And some of it can be invented and planned.

Our continuing intellectual problem will be to know when it is most useful to view the future deterministically, when it is best to view it stochastically (and hence as indeterminate), and when we can profitably view it teleologically.

That question is likely to take on the character of an intellectual dilemma. In a setting of rapid technological and social change, the possibilities for "accurate" prediction would seem to decline. But with improving predictive theory, we should also be able more sensitively to anticipate coming changes. And with increasing organizational capacities for large-scale decision and action, we should be able deliberately to shape more of the future than was once possible. No formula is available for resolving these competing views. It may be that the conceptual, methodological, and governmental issues that surround these images will continue to occupy us as we are carried along into the coming decades.

Some signs of the future

Despite the diversity within the community of futurist students, there is a striking consensus among them concerning some of the major historical changes that appear to be under way. Nearly all are by now persuaded that the industrial age is coming to an imminent end in the western developed nations, and with it the end of the age of the industrial city. For a profession that emerged in response to the industrial city, this forecast must surely be of fundamental interest.

Today, when history is speeding up so rapidly, these commentators agree on one thing if nothing else: that western society is at a major turning point and that future society will differ vastly from contemporary society. In an article in a recent issue of *Encounter,* Professor Brzezinski put it flatly and unambiguously:

> Ours is no longer the conventional revolutionary era; we are entering a novel metamorphic phase in human history. The world is on the eve of a transformation more dramatic in its historic and human consequences than that wrought by the French or the Russian revolutions. Viewed from the long perspective, these famous revolutions merely scratched the surface of the human condition. The changes they precipitated involved alterations in the distribution of power and property within society; they did not affect the essence of individual and social existence. Life—personal and organized—continued much as before, even though some of its external forms (primarily political) were substantially altered. Shocking though it may sound to their acolytes, by the year 2000 it will be accepted that Robespierre and Lenin were mild reformers.[1]

He then goes on to say that "Unlike the revolutions of the past, the developing metamorphosis will have no charismatic leaders with strident doctrines, but its impact will be more profound" and, it can be added, more subtle. The major current generators of these changes, he notes, include the computers and the new advances in electronic communication, which are fundamentally "altering the mores, the social structure, and the value of society." And the work of the futurists, he reports, already "indicates that men living in the developed world will undergo during the next decades a mutation potentially as basic as that experienced through the slow process of evolution from animal to human status."

It is not possible to present here a plausible and coherent scenario that might describe the unfolding of the revolutionary era that we will find ourselves in. But some events that already appear to be "in the cards" can be recounted.

Because the United States is farthest along the paths toward post-industrial status and because most studies of the future are still localized there, the evidence will be drawn mainly from American experience. Insofar as the path beyond the industrial age is deterministic, the American experience is a precursor of future events in other highly developed societies as well.

The most apparent signal of post-industrialism is the shift in the composition of occupations. Industrialization initially moved men out of farming and related extractive industries at a rapid rate. (In the United States the proportion of the labor force in primary industries fell from around 90 percent in 1800 to 75 percent in 1900 to about 5 percent today, and it is still falling.) In Britain the current proportion is under 4 percent. How would people have reacted to a forecaster 100 years ago who predicted that only 4 percent of the labor force could produce all the products of farming, forestry, and fishing?

There was initially a counterexpansion that absorbed the labor force in manufacturing and related jobs—the ratio went from about 5-10 percent in 1800 to 37 percent in 1900. It has fluctuated around that level throughout this century, but it is now declining both as a percentage of total employment and in actual number. (In Britain it has varied between 43 percent and 49 percent during the 1910-1964 period.) Recently in the United States there has actually been a net loss in numbers of manufacturing jobs during the past ten years, as the service occupations have been expanding. Now, for the first time in the history of the world, there is a nation which employs more people in service than in manufacturing occupations. That in itself is a revolutionary event of dramatic order.

Despite the reduction of manufacturing employment and despite the reduction of the work week (from sixty hours in 1900 to forty hours today) manufacturing productivity is still growing, repeating the history of agriculture, which reached its most productive stage only when it decanted its labor in favor of machines. The trends in productivity show no signs of abating. Someone at the RAND Corporation recently made the wild guess that America will eventually be able to satisfy *all* its needs with a mere 2 percent of its labor force. His guess is a cartoon, of course; but his point is right.

Behind the rise in manufacturing productivity and the move into the service occupations lies the knowledge explosion that continues to impel the changes. Modern manufactured goods are congealed information; they are the products of intensive, organized research-and-development work that employs highly trained minds and sophisticated techniques. The machines that produce the machines are themselves the product of similarly intensive intellectual inputs. The jobs they create require long periods of training, frequently university-based training.

The rising demand for these sorts of R & D workers is being paralleled by a rising demand for other sorts of highly trained specialists—the university teachers, physicians, lawyers, management consultants, and the large varieties of other skilled specialists that complex organization and complex society demand. It is the contributors to and the practitioners within the knowledge industries who are now finding themselves on the crest of the new history. Indeed, the knowledge industry is fast becoming the new center of influence and power, with the university and the "R & D" firm assuming the roles that corporations and labor unions have recently occupied.

A coming repetition of the agricultural and manufacturing revolutions will be hitting the service industries in force before long. One reason people have been able to find jobs in the services is that the productivity of these occupations has so far remained low. But the signs of a change are already clear in banking, bookkeeping, and inventory control, where computers have found a ready application; in retail distribution, where customer self-service and mail-order service have reduced the need for sales clerks; and even in machine repair, where it is becoming cheaper to discard worn-out parts and to replace them with plug-in components than to repair them. To the degree that cybernation can eventually take over the tedious repetitive service jobs, man-hour productivity will rise and demands for employees will fall.

Some futurists, most notably Donald Michael at the University of Michigan,[2] are confidently predicting that even middle-level white-collar management jobs will be rapidly falling before the competences of cybernation. As a result, the vast office staffs that have been performing these sorts of tasks are already being displaced. Similarly, routine personnel management jobs, engineering staff jobs, quality-control inspection jobs, and others are being better done by computers; and the bigger and faster machines that are now in the works will have far greater capacities than present models. As a result, the routine office-based paper-work occupations may soon go the way of the manual manufacturing occupations.

To be sure, ever since the cybernation revolution hit us in the mid-1950s, some persons have been heralding the time when the work of advanced societies would be largely consigned to machines, and men would be freed for nonwork activities. It is true that it has not happened quite as rapidly as some of them had thought, in part because we have not yet found an adequate alternative means for distributing income other than through employment, in part because many of the service wants of advanced societies are very far from being satisfied. There still remain large latent demands for professional and sub-professional aides in the health services, education, childrearing and, indeed, in the expanding knowledge industries themselves that could absorb unemployed labor for some time to come. Sport and entertainment are presently occupying increasing numbers of performers. As the volume of free spectator-hours increases with the declining work-week and extended vacations, these are likely to become major industries. But the prospect of massive nonemployment is, for the first time in history, becoming real. The United States may soon be passing the threshold at which a full employment economy becomes an anachronistic goal.

As Mario Salvadori has put it, in pre-industrial times "work was . . . a personal human necessity. A man who could not or would not work was the prey of the forces of nature, and his chances of remaining alive were minimal." Later, and especially during the *early* industrial era, work was considered "man's duty and lifted to the level of the most honored human activity, until it became man's pride." Then, in the late-industrial period, with the rise of the labor union and supporting national legislation, work became a right. Now, as Salvadori puts it, "We are . . . witnessing the beginning of a situation in which work is no longer a right but a status symbol."[3]

We have already reached the stage when the most highly skilled professionals work the longest hours and the least skilled laborers the shortest. If we should ever reach the stage when only 2 percent (or 20 percent, or even 50 percent) of the employables can work, it will clearly be the men with the rarest skills who will hold jobs. The very fact of their being employed will confer high social status, reversing a longstanding rule of social ranking. What then is to become of the rest of us? In the early transition period, how will we deal with the sense of guilt that idleness will raise? The Calvinist ethic now assures us that idleness is the work of the devil and that work is virtuous. Under the initial impact of enforced unemployment, we shall have to create a new ethic to replace the mores that have so strongly dominated the Judeo-Christian world for so long.

And how will people spend their time? Some will find satisfying volunteer service roles in helping others. Some will find creative outlets in the arts, sports, and the more traditional leisuretime activities. But, in addition, *learning* may become the major nonpaid occupation of large segments of the population. The signs are by now beginning to show in the expanding demand for adult educational programs, the rapid growth of educational television, the sales boom in books and magazines, and the growing interest in music, theater, and the traditional fine arts. A world that turns from making things to enjoying ideas may sound like a fantasy better suited to utopian or science-fiction literature than to responsible forecast. At this stage of things it is still too early to know how the librarians ought to classify it. It is as plausibly the one as the other.

It is equally plausible to expect a continuing rise in popular participation in politics and civic affairs, The long-term trend toward wider distribution of political power and active citizen involvement is being dramatically expressed today in the rebellions localized in the major cities of the world. The current search among the world's youth for meaningful forms of "participant democracy" is being interpreted by some as a transitional crisis condition that will somehow eventually find a stable resolution. Others see it as a preliminary precursor of a continuing style of intergenerational confrontation. Again, either forecast is plausible.

In a world where machines will do more of our work and institutional change will be rapid, surely different forms of meaningful occupation must evolve. Already the concept of "full employment" has been modified with the slow accretion of changing practices. Early retirement is displacing people from the labor force before their productive years have run out. Young people are entering the labor force at much later ages than their fathers, first devoting long periods to education. Their delayed entry is paid for in part by the scholarship systems. Britain already offers college grants to virtually everyone who can qualify for college. The United States may soon follow this example; even without universal grants, around 40 percent of American youth receive some college training, and the proportion is rising rapidly. In California, it is now nearly 80 percent. It is also true that the number of women in the labor force is also rising, particularly married women, more particularly well-educated married women whose children no longer require them at home. But that too may be in for a change as husbands' salaries rise sufficiently to provide satisfactory family incomes and as more women find productive voluntary outlets for their activities.

Few futurists doubt that family incomes will continue to rise far beyond the wage earners' present expectations.

Kahn and Wiener are using a middle-level projection of United States per capita income for the year 2000 of around $10,000, a trebling of the 1965 level of $3,500 in but 35 years. That is equivalent to a shift from around $1,400 to $4,100 at current official exchange rates. With an annual average growth in Gross National Product (GNP) of 3 percent in Britain, the 1966 per capita share of GNP would rise from about £590 to £1,400; at 4 percent it would rise to over £2,000—well over trebled in 35 years. These are per capita estimates. Multiply them by a modest four members per family, and they suggest average family incomes in the year 2000 of the order of $16,000 in the United States and £5,600 in Britain at 3 percent, and £8,120 at 4 percent growth rates. Extend these forecasts an additional 20 years and the average family income levels jump to over $31,000 in the United States and between £10,500 and £15,500 in Britain —all expressed in constant purchasing power of money.

These are mean estimates and ignore the questions of income distribution. They are also unrefined forecasts, as any such long-range quantitative estimates inevitably must be. But they do suggest a new scale for our thinking. And they also suggest what happens when large numbers get compounded at even modest growth rates over a few decades.

These forecasts have been adjusted for population increase which is also subject to the effects of compound interest rates operating on large numbers. So to emphasize the point, it is necessary to consider what could happen to GNP itself over the next decades.

In 1966 Britain's GNP was around £32,500 million. At a 3 percent growth rate that figure would more than double by the year 2000 to £84,400 million. At a 4 percent growth rate it would nearly quadruple to £122,000 million. At a 5 percent growth rate it would quintuple to £167,000 million. By present outlooks, a steady 5 percent growth rate is unlikely, but an average rate somewhat between 3 percent and 4 percent is probably a reasonable expectation. For a rough and conservative guess, let us accept that the 1966 level of GNP— £32,500 million—will go to £100,000 million in the next 35 years; a modest trebling. Then consider the levels of public expenditure that will be possible, rather, that will be *necessary* to maintain economic stability. Consider how much can then be allocated to education, motorways, housing, national parks, health services, the British Museum, and so on.

These estimated figures indicate that we are on the verge of unprecedented wealth in the developed nations, a level of affluence that few of us can yet begin to imagine. When combined with the new wealth of knowledge that is forthcoming, this affluence is sure to generate new opportunities, new priorities, and new problems. We must all soon ask how we will be using this new-found wealth and, far more important, what that wealth will do to the highly developed nations where hundreds of thousands might still be poor, and to a world where thousands of millions of people in Asia, Africa, and Latin America will still be absolutely poor and relatively destitute.

Behind the GNP curve lies the recent explosion in the arts, the sciences, and the technologies. This is a worldwide phenomenon, even though it is still heavily localized in but a few nations. Because knowledge is peculiarly ignorant of national boundaries, the scientists, artists, and technologists throughout the world have come to share a common body of information, theory, and method. They share a consensus on values and on the epistemological bases for valuation. In effect they share a common culture.

Unlike the commodities of other enterprises, knowledge has the peculiar properties of drawing upon infinite resources, of being infinitely expandable, and being enriched by consumption. Given the incentives of impelling intellectual pursuits, and barring political or celestial catastrophe, we can expect that the current knowledge explosion will continue. More, we can be confident that it will continue to expand at exponential rates. As more and more people tune into the knowledge channels—whether as students in organized schools, as workers in the knowledge industries, or as persons seeking an avocational substitute for paid work—we can also expect that rising proportions of the populations will share the non-national culture of the present intellectual elites.

The internationalizing effect of science is being abetted by the parallel internationalizing effect of the communications systems that science and technology have spawned. Men who follow the intellectual pursuits are now able to maintain virtually instantaneous contact with each other. As the speed of communication and transportation rise and as the costs fall, the links that unite them are being further strengthened. These links are not new ones, of course. For several hundred years men have been able to stay in touch with each other around the globe. What *is* new is the speed of communication that is now commonplace, the intimacy that high accessibility provokes, and the extension of these communication lines to nearly the whole of the western world's population.

Although it has been commonplace to note that radio, television, and jet airplanes have shrunk the world to a small fraction of its nineteenth-century size, the scale is still so new that the consequences to society of that contraction are nonetheless still obscure. For example, student revolts around the world certainly cannot be attributed simply to the communications channels that have united the students into a common movement of protest, but those channels were nonetheless a necessary condition to the scenario that has evolved.

Throughout, there can be little doubt about the influence that radio, telephone, and particularly television has had upon similar movements of social protest. Television has the powerful capacity for turning distant events into local ones, for breaking through language barriers, and for communicating meaning as well as information. As its coverage extends to larger spectra of events and to larger numbers of people, it cannot fail to introduce an international unifying force with qualities never available in the world before. Real-time and realistic communication among such diverse places as Morningside Heights, Boulevard St. Michel, and the suburbs of Saigon has a way of turning these places into neighborhoods within the same city.

Another effect of shrinking space and time has been the recent rise of the international business firm that makes the services of its headquarters' technical staff promptly available to all its branches, wherever they may be. Those global corporate networks are rapidly being bound together by data-transmission lines feeding into headquarters' computers that will further erode regional differences in products and practices. In turn, corporate mergers are creating smaller numbers of giants that span nations, further integrating the worldwide economy and speeding up the processes of modernization.

The international revolution of rising expectations, the international student movement, and the international business firms are but the more visible signs of the spatially extensive communities that span nations. They are being paralleled by growing networks of informal organizations that join individuals and groups who share interests. These are perhaps best typified by the contemporary invisible colleges—those loose collections of colleagues which become visible whenever and wherever their members happen to gather, but whose real locations are inside the communication channels their members inhabit. They are typified, too, in the societies of Hippies, musicians, and diplomats who similarly share cultures with others who are spatially dispersed. The spatial extent of these culturally defined communities is spreading rapidly, as the pace of cultural diffusion rises: witness the speed with which fashions in clothes, politics, and architecture get transplanted from one corner of the world to others.

But the internationalizing trends do not necessarily mean that the world is becoming homogenized: just the opposite is happening. There can be no doubt that nationalism is on the rise at the same time that the cultural and economic boundaries of nations are becoming more permeable. So, too, is regionalism, at the same time that national governments and national pride are becoming stronger. Indeed, so too is localism, as the current community-organization drives in both the American suburbs and central city ghettos suggest.

It looks as though we are evolving a very ambiguous and complex sort of place-related social organization, in which groups joined by common interests are finding coherence against a wide range of spatial scales. Similarly, we are evolving a very complex network of interest bonds that are defining voluntary communities of ever more diverse sorts. Put another way, the rising scale of the society, the increased ease of communication, and hence the emergence of a world society is making for a range of cultural diversity that has never been possible before.

It was pre-industrial society that was homogeneous. Members of village communities followed similar life styles, shared common beliefs, and conformed to traditional behavioral norms. Members of the new high-scale world society have the opportunity to choose among a multiplicity of options. They can selectively join any of thousands of subgroups, each with its own styles and value systems. They can selectively read in an ever-expanding literature, follow any of a growing number of religions and, for the near-future at least, choose careers from among a widening range of possibilities. The numbers of such options have been expanding during the industrial era. Nothing appears to suggest that this long-term trend will be diverted. Increasing affluence, higher levels of education, and rapid social change are all likely to accelerate the trend to diversity—despite the shrinkage of the globe. I am suggesting that the forecasts of a mass-society are likely to prove wrong. Growing diversity in a growing society will have the inevitable effect of turning what would otherwise be small minorities into large and potentially powerful ones. Post-industrial society is likely to comprise a pluralism of competing minorities, with far less conformity than any in the history of the planet.

The shape of the world-population growth curve over the millenia is well known, as are the frightening extrapolations into the future. There were about one-quarter billion people in the world at the time of Christ, one-half billion at the time the American colonies were being established, one billion in 1850, two billion in 1925, and there will be around four billion in the mid-1970s. The consensus forecast has been putting it at around six billion in the year 2000. But it may then stabilize there. Donald Bogue reports that the impact of contraception during the past few years has already reversed the long-term trend, and that the rate of population growth has been slackening since 1965. He is predicting that "from 1965 onward . . . the rate of world population growth may be expected to decline with each passing year. The rate of growth will slacken at such a pace that it will be zero or near zero at about the year 2000, so that population growth will not be regarded as a major social problem except in isolated and small 'retarded' areas."[4]

If his projection is nearer right than the straight extrapolative ones, and it seems that it is, then one of the two major doomsday threats will be eroded away. But the problems that accompany population growth will not disappear. The poor and populous nations of the world have been losing ground steadily, relative to the levels of living that are emerging in the highly developed nations. Because population growth rates in the African, Asian, and Latin American nations are likely to respond more slowly to the contraceptive revolution, their status will be relatively worse in the future than now, despite even acceleration in rates of economic development there. At the same time, levels of literacy, aspiration, and international political influence are likely to continue to rise, providing the makings for a new scale of international conflict among the have and have-not nations on an unprecedented scale. Needless to say, those latent conflicts will be exacerbated by the visible contrasts that television and air travel will expose.

Richard Meier has recently been projecting the future patterns of city growth in Asia and finds no way of avoiding forecasts of city sizes up to 40 million.[5] A few years ago Kingsley Davis prepared a forecast for Calcutta and concluded that the metropolitan area may have 36 to 66 million by the year 2000.[6] In contrast, nineteenth century Manchester might have been a very amiable environment, and twenty-first century Manchester may strike many as a very attractive alternative. It is likely that the city expansion processes in the less developed nations are going to push immigration policy up to the top of the policy agenda in the more developed ones.

Similarly, the disparities in stages of development within the developed nations are likely to generate the major domestic policy problems there. As measured against any absolute index of quality, life in the contemporary city is far more comfortable and far less riven by hardship than at any time in the past. Even at its worst, housing is cleaner, safer, and more sanitary than it was, say, at the start of this century. Hours of work have been cut dramatically. Disease rates have been drastically reduced; for some dread diseases they have been reduced to zero. Education levels have been raised for virtually all segments of the population. Incomes are up to levels that permit a quality of nutrition never before achieved by national populations at large. On all these indices, the future promises even more dramatic improvements.

And yet we are approaching the end of the century with large proportions of western populations living in poverty—poverty relative to current national norms and to current national capabilities. If poverty is defined as family incomes below half the national median, then the poor comprise 20 percent of the United States population today and about 16–17 percent in Britain. The combined effects of the various changes mentioned above do not necessarily mean that their relative status will improve during the next decades. In the absence of concerted efforts to counteract these effects, it is likely that those who are now poor will be relatively worse off than they are now, mirroring the growing relative deprivation of those in the less developed nations.

Those who have the social and cognitive skills that will permit entry into the affluent sectors of post-industrial society are likely to fare very well indeed during the next generations. Those who lack these skills may find the entry points are closed. In the short run, employers can be expected to demand higher and higher levels of education and training. In the United States even clerks are now being required to have twelve years of schooling, and to present themselves in middle-class modes of dress, behavior, and speech. A growing proportion of occupations requires college-level preparation. Admission into the modern credential-society is becoming increasingly difficult. It is more difficult, in turn, to find positive roles that also confer a sense of personal dignity.

Many in America who still live in pre-industrial status and who have so far been excluded from industrial society have recently been indignantly demanding that they too have access to the modern world. The recent wave of riots is the most outspoken statement of their dilemma. The American experience has not yet been repeated in the other developed nations, where poverty also persists, but where working-class status carries dignity and stability. One wonders, however, whether the present American experience may be an early-warning of future European experience. At this moment in history, America is closest to the post-industrial stage of development. When the European nations and Japan reach that stage in the 1970s and 80s, can we expect that working-class groups will maintain their present stability? From this perspective it looks as if this is the critical question for urban planners. Today, America's central urban policy issue is posed by the dilemma of a large pre-industrial, city-based population in a society about to leave the industrial age. It could soon happen here in Britain as well.

Some implications for city planning

There are a great many other portents of the future that we might have recorded here: the revolution under way in biology and the new possibilities for extending life spans and for genetic engineering, communication prospects that lasers are promising, possibilities for new kinds of air-supported and electrically propelled vehicles, new prospects for weather control, and so on. I have mentioned just a few of the prospects not with the intent of portraying what the future may be like, but rather as a way of suggesting that the social, political, and economic environments for urban life may be in for some quantum changes. If they are, then our concept of future time will also have to change, and with it, our perceptions of our professional roles.

The conception of the future that has been guiding the city planning movement in the past is different from the one emerging in the new explorations. City planning has never really been orientated to future change. Despite the long horizons and the utopian traditions that have marked this field throughout its history, it has been guided by a future-directed ideology that has looked backwards; our binoculars have had an extra set of prisms built-in, so that, when we have aimed them at the future, they have reversed the field of vision.

I find it a sobering reminder, for example, that virtually not one of us foresaw the current affluence. No one foresaw the effects of widespread automobile ownership—whether on suburbanization, on the changing functions of the central business districts, or on the ways in which people would use their leisure time.

This is understandable for, instead of systematic forecasts of social change, we have prepared portraits of desired long-range futures for the physical-spatial city, because those portraits were for cities that would be built in the image of the long-range past. With genuinely bold and daring leadership, typically with selfless devotion to the public welfare, we have been proposing designs for future cities that were frequently idealized reconstructions of pre-industrial towns that served pre-industrial societies. I am reminded of the numerous attempts to build locally scaled social neighborhoods in contemporary American cities; the postwar "self-contained" new towns in Britain; the anti-auto ideology, and the persisting efforts to reconstruct in industrial democratic societies the kinds of large-scale urban designs that characterized the monarchies of pre-industrial times.

None of us has yet thought through the coming effects on cities and urban societies that now lie implicit in new electronic-communication systems, computers, rising per capita wealth, place-free and low-cost nuclear energy, new airborne transport systems, new modes of retail distribution, new public-private nonprofit corporations, the new movements for participatory democracy, and so on. Nor have we felt the need to, for we have been conducting our affairs against a concept of the future and against a set of substantive models that have not called for these sorts of *qualitative* conjectures.

City planners early adopted the thoughtways and the analytical methods that engineers devised for the design of public works, and they then applied them to the design of cities. In that context, and in the sense that city plans take a long time to accomplish, our work has indeed been future-orientated.

Seeking a scale on future "requirements," in the engineering model, we have always attempted to make good long-range quantitative forecasts of the population sizes that the cities must accommodate. Recently we have acquired some considerable skill in forecasting future travel volumes, as a way of scaling future demand for highways. In this sense, too, our work has been future-orientated.

But our plans and scalar forecasts have typically been made against a series of assumptions and on modes of prediction that the new futurists are beginning to challenge. These assumptions include at least the following:

1. That social organization and social objectives will remain stable during the time-period under review.
2. That there is a societywide consensus on city-development goals.
3. Because these goals are stable, future goals will be like present goals, and that they are knowable by professionals.

The recent projective studies have made the first two of these assumptions highly questionable. If history is indeed at a turning point without prior precedent, and if cultural diversity is really on the rise, present patterns may not guide us well. These studies suggest that projections of qualitative change must precede quantitative forecasts. They suggest that extrapolations of past trends are no longer reasonable, if only because extrapolation implies that past determinants of trend lines will persist into the future. Similarly they point to some built-in deficiencies of our present quantitative methods. The traditional scientific canons cannot be formally applied to phenomena that cannot yet be either observed or measured; and that plays havoc with empirically derived parameters. Qualitative projection requires reasoned judgment—built upon rigorous theory when it exists, but openly speculative and conjectural when it does not.

The third assumption—that professionals can make decent judgments on future societal *objectives* by observing present ones—a central issue in all planning fields, is even more dubious. First, because so much of the future is unpredictable; second, because professionals are inherently plagued by so many biases that inhibit their comprehension of the wants of increasingly diverse minorities. I shall argue in Part II of this article [in *Town Planning Review*] that a great many decisions that professionals are accustomed to take are best left to the public itself.

I shall also contend that we have frequently asked the wrong questions and sought to control the wrong variables. In the city planning field, for example, we have been asking questions about optimum city size and about optimum city form. Yet, the shifts in recent and future interaction patterns suggest that settlement size is no longer a critical question. For increasing segments of the high-scale societies, it is no longer meaningful. Similarly, questions about overall metropolitan spatial arrangements are giving way to the more intricate ones concerned with inter-establishment linkages and the ranges of locational opportunity open to types of families and firms. Rather than the design of physical layouts of cities, the city planning task is turning to the design of the fiscal and institutional arrangements that might then control the city-building process and to the designs for social services. The detailed decisions can be left to the consumer.

And then the prime questions that will be raised by the move into post-industrialism are: Who is to pay? Who is to profit? and Who is to decide? The fruits of the coming affluence will inevitably be unequally distributed, and that is likely to become the dominant political fact of the time. It could well be that the distributional questions will also be the dominant ones for city planning.

It could also be that the political urgency of these questions will force an expansion of city planning's traditional preoccupation with the quality of the city to encompass the larger range of concerns with the quality of urban life. Even with a rising flow of wealth through both public and private channels, we shall still have deliberately to plan for the expansion of opportunity and personal freedom. The future is no more likely to be beneficent than perverse and tyrannical. Futurists have written both sorts of scenarios, and they are equally plausible.

In our traditional lines of work, we shall soon have to confront the dilemma posed by the huge sunk investment in the nineteenth and twentieth century cities. The physical plant that future generations will inherit is not likely to match their standards of acceptable quality or their capacities to buy better cities. Buildings and roads have too long a lifespan to suit the pace of historical change. The Americans dealt with that fact by simply leaving the old cities behind, and moving out to new settlements in the suburbs. That solved the individuals' problems, but left a social residue unresolved. How will the great cities of Europe deal with old plants that were built in the industrial age?

On the other side of that coin we shall have to confront the dilemma posed, on the one hand, by our fiscal capacities for building an amiable and beautiful environment and the public pressures to build quickly and, on the other, by the paucity of ideas with which to meet that challenge. The fitting criteria of aesthetic quality are not likely to be those that have guided urban designers in the past. Those persons who will be able to afford spaciousness and high geographic mobility will also be able to claim both, and these cannot be simultaneously supplied in the mediaeval, or nineteenth-century, or even the twentieth-century packages we have been offering. Multi-house and multi-car families will use far more space than we are accustomed to provide; and those demands will be met, whether we cooperate or not. At the same time, and integral with the city designs, they will be demanding opportunities for exciting educational activities, for productive social roles, and for an information-rich life. These opportunities, too, must also be created as necessities—at least as imperative as sewers and streets.

These will be calling for a speculative and inventive capacity that has been rare in our field. If Professor Brzezinski and the others are right about the degree of qualitative change that is before us, we shall find few guides by looking to the cities of the past. As Britton Harris has been contending, we shall have to invent the future city and the opportunities for a rich urban life, because the models have not yet emerged in the course of past history.[7]

There is likely to be a happy congruence between the expanding knowledge of human and social systems, and our capacity to plan for this congruence. Planning has until recently been only an idea. With improving theory and improving computational capability, planning is only now becoming an operational method for defining goals, reaching decisions, and taking actions. In the post-industrial era it is likely to become the normal mode of decision and action—in a wide array of human activities. We are now learning how to apply the idea of planning to the city. And when we do, it may well be that our most troubling questions will surround the issues of equity. The industrial age was dominated by the idea of efficiency. The post-industrial age is likely to be dominated by conflicts over equity. The overriding question for planners will be "How shall the social product of an increasingly affluent and increasingly capable society be distributed?" Or, as I put it above: "Who shall pay?, Who shall profit?, and Who shall decide?" It is these questions I shall discuss in the January issue of this journal.

References

1. Brzezinski, Z., "America in the Technetronic Era," *Encounter,* January 1968, pp. 16–17.

2. Michael, Donald N., *Cybernation: The Silent Conquest,* Santa Barbara, California: Center for the Study of Democratic Institutions, 1962.

3. Salvadori, Mario G., speaking on "The Impact of Science and Technology" at a private conference, 1964.

4. Bogue, Donald, "The End of the Population Explosion," *The Public Interest,* no. 7, Spring 1967, pp. 11–201.

5. Meier, Richard L., *Studies on the Future of Cities in Asia,* Berkeley: Center for Planning and Development Research, University of California, 1967.

6. Davis, Kingsley, "Urbanization in India," *India's Urban Future,* Roy Turner (ed.), Berkeley: University of California Press, 1962, p. 25.

7. Harris, Britton, *Inventing the Future City,* Catherine Bauer Wurster Memorial Lecture, University of California, Berkeley, 1966 (mimeographed).

DATE DUE

JAN			